In The Beginnings

The Story of the Original Earth, its Destruction, and its Restoration

A Defense of the Biblical Gap Theory of Creation

Steven E. Dill, D.V.M.

In The Beginnings
(3rd Edition—2nd Printing)
Copyright 2007, 2010, 2018 by Steven E. Dill
Louisville, Kentucky

ISBN 978-1-7326258-4-6

Website: www.GapTheoryOfCreation.com
E-mail: TheGapTheoryGuy@gmail.com

All rights reserved.
No part of this book may be reproduced, copied, or stored in a retrieval system by any means –
digital, electronic, mechanical, photocopy, or otherwise –
without written permission of the author,
except for brief quotations in noncommercial reviews.

(Note: Throughout the book, items printed in bold print
are my emphases unless otherwise noted.)

Greek and Hebrew words designated as "Strong's Number…"
are defined according to *Strong's Dictionary of the Hebrew Language*,
Copyright: James Strong, 1890, London: Hodder and Stroughton

Table of Contents

TABLE OF CONTENTS 3

DEDICATION 11

INTRODUCTION 13

MY THANKS 15

A FOREWORD FOR YOUNG READERS 19

CHAPTER ONE: THE TRUTH ABOUT TRUTH 25

    What Happened When? 25

    Divine Revelation 28

CHAPTER TWO: THE CREATION COMBO SPECIAL 37

    I. The Meaning of "Day" 39

    II. The Meaning of "Create" 50

    III. The Meaning of "Beginning" 51

    IV. How Genesis 1:1 Relates to the Rest of the Chapter 51

    Four Characteristics of the Gap Theory 54

    Concerning "Chaos" 55

CHAPTER THREE: APPARENT PROBLEMS 57

    Scientific Problem 1: You're Out of Order... 57
        (Figure 1) Biblical Order of Appearance... 58
        (Figure 2) Scientific Order of Appearance.. 59
        (Figure 3) Evolution and the Geologic Ages... 61
        (Figure 4) Biblical Order vs. Scientific Order (Part 1) 62
        (Figure 5) Biblical Order vs. Scientific Order (Part 2) 63
        (Figure 6) The "Day" Ages Compared to the Geological Ages 66

Scientific Problem 2: Missing "Missing Links" 67

The Rainbow Painting 68

Scientific Problem 3: Living Fossils 72

CHAPTER FOUR: DAY-AGE SOLUTIONS 75

The Biblical Meaning of "DAY" 75

YOM (Day) 75

LAYIL (Night) 77

YOM and *LAYIL* (Day and Night) 97

EREB (Evening) 102

BOQER (Morning) 113

EREB and *BOQER* (Evening and Morning) 133

CHOSHEK (Dark, Darkness) 138

OWR (Light) 144

Counting the Days 157

YOM ECHAD (One Day) 158

YOM RISHON (First Day) 166

YOM SHENIY (Second Day) 170

YOMIM SHENAYIM (Two Days) 172
   YOM = YEAR 173
   HEMERA (Day) 178

YOM SHELIYSHIY (Third Day) 186

YOMIM SHALOSH (Three Days) 190

YOM REBIY'IY (Fourth Day) 195

YOMIM ARBA (Four Days) 196

YOM CHAMIYSHIY (Fifth Day) 196

YOMIM CAMESH (Five Days)	197
YOM SHISHSHIY (Sixth Day)	197
YOMIM SHESH (Six Days)	198
YOM SHEBIY'IY (Seventh Day)	199
YOMIM SHEBAH (Seven Days)	204
If the Six "Days" are Ages, What are the Six "Nights"?	214
If the "Days" are Long Ages, Then How Did Certain Plants Reproduce?	215
The Universe is Only Six Seconds Old	215
The Really Big Problem: Day-Age Weakens the Gospel	216

CHAPTER FIVE: YOUNG-EARTH SOLUTIONS 219

The Young-Earth Theory	219
Was There Death Before Adam Sinned?	225
Who Introduced Sin into the World?	228
Them Bones, Them Bones, Them Dry Bones	233
Apparent Age	235
Church Doctrines Don't Necessarily Equal Bible Doctrines	236
In God (Can) We Trust?	237
Astronomy 101½	238
Why Not Flood-Geology?	244
Specimen Ridge	244
Green River Varves	248
Coral Reefs	249
My Sentiments on Sediments	251
Carbon 14	253

Japanese Plesiosaur 256

Paluxy River Footprints 256

Magnetic Field Decay 257

Mississippi River Delta 258

No Earthquakes; No Volcanoes 259

CHAPTER SIX: A CLOSER LOOK AT THE BIBLE 267

Twenty-Seven Correct Translations of Genesis 1:1-2a...267

Seeking Informational Correctness: Genesis 1:1 272

Seeking Informational Correctness: Genesis 1:2 279

King James Version Translations of *TOHUW* and *BOHUW* 288

The Context of Isaiah 34:11 and Jeremiah 4:23 292

CHAPTER SEVEN: THE RESTORATION THEORY 299

HAYAH in Genesis (KJV) as Some Form of "Became" 307

How My Thinking Evolved 315

The Scholars Speak 317

Without Form, and Void 339

Another Creation Account 340

The Meaning of *TOHUW* in Isaiah 45:18 342

The Uses of *BARA* for God's Creations 343

Objecting in Vain 349

Let There Be Logic 350

BARA vs. *ASAH*...352

Fifty Ways to Leave Your Theory 357

CHAPTER EIGHT: A CLOSER LOOK AT THE SIX DAYS 363

- The Six Days of Creation.. 363
- Detour into Darkness 368
- Back Into the Light 371
- What-If?.. 373
- What Was the Condition of the Earth Just Before the Restoration? 374
- Phony Photons 375
- The Canopy Theory 379
- Dry Land... 385
- Old Lights—New Functions 386
- Years... 387
- Seasons 387
- Days 387
- Signs 387
- Set in the Firmament of the Heavens 390
- The Invisible Attributes of God 390
- The Fine Tuning of the Universe 391

CHAPTER NINE: THE ORIGINAL EARTH 401

- To *HAYAH* or not to *HAYAH*: That is the Question 410
- Is Jeremiah 4:23-26 Literal or Figurative?.. 412
- Does God Speak Hebrew? 413
- A Look at Satan's World 414
- Whose Cities Were These? 416
- Let's Look at "Let".. 418

CHAPTER TEN: EARTH'S TWO BEGINNINGS (DUO-GENESIS) 423

- Does "The Beginning" = "The Creation?" 423
- Two Creation Accounts = One Creation 428
- Matthew 19 and Mark 10 430
- The Beginning of the Beginning 430
- The End of the Beginning 436
- Lucifer's Rebellion 437
- Satan: Prince of this World 439
- Who Had Authority Over the Earth When? 442
- Lucifer Caused the Original Earth to Become *TOHUW WA-BOHUW* 448
- Isaiah's and Jeremiah's Views of the Pre-Adamic Earth 449
- What Did Lucifer Do? 450
- When Did Satan Regain Authority Over the Earth? 451
- Let Light Shine 454
- Born of Water and The Spirit 456
- All Shook Up 459
- Two Creation Accounts = Two Beginnings 468
- Two Global Floods 471
- Multiple Descriptions of the Pre-Adamic Earth 479
- The Past Age 483
- Stop the Clock 487
- The Gap Theory Under The Electron Microscope 490
  - End of the AGES 500
  - *KATABALLO* in the Septuagint 502

CHAPTER ELEVEN: SCIENCE AND THE RESTORATION THEORY 507

- Living Fossils 510
- Does The Gap Theory Allow for Evolution? 511
- Was There A Big Bang? 511
- How Long Was the Earth *TOHUW WA-BOHUW* 515
- Pre-Adamic "Men" 518
- Pre-Adamic Evil and Death 519

CHAPTER TWELVE: THE MEANING OF *HAYAH* 527

- *HAYAH* Used for Dynamic Conditions of Being 529
- *HAYAH* in Genesis (KJV) 534
- *HAYAH* Translated as, "Was" or "Wast," in the King James Version 536
- *HAYAH* in Genesis 1:2 548
- The *QAL* stem 548
- The *QAL* Imperfect 549
- The *QAL* Imperfect of *HAYAH* in Genesis (KJV) 551
- The *WAW* Consecutive 554
- The *QAL* Perfect 558
- The *WAW* Conjunctive 559
- The *WAW* Conjunctive with the *QAL* Perfect of *HAYAH* in Genesis (KJV) 559
- The *QAL* Perfect *HAYAH* of Genesis 1:2 560
- *HAYAH* and the Preposition *le* 565
- Looking for *LAMEDH* in All the Wrong Places 566
- *HAYAH* with the *LAMEDH* (ל) 566
- *HAYAH* without the *LAMEDH* (ל) 568

Can *HAYETAH* Mean "Became"?..577

CHAPTER THIRTEEN: THE MEANING OF *WAW* 581

The *WAW* Coordinative, Consecutive, and Disjunctive 581

Five examples of *WAW* Disjunctives followed by *HAYAH* in Genesis................................587

A Divinely Revealed Pattern 591

The *WAW* Pattern 592

Genesis 1 – Stirred; Not Shaken 596

Jack Langford's Picture Frame Pattern 604

Jonah 3:3 609

Genesis 1:2 and Jonah 3:3 612

Closing comment on *HAYAH*..615

That's Very Un-Becoming of You 617

Summary of the Evidence for the Duo-Genesis Principle 632

TO THOSE WHO HAVEN'T PUT THEIR TRUST IN JESUS 635

BIBLE TRANSLATIONS 639

HEBREW AND GREEK DEFINITIONS 645

INDEX 647

SCRIPTURE REFERENCES 655

BIBLIOGRAPHY 695

Dedication

I dedicate this book to Dr. Arthur Custance. (1910-1985) Dr. Custance earned his M. A. in Hebrew and Greek at the University of Toronto. He earned his Ph.D. in Biblical archaeology and anthropology at the University of Ottawa. He was also a research scientist and an engineer, and became the head of Canada's Human Engineering Laboratories at the Defense Research Board at Ottawa. He was a member of the Evangelical Theological Society, a Member Emeritus of the Canadian Physiological Society, a Fellow of the Royal Anthropological Institute, and a member the New York Academy of Sciences. These qualifications put him into that rare category of people who truly are both scientists and theologians. For Dr. Custance, there were no true discrepancies between science and the Bible; only errors in human interpretations.

Dr. Custance did not introduce me to the Biblical Gap Theory, but he did introduce me to the truth of the Biblical Gap Theory. Before becoming a Christian, I was a Theistic Evolutionist. After I put my trust in Jesus Christ and began studying the Bible, I learned evolution was a lie. So, I began searching for the truth about the origin of the universe and the origin of life. Although I knew the Bible must reveal the truth, I couldn't find the truth because I was being deceived by Christians who did not know the truth… and who did not teach the truth. Their problem was they did not love THE truth—they loved THEIR truth. I eventually discovered Arthur Custance's book *Without Form and Void.*[1] It was the treasure chest of truth for me… and what a treasure it was! The more I partook of that treasure, the more treasure I discovered. I consider my book a continuation of his work. If I had never read his book, my book would have never been written.

Introduction

This book is about earth's two beginnings. Putting it as bluntly as I can, it is a defense of the Gap Theory of Creation. It is called the Gap Theory, or the Genesis Gap Theory, because it theorizes there was a gap of time between the earth's original creation in Genesis 1:1 and its later re-creation during the six twenty-four-hour days of Genesis 1:3-31. It is also called the Ruin-Restoration Theory, or simply the Restoration Theory, because it deals with the destruction of the original earth and its later restoration. This theory is very unpopular these days. I say this right at the start because I don't want you to waste your time reading it if you have pre-decided you hate the Gap Theory. Christians have become extremely divided over the "correct" interpretation of God's Word concerning creation, and it has become a very emotional topic. Christian creationists have divided themselves into camps huddled around various creation theories. These camps are so divided that people often want to know your stand on these theories before they're willing to accept you as a fellow creationist; sometimes, even as a fellow Christian. Many Christians have been labeled as heretics simply because they hold opinions about creation that differ from someone else's. I have been so-labeled, and if you come to believe what I believe, I suspect you will be too.

The purpose of this book is simple: I want you to know the truth about our Creator, Jesus Christ. This is especially my goal if you are not a believer in the Lord Jesus Christ. Even if you are not a believer in Christ, I suspect you have heard the Gospel, or at least heard OF the Gospel, but something has kept you from believing the Gospel. For many, that "something" is the belief that science and the Bible are in conflict. This problem is compounded by the fact there really are creationists who believe things contrary to science. **Much of the unbelievers' objection to Biblical creationism is because some creation theories are not only unscientific, but anti-scientific.** Some creationists put stumbling blocks between unbelievers and the Gospel. They require you to believe things not scientifically true. They also require you to believe things not Biblically true. Their attitude is that if you don't believe what THEY say about creation, then YOU are rejecting God's Word and YOU aren't fit to be saved; therefore, YOU deserve to burn in hell.

I want unbelievers to know two things about salvation. First, I want unbelievers to know we all deserve to burn in hell; Christian and non-Christian alike. Christians are not saved from eternal damnation because we are better people. We are saved only because we have put our trust in the promise Jesus made to us. Jesus knows we all have sinned. He knows none of us can stand in the presence of a Holy God. He knows the wage of sin is eternal death in the Lake of Fire. He also knows we cannot undo our sins or pay for our sins with good deeds, moral living, or by church membership or attendance. He promised He would pay the price for our sins by taking our place on the Cross. (We are the ones who should be crucified.) He asks us to quit relying on ourselves, and trust Him to do what we can't. It is the proverbial story of a loving father urging his child to jump from the window of a burning building: "Jump and I will catch you." That leap is the leap of faith into His arms. There is no other escape from eternal death. Jesus is our God, our King, our Creator, our Master, and our Savior, and as such, He will do what He promised. He will catch us if we jump. It is only by His Work, His Grace, His Love, and His Mercy that anyone can be saved. It is not because of who we are; it is because of who He is. Second, I want unbelievers to know there is a Biblical creation theory in total agreement with true scientific observations. That theory is the Gap Theory. Belief in the Gap Theory will not get you saved, but it can remove the so-called scientific barriers that have prevented so many from even considering the truth of the Gospel. If you are an unbeliever, I want this defense of the Gap Theory to be the scalpel God uses to cut away your cancer of distrust of the Bible. I want it to help you put your trust in God's declarations rather than in man's interpretations.

The Word of God reveals the truth about our Creator, but so do the Works of God. I believe God is smart enough, powerful enough, and sovereign enough to make His Works and His Words agree. If you read some of the comments from the various creationists' camps, you get a feeling this isn't true. There is so little agreement among creationists about science and Scripture, it makes you wonder if God didn't make a mistake when He created creationists. I believe all the bickering harms the Gospel of Jesus Christ more than it helps. I believe it ought to stop. I believe only truth can make it stop. I believe the Gap Theory is true. It would be nice if I could convince all the other creationists to agree with me about the Gap Theory, but that's not my goal. My goal is to help unbelievers learn about our Creator, so they will come to love and put their trust in our Creator. If a million Christian Young-Earth and Day-Age creationists come to believe in the Gap Theory because of what I have written, I will be happy for them, but will have little joy in that outcome alone. However, joy beyond measure will fill my heart if at least one unbeliever comes to trust in Jesus Christ as Savior because of this book.

My Thanks

Above all others, I thank my Lord and Savior Jesus Christ for bearing my sins on the Cross and giving me His righteousness and eternal life. I also thank Him for sending the Holy Spirit to live inside me, and for the Spirit's guidance and revelation in spiritual matters. Without those gifts, I could not understand even the simplest spiritual concept. To God alone, be the glory.

I also thank a group of fellow Gap Theory defenders who have read my book and have encouraged and enlightened me. Many of them are authors themselves and have Internet Websites defending the Ruin-Restoration Creation Account. We are a small group of Christians who perceive that today's most popular theories of creation (The Young-Earth Theory and The Day-Age Theory) often create stumbling blocks between many unbelievers and the Gospel. While we all have differences concerning some of the details of the creation account, we all seek to use "The Gap Theory," "The Genesis Gap Theory," "The Gap Fact," "The Ruin-Restoration Theory," "The Re-Creation Theory," or might I suggest, "The Duo-Genesis Interpretation," as a God-Given revelation to win people to Christ. Plain and simple, we seek the glorification of our Lord and Savior Jesus Christ. His glorification is vastly more important than people praising us for our words or our thoughts. Here are their names: David Bickell, Ken Brown, Gaines Johnson, Jack Langford, James Lowrance, Robert Luginbill, Ole Madsen, Joaozinho Martins, Len Thies, Brett Thomas, and John Thomas. I especially want to thank Gaines Johnson, James Lowrance, Jack Langford, and Joaozinho Martins for their valuable insights and teachings in their books. Here are their Websites:

(Note: Due to the ever-changing nature of the Internet, these Web addresses may not be current, or even still present. You can do an Internet search for their names or their books if you need to.)

David Bickell:
http://www.biblestudiesrightlydivided.blogspot.com

Ken Brown:
http://brownbible.com/index.php/en-us/newsletter/biblical-considerations/55-creation-science-and-genesis-1

Gaines Johnson:
http://www.kjvbible.org

Jack Langford:
http://separationtruth.com/Creation-Gap.html

James Lowrance:
https://www.createspace.com/3694891

Robert Luginbill:
http://www.ichthys.com/sr2-copy.htm

Ole Madsen:
http://www.creationdays.dk

Joaozinho Martins:
http://christianreading.com/jmartins

Len Thies:
http://www.lulu.com/shop/len-thies/who-in-hell-is-hell-prepared-for/ebook/product-2221092.html

Brett Thomas:
http://mystery-babylon.org/thegaptheory.html

John Thomas:
http://www.evogenesis.com

    Paul Glenn Cawley, of Paul Glenn Cawley Productions in Aliso Viejo, California also deserves my thanks. His enthusiastic encouragement has been… enthusiastically encouraging. Paul is a screenwriter, singer-songwriter, video director, film producer, founder of the Christian rock band *Guardian*, and a man with an intense love for Jesus Christ. His edifying words have been a pure blessing to me; not just in the area of professional writing, but on a personal level as well. I thank God for my friend Paul.

    A big thanks goes to Dr. Richard Fee of the University of Louisville. He personally introduced me to the writings of Sir Robert Anderson. (1841-1918) Sir Robert was a brilliant investigator in Scotland Yard, and a brilliant theologian who used his knowledge of the nature of evidence to defend the Gap Theory. As only a detective could discover, he found solid evidence for the Gap Theory that could hold up under the most scrutinizing cross-examination. Thank you, Richard, for defending the truth of the Gospel by defending the truth of the Bible.

I give a many-years-long thanks to Dr. Terry Pearson of Louisville, Kentucky. He is not only a friend, but one of my clients. I have been Terry and Pat's (his wife) veterinarian for many years. Terry told me about G. Campbell Morgan and his belief in the Gap Theory. You'll read about Dr. Morgan in Chapter Seven. Terry and Pat's friendship has been a cherished gift, even if their cats don't like me.

Milton Hobbs of Hephzibah, Georgia is another man I want to thank and acknowledge as being a great encourager. His prayers for me have continued to uphold and strengthen me. He has a real burden for presenting the truth of the Creation to his friends, neighbors, family, and brothers and sisters in Christ. He has seen how the false teachings of some of the other creation theories have negatively influenced the lives of believers.

I also thank someone I don't really know, but consider a friend. Eddy from the Netherlands informed me via e-mail that theologian James Montgomery Boice defended the Gap Theory. Because of Eddy, I can now add Dr. Boice to a long list of scholars who believed something we are told, "No scholars believe." I asked Eddy if I could print his full name and information in my book, but he declined the fame (or is it notoriety?) and regarded his input into my work as reward enough. He asked that I mention him only as Eddy from the Netherlands. Thank you Eddy from the Netherlands.

Speaking of the Netherlands, I also want to thank Ralph Wilms from Roermond. He thanked me for my book because, as a Christian, he had been taught Theistic Evolution was true. In addition, he had been taught the Gap Theory was false. As he investigated the evidence for himself, he realized the Gap Theory was the only way to explain the Creation. He said the Gap Theory really opened his eyes. I immediately liked Ralph because he reminded me of me, so many years ago.

Simon A. Hailes of Belfast wrote me a note during an online debate I was having with a Hebrew scholar attacking my book. Mr. Hailes informed us that English scholar and theologian John W. Burgon (1813-1888) believed and defended the Gap Theory. Burgon was known as a strong defender of Biblical inerrancy. Thank you, Simon for interceding on my behalf, and for letting my Hebrew scholar opponent know there were Biblical scholars who considered the Gap Theory interpretation as an inerrant revelation from God.

I have one more fan from a foreign country; André Pretorius from South Africa. Like me, he has a background in molecular biology and genetics, but the most exciting thing about André was he read the second edition of my book twice. Wow! That news was a great encouragement. It's one thing to read a book one time, (Sometimes we obligate ourselves to read a book once we start, even if we discover we don't like it.) but to read it a second time; now that's a compliment. He said he was anxiously awaiting my third edition. André, I hope this book encourages you as much as you encouraged me. I also hope it helps you convince others of the truth of the Restoration Interpretation.

Bob Bolander, pastor of Austin Bible Church in Austin, Texas also deserves my thanks. His church defends the Gap Theory. As we shared information about ourselves, I learned he had been friends with two men I knew while I was in the Navy: Scotty Allen, the pastor of the church in Portsmouth, Virginia where my wife and I attended. He also knew Jay Chappell, the director of the Christian Servicemen's Center in Stonington, Connecticut. Jay was a great mentor while I was stationed at New London.

Bill Kelly, a seminary student living in Bluffton, Indiana wrote and encouraged me concerning a lengthy online argument I was having with a Hebrew scholar who was offended by "my" Hebrew interpretations. This Hebrew scholar insisted the Hebrew scholars I quoted (who defended the Gap Theory) were all wrong, and he was right. Bill reassured me my arguments and conclusions were Biblically sound, and I wasn't misinterpreting the Hebrew. (Actually, I think Bill got word of my book from Bob Bolander.)

I especially thank God for a very special friend, Bob Handley of Irmo, South Carolina for his continual encouragement and support. Bob read the manuscript, and his whole-hearted approval was very uplifting. Although he found some typos and errors, I hold him guiltless if there are more. His proofreading efforts were a gift of love to me, to our Lord, and to you, the reader. He really wants you to know the Truth about our Lord Jesus Christ. Thank you, Bob for defending the Gap Theory (and my book) against some rather nasty and untruthful attacks on the Internet. Much of the additional material I have put into this 3rd edition has come from questions Bob has asked me about the Gap Theory. His questions prompted me to do more research, and to rewrite/reword previous answers so they would be more complete. No one has prompted me more than Bob Handley in spurring me on to keep perfecting my book. This book is not perfect, but it is a lot closer to it because of Bob Handley. The Biblical knowledge and wisdom Bob has attained over the years is evident to anyone who listens to him. The Church would benefit tremendously if we had a thousand Bob Handleys to mentor us. Bob, you have more than earned my utmost respect for your knowledge and your life.

Last and best: This book would not have been possible without the love, help, understanding, and encouragement of my wife, Linda. Over the years, she has continued to encourage me throughout all three editions. She was a valuable proofreader of the manuscript, ever looking for ways to improve the finished product. More than that, she is a valuable proofreader of my life and my Christian conduct, helping to improve that finished product as well. Thank you, Linda, for always being there, and for the sacrifices it took to get this book published. Thank you, Jesus, for giving me this wonderful woman to be my life partner. Without her, I could not have written this book.

A Foreword for Young Readers

Before I go into the details concerning the Gap Theory, I need to take a big step back and explain some things that might be new or confusing to some of my readers. I'm sure 99% of my readers understand these things, but there may be some young people who have never studied the issue of creation in depth, and they may not understand what this is all about. If you are a young person, and you are feeling a little bit confused by some of this stuff, don't feel alone. I remember when I was twelve years old, I was trying to read an article in a magazine about the discovery of DNA by Watson and Crick. Although I read the article several times, I never could comprehend all it was saying. I remember being awestruck by how important DNA was. But, I also remember feeling a little sad I couldn't understand it all. It never struck me that the article wasn't written for twelve-year-olds. Now, over half a century later, I am pleased to tell you that when I read articles about DNA, I am still awestruck, and I still feel a little sad I can't understand it all. If you have those feelings too, you have the makings of a scientist; don't give up.

The issue in this book concerns the different beliefs about the origin of the universe. How did the universe begin? Did it begin, or has it always been here? The issue also concerns the different beliefs about the origin of life; especially of human life. How did life begin? How did human beings come into existence? The reason these questions are so important is because they prompt us to ask some other questions; some extremely important questions: Is there a purpose for life? Is there a purpose for you? Are you part of some grand plan? If so, what is your part? How do you fulfill your purpose? What happens to you after you die?

As far back as historical records go, we have been asking these questions. As far back as historical records go, we have been proposing answers to these questions. Some answers have been based on the superstitions of primitive cultures. Some answers have been based on the scientific observations of modern cultures. Some answers have been based on the religious beliefs of a whole variety of cultures. When it comes to your answers, remember this: No matter what answers you believe, and no matter why you believe them, you will not be able to prove them to those who don't want to believe your answers.

Logic can't prove anything, science can't prove anything, religion can't prove anything, philosophy can't prove anything, education can't prove anything, teachers can't prove anything, parents can't prove anything, governments can't prove anything, and books can't prove anything (including this book) to anyone who doesn't want to believe it. The reason is because proof, like beauty, is a decision of the mind. Even if 99.999% of your culture believes something, that is no guarantee you will believe it too. Your beliefs are based on your beliefs, and whether those beliefs agree or disagree with the beliefs of your friends, family, neighbors, and culture is of little importance in the final analysis of YOUR mind. Of course, how much you agree or disagree with those around can have some staggering consequences in your life. If you believe it is not wrong to drive eighty miles-per-hour in a neighborhood with a twenty-five miles-per-hour speed limit, and if you believe it is not wrong to run stop signs and red lights, and if you believe it is not wrong to make crude finger-gestures and vulgar comments to the police officer who pulls you over, then you will quickly find yourself suffering from the consequences of your beliefs. **Beliefs have consequences!**

One of the first consequences of beliefs is we can believe something that is not true. "Truth" and "Belief" are not necessarily the same things. Beliefs are decisions determined in the mind. Truths are absolutes, independent of the mind. Truth is truth whether you believe it or not. Don't be deceived into believing there is such a thing as relative truth; "my truth" and "your truth." There is such a thing as relative belief, but if someone tells you truth is relative, ask them, "Is that absolutely true?" You see, we might have different beliefs about the dangers of drinking arsenic, but no matter what you believe about arsenic, the truth remains universal and constant; drink enough arsenic, and you will die. **Truth has greater consequences!**

Beliefs about the origin of the universe and the origin of life have consequences, too. Down through the ages, people have been persecuted, imprisoned, tortured, and even killed for having the "wrong beliefs." While most of you won't face consequences that dire, some of you may be flunked out of a college biology class if your beliefs about the origin of life don't agree with what your professors and universities believe. I have seen this happen. Some of you may find your Christian fellowships disrupted because you don't have the same beliefs about Biblical Creation that your pastor, your elders, and your Sunday School teachers have. I have seen this happen too.

No matter what you believe about beliefs, believe this: Your beliefs about our origin will play a major role in how you live your life. Your beliefs will have an impact on your values, your conduct, your goals, and your interactions with other people. It is extremely important for your beliefs to be well-thought out. It's easy to be flippant about this issue, but sooner or later, you need to answer the questions about origins, and you need to be able to defend your answers. So, let's start asking (and answering) the questions about our origin.

Has the universe always existed, or did it begin to exist at some time in the past?

Different cultures and different peoples have had different beliefs. Nearly all non-Bible-based cultures have believed the universe always existed in one form or another. They said the universe was infinite/eternal. Even today, they do not believe time, space, matter, and energy came into existence at some time and point in the past. They believe the material things of the universe existed in some form for an infinite number of years in the past. In that sense, they do not believe the universe was actually created. All the pagan "creation" stories have the "gods" or the "forces" using the eternally existing "stuff" ("chaos") to shape, form, make, mold, and fashion the things in the universe to be what they are. This "stuff" might have been formless, shapeless raw matter and energy. This "stuff" might have been the body parts of the "gods" themselves. A "god" wept, and the tears became the ocean. A "god" bled, and the blood became the sun. One "god" killed another "god," and the dead "god's" body became the earth. None of them spoke about creating from nothing; only of reshaping or reforming what was already there. Only the God of the ancient Hebrews, the God of Abraham, Isaac, and Jacob spoke about the universe being created from nothing. This was a new idea when Moses wrote about it in the Book of Genesis. This brings up a second question.

If the universe began to exist at some time in the past, what (Who) caused it to exist?

The answer to this question is a logical issue because it conforms to everything we have ever observed about causes and effects. (Logic must be based on cause and effect; otherwise, it is not logic.) Every effect we have ever observed, tested, measured, and detected has been caused by something else. We have never seen uncaused effects. We have never seen an effect cause itself. In fact, science must reject those notions because science is the study of natural causes and natural effects. Science proves:

1.) Natural effects are caused by natural causes.
2.) Natural effects don't cause themselves.

You can reject these conclusions, but your rejection cannot be based on science. This doesn't mean we can't philosophically or religiously create wild scenarios about things popping into existence without causes, or things happening without causes, but such scenarios wind up being nothing more than decisions inside tiny brains. They are not truths that exist independently of the mind. They are not based on scientific observations. They are not based on anything other than what people want to believe. In fact, there are some people who claim the universe doesn't even exist. They say they believe everything we experience is an illusion, and nothing is real. Apart from having no evidence for this, they don't realize how self-contradictory their belief is. (illogic in; illogic out) If the illusion is all that exists, then by definition, the illusion is the universe, and they have solved nothing. Just ask them, "How do you perceive the illusion if it doesn't exist? How do you perceive the illusion if YOU don't exist?" If they believe the universe is an illusion, ask them, "Has the illusion always existed, or did it begin to exist?" If they say the illusion began to exist, then ask them, "What caused the illusion of the universe to begin to exist?" If they say the illusion has always existed, ask them, "How do you know it has always existed? Have you always existed, too?" Then, if you really want them to squirm, tell them to give you all their money, their car, their smartphone, their computer, their big-screen TV, their house, and all their possessions. If they truly believe what they say they believe, then they have no need for material possessions—material possessions don't exist. Who needs something that doesn't exist? They might as well give them to someone who thinks they exist... namely, you. You will expose them as the Cosmic Hypocrites they are.

The answer to whether the universe has always existed or began to exist, has an immediate impact on some of our concepts and definitions. The most important of these concepts/definitions is the meanings of the words "eternal" and "infinite." If the universe has always existed, then time and space have always existed. If this is true, then "eternal" and "infinite" are synonyms; they mean the same thing. The "eternal past" is the same thing as an infinite number of years ago. However, if the universe began to exist at some time in the past, then there can't be infinite years in the past. Time started at some time. "Before" that, there was no time. The same is true of space. Space is finite. Science shows how space came into existence from a dimensionless point and has been expanding ever since. In order for space to be infinite in size, it would have to expand for infinite years. Since time is finite, space is finite. There is a limit to the size of space. However, if the universe came into existence, then "eternal" means something different than "infinite." Infinity is an abstract concept, not a physical reality, because there can be nothing materially infinite in a finite universe. We could speak of infinite years in the past, but if time began to exist, there is no such thing as infinite years in the past. We could speak of infinite space, but if space began to exist, there is no such thing as infinite space. The same is true when speaking of infinite matter and energy. Infinity is an abstract concept that has no reality in a strictly-material universe. On the other hand, "eternal" implies a type of existence that is other-than, outside-of, and beyond time-space-matter-energy. It speaks of something supernatural, something other-than, outside-of, and beyond nature. When we speak of God being eternal, we do not mean He has existed for an infinite number of years. Instead, He exists other-than, outside-of, and beyond time and space.

The reason this is so important is because all the pagan cosmogonies (cosmogony is the study of the origin of the cosmos—the universe) and all the theories of evolution are dependent on the idea that time-space-matter-energy are infinite in some form or fashion. Even the Big Bang Theory, which speaks of the universe coming into existence fourteen billion years ago, has now been reworded to say it was caused by an infinite "sea" of fluctuating "energy" called, "The Quantum Vacuum." This belief is nothing more than a modern re-write of the ancient Chaos Theory. This belief is nothing more than a decision in the minds of those who don't want to believe the truth of the Bible. The Bible, and the religions directly and indirectly based on the Bible, hold to a belief in a Supernatural God, Who is a Person, (a mind, and not just a force) Who is eternal, Who has all power, Who has all knowledge, Who is in Sovereign control of all things, and Who created the universe and everything in it FROM nothing, but FOR something. The purpose of this book is to help you discover that something.

I can't prove it to you if you aren't willing to believe it, but I want to persuade you that the God of the Bible created you for a purpose. From before the beginning of time and space, God had a plan for you. God knew you by name. You are not who you are, where you are, and when you are by accident. You are an individual in His eyes. You have worth in His eyes. You have value in His eyes. You are loved by your Creator! God has a purpose for you, and He has a destiny for you. I want you to believe the Bible provides the answers to the questions about your purpose and your destiny. Amid all the confusion and arguments about what the Bible teaches about the creation, I believe the Gap Theory provides answers that are logically, scientifically, philosophically, and theologically true and rational. I believe the Gap Theory confirms the Gospel of Jesus Christ. If you have faith in the Person and Work of Jesus Christ, then you will enjoy life with Him in a glorious and wonderful eternal existence. **Faith in Christ has the greatest consequence of all!**

Chapter One: The Truth About Truth

What Happened When?

What really happened in the beginning? What did God do when He created things? What does the Bible say about creation? Those are big questions, and frankly, I don't have all the answers! I know some of the details, but not all. Only God knows it all. I know creation wasn't by evolution. I know God created various kinds of living things, and I know they have remained reproductively faithful within the limits He set. I know Adam and Eve were real individuals; not poetic imagery. I also know they were the parents of us all. Biblical creationists all over the world would agree with these things, but there are disagreements on the details.

One point of disagreement, for instance, is what the word "kind" means in the Bible. God created lifeforms in categories He called, "kinds," and He gave them the ability to multiply after their kind. Since God created plants and animals to reproduce in kind, some believe all the members of a kind should be cross-fertile with all the other members of the same kind. Some assume God created only a few, or even just one species in each kind. They think the different species seen in any particular kind today are the result of subsequent mutations and natural selection. For example, they assume all the various species of owls are descendants of one, or a few, original species of owl. Likewise, all the various butterflies have descended from one, or a few, original species of butterfly. But, if you assume God created only one, or a few, species per kind, you soon find yourself in an awful plight trying to explain speciation, the development of new species. You find yourself accepting the vague concept of micro-evolution. I've heard a number of creationists admit micro-evolution is true. Evolutionists love such concessions. To them, the difference between micro-evolution and macro-evolution is only a matter of degree. What one evolutionist means by micro, may be the very same thing another evolutionist means by macro. Theistic evolutionists point to the tremendous variety of species and subspecies in the taxonomic groups, and then use this as evidence for evolution. After all, if God started with only one, or a few, species per kind, and today there are numerous species per kind, then there had to be some evolutionary (change over time) process down through the ages. Whether speciation is micro-evolution or macro-evolution is unimportant. Speciation is not proof for evolution unless you first prove evolution, and ONLY evolution, created the species seen within the kinds. You would need to prove a Creator couldn't have done it. In other words, you need to prove evolution is true before you could use speciation as proof for evolution. Many creationists have had a hard time trying to explain speciation.

Now, I'm not saying there isn't such a thing as speciation. There most certainly is, but what does it prove? God describes His creation of organisms in Genesis as "kinds," but we don't know how that relates to the scientific classification system. The scientific classification system is a human-created system based on our observations of physical features. It is not the same classification system as Biblical kinds. Speciation is a biologic phenomenon, but it doesn't prove evolution, and it doesn't violate God's command of reproducing in kind. I wouldn't get too worried about speciation because all newly developed species stay within the limits of their own kind. Speciation doesn't disprove the Bible; it just messes up man's classification system. Speciation is not evidence the Bible is wrong, because the Bible doesn't define kind in scientific terms. We don't know the actual limits God placed on reproductive variability. Kind could have a number of meanings. In some cases, it may refer to Species. In other cases, it may refer to Genus. It may even refer to Family or Order sometimes. I don't think we should assume kind refers only to Species. I don't think we should try to limit God's creative abilities. Neither should we question God's choice of the word "kind" simply because it doesn't describe the Linnaean system of taxonomy. This may seem like a ridiculous point to worry about, but believe me, there are many creationists who get hung up on what the word "kind" is supposed to mean. I don't know what lifeforms He originally created, but none of them was the result of evolution. If anything, the use of the word "kind" provides three arguments against evolution. First, God did not create just one primordial kind of life; He created kinds of life. He created kinds of herbs; kinds of grass; kinds of trees; kinds of sea creatures; kinds of birds; kinds of beasts of the earth; kinds of creeping animals, and kinds of livestock. According to the Bible, there was no one, single kind; no Common Ancestor. Second, by establishing reproductive limits, the Bible says living organisms will remain in kind. One kind can never become another kind. This alone disproves evolution. Third, when God created man, He did not assign him to a kind. God uses the word "kind" for all other lifeforms; plants, fish, birds, creeping things, and mammals, but He did not do that for man. There aren't kinds of men. There are kinds of birds because there are many genera and species of birds. There are kinds of fish because there are many genera and species of fish. There are kinds of mammals because there are many genera and species of mammals. The Bible never speaks about kinds of men; humans are unique. Yes, we can place them into a man-made classification system that includes apes, monkeys, prehistoric Hominidae, *etc.*, but there is no Divinely-Given classification system that does that. Even if you interpreted the Bible to allow for the evolution of other lifeforms, the Bible never allows for the evolution of humans.

    There are a lot of disagreements about the creation, but the biggest disagreement involves the time factor. When did God create? How old is the universe? I want to share my opinion with you, but I also want to share my motive. You see, while it is important to know WHAT someone believes, sometimes it's more important to know WHY he believes it. When you learn why someone believes something, you often learn why he accepts or rejects new information. Few are willing to let new evidence change their preconceived ideas. Why am I saying this? There are two reasons.

    First, because over the years I have learned that when it comes to believing something, motive trumps facts almost every time. Television celebrity Art Linkletter once hosted a television program that included a segment called, "Kids Say the Darnedest

Things." It was a humorous look at how young children expressed their thoughts about the world around them. Equally funny would have been a segment called, "Adults Believe the Darnedest Things." People will believe and defend some of the most ridiculous ideas as long as they are motivated to do so. I have named this phenomenon, "Mental Inertia." Its definition is: An idea believed tends to stay believed, and an idea rejected tends to stay rejected. Its corollary is: It takes less evidence to convince people they are right, than to convince them they are wrong. The clearest, plainest, most-obvious fact can be ignored and rejected by the slimmest of evidence, or even no evidence, if that fact threatens a cherished opinion. My hope is that you will check your motives when faced with any evidence in this book contrary to what you believe.

The second reason I mention this, is because I haven't always believed what I now believe. At one time, I was a theistic-evolutionist. My motive was I believed in evolution. God needed billions of years to evolve life on earth. Then I learned a remarkable truth: The Theory of Evolution is a lie. **The Theory of Evolution contradicts Scripture and science.** As a result, I became a Day-Age creationist. My motive was I still believed in an old universe. While I didn't believe God EVOLVED life over billions of years, I did believe He CREATED life over billions of years. I believed the billions of years of creation were divided into six great divisions of time called, "days." I continued my studies, and I learned more. Strangely, the more I learned, the less I knew. The Bible clearly says these "days" were literal twenty-four-hour days. **The Day-Age Theory contradicts Scripture.** This led me to reject not only the Day-Age belief the "days" were ages, it led me to reject the Day-Age belief the universe was old.

Most of the creation material I was studying at that time came from Young-Earth creationists. Because of this, I became a Young-Earth creationist. I believed the Bible taught the earth was young. Later, as I probed deeper into Scripture, I became less sure of earth's age. I began to realize the Bible revealed how the earth could be much older than what the Young-Earth creationists claimed. Plus, I began to realize science unquestioningly proved the universe was billions of years old. **The Young-Earth Theory contradicts science.** What I used to know I knew, I now know I didn't know. After much study, I realized the Gap Theory made the most sense. The Gap Theory resolved a lot of disagreements, and it didn't disagree with Scriptural revelation or scientific observations.

Well, let me clarify that statement. The Gap Theory I eventually accepted doesn't disagree with science or the Bible. Like most creation theories, the Gap Theory has numerous sub-theories and variations. Some of these sub-theories and variations truly disagree with science and Scripture. Because of this, I will not try to defend all forms of the Gap Theory. I will defend only the Gap Theory that agrees with the evidence of Scripture and the evidence of science. That evidence changed my preconceived ideas, and if you disagree with the Gap Theory, I hope it will change yours as well. If our goal is to find truth about the creation, then we need to examine all the evidence. We need to examine both scientific and Scriptural evidence, and we need to study how the different schools of thought explain that evidence.

We also need to look at how the ancient Hebrews viewed the Biblical Creation Account. Even though they didn't have the scientific data we have about the creation of the universe, they had something we don't; a complete understanding of the ancient Hebrew language. Where we have Hebrew scholars and seminary professors arguing and bickering over the meanings of words and phrases in the Bible, their ten-year old children would have understood the text intuitively. For that reason, I will later mention the interpretations of three highly regarded Jewish scholars.

First, I will give a very brief quote from Louis Ginzberg (1873-1953, the well-known Jewish scholar, historian, and professor) about the Jewish view of creation.

Second, I will quote what Nahmanides (A.D. 1194-1270, Jewish philosopher, scholar, and theologian, born in Spain) said about the Jewish view of creation.

Third, I will mention Rabbi Simeon ben Jochai's (c. A.D. 100-160) interpretation of the Jewish view of creation.

I mention these three Jewish men; one from modern times, one from the Middle Ages, and one from around the time of Christ, because a crucial issue in this debate is what the Hebrews themselves historically believed about their own Hebrew Scriptures.

Now, I may not have reached the same conclusions as some of my brothers and sisters in Christ, and my theory may not agree with their theories, but that doesn't mean they aren't Christians. They are just as saved and just as loved by God as I am. If you are a believer in the Lord Jesus Christ, and you think Genesis is best interpreted by saying, "In the beginning God laid an egg and the universe hatched out," then I praise God for you, and I praise God that you are trying to defend the Bible. Furthermore, I pray you can use such an interpretation to the glory of Jesus Christ, and share the Gospel. However, if you belong to a church, denomination, or organization that makes defending a Hatched-Egg Theory more important than defending the integrity of Biblical revelation, then I have a warning for you. Be careful you don't elevate your love for scholarly recognition above your love for truth.

Divine Revelation

I want to start by discussing the nature of Divine Revelation. What does the Bible reveal about creation? There are many opinions. I have one opinion. You may have another. What is the truth about creation? **Well, a funny thing about knowing the truth is you have to know the truth, to know whether it's true or not.** For instance, if I told you I was a veterinarian, you really wouldn't know it was true unless you first knew whether or not I was a veterinarian. If you knew I was a carpenter, then you'd know my claim of being a veterinarian was a lie. If you knew I really was a veterinarian, then you'd know my claim was true. You wouldn't know the truth about my claim unless you first knew what was true. However, if you knew I was an absolute truth-teller who would never lie, then you would know I was a veterinarian simply because I revealed it to you. You wouldn't need to know my occupation in order to know my occupation. Instead of knowing something about my occupation, you'd have to know something about me. You'd have to know I was an absolute truth-teller. (Which by the way, I am not; and that's the absolute truth.) Now, don't get me wrong! I'm not trying to be relativistic and say there's no such thing as truth. Quite the contrary; there is such a thing as real, objective, absolute, universal, timeless truth... and that's the problem. The only way we can know what is true about creation is by knowing what is revealed by the only One who knows and tells the truth. We can't know it by ourselves. Only God knows the truth about creation, and only by Divine Revelation is it possible for any of us to know even the tiniest portion of the truth. Regrettably, it is the meaning of that very same Divine Revelation that causes our disagreements. This is our dilemma: Either God is a poor revealer of truth or we are poor understanders of truth............

I hope you didn't have to ponder very long on which it is. There's nothing wrong with God. God revealed the truth to us quite well, thank you! Oh, He didn't intend to reveal every facet and detail about creation. He chose to reveal only a tiny fraction. That's all our little brains could understand. However, what He revealed is true and is knowable to the limits He chooses to let us know. Beyond that, we can't know the truth. Some don't like this. Some don't like the way God reveals information to us. Believe it or not, I've read the comments of more than one creationist expressing dissatisfaction with the way God revealed information about the creation in the Bible. They think the Bible doesn't reveal enough technical information, or that it is just a bunch of simplistic statements written for simplistic nomads. Phooey! I see nothing wrong with a God who intended to reveal information in a non-technical way. Not only is it not incorrect, but it is quite clever to be able to reveal information about the creation in a way both modern man and primitive man could understand. I see nothing wrong with a perfect God who intended to reveal only a portion of the truth. I see nothing wrong with a perfect God who says, "Okay, I'll let you know this much right now, but beyond that, you'll have to wait until you are able to understand more." I see nothing wrong with a perfect God who gives a perfect revelation of truth, yet prevents it from being fully understood until the time He sees appropriate. After all, this is what He did with the Messianic prophecies. Christ was perfectly revealed in the Old Testament, but no one, not even the prophets themselves, understood all that had been revealed. Even John the Baptist didn't know what had been revealed. John didn't fully understand Jesus until after Jesus revealed to him what He had fulfilled. The prophecies came first, Christ fulfilled the prophecies next, and understanding the prophecies came last. **It wasn't until Christ fulfilled the prophecies, that the prophecies about Christ were understood.** Divine Revelation often has the mysterious quality of being fully revealed but only partially understood until such time as the Holy Spirit chooses to let it be known.

God often holds back the understanding of revelation until more information has been revealed. The Jews were looking forward to Messiah coming as the Conquering King; not as the Suffering Savior. His saving ministry was fully revealed in the Old Testament, but the revelation of the Saving Messiah wasn't understood until after the Saving Messiah was revealed. It wasn't until after God came as Savior that the saving ministry of God was comprehended. God had repeatedly told them He alone would be their Savior.

Isaiah 43:11 "I, *even* I, *am* the LORD; and beside me *there is* no saviour." (KJV)

The Jews who believed in Jesus understood this. They understood that if God was their only Savior, and if Messiah was their only Savior, then Messiah had to be God. No one else could be their only Savior. Since Messiah was the child who was born and the son who was given, (Isaiah 9:6) then He had to be a man... but this meant God had to become a man. Messiah had to be the God-Man. They understood why Jesus was both God and man. He was LORD and Messiah. That's why they accepted Him as their King. This understanding escaped the Jews who didn't believe in Jesus. They rejected what God revealed in their own Sacred Scriptures. They didn't want a Suffering Messiah for King; they wanted a Conquering Messiah for King. Rather than accept The Son of David as King, they cried out, "We have no king but Caesar." (John 19:15) In doing this, they inadvertently exposed their rejection of God's Written Word. God had told them through Moses that only an Israelite could be their king.

Deuteronomy 17:15 "You shall surely set a king over you whom the LORD your God chooses, *one* from among yourselves; you may not put a foreigner over yourselves who is not your countryman." (NASB)

By claiming Caesar as their king, they rejected Messiah as their King. They rebelled against God's Written Revelation because it was contrary to what they wanted to believe. God told them three times their King had to be Jewish: "one from among you," "not a foreigner," and "your countryman." They rejected everything God commanded. Instead of believing what the Bible ACTUALLY said, they believed what they WANTED the Bible to say. They accepted only the truth that met their criteria. It had to agree with what they wanted to believe before they would believe it: Mental Inertia. The Bible reveals not just what they believed, but why they believed it. The Jewish leaders who rejected Christ were men of power and prestige in their culture. They were the educated elite. They were honored and respected by the people, and they didn't want to lose their standing. They couldn't acknowledge that an uneducated, carpenter's son from Galilee could be Messiah the Prince. They refused to believe the Written Word had revealed such a thing. Why did they reject Jesus? If they admitted Jesus was Messiah, then they would be admitting their rejection of the Written Word. This was their motive: Their faith was not in God's Written Word, but in their own interpretation of God's Written Word. They ignored the truth that

God was capable of revealing truth in ways other than how they thought the truth should be revealed. God's revelation took on a form other than a Written Word. God's revelation became a Living Word. All they had to do was look at how Christ lived. His life revealed His Deity.

When John the Baptist was in prison, he sent his disciples to question Jesus about His identity. John knew the Written Revelation, but he still wasn't absolutely sure who Jesus was. In response, Jesus didn't send John's disciples back to him with a theological treatise. Instead, He sent them back to tell John what they saw Him DOING. (Luke 7:19-23) His Deity was revealed in what He did. They already knew the prophecies, but they didn't understand them until they saw Jesus fulfilling them. The unbelieving Jews failed to learn the truth about their Messiah because they ignored what they saw with their eyes. They clung to their preconceived ideas of what Messiah was supposed to be. He was supposed to be the Conquering King, and yes, someday He will come as the Conquering King, but He first wanted to come as the Suffering Savior. Otherwise, He would be the King of an unsaved people He would have to cast into the Lake of Fire. Unless their sins were paid for, they could not be saved. He did not come with the intention of overthrowing Rome and restoring Israel at that time. He wanted to save Israel (and all peoples) from their sins first. God gave them eyes to see this, but they refused to use them. They chose to accept only the prophecies of Messiah the Conquering King. They chose to reject and ignore the prophecies revealing Him as the Suffering Savior. They chose to believe their own preconceived ideas of how Messiah should be revealed rather than how God chose to reveal Him. God gave them a chance to learn the truth by using their eyes, but they shut their eyes to the truth. They held to their presuppositions and failed to see what God revealed. They failed to understand Messiah because they failed to understand the two revelations (Written and Living) of Messiah.

Our problem with understanding the creation is similar. We don't understand the creation because we fail to understand the two revelations (Science and Scripture) of the creation. We ignore the same two things about God the unbelieving Jews ignored.

First, we ignore the fact God reveals truth in various portions of Holy Scripture. All the truth about the Messiah was not in one portion of Scripture alone. Likewise, all the truth about creation is not in Genesis alone. If I told you I worked with animals, you wouldn't know I was a veterinarian. I might be a marine biologist, a zookeeper, or a cowboy. I would have to reveal more about my profession before you knew what I did. If I wrote you a series of letters, and each letter contained a clue to my occupation, then you'd have to assemble the letters to get a better idea of my job. You'd be foolish to read only one letter and decide what I did for a living. The same is true of creation. We need to see what the entire Bible says about it. Some people think they can take one or two sentences out of Genesis and fully comprehend the vastness of our Creator's actions and purposes. How foolish! We must look at what the whole Bible reveals. We must let it speak for itself, and we must accept everything it teaches; not just those parts that seemingly defend our preconceived ideas.

The second thing we ignore about God is that He has given us eyes to observe His handiwork and brains to understand it. Genesis 1:1 revealed the truth about the space-time continuum, but who understood it until Albert Einstein was able to deliver that knowledge to us? Einstein and other physicists made the space-time continuum a scientifically observable phenomenon, but it had been true all along. God created the space-time continuum in the beginning. Space-time physics was just as true in the time of Adam as it is today. However, God's revelation of space-time physics wasn't understood because human eyes had never observed it. The space-time continuum was an unknown phenomenon of creation even though God revealed it through Moses. Oh, a few of the great historical theologians like Nahmanides wrote about it, but they were ignored. Only after science observed it, did we realize the Bible had revealed it from the very first sentence in Genesis. The first sentence in the Book of Genesis is not a simplistic statement made by primitive nomads. It is as profound and information-laden as Einstein's formula $e=mc^2$. It is a very well-worded message that on one level reveals historic information for primitive man, but on another level, reveals scientific information for modern man.

Let me explain this very briefly. It has long been recognized by Biblical scholars, even centuries before modern science, that the Bible says God created four things in the beginning: Time, Space, Matter, and Energy. These are the four components of the physical universe. Every physical thing that exists, and every physical thing that happens is because of the interaction of these four components. In other words, the Bible hinted at, but didn't spell out, how these four components have an interdependent relationship. Then, along came Albert Einstein. He discovered how these four components are related: $e=mc^2$. In his formula, we see the four components of the physical universe: "e" is ENERGY. "m" is MATTER—mass. "c" is the speed of light measured in meters per second. Meters are a measurement of SPACE, and seconds are a measurement of TIME. $e=mc^2$ shows how these four components are related... all four components must exist simultaneously, and all four components had to come into existence simultaneously, or else the universe wouldn't exist. If space exists, then time exists. If matter exists, then energy exists. Einstein revealed that all space, time, matter, and energy came into existence simultaneously in the beginning. God's Word agrees with God's Work.

This additional scientific revelation had to wait until scientific man used his eyes and his brain to observe the universe. Ironically, the space-time continuum was one of the first things God revealed to man, but one of the last things understood. It made sense once we understood the space-time continuum. There could have been no such thing as space or time before creation. Everything but God, was made by God. Nothing but God existed prior to creation. God is spirit, not space. God is eternal, not time. God has no time or space. There would have been no space or time until Jesus brought them both into existence as the space-time continuum. This insight gives us a better understanding of the universe. It is constrained by the confines of time and space. Genesis 1:1 also helps us understand our Creator. He is not constrained by space or time. His ways are not our ways.

The Bible revealed other clues about our universe, such as the relationship between matter and energy, the force of gravity, and the principles of thermodynamics. No one recognized these things until scientists came along and gave us a greater understanding of nature. Many creationists like to use the Second Law of Thermodynamics to prove evolution couldn't have happened. I am one of them. However, I haven't forgotten it was scientists and not theologians who discovered the Second Law of Thermodynamics. The principles of thermodynamics had been revealed in the Bible for centuries, but those portions of Scripture weren't understood by theologians until after scientists discovered the principles of thermodynamics. We had to observe our universe to see how thermodynamics worked before we realized the Bible already told us how thermodynamics worked. The Second Law of Thermodynamics says the universe is wearing out. The Bible says the heavens and the earth will, "wax old like a garment"—Psalms 102:26. In other words, the universe is wearing out. The Bible gave us clues to this phenomenon, but it wasn't understood until after people used their eyes to observe it. Careful, precise observations have added to our understanding of the creation. The heavens do indeed reveal His handiwork.

Because of this, I think it is wrong to discount scientists and their observations if we want to know more about our universe and its beginning. We cannot rely on Bible scholars alone. No matter how well and how carefully the Hebrew and Greek exegetes ply their craft, they cannot reveal all that can be known about creation. Everything there is to know about creation is not found in the Bible. The Bible doesn't mention neutrinos, bosons, or anti-matter, but God still created them… and He created us with the abilities to discover them. God didn't choose to reveal quantum physics, black-holes, fundamental forces, or quark dynamics in the Bible. However, He did reveal these things by giving us eyes and ears and brains, so we could discover them as we studied His handiwork. We have learned things about the creation by careful interpretation of His Word, and we have learned things about the creation by careful observation of His Work. As truth-seeking Christians, we must believe the Bible and science harmonize, but we must be very cautious. When I say the Bible and science harmonize, I mean what the Bible truly says (not necessarily what we interpret it to say) and what science truly reveals (not just how we interpret observations) will not be contradictory. They may be complementary, but not contradictory. We need to look at both revelations of the creation. We need to look at what God reveals about the creation from the Bible. We also need to look at what God reveals about the creation from scientific observations.

All Scriptures are God-breathed, but we have to be careful in our interpretations.

The heavens declare the glory of God, but we have to be careful in our observations.

What do scientific observations reveal about the creation? We need to see what scientists have observed. More specifically, we need to see what creation-scientists, Christian men and women who are true creationists and true scientists, say they have observed. Since we're dealing with such a small group of people who all say they're trying to glorify Christ, you'd think there wouldn't be much controversy. Alas, it is not so. Battle lines have been drawn and war wages between two major camps of creation-science. These are the Young-Earth and the Day-Age camps. There are other views of creation, but creationists today generally belong to one of these two camps. The Young-Earthers believe God created the universe somewhere in the range of 6,000-8,000 years ago. Young-Earthers have dating techniques that seem to prove the earth is quite young. The Day-Agers believe creation happened about 14 billion years ago with the earth being formed about 4.5 billion years ago. Day-Agers have dating techniques that seem to prove the earth is quite old. I have read the books and heard the arguments from both sides. Both camps have some seemingly good evidence for their beliefs. Both camps use some pretty flimsy arguments as well. So, how do we determine what's true?

The best way to find truth is to approach the Bible and science from as unbiased a position as possible. This doesn't guarantee we'll make correct conclusions, but it helps eliminate blind spots in our thinking. Often, we overlook an opponent's arguments simply because we already "know" he's wrong. I shouldn't presuppose one particular interpretation of science is right or wrong until I see what the Bible truly reveals. Likewise, I shouldn't presuppose one particular interpretation of the Bible is right or wrong until I see what science truly reveals. Evolution is wrong, but that doesn't mean science is wrong. We must not automatically reject what scientists tell us about the age of the universe just because it doesn't fit our interpretation of Scripture. We can reject it if it contradicts a Biblical truth, not just a Biblical belief. (A Biblical belief is not necessarily the same thing as Biblical truth.) The best way to discover the truth about the creation is to make certain our Biblical interpretations are correct and our scientific observations are valid.

I am a creation-scientist. This means I believe we should sift our interpretations of SCIENCE through the filter of true Biblical revelation. If there are a dozen scientific theories explaining how the universe got here, we can automatically exclude those that are truly contrary to truly revealed Biblical facts.

I am a creation-scientist. This means I believe we should sift our interpretations of the BIBLE through the filter of true scientific observation. If there are a dozen theological theories explaining how the universe got here, we can automatically exclude those that are truly contrary to truly observed scientific facts.

Now, I do not believe human observation and Divine Revelation are equal in authority. Much has been said about how the domain of religion and the domain of science reveal different aspects of creation. (Science explains "how" and the Bible explains "why.") Much has been said about how science and religion should stay in their respective domains and not overlap. Much of what has been said is pure human foolishness. Human observation is limited, but Divine Revelation is only as limited as God decides it to be. When God reveals something to us, we can be sure it is true, whether or not we can verify it by scientific observations. Miracles are true even if they seem to contradict all previous human experiences. Natural observation reveals that God can create a planet with grapes growing on it, and those grapes can be used to make wine. Miraculous observation reveals that God can make wine without grapes. When Jesus made wine directly from water, it wasn't to teach us our normal observations are wrong. It was to teach us our normal observations are limited. The Bible clearly reveals that God is not a God of deception. Generally, we can trust our observations, but not always our interpretations. The only reason I can have faith in true scientific observations is because God has declared that observation is a valid system of perception. **In fact, God has declared that NATURAL observation is a valid system of SPIRITUAL perception.** The Bible tells us we can learn things about God because He has made Himself known in His works. God is revealed by the works of His hands.

Psalms 19:1-3 "For the director of music. A Psalms of David. The heavens declare the glory of God; the skies proclaim the work of his hands. *{2}* Day after day they pour forth speech; night after night they display knowledge. *{3}* There is no speech or language where their voice is not heard." (NIV)

Romans 1:20 "For since the creation of the world His invisible attributes, His eternal power and divine nature, have been clearly seen, being understood through what has been made, so that they are without excuse." (NASB)

God reveals Himself in the physical universe. Why? I believe it is for the same reason He reveals Himself in the Written Word. He wants us to discover the truth about Him. Physical observations can reveal truth about God, provided we don't superimpose our philosophies and beliefs on what we observe. "He who has eyes, let him see; and he who has ears, let him hear," are not wasted words. **What the eyes see and the ears hear, the heart can twist.** We're all good at doing this. My faith in observation isn't founded on the assumption that observations are inherently reliable. My faith in observation is founded on the belief that God hasn't created an observable universe merely to trick us, confuse us, and lead us into ignorance. When I see a rock, I can be certain the rock exists, because I have first assumed God isn't a God of confusion and deception. When scientists make true scientific observations, I can be certain what they observe is true because of that same basic assumption. If you are a creationist, I implore you not to reject what scientists discover when they observe the universe. God just might be revealing His invisible attributes. He just might want you to discover the truth about Him. He just might want you to discover He is the God of Restoration.

I remember reading the comments of some creationists who were overjoyed when scientists discovered the Hubble Space Telescope had a defective lens soon after it was launched into orbit. They boldly claimed it was God's will for the Hubble Project to fail. In truth, they were afraid of what scientists might learn about the universe. They were afraid of what the universe might reveal about its origin. Can you believe that? They were afraid of what God's handiwork might display. How foolish! The things we have learned from the Hubble Telescope, once its lens was corrected, have been a tremendous scientific apologetic for the Bible. I would ask my readers to review their motives very carefully before they reject what scientists have observed in our universe that might indicate its age. What science has revealed about the age of the universe may provide the key needed to unlock the truth about creation… and, the truth about our Creator.

That, my friends, is all I'm going to say about the age of the universe for now. I'll reopen this subject later, but if you want more details, go to your local Christian bookstore. You will find plenty of books about the age of the universe. Be warned! Opinions vary tremendously. There are a great number of books defending the views of the Day-Age gang, and there are a great number of books defending the views of the Young-Earth gang. There are also a few others that don't quite fit either view. Some of them are quite interesting.

Chapter Two: The Creation Combo Special

I would like to present all the different beliefs about the Biblical account of creation, but I don't want to get tangled up in the theories, sub-theories, and variables fought over in the past. There's no future in reliving the past. It would be too complex, and it would make this book so long, even I wouldn't read it. So, instead of trying to examine every possible variable, let's look at four major questions concerning the creation account. It is the disagreement over these four questions about the creation that has led to the various creation theories. If we can determine how the Bible truly answers these four questions, then we will be much more likely to understand what the Bible truly reveals about the creation. Here are the four questions:

1. What does "day" mean?
2. What does "create" mean?
3. What does "beginning" mean?
4. How does Genesis 1:1 relate to the rest of the chapter?

Each of these four questions involves different aspects of creation. Each has multiple variables, and the variables aren't necessarily mutually exclusive. Pick one variable from each of these four questions and you can create your own creation theory. It would be too confusing and time consuming to sort through all the combinations. Instead, let's look at how some of the more prominent theories fit together. Here are the variables in outline form. A more detailed explanation of these variables follows the outline. Refer back to this outline if things get confusing. Hopefully, it will help keep it all in perspective.

I. THE MEANING OF "DAY"

A. Day-Age
    1. Progressive Creation Theory
    2. Punctuated Creation Theory
B. Twenty-Four-Hour Day
    1. Old-Universe
        a. Single Gap Theory
        b. Multiple Gaps Theory
    2. Young-Earth Theory
C. Days of Relativity
D. Days of Revelation
E. Days of Divine Decrees
F. Repeated Days/Framework Theory

II. THE MEANING OF "CREATE"

A. Form/Fashion/Shape Co-Eternal Matter and Energy
B. Creation *EX NIHILO*

III. THE MEANING OF "BEGINNING"

A. Long Period of Time
B. Instantaneous Point of Time

IV. HOW GENESIS 1:1 RELATES TO THE REST OF THE CHAPTER

A. Title
B. Summary
C. Creative Act
    1. First Part of Day One
    2. Before Day One

    Now let's look at the details:

I. The Meaning of "Day"

A1. Day-Age, Progressive Creation Theory

2 Peter 3:8 "But, beloved, be not ignorant of this one thing, that one day *is* with the Lord as a thousand years, and a thousand years as one day." (KJV)

    Day-Age creationists point to this verse as proof the word "day" is only symbolic. It can mean any period of time, including billions of years. According to this theory, Genesis describes the creation of the universe, the earth itself, and life on earth. Creation is a very slow process taking place over several billion years. The Big Bang Theory fits nicely with this theory. The creation is divided into smaller periods called, "days," that are themselves millions or billions of years long. The "days" represent general types or categories of God's creative acts. During the course of the "days" God gradually and progressively created, but did not evolve, the lifeforms that have lived on this planet. He gradually created new species and gradually destroyed old species. According to this theory, the geological strata were gradually formed during those long day-ages.

    This theory is very popular and is defended by a very large number of very good Christians. While it is a creation theory, it can be so close to Theistic Evolution you might confuse the two. In fact, if the Progressive Creation events were gradual enough, it would be impossible from the geological evidence to distinguish Progressive Creation from Theistic Evolution. (Theistic Evolution is the theory that life on earth actually evolved by natural forces, but it was all planned by God.) As scientific as this theory seems, it doesn't allow us to redefine the meaning of "day" in Genesis. The argument it can mean a long period of time is an extremely weak argument because it works only if you don't analyze it. It sounds good on the surface, but when you dig deeper, it falls apart. I don't think most Day-Age creationists have thoroughly investigated this argument before accepting it as "proof." Why doesn't this argument prove what they want it to? There are two reasons.

1.) The descriptions in Genesis are given from an earthly perspective, thereby forcing us to accept an earthly frame of reference in both space and time. These are earth days. God is outside of space and time. God is eternal and has no single frame of reference for time and space. He is not limited or restricted by space and time. He is omnipresent and omnitemporal. As such, He experiences all space-time frames simultaneously. (Actually, "experiences" is not the right word to describe God's relationship with space-time, but I don't know how else to describe it. Maybe in heaven there will be a word defining how God simultaneously causes and experiences space-time.) Peter is describing how God "views" time outside time and space; not how time passes inside time and space. **2 Peter 3:8 has nothing to do with when or how creation happened.** 2 Peter 3:8 is God's "view" of time. Outside of time, there can be no first, second, third, fourth, *etc.* days of time, or years of time, or ages of time, because there is no time. What would "the first day" of eternity mean? Or, what would the "second age" of eternity mean? Such time-dependent terms mean nothing in a timeless existence. The Genesis Creation Account, although given by God, is given from an earthly, time-space perspective. God describes the creation events of the six days as if you were standing on the earth and watching what was happening around you. You would see the sun, and then you would see the moon and the stars. You would see dawn, and then you would see dusk. You would see day, and then you would see night. Again, the six days of creation are viewed from inside time and space. Inside time and space, a day is still a day, and a thousand years is still a thousand years.

2.) Peter uses a literary device known as a simile. So does Moses in Psalms 90:4 where he revealed this same truth about God.

Psalms 90:4 "For a thousand years, in thy sight, are as yesterday when it is past, and *as* a watch in the night." (KJV)

Similes are used to show similarities between objects, ideas, events, *etc*. Similes express SIMILARITIES, but not EQUALITIES. The key to interpreting these verses is to recognize they are not saying one day is equal to one thousand years. (If they were, then both the Young-Earth Theory and the Day-Age Theory are still wrong. If each "day" equaled one thousand years, then the six "days" of creation would have been six thousand years, not 144 hours as the Young-Earthers tell us, and not fourteen billion years as the Day-Agers say.) As you can see, both Moses and Peter use the word "as" to compare how God "views" time, to how we view time. How God "views" time is similar but not equivalent to how we view time.

2 Peter 3:8 "But, beloved, be not ignorant of this one thing, that one day *is* with the Lord AS a thousand years, and a thousand years AS one day." (KJV)

Psalms 90:4 "For a thousand years, in thy sight, are AS yesterday when it is past, and *AS* a watch in the night." (KJV)

Since both men use a simile, and not an equality, we know they know one day is not equal to one thousand years. One day is one day, and a thousand years is a thousand years. They are not saying they are equal. They are not telling us a short period of time is a long period of time. They don't confuse the two periods of time. They know a short period of time is a short period of time, and a long period of time is a long period of time. **The point of these passages is to tell us something about God**, not something about the passage of time. Let me repeat:

THE POINT OF THESE PASSAGES IS
TO TELL US SOMETHING ABOUT GOD

In fact, point this is so important, I will repeat it again.

THE POINT OF THESE PASSAGES IS
TO TELL US SOMETHING ABOUT GOD

This point is so important, I will repeat it again… at the end of the book. At that point, I will tie it into what the Gap Theory reveals about God. When you see that connection, you will see why these verses have nothing to do with the creation of the universe, but with its destiny. These verses are telling us how God "causes/experiences" time in a way we can't experience. While God might "view" one day as a thousand years from His perspective outside of time and space, it is still one day inside time and space. God also "views" one day as a billion years. God also "views" one day as a millisecond. God also "views" one day as one day. What gives us the right to pick just one of these frames of reference, and say this is how God views time? To God, the fourteen billion years since the Big Bang has been only seven days. But, to God, the fourteen billion years since the Big Bang has been only seven seconds. To God, the seven seconds it takes you to read this sentence has been fourteen billion years. The Day-Age Theory depends on the idea that a long period of time inside time and space must ALWAYS be equivalent to a short period of time in God's frame of reference. That works only if God has a limited frame of reference for time. A "day" to God must always be a long period of physical time, or this argument for the Day-Age Theory is without merit. Again, Moses and Peter are not telling us something about creation. We miss their point if we try to use these verses to defend the Day-Age Theory.

Day-Age creationists point to two events in the Genesis account of creation to defend their belief the days are long ages. The first is found in Genesis 2:19.

Genesis 2:19 "And out of the ground the LORD God formed every beast of the field, and every fowl of the air; and brought *them* unto Adam to see what he would call them: and whatsoever Adam called every living creature, that *was* the name thereof." (KJV)

There are millions of species of animals (six million species of insects alone) and if Adam named them all, it would have taken decades, to do it. Day-Age creationists say there was no possibility Adam could have done it in less than one day. I would agree with them if God brought every species to Adam, but the Bible doesn't say He did that. What does "every" mean when it says Adam named every living creature? Does it mean he named every individual animal? Does it mean he named every Species of animals? Does it mean he named every Genus of animals? Does it mean he named every Family of animals? How about Order, Class, or Phylum? It doesn't say. Using the Bible's own "classification system," did God bring every "kind" of animal to Adam? No. It mentions how Adam named livestock, beasts of the field and the birds of the air. It doesn't mention fish of the sea, great whales, and things that creep along the ground. If God brought every living creature to Adam for him to name, Adam would have needed a magnifying glass and a microscope to accomplish the task. I don't get the impression God brought Humpback Whales or microscopic soil nematodes to Adam to be named.

If you still insist Adam named every land animal, I can still show you why it wouldn't have taken long for Adam to do it. I'm going to give a name to every land animal, and if you'll get a stopwatch, you can measure how long it takes. Ready? Here I go: worm... amphibian... arthropod... reptile... bird... mammal... there, I'm done! I just gave a name to every land animal. How long did it take me? You see the problem with their argument. Their conclusion collapses under the weight of its own assumption. It's a weak argument. How long it took Adam to name every animal depends on what "every" means. Weak arguments never make a strong defense.

Some Day-Age creationists say it would have taken Adam years to study the animals before he could have given them names. This assumes Adam needed years of study before he could call a cow, a "cow." They must know something about Adam that God never revealed in the Bible. How long did Adam study the animals before giving them names? The Bible doesn't tell us. Does the name of an animal always relate to some physical fact about the animal that requires study? Was Adam so dull-witted or so limited in vocabulary skills he couldn't have looked at an animal and instantly given it a name? Why would it take years? Their speculation about Adam's limited vocabulary ability does not provide a real defense for their theory. Speculation never does.

Day-Age creationists often point to another Genesis event that "proves" the sixth "day" was longer than one day. It was when God created Eve.

Genesis 2:21 "And the LORD God caused a deep sleep to fall upon Adam, and he slept: and he took one of his ribs, and closed up the flesh instead thereof;" (KJV)

Every surgeon knows it would take more than one day for the flesh to heal. Since it would have taken a minimum of ten to fourteen days for the surgery site to heal, Day-Age creationists believe "day" six was a long period of time. If the flesh healed in a "day," then this "day" couldn't have been one, literal twenty-four-hour day.

Really? You know, we're talking about Dr. God! Genesis 2:21 says God closed the flesh after taking Adam's rib. It doesn't say He put in stitches, or staples, or used surgical adhesive. I think I would be a little embarrassed if I tried to limit God's healing ability, just so I could defend my beliefs. Tell me then, how many days did it take Jesus to heal Malchus' ear in the Garden of Gethsemane after Simon Peter cut if off with his sword? (Luke 22:51) How many days did it take Lazarus to walk again after Jesus commanded him to come out of the tomb? (John 11:43) After being four-days-dead in the tomb, Lazarus' muscles, vascular supply, and nerves would have been rotting. Jesus bypassed not only the tissue regeneration phase of healing, He bypassed the physical therapy phase. By saying God couldn't have healed Adam instantaneously, Day-Age creationists allow atheists to ridicule Jesus. If God couldn't instantaneously heal Adam, why are we to believe Jesus instantaneously healed Malchus and Lazarus? Creationists should think before they argue.

I don't accept the Day-Age Theory because I am fully convinced these days were twenty-four-hour days. In addition, the Day-Age Theory has three problems with geology. I'll explain these problems in the next chapter, but for now, here they are:

1.) The order in which fossils appear in Geology does not match the order of creation in Genesis.
2.) It doesn't explain gaps in the fossil record.
3.) It doesn't explain Living Fossils. (Species once thought to be extinct for millions of years, but found to be alive today.)

A2. Day-Age, Punctuated Creation Theory

This is similar to the above theory. The universe is billions of years old, but in this case, God made it in bursts of creative acts. God periodically came to earth to create new lifeforms, and possibly to destroy older ones. Again, the six "days" of creation are six long ages representing six general types or categories of God's creative works. However, He didn't gradually or continually create new lifeforms during each "day." Instead, He would come from time to time during each period to create a few new things, and then quit for a while. As a result, life was directly created in a punctuated fashion; not gradually, and not by evolution. This creationists' theory is equivalent to the evolutionists' Punctuated Equilibria Theory of Evolution. (I'll explain Punctuated Equilibria later.) In fact, it becomes difficult to distinguish between Punctuated Evolution and Punctuated Creation if you rely on the physical evidence alone. This theory is also believed by a lot of good Christians. On the positive side, it explains the gaps in the fossil record, but it suffers from the other two geological problems. The "days" are still in the wrong order and it can't explain Living Fossils .

B1a. Twenty-Four-Hour Day, Single Gap Theory

According to this theory, the six days of Genesis refer to what God created long after He originally created the universe. The six days are literal twenty-four-hour days, but God didn't begin those six days until long after He first created the universe. Let me explain.

In Genesis 1, each day begins with, "and God said, let...," and each day ends with, "and the evening and the morning were the _____ day." Genesis 1:1 begins and ends with no such statements; therefore, the creation of the heavens and the earth is not part of the first day. It came before the first day. The six days of creation begin later with, "And God said, let there be light...." Simply put, Genesis 1:1 describes the original creation of the universe. This is followed by a gap of time after which God performs the creative acts mentioned in the six literal days of Genesis 1:3-31, the second creation. It may or may not be assumed God originally created the heavens and the earth by means of the Big Bang over billions of years. However, when it came to restoring the earth and creating the lifeforms now on it, those creative acts were done within 144 hours. This is an essential part of the Gap Theory. When we examine the science of this theory, we will see it poses no problems with the geological record.

B1b. Twenty-Four-Hour Day, Multiple Gaps Theory

This is somewhat of a combination of the last two theories. The "days" were literal days, but there wasn't a single gap of time between the original creation of the universe and a re-creation of the earth. There was no re-creation of the earth because there was no destruction of the earth. Instead, there were long gaps of time between each of the six literal twenty-four-hour days. This means the universe can be billions of years old. God initially performed creative acts during the twenty-four-hour period of the first day. Then there was a gap of millions or billions of years followed by another twenty-four-hour period of creation called, "the second day." This was followed by another gap of millions or billions of years, *etc.* The heavens, the earth, and all life were created in six literal twenty-four-hour days, but nothing in the Bible says they had to be consecutive days. All of God's creative acts were performed in six, literal, twenty-four-hour days, but millions or billions of years passed between each of those literal days. This theory explains gaps in the fossil record extremely well, but it has the same two problems with geology the Day-Age Punctuated Creation Theory has. It doesn't explain Living Fossils, and the order of the geological layers is not correct.

B2. Twenty-Four-Hour Day, Young-Earth Theory

This theory says God created the universe, the earth, and life on the earth in six twenty-four-hour days, sometime in the last few to several thousand years. Over a period of 144 hours, God started and finished all the works of creation. Most Young-Earth creationists believe the creation was somewhere around 6,000 to 8,000 years ago. Two versions of the Young-Earth Theory have been developed. The Historic Young-Earth Theory was one of the most accepted interpretations for millennia, but it fell into disfavor as scientific evidence seemed to indicate the universe was billions of years old. It has been replaced by the Modern Young-Earth Theory.

What is the difference between the Historic and the Modern Young-Earth Theories? Originally, the Historic Young-Earth Theory proposed that all the geologic strata and fossils were created between the time of Adam's Fall and the time of Noah's Flood. But, this caused a problem with the geologic strata. There wasn't enough time between Adam and the Flood to create all the fossils and all the strata. Science said it took millions of years. Today, Modern Young-Earth creationists recognize that problem, but explain the fossils by an idea called, "Flood-Geology." Flood-Geology is the belief that all the geologic strata and all the fossils were laid down by the Great Flood of Noah's day. (I'll tell you all about this in Chapter Five.) Historic Young-Earth creationists weren't Flood Geologists. Today, Young-Earthers are Flood-Geologists by necessity. If Flood-Geology falls apart, then the Young-Earth Theory falls apart. I believe Flood-Geology falls apart. In spite of its very many errors, very many, very good, very devoted, very intelligent, and very loving Christians believe it. I once believed it many years ago, but that was before I put it to the scientific and Biblical tests. When I did that, I discovered it was very wrong.

C. Days of Relativity

This is an interesting explanation of the six days of creation. According to the principles of relativity, the passage of time depends on your physical frame of reference. The Bible says:

2 Peter 3:8 "But, beloved, be not ignorant of this one thing, that one day *is* with the Lord as a thousand years, and a thousand years as one day." (KJV)

We see the same verse, 2 Peter 3:8, used to defend a different creation theory. (Isn't the Bible amazing?) It is similar to the Day-Age Theory, but if differs in that it doesn't compare God's "view" of time to our view of time. Instead, it allows for the same period of physical time to be viewed in more than one physical way. A thousand years in one physical frame of reference might be a day in another physical frame of reference, and this is the key, some say, to understanding the days of Genesis.

Although this verse has nothing to do with creation, Peter reveals something about time that wasn't known, and couldn't have been known, by the people of his day. Peter reveals that time is relative. He does this by using a second literary device known as a "parallelism." A parallelism is when a statement is made about something, and then a second statement is made that expresses the very same thought, but in slightly different words. For example:

Isaiah 42:13 "The LORD will go forth like a warrior, He will arouse *His* zeal like a man of war. He will utter a shout, yes, He will raise a war cry. He will prevail against His enemies." (NASB)

Actually, two parallelisms are used in this verse.

1.) Statement A—"Arousing His zeal like a man of war," is a parallel statement of Statement B—"going forth like a warrior."

2.) Statement A—"He will utter a shout," is a parallel statement of
Statement B—"He will raise a war cry."

In each parallelism, Statement A is the same thing as Statement B, and Statement B is the same thing as Statement A.

Peter does something a little different here. He does not express the two periods of time as a parallelism. Instead, he expresses them as a paradox. In order for them to be parallel, Peter would have had to say something like, "A day is as a thousand years, and a year is as a thousand centuries." Peter would have to say a short period of time is a long period of time, and a long period of time is an even longer period of time. He doesn't say that. He says a short period is a long period AND/BUT a long period is a short period. Something is the same thing as its opposite at the same time; that's a paradox. The paradox is solved if time is relative. If time was an absolute, then what Peter said couldn't be true. Peter revealed this principle of relativity long before Einstein was born. This is an example of how God often revealed true principles of science in the Bible long before they were discovered by man. Science has shown how the passage of time is relative based on relative velocity. The faster you travel, the slower you experience time. An astronaut traveling at near-light speed could go to a distant star and back in only a few years of his time, but hundreds or even thousands of years would pass on earth. The amount of time it takes the astronaut to complete his trip depends on which frame of reference is used. At his velocity relative to the earth, his time would run slower than earth time. A short period of physical time to the astronaut would be a long period of physical time to people on earth. Paradox solved!

Not only does velocity affect the passage of time, so does gravity. The greater the gravity, the slower time passes. Both kinds of time-dilation, velocity and gravity, have been verified in experiments using atomic clocks. Atomic clocks at sea-level, atomic clocks on tops of mountains, and atomic clocks in orbit around the earth will measure the same period of time differently. For example, one second at sea level might be equal to one second plus a few nanoseconds, a couple of hundred miles in orbit. It is the same period of time, but how long that period of time is, depends on the frame of reference.

This theory proposes that in the beginning, the passage of time on the earth was different than the passage of time in the rest of the universe. One way to accomplish this task is to assume that when God created the earth, He made gravity billions of times stronger on the earth than in the rest of the universe. That way, seven twenty-four-hour days would pass on earth, while at the same time, fourteen-billion years would pass in the rest of the universe.

I'm sure you physicists see a problem. How could the earth experience gravity that was billions of times stronger than it is today, yet remain the earth? Such a massive gravitational force would crush the earth into a dwarf-star. The excess heat due to the excess gravity would cause the elements to undergo fusion. Such an "earth" could not be covered by water because the hydrogen in the water would be fused into helium. Nor, could the "earth" be dark. The energy released by that hydrogen fusion would create the same light the sun creates.

I'm sure you astronomers see another problem. In order for the sun to provide light by day, and the moon to provide light by night, the supposed immense gravitational force would have to include the sun and the moon. They would have to be experiencing the exact same time-dilation as the earth. Unfortunately for the earth, if this were true, then the gravitational attraction between the moon and the earth, and the gravitational attraction between the earth and the sun, would be a billion times stronger. The moon would be instantly pulled to the earth, and together they would be instantly pulled into the sun. If the sun and the moon were created on Day Four, the earth would end on Day Four. God's pronouncement that Day Four was, "good," would make no sense.

I'm sure you biologists see yet another problem. This theory requires the same massive gravitational force for all six days, in order for the same degree of time-dilation to be experienced for all six days. Therefore, on Day Five, when God created fish and birds, they would have been subjected to gravity billions of times stronger than today. If that happened, fish would instantly be smashed to the bottom of the ocean and birds would crash to the ground, unable to fly. On Day Six, all the livestock, beasts of the field, and creeping things, would be flatter than pancakes. Adam would have had a hard time naming them, not just because they were flat, but because the extra gravity would cause an atmospheric pressure so high, Adam couldn't have forced air out of his lungs to speak their names. In fact, he wouldn't be able to live; the oxygen/carbon dioxide exchange system in hemoglobin would completely fail at that pressure. This idea doesn't work.

D. Days of Revelation

This theory proposes that God revealed the creation story to Moses over a six-day period, and then rested from His revelation on the seventh day. According to this theory, there weren't six days of creation; there were six days in which God revealed what He had created. In other words, God met with Moses over a six-day period to reveal the details of creation. It took six days for God to give an account to Moses about what He had created in the beginning. (Creation itself could have taken billions of years.) For example: On the third day, God gave the account to Moses that He had created vegetation, plants, and trees on the earth. God didn't create or make vegetation on the third day; He only revealed this account to Moses on the third day of their time together. This idea stems from an interpretation of Genesis 2:4.

Genesis 2:4 "This is the account of the heavens and the earth when they were created, in the day that the LORD God made earth and heaven." (NASB)

The word translated "account" is plural. It should say, "These are the accounts…" We're told to believe the six days are days of accounts, not days of creation. This would be an acceptable explanation if it didn't contradict Scripture. Exodus 20:11 and other passages clearly tell us the six days refer to what God made.

Exodus 20:11 "For in six days the LORD made the heavens and the earth, the sea and all that is in them, and rested on the seventh day; therefore the LORD blessed the Sabbath day and made it holy." (NASB)

Exodus 20:11 doesn't say, "In six days the Lord gave an account of making the heavens and the earth…" It says the Lord made the heavens and the earth in six days. Actually, Genesis 2:4 does reveal something interesting about the creation by using *TOWLEDAH*, (Strong's Number H8435) the Hebrew word for "generations," "genealogies," "histories," or "accounts." I'll come back to Genesis 2:4 later in the book, but for now, Genesis 2:4 cannot be used as evidence that God took six days to tell Moses the story of creation.

E. Days of Divine Decrees

This is another interesting idea. According to this interpretation, God made six great decrees before time began. Each decree began with, "Let there be…," or the equivalent statement. These decrees were made over a six-day period, so that one decree was made per day. Since God is eternal and omnipotent, as far as He was concerned, making the decree was as good as actually creating the thing He decreed. Since the decrees took six days, God views creation as being six days. The actual formation of the universe could have been any length of time.

Regrettably, this view contradicts itself. If these decrees were made before time, then there was no such thing as six days. "Six days" measures a passage of time, but if time wasn't yet created, days couldn't pass, and it couldn't have taken God six days to make the decrees. If six days of time had passed, then the time-space continuum was already created. Further, there is nothing indicating God is talking about anything else but twenty-four-hour earth days. The mention of mornings and evenings (sunrise and sunset) proves these are earth days viewed from an earthly reference; not from Heaven. (There are no nights in Heaven.) These are earth days, and it would be hard to have earth days if the earth wasn't yet created.

F. Repeated Days (Framework Theory)

Those who believe the Framework Theory think there were only three creation "days" and not six. It's called the Framework Theory because it is based on the way its proponents say Genesis 1 is constructed (framed). They see a symmetry in the way God created things. They say Genesis 1 is laid out in two sets of triads of "days." According to this theory, "day" four is a parallel description of "day" one; "day" five parallels "day" two; and "day" six is the same "day" as "day" three. Their rationale is that "day" one and "day" four both describe the creation of light. "Day" one says, "Let there be light," while "day" four says, "Let there be lights in the firmament…" "Day" two and "day" five describe what God did with the waters. "Day" two describes God separating the waters from the waters; while "day" five describes God letting the waters bring forth sea creatures. Finally, "day" three describes the emergence of dry land and the creation of plant life on dry land, while "day" six describes the creation of animal life on dry land. Technically, this theory doesn't exactly say what "day" means. It could mean a short period, but Framework creationists almost always insist the "days" are Day-Ages. One of the primary reasons this theory was proposed is because plants were made on "day" three but the sun wasn't made until "day" four. Proponents find it hard to believe plants could exist for millions of years before the sun. Making "day" four the same as "day" one alleviates this problem. In other words, "Day One-Four" came before "Day Two-Five," which came before "Day Three-Six." This parallelism theory sounds good, but it also contradicts Exodus 20:11. Whatever the "days" were, there were six of them, not three. To its credit, it fits the geological record a little better. It describes the sun, moon, and stars existing before plant life, and aquatic life coming before terrestrial life. So, while it seems to alleviate one problem, it creates another problem. If "day" five is the same "day" as "day" two, then it means fish and birds were created on the same "day" ("Day Two-Five") long before dry land and plants were created on "Day Three-Six." That's no problem for fish, but if birds were created on "Day Two-Five," then birds had to fly around for millions of years before they could build nests, lay eggs, or even sleep. I bet they were very tired by the time God created dry land on "Day Three-Six." (And hungry too. All the seed-eating and nectar-feeding birds wouldn't have been able to eat for millions of years.) The creation of birds before the appearance of dry land creates a huge scientific problem in the imagined symmetry of the Framework Theory. Birds are predominately land animals. If the symmetry of the Framework Theory was true, God would have created birds on "day" six with the rest of the land animals.

The Other Three Variables

The theories listed above are the major theories dealing with whether the "days" are long periods of time, literal twenty-four-hour days, or something else. What follows are some of the theories dealing with the other questions about creation. Remember, these other variables are independent of the meaning of "day." Sometimes people will make it seem as if you have to accept one particular meaning of "day" before you can accept some of these other variables. This isn't true. If you will take the time to meditate on these ideas, you will understand how you can blend many of them with almost any definition of "day." Taking into consideration just the four questions and the variables I listed, you can come up with 108 creation permutations. We won't do that.

II. The Meaning of "Create"

A. Form/Fashion/Shape Co-Eternal Matter and Energy

This idea says Genesis describes the formation of the universe and the earth, but not their actual creation. Matter and energy, time and space, the fundamental particles and the fundamental forces of nature were already present. In fact, they had been eternally present when God began to work on them to fashion a cosmos out of chaos.

(Note: "Chaos" has both a vague and a specific definition depending on how it is used. I do not like to apply the word "chaos" in reference to the creation because such a thing cannot exist from God's perspective. I am forced to use the word because it has become a traditionally accepted definition of *TOHUW WA-BOHUW*—"without form and void" in Genesis.—or *TOHU WAW BOHU*, or *TOHU VA-BOHU*, or *TOHU VAV BOHU*, or however your favorite Hebrew scholar transliterates and pronounces the Hebrew: תהו ובהו. I will say more about "chaos" at the end of this chapter.)

According to this view, "create" means to form out of preexisting matter and energy. Creation in this sense describes the new things God made from eternally preexisting matter and energy. Any interpretation of "day" could fit with this theory. We can describe God as working on co-eternal matter and energy over billions of years to form the universe. We can also describe God as quickly working on co-eternal matter and energy to form the universe in six days. This theory runs counter to what cosmologists and astrophysicists tell us about matter and energy. Since the universe is expanding and its entropy (thermodynamic disorder) is increasing, it cannot have been here for eternity. Simply put, nothing natural can be eternal. (And the Bible has been telling us this for thousands of years.)

B. Creation *EX NIHILO*

The Latin phrase *EX NIHILO* (out of nothing) describes how everything was created out of absolutely nothing by an eternal, supernatural God. (I say, "absolutely nothing," because atheists nowadays use a skewed definition of "nothing" in order to defend their rejection of God. They say God didn't create everything; they say "nothing" created everything. They define "nothing" as a Quantum Vacuum. They say the universe came out of a Quantum Vacuum. What is a Quantum Vacuum? It supposedly is an eternal and infinite "sea" of fluctuating energy fields producing virtual waves and virtual particles that cease to exist as quickly as they come into existence. In other words, their "nothing" is not nothing.) Proponents of the *EX NIHILO* Theory say there was no preexisting matter, energy, space, or time; God created them all out of nothing. This theory can also be blended with any definition of "day." God could have created everything out of nothing over billions of years, or He could have created everything out of nothing during six twenty-four-hour days.

III. The Meaning of "Beginning"

A. Long Period of Time

This view says "the beginning" refers to the creation of the universe over a long period of time. God initially created the raw materials, but put nothing into shape; nothing was complete. At first, there were no stars, planets, *etc*. Creation started with the creation of time, space, matter, and energy. This was followed by the creation/formation of the stars, the galaxies, the sun, the earth, and all the rest. This theory does not necessarily imply that after creating the raw matter and energy, God let nature run its course. It allows for God to perform creative acts in the process. Genesis 1:1 encompasses God's creative acts up to the point of the earth being without form, and void. This theory is usually combined with the Day-Age Theory because it fits extremely well with the Big Bang Theory. It also fits extremely well with the Gap Theory.

B. Instantaneous Point of Time

This view says "the beginning" was an instantaneous point of time. Genesis 1:1 describes an instantaneous creation of the universe. What the universe contained is not specified. Some say the stars, galaxies, the sun, *etc*. Others say nothing but space and the earth. They say the earth was created instantly, but it was created without form, void, and covered by water. Genesis 1:3-31 describes what God did after the initial creation of an otherwise complete universe. This theory does not fit with the Big Bang Theory. All theories that hold to an instantaneous, intact creation of the heavens and the earth must reject what astronomers and cosmologists have observed about the origin of stars and galaxies. They also must reject what we learn about the stars and galaxies from their present-day appearances, movements, and locations. **Where the stars appear today are not where they are today.** Where they appeared a thousand years ago was not where they were a thousand years ago. Where they appeared four thousand years ago was not where they were four thousand years ago. Where they appeared on Day Four was not where they were on Day Four. Their movements and velocities we measure today are not their actual movements and velocities of today. Likewise, their observed chemical compositions (based on luminosities and spectral analyses) are what they were thousands, millions, and billions of years ago. The things we see today are things from long, long ago.

IV. How Genesis 1:1 Relates to the Rest of the Chapter

A. Title

This theory says that, "In the beginning God created the heavens and the earth," is merely the title. Genesis 1:1 is not an act of creation. Those who believe this interpretation must also believe Genesis 1:2 is a subtitle. Otherwise, the Creation Account actually begins in Genesis 1:2 with the formless, void, dark, and water-covered earth already in existence. This view says Genesis 1:2 describes what earth was like when God began to "create," but it never describes how it got to be that way. A good example of this is seen in *The Moffatt Bible*. James Moffatt moved the verses around so the first part of Genesis is a title or introduction.

Genesis 1:1 "This is the story of how the universe was formed. When God began to form the universe, the world was void and vacant, darkness lay over the abyss." (MB)

Note the use of the words "formed" and "form," instead of "created" and "create." In other words, Genesis 1:1 is not an act of creation. The earth was already without form, and void when God began to form the universe. So, rather than being an act of creation, Genesis 1:1 is a title, and Genesis 1:2 is subtitle for the acts of creation that follow. This idea doesn't say what happened, or how God created things. The "creation" starts with the creation of light in a preexisting universe; the heavens, the earth, and the deep already exist. This idea can be combined with either the Day-Age Theory or the Young-Earth Theory. It blends nicely with the Co-Eternal Matter Theory, but it can also be combined with The *EX NIHILO* Theory if God had created everything out of nothing before Genesis 1:1, but didn't tell us about it in Scripture. This idea does not fit with the Gap Theory. The Gap Theory agrees Genesis 1:1 describes the original creation, but not the six-day restoration that followed much later.

B. Summary

This view holds that Genesis 1:1-2 is a summary of the events of the six "days." In other words, Genesis 1:1-2 and Genesis 1:3-31 are parallel descriptions of the same events. They describe the same creative acts but with a different emphasis. Genesis 1:1-2 is the summary, and Genesis 1:3-31 are the details. There is a Biblical problem with this idea. The summary doesn't agree with the details, but I'll talk more about that later. As it stands, this sub-theory can be combined with either the Day-Age Theory or the Young-Earth Theory, and with either the *EX NIHILO* Theory or the Co-Eternal Matter and Energy Theory. Genesis 1:1-2 could be a summary of what God did over billions of years, or Genesis 1:1-2 could be a summary of what God did over six literal days. The earth could have been created without form, and void, or the earth could have been without form, and void for all eternity. This idea doesn't fit the Gap Theory either.

C. A Creative Act

The thought here is that Genesis 1:1 describes a creative act or acts that chronologically came before the creative acts of Genesis 1:3-31. Genesis 1:1 doesn't say when it happened or how long it took, but it was a creative act of God. This was followed in time by His other acts of creating, making, and forming. The question then arises, "What is the chronological relationship between Genesis 1:1 and the six days of creation?" There are two possibilities:

C1. Genesis 1:1 Is the First Part of the First Day

Both the Young-Earth and the Day-Age Theories generally try to incorporate Genesis 1:1-2 into the six days of creation. They want to make Genesis 1:1-2 the first part of the first day, but that doesn't work. As I mentioned, Genesis 1:1 doesn't start with, "And God said let." It is not part of the first day. If God created the earth in Genesis 1:1, and it says He did, then Genesis 1:1-2 describe the original creation of the earth. What follows in Genesis 1:3-31 does not describe the original creation of the earth. Genesis 1:3-31 does not describe the earth's first beginning. It describes a subsequent beginning; the earth had begun before Genesis 1:3. Even if it was created in a formless and void condition, it still began before Genesis 1:3. The earth was already created before God said, "Let there be light." This being the case, Young-Earth and Day-Age creationists must admit there was a gap of time between Genesis 1:1 and Genesis 1:3. Young-Earthers will say it was a gap of hours or minutes or even seconds, while Day-Agers could allow the gap to be billions of years. In spite of this, Day-Agers denounce the Gap Theory. I've never been able to figure out how they can say that. If you ask them when the earth was created, they will say it was about nine billion years after the universe began. This seems to be a fairly long gap of time to me. Young-Earthers are a little more consistent, but they still can't say Genesis 1:3-31 describes earth's original beginning. Genesis 1:3-31 describes what God did to the earth already created in Genesis 1:1. So, how can they object to the idea of earth having two beginnings? It's no longer a matter of if there was a gap of time. It's only a matter of how long that gap was and what happened during that gap.

C2. Genesis 1:1 Came Before the First Day

The Gap Theory states that Genesis 1:1 came before the First Day, and describes a different (previous) creation than what is described in Genesis 1:3-31. There are, of course, different variations on this theme. There is the Ruin-Restoration version that describes how the first earth was judged because of Lucifer's sin, and then restored. There is the Raw-Gap-of-Time version that describes how God first created the raw materials of the universe, (time, space, matter, and energy) and then later used those raw materials to make, form, create, and fashion the universe, up to the point of the earth being without form, void, dark, and water-covered. In this second version, there is no mention of what happened (if anything) during this long gap of time. As far as the ages of the universe and the earth are concerned, there are different versions of the Gap Theory depending on how long ago you believe the original creation was, and how long you believe the gap was.

As we will see later, both Young-Earth creationists and Day-Age creationists sometimes shift their stance between three conflicting views of Genesis 1:1.

1.) Genesis 1:1 is a title.
2.) Genesis 1:1 is a summary.
3.) Genesis 1:1 is the first part of the first day of creation.

They do this to defend their theories against the Biblical and scientific evidence that contradicts their beliefs.

Four Characteristics of the Gap Theory

Creation theories can be quite complex and varied. Fortunately, I'm not going to investigate all the sub-theories and their various contortions. Instead, I will focus on the four characteristics that define the Gap Theory. If I can show how these are true, then I think the Gap Theory rises to the top of the creation theories. Here are the four characteristics of the Gap Theory.

1. THE MEANING OF "DAY"
    Twenty-Four-Hour Day
    Old-Universe

2. THE MEANING OF "CREATE"
    EX NIHILO Creation
    Dual-Creation

3. THE MEANING OF "BEGINNING"
    Long Period of Time

4. HOW GENESIS 1:1 RELATES TO THE REST OF THE CHAPTER
    Separate Creative Act
    Before the First Day

I also want to reveal some of the shortcomings of the Day-Age and Young-Earth Theories when they are sifted through the filters of science and Scripture. If these theories fail to pass these tests, then they should be rejected. For instance, if Scripture proves the six days were twenty-four-hour days, then the Day-Age Theory is wrong. If science proves the universe is billions of years old, then the Young-Earth Theory is wrong. In addition, I absolutely must show how the Gap Theory resolves the apparent conflicts between science and Scripture better than the other theories. If a theory has a problem with resolving these apparent conflicts, we can't put much faith in that theory. The Day-Age and the Young-

Earth Theories don't solve a lot of conflicts. In fact, they often create bigger conflicts than they resolve.

I now want to examine some problems that seem to arise when we compare the Biblical account of creation with the scientific account of creation. **THIS IS THE HEART OF THE MATTER: THE BIBLICAL ACCOUNT OF CREATION SEEMS TO DISAGREE WITH THE SCIENTIFIC ACCOUNT OF CREATION.** We need to see how the different creation theories explain this. When we do that, I think you will see how the Gap Theory is superior to both the Day-Age and the Young-Earth Theories. Both of those theories fail to pass through the filters of true Biblical revelation and true scientific observation.

Concerning "Chaos"

The meaning of the word "chaos" is about as nebulous as the thing it is supposed to describe. From ancient times, it had a meaning ranging from, "the empty void of nothingness," to "raw, unordered (random) matter and energy." In spite of the fact that numerous translators and theologians use "chaos" to describe the condition of the earth in Genesis 1:2, it is very much a pagan concept. In truth, the pagans had no real cosmogonies because they believed the universe was infinite and eternal; it never had a beginning; it was never created. The Hebrews possessed a written, Divinely inspired, cosmogony contrary to pagan beliefs. Only the Bible presented the notion that time and space themselves were created along with matter and energy.

From God's perspective, nothing He creates could be a chaos. He would both know and control every fundamental unit of matter, energy, time, and space. Nothing would be random, nothing would be without cause, and nothing would have properties or qualities apart from what He determined. Therefore, everything He created would be perfectly in tune with His plan and purpose. God could not create a chaos; therefore, God did not create the earth a chaos.

Whatever we don't know about the universe, this much we know: God knows everything about the universe. Everything He created was known and ordered by Him. Nothing was random or outside His control. From God's perspective, nothing He created was a chaos. He both created and controlled every fundamental unit of matter, and energy, and time, and space in His creation. Nothing was random, nothing was without cause, and nothing had properties or qualities apart from what He determined and maintained. Everything was what He intended it to be, everything was where He intended it to be, and everything did what He intended it to do! Everything He created was perfectly in tune with His plan and purpose. God cannot create something beyond His omnipotence, omnipresence, and omniscience. The creation may appear a chaos to us because of our limited knowledge and perception, but that does not make it a chaos. Words like "chaos," "random," and "chance," are words we use to describe things we don't understand. These words reveal our ignorance. (Or, is it our arrogance?) If we don't know, or can't explain why something happens, we say it must not have an explanation. We do not possess or enjoy the power, knowledge, and wisdom of God, and as such, we have no right to say His works were unordered, uncontrolled, or without meaning or purpose. In short, we are wrong to say *TOHUW WA-BOHUW* means chaos. It was true in the beginning, and it is true today—Everything is what God intends it to be, everything is where He intends it to be, and everything does what He intends it to do! Everything He creates is perfectly in tune with His plan and purpose.

Chapter Three: Apparent Problems

Scientific Problem 1: You're Out of Order

If the six days in the first chapter of Genesis represent a chronological account of the creation, and they certainly seem to be exactly that, then a problem arises when we compare the order of the creation of living organisms with the order of their appearance in the geological record. The order in which the Bible says things were created doesn't match the order in which geology says they appeared. **The geological strata do not fit the Genesis account of creation.** Let me show you. Look at the order of appearance of things according to the Bible.

(Figure 1) Biblical Order of Appearance

```
DAY 6
  Man
  Land Animals
  Land Mammals

DAY 5
  Birds
  Marine Animals
  Marine Mammals

DAY 4
  Stars
  Moon
  Sun

DAY 3
  Fruit Trees
  Seed Plants
  Land Plants
  Dry Land

DAY 2
  Clouds
  Atmosphere

DAY 1
  Light
  Ocean
  Earth
```

Now look at the order of appearance of these things according to scientific observations.

(Figure 2) Scientific Order of Appearance
(MYA=Million Years Ago; BYA=Billion Years Ago)

0 MYA	Man
25 MYA	
50 MYA	
75 MYA	
100 MYA	Marine Mammals
125 MYA	Fruit Trees
150 MYA	Birds
175 MYA	Seed Plants
200 MYA	
225 MYA	
250 MYA	
275 MYA	
300 MYA	
325 MYA	
350 MYA	
375 MYA	
400 MYA	Land Animals
425 MYA	Land Plants
450 MYA	
475 MYA	
500 MYA	
550 MYA	
600 MYA	Marine Animals
650 MYA	
700 MYA	
750 MYA	
800 MYA	
850 MYA	
900 MYA	
1.0 BYA	
2.0 BYA	
3.0 BYA	
4.0 BYA	Ocean
4.5 BYA	Moon
4.5 BYA	Dry Land
4.5 BYA	Clouds
4.5 BYA	Atmosphere
4.5 BYA	Earth
4.5 BYA	Sun
13.6 BYA	Stars
13.8 BYA	Light

Here is a table of information from my college biology textbook, *Biology*.[2] It shows the geological ages and the order of appearance of the various groups and types of plants and animals, both aquatic and terrestrial:

(Figure 3) Evolution and the Geologic Ages

From: *Biology* 2nd Edition by John W. Kimball Copyright 1969 Addison-Wesley Publishing Co.

ERAS	PERIODS / EPOCHS	AQUATIC LIFE	TERRESTRIAL LIFE	STARTING (millions of years ago)
Cenozoic	Quaternary / Recent / Pleistocene	All Modern Groups Present	Man in the New World; First Men	0.5
Cenozoic	Tertiary / Pliocene / Miocene / Oligocene / Eocene / Paleocene		Hominids and Pongids; Monkeys and Ancestor of Apes; Adaptive Radiation of Birds; Modern Mammals and Herbaceous Angiosperms	63 +/- 2
Mesozoic	Cretaceous	Modern Bony Fishes; Extinction of Ammonites, Pleiosaurs, and Icthyosaurs	Extinction of Dinosaurs, Pterosaurs, Rise of Woody Angiosperms, Snakes	135 +/- 5
Mesozoic	Jurassic	Pleiosaurs and Icthyosaurs Abundant; Ammonites Again Abundant; Skates, Rays, and Bony Fishes	Dinosaurs Dominant; First Lizards: Archaeopteryx Insects Abundant First Angiosperms	180 +/- 5
Mesozoic	Triassic	First Pleiosaurs and Icthyosaurs Ammonites Abundant at First Rise of Bony Fishes	Adaptive Radiation of Reptiles (Thecodonts, Therapsids, Turtles, Crocodiles, First Dinosaurs); First Mammals	230 +/- 10
Paleozoic	Permian	Extinction of Trilobites and Placoderms	Reptiles Abundant (Cotylosaurs, Pelycosaurs); Cycads and Conifers; Ginkgoes	280 +/-10
Paleozoic	Pennsylvanian	Ammonites, Bony Fishes	First Reptiles; Coal Swamps	310 +/- 10
Paleozoic	Mississippian	Adaptive Radiation of Sharks	Forests of Lycopsids, Sphenopsids, and Seed Ferns; Amphibians Abundant; Land Snails	345 +/- 10
Paleozoic	Devonian	Placoderms, Cartilaginous and Bony Fishes Ammonites, Nautiloids	Ferns, Lycopsids, and Sphenopsids; First Gymnosperms and Bryophytes; First Insects; First Amphibians	405 +/- 10
Paleozoic	Silurian	Adaptive Radiation of Ostracoderms; Eurypterids	First Land Plants (Psilopsids, Lycopsids) Arachnids (Scorpions)	425 +/- 10
Paleozoic	Ordovician	First Vertebrates (Ostracoderms) Nautiloids, Plinia, Other Mollusks Trilobites Abundant	None	500 +/- 10
Paleozoic	Cambrian	Trilobites Dominant First Eurypterids, Crustaceans, Mollusks, Echinoderms Sponges, Cnidarians, Annelids Tunicates	None	600 +/- 50
	Pre-Cambrian	Fossils Rare But many Protistan and Invertebrate Phyla Probably Present	None	

Now, let me remove the dates and simply compare the orders of appearance.

(Figure 4) Biblical Order vs. Scientific Order (Part 1)

Biblical Order vs. Scientific Order

Biblical	Scientific
Man	Man
Land Animals	Marine Mammals
Land Mammals	Fruit Trees
Birds	Birds
Marine Animals	Seed Plants
Marine Mammals	Land Mammals
Stars	Land Animals
Moon	Land Plants
Sun	Marine Animals
Fruit Trees	Ocean
Seed Plants	Moon
Land Plants	Dry Land
Dry Land	Clouds
Clouds	Atmosphere
Atmosphere	Earth
Light	Sun
Ocean	Stars
Earth	Light

Don't look too closely and things may seem to fit. Many Christian creationists gleefully say the scientific order of appearance matches the Biblical order of appearance. They say this because there are some points of agreement. Both accounts show that man is the pinnacle of God's creation. Both accounts say dry land came before land plants and land animals, and both say the oceans came before marine life. Amazing!

A major problem becomes apparent if you look at the details. If the Biblical order matches the scientific order, then we would be able to draw lines from one side of the chart to the other and have nothing but parallel, uncrossing lines. If we draw lines from one side to the other, and any lines cross, then the Biblical account doesn't match the scientific account. Here is what we get when we connect the lines according to the order of appearance.

(Figure 5) Biblical Order vs. Scientific Order (Part 2)

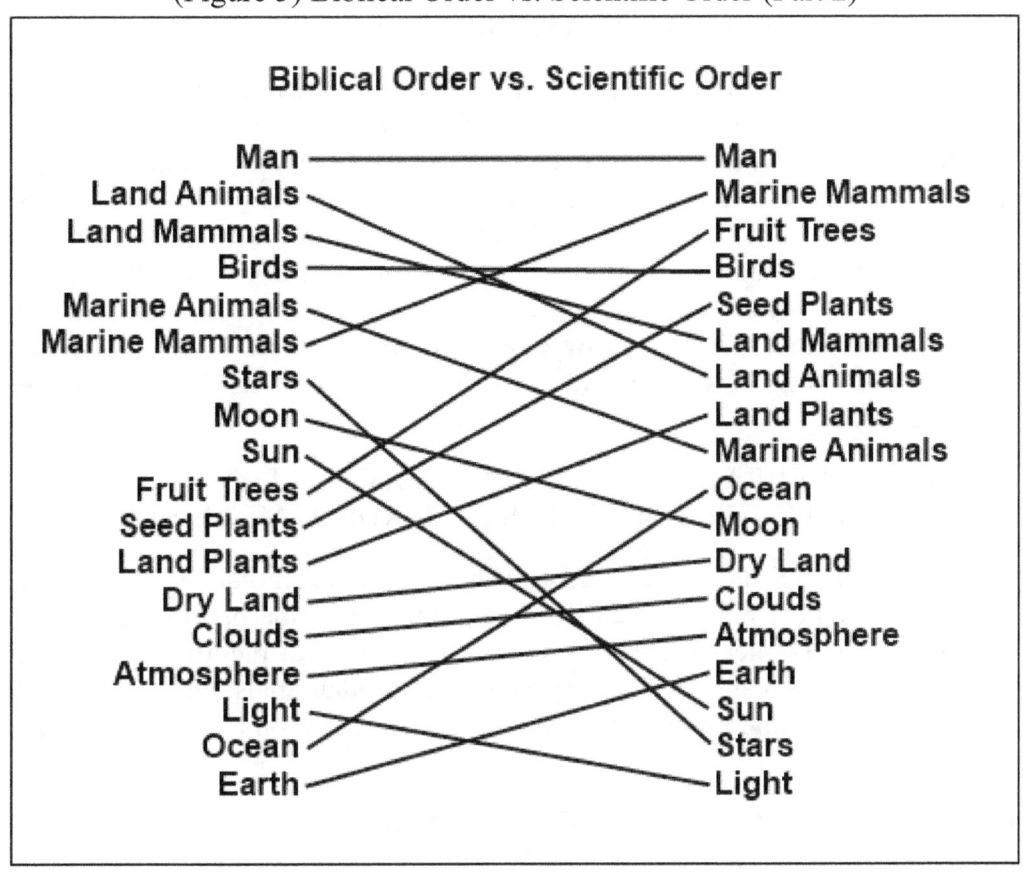

As you can see, the two accounts don't match. When any two lines cross, it means there is a discrepancy between the Biblical account and the scientific account; and there are lots of crossed lines, aren't there? Look at the appearance of the moon for example. The Biblical order of the appearance of the moon disagrees with the scientific order in respect to the appearance of the stars, fruit trees, seed plants, land plants, the oceans, and the atmosphere and clouds. That's six points of disagreement. The Biblical order of the appearance of fruit trees doesn't match the scientific order of the appearance of the sun, the stars, marine animals, land animals, land mammals, and birds. That's six more points of disagreement. Another major disagreement is how the Bible appears to place the water-covered earth even before the presence of light. That would mean the water-covered earth existed before the formation of the stars. Science disagrees with that idea. There are other disagreements.

THE BIBLE SAYS THE EARTH WAS COMPLETELY SUBMERGED IN WATER, AND DRY LAND APPEARED LATER

According to Genesis 1:2 and Genesis 1:9, the entire earth was under water before dry land was present. If you study the history of the earth according to science, you find no such condition. In fact, you find the opposite situation. Cosmologists and geologists say the earth was formed either by the accumulation of space debris or by gases from an explosion of the sun. In either case, the violent forces would have caused earth to be a molten mass. Only as it cooled, could a crust (dry land) form. Even after the crust formed, it would have been hundreds of degrees for millions of years. Oceans couldn't have formed until the crust cooled to a point that allowed liquid water to collect. According to scientists, dry land appeared long before there was surface water. The Bible and science seem to disagree on this point.

GEOLOGY REVEALS HOW BIRDS CAME AFTER LAND ANIMALS, WHILE THE BIBLE TELLS US, BIRDS CAME FIRST

The Bible says birds were created on Day Five. Land animals weren't created until Day Six. The geological record reveals that land animals came before birds. Something seems wrong. Is the Biblical record wrong? Is the geological record wrong? They both can't be right about this, can they? If birds came after land animals, then the Bible appears to be wrong. If birds came before land animals, then the geological record appears to be wrong.

GEOLOGY REVEALS THAT WHALES CAME AFTER LAND ANIMALS, BUT THE BIBLE SAYS THEY CAME BEFORE

Again, we see an apparent conflict between what the Bible says and what science reveals. Geology shows that land animals came before whales. According to the Bible, whales were created first. Whales were created on Day Five but land animals weren't created until Day Six. If whales came first, the Bible is right, but geology is wrong. If land animals came before whales, geology is right, but the Bible is wrong. Something doesn't seem to match.

GRASS AND TREES WERE CREATED BEFORE MARINE LIFE

The Bible says God created grass, trees, herbs, and seed-bearing plants on Day Three. The Bible also says God created sea creatures on Day Five. According to the Bible, trees and seed-bearing plants came before life in the oceans. Geology firmly teaches the opposite. The geological evidence proves the oceans teemed with life long before any land plants; especially seed-bearing plants, flowering plants, and fruit-bearing trees. Something seems out of place.

LAND PLANTS COME BEFORE THE SUN

Here we have another contradiction in theories. The Bible says God made land plants on the Third Day, but He didn't make the sun until Day Four. You can't blend this with science. Cosmologists and astronomers know the sun was present for billions of years before land plants. If the sun was created before land plants, then Day Four came before Day Three. That, of course, would mean God made a mistake.

WHAT HAPPENED WHEN?

The problem with the Day-Age Theory is that the beginnings and endings, and the durations of the "days" create scientific and Biblical contradictions. Look at Figure Six:

(Figure 6) The "Day" Ages Compared to the Geological Ages

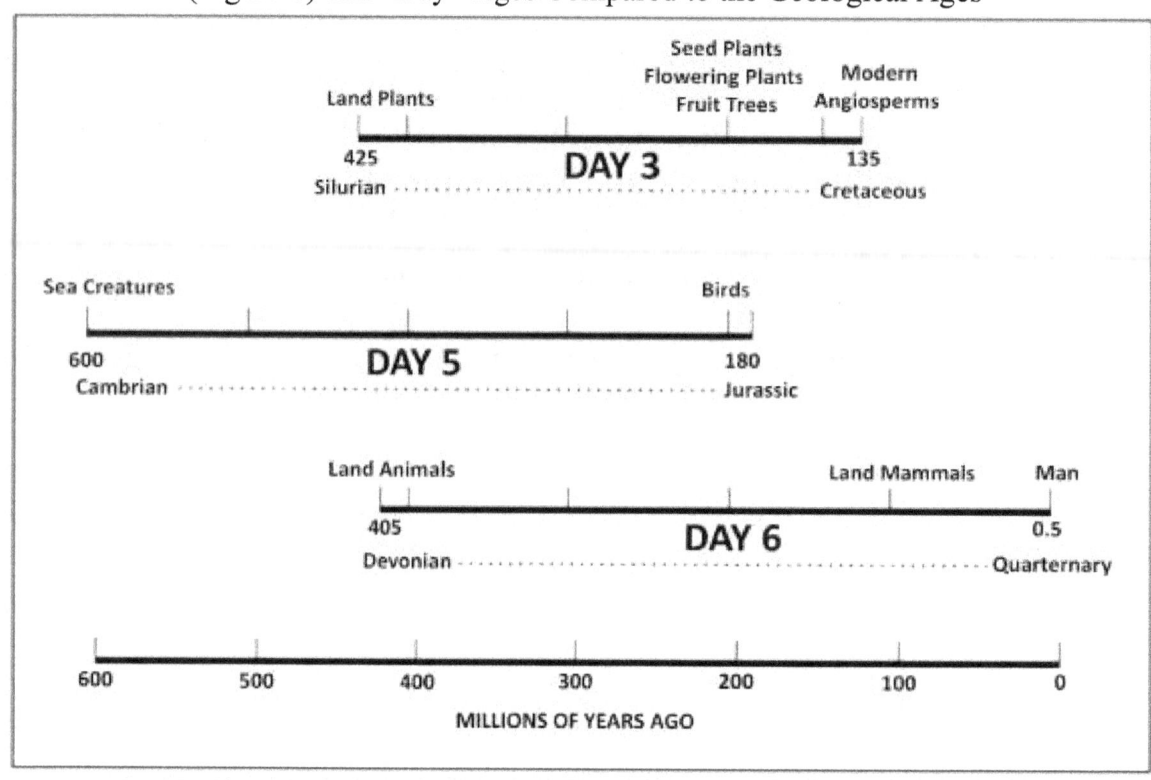

According to the Bible, land plants were created on "Day" Three. Since the first land plants appeared in the Silurian Period (425 million years ago) and the modern, flowering, seed-bearing angiosperms first appeared in the Cretaceous Period (135 million years ago), then we would have to believe "Day" Three lasted from the Silurian Period to the Cretaceous Period, or about 290 million years. If you look at the chart above, you see why this creates a problem. The Bible says God created sea creatures (fish, whales, *etc.*) and birds on "Day" Five. According to the Day-Age Theory, "Day" Five began around 600 million years ago in the Cambrian Period and ended around 180 million years ago in the Jurassic Period. That means "Day" Five was about 420 million years long. But, that also means "Day" Five started about 175 million years before "Day" Three started. It also means "Day" Three ended about 45 million years after "Day" Five ended. Why call it "Day" Five if it started before "Day" Three? Why call it "Day" Three if it ended after "Day" Five? Why would God list them in the order He did, and why call them the "Third Day" and the "Fifth Day" when it wasn't true. Did God lie? Did He get confused? Did He not study geology very well? Furthermore, "Day" Six overlaps both "Day" Three and "Day" Five. Look closely: "Day" Six happened during most of the same geologic periods as "Day" Three. Why would God call them the "Third Day" and the "Sixth Day" when they happened at the same time? Plus, what do you do with "Day" Four? It can't be put on this chart because the events of "Day" Four (The appearance of the sun, moon, and stars) happened billions of years before "Days" One, Two, and Three. Either that, or the sun, moon, and stars weren't created until after the end of the Cretaceous Period, long after the dinosaurs. "Day" Two can't be charted either because there was never a time when oceans came before the earth's crust. The same is true for "Day" One. There was never a time when the earth was dark and covered by water before light existed. How can Day-Age creationists say their interpretation of the Bible fits the scientific facts when it disagrees with the scientific facts?

    I think you get the idea. There are even more apparent discrepancies than the ones I've listed. Look back at all the lines that cross in the diagram and you'll see other problems. The Bible and science seemingly disagree on the appearance of land animals vs. seed plants, marine animals vs. land plants, birds vs. marine mammals, and others. **No wonder unbelievers laugh at the Bible. The Bible seems to contradict science right out of the starting block.** Whatever creation theory we come up with, it needs to explain these apparent contradictions, and it needs to explain them without creating bigger Biblical and scientific problems. Both the Young-Earth and the Day-Age Theories actually create more Biblical and scientific problems than they solve. One problem with the Day-Age Theory is it tries to reconcile the Genesis account with the fossil record because it assumes the fossils are a physical record of the six "days" of creation.

Scientific Problem 2: Missing "Missing Links"

    The fossil record is very important to both Day-Age creationists and evolutionists, but for different reasons. Day-Age creationists assume the fossils show the geologic ages in which God created the various lifeforms. For them, the fossils provide a record of what God created during the six Day-Ages. For evolutionists, the fossils provide a record of what evolved over those same long ages. About the only thing in common between the Day-Age Theory and the Theory of Evolution is the belief that species slowly changed over the ages. Day-Age creationists insist God slowly caused it. Evolutionists insist Darwinian evolution slowly caused it. Both theories agree life changed very gradually over very long periods of time. Unfortunately for both theories, this wasn't what the fossil record revealed. The fossil record didn't seem to provide the geologic evidence needed by both theories. Let's first look at how the fossil record affected the Theory of Evolution.

    According to Darwin, species changed in very small, very gradual steps, over very long periods of time. Although Darwin had no links connecting any of the biological groups together, he believed someday they would be discovered. Almost everyone in the scientific community agreed. A crucial point to remember is that Darwin and the evolutionists of his day didn't know how biological traits were produced or what caused biological traits to change. They also didn't know how traits were passed down to following generations. No one knew about DNA at the time. They simply believed that for some unexplained reason, biological traits changed very gradually over time. They also believed local environments changed very gradually over time. So, it made sense to them that once a very gradual biological change occurred, it would very gradually influence an organism's survival in its very gradually changing environmental niche. Gradualism was the paradigm of the day. This is where the phrase, "survival of the fittest," came into play. Darwinian evolutionists asserted there were two forces driving evolution forward. The first force produced change in heritable biological traits. The second force was the constantly changing environment. An organism with a trait that caused it to survive would be more likely to pass that trait on to the next generation. An organism with a trait that caused it to die wouldn't do as well. Over very long periods of time, species would very gradually change according to their ability to survive in their very gradually changing environmental niches. Those organisms with traits helping promote survivability would very gradually replace those organisms that didn't have those traits.

If what they asserted was true, then the fossil record would show very gradually changing biological TRAITS (not just SPECIES) as time passed. In fact, the changes in traits would be so gradual, even the Linnaean Classification System would eventually break down. (This is because evolution must happen at the intracellular, biomolecular level—by extremely tiny changes in DNA, RNA, amino acids, *etc*. The Linnaean Classification System only looks at the macro-anatomical features.) The traits of one Species would very gradually blur into the traits of another Species. One Genus would have traits that imperceptibly changed into the traits of another Genus. One Family's traits would change in such small gradations that it would be impossible to draw a definitive line where it changed into another Family. The same would be true for Order, Class, Phylum, and even Kingdom. Alas, the fossil record didn't reveal what they wanted.

The Rainbow Painting

I like explaining things with illustrations because sometimes it makes difficult concepts easier to grasp. Imagine you were an artist and you wanted to paint a picture of the visible color spectrum; a rainbow painting. You would start on the left edge of your canvass with red and work your way to the right with orange, then yellow, then green, then blue, then purple, and finally back to red. Let's also imagine your canvass was one hundred miles long. It's a big project. You would start with a can of paint that had 1,000,000 parts of pure red paint and nothing else. With that paint, you would paint a one-inch wide line from the top of the canvass to the bottom of the canvass. Next, you would get a new brush and a can of paint with 999,999 parts of red paint and one part of orange paint. With that paint, you would draw another one-inch line. This line would be touching the first line and be parallel to it for its entire length. Then you would get a new brush and a can of paint with 999,998 parts of red paint and two parts of orange. You would use this to paint your third one-inch line. For your fourth line, you would use paint that was 999,997 parts red and three parts orange. This process would continue until you painted one million one-inch lines. At that point, you would have a can of paint with 1,000,000 parts of orange paint and no red paint. Once you drew the pure orange line, you would go to your next can of paint. It would contain 999,999 parts of orange paint and one part of yellow paint. Very gradually, line by line, you would have one more part of yellow paint and one less part of orange paint in your paint cans. Once you completed the next million lines, you would have a can of pure yellow paint. Then you would use paint that was one part green and 999,999 parts yellow. You would continue this process color by color. You would add more and more green to your yellow, then more and more blue to your green, then more and more purple to your blue, and finally more and more red to your purple. Each can of paint would differ from its predecessor by one part per million. The total transition through all six colors (red, orange, yellow, green, blue, and purple) would require six million one-inch lines. Your color spectrum would evolve through six million transitions in the space of about a hundred miles.

Once you rested from your work, what would you expect to see? You would expect to see a rainbow with such insensibly fine gradations, you wouldn't be able to tell where red ended and orange began. You wouldn't be able to distinguish the 100% blue line from the 99.9999% blue/0.0001% purple line. You would be able to classify the colors into two "kingdoms," the warm colors (red, orange, and yellow) and the cool colors, (blue, green, and purple) but you wouldn't be able to tell when one "kingdom" ended and the other "kingdom" began. You would be able to see all six "phyla," (red, orange, yellow, green, blue, and purple) but you would find it difficult to see the lines of demarcation. You could create an entire classification scheme by labeling the colors as, "blue-green," "bluish green," "greenish blue," or "greenish blue-green," but it would be too confusing to decide when something was blue enough to be called, "bluish blue-green," instead of "greenish blue-green." In the end, your classification system would be inadequate because there would be insensibly fine transitions from one color to the next.

This is the kind of results you would expect from Darwinian Evolution, except it would be even harder to define species. In our rainbow painting example, we have six million steps in one hundred miles. In the case of living organisms, we are dealing with billions of DNA changes over hundreds of millions of years. Changes would have been much, much more gradual! Darwinists insisted the fossil record would eventually reveal this kind of evolution. They believed so many transitional fossils would be discovered, it would be plain for all to see how Darwinian Evolution explained the origins of species. So, if Darwinian Evolution is true, they should have found millions of insensibly finely gradated transitional fossils by now.

Is this what they found? No. A century and a half of intense searching passed, and they kept finding the same kind of fossils, of the same kind of organisms, with the same kind of traits, in the same kind of strata. In fact, this is how the Fossil Index System was made possible. The Fossil Index System was a way of determining when an organism lived, based on its features and its position in the fossil record. Because they kept finding the same kind of organisms, with the same kind of features, in the same geological strata all over the world, they assumed the fossil record was a chronological record of worldwide evolution. When they discovered particular fossils with particular traits, they were able to place them into a particular chronology. Each stratum had its own characteristic fossils with their own characteristic traits. But, if Darwinian evolution was true, then one would not expect to keep finding the same kind of organisms with the same kind of traits in the same kind of strata all over the world. Different species with different traits in different environments would show such gradual transitions that you wouldn't be able to tell when an index fossil started and when it ended. **The Fossil Index System seemed to indicate there had been abrupt changes in biologic traits as well as abrupt changes in environments.** Evolutionists knew if Darwinian Evolution was true, then the changes from one species to the next would be so gradual, there would be nothing but transitional fossils in the strata. It began to appear as if biological traits weren't gradually changing. Either that, or the ecological niches weren't gradually changing. Darwinian Evolution required both, but the fossil record provided neither. They kept finding Devonian strata with Devonian fossils, Permian strata with Permian fossils, Jurassic strata with Jurassic fossils, *etc.* The very fact these groupings kept appearing all over the world seemed to prove evolution happened in large, recognizable stages instead of small, imperceptible stages. This was a great discovery for the Fossil Index System, but it was a bad discovery for Darwinian Evolution. Evolutionists couldn't find the innumerable, insensibly fine gradations in the fossil record. They couldn't find the missing links.

Of course, many evolutionists claimed they found the missing links, but those discoveries always proved to be insufficient evidence because no one could unquestionably prove they were very gradual transitions from one major group to another. Oh, they might find an organism with a trait that appeared similar to the traits in other groups, but the transitions were still too large and still too abrupt to be universally accepted as proof, even by other evolutionists. You see, it wasn't just creationists who refuted Darwinism. By the mid-twentieth century, a number of well-known evolutionists also began doubting Darwin's model. Why did they doubt? For starters, it was discovered that biologic traits were the products of genetic instructions stored in strands of DNA. The only way to change biologic traits was to change the instructions. The only way to change the instructions was by random mutations. Because random mutations constantly occur and because environmental niches constantly change, there should be no fixity of species. Nothing should stay the same for very long. **Finding species that remained constant should be a very rare exception; not the overwhelming rule.** Finding the same kind of fossils, with the same kind of traits, in the same geological strata, all over the world was an awkward situation for gradualism. There were large gaps between the different organisms, and they couldn't find many (if any) truly transitional fossils. Darwin said the geological strata ought to show an uncountable number of transitional fossils with imperceptibly small changes. Unfortunately, they couldn't find that. This eventually became such an embarrassment for evolutionists, they quietly laid Darwinism to rest and created another Theory of Evolution. That theory is called Punctuated Equilibria. Simply stated, evolutionists now say evolution didn't happen very gradually over very long periods of time. Instead, it happened in very short periods of very rapid changes, with very long "quiet" periods of time in between. Very rapid bursts of evolution are separated by very long interludes of no-evolution. Because the changes were so rapid and the time periods were so short, there would be very few transitional organisms. That means there would be even fewer transitional fossils. Fish evolved to amphibians so quickly, it was unlikely any transitional forms would be found in the fossil record. Reptiles evolved to birds just as quickly. In fact, one evolutionist said a reptile laid an egg and a bird hatched out. Not much chance of finding transitional fossils in that case. This new theory could now be "proved" because it was based on the lack of evidence. The more transitional fossils you didn't find, the more "true" this theory became. Of course, real science is never strengthened by relying on the idea that the less evidence there is, the more scientific it becomes. Yet, this is what evolutionists have done over the past few decades.

So, how are gaps in the fossil record a problem for creationists? Well, they're not a problem for some creationists. Young-Earth creationists have no problem explaining this. God simply did not create lifeforms out of previous lifeforms. Gap Theory creationists agree. But, the Day-Age Theory initially said God very gradually created newer species from older species in very gradual steps over very long ages of time. If God had created life this way, then the fossil record should reveal billions of gradual transitional creations over hundreds of millions of years. Initially, Day-Age creationists believed that since God gradually created over very long periods of time, the fossil record would reveal very small, very gradual changes over time. In essence, they believed the fossil record would be identical to what Darwinian evolutionists were hoping for. The only difference was the creationists believed an intelligent Creator caused it, while the evolutionists believed the random physical forces of nature caused it. The creationists who believed this theory couldn't explain the gaps in the fossil record any better than the Darwinian Evolutionists. If God created life this way, then there should be uncountable numbers of created transitional forms among the fossils. Unfortunately for Day-Agers, their theory had a scientific problem: the missing links were missing. There were too many gaps in the fossil record. What could they do? Well, it wasn't long after the new Evolutionary Punctuated Equilibria Theory was formulated, that the new Creationist Punctuated Day-Age Theory was formulated. I'm sure this was a coincidence. Punctuated Day-Age creationists now say God didn't create new creatures gradually over long periods of time. Instead, He periodically created new species suddenly. Like the Punctuated-Equilibria crowd, the Punctuated Day-Age crowd uses the lack of transitional fossils as their "proof." Yes, it explains the gaps in the fossil record, but it still fails to explain the discrepancies in the order of appearance. It also fails to explain Living Fossils.

Scientific Problem 3: Living Fossils
(Yea, Though They Once Were Dead, Yet Shall They Live)

According to evolutionists and Day-Age creationists, the fossil layers are a record of the history of the appearance of life on earth. This was why gaps in the fossil record were so embarrassing. The fossil record kept ruining their theories. Nevertheless, evolutionists put a lot of stock in The Fossil Index System. They assumed simple organisms in the lower strata evolved into more complex organisms in the upper strata. Likewise, Day-Age creationists put a lot of stock in The Fossil Index System. They assumed God created simple organisms first and more complex organisms later. The Fossil Index System wasn't a bad system. Each specific stratum seemed to contain specific organisms regardless of where on earth the stratum was found. Nevertheless, there were problems with the system. One problem was that scientists kept discovering Living Fossils. These were organisms that died out millions of years ago according to the Fossil Index System, but were found to be alive today. The Coelacanth fish was a perfect example. This "primitive" fish was supposed to have died out seventy million years ago. They were found in strata older than seventy million years, but then they disappeared from later strata. So, it was assumed the Coelacanth became extinct seventy million years ago. Day-Age creationists were okay with this. God had created these "primitive" fish, and then they died out seventy million years ago. But, in 1938 a live Coelacanth was caught off the coast of South Africa. Many have been caught in other parts of the world since. The fossil record did not provide an accurate history of the Coelacanth fish. The same was true for numerous other Living Fossils that have been discovered. Examples are the Tuatara lizard, the Metasequoia tree, the Ginkgo tree, Neopilinia (a small marine mollusk), Lepidocaris (a crustacean), and over a hundred others. According to the fossil record, all these things were shown to have been extinct for millions of years. Yet, all these things are living today. Evolutionists either had to admit evolution was wrong, or admit the fossil record was less reliable than they had thought. They admitted the latter of course, but in doing so they cast doubt on Darwin's explanation for the origin of species. Day-Age creationists had to admit the same thing, but in doing so, they cast doubt on God's revelation of creation.

(Note: The term "Living Fossils" is no longer the preferred term for organisms that had been dead for millions of years according to the fossil record, yet are alive today. The new term is "Lazarus Fossils," as in the resurrection of Lazarus from the dead. (Scientists like to poke fun at the Bible, I guess.) These organisms appeared in the strata millions of years ago, but then suddenly disappeared for unknown reasons. They supposedly didn't go extinct; they just "died" to the geologic record for millions of years. Why they weren't fossilized is never explained except for, "imperfections in the fossil record." The lack of evidence again becomes the evidence.

The term "Living Fossils" is now used to indicate organisms that are virtually unchanged for millions of years. They resemble their ancestors to such a degree that scientists have to argue over their taxonomy. They are alive today, but they show only extremely slight differences in their anatomy. Why they haven't changed over those millions of years is not explained either, but they call it, "Non-Adaptive Radiation." Unfortunately, when I learned about these organisms, they were all called, "Living Fossils." I still use the term today because my mind has become a living fossil in its own right—it doesn't like to change over time. If you are offended by the term "Living Fossils," or if you think my use of this term negates the purpose of this book, then please mentally substitute the term "Lazarus Fossils" where appropriate. Actually, both Lazarus Fossils and Living Fossils are evidence that organisms don't gradually change over millions of years. Both are evidence that Darwinian evolution is not true.)

Day-Age creationists face the same problem. The fossil record is not a reliable record of when God created things during the six long Day-Ages. Again, the Biblical order does not match the scientific order. According to Day-Age thinking, God created Ginkgo trees 200 million years ago during "day" three of creation. The fossil record showed they died out even before land mammals appeared. This means they died out before "day" five. So, if they died out before "day" five but are alive today, then God must have gotten His "days" mixed up. He must have created trees after "day" five, or else Ginkgoes wouldn't be here. But if He did that, then the Bible is wrong when it says God created trees on "day" three. If you try to fit all the different Living Fossils into which "day" they were created, you get a terrible mess. Neopilinia was created on "day" five with the other marine animals. Their fossils, however, show they became extinct before seed plants appeared on "day" three. This means they became extinct even before they were created. Then somehow, they reappeared alive and well after being dead for 400 million years. The Day-Age Theory doesn't explain Living Fossils without having God being confused about what He created on which "day." The Gap Theory has a much better explanation.

Chapter Four: Day-Age Solutions

The most glaring problem Day-Age creationists face is the order of appearance of the lifeforms. The Biblical order doesn't match the geological order. The Day-Age Theory doesn't solve the problem. **Making the "days" long periods of time doesn't change their order.** Day-Agers can say the geological strata represent the six long ages, but they still must admit the ages are in the wrong order. According to them, God doesn't know the meaning of "first," "second," "third," *etc.* Apparently, God doesn't know the meaning of "day" either.

The Biblical Meaning of "DAY"

What does the Bible reveal about how we should translate "day" in Genesis 1? I believe we can discover its meaning if we simply examine how the word is used here and in other places in the Scriptures. I believe we can eliminate all creation theories that interpret the six "days" to be symbolic, to be ages, or to be anything other than regular twenty-four-hour earth days. Remember, God is describing things from an earthly perspective.

YOM (Day)

YOM (Strong's Number H3117) is the Hebrew word for "day." What does it mean? When used in reference to time, *YOM* can define four different periods.

1.) It is used for the daylight portion of a twenty-four-hour day.
2.) It is used of a complete twenty-four-hour day.
3.) It is used to describe an undetermined length of time.
4.) It is used to define a year. (I'll discuss this use later when I mention a passage where it is translated, "two years," but I think it means two days.)

Day-Agers believe the six "days" of creation cannot be literal twenty-four-hour days. They insist "day" is equivalent to "age." They say Genesis 1 is God's way of symbolically describing what He did during the billions of years between the Big Bang and the creation of man. Day-Agers defend their belief by telling us *YOM* can mean a long period of time. This is possible, although that's not its usual meaning. Nevertheless, because of this possibility, they feel justified in believing the "days" are long ages. Unfortunately for them, this possibility becomes impossible when you let the Bible interpret itself. (An important point to remember is that just because a word or phrase is used in a certain way, or with a certain meaning in historic Hebrew literature, it doesn't mean it has that same use or meaning in the Bible. What words and phrases mean and how they are used in the Bible is still the best way to determine their meaning in the Bible.)

So, what does *YOM* mean in Genesis 1? The answer is found in Genesis 1. You see, God defines the meaning of "day" in the text. God tells us exactly what period of time *YOM* describes. *YOM* is first used in Genesis 1:5. In fact, *YOM* is used twice in this verse with a different meaning each time.

Genesis 1:5 "And God called the light **DAY**, and the darkness He called night. And there was evening and there was morning, one **DAY**." (NASB)

In its first usage in Genesis 1:5, *YOM* was used as the name for a period of light. God called the light, "day." The word for "light" is *OWR*—Strong's Numbers H215 and H216. This means *YOM* and *OWR* are equivalent; they describe the same period of time. "Day" in this context is a period of light. The only way a "day" could be an age, is if the period of light was an age. I don't know how God could have made this any clearer. How long was that period of light? Genesis tells us when it says, "God called the light day." God tells us the light lasted a day. Was this a literal day or could it be "anything-you-want?" We only need to see what God called the other things He created during that week. Were they literal things or "anything-you-want" them to be?

Genesis 1:5b "...and the darkness He called night."
Genesis 1:8a "And God called the firmament Heaven."
Genesis 1:10a "And God called the dry *land* Earth;"
Genesis 1:10b "and the gathering together of the waters called He Seas:"

The context reveals these things were literal. The heavens were literal. The earth was literal. The waters were the literal. The dry land was the literal. The firmament (the atmosphere) was literal. The darkness was literal. The fish were literal. The birds were literal. The grass, and herbs, and trees, and flowers were literal. The night was literal. (We know this because the text mentions the literal moon and the literal stars) If you insist "day" can mean anything you want, then I can insist "night" can mean anything I want. I can insist "heaven" can mean anything I want. I can insist "earth" can mean anything I want. I can insist "seas" can mean anything I want. I can insist "fish," and "birds," and "animals," *etc.* can mean anything I want. I can come up with an interpretation of the Genesis Creation Account that describes how God created any number of exotic and weird worlds. All I have to do is insist the Words of God mean anything I want them to mean, and I can make Genesis say anything I want it to say. Since all these other things were literal, I see no justification in the context for saying "day" was not literal. In Genesis 1:5, "day" is a literal, time-and-space day.

The pattern is clear; *YOM* was a period of light. It was not a period of light-and-dark, light-and-dark, light-and-dark, as would be required if it were an age. To confirm this, God used "night" (*LAYIL*—Strong's Number H3915) to describe the period of time when it was dark (*CHOSHEK*—Strong's Number H2822). *LAYIL* describes a period of dark. This addition of *LAYIL* is important because it narrows down the definition of *YOM*. When used with *LAYIL*, *YOM* means the light portion of a twenty-four-hour day. The easiest way to determine the length of the "day" is by determining the length of the period of light. (*YOM* and *OWR* are equivalent.) The easiest way to determine the length of the "night" is by determining the length of the period of dark. (*LAYIL* and *CHOSHEK* are equivalent.) Day-Agers say the "days" (*YOM*) were periods of millions or billions of years, but this would mean the "nights" (*LAYIL*) were also periods of millions or billions of years. (There is one *YOM* for each *LAYIL*.) Unfortunately for their interpretation, they have no Biblical or scientific evidence to support it. The earth has never experienced light periods lasting millions or billions of years. The earth has never experienced dark periods lasting millions or billions of years. If their definition of "day" is correct, then Genesis 1:5 could be translated:

"And God called the light **AGE**, and the darkness He called **AGE**. And there was evening and there was morning, one **AGE**."

Day-Agers fail to look at the word "night." True, *YOM* can be used for a long period of time, but *LAYIL* is never used for a long period of time. *LAYIL* is used 235 times in the Bible and it is always the dark portion of a twenty-four-hour day when referring to time.

LAYIL (Night)

1.) Genesis 1:5 "And God called the light Day, and the darkness he called **Night**. And the evening and the morning were the first day." (KJV)

2.) Genesis 1:14 "And God said, Let there be lights in the firmament of the heaven to divide the day from the **night**; and let them be for signs, and for seasons, and for days, and years:" (KJV)

3.) Genesis 1:16 "And God made two great lights; the greater light to rule the day, and the lesser light to rule the **night**: *he made* the stars also." (KJV)

4.) Genesis 1:18 "And to rule over the day and over the **night**, and to divide the light from the darkness: and God saw that *it was* good." (KJV)

5.) Genesis 7:4 "For yet seven days, and I will cause it to rain upon the earth forty days and forty **nights**; and every living substance that I have made will I destroy from off the face of the earth." (KJV)

6.) Genesis 7:12 "And the rain was upon the earth forty days and forty **nights**." (KJV)

7.) Genesis 8:22 "While the earth remaineth, seedtime and harvest, and cold and heat, and summer and winter, and day and **night** shall not cease." (KJV)

8.) Genesis 14:15 "And he divided himself against them, he and his servants, by **night**, and smote them, and pursued them unto Hobah, which *is* on the left hand of Damascus." (KJV)

9.) Genesis 19:5 "And they called unto Lot, and said unto him, Where *are* the men which came in to thee this **night**? bring them out unto us, that we may know them." (KJV)

10.) Genesis 19:33 "And they made their father drink wine that **night**: and the firstborn went in, and lay with her father; and he perceived not when she lay down, nor when she arose." (KJV)

11.) Genesis 19:34 "And it came to pass on the morrow, that the firstborn said unto the younger, Behold, I lay yesternight with my father: let us make him drink wine this **night** also; and go thou in, *and* lie with him, that we may preserve seed of our father." (KJV)

12.) Genesis 19:35 "And they made their father drink wine that **night** also: and the younger arose, and lay with him; and he perceived not when she lay down, nor when she arose." (KJV)

13.) Genesis 20:3 "But God came to Abimelech in a dream by **night**, and said to him, Behold, thou *art but* a dead man, for the woman which thou hast taken; for she *is* a man's wife." (KJV)

14.) Genesis 26:24 "And the LORD appeared unto him the same **night**, and said, I *am* the God of Abraham thy father: fear not, for I *am* with thee, and will bless thee, and multiply thy seed for my servant Abraham's sake." (KJV)

15.) Genesis 30:15 "And she said unto her, *Is it* a small matter that thou hast taken my husband? and wouldest thou take away my son's mandrakes also? And Rachel said, Therefore he shall lie with thee to **night** for thy son's mandrakes." (KJV)

16.) Genesis 30:16 "And Jacob came out of the field in the evening, and Leah went out to meet him, and said, Thou must come in unto me; for surely I have hired thee with my son's mandrakes. And he lay with her that **night**." (KJV)

17.) Genesis 31:24 "And God came to Laban the Syrian in a dream by **night**, and said unto him, Take heed that thou speak not to Jacob either good or bad." (KJV)

18.) Genesis 31:39 "That which was torn *of beasts* I brought not unto thee; I bare the loss of it; of my hand didst thou require it, *whether* stolen by day, or stolen by **night**." (KJV)

19.) Genesis 31:40 "*Thus* I was; in the day the drought consumed me, and the frost by **night**; and my sleep departed from mine eyes." (KJV)

20.) Genesis 32:13 "And he lodged there that same **night**; and took of that which came to his hand a present for Esau his brother;" (KJV)

21.) Genesis 32:21 "So went the present over before him: and himself lodged that **night** in the company." (KJV)

22.) Genesis 32:22 "And he rose up that **night**, and took his two wives, and his two womenservants, and his eleven sons, and passed over the ford Jabbok." (KJV)

23.) Genesis 40:5 "And they dreamed a dream both of them, each man his dream in one **night**, each man according to the interpretation of his dream, the butler and the baker of the king of Egypt, which *were* bound in the prison." (KJV)

24.) Genesis 41:11 "And we dreamed a dream in one **night**, I and he; we dreamed each man according to the interpretation of his dream." (KJV)

25.) Genesis 46:2 "And God spake unto Israel in the visions of the **night**, and said, Jacob, Jacob. And he said, Here *am* I." (KJV)

26.) Exodus 10:13 "And Moses stretched forth his rod over the land of Egypt, and the LORD brought an east wind upon the land all that day, and all *that* **night**; *and* when it was morning, the east wind brought the locusts." (KJV)

27.) Exodus 11:4 "And Moses said, Thus saith the LORD, About mid**night** will I go out into the midst of Egypt:" (KJV)

28.) Exodus 12:8 "And they shall eat the flesh in that **night**, roast with fire, and unleavened bread; *and* with bitter *herbs* they shall eat it." (KJV)

29.) Exodus 12:12 "For I will pass through the land of Egypt this **night**, and will smite all the firstborn in the land of Egypt, both man and beast; and against all the gods of Egypt I will execute judgment: I *am* the LORD." (KJV)

30.) Exodus 12:29 "And it came to pass, that at mid**night** the LORD smote all the firstborn in the land of Egypt, from the firstborn of Pharaoh that sat on his throne unto the firstborn of the captive that *was* in the dungeon; and all the firstborn of cattle." (KJV)

31.) Exodus 12:30 "And Pharaoh rose up in the **night**, he, and all his servants, and all the Egyptians; and there was a great cry in Egypt; for *there was* not a house where *there was* not one dead." (KJV)

32.) Exodus 12:31 "And he called for Moses and Aaron by **night**, and said, Rise up, *and* get you forth from among my people, both ye and the children of Israel; and go, serve the LORD, as ye have said." (KJV)

33. and 34.) Exodus 12:42 "It *is* a **night** to be much observed unto the LORD for bringing them out from the land of Egypt: this *is* that **night** of the LORD to be observed of all the children of Israel in their generations." (KJV)

35. and 36.) Exodus 13:21 "And the LORD went before them by day in a pillar of a cloud, to lead them the way; and by **night** in a pillar of fire, to give them light; to go by day and **night**:" (KJV)

37.) Exodus 13:22 "He took not away the pillar of the cloud by day, nor the pillar of fire by **night**, *from* before the people." (KJV)

38. and 39.) Exodus 14:20 "And it came between the camp of the Egyptians and the camp of Israel; and it was a cloud and darkness *to them,* but it gave light by **night** *to these:* so that the one came not near the other all the **night**." (KJV)

40.) Exodus 14:21 "And Moses stretched out his hand over the sea; and the LORD caused the sea to go *back* by a strong east wind all that **night**, and made the sea dry *land,* and the waters were divided." (KJV)

41.) Exodus 24:18 "And Moses went into the midst of the cloud, and gat him up into the mount: and Moses was in the mount forty days and forty **nights**." (KJV)

42.) Exodus 34:28 "And he was there with the LORD forty days and forty **nights**; he did neither eat bread, nor drink water. And he wrote upon the tables the words of the covenant, the ten commandments." (KJV)

43.) Exodus 40:38 "For the cloud of the LORD *was* upon the tabernacle by day, and fire was on it by **night**, in the sight of all the house of Israel, throughout all their journeys." (KJV)

44.) Leviticus 6:9 "Command Aaron and his sons, saying, This *is* the law of the burnt offering: It *is* the burnt offering, because of the burning upon the altar all **night** unto the morning, and the fire of the altar shall be burning in it." (KJV)

45.) Leviticus 8:35 "Therefore shall ye abide *at* the door of the tabernacle of the congregation day and **night** seven days, and keep the charge of the LORD, that ye die not: for so I am commanded." (KJV)

46.) Numbers 9:16 "So it was alway: the cloud covered it *by day,* and the appearance of fire by **night**." (KJV)

47.) Numbers 9:21 "And *so* it was, when the cloud abode from even unto the morning, and *that* the cloud was taken up in the morning, then they journeyed: whether *it was* by day or by **night** that the cloud was taken up, they journeyed." (KJV)

48.) Numbers 11:9 "And when the dew fell upon the camp in the **night**, the manna fell upon it." (KJV)

49.) Numbers 11:32 "And the people stood up all that day, and all *that* **night**, and all the next day, and they gathered the quails: he that gathered least gathered ten homers: and they spread *them* all abroad for themselves round about the camp." (KJV)

50.) Numbers 14:1 "And all the congregation lifted up their voice, and cried; and the people wept that **night**." (KJV)

51.) Numbers 14:14 "And they will tell *it* to the inhabitants of this land: *for* they have heard that thou LORD *art* among this people, that thou LORD art seen face to face, and *that* thy cloud standeth over them, and *that* thou goest before them, by day time in a pillar of a cloud, and in a pillar of fire by **night**." (KJV)

52.) Numbers 22:8 "And he said unto them, Lodge here this **night**, and I will bring you word again, as the LORD shall speak unto me: and the princes of Moab abode with Balaam." (KJV)

53.) Numbers 22:19 "Now therefore, I pray you, tarry ye also here this **night**, that I may know what the LORD will say unto me more." (KJV)

54.) Numbers 22:20 "And God came unto Balaam at **night**, and said unto him, If the men come to call thee, rise up, *and* go with them; but yet the word which I shall say unto thee, that shalt thou do." (KJV)

55.) Deuteronomy 1:33 "Who went in the way before you, to search you out a place to pitch your tents *in,* in fire by **night**, to show you by what way ye should go, and in a cloud by day." (KJV)

56.) Deuteronomy 9:9 "When I was gone up into the mount to receive the tables of stone, *even* the tables of the covenant which the LORD made with you, then I abode in the mount forty days and forty **nights**, I neither did eat bread nor drink water:" (KJV)

57.) Deuteronomy 9:11 "And it came to pass at the end of forty days and forty **nights**, *that* the LORD gave me the two tables of stone, *even* the tables of the covenant." (KJV)

58.) Deuteronomy 9:18 "And I fell down before the LORD, as at the first, forty days and forty **nights**: I did neither eat bread, nor drink water, because of all your sins which ye sinned, in doing wickedly in the sight of the LORD, to provoke him to anger." (KJV)

59.) Deuteronomy 9:25 "Thus I fell down before the LORD forty days and forty **nights**, as I fell down *at the first;* because the LORD had said he would destroy you." (KJV)

60.) Deuteronomy 10:10 "And I stayed in the mount, according to the first time, forty days and forty **nights**; and the LORD hearkened unto me at that time also, *and* the LORD would not destroy thee." (KJV)

61.) Deuteronomy 16:1 "Observe the month of Abib, and keep the passover unto the LORD thy God: for in the month of Abib the LORD thy God brought thee forth out of Egypt by **night**." (KJV)

62.) Deuteronomy 23:10 "If there be among you any man, that is not clean by reason of uncleanness that chanceth him by **night**, then shall he go abroad out of the camp, he shall not come within the camp:" (KJV)

63.) Deuteronomy 28:66 "And thy life shall hang in doubt before thee; and thou shalt fear day and **night**, and shalt have none assurance of thy life:" (KJV)

64.) Joshua 1:8 "This book of the law shall not depart out of thy mouth; but thou shalt meditate therein day and **night**, that thou mayest observe to do according to all that is written therein: for then thou shalt make thy way prosperous, and then thou shalt have good success." (KJV)

65.) Joshua 2:2 "And it was told the king of Jericho, saying, Behold, there came men in hither to **night** of the children of Israel to search out the country." (KJV)

66.) Joshua 4:3 "And command ye them, saying, Take you hence out of the midst of Jordan, out of the place where the priests' feet stood firm, twelve stones, and ye shall carry them over with you, and leave them in the lodging place, where ye shall lodge this **night**." (KJV)

67.) Joshua 8:3 "So Joshua arose, and all the people of war, to go up against Ai: and Joshua chose out thirty thousand mighty men of valour, and sent them away by **night**." (KJV)

68.) Joshua 8:9 "Joshua therefore sent them forth: and they went to lie in ambush, and abode between Bethel and Ai, on the west side of Ai: but Joshua lodged that **night** among the people." (KJV)

69.) Joshua 8:13 "And when they had set the people, *even* all the host that *was* on the north of the city, and their liers in wait on the west of the city, Joshua went that **night** into the midst of the valley." (KJV)

70.) Joshua 10:9 "Joshua therefore came unto them suddenly, *and* went up from Gilgal all **night**." (KJV)

71.) Judges 6:25 "And it came to pass the same **night**, that the LORD said unto him, Take thy father's young bullock, even the second bullock of seven years old, and throw down the altar of Baal that thy father hath, and cut down the grove that *is* by it:" (KJV)

72.) Judges 6:27 "Then Gideon took ten men of his servants, and did as the LORD had said unto him: and *so* it was, because he feared his father's household, and the men of the city, that he could not do *it* by day, that he did *it* by **night**." (KJV)

73.) Judges 6:40 "And God did so that **night**: for it was dry upon the fleece only, and there was dew on all the ground." (KJV)

74.) Judges 7:9 "And it came to pass the same **night**, that the LORD said unto him, Arise, get thee down unto the host; for I have delivered it into thine hand." (KJV)

75.) Judges 9:32 "Now therefore up by **night**, thou and the people that *is* with thee, and lie in wait in the field:" (KJV)

76.) Judges 9:34 "And Abimelech rose up, and all the people that *were* with him, by **night**, and they laid wait against Shechem in four companies." (KJV)

77. and 78.) Judges 16:2 "*And it was told* the Gazites, saying, Samson is come hither. And they compassed *him* in, and laid wait for him all **night** in the gate of the city, and were quiet all the **night**, saying, In the morning, when it is day, we shall kill him." (KJV)

79. and 80.) Judges 16:3 "And Samson lay till mid**night**, and arose at mid**night**, and took the doors of the gate of the city, and the two posts, and went away with them, bar and all, and put *them* upon his shoulders, and carried them up to the top of an hill that *is* before Hebron." (KJV)

81.) Judges 19:25 "But the men would not hearken to him: so the man took his concubine, and brought her forth unto them; and they knew her, and abused her all the **night** until the morning: and when the day began to spring, they let her go." (KJV)

82.) Judges 20:5 "And the men of Gibeah rose against me, and beset the house round about upon me by **night**, *and* thought to have slain me: and my concubine have they forced, that she is dead." (KJV)

83.) Ruth 1:12 "Turn again, my daughters, go *your way;* for I am too old to have an husband. If I should say, I have hope, *if* I should have an husband also to **night**, and should also bear sons;" (KJV)

84.) Ruth 3:2 "And now *is* not Boaz of our kindred, with whose maidens thou wast? Behold, he winnoweth barley to **night** in the threshingfloor." (KJV)

85.) Ruth 3:8 "And it came to pass at mid**night**, that the man was afraid, and turned himself: and, behold, a woman lay at his feet." (KJV)

86.) Ruth 3:13 "Tarry this **night**, and it shall be in the morning, *that* if he will perform unto thee the part of a kinsman, well; let him do the kinsman's part: but if he will not do the part of a kinsman to thee, then will I do the part of a kinsman to thee, *as* the LORD liveth: lie down until the morning." (KJV)

87.) 1 Samuel 14:34 "And Saul said, Disperse yourselves among the people, and say unto them, Bring me hither every man his ox, and every man his sheep, and slay *them* here, and eat; and sin not against the LORD in eating with the blood. And all the people brought every man his ox with him that **night**, and slew *them* there." (KJV)

88.) 1 Samuel 14:36 "And Saul said, Let us go down after the Philistines by **night**, and spoil them until the morning light, and let us not leave a man of them. And they said, Do whatsoever seemeth good unto thee. Then said the priest, Let us draw near hither unto God." (KJV)

89.) 1 Samuel 15:11 "It repenteth me that I have set up Saul *to be* king: for he is turned back from following me, and hath not performed my commandments. And it grieved Samuel; and he cried unto the LORD all **night**." (KJV)

90.) 1 Samuel 15:16 "Then Samuel said unto Saul, Stay, and I will tell thee what the LORD hath said to me this **night**. And he said unto him, Say on." (KJV)

91.) 1 Samuel 19:10 "And Saul sought to smite David even to the wall with the javelin; but he slipped away out of Saul's presence, and he smote the javelin into the wall: and David fled, and escaped that **night**." (KJV)

92.) 1 Samuel 19:11 "Saul also sent messengers unto David's house, to watch him, and to slay him in the morning: and Michal David's wife told him, saying, If thou save not thy life to **night**, to morrow thou shalt be slain." (KJV)

93.) 1 Samuel 19:24 "And he stripped off his clothes also, and prophesied before Samuel in like manner, and lay down naked all that day and all that **night**. Wherefore they say, *Is* Saul also among the prophets?" (KJV)

94.) 1 Samuel 25:16 "They were a wall unto us both by **night** and day, all the while we were with them keeping the sheep." (KJV)

95.) 1 Samuel 26:7 "So David and Abishai came to the people by **night**: and, behold, Saul lay sleeping within the trench, and his spear stuck in the ground at his bolster: but Abner and the people lay round about him." (KJV)

96.) 1 Samuel 28:8 "And Saul disguised himself, and put on other raiment, and he went, and two men with him, and they came to the woman by **night**: and he said, I pray thee, divine unto me by the familiar spirit, and bring me *him* up, whom I shall name unto thee." (KJV)

97.) 1 Samuel 28:20 "Then Saul fell straightway all along on the earth, and was sore afraid, because of the words of Samuel: and there was no strength in him; for he had eaten no bread all the day, nor all the **night**." (KJV)

98.) 1 Samuel 28:25 "And she brought *it* before Saul, and before his servants; and they did eat. Then they rose up, and went away that **night**." (KJV)

99.) 1 Samuel 30:12 "And they gave him a piece of a cake of figs, and two clusters of raisins: and when he had eaten, his spirit came again to him: for he had eaten no bread, nor drunk *any* water, three days and three **nights**." (KJV)

100.) 1 Samuel 31:12 "All the valiant men arose, and went all **night**, and took the body of Saul and the bodies of his sons from the wall of Bethshan, and came to Jabesh, and burnt them there." (KJV)

101.) 2 Samuel 2:29 "And Abner and his men walked all that **night** through the plain, and passed over Jordan, and went through all Bithron, and they came to Mahanaim." (KJV)

102.) 2 Samuel 2:32 "And they took up Asahel, and buried him in the sepulchre of his father, which *was in* Bethlehem. And Joab and his men went all **night**, and they came to Hebron at break of day." (KJV)

103.) 2 Samuel 4:7 "For when they came into the house, he lay on his bed in his bedchamber, and they smote him, and slew him, and beheaded him, and took his head, and gat them away through the plain all **night**." (KJV)

104.) 2 Samuel 7:4 "And it came to pass that **night**, that the word of the LORD came unto Nathan, saying," (KJV)

105.) 2 Samuel 17:1 "Moreover Ahithophel said unto Absalom, Let me now choose out twelve thousand men, and I will arise and pursue after David this **night**:" (KJV)

106.) 2 Samuel 17:16 "Now therefore send quickly, and tell David, saying, Lodge not this **night** in the plains of the wilderness, but speedily pass over; lest the king be swallowed up, and all the people that *are* with him." (KJV)

107.) 2 Samuel 19:7 "Now therefore arise, go forth, and speak comfortably unto thy servants: for I swear by the LORD, if thou go not forth, there will not tarry one with thee this **night**: and that will be worse unto thee than all the evil that befell thee from thy youth until now." (KJV)

108.) 2 Samuel 21:10 "And Rizpah the daughter of Aiah took sackcloth, and spread it for her upon the rock, from the beginning of harvest until water dropped upon them out of heaven, and suffered neither the birds of the air to rest on them by day, nor the beasts of the field by **night**." (KJV)

109.) 1 Kings 3:5 "In Gibeon the LORD appeared to Solomon in a dream by **night**: and God said, Ask what I shall give thee." (KJV)

110.) 1 Kings 3:19 "And this woman's child died in the **night**; because she overlaid it." (KJV)

111.) 1 Kings 3:20 "And she arose at mid**night**, and took my son from beside me, while thine handmaid slept, and laid it in her bosom, and laid her dead child in my bosom." (KJV)

112.) 1 Kings 8:29 "That thine eyes may be open toward this house **night** and day, *even* toward the place of which thou hast said, My name shall be there: that thou mayest hearken unto the prayer which thy servant shall make toward this place." (KJV)

113.) 1 Kings 8:59 "And let these my words, wherewith I have made supplication before the LORD, be nigh unto the LORD our God day and **night**, that he maintain the cause of his servant, and the cause of his people Israel at all times, as the matter shall require:" (KJV)

114.) 1 Kings 19:8 "And he arose, and did eat and drink, and went in the strength of that meat forty days and forty **nights** unto Horeb the mount of God." (KJV)

115.) 2 Kings 6:14 "Therefore sent he thither horses, and chariots, and a great host: and they came by **night**, and compassed the city about." (KJV)

116.) 2 Kings 7:12 "And the king arose in the **night**, and said unto his servants, I will now show you what the Syrians have done to us. They know that we *be* hungry; therefore are they gone out of the camp to hide themselves in the field, saying, When they come out of the city, we shall catch them alive, and get into the city." (KJV)

117. 2 Kings 8:21 "So Joram went over to Zair, and all the chariots with him: and he rose by **night**, and smote the Edomites which compassed him about, and the captains of the chariots: and the people fled into their tents." (KJV)

118.) 2 Kings 19:35 "And it came to pass that **night**, that the angel of the LORD went out, and smote in the camp of the Assyrians an hundred fourscore and five thousand: and when they arose early in the morning, behold, they *were* all dead corpses." (KJV)

119.) 2 Kings 25:4 "And the city was broken up, and all the men of war *fled* by **night** by the way of the gate between two walls, which *is* by the king's garden: (now the Chaldees *were* against the city round about:) and *the king* went the way toward the plain." (KJV)

120.) 1 Chronicles 9:33 "And these *are* the singers, chief of the fathers of the Levites, *who remaining* in the chambers *were* free: for they were employed in *that* work day and **night**." (KJV)

121.) 1 Chronicles 17:3 "And it came to pass the same **night**, that the word of God came to Nathan, saying," (KJV)

122.) 2 Chronicles 1:7 "In that **night** did God appear unto Solomon, and said unto him, Ask what I shall give thee." (KJV)

123.) 2 Chronicles 6:20 "That thine eyes may be open upon this house day and **night**, upon the place whereof thou hast said that thou wouldest put thy name there; to hearken unto the prayer which thy servant prayeth toward this place." (KJV)

124.) 2 Chronicles 7:12 "And the LORD appeared to Solomon by **night**, and said unto him, I have heard thy prayer, and have chosen this place to myself for an house of sacrifice." (KJV)

125.) 2 Chronicles 21:9 "Then Jehoram went forth with his princes, and all his chariots with him: and he rose up by **night**, and smote the Edomites which compassed him in, and the captains of the chariots." (KJV)

126.) 2 Chronicles 35:14 "And afterward they made ready for themselves, and for the priests: because the priests the sons of Aaron *were busied* in offering of burnt offerings and the fat until **night**; therefore the Levites prepared for themselves, and for the priests the sons of Aaron." (KJV)

127.) Nehemiah 1:6 "Let thine ear now be attentive, and thine eyes open, that thou mayest hear the prayer of thy servant, which I pray before thee now, day and **night**, for the children of Israel thy servants, and confess the sins of the children of Israel, which we have sinned against thee: both I and my father's house have sinned." (KJV)

128.) Nehemiah 2:12 "And I arose in the **night**, I and some few men with me; neither told I *any* man what my God had put in my heart to do at Jerusalem: neither *was there any* beast with me, save the beast that I rode upon." (KJV)

129.) Nehemiah 2:13 "And I went out by **night** by the gate of the valley, even before the dragon well, and to the dung port, and viewed the walls of Jerusalem, which were broken down, and the gates thereof were consumed with fire." (KJV)

130.) Nehemiah 2:15 "Then went I up in the **night** by the brook, and viewed the wall, and turned back, and entered by the gate of the valley, and *so* returned." (KJV)

131.) Nehemiah 4:9 "Nevertheless we made our prayer unto our God, and set a watch against them day and **night**, because of them." (KJV)

132.) Nehemiah 4:22 "Likewise at the same time said I unto the people, Let every one with his servant lodge within Jerusalem, that in the **night** they may be a guard to us, and labour on the day." (KJV)

133.) Nehemiah 6:10 "Afterward I came unto the house of Shemaiah the son of Delaiah the son of Mehetabeel, who *was* shut up; and he said, Let us meet together in the house of God, within the temple, and let us shut the doors of the temple: for they will come to slay thee; yea, in the **night** will they come to slay thee." (KJV)

134.) Nehemiah 9:12 "Moreover thou leddest them in the day by a cloudy pillar; and in the **night** by a pillar of fire, to give them light in the way wherein they should go." (KJV)

135.) Nehemiah 9:19 "Yet thou in thy manifold mercies forsookest them not in the wilderness: the pillar of the cloud departed not from them by day, to lead them in the way; neither the pillar of fire by **night**, to show them light, and the way wherein they should go." (KJV)

136.) Esther 4:16 "Go, gather together all the Jews that are present in Shushan, and fast ye for me, and neither eat nor drink three days, **night** or day: I also and my maidens will fast likewise; and so will I go in unto the king, which *is* not according to the law: and if I perish, I perish." (KJV)

137.) Esther 6:1 "On that **night** could not the king sleep, and he commanded to bring the book of records of the chronicles; and they were read before the king." (KJV)

138.) Job 2:13 "So they sat down with him upon the ground seven days and seven **nights**, and none spake a word unto him: for they saw that *his* grief was very great." (KJV)

139.) Job 3:3 "Let the day perish wherein I was born, and the **night** *in which* it was said, There is a man child conceived." (KJV)

140.) Job 3:6 "As *for* that **night**, let darkness seize upon it; let it not be joined unto the days of the year, let it not come into the number of the months." (KJV)

141.) Job 3:7 "Lo, let that **night** be solitary, let no joyful voice come therein." (KJV)

142.) Job 4:13 "In thoughts from the visions of the **night**, when deep sleep falleth on men," (KJV)

143.) Job 5:14 "They meet with darkness in the daytime, and grope in the noonday as in the **night**." (KJV)

144.) Job 7:3 "So am I made to possess months of vanity, and wearisome **nights** are appointed to me." (KJV)

145.) Job 17:12 "They change the **night** into day: the light *is* short because of darkness." (KJV)

146.) Job 20:8 "He shall fly away as a dream, and shall not be found: yea, he shall be chased away as a vision of the **night**." (KJV)

147.) Job 24:14 "The murderer rising with the light killeth the poor and needy, and in the **night** is as a thief." (KJV)

148.) Job 27:20 "Terrors take hold on him as waters, a tempest stealeth him away in the **night**." (KJV)

149.) Job 30:17 "My bones are pierced in me in the **night** season: and my sinews take no rest." (KJV)

150.) Job 33:15 "In a dream, in a vision of the **night**, when deep sleep falleth upon men, in slumberings upon the bed;" (KJV)

151.) Job 34:20 "In a moment shall they die, and the people shall be troubled at mid**night**, and pass away: and the mighty shall be taken away without hand." (KJV)

152.) Job 34:25 "Therefore he knoweth their works, and he overturneth *them* in the **night**, so that they are destroyed." (KJV)

153.) Job 35:10 "But none saith, Where *is* God my maker, who giveth songs in the **night**;" (KJV)

154.) Job 36:20 "Desire not the **night**, when people are cut off in their place." (KJV)

155.) Psalms 1:2 "But his delight *is* in the law of the LORD; and in his law doth he meditate day and **night**." (KJV)

156.) Psalms 6:6 "I am weary with my groaning; all the **night** make I my bed to swim; I water my couch with my tears." (KJV)

157.) Psalms 16:7 "I will bless the LORD, who hath given me counsel: my reins also instruct me in the **night** seasons." (KJV)

158.) Psalms 17:3 "Thou hast proved mine heart; thou hast visited *me* in the **night**; thou hast tried me, *and* shalt find nothing; I am purposed *that* my mouth shall not transgress." (KJV)

159. and 160.) Psalms 19:2 "Day unto day uttereth speech, and **night** unto **night** showeth knowledge." (KJV)

161.) Psalms 22:2 "O my God, I cry in the daytime, but thou hearest not; and in the **night** season, and am not silent." (KJV)

162.) Psalms 32:4 "For day and **night** thy hand was heavy upon me: my moisture is turned into the drought of summer. Selah." (KJV)

163.) Psalms 42:3 "My tears have been my meat day and **night**, while they continually say unto me, Where *is* thy God?" (KJV)

164.) Psalms 42:8 "*Yet* the LORD will command his lovingkindness in the daytime, and in the **night** his song *shall be* with me, *and* my prayer unto the God of my life." (KJV)

165.) Psalms 55:10 "Day and **night** they go about it upon the walls thereof: mischief also and sorrow *are* in the midst of it." (KJV)

166.) Psalms 74:16 "The day *is* thine, the **night** also *is* thine: thou hast prepared the light and the sun." (KJV)

167.) Psalms 77:2 "In the day of my trouble I sought the Lord: my sore ran in the **night**, and ceased not: my soul refused to be comforted." (KJV)

168.) Psalms 77:6 "I call to remembrance my song in the **night**: I commune with mine own heart: and my spirit made diligent search." (KJV)

169.) Psalms 78:14 "In the daytime also he led them with a cloud, and all the **night** with a light of fire." (KJV)

170.) Psalms 88:1 "A Song *or* Psalms for the sons of Korah, to the chief Musician upon Mahalath Leannoth, Maschil of Heman the Ezrahite. O LORD God of my salvation, I have cried day *and* **night** before thee:" (KJV)

171.) Psalms 90:4 "For a thousand years in thy sight *are but* as yesterday when it is past, and *as* a watch in the **night**." (KJV)

172.) Psalms 91:5 "Thou shalt not be afraid for the terror by **night**; *nor* for the arrow *that* flieth by day;" (KJV)

173.) Psalms 92:2 "To show forth thy lovingkindness in the morning, and thy faithfulness every **night**," (KJV)

174.) Psalms 104:20 "Thou makest darkness, and it is **night**: wherein all the beasts of the forest do creep *forth*." (KJV)

175.) Psalms 105:39 "He spread a cloud for a covering; and fire to give light in the **night**." (KJV)

176.) Psalms 119:55 "I have remembered thy name, O LORD, in the **night**, and have kept thy law." (KJV)

177.) Psalms 119:62 "At mid**night** I will rise to give thanks unto thee because of thy righteous judgments." (KJV)

178.) Psalms 121:6 "The sun shall not smite thee by day, nor the moon by **night**." (KJV)

179.) Psalms 134:1 "A Song of degrees. Behold, bless ye the LORD, all *ye* servants of the LORD, which by **night** stand in the house of the LORD." (KJV)

180.) Psalms 136:9 "The moon and stars to rule by **night**: for his mercy *endureth* for ever." (KJV)

181.) Psalms 139:11 "If I say, Surely the darkness shall cover me; even the **night** shall be light about me." (KJV)

182.) Psalms 139:12 "Yea, the darkness hideth not from thee; but the **night** shineth as the day: the darkness and the light *are* both alike *to thee*." (KJV)

183.) Proverbs 7:9 "In the twilight, in the evening, in the black and dark **night**:" (KJV)

184.) Proverbs 31:15 "She riseth also while it is yet **night**, and giveth meat to her household, and a portion to her maidens." (KJV)

185. and 186.) Proverbs 31:18 "She perceiveth that her merchandise *is* good: her candle goeth not out by **night**." (KJV)

(Note: In Proverbs 31:18, the Hebrew word *LAYIL* is used twice. Literally, it says something like, "night by night.")

187.) Ecclesiastes 2:23 "For all his days *are* sorrows, and his travail grief; yea, his heart taketh not rest in the **night**. This is also vanity." (KJV)

188.) Ecclesiastes 8:16 "When I applied mine heart to know wisdom, and to see the business that is done upon the earth: (for also *there is that* neither day nor **night** seeth sleep with his eyes:)" (KJV)

189.) Song of Solomon 3:1 "By **night** on my bed I sought him whom my soul loveth: I sought him, but I found him not." (KJV)

190.) Song of Solomon 3:8 "They all hold swords, *being* expert in war: every man *hath* his sword upon his thigh because of fear in the **night**." (KJV)

191.) Song of Solomon 5:2 "I sleep, but my heart waketh: *it is* the voice of my beloved that knocketh, *saying*, Open to me, my sister, my love, my dove, my undefiled: for my head is filled with dew, *and* my locks with the drops of the **night**." (KJV)

192.) Isaiah 4:5 "And the LORD will create upon every dwelling place of mount Zion, and upon her assemblies, a cloud and smoke by day, and the shining of a flaming fire by **night**: for upon all the glory *shall be* a defence." (KJV)

193. and 194.) Isaiah 15:1 "The burden of Moab. Because in the **night** Ar of Moab is laid waste, *and* brought to silence; because in the **night** Kir of Moab is laid waste, *and* brought to silence;" (KJV)

195.) Isaiah 16:3 "Take counsel, execute judgment; make thy shadow as the **night** in the midst of the noonday; hide the outcasts; bewray not him that wandereth." (KJV)

196.) Isaiah 21:8 "And he cried, A lion: My lord, I stand continually upon the watchtower in the daytime, and I am set in my ward whole **nights**:" (KJV)

197. and 198.) Isaiah 21:11 "The burden of Dumah. He calleth to me out of Seir, Watchman, what of the **night**? Watchman, what of the **night**?" (KJV)

199.) Isaiah 21:12 "The watchman said, The morning cometh, and also the **night**: if ye will inquire, inquire ye: return, come." (KJV)

200.) Isaiah 26:9 "With my soul have I desired thee in the **night**; yea, with my spirit within me will I seek thee early: for when thy judgments *are* in the earth, the inhabitants of the world will learn righteousness." (KJV)

201.) Isaiah 27:3 "I the LORD do keep it; I will water it every moment: lest *any* hurt it, I will keep it **night** and day." (KJV)

202.) Isaiah 28:19 "From the time that it goeth forth it shall take you: for morning by morning shall it pass over, by day and by **night**: and it shall be a vexation only *to* understand the report." (KJV)

203.) Isaiah 29:7 "And the multitude of all the nations that fight against Ariel, even all that fight against her and her munition, and that distress her, shall be as a dream of a **night** vision." (KJV)

204.) Isaiah 30:29 "Ye shall have a song, as in the **night** *when* a holy solemnity is kept; and gladness of heart, as when one goeth with a pipe to come into the mountain of the LORD, to the mighty One of Israel." (KJV)

205.) Isaiah 34:10 "It shall not be quenched **night** nor day; the smoke thereof shall go up for ever: from generation to generation it shall lie waste; none shall pass through it for ever and ever." (KJV)

206.) Isaiah 38:12 "Mine age is departed, and is removed from me as a shepherd's tent: I have cut off like a weaver my life: he will cut me off with pining sickness: from day *even* to **night** wilt thou make an end of me." (KJV)

207.) Isaiah 38:13 "I reckoned till morning, *that,* as a lion, so will he break all my bones: from day *even* to **night** wilt thou make an end of me." (KJV)

208.) Isaiah 60:11 "Therefore thy gates shall be open continually; they shall not be shut day nor **night**; that *men* may bring unto thee the forces of the Gentiles, and *that* their kings *may be* brought." (KJV)

209.) Isaiah 62:6 "I have set watchmen upon thy walls, O Jerusalem, *which* shall never hold their peace day nor **night**: ye that make mention of the LORD, keep not silence." (KJV)

210.) Jeremiah 6:5 "Arise, and let us go by **night**, and let us destroy her palaces." (KJV)

211.) Jeremiah 9:1 "Oh that my head were waters, and mine eyes a fountain of tears, that I might weep day and **night** for the slain of the daughter of my people!" (KJV)

212.) Jeremiah 14:17 "Therefore thou shalt say this word unto them; Let mine eyes run down with tears **night** and day, and let them not cease: for the virgin daughter of my people is broken with a great breach, with a very grievous blow." (KJV)

213.) Jeremiah 16:13 "Therefore will I cast you out of this land into a land that ye know not, *neither* ye nor your fathers; and there shall ye serve other gods day and **night**; where I will not show you favour." (KJV)

214.) Jeremiah 31:35-36 "Thus saith the LORD, which giveth the sun for a light by day, *and* the ordinances of the moon and of the stars for a light by **night**, which divideth the sea when the waves thereof roar; The LORD of hosts *is* his name:" (KJV)

215. and 216.) Jeremiah 33:20 "Thus saith the LORD; If ye can break my covenant of the day, and my covenant of the **night**, and that there should not be day and **night** in their season;" (KJV)

217.) Jeremiah 33:25 "Thus saith the LORD; If my covenant *be* not with day and **night**, *and if* I have not appointed the ordinances of heaven and earth;" (KJV)

218.) Jeremiah 36:30 "Therefore thus saith the LORD of Jehoiakim king of Judah; He shall have none to sit upon the throne of David: and his dead body shall be cast out in the day to the heat, and in the **night** to the frost." (KJV)

219.) Jeremiah 39:4 "And it came to pass, *that* when Zedekiah the king of Judah saw them, and all the men of war, then they fled, and went forth out of the city by **night**, by the way of the king's garden, by the gate betwixt the two walls: and he went out the way of the plain." (KJV)

220.) Jeremiah 49:9 "If grapegatherers come to thee, would they not leave *some* gleaning grapes? if thieves by **night**, they will destroy till they have enough." (KJV)

221.) Jeremiah 52:7 "Then the city was broken up, and all the men of war fled, and went forth out of the city by **night** by the way of the gate between the two walls, which *was* by the king's garden; (now the Chaldeans *were* by the city round about:) and they went by the way of the plain." (KJV)

222.) Lamentations 1:2 "She weepeth sore in the **night**, and her tears *are* on her cheeks: among all her lovers she hath none to comfort *her:* all her friends have dealt treacherously with her, they are become her enemies." (KJV)

223.) Lamentations 2:18 "Their heart cried unto the Lord, O wall of the daughter of Zion, let tears run down like a river day and **night**: give thyself no rest; let not the apple of thine eye cease." (KJV)

224. and 225.) Lamentations 2:19 "Arise, cry out in the **night**: in the beginning of the watches pour out thine heart like water before the face of the Lord: lift up thy hands toward him for the life of thy young children, that faint for hunger in the top of every street." (KJV)

(Note: In Lamentations 2:19, the Hebrew word *LAYIL* is used twice. Literally, it says something like, "night by night.")

226.) Hosea 4:5 "Therefore shalt thou fall in the day, and the prophet also shall fall with thee in the **night**, and I will destroy thy mother." (KJV)

227.) Hosea 7:6 "For they have made ready their heart like an oven, whiles they lie in wait: their baker sleepeth all the **night**; in the morning it burneth as a flaming fire." (KJV)

228.) Amos 5:8 "*Seek him* that maketh the seven stars and Orion, and turneth the shadow of death into the morning, and maketh the day dark with **night**: that calleth for the waters of the sea, and poureth them out upon the face of the earth: The LORD *is* his name:" (KJV)

229.) Obadiah 1:5 "If thieves came to thee, if robbers by **night**, (how art thou cut off!) would they not have stolen till they had enough? if the grapegatherers came to thee, would they not leave *some* grapes?" (KJV)

230.) Jonah 1:17 "Now the LORD had prepared a great fish to swallow up Jonah. And Jonah was in the belly of the fish three days and three **nights**." (KJV)

231. and 232.) Jonah 4:10 "Then said the LORD, Thou hast had pity on the gourd, for the which thou hast not laboured, neither madest it grow; which came up in a **night**, and perished in a **night**:" (KJV)

233.) Micah 3:6 "Therefore **night** *shall be* unto you, that ye shall not have a vision; and it shall be dark unto you, that ye shall not divine; and the sun shall go down over the prophets, and the day shall be dark over them." (KJV)

234.) Zechariah 1:8 "I saw by **night**, and behold a man riding upon a red horse, and he stood among the myrtle trees that *were* in the bottom; and behind him *were there* red horses, speckled, and white." (KJV)

235.) Zechariah 14:7 "But it shall be one day which shall be known to the LORD, not day, nor **night**: but it shall come to pass, *that* at evening time it shall be light." (KJV)

In the Genesis account of creation, *LAYIL* is paired with *YOM*. It makes no sense to say "day" means billions of years when it is combined with the word "night" that always means the dark hours of a twenty-four-hour day. Furthermore, the words "day" and "night" (*YOM* and *LAYIL*) are combined in fifty-three other Biblical passages, as they are in Genesis 1. What do they mean when used together?

YOM and *LAYIL* (Day and Night)

1.) Genesis 1:5 "And God called the light **Day**, and the darkness he called **Night**. And the evening and the morning were the first **day**." (KJV)

2.) Genesis 1:14 "And God said, Let there be lights in the firmament of the heaven to divide the **day** from the **night**; and let them be for signs, and for seasons, and for **days**, and years:" (KJV)

3.) Genesis 1:16 "And God made two great lights; the greater light to rule the **day**, and the lesser light to rule the **night**: *he made* the stars also." (KJV)

4.) Genesis 1:18 "And to rule over the **day** and over the **night**, and to divide the light from the darkness: and God saw that *it was* good." (KJV)

5.) Genesis 7:4 "For yet seven **days**, and I will cause it to rain upon the earth forty **days** and forty **nights**; and every living substance that I have made will I destroy from off the face of the earth." (KJV)

6.) Genesis 7:12 "And the rain was upon the earth forty **days** and forty **nights**." (KJV)

7.) Genesis 8:22 "While the earth remaineth, seedtime and harvest, and cold and heat, and summer and winter, and **day** and **night** shall not cease." (KJV)

8.) Genesis 31:39 "That which was torn *of beasts* I brought not unto thee; I bare the loss of it; of my hand didst thou require it, *whether* stolen by **day**, or stolen by **night**." (KJV)

9.) Genesis 31:40 "*Thus* I was; in the **day** the drought consumed me, and the frost by **night**; and my sleep departed from mine eyes." (KJV)

10.) Exodus 10:13 "And Moses stretched forth his rod over the land of Egypt, and the LORD brought an east wind upon the land all that **day**, and all *that* **night**; *and* when it was morning, the east wind brought the locusts." (KJV)

11.) Exodus 24:18 "And Moses went into the midst of the cloud, and gat him up into the mount: and Moses was in the mount forty **days** and forty **nights**." (KJV)

12.) Exodus 34:28 "And he was there with the LORD forty **days** and forty **nights**; he did neither eat bread, nor drink water. And he wrote upon the tables the words of the covenant, the ten commandments." (KJV)

13.) Leviticus 8:35 "Therefore shall ye abide *at* the door of the tabernacle of the congregation **day** and **night** seven **days**, and keep the charge of the LORD, that ye die not: for so I am commanded." (KJV)

14.) Numbers 11:32 "And the people stood up all that **day**, and all *that* **night**, and all the next **day**, and they gathered the quails: he that gathered least gathered ten homers: and they spread *them* all abroad for themselves round about the camp." (KJV)

15.) Deuteronomy 9:9 "When I was gone up into the mount to receive the tables of stone, *even* the tables of the covenant which the LORD made with you, then I abode in the mount forty **days** and forty **nights**, I neither did eat bread nor drink water:" (KJV)

16.) Deuteronomy 9:11 "And it came to pass at the end of forty **days** and forty **nights**, *that* the LORD gave me the two tables of stone, *even* the tables of the covenant." (KJV)

17.) Deuteronomy 9:18 "And I fell down before the LORD, as at the first, forty **days** and forty **nights**: I did neither eat bread, nor drink water, because of all your sins which ye sinned, in doing wickedly in the sight of the LORD, to provoke him to anger." (KJV)

18.) Deuteronomy 9:25 "Thus I fell down before the LORD forty **days** and forty **nights**, as I fell down *at the first;* because the LORD had said he would destroy you." (KJV)

19.) Deuteronomy 10:10 "And I stayed in the mount, according to the first time, forty **days** and forty **nights**; and the LORD hearkened unto me at that time also, *and* the LORD would not destroy thee." (KJV)

20.) 1 Samuel 19:24 "And he stripped off his clothes also, and prophesied before Samuel in like manner, and lay down naked all that **day** and all that **night**. Wherefore they say, *Is* Saul also among the prophets?" (KJV)

21.) 1 Samuel 25:16 "They were a wall unto us both by **night** and **day**, all the while we were with them keeping the sheep." (KJV)

22.) 1 Samuel 28:20 "Then Saul fell straightway all along on the earth, and was sore afraid, because of the words of Samuel: and there was no strength in him; for he had eaten no bread all the **day**, nor all the **night**." (KJV)

23.) 1 Samuel 30:12 "And they gave him a piece of a cake of figs, and two clusters of raisins: and when he had eaten, his spirit came again to him: for he had eaten no bread, nor drunk *any* water, three **days** and three **nights**." (KJV)

24.) 1 Kings 8:29 "That thine eyes may be open toward this house **night** and **day**, *even* toward the place of which thou hast said, My name shall be there: that thou mayest hearken unto the prayer which thy servant shall make toward this place." (KJV)

25.) 1 Kings 8:59 "And let these my words, wherewith I have made supplication before the LORD, be nigh unto the LORD our God **day** and **night**, that he maintain the cause of his servant, and the cause of his people Israel at all times, as the matter shall require:" (KJV)

26.) 1 Kings 19:8 "And he arose, and did eat and drink, and went in the strength of that meat forty **days** and forty **nights** unto Horeb the mount of God." (KJV)

27.) Nehemiah 1:6 "Let thine ear now be attentive, and thine eyes open, that thou mayest hear the prayer of thy servant, which I pray before thee now, **day** and **night**, for the children of Israel thy servants, and confess the sins of the children of Israel, which we have sinned against thee: both I and my father's house have sinned." (KJV)

28.) Nehemiah 4:22 "Likewise at the same time said I unto the people, Let every one with his servant lodge within Jerusalem, that in the **night** they may be a guard to us, and labour on the **day**." (KJV)

29.) Esther 4:16 "Go, gather together all the Jews that are present in Shushan, and fast ye for me, and neither eat nor drink three **days**, **night** or **day**: I also and my maidens will fast likewise; and so will I go in unto the king, which *is* not according to the law: and if I perish, I perish." (KJV)

30.) Job 2:13 "So they sat down with him upon the ground seven **days** and seven **nights**, and none spake a word unto him: for they saw that *his* grief was very great." (KJV)

31.) Job 3:3 "Let the **day** perish wherein I was born, and the **night** *in which* it was said, There is a man child conceived." (KJV)

32.) Job 3:6 "As *for* that **night**, let darkness seize upon it; let it not be joined unto the **days** of the year, let it not come into the number of the months." (KJV)

33.) Job 17:12 "They change the **night** into **day**: the light *is* short because of darkness." (KJV)

34.) Psalms 19:2 "**Day** unto **day** uttereth speech, and **night** unto **night** showeth knowledge." (KJV)

35.) Psalms 42:3 "My tears have been my meat **day** and **night**, while they continually say unto me, Where *is* thy God?" (KJV)

36.) Psalms 74:16 "The **day** *is* thine, the **night** also *is* thine: thou hast prepared the light and the sun." (KJV)

37.) Psalms 77:2 "In the **day** of my trouble I sought the Lord: my sore ran in the **night**, and ceased not: my soul refused to be comforted." (KJV)

38.) Psalms 88:1 "A Song *or* Psalms for the sons of Korah, to the chief Musician upon Mahalath Leannoth, Maschil of Heman the Ezrahite. O LORD God of my salvation, I have cried **day** *and* **night** before thee:" (KJV)

39.) Psalms 90:4 "For a thousand years in thy sight *are but* as yester**day** when it is past, and *as* a watch in the **night**." (KJV)

40.) Psalms 139:12 "Yea, the darkness hideth not from thee; but the **night** shineth as the **day**: the darkness and the light *are* both alike *to thee*." (KJV)

41.) Ecclesiastes 2:23 "For all his **days** *are* sorrows, and his travail grief; yea, his heart taketh not rest in the **night**. This is also vanity." (KJV)

42.) Ecclesiastes 8:16 "When I applied mine heart to know wisdom, and to see the business that is done upon the earth: for also *there is that* neither **day** nor **night** seeth sleep with his eyes:" (KJV)

43.) Isaiah 27:3 "I the LORD do keep it; I will water it every moment: lest *any* hurt it, I will keep it **night** and **day**." (KJV)

44.) Isaiah 28:19 "From the time that it goeth forth it shall take you: for morning by morning shall it pass over, by **day** and by **night**: and it shall be a vexation only *to* understand the report." (KJV)

45.) Isaiah 38:12 "Mine age is departed, and is removed from me as a shepherd's tent: I have cut off like a weaver my life: he will cut me off with pining sickness: from **day** *even* to **night** wilt thou make an end of me." (KJV)

46.) Isaiah 38:13 "I reckoned till morning, *that,* as a lion, so will he break all my bones: from **day** *even* to **night** wilt thou make an end of me." (KJV)

47.) Isaiah 62:6 "I have set watchmen upon thy walls, O Jerusalem, *which* shall never hold their peace **day** nor **night**: ye that make mention of the LORD, keep not silence." (KJV)

48.) Jeremiah 33:20 "Thus saith the LORD; If ye can break my covenant of the **day**, and my covenant of the **night**, and that there should not be **day** and **night** in their season;" (KJV)

49.) Jeremiah 36:30 "Therefore thus saith the LORD of Jehoiakim king of Judah; He shall have none to sit upon the throne of David: and his dead body shall be cast out in the **day** to the heat, and in the **night** to the frost." (KJV)

50.) Hosea 4:5 "Therefore shalt thou fall in the **day**, and the prophet also shall fall with thee in the **night**, and I will destroy thy mother." (KJV)

51.) Amos 5:8 "*Seek him* that maketh the seven stars and Orion, and turneth the shadow of death into the morning, and maketh the **day** dark with **night**: that calleth for the waters of the sea, and poureth them out upon the face of the earth: The LORD *is* his name:" (KJV)

52.) Jonah 1:17 "Now the LORD had prepared a great fish to swallow up Jonah. And Jonah was in the belly of the fish three **days** and three **nights**." (KJV)

53.) Micah 3:6 "Therefore **night** *shall be* unto you, that ye shall not have a vision; and it shall be dark unto you, that ye shall not divine; and the sun shall go down over the prophets, and the **day** shall be dark over them." (KJV)

54.) Zechariah 14:7 "But it shall be one **day** which shall be known to the LORD, not **day**, nor **night**: but it shall come to pass, *that* at evening time it shall be light." (KJV)

     In every other portion of the Bible, when these words are used together to define a period of time, they refer to a twenty-four-hour period. Why would the Hebrew be translated differently in Genesis 1? This causes a difficulty for those who defend the Day-Age Theory. The Bible doesn't describe what God did during six days. The Bible describes what God did during six days AND six nights. Genesis 1:14-18 speaks about the lights made to rule the night. The addition of the word "night" is a big problem for those who believe the six days are six ages. *YOM* does not mean "age" in the first part of Genesis 1:5.

YOM is used a second time in Genesis 1:5. God says, "And there was evening and there was morning, one *YOM*." Some Day-Agers simply ignore the words "evening" and "morning" (*EREB*—Strong's Number H6153 and *BOQER*—Strong's Number H1242). Other Day-Agers have a different meaning for "evening and morning." They say these words are poetic, picturesque, non-literal imagery used to describe the beginning of a time period and the ending of a time period. They give an illustration by saying they could mean something like, "the dawn of a new age," or "I am in the sunset years of my life." This allows them to continue believing *EREB* and *BOQER* can define a long, unspecified period of time. Unfortunately, while they give illustrations of what these words MIGHT mean, they never give an example from Scripture that this is what they DO mean.

We are going to look at every *EREB* and *BOQER* in the Bible. First, we will look at them individually, then we will look at the passages where they are used together. Their combined use is extremely important in determining what "day" means, because context is extremely important in determining what any Hebrew word means. *EREB* and *BOQER* used together create a different context than when they are used alone. So, as we look at these words, be on the lookout for places where they mean the beginning or ending of any time period other than an actual evening, or morning, or day, or night. Look extra carefully at the verses where they are used together as they are in Genesis 1.

God says *YOM* One had an evening and *YOM* One had a morning. He said the same for the second through sixth days. The Genesis account of creation plainly shows *EREB* and *BOQER* describe short periods of time. What do *EREB* and *BOQER* mean?

EREB (Evening)

1.) Genesis 1:5 "And God called the light Day, and the darkness he called Night. And the **evening** and the morning were the first day." (KJV)

2.) Genesis 1:8 "And God called the firmament Heaven. And the **evening** and the morning were the second day." (KJV)

3.) Genesis 1:13 "And the **evening** and the morning were the third day." (KJV)

4.) Genesis 1:19 "And the **evening** and the morning were the fourth day." (KJV)

5.) Genesis 1:23 "And the **evening** and the morning were the fifth day." (KJV)

6.) Genesis 1:31 "And God saw every thing that he had made, and, behold, *it was* very good. And the **evening** and the morning were the sixth day." (KJV)

7.) Genesis 8:11 "And the dove came in to him in the **evening**; and, lo, in her mouth *was* an olive leaf plucked off: so Noah knew that the waters were abated from off the earth." (KJV)

8.) Genesis 19:1 "And there came two angels to Sodom at **even**; and Lot sat in the gate of Sodom: and Lot seeing *them* rose up to meet them; and he bowed himself with his face toward the ground;" (KJV)

9.) Genesis 24:11 "And he made his camels to kneel down without the city by a well of water at the time of the **evening**, *even* the time that women go out to draw *water*." (KJV)

10.) Genesis 24:63 "And Isaac went out to meditate in the field at the **eventide**: and he lifted up his eyes, and saw, and, behold, the camels *were* coming." (KJV)

11.) Genesis 29:23 "And it came to pass in the **evening**, that he took Leah his daughter, and brought her to him; and he went in unto her." (KJV)

12.) Genesis 30:16 "And Jacob came out of the field in the **evening**, and Leah went out to meet him, and said, Thou must come in unto me; for surely I have hired thee with my son's mandrakes. And he lay with her that night." (KJV)

13.) Genesis 49:27 "Benjamin shall ravin *as* a wolf: in the morning he shall devour the prey, and at **night** he shall divide the spoil." (KJV)

14.) Exodus 12:6 "And ye shall keep it up until the fourteenth day of the same month: and the whole assembly of the congregation of Israel shall kill it in the **evening**." (KJV)

15. and 16.) Exodus 12:18 "In the first *month,* on the fourteenth day of the month at **even**, ye shall eat unleavened bread, until the one and twentieth day of the month at **even**." (KJV)

17.) Exodus 16:6 "And Moses and Aaron said unto all the children of Israel, At **even**, then ye shall know that the LORD hath brought you out from the land of Egypt:" (KJV)

18.) Exodus 16:8 "And Moses said, *This shall be,* when the LORD shall give you in the **evening** flesh to eat, and in the morning bread to the full; for that the LORD heareth your murmurings which ye murmur against him: and what *are* we? your murmurings *are* not against us, but against the LORD." (KJV)

19.) Exodus 16:12 "I have heard the murmurings of the children of Israel: speak unto them, saying, At **even** ye shall eat flesh, and in the morning ye shall be filled with bread; and ye shall know that I *am* the LORD your God." (KJV)

20.) Exodus 16:13 "And it came to pass, that at **even** the quails came up, and covered the camp: and in the morning the dew lay round about the host." (KJV)

21.) Exodus 18:13 "And it came to pass on the morrow, that Moses sat to judge the people: and the people stood by Moses from the morning unto the **evening**." (KJV)

22.) Exodus 18:14 "And when Moses' father in law saw all that he did to the people, he said, What *is* this thing that thou doest to the people? why sittest thou thyself alone, and all the people stand by thee from morning unto **even**?" (KJV)

23.) Exodus 27:21 "In the tabernacle of the congregation without the veil, which *is* before the testimony, Aaron and his sons shall order it from **evening** to morning before the LORD: *it shall be* a statute for ever unto their generations on the behalf of the children of Israel." (KJV)

24.) Exodus 29:39 "The one lamb thou shalt offer in the morning; and the other lamb thou shalt offer at **even**:" (KJV)

25.) Exodus 29:41 "And the other lamb thou shalt offer at **even**, and shalt do thereto according to the meat offering of the morning, and according to the drink offering thereof, for a sweet savour, an offering made by fire unto the LORD." (KJV)

26.) Exodus 30:8 "And when Aaron *lighteth* the lamps at **even**, he shall burn incense upon it, a perpetual incense before the LORD throughout your generations." (KJV)

27.) Leviticus 6:20 "This *is* the offering of Aaron and of his sons, which they shall offer unto the LORD in the day when he is anointed; the tenth part of an ephah of fine flour for a meat offering perpetual, half of it in the morning, and half thereof at **night**." (KJV)

28.) Leviticus 11:24 "And for these ye shall be unclean: whosoever toucheth the carcase of them shall be unclean until the **even**." (KJV)

29.) Leviticus 11:25 "And whosoever beareth *ought* of the carcase of them shall wash his clothes, and be unclean until the **even**." (KJV)

30.) Leviticus 11:27 "And whatsoever goeth upon his paws, among all manner of beasts that go on *all* four, those *are* unclean unto you: whoso toucheth their carcase shall be unclean until the **even**." (KJV)

31.) Leviticus 11:28 "And he that beareth the carcase of them shall wash his clothes, and be unclean until the **even**: they *are* unclean unto you." (KJV)

32.) Leviticus 11:31 "These *are* unclean to you among all that creep: whosoever doth touch them, when they be dead, shall be unclean until the **even**." (KJV)

33.) Leviticus 11:32 "And upon whatsoever *any* of them, when they are dead, doth fall, it shall be unclean; whether *it be* any vessel of wood, or raiment, or skin, or sack, whatsoever vessel *it be,* wherein *any* work is done, it must be put into water, and it shall be unclean until the **even**; so it shall be cleansed." (KJV)

34.) Leviticus 11:39 "And if any beast, of which ye may eat, die; he that toucheth the carcase thereof shall be unclean until the **even**." (KJV)

35. and 36.) Leviticus 11:40 "And he that eateth of the carcase of it shall wash his clothes, and be unclean until the **even**: he also that beareth the carcase of it shall wash his clothes, and be unclean until the **even**." (KJV)

37.) Leviticus 14:46 "Moreover he that goeth into the house all the while that it is shut up shall be unclean until the **even**." (KJV)

38.) Leviticus 15:5 "And whosoever toucheth his bed shall wash his clothes, and bathe *himself* in water, and be unclean until the **even**." (KJV)

39.) Leviticus 15:6 "And he that sitteth on *any* thing whereon he sat that hath the issue shall wash his clothes, and bathe *himself* in water, and be unclean until the **even**." (KJV)

40.) Leviticus 15:7 "And he that toucheth the flesh of him that hath the issue shall wash his clothes, and bathe *himself* in water, and be unclean until the **even**." (KJV)

41.) Leviticus 15:8 "And if he that hath the issue spit upon him that is clean; then he shall wash his clothes, and bathe *himself* in water, and be unclean until the **even**." (KJV)

42. and 43.) Leviticus 15:10 "And whosoever toucheth any thing that was under him shall be unclean until the **even**: and he that beareth *any of* those things shall wash his clothes, and bathe *himself* in water, and be unclean until the **even**." (KJV)

44.) Leviticus 15:11"And whomsoever he toucheth that hath the issue, and hath not rinsed his hands in water, he shall wash his clothes, and bathe *himself* in water, and be unclean until the **even**." (KJV)

45.) Leviticus 15:16 "And if any man's seed of copulation go out from him, then he shall wash all his flesh in water, and be unclean until the **even**." (KJV)

46.) Leviticus 15:17 "And every garment, and every skin, whereon is the seed of copulation, shall be washed with water, and be unclean until the **even**." (KJV)

47.) Leviticus 15:18 "The woman also with whom man shall lie *with* seed of copulation, they shall *both* bathe *themselves* in water, and be unclean until the **even**." (KJV)

48.) Leviticus 15:19 "And if a woman have an issue, *and* her issue in her flesh be blood, she shall be put apart seven days: and whosoever toucheth her shall be unclean until the **even**." (KJV)

49.) Leviticus 15:21 "And whosoever toucheth her bed shall wash his clothes, and bathe *himself* in water, and be unclean until the **even**." (KJV)

50.) Leviticus 15:22 "And whosoever toucheth any thing that she sat upon shall wash his clothes, and bathe *himself* in water, and be unclean until the **even**." (KJV)

51.) Leviticus 15:23 "And if it *be* on *her* bed, or on any thing whereon she sitteth, when he toucheth it, he shall be unclean until the **even**." (KJV)

52.) Leviticus 15:27 "And whosoever toucheth those things shall be unclean, and shall wash his clothes, and bathe *himself* in water, and be unclean until the **even**." (KJV)

53.) Leviticus 17:15 "And every soul that eateth that which died *of itself,* or that which was torn *with beasts, whether it be* one of your own country, or a stranger, he shall both wash his clothes, and bathe *himself* in water, and be unclean until the **even**: then shall he be clean." (KJV)

54.) Leviticus 22:6 "The soul which hath touched any such shall be unclean until **even**, and shall not eat of the holy things, unless he wash his flesh with water." (KJV)

55.) Leviticus 23:5 "In the fourteenth *day* of the first month at **even** *is* the Lord's passover." (KJV)

56. 57. and 58.) Leviticus 23:32 "It *shall be* unto you a sabbath of rest, and ye shall afflict your souls: in the ninth *day* of the month at **even**, from **even** unto **even**, shall ye celebrate your sabbath." (KJV)

59.) Leviticus 24:3 "Without the veil of the testimony, in the tabernacle of the congregation, shall Aaron order it from the **evening** unto the morning before the LORD continually: *it shall be* a statute for ever in your generations." (KJV)

60.) Numbers 9:3 "In the fourteenth day of this month, at **even**, ye shall keep it in his appointed season: according to all the rites of it, and according to all the ceremonies thereof, shall ye keep it." (KJV)

61.) Numbers 9:5 "And they kept the passover on the fourteenth day of the first month at **even** in the wilderness of Sinai: according to all that the LORD commanded Moses, so did the children of Israel." (KJV)

62.) Numbers 9:11 "The fourteenth day of the second month at **even** they shall keep it, *and* eat it with unleavened bread and bitter *herbs*." (KJV)

63.) Numbers 9:15 "And on the day that the tabernacle was reared up the cloud covered the tabernacle, *namely,* the tent of the testimony: and at **even** there was upon the tabernacle as it were the appearance of fire, until the morning." (KJV)

64.) Numbers 9:21 "And *so* it was, when the cloud abode from **even** unto the morning, and *that* the cloud was taken up in the morning, then they journeyed: whether *it was* by day or by night that the cloud was taken up, they journeyed." (KJV)

65.) Numbers 19:7 "Then the priest shall wash his clothes, and he shall bathe his flesh in water, and afterward he shall come into the camp, and the priest shall be unclean until the **even**." (KJV)

66.) Numbers 19:8 "And he that burneth her shall wash his clothes in water, and bathe his flesh in water, and shall be unclean until the **even**." (KJV)

67.) Numbers 19:10 "And he that gathereth the ashes of the heifer shall wash his clothes, and be unclean until the **even**: and it shall be unto the children of Israel, and unto the stranger that sojourneth among them, for a statute for ever." (KJV)

68.) Numbers 19:19 "And the clean *person* shall sprinkle upon the unclean on the third day, and on the seventh day: and on the seventh day he shall purify himself, and wash his clothes, and bathe himself in water, and shall be clean at **even**." (KJV)

69.) Numbers 19:21 "And it shall be a perpetual statute unto them, that he that sprinkleth the water of separation shall wash his clothes; and he that toucheth the water of separation shall be unclean until **even**." (KJV)

70.) Numbers 19:22 "And whatsoever the unclean *person* toucheth shall be unclean; and the soul that toucheth *it* shall be unclean until **even**." (KJV)

71.) Numbers 28:4 "The one lamb shalt thou offer in the morning, and the other lamb shalt thou offer at **even**;" (KJV)

72.) Numbers 28:8 "And the other lamb shalt thou offer at **even**: as the meat offering of the morning, and as the drink offering thereof, thou shalt offer *it*, a sacrifice made by fire, of a sweet savour unto the LORD." (KJV)

73.) Deuteronomy 16:4 "And there shall be no leavened bread seen with thee in all thy coast seven days; neither shall there *any thing* of the flesh, which thou sacrificedst the first day at **even**, remain all night until the morning." (KJV)

74.) Deuteronomy 16:6 "But at the place which the LORD thy God shall choose to place his name in, there thou shalt sacrifice the passover at **even**, at the going down of the sun, at the season that thou camest forth out of Egypt." (KJV)

75.) Deuteronomy 23:11 "But it shall be, when **evening** cometh on, he shall wash *himself* with water: and when the sun is down, he shall come into the camp *again*." (KJV)

76. and 77.) Deuteronomy 28:67 "In the morning thou shalt say, Would God it were **even**! and at **even** thou shalt say, Would God it were morning! for the fear of thine heart wherewith thou shalt fear, and for the sight of thine eyes which thou shalt see." (KJV)

78.) Joshua 5:10 "And the children of Israel encamped in Gilgal, and kept the passover on the fourteenth day of the month at **even** in the plains of Jericho." (KJV)

79.) Joshua 7:6 "And Joshua rent his clothes, and fell to the earth upon his face before the ark of the LORD until the **eventide**, he and the elders of Israel, and put dust upon their heads." (KJV)

80.) Joshua 8:29 "And the king of Ai he hanged on a tree until **eventide**: and as soon as the sun was down, Joshua commanded that they should take his carcase down from the tree, and cast it at the entering of the gate of the city, and raise thereon a great heap of stones, *that remaineth* unto this day." (KJV)

81.) Joshua 10:26 "And afterward Joshua smote them, and slew them, and hanged them on five trees: and they were hanging upon the trees until the **evening**." (KJV)

82.) Judges 19:16 "And, behold, there came an old man from his work out of the field at **even**, which *was* also of mount Ephraim; and he sojourned in Gibeah: but the men of the place *were* Benjamites." (KJV)

83.) Judges 20:23 "And the children of Israel went up and wept before the LORD until **even**, and asked counsel of the LORD, saying, Shall I go up again to battle against the children of Benjamin my brother? And the LORD said, Go up against him." (KJV)

84.) Judges 20:26 "Then all the children of Israel, and all the people, went up, and came unto the house of God, and wept, and sat there before the LORD, and fasted that day until **even**, and offered burnt offerings and peace offerings before the LORD." (KJV)

85.) Judges 21:2 "And the people came to the house of God, and abode there till **even** before God, and lifted up their voices, and wept sore;" (KJV)

86.) Ruth 2:17 "So she gleaned in the field until **even**, and beat out that she had gleaned: and it was about an ephah of barley." (KJV)

87.) 1 Samuel 14:24 "And the men of Israel were distressed that day: for Saul had adjured the people, saying, Cursed *be* the man that eateth *any* food until **evening**, that I may be avenged on mine enemies. So none of the people tasted *any* food." (KJV)

88.) 1 Samuel 20:5 "And David said unto Jonathan, Behold, to morrow *is* the new moon, and I should not fail to sit with the king at meat: but let me go, that I may hide myself in the field unto the third *day* at **even**." (KJV)

89.) 1 Samuel 30:17 "And David smote them from the twilight even unto the **evening** of the next day: and there escaped not a man of them, save four hundred young men, which rode upon camels, and fled." (KJV)

90.) 2 Samuel 1:12 "And they mourned, and wept, and fasted until **even**, for Saul, and for Jonathan his son, and for the people of the LORD, and for the house of Israel; because they were fallen by the sword." (KJV)

91.) 2 Samuel 11:2 "And it came to pass in an **eveningtide**, that David arose from off his bed, and walked upon the roof of the king's house: and from the roof he saw a woman washing herself; and the woman *was* very beautiful to look upon." (KJV)

92.) 2 Samuel 11:13 "And when David had called him, he did eat and drink before him; and he made him drunk: and at **even** he went out to lie on his bed with the servants of his lord, but went not down to his house." (KJV)

93.) 1 Kings 17:6 "And the ravens brought him bread and flesh in the morning, and bread and flesh in the **evening**; and he drank of the brook." (KJV)

94.) 1 Kings 22:35 "And the battle increased that day: and the king was stayed up in his chariot against the Syrians, and died at **even**: and the blood ran out of the wound into the midst of the chariot." (KJV)

95.) 2 Kings 16:15 "And king Ahaz commanded Urijah the priest, saying, Upon the great altar burn the morning burnt offering, and the **evening** meat offering, and the king's burnt sacrifice, and his meat offering, with the burnt offering of all the people of the land, and their meat offering, and their drink offerings; and sprinkle upon it all the blood of the burnt offering, and all the blood of the sacrifice: and the brazen altar shall be for me to inquire *by*." (KJV)

96.) 1 Chronicles 16:40 "To offer burnt offerings unto the LORD upon the altar of the burnt offering continually morning and **evening**, and *to do* according to all that is written in the law of the LORD, which he commanded Israel;" (KJV)

97.) 1 Chronicles 23:30 "And to stand every morning to thank and praise the LORD, and likewise at **even**;" (KJV)

98.) 2 Chronicles 2:4 "Behold, I build an house to the name of the LORD my God, to dedicate *it* to him, *and* to burn before him sweet incense, and for the continual showbread, and for the burnt offerings morning and **evening**, on the sabbaths, and on the new moons, and on the solemn feasts of the LORD our God. This *is an ordinance* for ever to Israel." (KJV)

99. 100. 101. and 102.) 2 Chronicles 13:11 "And they burn unto the LORD every morning and every **evening** burnt sacrifices and sweet incense: the showbread also *set they in order* upon the pure table; and the candlestick of gold with the lamps thereof, to burn every **evening**: for we keep the charge of the LORD our God; but ye have forsaken him." (KJV)

(Note: In 2 Chronicles 13:11, the Hebrew word *EREB* is used twice in each of the mentions of "evening" in the English. Literally, it says something like, "evening by evening," both times it is used.)

103.) 2 Chronicles 18:34 "And the battle increased that day: howbeit the king of Israel stayed *himself* up in *his* chariot against the Syrians until the **even**: and about the time of the sun going down he died." (KJV)

104.) 2 Chronicles 31:3 "*He appointed* also the king's portion of his substance for the burnt offerings, *to wit,* for the morning and **evening** burnt offerings, and the burnt offerings for the sabbaths, and for the new moons, and for the set feasts, as *it is* written in the law of the LORD." (KJV)

105.) Ezra 3:3 "And they set the altar upon his bases; for fear *was* upon them because of the people of those countries: and they offered burnt offerings thereon unto the LORD, *even* burnt offerings morning and **evening**." (KJV)

106.) Ezra 9:4 "Then were assembled unto me every one that trembled at the words of the God of Israel, because of the transgression of those that had been carried away; and I sat astonied until the **evening** sacrifice." (KJV)

107.) Ezra 9:5 "And at the **evening** sacrifice I arose up from my heaviness; and having rent my garment and my mantle, I fell upon my knees, and spread out my hands unto the LORD my God," (KJV)

108.) Esther 2:14 "In the **evening** she went, and on the morrow she returned into the second house of the women, to the custody of Shaashgaz, the king's chamberlain, which kept the concubines: she came in unto the king no more, except the king delighted in her, and that she were called by name." (KJV)

109.) Job 4:20 "They are destroyed from morning to **evening**: they perish for ever without any regarding *it*." (KJV)

110.) Job 7:4 "When I lie down, I say, When shall I arise, and the **night** be gone? and I am full of tossings to and fro unto the dawning of the day." (KJV)

111.) Psalms 30:5 "For his anger *endureth but* a moment; in his favour *is* life: weeping may endure for a **night**, but joy *cometh* in the morning." (KJV)

112.) Psalms 55:17 "**Evening**, and morning, and at noon, will I pray, and cry aloud: and he shall hear my voice." (KJV)

113.) Psalms 59:6 "They return at **evening**: they make a noise like a dog, and go round about the city." (KJV)

114.) Psalms 59:14 "And at **evening** let them return; *and* let them make a noise like a dog, and go round about the city." (KJV)

115.) Psalms 65:8 "They also that dwell in the uttermost parts are afraid at thy tokens: thou makest the outgoings of the morning and **evening** to rejoice." (KJV)

116.) Psalms 90:6 "In the morning it flourisheth, and groweth up; in the **evening** it is cut down, and withereth." (KJV)

This verse needs some explaining in order to figure out what length of time periods it describes. Since it also uses "morning," (*BOQER*) I'll wait to explain it when I get to the section where we see *EREB* and *BOQER* used together.

117.) Psalms 104:23 "Man goeth forth unto his work and to his labour until the **evening**." (KJV)

118.) Psalms 141:2 "Let my prayer be set forth before thee *as* incense; *and* the lifting up of my hands *as* the **evening** sacrifice." (KJV)

119.) Proverbs 7:9 "In the twilight, in the **evening**, in the black and dark night:" (KJV)

120.) Ecclesiastes 11:6 "In the morning sow thy seed, and in the **evening** withhold not thine hand: for thou knowest not whether shall prosper, either this or that, or whether they both *shall be* alike good." (KJV)

121.) Isaiah 17:14 "And behold at **eveningtide** trouble; *and* before the morning he *is* not. This *is* the portion of them that spoil us, and the lot of them that rob us." (KJV)

122.) Jeremiah 6:4 "Prepare ye war against her; arise, and let us go up at noon. Woe unto us! for the day goeth away, for the shadows of the **evening** are stretched out." (KJV)

123.) Ezekiel 12:4 "Then shalt thou bring forth thy stuff by day in their sight, as stuff for removing: and thou shalt go forth at **even** in their sight, as they that go forth into captivity." (KJV)

124.) Ezekiel 12:7 "And I did so as I was commanded: I brought forth my stuff by day, as stuff for captivity, and in the **even** I digged through the wall with mine hand; I brought *it* forth in the twilight, *and* I bare *it* upon *my* shoulder in their sight." (KJV)

125.) Ezekiel 24:18 "So I spake unto the people in the morning: and at **even** my wife died; and I did in the morning as I was commanded." (KJV)

126.) Ezekiel 33:22 "Now the hand of the LORD was upon me in the **evening**, afore he that was escaped came; and had opened my mouth, until he came to me in the morning; and my mouth was opened, and I was no more dumb." (KJV)

127.) Ezekiel 46:2 "And the prince shall enter by the way of the porch of *that* gate without, and shall stand by the post of the gate, and the priests shall prepare his burnt offering and his peace offerings, and he shall worship at the threshold of the gate: then he shall go forth; but the gate shall not be shut until the **evening**." (KJV)

128.) Daniel 8:14 "And he said unto me, Unto two thousand and three hundred **days**; then shall the sanctuary be cleansed." (KJV)

(Note: The Hebrew literally says 2,300 "evening-morning" (*EREB-BOQER*, each in the singular.) The *King James Bible* lumps "evening-morning" together and call them, "days," because there are 2,300 of them.)

129.) Daniel 8:26 "And the vision of the **evening** and the morning which was told *is* true: wherefore shut thou up the vision; for it *shall be* for many days." (KJV)

130.) Daniel 9:21 "Yea, whiles I *was* speaking in prayer, even the man Gabriel, whom I had seen in the vision at the beginning, being caused to fly swiftly, touched me about the time of the **evening** oblation." (KJV)

131.) Habakkuk 1:8 "Their horses also are swifter than the leopards, and are more fierce than the **evening** wolves: and their horsemen shall spread themselves, and their horsemen shall come from far; they shall fly as the eagle *that* hasteth to eat." (KJV)

132.) Zephaniah 2:7 "And the coast shall be for the remnant of the house of Judah; they shall feed thereupon: in the houses of Ashkelon shall they lie down in the **evening**: for the LORD their God shall visit them, and turn away their captivity." (KJV)

133.) Zephaniah 3:3 "Her princes within her *are* roaring lions; her judges *are* **evening** wolves; they gnaw not the bones till the morrow." (KJV)

134.) Zechariah 14:7 "But it shall be one day which shall be known to the LORD, not day, nor night: but it shall come to pass, *that* at **evening** time it shall be light." (KJV)

Did you see any verses describing the "sunset" of anybody's years? No? Well, I didn't either. *EREB* is used 134 times in the Bible and it means the short period of time we call evening, dusk, or twilight. *EREB* does not refer to a long period of time. When used in reference to a measurable period of time, the Bible never uses *EREB* to describe anything but the twilight portion of a twenty-four-hour day. What grammatical basis is there for saying *EREB* means a short period of time everywhere in the Bible except in the first chapter of Genesis?

BOQER (Morning)

1.) Genesis 1:5 "And God called the light Day, and the darkness he called Night. And the evening and the **morning** were the first day." (KJV)

2.) Genesis 1:8 "And God called the firmament Heaven. And the evening and the **morning** were the second day." (KJV)

3.) Genesis 1:13 "And the evening and the **morning** were the third day." (KJV)

4.) Genesis 1:19 "And the evening and the **morning** were the fourth day." (KJV)

5.) Genesis 1:23 "And the evening and the **morning** were the fifth day." (KJV)

6.) Genesis 1:31 "And God saw every thing that he had made, and, behold, *it was* very good. And the evening and the **morning** were the sixth day." (KJV)

7.) Genesis 19:27 "And Abraham gat up early in the **morning** to the place where he stood before the LORD:" (KJV)

8.) Genesis 20:8 "Therefore Abimelech rose early in the **morning**, and called all his servants, and told all these things in their ears: and the men were sore afraid." (KJV)

9.) Genesis 21:14 "And Abraham rose up early in the **morning**, and took bread, and a bottle of water, and gave *it* unto Hagar, putting *it* on her shoulder, and the child, and sent her away: and she departed, and wandered in the wilderness of Beersheba." (KJV)

10.) Genesis 22:3 "And Abraham rose up early in the **morning**, and saddled his ass, and took two of his young men with him, and Isaac his son, and clave the wood for the burnt offering, and rose up, and went unto the place of which God had told him." (KJV)

11.) Genesis 24:54 "And they did eat and drink, he and the men that *were* with him, and tarried all night; and they rose up in the **morning**, and he said, Send me away unto my master." (KJV)

12.) Genesis 26:31 "And they rose up betimes in the **morning**, and sware one to another: and Isaac sent them away, and they departed from him in peace." (KJV)

13.) Genesis 28:18 "And Jacob rose up early in the **morning**, and took the stone that he had put *for* his pillows, and set it up *for* a pillar, and poured oil upon the top of it." (KJV)

14.) Genesis 29:25 "And it came to pass, that in the **morning**, behold, it *was* Leah: and he said to Laban, What *is* this thou hast done unto me? did not I serve with thee for Rachel? wherefore then hast thou beguiled me?" (KJV)

15.) Genesis 31:55 "And early in the **morning** Laban rose up, and kissed his sons and his daughters, and blessed them: and Laban departed, and returned unto his place." (KJV)

16.) Genesis 40:6 "And Joseph came in unto them in the **morning**, and looked upon them, and, behold, they *were* sad." (KJV)

17.) Genesis 41:8 "And it came to pass in the **morning** that his spirit was troubled; and he sent and called for all the magicians of Egypt, and all the wise men thereof: and Pharaoh told them his dream; but *there was* none that could interpret them unto Pharaoh." (KJV)

18.) Genesis 44:3 "As soon as the **morning** was light, the men were sent away, they and their asses." (KJV)

19.) Genesis 49:27 "Benjamin shall ravin *as* a wolf: in the **morning** he shall devour the prey, and at night he shall divide the spoil." (KJV)

20.) Exodus 7:15 "Get thee unto Pharaoh in the **morning**; lo, he goeth out unto the water; and thou shalt stand by the river's brink against he come; and the rod which was turned to a serpent shalt thou take in thine hand." (KJV)

21.) Exodus 8:20 "And the LORD said unto Moses, Rise up early in the **morning**, and stand before Pharaoh; lo, he cometh forth to the water; and say unto him, Thus saith the LORD, Let my people go, that they may serve me." (KJV)

22.) Exodus 9:13 "And the LORD said unto Moses, Rise up early in the **morning**, and stand before Pharaoh, and say unto him, Thus saith the LORD God of the Hebrews, Let my people go, that they may serve me." (KJV)

23.) Exodus 10:13 "And Moses stretched forth his rod over the land of Egypt, and the LORD brought an east wind upon the land all that day, and all *that* night; *and* when it was **morning**, the east wind brought the locusts." (KJV)

24. and 25.) Exodus 12:10 "And ye shall let nothing of it remain until the **morning**; and that which remaineth of it until the **morning** ye shall burn with fire." (KJV)

26.) Exodus 12:22 "And ye shall take a bunch of hyssop, and dip *it* in the blood that *is* in the basin, and strike the lintel and the two side posts with the blood that *is* in the basin; and none of you shall go out at the door of his house until the **morning**." (KJV)

27.) Exodus 14:24 "And it came to pass, that in the **morning** watch the LORD looked unto the host of the Egyptians through the pillar of fire and of the cloud, and troubled the host of the Egyptians," (KJV)

28.) Exodus 14:27 "And Moses stretched forth his hand over the sea, and the sea returned to his strength when the **morning** appeared; and the Egyptians fled against it; and the LORD overthrew the Egyptians in the midst of the sea." (KJV)

29.) Exodus 16:7 "And in the **morning**, then ye shall see the glory of the LORD; for that he heareth your murmurings against the LORD: and what *are* we, that ye murmur against us?" (KJV)

30.) Exodus 16:8 "And Moses said, *This shall be,* when the LORD shall give you in the evening flesh to eat, and in the **morning** bread to the full; for that the LORD heareth your murmurings which ye murmur against him: and what *are* we? your murmurings *are* not against us, but against the LORD." (KJV)

31.) Exodus 16:12 "I have heard the murmurings of the children of Israel: speak unto them, saying, At even ye shall eat flesh, and in the **morning** ye shall be filled with bread; and ye shall know that I *am* the LORD your God." (KJV)

32.) Exodus 16:13 "And it came to pass, that at even the quails came up, and covered the camp: and in the **morning** the dew lay round about the host." (KJV)

33.) Exodus 16:19 "And Moses said, Let no man leave of it till the **morning**." (KJV)

34.) Exodus 16:20 "Notwithstanding they hearkened not unto Moses; but some of them left of it until the **morning**, and it bred worms, and stank: and Moses was wroth with them." (KJV)

35. and 36.) Exodus 16:21 "And they gathered it every **morning**, every man according to his eating: and when the sun waxed hot, it melted." (KJV)

(Note: In Exodus 16:21, the Hebrew word *BOQER* is used twice. Literally, it says something like, "morning by morning.")

37.) Exodus 16:23 "And he said unto them, This *is that* which the LORD hath said, To morrow *is* the rest of the holy sabbath unto the LORD: bake *that* which ye will bake *to day,* and seethe that ye will seethe; and that which remaineth over lay up for you to be kept until the **morning**." (KJV)

38.) Exodus 16:24 "And they laid it up till the **morning**, as Moses bade: and it did not stink, neither was there any worm therein." (KJV)

39.) Exodus 18:13 "And it came to pass on the morrow, that Moses sat to judge the people: and the people stood by Moses from the **morning** unto the evening." (KJV)

40.) Exodus 18:14 "And when Moses' father in law saw all that he did to the people, he said, What *is* this thing that thou doest to the people? why sittest thou thyself alone, and all the people stand by thee from **morning** unto even?" (KJV)

41.) Exodus 19:16 "And it came to pass on the third day in the **morning**, that there were thunders and lightnings, and a thick cloud upon the mount, and the voice of the trumpet exceeding loud; so that all the people that *was* in the camp trembled." (KJV)

42.) Exodus 23:18 "Thou shalt not offer the blood of my sacrifice with leavened bread; neither shall the fat of my sacrifice remain until the **morning**." (KJV)

43.) Exodus 24:4 "And Moses wrote all the words of the LORD, and rose up early in the **morning**, and builded an altar under the hill, and twelve pillars, according to the twelve tribes of Israel." (KJV)

44.) Exodus 27:21 "In the tabernacle of the congregation without the veil, which *is* before the testimony, Aaron and his sons shall order it from evening to **morning** before the LORD: *it shall be* a statute for ever unto their generations on the behalf of the children of Israel." (KJV)

45.) Exodus 29:34 "And if ought of the flesh of the consecrations, or of the bread, remain unto the **morning**, then thou shalt burn the remainder with fire: it shall not be eaten, because it *is* holy." (KJV)

46.) Exodus 29:39 "The one lamb thou shalt offer in the **morning**; and the other lamb thou shalt offer at even:" (KJV)

47.) Exodus 29:41 "And the other lamb thou shalt offer at even, and shalt do thereto according to the meat offering of the **morning**, and according to the drink offering thereof, for a sweet savour, an offering made by fire unto the LORD." (KJV)

48. and 49.) Exodus 30:7 "And Aaron shall burn thereon sweet incense every **morning**: when he dresseth the lamps, he shall burn incense upon it." (KJV)

(Note: In Exodus 30:7, the Hebrew word *BOQER* is used twice. Literally, it says something like, "morning by morning.")

50. and 51.) Exodus 34:2 "And be ready in the **morning**, and come up in the **morning** unto mount Sinai, and present thyself there to me in the top of the mount." (KJV)

52.) Exodus 34:4 "And he hewed two tables of stone like unto the first; and Moses rose up early in the **morning**, and went up unto mount Sinai, as the LORD had commanded him, and took in his hand the two tables of stone." (KJV)

53.) Exodus 34:25 "Thou shalt not offer the blood of my sacrifice with leaven; neither shall the sacrifice of the feast of the passover be left unto the **morning**." (KJV)

54. and 55.) Exodus 36:3 "And they received of Moses all the offering, which the children of Israel had brought for the work of the service of the sanctuary, to make it *withal*. And they brought yet unto him free offerings every **morning**." (KJV)

(Note: In Exodus 36:3, the Hebrew word *BOQER* is used twice. Literally, it says something like, "morning by morning.")

56.) Leviticus 6:9 "Command Aaron and his sons, saying, This *is* the law of the burnt offering: It *is* the burnt offering, because of the burning upon the altar all night unto the **morning**, and the fire of the altar shall be burning in it." (KJV)

57. and 58.) Leviticus 6:12 "And the fire upon the altar shall be burning in it; it shall not be put out: and the priest shall burn wood on it every **morning**, and lay the burnt offering in order upon it; and he shall burn thereon the fat of the peace offerings." (KJV)

(Note: In Leviticus 6:12, the Hebrew word *BOQER* is used twice. Literally, it says something like, "morning by morning.")

59.) Leviticus 6:20 "This *is* the offering of Aaron and of his sons, which they shall offer unto the LORD in the day when he is anointed; the tenth part of an ephah of fine flour for a meat offering perpetual, half of it in the **morning**, and half thereof at night." (KJV)

60.) Leviticus 7:15 "And the flesh of the sacrifice of his peace offerings for thanksgiving shall be eaten the same day that it is offered; he shall not leave any of it until the **morning**." (KJV)

61.) Leviticus 9:17 "And he brought the meat offering, and took an handful thereof, and burnt *it* upon the altar, beside the burnt sacrifice of the **morning**." (KJV)

62.) Leviticus 19:13 "Thou shalt not defraud thy neighbour, neither rob *him:* the wages of him that is hired shall not abide with thee all night until the **morning**." (KJV)

63.) Leviticus 22:30 "On the same day it shall be eaten up; ye shall leave none of it until the **morrow**: I *am* the LORD." (KJV)

64.) Leviticus 24:3 "Without the veil of the testimony, in the tabernacle of the congregation, shall Aaron order it from the evening unto the **morning** before the LORD continually: *it shall be* a statute for ever in your generations." (KJV)

65.) Numbers 9:12 "They shall leave none of it unto the **morning**, nor break any bone of it: according to all the ordinances of the passover they shall keep it." (KJV)

66.) Numbers 9:15 "And on the day that the tabernacle was reared up the cloud covered the tabernacle, *namely,* the tent of the testimony: and at even there was upon the tabernacle as it were the appearance of fire, until the **morning**." (KJV)

67. and 68.) Numbers 9:21 "And *so* it was, when the cloud abode from even unto the **morning**, and *that* the cloud was taken up in the **morning**, then they journeyed: whether *it was* by day or by night that the cloud was taken up, they journeyed." (KJV)

69.) Numbers 14:40 "And they rose up early in the **morning**, and gat them up into the top of the mountain, saying, Lo, we *be here,* and will go up unto the place which the LORD hath promised: for we have sinned." (KJV)

70.) Numbers 16:5 "And he spake unto Korah and unto all his company, saying, Even to **morrow** the LORD will show who *are* his, and *who is* holy; and will cause *him* to come near unto him: even *him* whom he hath chosen will he cause to come near unto him." (KJV)

71.) Numbers 22:13 "And Balaam rose up in the **morning**, and said unto the princes of Balak, Get you into your land: for the LORD refuseth to give me leave to go with you." (KJV)

72.) Numbers 22:21 "And Balaam rose up in the **morning**, and saddled his ass, and went with the princes of Moab." (KJV)

73.) Numbers 22:41 "And it came to pass on the **morrow**, that Balak took Balaam, and brought him up into the high places of Baal, that thence he might see the utmost *part* of the people." (KJV)

74.) Numbers 28:4 "The one lamb shalt thou offer in the **morning**, and the other lamb shalt thou offer at even;" (KJV)

75.) Numbers 28:8 "And the other lamb shalt thou offer at even: as the meat offering of the **morning**, and as the drink offering thereof, thou shalt offer *it,* a sacrifice made by fire, of a sweet savour unto the LORD." (KJV)

76.) Numbers 28:23 "Ye shall offer these beside the burnt offering in the **morning**, which *is* for a continual burnt offering." (KJV)

77.) Deuteronomy 16:4 "And there shall be no leavened bread seen with thee in all thy coast seven days; neither shall there *any thing* of the flesh, which thou sacrificedst the first day at even, remain all night until the **morning**." (KJV)

78.) Deuteronomy 16:7 "And thou shalt roast and eat *it* in the place which the LORD thy God shall choose: and thou shalt turn in the **morning**, and go unto thy tents." (KJV)

79. and 80.) Deuteronomy 28:67 "In the **morning** thou shalt say, Would God it were even! and at even thou shalt say, Would God it were **morning**! for the fear of thine heart wherewith thou shalt fear, and for the sight of thine eyes which thou shalt see." (KJV)

81.) Joshua 3:1 "And Joshua rose early in the **morning**; and they removed from Shittim, and came to Jordan, he and all the children of Israel, and lodged there before they passed over." (KJV)

82.) Joshua 6:12 "And Joshua rose early in the **morning**, and the priests took up the ark of the LORD." (KJV)

83.) Joshua 7:14 "In the **morning** therefore ye shall be brought according to your tribes: and it shall be, *that* the tribe which the LORD taketh shall come according to the families *thereof;* and the family which the LORD shall take shall come by households; and the household which the LORD shall take shall come man by man." (KJV)

84.) Joshua 7:16 "So Joshua rose up early in the **morning**, and brought Israel by their tribes; and the tribe of Judah was taken:" (KJV)

85.) Joshua 8:10 "And Joshua rose up early in the **morning**, and numbered the people, and went up, he and the elders of Israel, before the people to Ai." (KJV)

86.) Judges 6:28 "And when the men of the city arose early in the **morning**, behold, the altar of Baal was cast down, and the grove was cut down that *was* by it, and the second bullock was offered upon the altar *that was* built." (KJV)

87.) Judges 6:31 "And Joash said unto all that stood against him, Will ye plead for Baal? will ye save him? he that will plead for him, let him be put to death whilst *it is yet* **morning**: if he *be* a god, let him plead for himself, because *one* hath cast down his altar." (KJV)

88.) Judges 9:33 "And it shall be, *that* in the **morning**, as soon as the sun is up, thou shalt rise early, and set upon the city: and, behold, *when* he and the people that *is* with him come out against thee, then mayest thou do to them as thou shalt find occasion." (KJV)

89.) Judges 16:2 "*And it was told* the Gazites, saying, Samson is come hither. And they compassed *him* in, and laid wait for him all night in the gate of the city, and were quiet all the night, saying, In the **morning**, when it is day, we shall kill him." (KJV)

90.) Judges 19:5 "And it came to pass on the fourth day, when they arose early in the **morning**, that he rose up to depart: and the damsel's father said unto his son in law, Comfort thine heart with a morsel of bread, and afterward go your way." (KJV)

91.) Judges 19:8 "And he arose early in the **morning** on the fifth day to depart: and the damsel's father said, Comfort thine heart, I pray thee. And they tarried until afternoon, and they did eat both of them." (KJV)

92.) Judges 19:25 "But the men would not hearken to him: so the man took his concubine, and brought her forth unto them; and they knew her, and abused her all the night until the **morning**: and when the day began to spring, they let her go." (KJV)

93.) Judges 19:26 "Then came the woman in the dawning of the **day**, and fell down at the door of the man's house where her lord *was,* till it was light." (KJV)

94.) Judges 19:27 "And her lord rose up in the **morning**, and opened the doors of the house, and went out to go his way: and, behold, the woman his concubine was fallen down *at* the door of the house, and her hands *were* upon the threshold." (KJV)

95.) Judges 20:19 "And the children of Israel rose up in the **morning**, and encamped against Gibeah." (KJV)

96.) Ruth 2:7 "And she said, I pray you, let me glean and gather after the reapers among the sheaves: so she came, and hath continued even from the **morning** until now, that she tarried a little in the house." (KJV)

97. and 98.) Ruth 3:13 "Tarry this night, and it shall be in the **morning**, *that* if he will perform unto thee the part of a kinsman, well; let him do the kinsman's part: but if he will not do the part of a kinsman to thee, then will I do the part of a kinsman to thee, *as* the LORD liveth: lie down until the **morning**." (KJV)

99.) Ruth 3:14 "And she lay at his feet until the **morning**: and she rose up before one could know another. And he said, Let it not be known that a woman came into the floor." (KJV)

100.) 1 Samuel 1:19 "And they rose up in the **morning** early, and worshipped before the LORD, and returned, and came to their house to Ramah: and Elkanah knew Hannah his wife; and the LORD remembered her." (KJV)

101.) 1 Samuel 3:15 "And Samuel lay until the **morning**, and opened the doors of the house of the LORD. And Samuel feared to show Eli the vision." (KJV)

102.) 1 Samuel 5:4 "And when they arose early on the morrow **morning**, behold, Dagon *was* fallen upon his face to the ground before the ark of the LORD; and the head of Dagon and both the palms of his hands *were* cut off upon the threshold; only *the stump of* Dagon was left to him." (KJV)

103.) 1 Samuel 9:19 "And Samuel answered Saul, and said, I *am* the seer: go up before me unto the high place; for ye shall eat with me to day, and to **morrow** I will let thee go, and will tell thee all that *is* in thine heart." (KJV)

104.) 1 Samuel 11:11 "And it was *so* on the morrow, that Saul put the people in three companies; and they came into the midst of the host in the **morning** watch, and slew the Ammonites until the heat of the day: and it came to pass, that they which remained were scattered, so that two of them were not left together." (KJV)

105.) 1 Samuel 14:36 "And Saul said, Let us go down after the Philistines by night, and spoil them until the **morning** light, and let us not leave a man of them. And they said, Do whatsoever seemeth good unto thee. Then said the priest, Let us draw near hither unto God." (KJV)

106.) 1 Samuel 15:12 "And when Samuel rose early to meet Saul in the **morning**, it was told Samuel, saying, Saul came to Carmel, and, behold, he set him up a place, and is gone about, and passed on, and gone down to Gilgal." (KJV)

107.) 1 Samuel 17:20 "And David rose up early in the **morning**, and left the sheep with a keeper, and took, and went, as Jesse had commanded him; and he came to the trench, as the host was going forth to the fight, and shouted for the battle." (KJV)

108.) 1 Samuel 19:2 "But Jonathan Saul's son delighted much in David: and Jonathan told David, saying, Saul my father seeketh to kill thee: now therefore, I pray thee, take heed to thyself until the **morning**, and abide in a secret *place,* and hide thyself:" (KJV)

109.) 1 Samuel 19:11 "Saul also sent messengers unto David's house, to watch him, and to slay him in the **morning**: and Michal David's wife told him, saying, If thou save not thy life to night, to morrow thou shalt be slain." (KJV)

110.) 1 Samuel 20:35 "And it came to pass in the **morning**, that Jonathan went out into the field at the time appointed with David, and a little lad with him." (KJV)

111.) 1 Samuel 25:22 "So and more also do God unto the enemies of David, if I leave of all that *pertain* to him by the **morning** light any that pisseth against the wall." (KJV)

112.) 1 Samuel 25:34 "For in very deed, *as* the LORD God of Israel liveth, which hath kept me back from hurting thee, except thou hadst hasted and come to meet me, surely there had not been left unto Nabal by the **morning** light any that pisseth against the wall." (KJV)

113.) 1 Samuel 25:36 "And Abigail came to Nabal; and, behold, he held a feast in his house, like the feast of a king; and Nabal's heart *was* merry within him, for he *was* very drunken: wherefore she told him nothing, less or more, until the **morning** light." (KJV)

114.) 1 Samuel 25:37 "But it came to pass in the **morning**, when the wine was gone out of Nabal, and his wife had told him these things, that his heart died within him, and he became *as* a stone." (KJV)

115. and 116.) 1 Samuel 29:10 "Wherefore now rise up early in the **morning** with thy master's servants that are come with thee: and as soon as ye be up early in the **morning**, and have light, depart." (KJV)

117.) 1 Samuel 29:11 "So David and his men rose up early to depart in the **morning**, to return into the land of the Philistines. And the Philistines went up to Jezreel." (KJV)

118.) 2 Samuel 2:27 "And Joab said, *As* God liveth, unless thou hadst spoken, surely then in the **morning** the people had gone up every one from following his brother." (KJV)

119.) 2 Samuel 11:14 "And it came to pass in the **morning**, that David wrote a letter to Joab, and sent *it* by the hand of Uriah." (KJV)

120. and 121.) 2 Samuel 13:4 "And he said unto him, Why *art* thou, *being* the king's son, lean from **day** to **day**? wilt thou not tell me? And Amnon said unto him, I love Tamar, my brother Absalom's sister." (KJV)

Since this verse is in *King James* English, its meaning seems a bit vague to me. What does it mean to be, "lean from day to day," or more accurately, "lean, morning by morning?" Does this refer to regular mornings or does "day to day" mean an age? Here is the same verse in the NIV:

2 Samuel 13:4 "He asked Amnon, 'Why do you, the king's son, look so haggard **morning after morning**? Won't you tell me?' Amnon said to him, 'I'm in love with Tamar, my brother Absalom's sister.'" (NIV)

122.) 2 Samuel 17:22 "Then David arose, and all the people that *were* with him, and they passed over Jordan: by the **morning** light there lacked not one of them that was not gone over Jordan." (KJV)

123. and 124.) 2 Samuel 23:4 "And *he shall be* as the light of the **morning**, *when* the sun riseth, *even* a **morning** without clouds; *as* the tender grass *springing* out of the earth by clear shining after rain." (KJV)

125.) 2 Samuel 24:11 "For when David was up in the **morning**, the word of the LORD came unto the prophet Gad, David's seer, saying," (KJV)

126.) 2 Samuel 24:15 "So the LORD sent a pestilence upon Israel from the **morning** even to the time appointed: and there died of the people from Dan even to Beersheba seventy thousand men." (KJV)

127. and 128.) 1 Kings 3:21 "And when I rose in the **morning** to give my child suck, behold, it was dead: but when I had considered it in the **morning**, behold, it was not my son, which I did bear." (KJV)

129.) 1 Kings 17:6 "And the ravens brought him bread and flesh in the **morning**, and bread and flesh in the evening; and he drank of the brook." (KJV)

130.) 1 Kings 18:26 "And they took the bullock which was given them, and they dressed *it,* and called on the name of Baal from **morning** even until noon, saying, O Baal, hear us. But *there was* no voice, nor any that answered. And they leaped upon the altar which was made." (KJV)

131.) 2 Kings 3:20 "And it came to pass in the **morning**, when the meat offering was offered, that, behold, there came water by the way of Edom, and the country was filled with water." (KJV)

132.) 2 Kings 3:22 "And they rose up early in the **morning**, and the sun shone upon the water, and the Moabites saw the water on the other side *as* red as blood:" (KJV)

133.) 2 Kings 7:9 "Then they said one to another, We do not well: this day *is* a day of good tidings, and we hold our peace: if we tarry till the **morning** light, some mischief will come upon us: now therefore come, that we may go and tell the king's household." (KJV)

134.) 2 Kings 10:8 "And there came a messenger, and told him, saying, They have brought the heads of the king's sons. And he said, Lay ye them in two heaps at the entering in of the gate until the **morning**." (KJV)

135.) 2 Kings 10:9 "And it came to pass in the **morning**, that he went out, and stood, and said to all the people, Ye *be* righteous: behold, I conspired against my master, and slew him: but who slew all these?" (KJV)

136.) 2 Kings 16:15 "And king Ahaz commanded Urijah the priest, saying, Upon the great altar burn the **morning** burnt offering, and the evening meat offering, and the king's burnt sacrifice, and his meat offering, with the burnt offering of all the people of the land, and their meat offering, and their drink offerings; and sprinkle upon it all the blood of the burnt offering, and all the blood of the sacrifice: and the brazen altar shall be for me to inquire *by*." (KJV)

137.) 2 Kings 19:35 "And it came to pass that night, that the angel of the LORD went out, and smote in the camp of the Assyrians an hundred fourscore and five thousand: and when they arose early in the **morning**, behold, they *were* all dead corpses." (KJV)

138. and 139.) 1 Chronicles 9:27 "And they lodged round about the house of God, because the charge *was* upon them, and the opening thereof every **morning** *pertained* to them." (KJV)

(Note: In 1 Chronicles 9:27, the Hebrew word *BOQER* is used twice. Literally, it says something like, "morning by morning.")

140.) 1 Chronicles 16:40 "To offer burnt offerings unto the LORD upon the altar of the burnt offering continually **morning** and evening, and *to do* according to all that is written in the law of the LORD, which he commanded Israel;" (KJV)

141. and 142.) 1 Chronicles 23:30 "And to stand every **morning** to thank and praise the LORD, and likewise at even;" (KJV)

(Note: In 1 Chronicles 23:30, the Hebrew word *BOQER* is used twice. Literally, it says something like, "morning by morning.")

143.) 2 Chronicles 2:4 "Behold, I build an house to the name of the LORD my God, to dedicate *it* to him, *and* to burn before him sweet incense, and for the continual showbread, and for the burnt offerings **morning** and evening, on the sabbaths, and on the new moons, and on the solemn feasts of the LORD our God. This *is an ordinance* for ever to Israel." (KJV)

144. and 145.) 2 Chronicles 13:11 "And they burn unto the LORD every **morning** and every evening burnt sacrifices and sweet incense: the showbread also *set they in order* upon the pure table; and the candlestick of gold with the lamps thereof, to burn every evening: for we keep the charge of the LORD our God; but ye have forsaken him." (KJV)

(Note: In 2 Chronicles 13:11, the Hebrew word *BOQER* is used twice. Literally, it says something like, "morning by morning.")

146.) 2 Chronicles 20:20 "And they rose early in the **morning**, and went forth into the wilderness of Tekoa: and as they went forth, Jehoshaphat stood and said, Hear me, O Judah, and ye inhabitants of Jerusalem; Believe in the LORD your God, so shall ye be established; believe his prophets, so shall ye prosper." (KJV)

147.) 2 Chronicles 31:3 "*He appointed* also the king's portion of his substance for the burnt offerings, *to wit,* for the **morning** and evening burnt offerings, and the burnt offerings for the sabbaths, and for the new moons, and for the set feasts, as *it is* written in the law of the LORD." (KJV)

148.) Ezra 3:3 "And they set the altar upon his bases; for fear *was* upon them because of the people of those countries: and they offered burnt offerings thereon unto the LORD, *even* burnt offerings **morning** and evening." (KJV)

149.) Esther 2:14 "In the evening she went, and on the **morrow** she returned into the second house of the women, to the custody of Shaashgaz, the king's chamberlain, which kept the concubines: she came in unto the king no more, except the king delighted in her, and that she were called by name." (KJV)

150.) Esther 5:14 "Then said Zeresh his wife and all his friends unto him, Let a gallows be made of fifty cubits high, and to **morrow** speak thou unto the king that Mordecai may be hanged thereon: then go thou in merrily with the king unto the banquet. And the thing pleased Haman; and he caused the gallows to be made." (KJV)

151.) Job 1:5 "And it was so, when the days of *their* feasting were gone about, that Job sent and sanctified them, and rose up early in the **morning**, and offered burnt offerings *according* to the number of them all: for Job said, It may be that my sons have sinned, and cursed God in their hearts. Thus did Job continually." (KJV)

152.) Job 4:20 "They are destroyed from **morning** to evening: they perish for ever without any regarding *it*." (KJV)

153.) Job 7:18 "And *that* thou shouldest visit him every **morning**, *and* try him every moment?" (KJV)

154.) Job 11:17 "And *thine* age shall be clearer than the noonday; thou shalt shine forth, thou shalt be as the **morning**." (KJV)

155.) Job 24:17 "For the **morning** *is* to them even as the shadow of death: if *one* know *them, they are in* the terrors of the shadow of death." (KJV)

156.) Job 38:7 "When the **morning** stars sang together, and all the sons of God shouted for joy?" (KJV)

157.) Job 38:12 "Hast thou commanded the **morning** since thy days; *and* caused the dayspring to know his place;" (KJV)

158. and 159.) Psalms 5:3 "My voice shalt thou hear in the **morning**, O LORD; in the **morning** will I direct *my prayer* unto thee, and will look up." (KJV)

160.) Psalms 30:5 "For his anger *endureth but* a moment; in his favour *is* life: weeping may endure for a night, but joy *cometh* in the **morning**." (KJV)

161.) Psalms 46:5 "God *is* in the midst of her; she shall not be moved: God shall help her, *and that* right **early**." (KJV)

162.) Psalms 49:14 "Like sheep they are laid in the grave; death shall feed on them; and the upright shall have dominion over them in the **morning**; and their beauty shall consume in the grave from their dwelling." (KJV)

163.) Psalms 55:17 "Evening, and **morning**, and at noon, will I pray, and cry aloud: and he shall hear my voice." (KJV)

164.) Psalms 59:16 "But I will sing of thy power; yea, I will sing aloud of thy mercy in the **morning**: for thou hast been my defence and refuge in the day of my trouble." (KJV)

165.) Psalms 65:8 "They also that dwell in the uttermost parts are afraid at thy tokens: thou makest the outgoings of the **morning** and evening to rejoice." (KJV)

166.) Psalms 73:14 "For all the day long have I been plagued, and chastened every **morning**." (KJV)

167.) Psalms 88:13 "But unto thee have I cried, O LORD; and in the **morning** shall my prayer prevent thee." (KJV)

168.) Psalms 90:5 "Thou carriest them away as with a flood; they are *as* a sleep: in the **morning** *they are* like grass *which* groweth up." (KJV)

169.) Psalms 90:6 "In the **morning** it flourisheth, and groweth up; in the evening it is cut down, and withereth." (KJV)

170.) Psalms 90:14 "O satisfy us **early** with thy mercy; that we may rejoice and be glad all our days." (KJV)

171.) Psalms 92:2 "To show forth thy lovingkindness in the **morning**, and thy faithfulness every night," (KJV)

172.) Psalms 101:8 "I will **early** destroy all the wicked of the land; that I may cut off all wicked doers from the city of the LORD." (KJV)

173. and 174.) Psalms 130:6 "My soul *waiteth* for the Lord more than they that watch for the **morning**: *I say, more than* they that watch for the **morning**." (KJV)

175.) Psalms 143:8 "Cause me to hear thy lovingkindness in the **morning**; for in thee do I trust: cause me to know the way wherein I should walk; for I lift up my soul unto thee." (KJV)

176.) Proverbs 7:18 "Come, let us take our fill of love until the **morning**: let us solace ourselves with loves." (KJV)

177.) Proverbs 27:14 "He that blesseth his friend with a loud voice, rising early in the **morning**, it shall be counted a curse to him." (KJV)

178.) Ecclesiastes 10:16 "Woe to thee, O land, when thy king *is* a child, and thy princes eat in the **morning**!" (KJV)

179.) Ecclesiastes 11:6 "In the **morning** sow thy seed, and in the evening withhold not thine hand: for thou knowest not whether shall prosper, either this or that, or whether they both *shall be* alike good." (KJV)

180.) Isaiah 5:11 "Woe unto them that rise up early in the **morning**, *that* they may follow strong drink; that continue until night, *till* wine inflame them!" (KJV)

181.) Isaiah 17:11 "In the day shalt thou make thy plant to grow, and in the **morning** shalt thou make thy seed to flourish: *but* the harvest *shall be* a heap in the day of grief and of desperate sorrow." (KJV)

Anti-Gap Theory creationists have used this verse to prove *BOQER* does not always mean a literal morning. There is no way someone can make a seed literally grow and flourish on the same day it is planted. Therefore, both "day" (*YOM*) and "morning" (*BOQER*) in this verse can't mean a literal day or a literal morning. When they say this, it just proves they haven't looked at the context. Let's not make the same mistake; let's look at the context.

Isaiah 17:7-11 "In that day man will look to his Maker, and his eyes will look on the Holy One of Israel. {8} He will not look to the altars, the work of his hands, and he will not look on what his own fingers have made, either the Asherim or the altars of incense. {9} In that day their strong cities will be like the deserted places of the wooded heights and the hilltops, which they deserted because of the children of Israel, and there will be desolation. {10} For you have forgotten the God of your salvation and have not remembered the Rock of your refuge; therefore, though you plant pleasant plants and sow the vine-branch of a stranger, {11} though you make them grow on the day that you plant them, and make them blossom in the morning that you sow, yet the harvest will flee away in a day of grief and incurable pain." (ESV)

Isaiah is warning Israel of God's judgment upon them because they have forgotten Him. In this warning, Isaiah is using non-literal imagery, and although the imagery is non-literal, the fact of God's pending judgment is absolutely true and literal. (God's warnings of judgment always refer to literal judgment, even if the warnings use non-literal language.) These people have forgotten God, and have put their trust in what THEY have done to secure their own peace and prosperity. They have built all kinds of altars to all kinds of gods. They have built strong cities. They have planted all kinds of good and exotic plants. Isaiah comes along and tells them that all they have done for themselves will not save them. He then uses hyperbole to drive the point home. Even if they could make their seeds sprout, grow, and produce a crop in one literal day, it would avail them nothing. The harvest will still be grief and incurable pain. So, while the passage uses hyperbole, (the ability to grow and harvest plants in a day) the references to "day" (*YOM*) and "morning" (*BOQER*) still refer to a literal day and a literal morning. Otherwise, it wouldn't be hyperbole. If "day" and "morning" mean a long period of time, then Isaiah's hyperbole makes no sense… "though you make them grow and make them blossom over a long period of time, yet the harvest will flee away in a long period of time of grief and pain." He is not saying there are plants that can be planted and harvested in one day, but he is saying that even if Israel could do that, it would be of no avail. He is still using "morning and "day" to define a literal morning and a literal day.

182.) Isaiah 17:14 "And behold at eveningtide trouble; *and* before the **morning** he *is* not. This *is* the portion of them that spoil us, and the lot of them that rob us." (KJV)

183.) Isaiah 21:12 "The watchman said, The **morning** cometh, and also the night: if ye will inquire, inquire ye: return, come." (KJV)

184. and 185.) Isaiah 28:19 "From the time that it goeth forth it shall take you: for **morning** by **morning** shall it pass over, by day and by night: and it shall be a vexation only *to* understand the report." (KJV)

186.) Isaiah 33:2 "O LORD, be gracious unto us; we have waited for thee: be thou their arm every **morning**, our salvation also in the time of trouble." (KJV)

187.) Isaiah 37:36 "Then the angel of the LORD went forth, and smote in the camp of the Assyrians a hundred and fourscore and five thousand: and when they arose early in the **morning**, behold, they *were* all dead corpses." (KJV)

188.) Isaiah 38:13 "I reckoned till **morning**, *that,* as a lion, so will he break all my bones: from day *even* to night wilt thou make an end of me." (KJV)

189. and 190.) Isaiah 50:4 "The Lord GOD hath given me the tongue of the learned, that I should know how to speak a word in season to *him that is* weary: he wakeneth **morning** by **morning**, he wakeneth mine ear to hear as the learned." (KJV)

191.) Jeremiah 20:16 "And let that man be as the cities which the LORD overthrew, and repented not: and let him hear the cry in the **morning**, and the shouting at noontide;" (KJV)

192.) Jeremiah 21:12 "O house of David, thus saith the LORD; Execute judgment in the **morning**, and deliver *him that is* spoiled out of the hand of the oppressor, lest my fury go out like fire, and burn that none can quench *it,* because of the evil of your doings." (KJV)

193.) Lamentations 3:23 "*They are* new every **morning**: great *is* thy faithfulness." (KJV)

194.) Ezekiel 12:8 "And in the **morning** came the word of the LORD unto me, saying," (KJV)

195. and 196.) Ezekiel 24:18 "So I spake unto the people in the **morning**: and at even my wife died; and I did in the **morning** as I was commanded." (KJV)

197.) Ezekiel 33:22 "Now the hand of the LORD was upon me in the evening, afore he that was escaped came; and had opened my mouth, until he came to me in the **morning**; and my mouth was opened, and I was no more dumb." (KJV)

198. and 199.) Ezekiel 46:13 "Thou shalt daily prepare a burnt offering unto the LORD *of* a lamb of the first year without blemish: thou shalt prepare it every **morning**." (KJV)

(Note: In Ezekiel 46:13, the Hebrew word *BOQER* is used twice. Literally, it says something like, "morning by morning.")

200. and 201.) Ezekiel 46:14 "And thou shalt prepare a meat offering for it every **morning**, the sixth part of an ephah, and the third part of an hin of oil, to temper with the fine flour; a meat offering continually by a perpetual ordinance unto the LORD." (KJV)

(Note: In Ezekiel 46:14, the Hebrew word *BOQER* is used twice. Literally, it says something like, "morning by morning.")

202. and 203.) Ezekiel 46:15 "Thus shall they prepare the lamb, and the meat offering, and the oil, every **morning** *for* a continual burnt offering." (KJV)

(Note: In Ezekiel 46:15, the Hebrew word *BOQER* is used twice. Literally, it says something like, "morning by morning.")

204.) Daniel 8:14 "And he said unto me, Unto two thousand and three hundred **days**; then shall the sanctuary be cleansed." (KJV)

(Note: The Hebrew literally says 2,300 "evening-morning" (*EREB-BOQER*, each in the singular.) The *King James Bible* lumps "evening-morning" together and call them, "days," because there are 2,300 of them.)

205.) Daniel 8:26 "And the vision of the evening and the **morning** which was told *is* true: wherefore shut thou up the vision; for it *shall be* for many days." (KJV)

206.) Hosea 6:4 "O Ephraim, what shall I do unto thee? O Judah, what shall I do unto thee? for your goodness *is* as a **morning** cloud, and as the early dew it goeth away." (KJV)

207.) Hosea 7:6 "For they have made ready their heart like an oven, whiles they lie in wait: their baker sleepeth all the night; in the **morning** it burneth as a flaming fire." (KJV)

208.) Hosea 13:3 "Therefore they shall be as the **morning** cloud, and as the early dew that passeth away, as the chaff *that* is driven with the whirlwind out of the floor, and as the smoke out of the chimney." (KJV)

209.) Amos 4:4 "Come to Bethel, and transgress; at Gilgal multiply transgression; and bring your sacrifices every **morning**, *and* your tithes after three years:" (KJV)

210.) Amos 5:8 "*Seek him* that maketh the seven stars and Orion, and turneth the shadow of death into the **morning**, and maketh the day dark with night: that calleth for the waters of the sea, and poureth them out upon the face of the earth: The LORD *is* his name:" (KJV)

211.) Micah 2:1 "Woe to them that devise iniquity, and work evil upon their beds! when the **morning** is light, they practice it, because it is in the power of their hand." (KJV)

212.) Zephaniah 3:3 "Her princes within her *are* roaring lions; her judges *are* evening wolves; they gnaw not the bones till the **morrow**." (KJV)

213. and 214.) Zephaniah 3:5 "The just LORD *is* in the midst thereof; he will not do iniquity: every **morning** doth he bring his judgment to light, he faileth not; but the unjust knoweth no shame." (KJV)

(Note: In Zephaniah 3:5, the Hebrew word *BOQER* is used twice. Literally, it says, "morning by morning.")

Did you see all those verses where *BOQER* is used to describe a period of time where it means something like the "dawn" of a new age? You didn't see them? I didn't see them either, but according to Day-Age creationists they must be there someplace. Go back and read all those verses again and again and again. Maybe with enough determination and imagination, you'll eventually see them.

BOQER is used 214 times in the Bible, and it refers to sunrise, dawn, or the beginning of the light portion of a twenty-four-hour day. Again, when used to describe a measurable period of time, it always means a short period of time. It is never used for a long period of time in the rest of the Bible. What gives anyone the right to give it a unique meaning in Genesis 1?

EREB and *BOQER* (Evening and Morning)

EREB and *BOQER* are combined in 44 Biblical passages. When used together, do these words mean an age or an ordinary day?

1.) Genesis 1:5 "And God called the light Day, and the darkness he called Night. And the **evening** and the **morning** were the first day." (KJV)

2.) Genesis 1:8 "And God called the firmament Heaven. And the **evening** and the **morning** were the second day." (KJV)

3.) Genesis 1:13 "And the **evening** and the **morning** were the third day." (KJV)

4.) Genesis 1:19 "And the **evening** and the **morning** were the fourth day." (KJV)

5.) Genesis 1:23 "And the **evening** and the **morning** were the fifth day." (KJV)

6.) Genesis 1:31 "And God saw every thing that he had made, and, behold, *it was* very good. And the **evening** and the **morning** were the sixth day." (KJV)

7.) Genesis 49:27 "Benjamin shall ravin *as* a wolf: in the **morning** he shall devour the prey, and at **night** he shall divide the spoil." (KJV)

8.) Exodus 16:8 "And Moses said, *This shall be,* when the LORD shall give you in the **evening** flesh to eat, and in the **morning** bread to the full; for that the LORD heareth your murmurings which ye murmur against him: and what *are* we? your murmurings *are* not against us, but against the LORD." (KJV)

9.) Exodus 16:12 "I have heard the murmurings of the children of Israel: speak unto them, saying, At **even** ye shall eat flesh, and in the **morning** ye shall be filled with bread; and ye shall know that I *am* the LORD your God." (KJV)

10.) Exodus 16:13 "And it came to pass, that at **even** the quails came up, and covered the camp: and in the **morning** the dew lay round about the host." (KJV)

11.) Exodus 18:13 "And it came to pass on the morrow, that Moses sat to judge the people: and the people stood by Moses from the **morning** unto the **evening**." (KJV)

12.) Exodus 18:14 "And when Moses' father in law saw all that he did to the people, he said, What *is* this thing that thou doest to the people? why sittest thou thyself alone, and all the people stand by thee from **morning** unto **even**?" (KJV)

13.) Exodus 27:21 "In the tabernacle of the congregation without the veil, which *is* before the testimony, Aaron and his sons shall order it from **evening** to **morning** before the LORD: *it shall be* a statute for ever unto their generations on the behalf of the children of Israel." (KJV)

14.) Exodus 29:39 "The one lamb thou shalt offer in the **morning**; and the other lamb thou shalt offer at **even**:" (KJV)

15.) Exodus 29:41 "And the other lamb thou shalt offer at **even**, and shalt do thereto according to the meat offering of the **morning**, and according to the drink offering thereof, for a sweet savour, an offering made by fire unto the LORD." (KJV)

16.) Leviticus 6:20 "This *is* the offering of Aaron and of his sons, which they shall offer unto the LORD in the day when he is anointed; the tenth part of an ephah of fine flour for a meat offering perpetual, half of it in the **morning**, and half thereof at **night**." (KJV)

17.) Leviticus 24:3 "Without the veil of the testimony, in the tabernacle of the congregation, shall Aaron order it from the **evening** unto the **morning** before the LORD continually: *it shall be* a statute for ever in your generations." (KJV)

18.) Numbers 9:15 "And on the day that the tabernacle was reared up the cloud covered the tabernacle, *namely,* the tent of the testimony: and at **even** there was upon the tabernacle as it were the appearance of fire, until the **morning**." (KJV)

19.) Numbers 9:21 "And *so* it was, when the cloud abode from **even** unto the **morning**, and *that* the cloud was taken up in the **morning**, then they journeyed: whether *it was* by day or by night that the cloud was taken up, they journeyed." (KJV)

20.) Numbers 28:4 "The one lamb shalt thou offer in the **morning**, and the other lamb shalt thou offer at **even**;" (KJV)

21.) Numbers 28:8 "And the other lamb shalt thou offer at **even**: as the meat offering of the **morning**, and as the drink offering thereof, thou shalt offer *it,* a sacrifice made by fire, of a sweet savour unto the LORD." (KJV)

22.) Deuteronomy 16:4 "And there shall be no leavened bread seen with thee in all thy coast seven days; neither shall there *any thing* of the flesh, which thou sacrificedst the first day at **even**, remain all night until the **morning**." (KJV)

23.) Deuteronomy 28:67 "In the **morning** thou shalt say, Would God it were **even**! and at **even** thou shalt say, Would God it were **morning**! for the fear of thine heart wherewith thou shalt fear, and for the sight of thine eyes which thou shalt see." (KJV)

24.) 1 Kings 17:6 "And the ravens brought him bread and flesh in the **morning**, and bread and flesh in the **evening**; and he drank of the brook." (KJV)

25.) 2 Kings 16:15 "And king Ahaz commanded Urijah the priest, saying, Upon the great altar burn the **morning** burnt offering, and the **evening** meat offering, and the king's burnt sacrifice, and his meat offering, with the burnt offering of all the people of the land, and their meat offering, and their drink offerings; and sprinkle upon it all the blood of the burnt offering, and all the blood of the sacrifice: and the brazen altar shall be for me to inquire *by*." (KJV)

26.) 1 Chronicles 16:40 "To offer burnt offerings unto the LORD upon the altar of the burnt offering continually **morning** and **evening**, and *to do* according to all that is written in the law of the LORD, which he commanded Israel;" (KJV)

27.) 1 Chronicles 23:30 "And to stand every **morning** to thank and praise the LORD, and likewise at **even**;" (KJV)

28.) 2 Chronicles 2:4 "Behold, I build an house to the name of the LORD my God, to dedicate *it* to him, *and* to burn before him sweet incense, and for the continual showbread, and for the burnt offerings **morning** and **evening**, on the sabbaths, and on the new moons, and on the solemn feasts of the LORD our God. This *is an ordinance* for ever to Israel." (KJV)

29.) 2 Chronicles 13:11 "And they burn unto the LORD every **morning** and every **evening** burnt sacrifices and sweet incense: the showbread also *set they in order* upon the pure table; and the candlestick of gold with the lamps thereof, to burn every **evening**: for we keep the charge of the LORD our God; but ye have forsaken him." (KJV)

30.) 2 Chronicles 31:3 "*He appointed* also the king's portion of his substance for the burnt offerings, *to wit*, for the **morning** and **evening** burnt offerings, and the burnt offerings for the sabbaths, and for the new moons, and for the set feasts, as *it is* written in the law of the LORD." (KJV)

31.) Ezra 3:3 "And they set the altar upon his bases; for fear *was* upon them because of the people of those countries: and they offered burnt offerings thereon unto the LORD, *even* burnt offerings **morning** and **evening**." (KJV)

32.) Esther 2:14 "In the **evening** she went, and on the **morrow** she returned into the second house of the women, to the custody of Shaashgaz, the king's chamberlain, which kept the concubines: she came in unto the king no more, except the king delighted in her, and that she were called by name." (KJV)

33.) Job 4:20 "They are destroyed from **morning** to **evening**: they perish for ever without any regarding *it*." (KJV)

34.) Psalms 30:5 "For his anger *endureth but* a moment; in his favour *is* life: weeping may endure for a **night**, but joy *cometh* in the **morning**." (KJV)

35.) Psalms 55:17 "**Evening**, and **morning**, and at noon, will I pray, and cry aloud: and he shall hear my voice." (KJV)

36.) Psalms 65:8 "They also that dwell in the uttermost parts are afraid at thy tokens: thou makest the outgoings of the **morning** and **evening** to rejoice." (KJV)

37.) Psalms 90:6 "In the **morning** it flourisheth, and groweth up; in the **evening** it is cut down, and withereth." (KJV)

      Some like to attack the literal, twenty-four-hour day interpretation of Genesis because Psalms 90:6 mentions plants that grow, flourish, and whither in one day. There are no plants that grow, flourish, and wither in the time span of a literal morning and evening. Therefore, we are not looking at literal plants. Now, I know there are flowers that bloom for a day and then the petals fall, but the plant itself doesn't do this. So, does this mean "morning and evening" can't be a literal twenty-four-hour day in Genesis 1? Does this mean "morning and evening" describes a long period of time in Genesis 1? No; this is poetry. Genesis 1 is not. This passage contains non-literal imagery. Genesis 1 does not. These "plants" don't exist. The plants in Genesis 1 do. Does a poetic definition of a word always define the prosaic definition of a word? Not in English; not in Hebrew; probably not an any language. The non-literal (poetry) meaning of "morning and evening" here in Psalms 90:6, does not change the literal (prose) meaning of "morning and evening" in Genesis 1:3-31. If anything, it does the complete opposite of what the Day-Age Theory requires. Psalms 90:6 uses morning and evening to describe a short period of time, the lives of men, not long ages. If you remember, back in Chapter Two, we looked at Psalms 90:4, and saw how it used a simile, a literary device, to explain that God "views" time differently than the way we view time. Psalms 90:6 is a continuation of that simile. We need some context to decipher this verse.

Psalms 90:1-6 "A Prayer of Moses the man of God. Lord, thou hast been our dwelling place in all generations. *{2}* Before the mountains were brought forth, or ever thou hadst formed the earth and the world, even from everlasting to everlasting, thou *art* God. *{3}* Thou turnest man to destruction; and sayest, Return, ye children of men. *{4}* For a thousand years in thy sight *are but* as yesterday when it is past, and *as* a watch in the night. *{5}* Thou carriest them away as with a flood; they are *as* a sleep: in the morning *they are* like grass *which* groweth up. *{6}* In the morning it flourisheth, and groweth up; in the evening it is cut down, and withereth." (KJV)

There is no comparison, only contrast, between what Psalms 90 says about a "day," and what Genesis 1 says about a "day." The perspectives are different. Psalms 90 describes how God "views" time. Genesis 1 describes how man views time. (God is describing the creation in Genesis, but it is written from an earth-bound, inside time-and-space, frame of reference.) Psalms 90 tells us God is not limited to that frame of reference. In fact, God is not limited to any frame of reference for time. Every "long period" of time to us is a "short period" of time to God. Every "short period" of time to us is a "long period" of time to God. This is what Psalms 90 reveals. Psalms 90 is a poetic description of how God "views" time; not how time passes in the literal time-and-space universe. Still, even in poetry, it conveys the idea that a "day" is a short period of time. (Otherwise, it would be saying, "a long period of time to God is like an age to God.") Men's physical lives are very short from God's perspective; we don't live for ages. "Morning and evening" describe a short period of time in Psalms 90. Therefore, "morning and evening" cannot be used in Genesis 1 to describe a long period of time.

38.) Ecclesiastes 11:6 "In the **morning** sow thy seed, and in the **evening** withhold not thine hand: for thou knowest not whether shall prosper, either this or that, or whether they both *shall be* alike good." (KJV)

39.) Isaiah 17:14 "And behold at **eveningtide** trouble; *and* before the **morning** he *is* not. This *is* the portion of them that spoil us, and the lot of them that rob us." (KJV)

40.) Ezekiel 24:18 "So I spake unto the people in the **morning**: and at **even** my wife died; and I did in the morning as I was commanded." (KJV)

41.) Ezekiel 33:22 "Now the hand of the LORD was upon me in the **evening**, afore he that was escaped came; and had opened my mouth, until he came to me in the **morning**; and my mouth was opened, and I was no more dumb." (KJV)

42.) Daniel 8:14 "And he said unto me, Unto two thousand and three hundred **days**; then shall the sanctuary be cleansed." (KJV)

(Note: The Hebrew literally says 2,300 "evening-morning" (*EREB-BOQER*, each in the singular.) The *King James Bible* lumps "evening-morning" together and call them, "days," because there are 2,300 of them.)

43.) Daniel 8:26 "And the vision of the **evening** and the **morning** which was told *is* true: wherefore shut thou up the vision; for it *shall be* for many days." (KJV)

44.) Zephaniah 3:3 "Her princes within her *are* roaring lions; her judges *are* **evening** wolves; they gnaw not the bones till the **morrow**." (KJV)

Every time these words are used together to describe physical time, they refer to short periods of time. Why would "evening and morning" have a different meaning in Genesis 1?

CHOSHEK (Dark, Darkness)

In its literal meaning, *CHOSHEK* designates physical darkness or the absence of light. If used figuratively, it can mean misery, destruction, death, ignorance, sorrow, or wickedness. In some places it is used literally, while in other places it is used figuratively. Here is how **CHOSHEK** (in bold print) is translated in the *King James Bible*.

1.) Genesis 1:2 "And the earth was without form, and void; and **darkness** *was* upon the face of the deep. And the Spirit of God moved upon the face of the waters." (KJV)

2. and 3.) Genesis 1:4-5 "And God saw the light, that *it was* good: and God divided the light from the **darkness**. {5} And God called the light Day, and the **darkness** he called Night. And the evening and the morning were the first day." (KJV)

4.) Genesis 1:18 "And to rule over the day and over the night, and to divide the light from the **darkness**: and God saw that *it was* good." (KJV)

5. 6. and 7.) Exodus 10:21-22 "And the LORD said unto Moses, Stretch out thine hand toward heaven, that there may be **darkness** over the land of Egypt, even **darkness** *which* may be felt. {22} And Moses stretched forth his hand toward heaven; and there was a thick **darkness** in all the land of Egypt three days:" (KJV)

8.) Exodus 14:20 "And it came between the camp of the Egyptians and the camp of Israel; and it was a cloud and **darkness** *to them*, but it gave light by night *to these*: so that the one came not near the other all the night." (KJV)

9.) Deuteronomy 4:11 "And ye came near and stood under the mountain; and the mountain burned with fire unto the midst of heaven, with **darkness**, clouds, and thick darkness." (KJV)

10.) Deuteronomy 5:23 "And it came to pass, when ye heard the voice out of the midst of the **darkness**, (for the mountain did burn with fire,) that ye came near unto me, *even* all the heads of your tribes, and your elders;" (KJV)

11.) Joshua 2:5 "And it came to pass *about the time* of shutting of the gate, when it was **dark**, that the men went out: whither the men went I wot not: pursue after them quickly; for ye shall overtake them." (KJV)

12.) 1 Samuel 2:9 "He will keep the feet of his saints, and the wicked shall be silent in **darkness**; for by strength shall no man prevail." (KJV)

13.) 2 Samuel 22:12 "And he made **darkness** pavilions round about him, dark waters, *and* thick clouds of the skies." (KJV)

14.) 2 Samuel 22:29 "For thou *art* my lamp, O LORD: and the LORD will lighten my **darkness**." (KJV)

15. and 16.) Job 3:4-5 "Let that day be **darkness**; let not God regard it from above, neither let the light shine upon it. *{5}* Let **darkness** and the shadow of death stain it; let a cloud dwell upon it; let the blackness of the day terrify it." (KJV)

17.) Job 5:14 "They meet with **darkness** in the daytime, and grope in the noonday as in the night." (KJV)

18.) Job 10:21 "Before I go *whence* I shall not return, *even* to the land of **darkness** and the shadow of death;" (KJV)

19.) Job 12:22 "He discovereth deep things out of **darkness**, and bringeth out to light the shadow of death." (KJV)

20.) Job 12:25 "They grope in the **dark** without light, and he maketh them to stagger like *a* drunken *man*." (KJV)

21. and 22.) Job 15:22-23 "He believeth not that he shall return out of **darkness**, and he is waited for of the sword. *{23}* He wandereth abroad for bread, *saying*, Where *is it*? he knoweth that the day of **darkness** is ready at his hand." (KJV)

23.) Job 15:30 "He shall not depart out of **darkness**; the flame shall dry up his branches, and by the breath of his mouth shall he go away." (KJV)

24. and 25.) Job 17:12-13 "They change the night into day: the light *is* short because of **darkness**. *{13}* If I wait, the grave *is* mine house: I have made my bed in the **darkness**." (KJV)

26.) Job 18:18 "He shall be driven from light into **darkness**, and chased out of the world." (KJV)

27.) Job 19:8 "He hath fenced up my way that I cannot pass, and he hath set **darkness** in my paths." (KJV)

28.) Job 20:26 "All **darkness** *shall be* hid in his secret places: a fire not blown shall consume him; it shall go ill with him that is left in his tabernacle." (KJV)

29.) Job 22:11 "Or **darkness**, *that* thou canst not see; and abundance of waters cover thee." (KJV)

30.) Job 23:17 "Because I was not cut off before the **darkness**, *neither* hath he covered the darkness from my face." (KJV)

31.) Job 24:16 "In the **dark** they dig through houses, *which* they had marked for themselves in the daytime: they know not the light." (KJV)

32.) Job 26:10 "He hath compassed the waters with bounds, until the day and **night** come to an end." (KJV)

33. and 34.) Job 28:3 "He setteth an end to **darkness**, and searcheth out all perfection: the stones of **darkness**, and the shadow of death." (KJV)

35.) Job 29:3 "When his candle shined upon my head, *and when* by his light I walked *through* **darkness**;" (KJV)

36.) Job 34:22 "*There is* no **darkness**, nor shadow of death, where the workers of iniquity may hide themselves." (KJV)

37.) Job 37:19 "Teach us what we shall say unto him; *for* we cannot order *our speech* by reason of **darkness**." (KJV)

38.) Job 38:19 "Where is the way *where* light dwelleth? and *as for* **darkness**, where *is* the place thereof," (KJV)

39.) Psalms 18:11 "He made **darkness** his secret place; his pavilion round about him *were* dark waters *and* thick clouds of the skies." (KJV)

40.) Psalms 18:28 "For thou wilt light my candle: the LORD my God will enlighten my **darkness**." (KJV)

41.) Psalms 35:6 "Let their way be **dark** and slippery: and let the angel of the LORD persecute them." (KJV)

42.) Psalms 88:12 "Shall thy wonders be known in the **dark**? and thy righteousness in the land of forgetfulness?" (KJV)

43.) Psalms 104:20 "Thou makest **darkness**, and it is night: wherein all the beasts of the forest do creep *forth*." (KJV)

44.) Psalms 105:28 "He sent **darkness**, and made it dark; and they rebelled not against his word." (KJV)

45.) Psalms 107:10 "Such as sit in **darkness** and in the shadow of death, *being* bound in affliction and iron;" (KJV)

46.) Psalms 107:14 "He brought them out of **darkness** and the shadow of death, and brake their bands in sunder." (KJV)

47.) Psalms 112:4 "Unto the upright there ariseth light in the **darkness**: *he is* gracious, and full of compassion, and righteous." (KJV)

48. and 49.) Psalms 139:11-12 "If I say, Surely the **darkness** shall cover me; even the night shall be light about me. *{12}* Yea, the **darkness** hideth not from thee; but the night shineth as the day: the darkness and the light *are* both alike to *thee*." (KJV)

50.) Proverbs 2:13 "Who leave the paths of uprightness, to walk in the ways of **darkness**;" (KJV)

51.) Proverbs 20:20 "Whoso curseth his father or his mother, his lamp shall be put out in obscure **darkness**." (KJV)

52. and 53.) Ecclesiastes 2:13-14 "Then I saw that wisdom excelleth folly, as far as light excelleth **darkness**. *{14}* The wise man's eyes are in his head; but the fool walketh in **darkness**: and I myself perceived also that one event happeneth to them all." (KJV)

54.) Ecclesiastes 5:17 "All his days also he eateth in **darkness**, and he hath much sorrow and wrath with his sickness." (KJV)

55. and 56.) Ecclesiastes 6:4 "For he cometh in with vanity, and departeth in **darkness**, and his name shall be covered with **darkness**." (KJV)

57.) Ecclesiastes 11:8 "But if a man live many years, *and* rejoice in them all; yet let him remember the days of **darkness**; for they shall be many. All that cometh *is* vanity." (KJV)

58. and 59.) Isaiah 5:20 "Woe unto them that call evil good, and good evil; that put **darkness** for light, and light for **darkness**; that put bitter for sweet, and sweet for bitter!" (KJV)

60.) Isaiah 5:30 "And in that day they shall roar against them like the roaring of the sea: and if *one* look unto the land, behold **darkness** *and* sorrow, and the light is darkened in the heavens thereof." (KJV)

61.) Isaiah 9:2 "The people that walked in **darkness** have seen a great light: they that dwell in the land of the shadow of death, upon them hath the light shined." (KJV)

62.) Isaiah 29:18 "And in that day shall the deaf hear the words of the book, and the eyes of the blind shall see out of obscurity, and out of **darkness**." (KJV)

63.) Isaiah 42:7 "To open the blind eyes, to bring out the prisoners from the prison, *and* them that sit in **darkness** out of the prison house." (KJV)

64.) Isaiah 45:3 "And I will give thee the treasures of **darkness**, and hidden riches of secret places, that thou mayest know that I, the LORD, which call *thee* by thy name, *am* the God of Israel." (KJV)

65.) Isaiah 45:7 "I form the light, and create **darkness**: I make peace, and create evil: I the LORD do all these *things*." (KJV)

66.) Isaiah 45:19 "I have not spoken in secret, in a **dark** place of the earth: I said not unto the seed of Jacob, Seek ye me in vain: I the LORD speak righteousness, I declare things that are right." (KJV)

67.) Isaiah 47:5 "Sit thou silent, and get thee into **darkness**, O daughter of the Chaldeans: for thou shalt no more be called, The lady of kingdoms." (KJV)

68.) Isaiah 49:9 "That thou mayest say to the prisoners, Go forth; to them that *are* in **darkness**, Show yourselves. They shall feed in the ways, and their pastures *shall be* in all high places." (KJV)

69.) Isaiah 58:10 "And *if* thou draw out thy soul to the hungry, and satisfy the afflicted soul; then shall thy light rise in **obscurity**, and thy darkness *be* as the noon day:" (KJV)

70.) Isaiah 59:9 "Therefore is judgment far from us, neither doth justice overtake us: we wait for light, but behold **obscurity**; for brightness, *but* we walk in darkness." (KJV)

71.) Isaiah 60:2 "For, behold, the **darkness** shall cover the earth, and gross darkness the people: but the LORD shall arise upon thee, and his glory shall be seen upon thee." (KJV)

72.) Lamentations 3:2 "He hath led me, and brought *me into* **darkness**, but not *into* light." (KJV)

73.) Ezekiel 8:12 "Then said he unto me, Son of man, hast thou seen what the ancients of the house of Israel do in the **dark**, every man in the chambers of his imagery? for they say, The LORD seeth us not; the LORD hath forsaken the earth." (KJV)

74.) Ezekiel 32:8 "All the bright lights of heaven will I make dark over thee, and set **darkness** upon thy land, saith the Lord GOD." (KJV)

75.) Joel 2:2 "A day of **darkness** and of gloominess, a day of clouds and of thick darkness, as the morning spread upon the mountains: a great people and a strong; there hath not been ever the like, neither shall be any more after it, *even* to the years of many generations." (KJV)

76.) Joel 2:31 "The sun shall be turned into **darkness**, and the moon into blood, before the great and the terrible day of the LORD come." (KJV)

77.) Amos 5:18 "Woe unto you that desire the day of the LORD! to what end *is* it for you? the day of the LORD *is* **darkness**, and not light." (KJV)

78.) Amos 5:20 "*Shall* not the day of the LORD *be* **darkness**, and not light? even very dark, and no brightness in it?" (KJV)

79.) Micah 7:8 "Rejoice not against me, O mine enemy: when I fall, I shall arise; when I sit in **darkness**, the LORD *shall be* a light unto me." (KJV)

80.) Nahum 1:8 "But with an overrunning flood he will make an utter end of the place thereof, and **darkness** shall pursue his enemies." (KJV)

81.) Zephaniah 1:15 "That day *is* a day of wrath, a day of trouble and distress, a day of wasteness and desolation, a day of **darkness** and gloominess, a day of clouds and thick darkness," (KJV)

When *CHOSHEK* is used to define a period of literal darkness, it never defines an age. In fact, the longest period of darkness mentioned in the Bible was the three days God brought down upon Egypt just before the Exodus. Since *CHOSHEK* is never used for an age of time anywhere else in the Bible, it should not be interpreted that the six nights in Genesis were ages. (I believe this hints that the Pre-Adamic darkness in Genesis 1:2 was a short period of time as well.)

OWR (Light)

As was true for *CHOSHEK*, so it is for *OWR*. It is used both literally and figuratively in the Bible. Figuratively, it describes knowledge, joy, approval, righteousness, health, blessing, *etc*. Literally, it describes light; either physical/photonic light or Divine/Spiritual light. Even when it describes physical light, it doesn't necessarily describe a period of time. For instance, it is used to describe the light from an oil lamp, a candle, or a fire, but that doesn't define a specific length of time. However, when it is used in connection with a period of time, it never describes long ages. **Since God called the light, "day," and He called the darkness, "night," all we need to do is figure out how long the periods of light and dark were, and then we will know how long the days and nights were in the Genesis Creation Account**. Personally, I think it is foolish to believe the "days" were millions or billions of years long unless you also believe the "nights" were millions or billions of years long. They both describe the same period of time; a short period of time.

As I we did for *CHOSHEK*, so we will do for *OWR*. We will look at all its uses in the Bible. The significant point we need to observe is how it is used in connection to the passage of a period of physical time. As you read all these verses, look for the places where *OWR* is used to describe a period of millions or billions of years of physical light. I'll give you a little hint up front: you won't find any such verses.

(Note: Two forms of *OWR* are used for "light" in the Old Testament, but they are essentially the same word. *OWR* is listed as Strong's Number H215 and Strong's Number H216. Not knowing Hebrew, I don't know the difference between them. Whether this reflects differences in ancient manuscripts or differences in modern interpretations, I am willingly clueless. I will mark the Strong's Numbers after each use. Truthfully, it makes no difference since neither form is used to describe long periods of time.)

1. and 2.) Genesis 1:3 "And God said, Let there be **light:**[H216] and there was **light.**"[H216] (KJV)

3. and 4.) Genesis 1:4 "And God saw the **light,**[H216] that it *was* good: and God divided the **light**[H216] from the darkness." (KJV)

5.) Genesis 1:5 "And God called the **light**[H216] Day, and the darkness he called Night. And the evening and the morning were the first day." (KJV)

6.) Genesis 1:15 "And let them be for lights in the firmament of the heaven to give **light**[H215] upon the earth: and it was so." (KJV)

7.) Genesis 1:17 "And God set them in the firmament of the heaven to give **light**[H215] upon the earth," (KJV)

8.) Genesis 1:18 "And to rule over the day and over the night, and to divide the **light**[H216] from the darkness: and God saw that it *was* good." (KJV)

9.) Genesis 44:3 "As soon as the morning was **light,**[H215] the men were sent away, they and their asses." (KJV)

10.) Exodus 10:23 "They saw not one another, neither rose any from his place for three days: but all the children of Israel had **light**[H216] in their dwellings." (KJV)

11.) Exodus 13:21 "And the LORD went before them by day in a pillar of a cloud, to lead them the way; and by night in a pillar of fire, to give them **light;**[H215] to go by day and night:" (KJV)

12.) Exodus 14:20 "And it came between the camp of the Egyptians and the camp of Israel; and it was a cloud and darkness *to them*, but it gave **light**[H215] by night *to these*: so that the one came not near the other all the night." (KJV)

13.) Exodus 25:37 "And thou shalt make the seven lamps thereof: and they shall light the lamps thereof, that they may give **light**[H215] over against it." (KJV)

14.) Numbers 6:25 "The LORD make his face **shine**[H215] upon thee, and be gracious unto thee:" (KJV)

15.) Numbers 8:2 "Speak unto Aaron, and say unto him, When thou lightest the lamps, the seven lamps shall give **light**[H215] over against the candlestick." (KJV)

16.) Judges 16:2 "*And it was told* the Gazites, saying, Samson is come hither. And they compassed *him* in, and laid wait for him all night in the gate of the city, and were quiet all the night, saying, In the morning, when it is **day,**[H216] we shall kill him." (KJV)

17.) Judges 19:26 "Then came the woman in the dawning of the day, and fell down at the door of the man's house where her lord *was*, till it was **light."**[H216](KJV)

18.) 1 Samuel 14:27 "But Jonathan heard not when his father charged the people with the oath: wherefore he put forth the end of the rod that *was* in his hand, and dipped it in an honeycomb, and put his hand to his mouth; and his eyes were **enlightened."**[H215](KJV)

19.) 1 Samuel 14:29 "Then said Jonathan, My father hath troubled the land: see, I pray you, how mine eyes have been **enlightened,**[H215] because I tasted a little of this honey." (KJV)

20.) 1 Samuel 14:36 "And Saul said, Let us go down after the Philistines by night, and spoil them until the morning **light,**[H216] and let us not leave a man of them. And they said, Do whatsoever seemeth good unto thee. Then said the priest, Let us draw near hither unto God." (KJV)

21.) 1 Samuel 25:34 "For in very deed, *as* the LORD God of Israel liveth, which hath kept me back from hurting thee, except thou hadst hasted and come to meet me, surely there had not been left unto Nabal by the morning **light**[H216] any that pisseth against the wall." (KJV)

22.) 1 Samuel 25:36 "And Abigail came to Nabal; and, behold, he held a feast in his house, like the feast of a king; and Nabal's heart *was* merry within him, for he *was* very drunken: wherefore she told him nothing, less or more, until the morning **light."**[H216](KJV)

23.) 1 Samuel 29:10 "Wherefore now rise up early in the morning with thy master's servants that are come with thee: and as soon as ye be up early in the morning, and have **light,**[H216] depart." (KJV)

24.) 2 Samuel 2:32 "And they took up Asahel, and buried him in the sepulchre of his father, which *was in* Bethlehem. And Joab and his men went all night, and they came to Hebron at break of **day."**[H215](KJV)

25.) 2 Samuel 17:22 "Then David arose, and all the people that *were* with him, and they passed over Jordan: by the morning **light**[H216] there lacked not one of them that was not gone over Jordan." (KJV)

26.) 2 Samuel 23:4 "And *he shall be* as the **light**[H216] of the morning, *when* the sun riseth, *even* a morning without clouds; *as* the tender grass *springing* out of the earth by clear shining after rain." (KJV)

27.) 2 Kings 7:9 "Then they said one to another, We do not well: this day *is* a day of good tidings, and we hold our peace: if we tarry till the morning **light,**[H216] some mischief will come upon us: now therefore come, that we may go and tell the king's household." (KJV)

28.) Ezra 9:8 "And now for a little space grace hath been *shewed* from the LORD our God, to leave us a remnant to escape, and to give us a nail in his holy place, that our God may **lighten**[H215] our eyes, and give us a little reviving in our bondage" (KJV)

29.) Nehemiah 8:3 "And he read therein before the street that *was* before the water gate from the **morning**[H216] until midday, before the men and the women, and those that could understand; and the ears of all the people *were attentive* unto the book of the law." (KJV)

30.) Nehemiah 9:12 "Moreover thou leddest them in the day by a cloudy pillar; and in the night by a pillar of fire, to give them **light**[H215] in the way wherein they should go." (KJV)

31.) Nehemiah 9:19 "Yet thou in thy manifold mercies forsookest them not in the wilderness: the pillar of the cloud departed not from them by day, to lead them in the way; neither the pillar of fire by night, to shew them **light,**[H215] and the way wherein they should go." (KJV)

32.) Job 3:9 "Let the stars of the twilight thereof be dark; let it look for **light,**[H216] but *have* none; neither let it see the dawning of the day:" (KJV)

33.) Job 3:16 "Or as an hidden untimely birth I had not been; as infants *which* never saw **light.**"[H216] (KJV)

34.) Job 3:20 "Wherefore is **light**[H216] given to him that is in misery, and life unto the bitter *in* soul;" (KJV)

35.) Job 12:22 "He discovereth deep things out of darkness, and bringeth out to **light**[H216] the shadow of death." (KJV)

36.) Job 12:25 "They grope in the dark without **light,**[H216] and he maketh them to stagger like *a* drunken *man*." (KJV)

37.) Job 17:12 "They change the night into day: the **light**[H216] *is* short because of darkness." (KJV)

38.) Job 18:5 "Yea, the **light**[H216] of the wicked shall be put out, and the spark of his fire shall not shine." (KJV)

39.) Job 18:6 "The **light**[H216] shall be dark in his tabernacle, and his candle shall be put out with him." (KJV)

40.) Job 18:18 "He shall be driven from **light**[H216] into darkness, and chased out of the world." (KJV)

41.) Job 22:28 "Thou shalt also decree a thing, and it shall be established[5] unto thee: and the **light**[H216] shall shine upon thy ways." (KJV)

42.) Job 24:13 "They are of those that rebel against the **light;**[H216] they know not the ways thereof, nor abide in the paths thereof." (KJV)

43.) Job 24:14 "The murderer rising with the **light**[H216] killeth the poor and needy, and in the night is as a thief." (KJV)

44.) Job 24:16 "In the dark they dig through houses, *which* they had marked for themselves in the daytime: they know not the **light.**"[H216] (KJV)

45.) Job 25:3 "Is there any number of his armies? and upon whom doth not his **light**[H216] arise?" (KJV)

46.) Job 26:10 "He hath compassed the waters with bounds, until the **day**[H216] and night come to an end." (KJV)

47.) Job 28:11 "He bindeth the floods from overflowing; and *the thing that is* hid[7] bringeth he forth to **light.**"[H216] (KJV)

48.) Job 29:3 "When his candle shined upon my head, *and when* by his **light**[H216] I walked *through* darkness;" (KJV)

49.) Job 29:24 "If I laughed on them, they believed it not; and the **light**[H216] of my countenance they cast not down." (KJV)

50.) Job 30:26 "When I looked for good, then evil came *unto me*: and when I waited for **light,**[H216] there came darkness." (KJV)

51.) Job 31:26 "If I beheld the **sun**[H216] when it shined, or the moon walking *in* brightness;" (KJV)

52.) Job 33:28 "He will deliver his soul from going into the pit, and his life shall see the **light."**[H216](KJV)

53. and 54.) Job 33:30 "To bring back his soul from the pit, to be **enlightened**[H215] with the **light**[H216] of the living." (KJV)

55.) Job 36:30 "Behold, he spreadeth his **light**[H216] upon it, and covereth the bottom of the sea." (KJV)

56.) Job 36:32 "With clouds he covereth the **light;**[H216] and commandeth it *not to shine* by *the cloud* that cometh betwixt." (KJV)

57.) Job 37:3 "He directeth it under the whole heaven, and his **lightning**[H216] unto the ends of the earth." (KJV)

58.) Job 37:11 "Also by watering he wearieth the thick cloud: he scattereth his **bright**[H216] cloud:" (KJV)

59.) Job 37:15 "Dost thou know when God disposed them, and caused the **light**[H216] of his cloud to shine?" (KJV)

60.) Job 37:21 "And now *men* see not the bright **light**[H216] which *is* in the clouds: but the wind passeth, and cleanseth them." (KJV)

61.) Job 38:15 "And from the wicked their **light**[H216] is withholden, and the high arm shall be broken." (KJV)

62.) Job 38:19 "Where *is* the way *where* **light**[H216] dwelleth? and *as for* darkness, where *is* the place thereof," (KJV)

63.) Job 38:24 "By what way is the **light**[H216] parted, *which* scattereth the east wind upon the earth?" (KJV)

64.) Job 41:18 "By his neesings a **light**[H216] doth shine, and his eyes *are* like the eyelids of the morning." (KJV)

65.) Job 41:32 "He maketh a path to **shine**[H215] after him; *one* would think the deep *to be* hoary." (KJV)

66.) Psalms 4:6 "*There be* many that say, Who will shew us *any* good? LORD, lift thou up the **light**[H216] of thy countenance upon us." (KJV)

67.) Psalms 13:3 "Consider *and* hear me, O LORD my God: **lighten**[H215] mine eyes, lest I sleep the *sleep of death*;" (KJV)

68.) Psalms 18:28 "For thou wilt **light**[H215] my candle: the LORD my God will enlighten my darkness." (KJV)

69.) Psalms 19:8 "The statutes of the LORD *are* right, rejoicing the heart: the commandment of the LORD *is* pure, **enlightening**[H215] the eyes." (KJV)

70.) Psalms 27:1 "*A Psalm* of David. The LORD *is* my **light**[H216] and my salvation; whom shall I fear? the LORD *is* the strength of my life; of whom shall I be afraid?" (KJV)

71.) Psalms 31:16 "Make thy face to **shine**[H215] upon thy servant: save me for thy mercies' sake." (KJV)

72. and 73.) Psalms 36:9 "For with thee *is* the fountain of life: in thy **light**[H216] shall we see **light.**"[H216](KJV)

74.) Psalms 37:6 "And he shall bring forth thy righteousness as the **light,**[H216] and thy judgment as the noonday." (KJV)

75.) Psalms 38:10 "My heart panteth, my strength faileth me: as for the **light**[H216] of mine eyes, it also is gone from me." (KJV)

76.) Psalms 43:3 "O send out thy **light**[H216] and thy truth: let them lead me; let them bring me unto thy holy hill, and to thy tabernacles." (KJV)

77.) Psalms 44:3 "For they got not the land in possession by their own sword, neither did their own arm save them: but thy right hand, and thine arm, and the **light**[H216] of thy countenance, because thou hadst a favour unto them." (KJV)

78.) Psalms 49:19 "He shall go to the generation of his fathers; they shall never see **light.**"[H216](KJV)

79.) Psalms 56:13 "For thou hast delivered my soul from death: *wilt* not *thou deliver* my feet from falling, that I may walk before God in the **light**[H216] of the living?" (KJV)

80.) Psalms 67:1 "To the chief Musician on Neginoth, A Psalm or Song. God be merciful unto us, and bless us; and cause his face to **shine**[H215] upon us; Selah." (KJV)

81.) Psalms 76:4 "Thou *art* more **glorious**[H215] *and* excellent than the mountains of prey." (KJV)

82.) Psalms 77:18 "The voice of thy thunder *was* in the heaven: the lightnings **lightened**[H215] the world: the earth trembled and shook." (KJV)

83.) Psalms 78:14 "In the daytime also he led them with a cloud, and all the night with a **light**[H216] of fire." (KJV)

84.) Psalms 80:3 "Turn us again, O God, and cause thy face to **shine;**[H215] and we shall be saved." (KJV)

85.) Psalms 80:7 "Turn us again, O God of hosts, and cause thy face to **shine;**[H215] and we shall be saved." (KJV)

86.) Psalms 80:19 "Turn us again, O LORD God of hosts, cause thy face to **shine;**[H215] and we shall be saved." (KJV)

87.) Psalms 89:15 "Blessed *is* the people that know the joyful sound: they shall walk, O LORD, in the **light**[H216] of thy countenance." (KJV)

88.) Psalms 97:4 "His lightnings **enlightened**[H215] the world: the earth saw, and trembled." (KJV)

89.) Psalms 97:11 "**Light**[H216] is sown for the righteous, and gladness for the upright in heart." (KJV)

90.) Psalms 104:2 "Who coverest *thyself* with **light**[H216] as *with* a garment: who stretchest out the heavens like a curtain:" (KJV)

91.) Psalms 105:39 "He spread a cloud for a covering; and fire to give **light**[H215] in the night." (KJV)

92.) Psalms 112:4 "Unto the upright there ariseth **light**[H216] in the darkness: *he is* gracious, and full of compassion, and righteous." (KJV)

93.) Psalms 118:27 "God is the LORD, which hath shewed us **light:**[H215] bind the sacrifice with cords, *even* unto the horns of the altar." (KJV)

94.) Psalms 119:105 "NUN. Thy word *is* a lamp unto my feet, and a **light**[H216] unto my path." (KJV)

95.) Psalms 119:130 "The entrance of thy words giveth **light;**[H215] it giveth understanding unto the simple." (KJV)

96.) Psalms 119:135 "Make thy face to **shine**[H215] upon thy servant; and teach me thy statutes." (KJV)

97.) Psalms 136:7 "To him that made great **lights:**[H216] for his mercy *endureth* for ever:" (KJV)

98.) Psalms 139:11 "If I say, Surely the darkness shall cover me; even the night shall be **light**[H216] about me." (KJV)

99.) Psalms 139:12 "Yea, the darkness hideth not from thee; but the night **shineth**[H215] as the day: the darkness and the light *are* both alike *to thee*." (KJV)

100.) Psalms 148:3 "Praise ye him, sun and moon: praise him, all ye stars of **light.**"[H216] (KJV)

101. and 102.) Proverbs 4:18 "But the path of the just is as the shining **light,**[H216] that **shineth**[H215] more and more unto the perfect day." (KJV)

103.) Proverbs 6:23 "For the commandment *is* a lamp; and the law *is* **light;**[H216] and reproofs of instruction *are* the way of life:" (KJV)

104.) Proverbs 13:9 "The **light**[H216] of the righteous rejoiceth: but the lamp of the wicked shall be put out." (KJV)

105.) Proverbs 16:15 "In the **light**[H216] of the king's countenance is life; and his favour *is* as a cloud of the latter rain." (KJV)

106.) Proverbs 29:13 "The poor and the deceitful man meet together: the LORD **lighteneth**[H215] both their eyes." (KJV)

107.) Ecclesiastes 2:13 "Then I saw that wisdom excelleth folly, as far as **light**[H216] excelleth darkness." (KJV)

108.) Ecclesiastes 8:1 "Who *is* as the wise *man*? and who knoweth the interpretation of a thing? a man's wisdom maketh his face to **shine,**[H215] and the boldness of his face shall be changed." (KJV)

109.) Ecclesiastes 11:7 "Truly the **light**[H216] *is* sweet, and a pleasant *thing it is* for the eyes to behold the sun:" (KJV)

110.) Ecclesiastes 12:2 "While the sun, or the **light,**[H216] or the moon, or the stars, be not darkened, nor the clouds return after the rain:" (KJV)

111.) Isaiah 2:5 "O house of Jacob, come ye, and let us walk in the **light**[H216] of the LORD." (KJV)

112. and 113.) Isaiah 5:20 "Woe unto them that call evil good, and good evil; that put darkness for **light,**[H216] and **light**[H216] for darkness; that put bitter for sweet, and sweet for bitter!" (KJV)

114.) Isaiah 5:30 "And in that day they shall roar against them like the roaring of the sea: and if *one* look unto the land, behold darkness *and* sorrow, and the **light**[H216] is darkened in the heavens thereof." (KJV)

115. and 116.) Isaiah 9:2 "The people that walked in darkness have seen a great **light:**[H216] they that dwell in the land of the shadow of death, upon them hath the **light**[H216] shined." (KJV)

117.) Isaiah 10:17 "And the **light**[H216] of Israel shall be for a fire, and his Holy One for a flame: and it shall burn and devour his thorns and his briers in one day;" (KJV)

118. and 119.) Isaiah 13:10 "For the stars of heaven and the constellations thereof shall not give their **light:**[H216] the sun shall be darkened in his going forth, and the moon shall not cause her **light**[H216] to shine." (KJV)

120.) Isaiah 27:11 "When the boughs thereof are withered, they shall be broken off: the women come, *and* set them on **fire:**[H215] for it *is* a people of no understanding: therefore he that made them will not have mercy on them, and he that formed them will shew them no favour." (KJV)

121. 122. 123. and 124.) Isaiah 30:26 "Moreover the **light**[H216] of the moon shall be as the **light**[H216] of the sun, and the **light**[H216] of the sun shall be sevenfold, as the **light**[H216] of seven days, in the day that the LORD bindeth up the breach of his people, and healeth the stroke of their wound." (KJV)

125.) Isaiah 42:6 "I the LORD have called thee in righteousness, and will hold thine hand, and will keep thee, and give thee for a covenant of the people, for a **light**[H216] of the Gentiles;" (KJV)

126.) Isaiah 42:16 "And I will bring the blind by a way *that* they knew not; I will lead them in paths *that* they have not known: I will make darkness **light**[H216] before them, and crooked things straight. These things will I do unto them, and not forsake them." (KJV)

127.) Isaiah 45:7 "I form the **light**,[H216] and create darkness: I make peace, and create evil: I the LORD do all these *things*." (KJV)

128.) Isaiah 49:6 "And he said, It is a light thing that thou shouldest be my servant to raise up the tribes of Jacob, and to restore the preserved of Israel: I will also give thee for a **light**[H216] to the Gentiles, that thou mayest be my salvation unto the end of the earth." (KJV)

129.) Isaiah 51:4 "Hearken unto me, my people; and give ear unto me, O my nation: for a law shall proceed from me, and I will make my judgment to rest for a **light**[H216] of the people." (KJV)

130.) Isaiah 58:8 "Then shall thy **light**[H216] break forth as the morning, and thine health shall spring forth speedily: and thy righteousness shall go before thee; the glory of the LORD shall be thy rereward." (KJV)

131.) Isaiah 58:10 "And *if* thou draw out thy soul to the hungry, and satisfy the afflicted soul; then shall thy **light**[H216] rise in obscurity, and thy darkness *be* as the noonday:" (KJV)

132.) Isaiah 59:9 "Therefore is judgment far from us, neither doth justice overtake us: we wait for **light**,[H216] but behold obscurity; for brightness, *but* we walk in darkness." (KJV)

133. and 134.) Isaiah 60:1 "Arise, **shine**;[H215] for thy **light**[H216] is come, and the glory of the LORD is risen upon thee." (KJV)

135.) Isaiah 60:3 "And the Gentiles shall come to thy **light**,[H216] and kings to the brightness of thy rising." (KJV)

136. 137. and 138.) Isaiah 60:19 "The sun shall be no more thy **light**[H216] by day; neither for brightness shall the moon give **light**[H215] unto thee: but the LORD shall be unto thee an everlasting **light**,[H216] and thy God thy glory." (KJV)

139.) Isaiah 60:20 "Thy sun shall no more go down; neither shall thy moon withdraw itself: for the LORD shall be thine everlasting **light,**[H216] and the days of thy mourning shall be ended." (KJV)

140.) Jeremiah 4:23 "I beheld the earth, and, lo, *it was* without form, and void; and the heavens, and they had no **light."**[H216](KJV)

141.) Jeremiah 13:16 "Give glory to the LORD your God, before he cause darkness, and before your feet stumble upon the dark mountains, and, while ye look for **light,**[H216] he turn it into the shadow of death, *and* make *it* gross darkness." (KJV)

142.) Jeremiah 25:10 "Moreover I will take from them the voice of mirth, and the voice of gladness, the voice of the bridegroom, and the voice of the bride, the sound of the millstones, and the **light**[H216] of the candle." (KJV)

143. and 144.) Jeremiah 31:35 "Thus saith the LORD, which giveth the sun for a **light**[H216] by day, *and* the ordinances of the moon and of the stars for a **light**[H216] by night, which divideth the sea when the waves thereof roar; The LORD of hosts *is* his name:" (KJV)

145.) Lamentations 3:2 "He hath led me, and brought *me into* darkness, but not *into* **light."**[H216](KJV)

146. and 147.) Ezekiel 32:7 "And when I shall put thee out, I will cover the heaven, and make the stars thereof dark; I will cover the sun with a cloud, and the moon shall not **give**[H215] her **light."**[H216](KJV)

148.) Ezekiel 32:8 "All the **bright**[H216] lights of heaven will I make dark over thee, and set darkness upon thy land, saith the Lord GOD." (KJV)

149.) Ezekiel 43:2 "And, behold, the glory of the God of Israel came from the way of the east: and his voice *was* like a noise of many waters: and the earth **shined**[H215] with his glory." (KJV)

150.) Daniel 9:17 "Now therefore, O our God, hear the prayer of thy servant, and his supplications, and cause thy face to **shine**[H215] upon thy sanctuary that is desolate, for the Lord's sake." (KJV)

151.) Hosea 6:5 "Therefore have I hewed *them* by the prophets; I have slain them by the words of my mouth: and thy judgments *are as* the **light**[H216] *that* goeth forth." (KJV)

152.) Amos 5:18 "Woe unto you that desire the day of the LORD! to what end *is it* for you? the day of the LORD is darkness, and not **light.**[H216](KJV)

153.) Amos 5:20 "*Shall* not the day of the LORD *be* darkness, and not **light?**[H216] even very dark, and no brightness in it?" (KJV)

154.) Amos 8:9 "And it shall come to pass in that day, saith the Lord GOD, that I will cause the sun to go down at noon, and I will darken the earth in the **clear**[H216] day:" (KJV)

155.) Micah 2:1 "Woe to them that devise iniquity, and work evil upon their beds! when the morning is **light,**[H216] they practise it, because it is in the power of their hand." (KJV)

156.) Micah 7:8 "Rejoice not against me, O mine enemy: when I fall, I shall arise; when I sit in darkness, the LORD *shall be* a **light**[H216] unto me." (KJV)

157.) Micah 7:9 "I will bear the indignation of the LORD, because I have sinned against him, until he plead my cause, and execute judgment for me: he will bring me forth to the **light,**[H216] *and* I shall behold his righteousness." (KJV)

158.) Habakkuk 3:4 "And *his* brightness was as the **light;**[H216] he had horns *coming* out of his hand: and there *was* the hiding of his power." (KJV)

159.) Habakkuk 3:11 "The sun *and* moon stood still in their habitation: at the **light**[H216] of thine arrows they went, *and* at the shining of thy glittering spear." (KJV)

160.) Zephaniah 3:5 "The just LORD *is* in the midst thereof; he will not do iniquity: every morning doth he bring his judgment to **light,**[H216] he faileth not; but the unjust knoweth no shame." (KJV)

161.) Zechariah 14:6 "And it shall come to pass in that day, *that* the **light**[H216] shall not be clear, *nor* dark:" (KJV)

162.) Zechariah 14:7 "But it shall be one day which shall be known to the LORD, not day, nor night: but it shall come to pass, *that* at evening time it shall be **light.**[H216](KJV)

163.) Malachi 1:10 "Who *is there* even among you that would shut the doors *for nought*? neither do ye **kindle**[H215] *fire* on mine altar for nought. I have no pleasure in you, saith the LORD of hosts, neither will I accept an offering at your hand." (KJV)

OWR figuratively describes how Jonathan's eyes lit up after eating some honey, but I don't think we can use that as a way of proving *OWR* describes a literal period of physical time lasting millions or billions of years. Day-Age creationists have no grammatical basis for their belief the "days" are ages, because the Bible never mentions a period of light lasting for ages.

Counting the Days

The Day-Age defenders look at the word "day," but not its modifiers. The first chapter of Genesis uses a cardinal number (one) for the first day and ordinal numbers (second, third, fourth, *etc.*) for the other days. This is significant. It's as if God anticipated the Non-Literal Day crowd, and wanted to make it clear He is talking about ordinary days. After saying *YOM* had a period of light and a period of dark (ordinary days have a period of light and a period of dark), after saying it had an evening and a morning (ordinary days have an evening and a morning), He then gives the MEASURABLE LENGTH OF TIME it encompassed. He said it was, "one day." God gives no hint He is talking about long ages. If He meant long ages, then He would have used *YOM* in the plural, which can mean a long, unspecified period of time. (Such as, "All the days of Noah.") Instead, He used words that mean literal, twenty-four-hour days everywhere else in the Bible. When an ordinal or cardinal are combined with *YOM*, the meaning becomes specific. Throughout the entire Bible, when these seven numerical modifiers are added to the Hebrew word for "day" (*YOM* in the singular—as used in Genesis 1) it means a twenty-four-hour period.

Another significance of using the cardinal number for Day One instead of the ordinal number is that it was not the FIRST day. Ordinal numbers describe a sequential relationship; cardinal numbers don't. The significance of this is aimed more at Young-Earth defenders than Day-Age defenders. Young-Earth defenders believe Genesis 1:1-2 is part of the same twenty-four-hour period as Genesis 1:3-5. They think Genesis 1:1-5 describes the very first twenty-four-hour period of time. This seems reasonable at first. After using the word "beginning" (the beginning of time and space) in Genesis 1:1, it would be easy to think Genesis 1:3-5 described the very first day of time. But our reasoning doesn't always match God's reasoning. He doesn't say it was the first day. He knows the difference between cardinal numbers and ordinal numbers. He describes Day One in a different way than the second through seventh days. There must be something different about Day One, or else He wouldn't describe it differently. Yes, Day One was the first day of the seven-day week, but if it was called, "the first day," then it might be misconstrued as the first day of time. (Since the text had just mentioned, "the beginning.") If the events described in Genesis 1:3-5 were on the very first day of time, then using the ordinal number would be more appropriate because it was both the first day of time and the first day of the week. If it was the first day, it should be called the "first day." But, God didn't call it the "first day;" He said it was "one day." He used a cardinal instead of an ordinal for Day One because He was describing WHAT it was, not WHEN it was. **"One day" describes how long it was; not how long ago it was.** I believe this is a clue. God did not intend for us to interpret this day as the first day of creation. I think our interpretation should be this: Yes, it was a literal, twenty-four-hour period of time. It was one day, but it was not the first day. There had been an unspecified period of time prior to the six days of restoration. Genesis 1:3-31 describes a second beginning. (Genesis 1:1 describes the first beginning.) There have been two beginnings; Duo-Genesis. Genesis 1:3-5 is Day One of the new beginning. Let's look at how the Bible uses *YOM* when combined with the numbers one through seven.

(Note: In the following sections, I will list all the verses using *YOM* when combined with both the cardinal and ordinal numbers one through seven. Included in this list are verses that use *YOM*, the singular form of "day," as well as *YOMIM*, the plural form of "day." Although only the singular form is used when describing each of the six days in Genesis 1, I am including the plural form because for some reason the singular form is translated as a plural ("days") and the plural form is translated as a singular ("day") in various places. I don't want to leave out any such translations, lest I be accused of deception. Besides, they all seem to refer to regular, twenty-four-hour days. However, even if I am wrong about the plural form, the word is in the singular in Genesis 1. So, while *YOM* can indicate a long, undetermined period of time in some places in Scripture, it never does so unless the context allows it. **YOM plus a number, set in a context that describes sunsets and sunrises, (a period of dark followed by a period of light) ALWAYS indicates a regular, twenty-four-hour day**. My point is that the exact form of *YOM*, combined with these same numbers, and with the same context as Genesis 1, is always used to describe twenty-four-hour days everywhere else in Scripture. Since this is the case, no one has the right to change the meaning of the days in the creation account.)

YOM ECHAD (One Day)
(*YOM*—Strong's Number H3117 and
ECHAD—Strong's Number H259)

1.) Genesis 1:5 "And God called the light Day, and the darkness he called Night. And the evening and the morning were the **first day**." (KJV)

2.) Genesis 27:44 "And tarry with him a **few days**, until thy brother's fury turn away;" (KJV)

3.) Genesis 27:45 "Until thy brother's anger turn away from thee, and he forget *that* which thou hast done to him: then I will send, and fetch thee from thence: why should I be deprived also of you both in **one day**?" (KJV)

4.) Genesis 29:20 "And Jacob served seven years for Rachel; and they seemed unto him *but* a **few days**, for the love he had to her." (KJV)

5.) Genesis 33:13 "And he said unto him, My lord knoweth that the children *are* tender, and the flocks and herds with young *are* with me: and if men should overdrive them **one day**, all the flock will die." (KJV)

6.) Exodus 12:18 "In the first *month,* on the fourteenth day of the month at even, ye shall eat unleavened bread, until the **one** and twentieth **day** of the month at even." (KJV)

7.) Exodus 40:2 "On the **first day** of the first month shalt thou set up the tabernacle of the tent of the congregation." (KJV)

8.) Leviticus 22:28 "And *whether it be* cow or ewe, ye shall not kill it and her young both in **one day**." (KJV)

9.) Numbers 7:11 "And the LORD said unto Moses, They shall offer their offering, each prince on his **day**, for the dedicating of the altar." (KJV)

10.) Numbers 11:19 "Ye shall not eat **one day**, nor two days, nor five days, neither ten days, nor twenty days;" (KJV)

11.) 1 Samuel 2:34 "And this *shall be* a sign unto thee, that shall come upon thy two sons, on Hophni and Phinehas; in **one day** they shall die both of them." (KJV)

12.) 1 Samuel 9:15 "Now the LORD had told Samuel in his ear **a day** before Saul came, saying," (KJV)

13.) 1 Samuel 27:1 "And David said in his heart, I shall now perish **one day** by the hand of Saul: *there is* nothing better for me than that I should speedily escape into the land of the Philistines; and Saul shall despair of me, to seek me any more in any coast of Israel: so shall I escape out of his hand." (KJV)

14.) 1 Kings 4:22 "And Solomon's provision for **one day** was thirty measures of fine flour, and threescore measures of meal," (KJV)

15.) 1 Kings 20:29 "And they pitched one over against the other seven days. And *so* it was, that in the seventh day the battle was joined: and the children of Israel slew of the Syrians an hundred thousand footmen in **one day**." (KJV)

16.) 2 Chronicles 28:6 "For Pekah the son of Remaliah slew in Judah an hundred and twenty thousand in **one day**, *which were* all valiant men; because they had forsaken the LORD God of their fathers." (KJV)

17.) Ezra 3:6 "From the **first day** of the seventh month began they to offer burnt offerings unto the LORD. But the foundation of the temple of the LORD was not *yet* laid." (KJV)

18.) Ezra 10:13 "But the people *are* many, and *it is* a time of much rain, and we are not able to stand without, neither *is this* a work of **one day** or two: for we are many that have transgressed in this thing." (KJV)

19.) Ezra 10:16 "And the children of the captivity did so. And Ezra the priest, *with* certain chief of the fathers, after the house of their fathers, and all of them by *their* names, were separated, and sat down in the **first day** of the tenth month to examine the matter." (KJV)

20.) Ezra 10:17 "And they made an end with all the men that had taken strange wives by the **first day** of the first month." (KJV)

21.) Nehemiah 5:18 "Now *that* which was prepared *for me* **daily** *was* one ox *and* six choice sheep; also fowls were prepared for me, and once in ten days store of all sorts of wine: yet for all this required not I the bread of the governor, because the bondage was heavy upon this people." (KJV)

22.) Nehemiah 8:2 "And Ezra the priest brought the law before the congregation both of men and women, and all that could hear with understanding, upon the **first day** of the seventh month." (KJV)

23.) Esther 3:13 "And the letters were sent by posts into all the king's provinces, to destroy, to kill, and to cause to perish, all Jews, both young and old, little children and women, in **one day**, *even* upon the thirteenth *day* of the twelfth month, which is the month Adar, and *to take* the spoil of them for a prey." (KJV)

24.) Esther 8:12 "Upon **one day** in all the provinces of king Ahasuerus, *namely,* upon the thirteenth *day* of the twelfth month, which *is* the month Adar." (KJV)

25.) Isaiah 9:14 "Therefore the LORD will cut off from Israel head and tail, branch and rush, in **one day**." (KJV)

26.) Isaiah 10:17 "And the light of Israel shall be for a fire, and his Holy One for a flame: and it shall burn and devour his thorns and his briers in **one day**;" (KJV)

27.) Isaiah 47:9 "But these two *things* shall come to thee in a moment in **one day**, the loss of children, and widowhood: they shall come upon thee in their perfection for the multitude of thy sorceries, *and* for the great abundance of thine enchantments." (KJV)

28) Isaiah 66:8 "Who hath heard such a thing? who hath seen such things? Shall the earth be made to bring forth in **one day**? *or* shall a nation be born at once? for as soon as Zion travailed, she brought forth her children." (KJV)

29.) Daniel 10:13 "But the prince of the kingdom of Persia withstood me **one** and twenty **days**: but, lo, Michael, one of the chief princes, came to help me; and I remained there with the kings of Persia." (KJV)

30.) Daniel 11:20 "Then shall stand up in his estate a raiser of taxes *in* the glory of the kingdom: but within **few days** he shall be destroyed, neither in anger, nor in battle." (KJV)

31.) Jonah 3:4 "And Jonah began to enter into the city **a day's** journey, and he cried, and said, Yet forty days, and Nineveh shall be overthrown." (KJV)

32.) Haggai 1:1 "In the second year of Darius the king, in the sixth month, in the **first day** of the month, came the word of the LORD by Haggai the prophet unto Zerubbabel the son of Shealtiel, governor of Judah, and to Joshua the son of Josedech, the high priest, saying," (KJV)

33.) Zechariah 3:9 "or behold the stone that I have laid before Joshua; upon one stone *shall be* seven eyes: behold, I will engrave the graving thereof, saith the LORD of hosts, and I will remove the iniquity of that land in **one day**." (KJV)

34.) Zechariah 14:7 "But it shall be **one day** which shall be known to the LORD, not day, nor night: but it shall come to pass, *that* at evening time it shall be light." (KJV)

It appears my interpretation of *YOM ECHAD* in Genesis 1:5 as "one day" is in jeopardy. *YOM ECHAD* is translated, "first day," in Exodus 40:2, Ezra 3:6, Ezra 10:16, Ezra 10:17, Nehemiah 8:2, and Haggai 1:1. If it can be translated, "first day," in those passages, why can't it be translated, "first day," in Genesis 1:5? The answer is simple. Language is used to communicate ideas, concepts, and information. How a word or a phrase is translated depends mainly on the knowledge, beliefs, and preferences of the translator. This means it is possible to communicate the same idea, concept, or information in a variety of ways. The passages in Exodus, Ezra, Nehemiah, and Haggai are set in a different context than the passage in Genesis 1:5. Exodus 40:2 actually says, "day one of the first month," Ezra 3:6 says, "day one of the seventh month." Ezra 10:16 says, "day one of the tenth month." Ezra 10:17 says, "day one of the first month." Nehemiah 8:2 says, "day one of the seventh month." Haggai 1:1 says, "day one of the sixth month." All six of those passages include the designation of another period of time, namely the month in question, into which we place day one. (Which means all six of those passages speak of regular, ordinary days; not ages, unless you can explain what the "first age" of the month means, or the "second age", or the "third age," *etc*.) I totally agree day one of the seventh month is the first day of the seventh month. Translating a cardinal number as an ordinal number is not an exact translation, but it does convey the same idea as long as the context is clearly revealed. As long as we are told what other period of time day one fits into, then we understand what period of time that first day describes. Genesis 1:5 has no designation of another time period. God reveals Day One as a regular, twenty-four-hour period of light and dark, day and night, sunrise and sunset. However, He does not give us a time period into which we can place that day. This means there is no justification for insisting it is the very first day of all creation. All the other days are placed into the time frame of Day One, but the time frame of Day One is not revealed. All we know is it was sometime after the beginning. How long after is not specified. Again, I believe if God had intended for us to interpret this day as the very first day of all creation, then He would have revealed it in the very same way He revealed the other six days. He would have said, "first day," instead of, "one day." He didn't reveal it that way, so I won't interpret it that way.

You can find other instances of "first day" (using *ECHAD*) in the KJV, such as in Leviticus 23:24, but again, the wording and context are not the same as in Genesis 1:5. Leviticus 23:24 says, "On the FIRST *day* of the month." The word "day" is in italics and not in the original Hebrew. (In the *King James Version*, italics are used to indicate the words that are not in the original Hebrew or Greek, but have been added by the English translators to help the text make more sense to English readers.) The Hebrew actually says, "On the ONE of the month." *ECHAD* and *YOM* are also combined in their plural forms and are translated, "a few days." This is seen in Genesis 27:44, Genesis 29:20, and Daniel 11:20. There are some other things to consider. For instance, Exodus 12:15 says, "first day," in the KJV, but *ECHAD* is not used in this verse. *YOM* is used with a different word for "first." In addition, some manuscripts have *ECHAD* in Ezra 3:6 while other manuscripts don't. I found it listed in some translations but not in others. I don't know why. There are a few other minor variations, such as "same day" and "each day" when *YOM* is used with other numerical modifiers. *ECHAD* is also combined with other numbers, such as "twenty and one"—21 days. (Exodus 12:18 and Daniel 10:13) However, they always refer to a real twenty-four-hour day; never to an extended period of time. Genesis 1:3-5 was one day; not an age! Let's look at three passages using *YOM ECHAD* that might be a problem for my interpretation.

Numbers 7:11 "And the LORD said unto Moses, They shall offer their offering, each prince on his **day**, for the dedicating of the altar." (KJV)

The situation in Numbers 7:11 requires a brief explanation. After Moses set up the Tabernacle, the different leaders (princes) of the tribes were to provide the offerings for it. Each tribe was to provide the offerings on a different day. Thus, each prince had a particular day (not age) on which he was to bring his tribe's offerings. A closer look at the Hebrew wording shows that a better translation would be:

Numbers 7:11 "And the LORD said unto Moses, They shall offer their offering, each prince on **his one day** for the dedicating of the altar."

1 Samuel 27:1 "And David said in his heart, I shall now perish **one day** by the hand of Saul: *there is* nothing better for me than that I should speedily escape into the land of the Philistines; and Saul shall despair of me, to seek me any more in any coast of Israel: so shall I escape out of his hand." (KJV)

     1 Samuel 27:1 is a verse Day-Age creationists use to refute the idea *YOM* plus a number means a regular twenty-four-hour day. David is running from King Saul, who is trying to kill him. Since David does not refer to a specific day, the critics say *YOM ECHAD* doesn't mean a literal day. But, David is merely expressing the thought that, "One day, I will perish at the hand of Saul." The thought might also be, "Some day, I will perish by the hand of Saul." Even without specifying an exact date, David would have been thinking in terms of, "Some LITERAL DAY, I will perish at the hand of Saul." David knew if Saul killed him, it would not take an age to die. Once you're killed, you're dead on that day. David was worried that ONE LITERAL DAY, Saul was going to kill him if he had the chance.

Zechariah 14:7 "But it shall be **one day** which shall be known to the LORD, not day, nor night: but it shall come to pass, *that* at evening time it shall be light." (KJV)

     Day-Age creationists say Zechariah 14:7 proves I am wrong about *YOM ECHAD*. According to Hebrew scholars, *ECHAD* can mean "unique;" not just "one" or "first." This is true, and we see this truth revealed in other translations.

Zechariah 14:7 "It will be a **unique day**, without daytime or nighttime—a day known to the LORD. When evening comes, there will be light." (NIV)

Zechariah 14:7 "For it will be a **unique day** which is known to the LORD, neither day nor night, but it will come about that at evening time there will be light." (NASB)

Zechariah 14:7 "And there shall be a **unique day**, which is known to the LORD, neither day nor night, but at evening time there shall be light." (ESV)

Zechariah 14:7 "There will be **no other day** like it, and the LORD knows when it will come. There will be no day or night; even at evening it will still be light." (NCV)

     So, while their claim *ECHAD* can mean "unique" is true, it doesn't negate my argument. Used in this fashion, *ECHAD* is neither an ordinal nor a cardinal number. It's the same word, but it has an entirely different meaning and function. Words that are spelled the same and sound the same, don't always have the same meaning, even if they are related. This is especially true in the ancient Hebrew language, which had a surprisingly small number of words when compared to other languages. One online site said it had only about 8,000.

> "Biblical Hebrew had a remarkably small number of words – 8,000 at most, with 1,700 used only once as compared to modern English which has over 450,000. As a basis of comparison, French, Spanish and Arabic each have about 175,000 words."[3]

This means ancient Hebrew words generally conveyed a larger number of different meanings, shades of meanings, ideas, thoughts, and concepts. For example, *The King James Bible* has over a dozen translations for the word *ECHAD*, while *The New American Standard Bible* has over twenty. My argument is that when the singular form of *YOM* is modified by these seven ordinal or seven cardinal numbers, it always refers to a regular day. One must always keep in mind that just because a word CAN have a particular meaning, it does not mean the word MUST have that particular meaning. The fact *ECHAD* can mean "unique" does not eliminate the possibility it can mean "one." There are plenty of translations besides the *King James* that interpret it as "one day."

Zechariah 14:7 "And it shall be **one day** which is known to Jehovah, not day, and not night; and it shall come to pass, at eventide it shall be light." (DBY)

Zechariah 14:7 "And there hath been **one day**, It is known to Jehovah, not day nor night, And it hath been at evening-time -- there is light." (YLT)

Zechariah 14:7 "There will be **one day**—a day known to the LORD—with no difference between day and night. It will be light even in the evening." (GW)

Zechariah 14:7 But it shall be **one day** which shall be known to *the LORD* Yah Veh, not day, nor night: *but* and so be it *shall come to pass*, that at evening time it shall be light. (ERRB)

Zechariah 14:7 "It will be **a day** known only to Yahweh, without day or night, but there will be light at evening." (HCSB)

Zechariah 14:7 "And it shall be **a day** by itself, The same, shall be known unto Yahweh—Not day, nor night,—But it shall come to pass, that, at evening time, there shall be light." (EMP)

Zechariah 14:7 "And it shall be **one day** which is known to יהוה, neither day nor night, but at evening time there shall be light." (SCRIP)

Nevertheless, let's look at their argument to see if it has any merit. According to these Gap Theory opponents, this "unique day" is not like ordinary days because it will not have days or nights like ordinary days. Since *YOM ECHAD* means a "unique day," these scholars leap to the conclusion that this "day" is a long age. That's a big leap without first determining why the day is unique.

These Gap Theory opponents say it will be unique because when evening time comes, it will still be light. That's never happened before… or so say these Gap Theory opponents. My questions to them is, "Have you ever been to the Arctic Circle in summer?" I haven't been to the Arctic Circle, but I have been to Mount McKinley (Denali) in June. I remember standing outside at near-midnight, in the light, long after "evening time" had come.

So, why is this day unique? Light at evening time is unusual, but not unique. What is unique about this day? Certainly, it would be unique if it really means an age, but that's the conclusion they use to prove their assumption. Does this speak of an ordinary day or of an age? We need to figure out how long of a time period the *YOM* in Zechariah 14:7 describes. The answer requires us to go up three verses to Zechariah 14:4 to see the context.

Zechariah 14:4 "And his feet shall stand in **that day** upon the mount of Olives, which *is* before Jerusalem on the east, and the mount of Olives shall cleave in the midst thereof toward the east and toward the west, *and there shall be* a very great valley; and half of the mountain shall remove toward the north, and half of it toward the south." (KJV)

Zechariah 14:4 speaks of the DAY the Lord returns to earth by coming down to the Mount of Olives. How long will it take Him to descend? A year? A hundred years? A thousand years? No. It will be a sudden event. In fact, Acts 1:9-12 reveals just how short this time period will be:

Acts 1:9-12 "And when he had spoken these things, while they beheld, he was taken up; and a cloud received him out of their sight. *{10}* And while they looked stedfastly toward heaven as he went up, behold, two men stood by them in white apparel; *{11}* Which also said, Ye men of Galilee, why stand ye gazing up into heaven? **this same Jesus, which is taken up from you into heaven, shall so come in like manner as ye have seen him go into heaven.** *{12}* Then returned they unto Jerusalem from the mount called Olivet, which is from Jerusalem a sabbath day's journey." (KJV)

Jesus will descend to the Mount of Olives just as His disciples saw Him ascend from the Mount of Olives. It won't take an age. They weren't standing there looking up for days and weeks and months and years. It was probably only a few minutes. It happened quickly and it happened on an ordinary day. The same thing will happen when He returns. It won't take Jesus hundreds or thousands of years to descend upon the Mount of Olives. People won't look up and see Jesus slowly descending over years or decades or centuries of time. It will be sudden and it will be on an ordinary day. There is a particular day (a literal day) known only to God, when Jesus will descend upon the Mount of Olives. It is a unique day, but not because it is an age of time; it is unique because it is the day the Lord returns to set up His Kingdom. We don't know when that day will be, but it will be on some ordinary, calendar day in the future. Zechariah 14:7 tells us the Lord will return one day. His return will happen *YOM ECHAD* (One Day) in the future. Zechariah 14:7 does not refer to an age of time.

YOM RISHON (First Day)
(*YOM*—Strong's Number H3117 and
RISHON—Strong's Number H7223)

An interesting thought about using *RISHON* in relation to time is it carries the idea of an initial condition or state. Here is how *RISHON* is translated when describing periods of time called, "day" or "days." (*YOM* or *YOMIM*)

1. and 2.) Exodus 12:15 "Seven days shall ye eat unleavened bread; even the **first day** ye shall put away leaven out of your houses: for whosoever eateth leavened bread from the **first day** until the seventh day, that soul shall be cut off from Israel." (KJV)

3.) Exodus 12:16 "And in the **first day** *there shall be* an holy convocation, and in the seventh day there shall be an holy convocation to you; no manner of work shall be done in them, save *that* which every man must eat, that only may be done of you." (KJV)

4.) Leviticus 23:7 "In the **first day** ye shall have an holy convocation: ye shall do no servile work therein." (KJV)

5.) Leviticus 23:35 "On the **first day** *shall be* an holy convocation: ye shall do no servile work *therein.*" (KJV)

6.) Leviticus 23:39 "Also in the fifteenth day of the seventh month, when ye have gathered in the fruit of the land, ye shall keep a feast unto the LORD seven days: on the **first day** *shall be* a sabbath, and on the eighth day *shall be* a sabbath." (KJV)

7.) Leviticus 23:40 "And ye shall take you on the **first** day the boughs of goodly trees, branches of palm trees, and the boughs of thick trees, and willows of the brook; and ye shall rejoice before the LORD your God seven days." (KJV)

8.) Numbers 6:12 "And he shall consecrate unto the LORD the days of his separation, and shall bring a lamb of the first year for a trespass offering: but the **days that were before** shall be lost, because his separation was defiled." (KJV)

It looks as if this verse destroys my argument that a numerical modifier added to *YOM* always makes it mean a regular, twenty-four-hour day. In this case *RISHON* is translated, "before," rather than, "first." In relation to time, it means "first," but it also means "primary," "beginning," "former," "past," and other ideas related to an initial (first) condition. (It also means "first" in the sense of "best," "chief," and "foremost," but it isn't connected to the concept of time in those uses.) I think my argument still stands because this verse does not use *YOM* in the singular. It uses *YOMIM* in the plural. There is a difference between the meaning of the word "day" and the meaning of the word "days." Instead of destroying my argument about the meaning of "day" in the Genesis Creation Account, it actually strengthens it. You see, using the plural of the word "day" was the way the ancient Hebrews expressed the idea of a long, unspecified period of time.

Genesis 3:17 "And unto Adam he said, Because thou hast hearkened unto the voice of thy wife, and hast eaten of the tree, of which I commanded thee, saying, Thou shalt not eat of it: cursed *is* the ground for thy sake; in sorrow shalt thou eat *of* it all the **days** of thy life;" (KJV)

Genesis 5:4 "And the **days** of Adam after he had begotten Seth were eight hundred years: and he begat sons and daughters:" (KJV)

Genesis 6:4 "There were giants in the earth in those **days**; and also after that, when the sons of God came in unto the daughters of men, and they bare *children* to them, the same *became* mighty men which *were* of old, men of renown." (KJV)

Genesis 14:1 "And it came to pass in the **days** of Amraphel king of Shinar, Arioch king of Ellasar, Chedorlaomer king of Elam, and Tidal king of nations;" (KJV)

Genesis 49:1 "And Jacob called unto his sons, and said, Gather yourselves together, that I may tell you *that* which shall befall you in the last **days**." (KJV)

The author of these passages of Scripture was Moses himself. This means Moses knew which form of *YOM* to use to express the idea of a long, unspecified period of time. Moses readily used the plural *YOMIM* to express this idea throughout the Pentateuch, but he didn't use it in the Genesis Creation Account! If the "days" were ages, he would have used the plural, and the Bible would say these were: "The first days," "the second days," "the third days," *etc*. If the Bible said that, then we could translate them as "the first age," "the second age," and on up to "the seventh age." The Bible doesn't say that, so we have no right to say that. Moses used the singular of *YOM* in the Genesis Creation Account because each "day" was a day, not an age. As we look down this list, we will see other instances of *RISHON* used with *YOM* and *YOMIM*.

9.) Numbers 7:12 "And he that offered his offering the **first day** was Nahshon the son of Amminadab, of the tribe of Judah:" (KJV)

10.) Numbers 28:18 "In the **first day** *shall be* an holy convocation; ye shall do no manner of servile work *therein:*" (KJV)

11.) Deuteronomy 4:32 "For ask now of the **days that are past**, which were before thee, since the day that God created man upon the earth, and *ask* from the one side of heaven unto the other, whether there hath been *any such thing* as this great thing *is,* or hath been heard like it?" (KJV) (This is another case where *YOMIM* is used.)

12.) Deuteronomy 10:10 "And I stayed in the mount, according to the **first time**, forty days and forty nights; and the LORD hearkened unto me at that time also, *and* the LORD would not destroy thee." (KJV) (*YOMIM* is also used here.)

13.) Deuteronomy 16:4 "And there shall be no leavened bread seen with thee in all thy coast seven days; neither shall there *any thing* of the flesh, which thou sacrificedst the **first day** at even, remain all night until the morning." (KJV)

14.) Judges 20:22 "And the people the men of Israel encouraged themselves, and set their battle again in array in the place where they put themselves in array the **first day**." (KJV)

15.) 2 Samuel 19:20 "For thy servant doth know that I have sinned: therefore, behold, I am come the **first** this **day** of all the house of Joseph to go down to meet my lord the king." (KJV)

16.) Nehemiah 8:18 "Also day by day, from the **first day** unto the last day, he read in the book of the law of God. And they kept the feast seven days; and on the eighth day *was* a solemn assembly, according unto the manner." (KJV)

17.) Ecclesiastes 7:10 "Say not thou, What is *the cause* that the **former days** were better than these? for thou dost not enquire wisely concerning this." (KJV) (*YOMIM* is used here.)

18.) Daniel 10:12 "Then said he unto me, Fear not, Daniel: for from the **first day** that thou didst set thine heart to understand, and to chasten thyself before thy God, thy words were heard, and I am come for thy words." (KJV)

Another interesting thought about using *RISHON* (Strong's Number H7223) in relation to time, is it carries the same idea of an initial condition or state as the word *RESHITH*—Strong's Number H7225. As you can tell from the Strong's numbers, these words are related. In fact, they are derived from the same Hebrew root word meaning "first," "head," "chief," or "beginning." Is the word *RESHITH* used in the creation account? Yes... it's the first word in the Bible:

Genesis 1:1 "In the **beginning**[H7225] God[H430] created[H1254] the[H853] heaven[H8064] and the[H853] earth[H776]." (KJV)

Genesis 1:1 בְּרֵאשִׁית[H7225] בָּרָא[H1254] אֱלֹהִים[H430] אֵת[H853] הַשָּׁמַיִם[H8064] וְאֵת[H853] הָאָרֶץ[H776]

RESHITH is used for the **beginning** of creation in Genesis 1:1, but *RISHON* is not used for the **first** day in Genesis 1:5. Rather than *RISHON*, *ECHAD* is used.

Genesis 1:5 "And God[H430] called[H7121] the light[H216] Day,[H3117] and the darkness[H2822] he called[H7121] Night.[H3915] And the evening[H6153] and the morning[H1242] were[H1961] the **first**[H259] day.[H3117]" (KJV)

Genesis 1:5 וַיִּקְרָא[H7121] אֱלֹהִים[H430] לָאוֹר[H216] יוֹם[H3117] וְלַחֹשֶׁךְ[H2822] קָרָא[H7121] לָיְלָה[H3915] וַיְהִי[H1961] עֶרֶב[H6153] וַיְהִי[H1961] בֹקֶר[H1242] יוֹם[H3117] **אֶחָד**[H259]

This implies it was not the initial, first, chief, or beginning day. The Bible uses *ECHAD* (one) instead of *RISHON* (first) to describe the day on which God said, "Let there be light." If Day One of the Genesis creation week was the first day of all time, then *RISHON* would have been the perfect word to convey that idea. Moses would have used *RISHON* instead of *ECHAD*. That way there would be no confusion Genesis 1:5 was the initial, first, chief, or beginning day of all time. That would have made it clear that Genesis 1:1 and Genesis 1:5 were describing the same period of time. Moses didn't use *RISHON*. From this, I conclude Day One wasn't the first day of all time. The first day of the creation week was not the first day of the universe; it was not the first day of the time-space continuum. There had been days before that day. How many days? The Bible doesn't tell us, but it does let us know that Genesis 1:1-2 is not part of the seven-day creation week. The heavens and earth were created before the creation week. The two indicators that "one day" does not mean "first age" in Genesis 1 are:

1.) Moses did not use *RISHON*.
2.) Moses did not use *YOMIM*.

It's not a very convincing argument to say that because *YOMIM RISHON* doesn't necessarily mean a twenty-four-hour day, then *YOM ECHAD* must not mean a twenty-four-hour day. Moses used *RISHON* in other places to indicate "first." Moses used *YOMIM* in other places to indicate "age." Moses used neither in Genesis 1. Day One was neither the "**first** day" of all time, nor the "first **age**" of all time. It was **one day** in time... which is exactly what *YOM ECHAD* means. This alone disproves the Young-Earth and Day-Age Theories. Those theories interpret Genesis as if Genesis 1:3-5 was the first day or the first age of all time. The Gap Theory says it was *YOM ECHAD* (one day) in time. The Gap Theory interprets the Bible exactly as the Bible reads.

Since *YOM ECHAD* (One Day) and *YOM RISHON* (First Day) are never used to describe an age of time anywhere else in the Bible, what clue do we have that the days of the Genesis Creation Account describe long ages?

YOM SHENIY (Second Day)
(*YOM*—Strong's Number H3117 and
SHENIY—Strong's Number H8145)

1.) Genesis 1:8 "And God called the firmament Heaven. And the evening and the morning were the **second day**." (KJV)

2.) Exodus 2:13 "And when he went out the **second day**, behold, two men of the Hebrews strove together: and he said to him that did the wrong, Wherefore smitest thou thy fellow?" (KJV)

3.) Leviticus 13:5 "And the priest shall look on him the seventh day: and, behold, *if* the plague in his sight be at a stay, *and* the plague spread not in the skin; then the priest shall shut him up seven **days more**:" (KJV)

4.) Leviticus 13:33 "He shall be shaven, but the scall shall he not shave; and the priest shall shut up *him that hath* the scall seven **days more**:" (KJV)

5.) Leviticus 13:54 "Then the priest shall command that they wash *the thing* wherein the plague *is,* and he shall shut it up seven **days more**:" (KJV)

6.) Numbers 7:18 "On the **second day** Nethaneel the son of Zuar, prince of Issachar, did offer:" (KJV)

7.) Numbers 29:17 "And on the **second day** *ye shall offer* twelve young bullocks, two rams, fourteen lambs of the first year without spot:" (KJV)

8.) Joshua 6:14 "And the **second day** they compassed the city once, and returned into the camp: so they did six days." (KJV)

9.) Joshua 10:32 "And the LORD delivered Lachish into the hand of Israel, which took it on the **second day**, and smote it with the edge of the sword, and all the souls that *were* therein, according to all that he had done to Libnah." (KJV)

10.) Judges 20:24 "And the children of Israel came near against the children of Benjamin the **second day**." (KJV)

11.) Judges 20:25 "And Benjamin went forth against them out of Gibeah the **second day**, and destroyed down to the ground of the children of Israel again eighteen thousand men; all these drew the sword." (KJV)

12.) 1 Samuel 20:34 "So Jonathan arose from the table in fierce anger, and did eat no meat the **second day** of the month: for he was grieved for David, because his father had done him shame." (KJV)

13.) Nehemiah 8:13 "And on the **second day** were gathered together the chief of the fathers of all the people, the priests, and the Levites, unto Ezra the scribe, even to understand the words of the law." (KJV)

14.) Esther 7:2 "And the king said again unto Esther on the **second day** at the banquet of wine, What *is* thy petition, queen Esther? and it shall be granted thee: and what *is* thy request? and it shall be performed, *even* to the half of the kingdom." (KJV)

15.) Jeremiah 41:4 "And it came to pass the **second day** after he had slain Gedaliah, and no man knew *it*," (KJV)

16.) Ezekiel 43:22 "And on the **second day** thou shalt offer a kid of the goats without blemish for a sin offering; and they shall cleanse the altar, as they did cleanse *it* with the bullock." (KJV)

As is the case of "first day," there are verses translated, "second day of the month," in the KJV when the word "day" is in italics and not in the original. Two such examples are 1 Samuel 20:27 and 2 Chronicles 3:2. Various other modifiers are used with *YOM* that result in a translation of "next day," but *SHENIY* (Strong's Number H8145) is not used. Again, in all of these usages, *YOM* still refers to a regular day. The second day of creation was one day; not an age!

SHENIY can also mean "more" or "again," and is used with *YOM*, in Leviticus 13:5, Leviticus 13:33, and Leviticus 13:54, where it says, "seven days **more**." Even with that, the Scriptures are talking about literal days, not ages.

YOMIM SHENAYIM (Two Days)
(*YOMIM*—Strong's Number H3117 and
SHENAYIM—Strong's Number H8147)

1.) Numbers 7:78 "On the **twelfth day** Ahira the son of Enan, prince of the children of Naphtali, *offered:*" (KJV) (Literally, "the ten and **two day**.")

2.) 2 Samuel 1:1 "Now it came to pass after the death of Saul, when David was returned from the slaughter of the Amalekites, and David had abode **two days** in Ziklag;" (KJV)

3.) 2 Samuel 19:34 "And Barzillai said unto the king, How **long** have I to live, that I should go up with the king unto Jerusalem?" (KJV) (Literally, "How many **more days/years** have I to live?")

(Note: Some study references have *SHAWNAW*—Strong's Number H8141 modifying *YOMIM* instead of *SHENAYIM*—Strong's Number H8147 in 2 Samuel 19:34. *SHAWNAW* generally means "year." *SHENAYIM* generally means "two." *SHENAYIM* is the Dual Form of *SHENIY*—Strong's Number H8145, which generally means "second." (The Dual Form implies the idea of a pair. It is often used to describe a pair, a couple, or both of two things. I'll explain more about the use of the Dual Form when I talk about the meaning of "heaven" vs. "heavens.") These words must be related, but I don't know why the references vary. Again, I suspect it reflects a difference in ancient manuscripts. Regardless of the reason, Barzillai is asking, "How many **more years/days** (plural) have I to live?" I think Barzillai is concerned about the short time he has left; he is not speaking about long ages. The Bible says he was very old, (eighty years old) and the text seems to indicate he was in bad health. He was unable to taste food and drink, and his hearing may have been impaired. He told King David he wanted to return to his home city so he could die and be buried in his family's grave. Since Barzillai uses *YOMIM* to describe the short time he has left to live, I don't think *YOMIM* means an age of millions of years. Plus, this verse doesn't use *YOM* in the singular as it does in the Genesis Creation Account. It also doesn't use *SHENIY* or *SHAWNAW* as an ordinal or cardinal number. Instead, it uses them to mean, "more." This verse doesn't change the meaning of "day" in Genesis.)

4.) 2 Chronicles 21:19 "And it came to pass, that in process of time, after the end of **two years**, his bowels fell out by reason of his sickness: so he died of sore diseases. And his people made no burning for him, like the burning of his fathers." (KJV)

Some Day-Age creationists say my claim that "two days" always refers to regular days is in error because 2 Chronicles 21:19 uses "two days" in the Hebrew, but it describes a two-year period of time. Before we look at this passage, let's look at the last two verses that use *YOMIM SHENAYIM.*

5.) Nehemiah 6:15 "So the wall was finished in the twenty and fifth *day* of *the month* Elul, in fifty and **two days**." (KJV)

6.) Esther 9:27 "The Jews ordained, and took upon them, and upon their seed, and upon all such as joined themselves unto them, so as it should not fail, that they would keep these **two days** according to their writing, and according to their *appointed* time every year;" (KJV)

Every passage seems to indicate that "days" are days… except for 2 Chronicles 21:19. Let's look at the context.

2 Chronicles 21:16-19 "Moreover the LORD stirred up against Jehoram the spirit of the Philistines, and of the Arabians, that *were* near the Ethiopians: *{17}* And they came up into Judah, and brake into it, and carried away all the substance that was found in the king's house, and his sons also, and his wives; so that there was never a son left him, save Jehoahaz, the youngest of his sons. *{18}* And after all this the LORD smote him in his bowels with an incurable disease. *{19}* And it came to pass, that in process of time, after the end of **two years**, his bowels fell out by reason of his sickness: so he died of sore diseases. And his people made no burning for him, like the burning of his fathers." (KJV)

This passage of Scripture tells how God brought judgment and death to King Jehoram, a very wicked king of Judah. "After the end of **two years**" his bowels came out of him and he died. (Wow, what a disgusting topic!) I certainly need to explain this verse, because my critics are correct when they say this verse says, "two years," in virtually every translation. That means I have to contradict virtually every Hebrew translator. That means I think I know something about Hebrew that virtually every Hebrew translator doesn't know… or else I think I know something about Jehoram's medical condition that virtually every Hebrew translator doesn't know. I think you can guess which it is, but before we get to that, we need to take a detour to verify *YOM* can be translated, "year."

YOM = YEAR

There are numerous examples in the Bible where the word *YOM* (in both its singular form and plural form) is translated, "year" or "years," in the *King James Bible*.

1. and 2.) Exodus 13:10 "Thou shalt therefore keep this ordinance in his season from **year** to **year**." (KJV)

3.) Leviticus 25:29 "And if a man sell a dwelling house in a walled city, then he may redeem it within a whole year after it is sold; *within* a full **year** may he redeem it." (KJV)

(Note: The first "year," translated, "whole year," is not *YOM*, but the usual word for "year," *SHAWNAW* Strong's Number H8141. The second "year," translated, "**full year**" is *YOMIM*. I don't know the significance of using both of them together like this. I'm sure a Hebrew scholar could tell you. I suspect it might be saying something like, "a year to the day," making it a whole or full year, but that's only speculation on my part.)

4. and 5.) Joshua 13:1 "Now Joshua was old *and* stricken in **years**; and the LORD said unto him, Thou art old *and* stricken in **years**, and there remaineth yet very much land to be possessed." (KJV)

6.) Judges 17:10 "And Micah said unto him, Dwell with me, and be unto me a father and a priest, and I will give thee ten *shekels* of silver by the **year**, and a suit of apparel, and thy victuals. So the Levite went in." (KJV)

7. 8. and 9.) 1 Samuel 2:19 "Moreover his mother made him a little coat, and brought *it* to him from **year** to **year**, when she came up with her husband to offer the **yearly** sacrifice." (KJV)

10.) 1 Samuel 27:7 "And the time that David dwelt in the country of the Philistines was a full **year** and four months." (KJV)

11.) 2 Samuel 13:23 "And it came to pass after two full **years**, that Absalom had sheepshearers in Baalhazor, which *is* beside Ephraim: and Absalom invited all the king's sons." (KJV)

"Look," a Day-Age creationist will say, "This verse has the number two combined with *YOM* and is translated, 'years,' not, 'days.' Doesn't this prove the Gap Theory is wrong?" No. It changes nothing. It doesn't say, "two years." The number two (*SHENAYIM*) is not used. Neither an ordinal nor a cardinal number is connected to *YOM*. Instead it uses *SHAWNAW* (years) in the Dual Form. Furthermore, it uses *YOMIM* rather than *YOM*. Then, like Leviticus 25:29, it links *YOMIM* with *SHAWNAW*. (The word "days" is linked to the word "years." Again, I don't know the significance, but it may be saying something like... "a pair of years to the day." This is my speculation only.) Because this verse doesn't use the number "two," and because this verse doesn't use *YOM* in the same form as it is used in Genesis 1, this verse cannot be used to alter the meaning of "day" in the creation account.

12.) 2 Samuel 14:26 "And when he polled his head, (for it was at every **year's** end that he polled *it:* because *the hair* was heavy on him, therefore he polled it:) he weighed the hair of his head at two hundred shekels after the king's weight." (KJV)

13.) 2 Samuel 14:28 "So Absalom dwelt two full **years** in Jerusalem, and saw not the king's face." (KJV)

14.) 1 Kings 1:1 "Now king David was old *and* stricken in **years**; and they covered him with clothes, but he gat no heat." (KJV)

15.) 2 Chronicles 21:19 "And it came to pass, that in process of time, after the end of two **years**, his bowels fell out by reason of his sickness: so he died of sore diseases. And his people made no burning for him, like the burning of his fathers." (KJV)

Here is our verse in question again, but before we finally examine it, we need to look at one last verse that translates *YOM* as "years."

16.) Amos 4:4 "Come to Bethel, and transgress; at Gilgal multiply transgression; and bring your sacrifices every morning, *and* your tithes after three **years**:" (KJV)

Surely, here is a passage of Scripture that uses a number (in this case a cardinal number) with *YOMIM*, but it means "years," not "days." Well, maybe not. We will look at Amos 4:4 when we get to the section dealing with how the number three is used with *YOM*.

Okay, we have seen how *YOM* can be translated, "year" or "years," in certain passages, but none of those passages uses *YOM* and numerical modifiers the same way they are used in Genesis 1. The fact they are different forms of the words, used in different ways, means they can't be used to defend the Day-Age Theory.

So, now we need to go back and examine 2 Chronicles 21:19 to see why "two days" is translated, "two years." We need to look at the Hebrew words used in this passage. The word translated, "years," is *YOMIM*. Normally, that's the word "days." Why translate "days" as "years," if it always means an ordinary day when combined with a numerical modifier as I claim? (So far, my critics have a good point.) Let's go on to the next word. The word "two" isn't exactly in the same form as it is in Genesis 1:8. In Genesis 1:8, the word is *SHENIY* (Strong's Number H8145), but in 2 Chronicles 21:19 it is *SHENAYIM*. Again, *SHENAYIM* is the Dual Form of *SHENIY*. Even with that special usage, it is accurately translated as the number two elsewhere. Besides 2 Chronicles 21:19, it is used in connection with *YOMIM* (days) in three other passages of Scripture that talk about literal days.

2 Samuel 1:1 "Now it came to pass after the death of Saul, when David was returned from the slaughter of the Amalekites, and David had abode **two days** in Ziklag;" (KJV)

Nehemiah 6:15 "So the wall was finished in the twenty and fifth *day* of *the month* Elul, in fifty and **two days**." (KJV)

Esther 9:27 "The Jews ordained, and took upon them, and upon their seed, and upon all such as joined themselves unto them, so as it should not fail, that they would keep these **two days** according to their writing, and according to their *appointed* time every year;" (KJV)

It is also used in combination with the number "ten," as in "two plus ten" to make the number "twelve."

Numbers 7:78 "On the **twelfth day** Ahira the son of Enan, prince of the children of Naphtali, *offered*:" (KJV)

Okay, if *YOMIM SHENAYIM* is used in connection with literal days elsewhere in Scripture, why is it translated as two "years" in 2 Chronicles 21:19 in virtually every translation? I don't know, but I suspect it is because the translators wanted to make it fit the context of the passage… or at least the context they presupposed. What is the context? Most translators think the context is the last two years of Jehoram's reign. He had been King of Judah for eight years, and his reign was filled with wickedness, murder, and war. (He murdered his six brothers and other potential political rivals, he married the wicked daughter of Ahab and Jezebel, he rejected God, and he instituted Baal worship in Judah.) During his reign, neighboring nations went to war with him and succeeded in plundering Judah and taking his wives and all his sons except his youngest, Jehoahaz. Then, "after all this," the Lord struck Jehoram with a terminal intestinal disease.

2 Chronicles 21:18 "And after all this the LORD smote him in his bowels with an incurable disease." (KJV)

We don't know when the Lord smote him with this disease. It doesn't say, "after two years; it just says, "after all this." To what is "all this" referring? It seems to me it is referring to the attack and sacking of Jerusalem by the foreign nations. The context implies this was after his wives and all his sons but Jehoahaz were carried off. The Bible doesn't give a date for when this disease struck him. It doesn't say it was two years before he died. I think most scholars try to make this a long period of time because Elijah the Prophet sent Jehoram a warning letter before "all this" happened. (2 Chronicles 21:12-15) Elijah told him of the disasters that would befall Judah, Jehoram's family, and of Jehoram's intestinal disease itself. It is extremely difficult to think "all this" could happen in two days. So, I think virtually all translators have assumed the context is focused on the timing of Elijah's warning. (They have not considered the context could be focused on the timing of Jehoram's medical condition.) Therefore, the most common interpretation is that "all this" happened over the last two years of Jehoram's reign. But, while Elijah's warning may have come to Jehoram two years before "all this" happened, Elijah didn't say when the intestinal disease would strike. God may warn someone of a judgment, but withhold that judgment for a long period of time. (In fact, this is the most common way God warns people of judgment.) While God may have warned Jehoram two years before the disease, it doesn't mean God struck him with the disease at the time of the warning. The context is two years only if you presuppose the disease struck him when he first got the warning from Elijah. It may be grammatically correct to do that, but to be informationally correct, we need to know something about Jehoram's disease.

There is another possible context. The passage may not be talking about the last two years of Jehoram's life, but about the last two days of Jehoram's life. It may well have been that God didn't strike Jehoram with this disease until his last two days. Again, there is nothing in the chapter that tells us when this disease struck. Since I am not a scholar of either the Hebrew language or Hebrew history, I have to rely on the knowledge of others who are scholars. Here is Keil and Delitzsch's comment about this passage of Scripture:

"2 Chronicles 21:19—And it came to pass in days after days (*i.e.*, when a number of days had passed), and that at the time (וּכְעֵת (emit eh) of the expiration of the end in **two days**, then his bowels went out during his sickness, and he died in sore pains (תַּחֲלָאִים, phenomena of disease, *i.e.*, pains)."[4]

According to these two eminent Hebrew scholars, *YOMIM SHENAYIM* means "two days." Is there another scholarly work that translates it the same way? Yes. *The Apostolic Bible Polyglot* translates it "two days."

2 Chronicles 21:19 "And it happened from days unto days, and as [²came ¹his time] in [²**days** ¹**two**], there came forth his innards with his belly in his sickness. And he died in [²sicknesses ¹severe], and [²did not make ⁴to him ¹his people ³a funeral], nor a burning according to the burning of his fathers." (ABP)

I could rest my case by relying on these scholars alone. Still, it might be easy for someone to accuse these scholars of not understanding ancient Hebrew. However, there was another group of scholars who made this same translation, and no one can accuse them of not understanding ancient Hebrew. They were the translators of the Septuagint. The Septuagint was a translation of the Hebrew Bible (Old Testament) into the Greek during the 3rd century B.C. It was done by approximately seventy (hence the name Septuagint) Hebrew-Greek scholars for the purpose of letting the Greek-speaking Jews have the

Scriptures in a language they could read. History tells us these were the best and brightest Hebrew-Greek scholars in Israel at the time; they knew the Bible very well. It would be difficult to claim they didn't understand ancient Hebrew, because they were ancient Hebrews. In fact, the Septuagint had been around for over two hundred years when Jesus was born. Paul studied it and quoted it. So, how did the translators of the Septuagint translate 2 Chronicles 21:19?

2 Chronicles 21:19 "καὶ ἐγένετο ἐξ ἡμερῶν εἰς ἡμέρας, καὶ ὡς ἦλθεν καιρὸς τῶν ἡμερῶν **ἡμέρας δύο**, ἐξῆλθεν ἡ κοιλία αὐτοῦ μετὰ τῆς νόσου, καὶ ἀπέθανεν ἐν μαλακίᾳ πονηρᾷ. καὶ οὐκ ἐποίησεν ὁ λαὸς αὐτοῦ ἐκφορὰν καθὼς ἐκφορὰν πατέρων αὐτοῦ."

If you're like me and can't read ancient Greek, this is just a bunch of squiggles. *HEMERA DUO* (ἡμέρας δύο) is the Greek translation of the Hebrew *YOMIM SHENAYIM*. You probably recognize *DUO* as "two." *HEMERA* is the Greek word for "day." This means these seventy distinguished Bible scholars, whose native language was ancient Hebrew, and who were Israel's greatest Greek scholars of their day, apparently thought this passage of Scripture said, "two days."

(Note: If you look at English translations of the Septuagint, you will discover they do the same thing to the Greek they do to the Hebrew. They translate it as "two years." But again, this isn't because the Greek necessarily says, "two years;" it's because the translators are making it fit the long-accepted translation based on the long-accepted presupposed context. Nowhere in the New Testament is *HEMERA DUO* translated, "two years." It is always translated, "two days.")

What I think happened was the Lord struck King Jehoram with some kind of severe inflammatory intestinal disease sometime after the sacking of Judah. I suspect it was a severe case of intestinal parasites. After two days of this, he suffered an intestinal prolapse and died in great pain. I have treated parasite-induced intestinal prolapses in animals. It comes on very suddenly, it is very painful, and if not corrected (usually by surgery) the patient can only live a day or two. They never live a year or two. 2 Chronicles 21:19 describes King Jehoram's last two days; not his last two years.

Since *YOM SHENIY* (Second Day) and *YOMIM SHENAYIM* (Two Days) are never used to describe an age of time anywhere else in the Bible, what clue do we have that the days of the Genesis Creation Account describe long ages?

HEMERA (Day)

An immediate objection is raised: Since *HEMERA* is the Greek equivalent of the Hebrew *YOM* when the New Testament describes Old Testament historical events, couldn't we conclude that since *HEMERA* can mean a long period of time, then *YOM* can mean a long period of time as well? To answer that, let me first acknowledge it is true; *HEMERA* is translated, "day," "age," "years," and other indefinite periods of time in the New Testament. Here are a few examples:

1.) Matthew 2:1 "Now when Jesus was born in Bethlehem of Judaea in the **days** of Herod the king, behold, there came wise men from the east to Jerusalem," (KJV)

2.) Luke 1:7 "And they had no child, because that Elisabeth was barren, and they both were *now* well stricken in **years**." (KJV)

3.) Luke 1:18 "And Zacharias said unto the angel, Whereby shall I know this? for I am an old man, and my wife well stricken in **years**." (KJV)

4.) 2 Timothy 3:1 "This know also, that in the last **days** perilous times shall come." (KJV)

And there are many more examples of this, but it proves nothing. I am not saying *HEMERA* cannot mean a long period of time. I am not saying *YOM* cannot mean a long period of time. They both can mean a full day, the daylight portion of a day, a year, and an indefinite period of time. What I am saying is when these words are combined with a numerical modifier, set in the context of evenings and mornings, as they are in Genesis 1, they always refer to ordinary days in the Bible. **You cannot ignore the context of Genesis 1 while trying to interpret Genesis 1.** Here is how *HEMERA* is used when it is combined with a numerical modifier.

One Day

1.) Acts 21:7 "And when we had finished our course from Tyre, we came to Ptolemais, and saluted the brethren, and abode with them **one day**." (KJV)

2.) Acts 28:13 "And from thence we fetched a compass, and came to Rhegium: and after **one day** the south wind blew, and we came the next day to Puteoli:" (KJV)

3.) Romans 14:5 "One man esteemeth **one day** above another: another esteemeth every day alike. Let every man be fully persuaded in his own mind." (KJV)

4.) 1 Corinthians 10:8 "Neither let us commit fornication, as some of them committed, and fell in **one day** three and twenty thousand." (KJV)

5.) 2 Peter 3:8 "But, beloved, be not ignorant of this one thing, that **one day** is with the Lord as a thousand years, and a thousand years as **one day**." (KJV)

6.) Revelation 18:8 "Therefore shall her plagues come in **one day**, death, and mourning, and famine; and she shall be utterly burned with fire: for strong is the Lord God who judgeth her." (KJV)

First Day

1.) Mark 14:12 "And the **first day** of unleavened bread, when they killed the passover, his disciples said unto him, Where wilt thou that we go and prepare that thou mayest eat the passover?" (KJV)

2.) Acts 20:18 "And when they were come to him, he said unto them, Ye know, from the **first day** that I came into Asia, after what manner I have been with you at all seasons," (KJV)

3.) Philippians 1:5 "For your fellowship in the gospel from the **first day** until now;" (KJV)

Two Days

1.) Matthew 26:2 "Ye know that after **two days** is *the feast of* the passover, and the Son of man is betrayed to be crucified." (KJV)

2.) Mark 14:1 "After **two days** was *the feast of* the passover, and of unleavened bread: and the chief priests and the scribes sought how they might take him by craft, and put *him* to death." (KJV)

3.) John 4:40 "So when the Samaritans were come unto him, they besought him that he would tarry with them: and he abode there **two days**." (KJV)

4.) John 4:43 "Now after **two days** he departed thence, and went into Galilee." (KJV)

5.) John 11:6 "When he had heard therefore that he was sick, he abode **two days** still in the same place where he was." (KJV)

Three Days

1. and 2.) Matthew 12:40 "For as Jonas was **three days** and three nights in the whale's belly; so shall the Son of man be **three days** and three nights in the heart of the earth." (KJV)

3.) Matthew 15:32 "Then Jesus called his disciples unto him, and said, I have compassion on the multitude, because they continue with me now **three days**, and have nothing to eat: and I will not send them away fasting, lest they faint in the way." (KJV)

4.) Matthew 26:61 "And said, This fellow said, I am able to destroy the temple of God, and to build it in **three days**." (KJV)

5.) Matthew 27:40 "And saying, Thou that destroyest the temple, and buildest it in **three days**, save thyself. If thou be the Son of God, come down from the cross." (KJV)

6.) Matthew 27:63 "Saying, Sir, we remember that that deceiver said, while he was yet alive, After **three days** I will rise again." (KJV)

7.) Mark 8:2 "I have compassion on the multitude, because they have now been with me **three days**, and have nothing to eat:" (KJV)

8.) Mark 8:31 "And he began to teach them, that the Son of man must suffer many things, and be rejected of the elders, and of the chief priests, and scribes, and be killed, and after **three days** rise again." (KJV)

9.) Mark 14:58 "We heard him say, I will destroy this temple that is made with hands, and within **three days** I will build another made without hands." (KJV)

10.) Mark 15:29 "And they that passed by railed on him, wagging their heads, and saying, Ah, thou that destroyest the temple, and buildest it in **three days**," (KJV)

11.) Luke 2:46 "And it came to pass, that after **three days** they found him in the temple, sitting in the midst of the doctors, both hearing them, and asking them questions." (KJV)

12.) John 2:19 "Jesus answered and said unto them, Destroy this temple, and in **three days** I will raise it up." (KJV)

13.) John 2:20 "Then said the Jews, Forty and six years was this temple in building, and wilt thou rear it up in **three days**?" (KJV)

14.) Acts 9:9 "And he was **three days** without sight, and neither did eat nor drink." (KJV)

15.) Acts 25:1 "Now when Festus was come into the province, after **three days** he ascended from Caesarea to Jerusalem." (KJV)

16.) Acts 28:7 "In the same quarters were possessions of the chief man of the island, whose name was Publius; who received us, and lodged us **three days** courteously." (KJV)

17.) Acts 28:12 "And landing at Syracuse, we tarried there **three days**." (KJV)

18.) Acts 28:17 "And it came to pass, that after **three days** Paul called the chief of the Jews together: and when they were come together, he said unto them, Men and brethren, though I have committed nothing against the people, or customs of our fathers, yet was I delivered prisoner from Jerusalem into the hands of the Romans." (KJV)

19.) Revelation 11:9 "And they of the people and kindreds and tongues and nations shall see their dead bodies **three days** and an half, and shall not suffer their dead bodies to be put in graves." (KJV)

20.) Revelation 11:11 "And after **three days** and an half the Spirit of life from God entered into them, and they stood upon their feet; and great fear fell upon them which saw them." (KJV)

Third Day

1.) Matthew 16:21 "From that time forth began Jesus to shew unto his disciples, how that he must go unto Jerusalem, and suffer many things of the elders and chief priests and scribes, and be killed, and be raised again the **third day**." (KJV)

2.) Matthew 17:23 "And they shall kill him, and the **third day** he shall be raised again. And they were exceeding sorry." (KJV)

3.) Matthew 20:19 "And shall deliver him to the Gentiles to mock, and to scourge, and to crucify him: and the **third day** he shall rise again." (KJV)

4.) 27:64 "Command therefore that the sepulchre be made sure until the **third day**, lest his disciples come by night, and steal him away, and say unto the people, He is risen from the dead: so the last error shall be worse than the first." (KJV)

5.) Mark 9:31 "For he taught his disciples, and said unto them, The Son of man is delivered into the hands of men, and they shall kill him; and after that he is killed, he shall rise the **third day**." (KJV)

6.) Mark 10:34 "And they shall mock him, and shall scourge him, and shall spit upon him, and shall kill him: and the **third day** he shall rise again." (KJV)

7.) Luke 9:22 "Saying, The Son of man must suffer many things, and be rejected of the elders and chief priests and scribes, and be slain, and be raised the **third day**." (KJV)

8.) Luke 18:33 "And they shall scourge him, and put him to death: and the **third day** he shall rise again." (KJV)

9.) Luke 24:7 "Saying, The Son of man must be delivered into the hands of sinful men, and be crucified, and the **third day** rise again." (KJV)

10.) Luke 24:21 "But we trusted that it had been he which should have redeemed Israel: and beside all this, to day is the **third day** since these things were done." (KJV)

11.) Luke 24:46 "And said unto them, Thus it is written, and thus it behoved Christ to suffer, and to rise from the dead the **third day**:" (KJV)

12.) John 2:1 "And the **third day** there was a marriage in Cana of Galilee; and the mother of Jesus was there:" (KJV)

13.) Acts 10:40 "Him God raised up the **third day**, and shewed him openly;" (KJV)

14.) 1 Corinthians 15:4 "And that he was buried, and that he rose again the **third day** according to the scriptures:" (KJV)

Four Days

1.) John 11:17 "Then when Jesus came, he found that he had lain in the grave **four days** already." (KJV)

2.) Acts 10:30 "And Cornelius said, **Four days** ago I was fasting until this hour; and at the ninth hour I prayed in my house, and, behold, a man stood before me in bright clothing," (KJV)

Five Days

1.) Acts 20:6 "And we sailed away from Philippi after the days of unleavened bread, and came unto them to Troas in **five days**; where we abode seven days." (KJV)

2.) Acts 24:1 "And after **five days** Ananias the high priest descended with the elders, and with a certain orator named Tertullus, who informed the governor against Paul." (KJV)

Six Days

1.) Matthew 17:1 "And after **six days** Jesus taketh Peter, James, and John his brother, and bringeth them up into an high mountain apart," (KJV)

2.) Mark 9:2 "And after **six days** Jesus taketh with him Peter, and James, and John, and leadeth them up into an high mountain apart by themselves: and he was transfigured before them." (KJV)

3.) Luke 13:14 "And the ruler of the synagogue answered with indignation, because that Jesus had healed on the sabbath day, and said unto the people, There are **six days** in which men ought to work: in them therefore come and be healed, and not on the sabbath day." (KJV)

4.) John 12:1 "Then Jesus **six days** before the passover came to Bethany, where Lazarus was which had been dead, whom he raised from the dead." (KJV)

Seven Days

1.) Acts 20:6 "And we sailed away from Philippi after the days of unleavened bread, and came unto them to Troas in five days; where we abode **seven days**." (KJV)

2.) Acts 21:4 "And finding disciples, we tarried there **seven days**: who said to Paul through the Spirit, that he should not go up to Jerusalem." (KJV)

3.) Acts 21:27 "And when the **seven days** were almost ended, the Jews which were of Asia, when they saw him in the temple, stirred up all the people, and laid hands on him," (KJV)

4.) Acts 28:14 "Where we found brethren, and were desired to tarry with them **seven days**: and so we went toward Rome." (KJV)

5.) Hebrews 11:30 "By faith the walls of Jericho fell down, after they were compassed about **seven days**." (KJV)

Seventh Day

1.) Hebrews 4:4 "For he spake in a certain place of the **seventh day** on this wise, And God did rest the **seventh day** from all his works." (KJV)

Eight Days

1.) Luke 2:21 "And when **eight days** were accomplished for the circumcising of the child, his name was called JESUS, which was so named of the angel before he was conceived in the womb." (KJV)

2.) Luke 9:28 "And it came to pass about an **eight days** after these sayings, he took Peter and John and James, and went up into a mountain to pray." (KJV)

3.) John 20:26 "And after **eight days** again his disciples were within, and Thomas with them: then came Jesus, the doors being shut, and stood in the midst, and said, Peace be unto you." (KJV)

Eighth Day

1.) Luke 1:59 "And it came to pass, that on the **eighth day** they came to circumcise the child; and they called him Zacharias, after the name of his father." (KJV)

2.) Acts 7:8 "And he gave him the covenant of circumcision: and so Abraham begat Isaac, and circumcised him the **eighth day**; and Isaac begat Jacob; and Jacob begat the twelve patriarchs." (KJV)

Ten Days

1.) Acts 25:6 "And when he had tarried among them more than **ten days**, he went down unto Caesarea; and the next day sitting on the judgment seat commanded Paul to be brought." (KJV)

2.) Revelation 2:10 "Fear none of those things which thou shalt suffer: behold, the devil shall cast some of you into prison, that ye may be tried; and ye shall have tribulation **ten days**: be thou faithful unto death, and I will give thee a crown of life." (KJV)

Twelve Days

1.) Acts 24:11 "Because that thou mayest understand, that there are yet but **twelve days** since I went up to Jerusalem for to worship." (KJV)

Fourteenth Day

1.) Acts 27:33 "And while the day was coming on, Paul besought them all to take meat, saying, This day is the **fourteenth day** that ye have tarried and continued fasting, having taken nothing." (KJV)

Fifteen Days

1.) Galatians 1:18 "Then after three years I went up to Jerusalem to see Peter, and abode with him **fifteen days**." (KJV)

Forty Days

1.) Matthew 4:2 "And when he had fasted **forty days** and forty nights, he was afterward an hungred." (KJV)

2.) Mark 1:13 "And he was there in the wilderness **forty days**, tempted of Satan; and was with the wild beasts; and the angels ministered unto him." (KJV)

3.) Luke 4:2 "Being **forty days** tempted of the devil. And in those days he did eat nothing: and when they were ended, he afterward hungered." (KJV)

4.) Acts 1:3 "To whom also he shewed himself alive after his passion by many infallible proofs, being seen of them **forty days**, and speaking of the things pertaining to the kingdom of God:" (KJV)

One-Thousand-Two-Hundred-Sixty Days

1.) Revelation 11:3 "And I will give power unto my two witnesses, and they shall prophesy a **thousand two hundred and threescore days**, clothed in sackcloth." (KJV)

2.) Revelation 12:6 "And the woman fled into the wilderness, where she hath a place prepared of God, that they should feed her there a **thousand two hundred and threescore days**." (KJV)

As you can see, everywhere *HEMERA* is combined with a numerical modifier, it refers to ordinary, twenty-four-hour days. Since the Greek *HEMERA DUO* is equivalent to the Hebrew *YOMIM SHENAYIM*, and since the Hebrew-Greek scholars who translated 2 Chronicles 21:19 in the Septuagint say it means, "two days," then I conclude 2 Chronicles 21:19 should be translated, "two days," not, "two years." This Day-Age argument fails.

YOM SHELIYSHIY (Third Day)
(*YOM*—Strong's Number H3117 and
SHELIYSHIY—Strong's Number H7992)

1.) Genesis 1:13 "And the evening and the morning were the **third day**." (KJV)

2.) Genesis 22:4 "Then on the **third day** Abraham lifted up his eyes, and saw the place afar off." (KJV)

3.) Genesis 31:22 "And it was told Laban on the **third day** that Jacob was fled." (KJV)

4.) Genesis 34:25 "And it came to pass on the **third day**, when they were sore, that two of the sons of Jacob, Simeon and Levi, Dinah's brethren, took each man his sword, and came upon the city boldly, and slew all the males." (KJV)

5.) Genesis 40:20 "And it came to pass the **third day**, *which was* Pharaoh's birthday, that he made a feast unto all his servants: and he lifted up the head of the chief butler and of the chief baker among his servants." (KJV)

6.) Genesis 42:18 "And Joseph said unto them the **third day**, This do, and live; *for* I fear God:" (KJV)

7. and 8.) Exodus 19:11 "And be ready against the **third day**: for the **third day** the LORD will come down in the sight of all the people upon mount Sinai." (KJV)

9.) Exodus 19:16 "And it came to pass on the **third day** in the morning, that there were thunders and lightnings, and a thick cloud upon the mount, and the voice of the trumpet exceeding loud; so that all the people that *was* in the camp trembled." (KJV)

10.) Leviticus 7:17 "But the remainder of the flesh of the sacrifice on the **third day** shall be burnt with fire." (KJV)

11.) Leviticus 7:18 "And if *any* of the flesh of the sacrifice of his peace offerings be eaten at all on the **third day**, it shall not be accepted, neither shall it be imputed unto him that offereth it: it shall be an abomination, and the soul that eateth of it shall bear his iniquity." (KJV)

12.) Leviticus 19:6 "It shall be eaten the same day ye offer it, and on the morrow: and if ought remain until the **third day**, it shall be burnt in the fire." (KJV)

13.) Leviticus 19:7 "And if it be eaten at all on the **third day**, it *is* abominable; it shall not be accepted." (KJV)

14.) Numbers 7:24 "On the **third day** Eliab the son of Helon, prince of the children of Zebulun, *did offer:*" (KJV)

15. and 16.) Numbers 19:12 "He shall purify himself with it on the **third day**, and on the seventh day he shall be clean: but if he purify not himself the **third day**, then the seventh day he shall not be clean." (KJV)

17.) Numbers 19:19 "And the clean *person* shall sprinkle upon the unclean on the **third day**, and on the seventh day: and on the seventh day he shall purify himself, and wash his clothes, and bathe himself in water, and shall be clean at even." (KJV)

18.) Numbers 29:20 "And on the **third day** eleven bullocks, two rams, fourteen lambs of the first year without blemish;" (KJV)

19.) Numbers 31:19 "And do ye abide without the camp seven days: whosoever hath killed any person, and whosoever hath touched any slain, purify *both* yourselves and your captives on the **third day**, and on the seventh day." (KJV)

20.) Joshua 9:17 "And the children of Israel journeyed, and came unto their cities on the **third day**. Now their cities *were* Gibeon, and Chephirah, and Beeroth, and Kirjathjearim." (KJV)

21.) Judges 20:30 "And the children of Israel went up against the children of Benjamin on the **third day**, and put themselves in array against Gibeah, as at other times." (KJV)

22.) 1 Samuel 30:1 "And it came to pass, when David and his men were come to Ziklag on the **third day**, that the Amalekites had invaded the south, and Ziklag, and smitten Ziklag, and burned it with fire;" (KJV)

23.) 2 Samuel 1:2 "It came even to pass on the **third day**, that, behold, a man came out of the camp from Saul with his clothes rent, and earth upon his head: and *so* it was, when he came to David, that he fell to the earth, and did obeisance." (KJV)

24.) 1 Kings 3:18 "And it came to pass the **third day** after that I was delivered, that this woman was delivered also: and we *were* together; *there was* no stranger with us in the house, save we two in the house." (KJV)

25. and 26.) 1 Kings 12:12 "So Jeroboam and all the people came to Rehoboam the **third day**, as the king had appointed, saying, Come to me again the **third day**." (KJV)

27.) 2 Kings 20:5 "Turn again, and tell Hezekiah the captain of my people, Thus saith the LORD, the God of David thy father, I have heard thy prayer, I have seen thy tears: behold, I will heal thee: on the **third day** thou shalt go up unto the house of the LORD." (KJV)

28.) 2 Kings 20:8 "And Hezekiah said unto Isaiah, What *shall be* the sign that the LORD will heal me, and that I shall go up into the house of the LORD the **third day**?" (KJV)

29. and 30.) 2 Chronicles 10:12 "So Jeroboam and all the people came to Rehoboam on the **third day**, as the king bade, saying, Come again to me on the **third day**." (KJV)

31.) Esther 5:1 "Now it came to pass on the **third day**, that Esther put on *her* royal *apparel,* and stood in the inner court of the king's house, over against the king's house: and the king sat upon his royal throne in the royal house, over against the gate of the house." (KJV)

32.) Hosea 6:2 "After two days will he revive us: in the **third day** he will raise us up, and we shall live in his sight." (KJV)

Like the case of "one day" and "second day," there are some cases of "third day" that don't use the word *YOM*, and there are some other cases where other words are used for "third" instead of *SHELIYSHIY*. Even with those differences, they always refer to a regular twenty-four-hour day. The third day of creation was one day; not an age!

Wait! Day-Agers point to Hosea 6:2 as an exception to the rule. They say Hosea 6:2 proves *YOM* can mean an age. Let's look at Hosea 6:2 in context.

Hosea 6:1-3 "Come, let us return to the LORD. He has torn us to pieces but he will heal us; he has injured us but he will bind up our wounds. *{2}* After two days he will revive us; on the **third day** he will restore us, that we may live in his presence. *{3}* Let us acknowledge the LORD; let us press on to acknowledge him. As surely as the sun rises, he will appear; he will come to us like the winter rains, like the spring rains that water the earth." (NIV)

Day-Agers point out the restoration of Israel did not take place within three literal days. Therefore, an ordinal before *YOM* can mean an extended period of time. I disagree! Look carefully at what the text reveals. (In other words, look at the context.) Hosea demands that Israel first return to the Lord. Hosea tells Israel that if they would truly acknowledge the Lord, then He would restore them within three days. Israel only had to acknowledge God, and by the third day it would be restored. The problem wasn't with God. The problem was with Israel. The people didn't denounce their evil. They didn't acknowledge the Lord. They didn't return to the Lord. The restoration did not come within three days because Israel failed to do as Hosea demanded. Hosea gives no hint God is talking about anything but literal twenty-four-hour days. No symbolism is indicated. His wording in the text includes such concrete images as the sun rising, the winter rains, the earth, and the spring rains. As you read the rest of the chapter you see Hosea mentions the early dew, flashes of lightning, and the morning fog. Nothing in this chapter is symbolic of anything. Rather than being symbolic, God is announcing He will respond to repentance immediately. "As surely as the sun rises," He will respond. He will not postpone His response if Israel returns to Him. Why would God ask His beloved people to acknowledge Him, and then after they do, make them wait three "ages" to be restored? Rather than proving these days are long periods of time, Hosea proves God is willing to work in very short periods of time to bless His people. God told Hosea He was ready to restore Israel within seventy-two hours. True, the restoration of Israel did not come within three literal days, but the sad thing is, it could have. (As a point of history, however, this prophetic passage was fulfilled. After three days in the tomb, Christ restored those Jews who acknowledged Him.)

YOMIM SHALOSH (Three Days)
(*YOMIM*—Strong's Number H3117 and
SHALOSH—Strong's Number H7969)

1.) Genesis 30:36 "And he set **three days**' journey betwixt himself and Jacob: and Jacob fed the rest of Laban's flocks." (KJV)

2.) Genesis 40:12 "And Joseph said unto him, This *is* the interpretation of it: The three branches *are* **three days**:" (KJV)

3.) Genesis 40:13 "Yet within **three days** shall Pharaoh lift up thine head, and restore thee unto thy place: and thou shalt deliver Pharaoh's cup into his hand, after the former manner when thou wast his butler." (KJV)

4.) Genesis 40:18 "And Joseph answered and said, This *is* the interpretation thereof: The three baskets *are* **three days**:" (KJV)

5.) Genesis 40:19 "Yet within **three days** shall Pharaoh lift up thy head from off thee, and shall hang thee on a tree; and the birds shall eat thy flesh from off thee." (KJV)

6.) Genesis 42:17 "And he put them all together into ward **three days**." (KJV)

7.) Exodus 3:18 "And they shall hearken to thy voice: and thou shalt come, thou and the elders of Israel, unto the king of Egypt, and ye shall say unto him, The LORD God of the Hebrews hath met with us: and now let us go, we beseech thee, **three days**' journey into the wilderness, that we may sacrifice to the LORD our God." (KJV)

8.) Exodus 5:3 "And they said, The God of the Hebrews hath met with us: let us go, we pray thee, **three days**' journey into the desert, and sacrifice unto the LORD our God; lest he fall upon us with pestilence, or with the sword." (KJV)

9.) Exodus 8:27 "We will go **three days**' journey into the wilderness, and sacrifice to the LORD our God, as he shall command us." (KJV)

10.) Exodus 10:22 "And Moses stretched forth his hand toward heaven; and there was a thick darkness in all the land of Egypt **three days**:" (KJV)

11.) Exodus 10:23 "They saw not one another, neither rose any from his place for **three days**: but all the children of Israel had light in their dwellings." (KJV)

12.) Exodus 15:22 "So Moses brought Israel from the Red sea, and they went out into the wilderness of Shur; and they went **three days** in the wilderness, and found no water." (KJV)

13.) Exodus 19:15 "And he said unto the people, Be ready against the **third day**: come not at *your* wives." (KJV)

14.) Leviticus 12:4 "And she shall then continue in the blood of her purifying **three** and thirty **days**; she shall touch no hallowed thing, nor come into the sanctuary, until the days of her purifying be fulfilled." (KJV)

15. and 16.) Numbers 10:33 "And they departed from the mount of the LORD **three days'** journey: and the ark of the covenant of the LORD went before them in the **three days'** journey, to search out a resting place for them." (KJV)

17.) Numbers 33:8 "And they departed from before Pihahiroth, and passed through the midst of the sea into the wilderness, and went **three days'** journey in the wilderness of Etham, and pitched in Marah." (KJV)

18.) Joshua 1:11 "Pass through the host, and command the people, saying, Prepare you victuals; for within **three days** ye shall pass over this Jordan, to go in to possess the land, which the LORD your God giveth you to possess it." (KJV)

19.) Joshua 2:16 "And she said unto them, Get you to the mountain, lest the pursuers meet you; and hide yourselves there **three days**, until the pursuers be returned: and afterward may ye go your way." (KJV)

20.) Joshua 2:22 "And they went, and came unto the mountain, and abode there **three days**, until the pursuers were returned: and the pursuers sought *them* throughout all the way, but found *them* not." (KJV)

21.) Joshua 3:2 "And it came to pass after **three days**, that the officers went through the host;" (KJV)

22.) Joshua 9:16 "And it came to pass at the end of **three days** after they had made a league with them, that they heard that they *were* their neighbours, and *that* they dwelt among them." (KJV)

23.) Judges 14:14 "And he said unto them, Out of the eater came forth meat, and out of the strong came forth sweetness. And they could not in **three days** expound the riddle." (KJV)

24.) Judges 19:4 "And his father in law, the damsel's father, retained him; and he abode with him **three days**: so they did eat and drink, and lodged there." (KJV)

25.) 1 Samuel 9:20 "And as for thine asses that were lost **three days** ago, set not thy mind on them; for they are found. And on whom *is* all the desire of Israel? *Is it* not on thee, and on all thy father's house?" (KJV)

26.) 1 Samuel 30:12 "And they gave him a piece of a cake of figs, and two clusters of raisins: and when he had eaten, his spirit came again to him: for he had eaten no bread, nor drunk *any* water, **three days** and three nights." (KJV)

27.) 1 Samuel 30:13 "And David said unto him, To whom *belongest* thou? and whence *art* thou? And he said, I *am* a young man of Egypt, servant to an Amalekite; and my master left me, because **three days** agone I fell sick." (KJV)

28.) 2 Samuel 20:4 "Then said the king to Amasa, Assemble me the men of Judah within **three days**, and be thou here present." (KJV)

29.) 2 Samuel 24:13 "So Gad came to David, and told him, and said unto him, Shall seven years of famine come unto thee in thy land? or wilt thou flee three months before thine enemies, while they pursue thee? or that there be **three days**' pestilence in thy land? now advise, and see what answer I shall return to him that sent me." (KJV)

30.) 1 Kings 12:5 "And he said unto them, Depart yet *for* **three days**, then come again to me. And the people departed." (KJV)

31.) 2 Kings 2:17 "And when they urged him till he was ashamed, he said, Send. They sent therefore fifty men; and they sought **three days**, but found him not." (KJV)

32.) 1 Chronicles 12:39 "And there they were with David **three days**, eating and drinking: for their brethren had prepared for them." (KJV)

33.) 1 Chronicles 21:12 "Either three years' famine; or three months to be destroyed before thy foes, while that the sword of thine enemies overtaketh *thee;* or else **three days** the sword of the LORD, even the pestilence, in the land, and the angel of the LORD destroying throughout all the coasts of Israel. Now therefore advise thyself what word I shall bring again to him that sent me." (KJV)

34.) 2 Chronicles 10:5 "And he said unto them, Come again unto me after **three days**. And the people departed." (KJV)

35.) 2 Chronicles 20:25 "And when Jehoshaphat and his people came to take away the spoil of them, they found among them in abundance both riches with the dead bodies, and precious jewels, which they stripped off for themselves, more than they could carry away: and they were **three days** in gathering of the spoil, it was so much." (KJV)

36.) Ezra 8:15 "And I gathered them together to the river that runneth to Ahava; and there abode we in tents **three days**: and I viewed the people, and the priests, and found there none of the sons of Levi." (KJV)

37.) Ezra 8:32 "And we came to Jerusalem, and abode there **three days**." (KJV)

38.) Ezra 10:8 "And that whosoever would not come within **three days**, according to the counsel of the princes and the elders, all his substance should be forfeited, and himself separated from the congregation of those that had been carried away." (KJV)

39.) Ezra 10:9 "Then all the men of Judah and Benjamin gathered themselves together unto Jerusalem within **three days**. It *was* the ninth month, on the twentieth *day* of the month; and all the people sat in the street of the house of God, trembling because of *this* matter, and for the great rain." (KJV)

40.) Nehemiah 2:11 "So I came to Jerusalem, and was there **three days**." (KJV)

41.) Esther 4:16 "Go, gather together all the Jews that are present in Shushan, and fast ye for me, and neither eat nor drink **three days**, night or day: I also and my maidens will fast likewise; and so will I go in unto the king, which *is* not according to the law: and if I perish, I perish." (KJV)

42.) Esther 9:17 "On the **thirteenth day** of the month Adar; and on the fourteenth day of the same rested they, and made it a day of feasting and gladness." (KJV) (Literally, "three and ten day.")

43.) Amos 4:4 "Come to Bethel, and transgress; at Gilgal multiply transgression; and bring your sacrifices every morning, *and* your tithes after **three years**:" (KJV)

All right, here is the previously mentioned verse Day-Age creationists use to prove how a number plus *YOM* can mean a long period of time. Well, I hate to be arrogant, but the *King James* translators just flat out blew it on this one! I think someone was sleepy when making this translation, and didn't bother looking at the context. I'm sure the translator was reading along and came across this verse that mentioned bringing in tithes every three days, and he thought, "What? That doesn't make sense. A tithe is one-tenth of your annual income. If you brought in your tithe every three days, then after thirty days you would have given all your income and couldn't give any more… it must mean every three years, not days."

Well, at least that's how I like to think it happened. Read the chapter and you will see why this means three days. Look at what God is saying: He is going to judge Israel, the Northern Kingdom. They have oppressed the poor and needy. They have rejected all of His warnings. They have become so wicked, that even their attempts to be religious only add to their sin. They refuse to go to Jerusalem to offer their sacrifices as God commanded. Instead, they go to Bethel and Gilgal, two centers of pagan worship. The more they go there, the more they multiply their sin. The more they offer, the more they offend. They are trying to buy God's favor, but only earn God's wrath. They offer sacrifices daily; something far beyond what God commanded. They bring in a tithe every three days instead of every year, but it will not turn aside God's anger. It only makes it worse. The context clearly reveals how these people are trying to impress God by offering more sacrifices and tithes than He commanded. But, that won't help them. So, if "super-tithing" doesn't impress God, then bringing in a tithe every three years would not impress God either. That's less than He commanded. Even they would realize tithing every three years would anger Him. Common sense and a comparison of translations will show this verse says, "three days."

Amos 4:4 "Come to Bethel, and transgress; to Gilgal, and multiply transgression; bring your sacrifices every morning, your tithes every **three days**;" (ESV)

Amos 4:4 "Enter Bethel and transgress; In Gilgal multiply transgression! Bring your sacrifices every morning, Your tithes every **three days**." (NASB)

Amos 4:4 "Come to Bethel, and transgress; at Gilgal multiply transgression; and bring your sacrifices in the morning, your tithes every **three days**," (DBY)

Amos 4:4 "Enter ye Bethel, and transgress, At Gilgal, cause transgression, to abound,—Yea, carry in, every morning, your sacrifices, every **three days**, your tithes;" (EMP)

YOMIM SHALOSH in Amos 4:4 means, "three days." It means the same in the last two verses in the Bible where these words are used.

44.) Jonah 1:17 "Now the LORD had prepared a great fish to swallow up Jonah. And Jonah was in the belly of the fish **three days** and three nights." (KJV)

45.) Jonah 3:3 "So Jonah arose, and went unto Nineveh, according to the word of the LORD. Now Nineveh was an exceeding great city of **three days**' journey." (KJV)

Since *YOM SHELIYSHIY* (Third Day) and *YOMIM SHALOSH* (Three Days) are never used to describe an age of time anywhere else in the Bible, what clue do we have that the days of the Genesis Creation Account describe long ages?

YOM REBIY'IY (Fourth Day)
(*YOM*—Strong's Number H3117 and
REBIY'IY—Strong's Number H7243)

1.) Genesis 1:19 "And the evening and the morning were the **fourth day**." (KJV)

2.) Numbers 7:30 "On the **fourth day** Elizur the son of Shedeur, prince of the children of Reuben, *did offer:*" (KJV)

3.) Numbers 29:23 "And on the **fourth day** ten bullocks, two rams, *and* fourteen lambs of the first year without blemish:" (KJV)

4.) Judges 19:5 "And it came to pass on the **fourth day**, when they arose early in the morning, that he rose up to depart: and the damsel's father said unto his son in law, Comfort thine heart with a morsel of bread, and afterward go your way." (KJV)

5.) 2 Chronicles 20:26 "And on the **fourth day** they assembled themselves in the valley of Berachah; for there they blessed the LORD: therefore the name of the same place was called, The valley of Berachah, unto this day." (KJV)

6.) Ezra 8:33 "Now on the **fourth day** was the silver and the gold and the vessels weighed in the house of our God by the hand of Meremoth the son of Uriah the priest; and with him *was* Eleazar the son of Phinehas; and with them *was* Jozabad the son of Jeshua, and Noadiah the son of Binnui, Levites;" (KJV)

7.) Nehemiah 9:1 "Now in the twenty and **fourth day** of this month the children of Israel were assembled with fasting, and with sackclothes, and earth upon them." (KJV)

8.) Nehemiah 9:3 "And they stood up in their place, and read in the book of the law of the LORD their God *one* **fourth part of the day**; and *another* fourth part they confessed, and worshipped the LORD their God." (KJV)

YOMIM ARBA (Four Days)
(*YOMIM*—Strong's Number H3117 and
ARBA—Strong's Number H702)

1.) Judges 11:40 "*That* the daughters of Israel went yearly to lament the daughter of Jephthah the Gileadite **four days** in a year." (KJV)

2.) 1 Kings 8:65 "And at that time Solomon held a feast, and all Israel with him, a great congregation, from the entering in of Hamath unto the river of Egypt, before the LORD our God, seven days and seven days, *even* **four**teen **days**." (KJV) (Literally, "four and ten day.")

3.) Esther 9:15 "For the Jews that *were* in Shushan gathered themselves together on the **four**teenth **day** also of the month Adar, and slew three hundred men at Shushan; but on the prey they laid not their hand." (KJV) (Literally, "four and ten day.")

4.) Esther 9:19 "Therefore the Jews of the villages, that dwelt in the unwalled towns, made the **four**teenth **day** of the month Adar *a day of* gladness and feasting, and a good day, and of sending portions one to another." (KJV) (Literally, "four and ten day.")

5.) Esther 9:21 "To stablish *this* among them, that they should keep the **four**teenth **day** of the month Adar, and the fifteenth day of the same, yearly," (KJV) (Literally, "four and ten day.")

Since *YOM REBIY'IY* (Fourth Day) and *YOMIM ARBA* (Four Days) are never used to describe an age of time anywhere else in the Bible, what clue do we have that the days of the Genesis Creation Account describe long ages?

YOM CHAMIYSHIY (Fifth Day)
(*YOM*—Strong's Number H3117 and
CHAMIYSHIY—Strong's Number H2549)

1.) Genesis 1:23 "And the evening and the morning were the **fifth day**." (KJV)

2.) Numbers 7:36 "On the **fifth day** Shelumiel the son of Zurishaddai, prince of the children of Simeon, *did offer:*" (KJV)

3.) Numbers 29:26 "And on the **fifth day** nine bullocks, two rams, *and* fourteen lambs of the first year without spot:" (KJV)

4.) Judges 19:8 "And he arose early in the morning on the **fifth day** to depart: and the damsel's father said, Comfort thine heart, I pray thee. And they tarried until afternoon, and they did eat both of them." (KJV)

YOMIM CAMESH (Five Days)
(*YOMIM*—Strong's Number H3117 and
CAMESH—Strong's Number H2568)

1.) Numbers 11:19 "Ye shall not eat one day, nor two days, nor **five days**, neither ten days, nor twenty days;" (KJV)

2.) Esther 9:21 "To stablish *this* among them, that they should keep the fourteenth day of the month Adar, and the **fif**teenth **day** of the same, yearly," (KJV) (Literally, "five and ten day.")

Since *YOM CHAMIYSHIY* (Fifth Day) and *YOMIM CAMESH* (Five Days) are never used to describe an age of time anywhere else in the Bible, what clue do we that have the days of the Genesis Creation Account describe long ages?

YOM SHISHSHIY (Sixth Day)
(*YOM*—Strong's Number H3117 and
SHISHSHIY—Strong's Number H8345)

1.) Genesis 1:31 "And God saw every thing that he had made, and, behold, *it was* very good. And the evening and the morning were the **sixth day**." (KJV)

2.) Exodus 16:5 "And it shall come to pass, that on the **sixth day** they shall prepare *that* which they bring in; and it shall be twice as much as they gather daily." (KJV)

3.) Exodus 16:22 "And it came to pass, *that* on the **sixth day** they gathered twice as much bread, two omers for one *man:* and all the rulers of the congregation came and told Moses." (KJV)

4.) Exodus 16:29 "See, for that the LORD hath given you the sabbath, therefore he giveth you on the **sixth day** the bread of two days; abide ye every man in his place, let no man go out of his place on the seventh day." (KJV)

5.) Numbers 7:42 "On the **sixth day** Eliasaph the son of Deuel, prince of the children of Gad, *offered:*" (KJV)

6.) Numbers 29:29 "And on the **sixth day** eight bullocks, two rams, *and* fourteen lambs of the first year without blemish:" (KJV)

YOMIM SHESH (Six Days)
(*YOMIM*—Strong's Number H3117 and
SHESH—Strong's Number H8337)

1.) Exodus 16.26 "**Six days** ye shall gather it; but on the seventh day, *which is* the sabbath, in it there shall be none." (KJV)

2.) Exodus 20:9 "**Six days** shalt thou labour, and do all thy work:" (KJV)

3.) Exodus 20:11 "For *in* **six days** the LORD made heaven and earth, the sea, and all that in them *is,* and rested the seventh day: wherefore the LORD blessed the sabbath day, and hallowed it." (KJV)

4.) Exodus 23:12 "**Six days** thou shalt do thy work, and on the seventh day thou shalt rest: that thine ox and thine ass may rest, and the son of thy handmaid, and the stranger, may be refreshed." (KJV)

5.) Exodus 24:16 "And the glory of the LORD abode upon mount Sinai, and the cloud covered it **six days**: and the seventh day he called unto Moses out of the midst of the cloud." (KJV)

6.) Exodus 31:15 "**Six days** may work be done; but in the seventh *is* the sabbath of rest, holy to the LORD: whosoever doeth *any* work in the sabbath day, he shall surely be put to death." (KJV)

7.) Exodus 31:17 "It *is* a sign between me and the children of Israel for ever: for *in* **six days** the LORD made heaven and earth, and on the seventh day he rested, and was refreshed." (KJV)

8.) Exodus 34:21 "**Six days** thou shalt work, but on the seventh day thou shalt rest: in earing time and in harvest thou shalt rest." (KJV)

9.) Exodus 35:2 "**Six days** shall work be done, but on the seventh day there shall be to you an holy day, a sabbath of rest to the LORD: whosoever doeth work therein shall be put to death." (KJV)

10.) Leviticus 12:5 "But if she bear a maid child, then she shall be unclean two weeks, as in her separation: and she shall continue in the blood of her purifying threescore and **six days**." (KJV)

11.) Leviticus 23:3 "**Six days** shall work be done: but the seventh day *is* the sabbath of rest, an holy convocation; ye shall do no work *therein:* it *is* the sabbath of the LORD in all your dwellings." (KJV)

12.) Deuteronomy 5:13 "**Six days** thou shalt labour, and do all thy work:" (KJV)

13.) Deuteronomy 16:8 "**Six days** thou shalt eat unleavened bread: and on the seventh day *shall be* a solemn assembly to the LORD thy God: thou shalt do no work *therein.*" (KJV)

14.) Joshua 6:3 "And ye shall compass the city, all *ye* men of war, *and* go round about the city once. Thus shalt thou do **six days**." (KJV)

15.) Joshua 6:14 "And the second day they compassed the city once, and returned into the camp: so they did **six days**." (KJV)

16.) 2 Chronicles 29:17 "Now they began on the first day of the first month to sanctify, and on the eighth day of the month came they to the porch of the LORD: so they sanctified the house of the LORD in eight days; and in the **six**teenth **day** of the first month they made an end." (KJV) (literally, "six and ten day.")

17.) Ezekiel 46:1 "Thus saith the Lord GOD; The gate of the inner court that looketh toward the east shall be shut the **six** working **days**; but on the sabbath it shall be opened, and in the day of the new moon it shall be opened." (KJV)

Since *YOM SHISHSHIY* (Sixth Day) and *YOMIM SHESH* (Six Days) are never used to describe an age of time anywhere else in the Bible, what clue do we have that the days of the Genesis Creation Account describe long ages?

YOM SHEBIY'IY (Seventh Day)
(*YOM*—Strong's Number H3117 and
SHEBIY'IY—Strong's Number H7637)

1. and 2.) Genesis 2:2 "And on the **seventh day** God ended his work which he had made; and he rested on the **seventh day** from all his work which he had made." (KJV)

3.) Genesis 2:3 "And God blessed the **seventh day**, and sanctified it: because that in it he had rested from all his work which God created and made." (KJV)

4.) Exodus 12:15 "Seven days shall ye eat unleavened bread; even the first day ye shall put away leaven out of your houses: for whosoever eateth leavened bread from the first day until the **seventh day**, that soul shall be cut off from Israel." (KJV)

5.) Exodus 12:16 "And in the first day *there shall be* an holy convocation, and in the **seventh day** there shall be an holy convocation to you; no manner of work shall be done in them, save *that* which every man must eat, that only may be done of you." (KJV)

6.) Exodus 13:6 "Seven days thou shalt eat unleavened bread, and in the **seventh day** *shall be* a feast to the LORD." (KJV)

7.) Exodus 16:26 "Six days ye shall gather it; but on the **seventh day**, *which is* the sabbath, in it there shall be none." (KJV)

8.) Exodus 16:27 "And it came to pass, *that* there went out *some* of the people on the **seventh day** for to gather, and they found none." (KJV)

9.) Exodus 16:29 "See, for that the LORD hath given you the sabbath, therefore he giveth you on the sixth day the bread of two days; abide ye every man in his place, let no man go out of his place on the **seventh day**." (KJV)

10.) Exodus 16:30 "So the people rested on the **seventh day**." (KJV)

11.) Exodus 20:10 "But the **seventh day** *is* the sabbath of the LORD thy God: *in it* thou shalt not do any work, thou, nor thy son, nor thy daughter, thy manservant, nor thy maidservant, nor thy cattle, nor thy stranger that *is* within thy gates:" (KJV)

12.) Exodus 20:11 "For *in* six days the LORD made heaven and earth, the sea, and all that in them *is,* and rested the **seventh day**: wherefore the LORD blessed the sabbath day, and hallowed it." (KJV)

13.) Exodus 23:12 "Six days thou shalt do thy work, and on the **seventh day** thou shalt rest: that thine ox and thine ass may rest, and the son of thy handmaid, and the stranger, may be refreshed." (KJV)

14.) Exodus 24:16 "And the glory of the LORD abode upon mount Sinai, and the cloud covered it six days: and the **seventh day** he called unto Moses out of the midst of the cloud." (KJV)

15.) Exodus 31:15 "Six days may work be done; but in the **seventh** *is* the sabbath of rest, holy to the LORD: whosoever doeth *any* work in the sabbath day, he shall surely be put to death." (KJV)

16.) Exodus 31:17 "It *is* a sign between me and the children of Israel for ever: for *in* six days the LORD made heaven and earth, and on the **seventh day** he rested, and was refreshed." (KJV)

17.) Exodus 34:21 "Six days thou shalt work, but on the **seventh day** thou shalt rest: in earing time and in harvest thou shalt rest." (KJV)

18.) Exodus 35:2 "Six days shall work be done, but on the **seventh day** there shall be to you an holy day, a sabbath of rest to the LORD: whosoever doeth work therein shall be put to death." (KJV)

19.) Leviticus 13:5 "And the priest shall look on him the **seventh day**: and, behold, *if* the plague in his sight be at a stay, *and* the plague spread not in the skin; then the priest shall shut him up seven days more:" (KJV)

20.) Leviticus 13:6 "And the priest shall look on him again the **seventh day**: and, behold, *if* the plague *be* somewhat dark, *and* the plague spread not in the skin, the priest shall pronounce him clean: it *is but* a scab: and he shall wash his clothes, and be clean." (KJV)

21.) Leviticus 13:27 "And the priest shall look upon him the **seventh day**: *and* if it be spread much abroad in the skin, then the priest shall pronounce him unclean: it *is* the plague of leprosy." (KJV)

22.) Leviticus 13:32 "And in the **seventh day** the priest shall look on the plague: and, behold, *if* the scall spread not, and there be in it no yellow hair, and the scall *be* not in sight deeper than the skin;" (KJV)

23.) Leviticus 13:34 "And in the **seventh day** the priest shall look on the scall: and, behold, *if* the scall be not spread in the skin, nor *be* in sight deeper than the skin; then the priest shall pronounce him clean: and he shall wash his clothes, and be clean." (KJV)

24.) Leviticus 13:51 "And he shall look on the plague on the **seventh day**: if the plague be spread in the garment, either in the warp, or in the woof, or in a skin, *or* in any work that is made of skin; the plague *is* a fretting leprosy; it *is* unclean." (KJV)

25.) Leviticus 14:9 "But it shall be on the **seventh day**, that he shall shave all his hair off his head and his beard and his eyebrows, even all his hair he shall shave off: and he shall wash his clothes, also he shall wash his flesh in water, and he shall be clean." (KJV)

26.) Leviticus 14:39 "And the priest shall come again the **seventh day**, and shall look: and, behold, *if* the plague be spread in the walls of the house;" (KJV)

27.) Leviticus 23:3 "Six days shall work be done: but the **seventh day** *is* the sabbath of rest, an holy convocation; ye shall do no work *therein:* it *is* the sabbath of the LORD in all your dwellings." (KJV)

28.) Leviticus 23:8 "But ye shall offer an offering made by fire unto the LORD seven days: in the **seventh day** *is* an holy convocation: ye shall do no servile work *therein.*" (KJV)

29.) Numbers 6:9 "And if any man die very suddenly by him, and he hath defiled the head of his consecration; then he shall shave his head in the day of his cleansing, on the **seventh day** shall he shave it." (KJV)

30.) Numbers 7:48 "On the **seventh day** Elishama the son of Ammihud, prince of the children of Ephraim, *offered:*" (KJV)

31. and 32.) Numbers 19:12 "He shall purify himself with it on the third day, and on the **seventh day** he shall be clean: but if he purify not himself the third day, then the **seventh day** he shall not be clean." (KJV)

33. and 34.) Numbers 19:19 "And the clean *person* shall sprinkle upon the unclean on the third day, and on the **seventh day**: and on the **seventh day** he shall purify himself, and wash his clothes, and bathe himself in water, and shall be clean at even." (KJV)

35.) Numbers 28:25 "And on the **seventh day** ye shall have an holy convocation; ye shall do no servile work." (KJV)

36.) Numbers 29:32 "And on the **seventh day** seven bullocks, two rams, *and* fourteen lambs of the first year without blemish:" (KJV)

37.) Numbers 31:19 "And do ye abide without the camp seven days: whosoever hath killed any person, and whosoever hath touched any slain, purify *both* yourselves and your captives on the third day, and on the **seventh day**." (KJV)

38.) Numbers 31:24 "And ye shall wash your clothes on the **seventh day**, and ye shall be clean, and afterward ye shall come into the camp." (KJV)

39.) Deuteronomy 5:14 "But the **seventh day** *is* the sabbath of the LORD thy God: *in it* thou shalt not do any work, thou, nor thy son, nor thy daughter, nor thy manservant, nor thy maidservant, nor thine ox, nor thine ass, nor any of thy cattle, nor thy stranger that *is* within thy gates; that thy manservant and thy maidservant may rest as well as thou." (KJV)

40.) Deuteronomy 16:8 "Six days thou shalt eat unleavened bread: and on the **seventh day** *shall be* a solemn assembly to the LORD thy God: thou shalt do no work *therein.*" (KJV)

41.) Joshua 6:4 "And seven priests shall bear before the ark seven trumpets of rams' horns: and the **seventh day** ye shall compass the city seven times, and the priests shall blow with the trumpets." (KJV)

42.) Joshua 6:15 "And it came to pass on the **seventh day**, that they rose early about the dawning of the day, and compassed the city after the same manner seven times: only on that day they compassed the city seven times." (KJV)

43.) Judges 14:17 "And she wept before him the seven days, while their feast lasted: and it came to pass on the **seventh day**, that he told her, because she lay sore upon him: and she told the riddle to the children of her people." (KJV)

44.) Judges 14:18 "And the men of the city said unto him on the **seventh day** before the sun went down, What *is* sweeter than honey? and what *is* stronger than a lion? And he said unto them, If ye had not plowed with my heifer, ye had not found out my riddle." (KJV)

45.) 2 Samuel 12:18 "And it came to pass on the **seventh day**, that the child died. And the servants of David feared to tell him that the child was dead: for they said, Behold, while the child was yet alive, we spake unto him, and he would not hearken unto our voice: how will he then vex himself, if we tell him that the child is dead?" (KJV)

46.) 1 Kings 20:29 "And they pitched one over against the other seven days. And *so* it was, that in the **seventh day** the battle was joined: and the children of Israel slew of the Syrians an hundred thousand footmen in one day." (KJV)

47.) Esther 1:10 "On the **seventh day**, when the heart of the king was merry with wine, he commanded Mehuman, Biztha, Harbona, Bigtha, and Abagtha, Zethar, and Carcas, the seven chamberlains that served in the presence of Ahasuerus the king," (KJV)

There is one more *YOM SHEBIY'IY* (Judges 14:15) I didn't list in the above group because it is controversial. Ah-Ha! Finally, here is a real controversy! If you are a Day-Ager and you want to use a Bible verse to destroy all I have presented so far, then here is your verse. This is the one verse that might be used to show "seventh day" does not mean "seventh day." How can you use this verse to prove "seventh day" doesn't mean "seventh day?" Well, for some reason, some of the translations say, "fourth day," instead of, "seventh day."

Judges 14:15 "And it came to pass on the **seventh day**, that they said unto Samson's wife, Entice thy husband, that he may declare unto us the riddle, lest we burn thee and thy father's house with fire: have ye called us to take that we have? is it not so?" (KJV)

Judges 14:15 "Then it came about on the **fourth day** that they said to Samson's wife, 'Entice your husband, that he may tell us the riddle, lest we burn you and your father's house with fire. Have you invited us to impoverish us? Is this not so?'" (NASB)

      I've looked at several translations and there seems to be a fairly even split over what Judges 14:15 tells us. Is it "seventh" or is it "fourth?" I don't know. I suspect the difference arises from which ancient manuscript you use for your translation. Of course, even if you decide to blast my arguments by claiming Judges 14:15 speaks of a "fourth day" instead of a "seventh day," you're still stuck with the fact it means an ordinary day. "Day" doesn't mean "age" in that context either.

YOMIM SHEBAH (Seven Days)
(*YOMIM*—Strong's Number H3117 and
SHEBAH—Strong's Number H7651)

1.) Genesis 7:4 "For yet **seven days**, and I will cause it to rain upon the earth forty days and forty nights; and every living substance that I have made will I destroy from off the face of the earth." (KJV)

2.) Genesis 7:10 "And it came to pass after **seven days**, that the waters of the flood were upon the earth." (KJV)

3.) Genesis 8:10 "And he stayed yet other **seven days**; and again he sent forth the dove out of the ark;" (KJV)

4.) Genesis 8:12 "And he stayed yet other **seven days**; and sent forth the dove; which returned not again unto him any more." (KJV)

5.) Genesis 31:23 "And he took his brethren with him, and pursued after him **seven days'** journey; and they overtook him in the mount Gilead." (KJV)

6.) Genesis 50:10 "And they came to the threshingfloor of Atad, which *is* beyond Jordan, and there they mourned with a great and very sore lamentation: and he made a mourning for his father **seven days**." (KJV)

7.) Exodus 7:25 "And **seven days** were fulfilled, after that the LORD had smitten the river." (KJV)

8.) Exodus 12:15 "**Seven days** shall ye eat unleavened bread; even the first day ye shall put away leaven out of your houses: for whosoever eateth leavened bread from the first day until the seventh day, that soul shall be cut off from Israel." (KJV)

9.) Exodus 12:19 "**Seven days** shall there be no leaven found in your houses: for whosoever eateth that which is leavened, even that soul shall be cut off from the congregation of Israel, whether he be a stranger, or born in the land." (KJV)

10.) Exodus 13:6 "**Seven days** thou shalt eat unleavened bread, and in the seventh day *shall be* a feast to the LORD." (KJV)

11.) Exodus 13:7 "Unleavened bread shall be eaten **seven days**; and there shall no leavened bread be seen with thee, neither shall there be leaven seen with thee in all thy quarters." (KJV)

12.) Exodus 22:30 "Likewise shalt thou do with thine oxen, *and* with thy sheep: **seven days** it shall be with his dam; on the eighth day thou shalt give it me." (KJV)

13.) Exodus 23:15 "Thou shalt keep the feast of unleavened bread: (thou shalt eat unleavened bread **seven days**, as I commanded thee, in the time appointed of the month Abib; for in it thou camest out from Egypt: and none shall appear before me empty:)" (KJV)

14.) Exodus 29:30 "*And* that son that is priest in his stead shall put them on **seven days**, when he cometh into the tabernacle of the congregation to minister in the holy *place*." (KJV)

15.) Exodus 29:35 "And thus shalt thou do unto Aaron, and to his sons, according to all *things* which I have commanded thee: **seven days** shalt thou consecrate them." (KJV)

16.) Exodus 29:37 "**Seven days** thou shalt make an atonement for the altar, and sanctify it; and it shall be an altar most holy: whatsoever toucheth the altar shall be holy." (KJV)

17.) Exodus 34:18 "The feast of unleavened bread shalt thou keep. **Seven days** thou shalt eat unleavened bread, as I commanded thee, in the time of the month Abib: for in the month Abib thou camest out from Egypt." (KJV)

18. and 19.) Leviticus 8:33 "And ye shall not go out of the door of the tabernacle of the congregation *in* **seven days**, until the days of your consecration be at an end: for **seven days** shall he consecrate you." (KJV)

20.) Leviticus 8:35 "Therefore shall ye abide *at* the door of the tabernacle of the congregation day and night **seven days**, and keep the charge of the LORD, that ye die not: for so I am commanded." (KJV)

21.) Leviticus 12:2 "Speak unto the children of Israel, saying, If a woman have conceived seed, and born a man child: then she shall be unclean **seven days**; according to the days of the separation for her infirmity shall she be unclean." (KJV)

22.) Leviticus 13:4 "If the bright spot *be* white in the skin of his flesh, and in sight *be* not deeper than the skin, and the hair thereof be not turned white; then the priest shall shut up *him that hath* the plague **seven days**:" (KJV)

23.) Leviticus 13:5 "And the priest shall look on him the seventh day: and, behold, *if* the plague in his sight be at a stay, *and* the plague spread not in the skin; then the priest shall shut him up **seven days** more:" (KJV)

24.) Leviticus 13:21 "But if the priest look on it, and, behold, *there be* no white hairs therein, and *if* it *be* not lower than the skin, but *be* somewhat dark; then the priest shall shut him up **seven days**:" (KJV)

25.) Leviticus 13:26 "But if the priest look on it, and, behold, *there be* no white hair in the bright spot, and it *be* no lower than the *other* skin, but *be* somewhat dark; then the priest shall shut him up **seven days**:" (KJV)

26.) Leviticus 13:31 "And if the priest look on the plague of the scall, and, behold, it *be* not in sight deeper than the skin, and *that there is* no black hair in it; then the priest shall shut up *him that hath* the plague of the scall **seven days**:" (KJV)

27.) Leviticus 13:33 "He shall be shaven, but the scall shall he not shave; and the priest shall shut up *him that hath* the scall **seven days** more:" (KJV)

28.) Leviticus 13:50 "And the priest shall look upon the plague, and shut up *it that hath* the plague **seven days**:" (KJV)

29.) Leviticus 13:54 "Then the priest shall command that they wash *the thing* wherein the plague *is,* and he shall shut it up **seven days** more:" (KJV)

30.) Leviticus 14:8 "And he that is to be cleansed shall wash his clothes, and shave off all his hair, and wash himself in water, that he may be clean: and after that he shall come into the camp, and shall tarry abroad out of his tent **seven days**." (KJV)

31.) Leviticus 14:38 "Then the priest shall go out of the house to the door of the house, and shut up the house **seven days**:" (KJV)

32.) Leviticus 15:13 "And when he that hath an issue is cleansed of his issue; then he shall number to himself **seven days** for his cleansing, and wash his clothes, and bathe his flesh in running water, and shall be clean." (KJV)

33.) Leviticus 15:19 "And if a woman have an issue, *and* her issue in her flesh be blood, she shall be put apart **seven days**: and whosoever toucheth her shall be unclean until the even." (KJV)

34.) Leviticus 15:24 "And if any man lie with her at all, and her flowers be upon him, he shall be unclean **seven days**; and all the bed whereon he lieth shall be unclean." (KJV)

35.) Leviticus 15:28 "But if she be cleansed of her issue, then she shall number to herself **seven days**, and after that she shall be clean." (KJV)

36.) Leviticus 22:27 "When a bullock, or a sheep, or a goat, is brought forth, then it shall be **seven days** under the dam; and from the eighth day and thenceforth it shall be accepted for an offering made by fire unto the LORD." (KJV)

37.) Leviticus 23:6 "And on the fifteenth day of the same month *is* the feast of unleavened bread unto the LORD: **seven days** ye must eat unleavened bread." (KJV)

38.) Leviticus 23:8 "But ye shall offer an offering made by fire unto the LORD **seven days**: in the seventh day *is* an holy convocation: ye shall do no servile work *therein.*" (KJV)

39.) Leviticus 23:34 "Speak unto the children of Israel, saying, The fifteenth day of this seventh month *shall be* the feast of tabernacles *for* **seven days** unto the LORD." (KJV)

40.) Leviticus 23:36 "**Seven days** ye shall offer an offering made by fire unto the LORD: on the eighth day shall be an holy convocation unto you; and ye shall offer an offering made by fire unto the LORD: it *is* a solemn assembly; *and* ye shall do no servile work *therein.*" (KJV)

41.) Leviticus 23:39 "Also in the fifteenth day of the seventh month, when ye have gathered in the fruit of the land, ye shall keep a feast unto the LORD **seven days**: on the first day *shall be* a sabbath, and on the eighth day *shall be* a sabbath." (KJV)

42.) Leviticus 23:40 "And ye shall take you on the first day the boughs of goodly trees, branches of palm trees, and the boughs of thick trees, and willows of the brook; and ye shall rejoice before the LORD your God **seven days**." (KJV)

43.) Leviticus 23:41 "And ye shall keep it a feast unto the LORD **seven days** in the year. *It shall be* a statute for ever in your generations: ye shall celebrate it in the seventh month." (KJV)

44.) Leviticus 23:42 "Ye shall dwell in booths **seven days**; all that are Israelites born shall dwell in booths:" (KJV)

45. and 46.) Numbers 12:14 "And the LORD said unto Moses, If her father had but spit in her face, should she not be ashamed **seven days**? let her be shut out from the camp **seven days**, and after that let her be received in *again*." (KJV)

47.) Numbers 12:15 "And Miriam was shut out from the camp **seven days**: and the people journeyed not till Miriam was brought in *again*." (KJV)

48.) Numbers 19:11 "He that toucheth the dead body of any man shall be unclean **seven days**." (KJV)

49.) Numbers 19:14 "This *is* the law, when a man dieth in a tent: all that come into the tent, and all that *is* in the tent, shall be unclean **seven days**." (KJV)

50.) Numbers 19:16 "And whosoever toucheth one that is slain with a sword in the open fields, or a dead body, or a bone of a man, or a grave, shall be unclean **seven days**." (KJV)

51.) Numbers 28:17 "And in the fifteenth day of this month *is* the feast: **seven days** shall unleavened bread be eaten." (KJV)

52.) Numbers 28:24 "After this manner ye shall offer daily, throughout the **seven days**, the meat of the sacrifice made by fire, of a sweet savour unto the LORD: it shall be offered beside the continual burnt offering, and his drink offering." (KJV)

53.) Numbers 29:12 "And on the fifteenth day of the seventh month ye shall have an holy convocation; ye shall do no servile work, and ye shall keep a feast unto the LORD **seven days**:" (KJV)

54.) Numbers 31:19 "And do ye abide without the camp **seven days**: whosoever hath killed any person, and whosoever hath touched any slain, purify *both* yourselves and your captives on the third day, and on the seventh day." (KJV)

55.) Deuteronomy 16:3 "Thou shalt eat no leavened bread with it; **seven days** shalt thou eat unleavened bread therewith, *even* the bread of affliction; for thou camest forth out of the land of Egypt in haste: that thou mayest remember the day when thou camest forth out of the land of Egypt all the days of thy life." (KJV)

56.) Deuteronomy 16:4 "And there shall be no leavened bread seen with thee in all thy coast **seven days**; neither shall there *any thing* of the flesh, which thou sacrificedst the first day at even, remain all night until the morning." (KJV)

57.) Deuteronomy 16:13 "Thou shalt observe the feast of tabernacles **seven days**, after that thou hast gathered in thy corn and thy wine:" (KJV)

58.) Deuteronomy 16:15 "**Seven days** shalt thou keep a solemn feast unto the LORD thy God in the place which the LORD shall choose: because the LORD thy God shall bless thee in all thine increase, and in all the works of thine hands, therefore thou shalt surely rejoice." (KJV)

59.) Judges 14:12 "And Samson said unto them, I will now put forth a riddle unto you: if ye can certainly declare it me within the **seven days** of the feast, and find *it* out, then I will give you thirty sheets and thirty change of garments:" (KJV)

60.) Judges 14:17 "And she wept before him the **seven days**, while their feast lasted: and it came to pass on the seventh day, that he told her, because she lay sore upon him: and she told the riddle to the children of her people." (KJV)

61.) 1 Samuel 10:8 "And thou shalt go down before me to Gilgal; and, behold, I will come down unto thee, to offer burnt offerings, *and* to sacrifice sacrifices of peace offerings: **seven days** shalt thou tarry, till I come to thee, and shew thee what thou shalt do." (KJV)

62.) 1 Samuel 11:3 "And the elders of Jabesh said unto him, Give us **seven days**' respite, that we may send messengers unto all the coasts of Israel: and then, if *there be* no man to save us, we will come out to thee." (KJV)

63.) 1 Samuel 13:8 "And he tarried **seven days**, according to the set time that Samuel *had appointed:* but Samuel came not to Gilgal; and the people were scattered from him." (KJV)

64.) 1 Samuel 31:13 "And they took their bones, and buried *them* under a tree at Jabesh, and fasted **seven days**." (KJV)

65. and 66.) 1 Kings 8:65 "And at that time Solomon held a feast, and all Israel with him, a great congregation, from the entering in of Hamath unto the river of Egypt, before the LORD our God, **seven days** and **seven days**, *even* fourteen days." (KJV)

67.) 1 Kings 16:15 "In the twenty and seventh year of Asa king of Judah did Zimri reign **seven days** in Tirzah. And the people *were* encamped against Gibbethon, which *belonged* to the Philistines." (KJV)

68.) 1 Kings 20:29 "And they pitched one over against the other **seven days**. And *so* it was, that in the seventh day the battle was joined: and the children of Israel slew of the Syrians an hundred thousand footmen in one day." (KJV)

69.) 2 Kings 3:9 "So the king of Israel went, and the king of Judah, and the king of Edom: and they fetched a compass of **seven days**' journey: and there was no water for the host, and for the cattle that followed them." (KJV)

70.) 1 Chronicles 9:25 "And their brethren, *which were* in their villages, *were* to come after **seven days** from time to time with them." (KJV)

71.) 1 Chronicles 10:12 "They arose, all the valiant men, and took away the body of Saul, and the bodies of his sons, and brought them to Jabesh, and buried their bones under the oak in Jabesh, and fasted **seven days**." (KJV)

72.) 2 Chronicles 7:8 "Also at the same time Solomon kept the feast **seven days**, and all Israel with him, a very great congregation, from the entering in of Hamath unto the river of Egypt." (KJV)

73.) 2 Chronicles 7:9 "And in the eighth day they made a solemn assembly: for they kept the dedication of the altar **seven days**, and the feast **seven days**." (KJV)

74.) 2 Chronicles 30:21 "And the children of Israel that were present at Jerusalem kept the feast of unleavened bread **seven days** with great gladness: and the Levites and the priests praised the LORD day by day, *singing* with loud instruments unto the LORD." (KJV)

75.) 2 Chronicles 30:22 "And Hezekiah spake comfortably unto all the Levites that taught the good knowledge of the LORD: and they did eat throughout the feast **seven days**, offering peace offerings, and making confession to the LORD God of their fathers." (KJV)

76. and 77.) 2 Chronicles 30:23 "And the whole assembly took counsel to keep other **seven days**: and they kept *other* **seven days** with gladness." (KJV)

78.) 2 Chronicles 35:17 "And the children of Israel that were present kept the passover at that time, and the feast of unleavened bread **seven days**." (KJV)

79.) Ezra 6:22 "And kept the feast of unleavened bread **seven days** with joy: for the LORD had made them joyful, and turned the heart of the king of Assyria unto them, to strengthen their hands in the work of the house of God, the God of Israel." (KJV)

80.) Nehemiah 8:18 "Also day by day, from the first day unto the last day, he read in the book of the law of God. And they kept the feast **seven day**s; and on the eighth day *was* a solemn assembly, according unto the manner." (KJV)

81.) Esther 1:5 "And when these days were expired, the king made a feast unto all the people that were present in Shushan the palace, both unto great and small, **seven days**, in the court of the garden of the king's palace;" (KJV)

82.) Job 2:13 "So they sat down with him upon the ground **seven days** and seven nights, and none spake a word unto him: for they saw that *his* grief was very great." (KJV)

83.) Isaiah 30:26 "Moreover the light of the moon shall be as the light of the sun, and the light of the sun shall be sevenfold, as the light of **seven days**, in the day that the LORD bindeth up the breach of his people, and healeth the stroke of their wound." (KJV)

84.) Ezekiel 3:15 "Then I came to them of the captivity at Telabib, that dwelt by the river of Chebar, and I sat where they sat, and remained there astonished among them **seven days**." (KJV)

85.) Ezekiel 3:16 "And it came to pass at the end of **seven days**, that the word of the LORD came unto me, saying," (KJV)

86.) Ezekiel 43:25 "**Seven days** shalt thou prepare every day a goat *for* a sin offering: they shall also prepare a young bullock, and a ram out of the flock, without blemish." (KJV)

87.) Ezekiel 43:26 "**Seven days** shall they purge the altar and purify it; and they shall consecrate themselves." (KJV)

88.) Ezekiel 44:26 "And after he is cleansed, they shall reckon unto him **seven days**." (KJV)

89.) Ezekiel 45:21 "In the first *month,* in the fourteenth day of the month, ye shall have the passover, a feast of **seven days**; unleavened bread shall be eaten." (KJV)

90.) Ezekiel 45:23 "And **seven days** of the feast he shall prepare a burnt offering to the LORD, seven bullocks and seven rams without blemish daily the **seven days**; and a kid of the goats daily *for* a sin offering." (KJV)

91.) Ezekiel 45:25 "In the seventh *month,* in the fifteenth day of the month, shall he do the like in the feast of the **seven days**, according to the sin offering, according to the burnt offering, and according to the meat offering, and according to the oil." (KJV)

Since *YOM SHEBIY'IY* (Seventh Day) and *YOMIM SHEBAH* (Seven Days) are never used to describe an age of time anywhere else in the Bible, what clue do we have that the days of the Genesis Creation Account describe long ages?

Ask yourself this question: When you want to describe something that can be measured in units, what units of measure do you generally use? You use the one that best fits the item or situation. For instance, if you wanted to describe the displacement of a battleship, what unit of weight would you use? Since a battleship can weigh 45,000 tons or more, I don't think you would say the battleship weighs 1,440,000,000 ounces. On the other hand, if you were describing the weight of a butterfly, would you say it weighs one-half gram or would you say it weighs 0.00000052 ton? I'm sure you would use grams. If you wanted to describe the length of a football field, you would say it was 100 yards, not 0.0000000000000097 light-years. In our language and culture, we most commonly use the units of measure that best fit the things we are measuring in the context of what we are describing. Now, I'm going to speculate that all languages and cultures are similar in this respect. So, that means I'm extending my speculation to the ancient Hebrew people. I speculate that the measurements used in the Old Testament are best put into the context of ancient Hebrew language and culture. This means we can look at the units of measure mentioned in any context and get an idea about what range of time, weight, or length the Bible is talking about by looking at it from their culture.

What does the word "day" mean in Genesis 1 when it is combined with a number in their culture? When we compare it to every other place in Scripture where the same form of those numbers are used with the same form of "day," it always means a regular, twenty-four-hour day. *YOM ECHAD* (One Day) is used 34 times in the Old Testament. *YOM SHENIY* (Second Day) is used 16 times. *YOM SHELIYSHIY* (Third Day) is used 32 times. *YOM REBIY'IY* (Fourth Day) is used 8 times. *YOM CHAMIYSHIY* (Fifth Day) is used 4 times. *YOM SHISHSHIY* (Sixth Day) is used 6 times. *YOM SHEBIY'IY* (Seventh Day) is used either 47 or 48 times. These are the very words used to describe the days in Genesis 1. These are the very words the ancient Hebrews used to describe regular, ordinary, everyday twenty-four-hour days. All total, *YOM* is combined with these numbers about

148 times. God gives no clues anywhere in the Bible these are anything other than Hebrew days; real twenty-four-hour days. In every other portion of the Bible, when these modifiers are attached to "day," it refers to a twenty-four-hour period. God gives no clues He is using *YOM* in any other way for the seven days in the Genesis Creation Account. If He intended for us to interpret the seven days as anything but seven literal twenty-four-hour periods, He would have given us a clue. He would have included some kind of literary device to indicate His intended meaning. In other words, the context would contain something to show He was speaking in symbolic, figurative terms. Does the Genesis Creation Account contain any such indicators? No! There is nothing in the account to hint the context is anything else but the real, physical, time-and-space heavens and earth. The heavens are the real physical heavens. The earth is the real physical earth. The ocean is the real physical ocean. The dry land is the real physical dry land. The sun, the moon, the stars, the light, the dark, the fish, the birds, the plants, the animals, and Adam and Eve are all the real deal. Nothing about them is figurative, non-literal, or mystical. There are no clues that God intends for us to interpret the Genesis Creation Account in a mystical, magical fashion. Everything in Genesis shouts, "Hey, people. These are days; not ages!"

The Bible clearly describes the first *YOM* as a regular day. It does the same for the second *YOM* and the third *YOM*. Now, even if I tried to close my eyes and pretend I didn't see God's clear definition of *YOM* for the first three days, I could no longer pretend *YOM* was an age by the time I got to the fourth *YOM*. Why? It's because the Bible mentions a greater light during the DAY and a lesser light during the NIGHT on the fourth *YOM*. What were these two lights? They were the sun and the moon. On the fourth *YOM*, God connects the sun with the light period—the day. He connects the moon and stars with the dark period—the night. Even if *YOM* was a long period of time for the first three days, it couldn't be a long period of time for the last three days. By adding this information about the sun, the moon, and the stars, we cannot mistake God's intent. God is talking about regular days and regular nights. This creates a conflict with the Day-Age Theory. Up to this point, the only life God had created (restored) was land vegetation. (Day Three) It was days five and six when God created life in the oceans and animal life on the land. Day-Agers contend that "days" five and six had to be a period of about 400 million years. By pointing out how these periods of time were marked by the presence of the sun during the day, and the moon and stars during the night, God says these were two days. I'll leave it to you to decide whom you want to believe.

YOM by itself can mean an age of time. However, when *YOM* is used in context with modifiers and companion words with specific meanings, then *YOM* takes on that same specific meaning. This is exactly what we see in our language. Let me give you an example. Let's say I looked out my window and told you, "There's a pig in my garden." Without looking out my window, what image comes to mind? Well, you'd probably think of a four-footed animal with a short snout and a curly tail. That's the most common meaning of the word "pig." Ah, but in the 1960's, "pig" was a derogatory word for "policeman." Couldn't someone argue I was looking at a police officer in my garden? Yes. Even though "policeman" is not the usual definition of "pig," such an argument could be grammatically correct. Now, if I said, "There's a pig and a cow in my garden," wouldn't it make the definition of "pig" be a little more specific? Of course it would. As soon as I added a companion word with such a specific meaning, it would be difficult to think I was telling you there was a police officer and a cow in my garden. Furthermore, if I said, "There's a pig and a cow in my garden; and I'm talking porcine and bovine," then it would be impossible to mistake my meaning. Finally, if I said, "There's a small animal called a pig and a large animal called a cow in my garden," then only a fool would think I was talking about a police officer.

This is exactly what God does with the word *YOM* (day). Its most common meaning is an ordinary day. To make this meaning clear to us, He adds the specific companion word, *LAYIL* (night). He then adds two more companion words, *BOQER* (morning) and *EREB* (evening) to make His meaning more exact. Finally, to make His meaning impossible to mistranslate, He adds two more companion words, *OWR* (light) and *CHOSHEK* (dark). The creation account in Genesis cannot be subjected to twisted interpretations. Night always means night. Morning always means morning. Evening always means evening. When used in reference to time, all of these words refer to portions of the normal twenty-four-hour day. By adding the words "light" and "dark" in reference to measurable periods of time, God makes it evident He's talking about real days and nights. By referring to them as one day, and as the second day, and the third day, on up to the seventh day, He makes it evident He's talking about a real seven-day week. By mentioning the sun in the day and the moon at night, it means these are not ages. It is glaringly obvious that "day" can only be translated in the same way its companion words are, and that is a literal day. Clearly, six literal days are not compatible with the Day-Age Theory. So, who's wrong; God or the Day-Agers?

If the Six "Days" are Ages, What are the Six "Nights"?

If the Day-Age Theory is correct, then the six day-ages of creation span fourteen billion years. This interpretation of "day" creates another problem. According to Day-Agers each "day" was about two billion years long on the average. But according to the Bible, each "day" had ONE day and ONE night. Each "day" had ONE morning and ONE evening. Each "day" is said to consist of a single period of dark and a single period of light. Each "day" had a period of time when the sun dominated the light portion and each "day" had a period of time when the moon dominated the dark portion. The Bible says each "day" had an evening (*EREB* in the singular) and a morning (*BOQER* in the singular). It doesn't say each "day" had evenings and mornings. Each "day" consisted of one *YOM* (day in the singular) and one *LAYIL* (night in the singular). Each "day" had a single period of *OWR* (light) and a single period of *CHOSHEK* (dark). Each single light period followed each single dark period. God used the singular forms to describe each period of light and each period of dark. The Hebrew can't be translated that each "day" had billions of mornings and billions of evenings unless the plural forms of these words were used. God didn't use the plural forms. Since there were six instances of the singular forms, then there were six singular periods of light and six singular periods of dark. If each "day-age" consisted of a single period of light (day) and a single period of dark (night), then we would be forced to believe the absurd notion that each light period would have been a billion years long and each dark period would have been a billion years long. Now, what would happen to living things if the earth was subjected to periods of total darkness lasting a billion years? What would happen to living things if the earth was subjected to periods of total light lasting a billion years? The earth would be a frozen ball of ice for a billion years and then it would be molten for a billion years. No lifeform could withstand a billion years of constant darkness or a billion years of constant light. Now, I admit no one believes the periods of light and periods of dark lasted a billion years. Yet once you accept the notion each "day" had billions of days and billions of nights, you have to wonder why God said each day had only one day and one night. The Day-Age Theory doesn't fit well through the filter of Scripture.

If the "Days" are Long Ages, Then How Did Certain Plants Reproduce?

As I have mentioned, the Day-Age Theory has a problem with the order of strata seen in the geological layers. Making the "days" into long ages doesn't correct the incorrect order of geologic appearance. Besides not correcting the geology problem, it creates an even bigger biology problem. If the Day-Age Theory is true, then the "days" of Genesis 1 were extremely long periods of time. If the "days" represent billions of years, then a problem arises with the survival of many species. There are numerous species of plants that require animals in order to reproduce. Thousands of flowering plants require an animal (bees, butterflies, wasps, hummingbirds, *etc.*) to pollinate them. Sometimes it's species specific. There is a species of Yucca plant, for instance, that requires a particular species of Yucca moth to carry its pollen. Only that Yucca moth has the ability to do this. Certain fig trees need certain fig-wasps to do their pollinating. The seeds of many seed-bearing plants must pass through the digestive tracts of animals to be softened before they can germinate. All of these plants, created on Day Three, would have had to wait millions of years before the necessary animals were created on days five and six. How could they have survived millions of years without being able to reproduce?

The Universe is Only Six Seconds Old

In spite of all the Biblical evidence the seven *YOM*s of the Genesis Creation Account were literal, twenty-four-hour days, there are plenty of scholars who believe the "days" are long periods of time. They ignore the evidence, and base their belief on this one desperate line of reasoning: There is nothing in the context that indicates the "days" cannot be long periods of time. Well, they're right except for the part where they say there is nothing in the context that indicates the "days" cannot be long periods of time. The truth of the matter is this: There is nothing in the context that indicates the days are anything but literal, twenty-four-hour days. Using their logic, I could insist *YOM* means a second. The heavens and the earth and all that is in them were created in six seconds. God then rested on the seventh second. There is nothing in the context that indicates the "days" cannot be seconds. With such a creative creation interpretation, I could insist the universe was created six seconds ago. Everything in it that indicates a greater age is merely an illusion created by God to give the appearance of age. (I'll talk about Apparent Age in the next chapter.) That means everything you think happened in the past, never really happened. That means you came into existence with this book in your hand and a "created memory" of having read it up to this point. There is nothing in the context of the Genesis Creation Account that could disprove this idea, but you would have to be a fool to believe it.

The Really Big Problem: Day-Age Weakens the Gospel

In addition to creating more scientific problems, the Day-Age Theory creates a bigger Biblical problem. According to Hebrew scholars, it is risky to interpret a word or phrase in a unique fashion if it is defined throughout the Bible in a different way. There is a danger in accepting a unique definition as a way of defending your favorite doctrine. Once you do it, you have no basis for objecting to someone else's unique definition as a way of defending their favorite doctrine. To defend the Day-Age Theory, you have to accept these unique meanings of words:

1.) *LAYIL* would have to have a unique meaning. (One night must equal an age.)
2.) *EREB* would have to have a unique meaning. (One evening must equal an age.)
3.) *BOQER* would have to have a unique meaning. (One morning must equal an age.)

That's the only way one *YOM* in the Genesis Creation Account could equal an age.

Furthermore:

4.) The combination of *YOM* and *LAYIL* would have to have a unique meaning.
5.) The combination of *EREB* and *BOQER* would have to have a unique meaning.
6.) The combination of a numerical modifier and *YOM* would have to have a unique meaning.

If we allow these words to mean something other than what they plainly mean, then we find ourselves with some real problems in trying to understand the Bible's account of creation. As bad as it is to have a theological problem with creation, an even bigger theological problem arises if we permit this same kind of liberty with word usage elsewhere in the Bible.

Jesus said He would be in the grave three days and three nights (Matthew 12:40). What if someone said these were three ages? On what grammatical basis could you prove their interpretation was wrong? If you insisted "day" in Genesis meant an age, how could you say they were wrong if they insisted "day" in Matthew also meant an age? You couldn't! You'd have no right to say they were wrong. Their New Testament Day-Age Theory would be just as valid as your Old Testament Day-Age Theory, but what would that mean to Christianity? It would mean Jesus is not alive today. It would mean He is still dead and in the grave. It would mean His disciples and followers didn't really see Him alive after the crucifixion. It would mean everything we believe as Christians is a lie. It would mean the Gospel accounts are not true. It would mean Paul's epistles are based on a lie. None of the New Testament could be considered reliable or historical. It would mean the New Testament writers were lying to us.

Dear, dear Day-Age creationists friends, it is a dangerous thing to allow man's interpretations to overshadow God's declarations. We are in real danger of turning the resurrection of Christ into a meaningless yarn if we can't trust God to define the meaning of "day." **We give ammunition to the atheists when we present "Biblical" arguments that are not Biblically true.** The six days of creation in Genesis must be regular twenty-four-hour days. If "day" can mean something else in the creation accounts, then "day" can mean something else in the resurrection accounts. If that is possible, then we have no defense for the visible, physical resurrection of Our Lord three days after His crucifixion.

Chapter Five: Young-Earth Solutions

The geological record and the Biblical record don't match, or at least they don't seem to match. Now, I hope you're astute enough to see where I'm going with these geological problems. The difficulty is that most people think the geological strata and the six days of Genesis are records of the same event. They assume geology is the PHYSICAL RECORD of the six days of creation and the Bible is the WRITTEN RECORD of the six days of creation. But, what if they aren't the same event? What if the geological strata are a historical record of something other than the six days of Genesis? If this were so, then we wouldn't necessarily expect the Biblical order of appearances to match the geological order of appearances. There are two ways this problem can be resolved.

The first solution is Flood-Geology. If Young-Earth/Flood-Geologists are correct, then the geological strata have nothing to do with the order of creation in Genesis 1. Regardless of the sequence of creation, things got jumbled up during the Flood. The six days of Genesis record the order of creation, but geology records the results of the Flood. This is why Young-Earthers must be Flood-Geologists. If the geological strata were not caused by the Flood, then Young-Earthers have the very same problems with geology the Day-Agers have.

The second solution is the Restoration Theory. I believe the Gap Theory resolves these problems in a better way. Here's how: The geological strata record the original creation (Genesis 1:1) over a long period of time, while the six days of Genesis record the restoration (Genesis 1:3-31) that happened over a short period of time. The orders of appearance don't match because they are two different creations. Geology is a physical record of the first beginning, and the six days of Genesis are a written record of the second beginning. Earth has had two beginnings. More on that later; let's now look at the Young-Earth Theory.

The Young-Earth Theory

Many, many, many... very many Christians today believe the Young-Earth Theory. In fact, some believe it so strongly, they consider those who don't believe it to be false Christians. Few, few, few... very few Christians today realize the Modern Young-Earth Theory differs from the Historic Young-Earth Theory. Actually, there were two versions of the Historic Young-Earth Theory that differed only in their explanations of fossils.

The Historic Young-Earth Theory had a problem with the fossils. It was the same problem the Day-Age Theory had. The order of the creation of those organisms in Genesis did not match the order of the appearance of their fossils found in the geologic strata. Initially that was no problem. One version of the Historic Young-Earth Theory said the fossils had no biological significance. They were merely geological oddities, strange rocks, created in the strata by God for the purpose of making people think they were the remains of ancient lifeforms. That way He could damn them to hell for thinking they were the remains of ancient lifeforms.

It probably doesn't surprise you that very few Historic Young-Earth creationists favored this version. It was ludicrous! Most defenders of the Historic Young-Earth Theory realized the fossils had to be the remains of once-living plants and animals. So, the other version of the Historic Young-Earth Theory said the fossils were the remains of organisms that died after Adam fell. (No death before Adam sinned.) Their version of the Young-Earth Theory stated that all the fossiliferous strata were laid down between the fall of Adam and the time of Noah. Granted, this allowed only about 1,600 years for all the mountains, valleys, canyons, and geologic strata to form, but that could be explained. It had to do with God cursing the ground because of Adam's sin. God's curse of the ground (from the time of Adam to the time of Noah) apparently involved tremendous geologic forces capable of shaping the face of the earth. (Besides, it was 1,600X easier than doing it all in one year as proposed by the Modern Young-Earth/Flood-Geology Theory.) As difficult as it was to explain geology with this theory, it eliminated the problem with the order of the appearance of the fossils. The fossils were laid down after the six days, so they had no connection with the six days.

Most Young-Earth creationists today think the Young-Earth Theory has been the most popular and accepted theory from time immemorial. Now, the Historic Young-Earth Theory had been around for millennia, but even then, it was not as widely accepted as some think. Even though it was commonly believed, the Historic Young-Earth Theory was largely abandoned by the 1800's because it didn't agree with science. Most Young-Earth Theory defenders today don't realize their version of creation, the Modern Young-Earth Theory, had its origin in the mid 1800's to early 1900's—it's not an ancient interpretation. It flowed from the mind of Ellen White (1827-1915). Ellen White was the "Prophetess" and spiritual leader of The Seventh-Day Adventist cult. (The Seventh-Day Adventist Church of today is not what it was a hundred years ago. From what I've been told, it is now considered to be more in line with accepted Christianity. Nevertheless, at the time of Ellen White, it was very much a cult.) Ellen White came up with the Modern Young-Earth Theory by explaining how the geologic strata and fossils were created. Unlike the Historic Young-Earth Theory, Ellen White said all the strata and fossils were created by Noah's Flood. This phenomenon was called, "Flood-Geology."

Ellen White's theory didn't agree with science either, but that didn't slow her down. She added a new twist by using Flood-Geology to explain the strata and fossils. I'm not saying the belief that Noah's Flood altered and shaped the face of the earth to some degree was new, but the idea it was solely responsible for ALL of geology was a radical concept. Certainly, many Christians before the 18th century believed fossils may have been deposited by Noah's Flood, but they had no grasp of the enormous amounts of strata that would have had to be upturned and deposited at that same time. To them, fossils seemed like a surface phenomenon only. They had no idea the fossil-bearing strata were so very thick. (The average thickness of sedimentary rock on land is over one mile. There are places on earth with over twelve miles of sediment.[5]) On the average, in order to deposit a one-mile thick layer of sediment ON the entire surface of the earth, the waters of the Noah's Flood had to first scour a one-mile deep layer of soil and rock FROM the entire surface of the earth. Imagine the force it would take for water to suspend and carry the entire weight of all the sedimentary layers now deposited on the earth. The waters of Noah's Flood had to be insanely tumultuous and violent. Whether or not Flood-Geology had been proposed before, it sprang into popularity when Ellen White made it an essential doctrine for her religion. Reject it, and you reject her. Reject her, and you burn for eternity. (So she claimed.)

At this point you are probably wondering how she came up with Flood-Geology. The answer is simple: She claimed God "took her back" to witness the Creation and the Flood in "visions." In fact, she said she had hundreds of "visions" where God directly revealed things to her; things He didn't reveal to the apostles or prophets. God "took her back" 6,000 years ago so she could witness the Creation for herself. God "took her back" to the time of Noah so she could see why He flooded the earth. According to White, it was because humans were crossbreeding with animals and producing tainted offspring. She called this, "The Amalgamation." That's why God picked Noah and his family (apparently, they were the last of the pure Adamic blood) and why He picked two (untainted) animals of each species to repopulate the earth. Of course, "Amalgamation" is biological impossible… but what does science mean when you have such a juicy theory. God "told" her this is what happened. God also "told" her how coal was formed during the Flood. He "told" her that vast amounts of trees were buried by the sediment brought on by the Flood. The wood quickly petrified and then turned to coal. It sounds interesting, but there is a problem with this explanation. Petrified wood is created when minerals (iron, calcite, manganese, copper, silicates, *etc*.) leach into wood and replace all the organic material. While coal is almost pure carbon, there is no carbon in petrified wood. Petrified wood cannot turn into coal because it has no carbon. Again, God "told" her something scientifically impossible. God also "told" her the Amalgamation continued after the Flood, and He "told" her that some humans are not fully human:

> "Since the flood there has been amalgamation of man and beast, as may be seen in the almost endless varieties of species of animals, and in certain races of men."[6]

Ellen White believed, "certain races of men," were not fully human. (Don't ask me what races she was talking about… I'll let you fill in the blanks.) Since God "told" her this, I guess God forgot He told Luke something different; all men come from one bloodline.

Acts 17:26 "And hath made of one blood all nations of men for to dwell on all the face of the earth, and hath determined the times before appointed, and the bounds of their habitation;" (KJV)

Ellen White's unscientific and blasphemous teachings about the Creation and the Flood were picked up by one of her Seventh-Day Adventist cult followers, George McCready Price. (1870-1963) Price was an amateur geologist who defended and expanded White's Young-Earth and Flood-Geology Theories. Although ignored by real geologists and by real Christians, his writings gave birth to the Modern Young-Earth/Creation-Science movement in the early 1960's when some Young-Earth creationists began using Price's material as the foundation for their own books, lectures, and teachings. Virtually all of today's Modern Young-Earth/Flood-Geology organizations teach and defend Ellen White's views and beliefs about the creation and the Flood. (Do an Internet search on "Ellen White, George McCready Price, and Flood-Geology" to confirm this for yourself.) A cult has wormed its way into the Church, and the worst part is it has been kept secret. Most Modern Young-Earth defenders don't know the truth about the origin of their beliefs, but many do. Her lie has deceived millions of Bible-believing Christians.

Many say the Young-Earth Theory was never challenged until the coming of the age of science. This isn't so. Long before our modern scientific age, people wondered about the age of the earth. For as long as historical records have shown, there have been different cosmologies, religions, and philosophies trying to answer why and how and when we got here. Christians aren't the only people who have wondered about the age of the earth. The problem is that humanity hasn't been able to agree on what source of information is reliable. Do we trust the ancient pagan religions? Do we trust the Chinese calendar? Do we trust the ancient Greek philosophers? Do we trust science? How about the Mayan calendars? Where do we find truth? As Christians, we know we have THE source of truth, but that source of truth doesn't actually tell us when God created the heavens and the earth. This may shock you, but it is true. The Bible does not say! There is no statement in the Bible that says God created the universe on any particular date. **All creation chronologies derived from the Bible are Biblical INTERPRETATIONS, not Biblical DECLARATIONS.**

Oh, I know Young-Earth creationists will disagree. They say they believe what the Bible "literally" says. Let's check their claim. If you take your handy exhaustive concordance of the *King James Bible* (The 1769 version) and look up the word "thousand," you will see it is used 521 times. If you narrow the search to "thousand years," you will find only 10 matches. Here are those verses:

1.) Psalms 90:4 "For a **thousand years** in thy sight *are but* as yesterday when it is past, and *as* a watch in the night." (KJV)

2.) Ecclesiastes 6:6 "Yea, though he live a **thousand years** twice *told,* yet hath he seen no good: do not all go to one place?" (KJV)

3. and 4.) 2 Peter 3:8 "But, beloved, be not ignorant of this one thing, that one day *is* with the Lord as a **thousand years**, and a **thousand years** as one day." (KJV)

5. – 10.) Revelation 20:2-7 "And he laid hold on the dragon, that old serpent, which is the Devil, and Satan, and bound him a **thousand years**, *{3}* And cast him into the bottomless pit, and shut him up, and set a seal upon him, that he should deceive the nations no more, till the **thousand years** should be fulfilled: and after that he must be loosed a little season. *{4}* And I saw thrones, and they sat upon them, and judgment was given unto them: and *I saw* the souls of them that were beheaded for the witness of Jesus, and for the word of God, and which had not worshipped the beast, neither his image, neither had received *his* mark upon their foreheads, or in their hands; and they lived and reigned with Christ a **thousand years**. *{5}* But the rest of the dead lived not again until the **thousand years** were finished. This *is* the first resurrection. *{6}* Blessed and holy *is* he that hath part in the first resurrection: on such the second death hath no power, but they shall be priests of God and of Christ, and shall reign with him a **thousand years**. *{7}* And when the **thousand years** are expired, Satan shall be loosed out of his prison," (KJV)

    As you can see, there is not a single verse in Scripture that uses "thousand" and "years" in connection with the age of the earth. Six of those uses are in the Book of the Revelation of Jesus Christ where it refers to the future thousand-year reign of Christ and the binding of Satan; they don't describe the creation. The other "thousand years" verses don't say anything about when the earth was created either. The Bible doesn't literally say the earth is "six-thousand," "eight-thousand," "ten-thousand," or "any-thousand years old." Those words are not in the Bible. When a Young-Earth creationist tells you his interpretation is the "literal" interpretation of the Bible, you can now show him he is wrong. The Bible doesn't literally say that. So, while there is not a single declaration that the earth is young in God's WORD, there are multiple declarations that the earth is old in God's WORK.

    All the creation chronologies generated by Young-Earth creationists are derived from interpretations of Scripture. The most famous of these creation chronologies is the 1650 Ussher Chronology. James Ussher (1581-1656) was the Archbishop of Armagh (Northern Ireland). By looking at the genealogies in the Old Testament and comparing them with some known historical events, Archbishop Ussher decided the universe was created on October 23, 4004 B.C. There have been others who have done similar chronologies with other specific dates, but Ussher's date has been the accepted view by many Christians. After all, it seems reasonable that you could look at the genealogies ("so-in-so" begat "so-in-so") in the Old Testament and calculate the age of the earth. It's not that easy.

    The reliability of this dating technique has been disputed for as long as it has been proposed. It is argued that "begat" (*YALAD*—Strong's Number H3502) doesn't necessarily mean being the direct father of someone. It can mean grandfather, great-grandfather, great-great-grandfather, *etc.* This means there could be gaps in the names mentioned in the genealogies.

It's tempting to exploit this idea, but I'm not going to get into this argument. At best, it is a weak argument. Even if there are gaps in the genealogies, I don't think we could get millions of years from Adam to me. That would require a tremendous number of gaps and/or extremely long gaps. It still seems we would be looking in the range of thousands of years. So, while I won't argue the meaning of "begat," I will point out the problem with Ussher's conclusion. Deriving dates from the genealogies can only determine the time of the creation of Adam; not the creation of the heavens and the earth. Ussher first assumed there was no gap of time between Genesis 1:1 and Genesis 1:3. The Gap Theory and the idea the universe was very old were discussed long before Ussher was born. In fact, as we will see later, the Gap Theory predates the Christian Church. Ussher rejected an old earth out of hand. His logic was based on circular reasoning. He assumed the earth was young, (no long gap of time before Adam) and since he concluded the earth was young, he believed his original assumption was correct. This kind of chronology didn't disprove the Gap Theory because it was based on the assumption, not on the evidence, the Gap Theory was untrue. It didn't prove the earth was young; it merely ignored the possibility of the earth being old.

Why is this important? Because Young-Earth creationists still use this same faulty logic. They insist the Gap Theory can't be true because the genealogies prove the universe is young. Their "proof" doesn't prove anything. They don't seem to understand how the gap came before the genealogies and has nothing to do with the genealogies. They bring circular reasoning to their defense. They believe that since Adam was created on the sixth day of all time, (six literal days after the beginning of time and space) and since the genealogies prove Adam was created six thousand years ago, then the time since the creation must be six thousand years. But, that is not a logical argument, nor a Biblical necessity. As we have seen, there is no verse in the Bible that connects "days" with "thousands" when describing creation. Their connection is entirely man-made. Six twenty-four-hour days don't prove the universe is young unless you first assume there was no long gap of time before the six twenty-four-hour days. Let me give an event from my life to show you how they err.

One summer, I decided to put a new roof on my house. Being somewhat handy with tools, and desiring to save myself a bunch of money, I decided I would do it myself. I tore off the old shingles, laid down new tar paper, and hammered all the new shingles into place. I must say I did a very nice job, too. In fact, I put more care into the project than most professional roofers; it was my house! It took me seven days to complete this project, but it was a job done well; it was very good. Now, here's my question: In what year did I re-roof my house; how long ago was it?

You can't know, can you? The fact it took seven days doesn't tell you when it happened. "Seven days" describes a period of time, not a point in time. There is insufficient data to be able to determine a date. The only way the seven days could be used to calculate a date would be if you knew it was seven days from a reference date. Without a reference date, you wouldn't know if it was last year or ten years ago. I would have to supply you with a starting date before you could calculate when it happened. If I didn't give you a starting date, then a seven-day time period doesn't solve anything. The Bible doesn't give us a starting date for the seven days of creation. **The seven days in Genesis describe a period of time, not a point in time.** The fact it was seven days doesn't tell us when it happened. It doesn't prove the earth is young unless you first know there was no gap of time before the seven days started. Young-Earth creationists assume there was no gap of time before the seven days started. Then, based on that assumption, they conclude their assumption is correct. This is circular reasoning on a par with the circular reasoning of evolutionists. (By the way, I did my roofing project during the summer of 1981… I thought some might want the answer.)

Was There Death Before Adam Sinned?

There are other flawed arguments Young-Earthers use against the Gap Theory. Over the years, I have seen Young-Earth creationists repeatedly try to destroy the Gap Theory by using an argument that "proves" they are right. Let me refute this argument. Young-Earth creationists insist the Restoration Theory is wrong because it means death reigned before Adam. Gap Theory creationists look at the geological strata and say all those fossils (dead things) were formed before Adam was created. Young-Earth creationists become indignant when they hear this. They believe there was no death before Adam sinned. "By one man sin entered into the world, and death by sin," they'll quote. According to them, Romans 5:12 and 1 Corinthians 15:21 prove there was no death before Adam sinned. If you question them, however, most Young-Earth creationists admit some kind of death must have existed before Adam's fall. For example, plants died when eaten.

Sadly, some Young-Earth creationists violently object even to this idea. They say plants don't actually have life, therefore they cannot die. They cite several verses as a way of defending their belief.

Genesis 1:21 "And God created great whales, and every **living creature** that moveth, which the waters brought forth abundantly, after their kind, and every winged fowl after his kind: and God saw that *it was* good." (KJV)

Genesis 1:24 "And God said, Let the earth bring forth the **living creature** after his kind, cattle, and creeping thing, and beast of the earth after his kind: and it was so." (KJV)

Genesis 2:7 "And the LORD God formed man *of* the dust of the ground, and breathed into his nostrils the **breath** of **life**; and man became a **living soul**." (KJV)

Genesis 2:19 "And out of the ground the LORD God formed every beast of the field, and every fowl of the air; and brought *them* unto Adam to see what he would call them: and whatsoever Adam called every **living creature**, that *was* the name thereof." (KJV)

The Hebrew word for "life" and "living" is *CHAY* (Strong's Number H2416). "Breath" is *NESHAMAH* (Strong's Number H5397). The word for "creature," "soul," or "being" is *NEPHESH* (Strong's Number H5315). Since these words are used in connection with animals and man, but never with plants, these Young-Earth creationists say plants do not have life. Because they do not have life, they cannot die. They explain it this way: Plants are destroyed when eaten, but they don't die. In order to defend their idea of, "No-Death-Before-Adam-Sinned," they say plants cannot die... I can't wait to get to heaven to hear them tell Jesus how ignorant He was when He made the following statement:

John 12:24 "I tell you the truth, unless a kernel of wheat falls to the ground and **dies**, it remains only a single seed. But if it **dies**, it produces many seeds." (NIV)

Jesus thought seeds could die. But, the only way something can die is if it was alive. Rocks can be destroyed without dying. Automobiles can be destroyed without dying. Computers can be destroyed without dying. Seeds don't fit that category according to Jesus. Jesus said seeds can die. That means Jesus thought seeds were alive. That means seeds have life... and He should know. But, how can seeds have life if plants don't have life? Seeds come from plants. How can living seeds come from non-living plants? This is what has to happen if seeds have life but plants don't. In order to believe this Young-Earth nonsense, you have to believe life can arise from non-life. But, that is abiogenesis. That's the very thing evolutionists use to explain the origin of life. Evolutionists say life arose from a mixture of non-living chemicals, and if plants don't have life, that's all they are; a mixture of non-living chemicals. These Young-Earth creationists are so entrenched in the belief there was no death before Adam sinned, they wind up believing in abiogenesis just like the evolutionists. Young-Earth creationists are willing to reject the teachings of Jesus and the facts of biology, just so they can defend their anti-Biblical, anti-scientific interpretation of creation. They reject the Words of God and they reject the works of God. Why would any Christian be willing to defend a theory that rejects the teachings of Jesus? Please, Young-Earth creationists, be careful what you believe. In the eyes of unbelievers, you are making Jesus look foolish.

This "Animals-Die-but-Plants-Don't" explanation is purely a human invention. It is not found in the Bible. Furthermore, it is based firmly on science from the 1700's. Back then, science divided living organisms into two Kingdoms: Plants and Animals. Today we know there are many living organisms that are neither plant nor animal. In fact, science recognizes at least six Kingdoms: Plant, Fungi, Eubacteria, Archaebacteria, Protista, and Animal. Some even describe eight Kingdoms rather than six. There are enough differences between each of these groups that scientists know all living organisms don't fit into the simple plant-or-animal classification system. What do Young-Earth creationists say about these other organisms? They say they are not alive either. How sad! Even atheists know all kingdoms of life have life.

Jesus believed seeds could die. In fact, Jesus taught that seeds must die in order for plants to grow. The outer-part (the seed-coat) must be broken open. Then, the inner-part (the endosperm) must be broken down to supply what is necessary for the seed to produce new life. Being broken open and broken down, is a pretty good description of death. Jesus obviously knew about plant life, death, and reproduction. More importantly, He used seed death to explain His own death on the cross. Seed death produces new life. His death produces new life. Jesus believed plants could die. Jesus believed plants had life. I believe what Jesus believed, not what Young-Earth creationist say.

John 12:23-24 "And Jesus answered them, saying, 'The hour has come for the Son of Man to be glorified. {24} Truly, truly, I say to you, unless a grain of wheat falls into the earth and **dies**, it remains by itself alone; but if it **dies**, it bears much fruit.'" (NASB)

If plant death is not literal, then His death was not literal. If plants don't literally die, then seeds don't literally die. If seeds don't literally die, then He didn't literally die. If He didn't literally die, then we aren't literally saved. Did plants die before Adam sinned? If not, then Jesus was mistaken about seed-death. Worse than that, Jesus was mistaken about His own death. Was there death before Adam sinned? I think the answer is obvious!

Okay, so much for plant death. Did animals experience death too? Yes! Cows didn't carry microscopes to pick off the microscopic mites living on the blades of grass before they ate. These mites would have been swallowed along with the plants, and they would have been killed by the cow's digestion system. Insects, earthworms, and other soil-living creatures got squished as great herds of buffalo crossed the plains. Plankton-feeding whales would have swallowed the plants and animals that constitute plankton. Whales have no mechanism by which they could filter out the animals. After being swallowed, those animals would have been digested. Once something is digested, it's dead. The outer-most layer of epithelial tissue (skin) consists of dead cells. If those skin cells were alive, we would be in excruciating pain every time something touched us, and worse than that, we would dehydrate within hours. The layer of dead cells acts as a fluid barrier to prevent desiccation. If those cells weren't dead, we soon would be! Furthermore, those dead cells are constantly being rubbed off and replaced by the growing cells beneath them. Epithelial cells aren't the only cells continually dying in order for animals to live. Red blood cells have a constant turnover rate. White blood cells do the same. Osteoclasts are cells that continually kill old bone cells so new bone cells can be made by osteoblasts. If this didn't happen, bones couldn't grow. Baby animals couldn't become adult animals if living cells didn't die. If you study embryological development, you'll discover that certain embryonic cells have to die in order for further development to take place. The same is true for metamorphosis. Caterpillar and tadpole cells must die in order for butterflies and frogs to live. Animal cells must die for animals to live.

"Yes," the Young-Earth creationists reply, "But, that's cell-death; that's not real death." This is their counter-argument, and it seems like a strong argument. Unfortunately, it is a very subtle and dangerous lie. Why? Because it comes from Satan, and it is meant to deceive. It is an argument that destroys the sanctity of human life. If animal-cell-death is not the same as real animal-death, then embryonic human-cell-death is not the same as real human-death. How can you argue for the sanctity of human life at conception if the first human cell has no life? If you admit that cell death is not real death, then how can you defend the unborn? When does a human become a human? At the two-cell stage? At the eight-cell stage? At the 256-cell stage? At the 1,024-cell stage? When can babies be murdered, and God wouldn't consider it death? This argument provides ammunition for pro-abortionists to claim that killing human cells *en utero* is not the same as killing humans. "It's cell death; not real death." (Surely, they don't die.) It is a lie that defends the destruction of life. Young-Earth creationists ought to think about the implications of their belief.

Many Young-Earth creationists take this no-death theory one step further and say the Second Law of Thermodynamics didn't exist before sin. (The Second Law of Thermodynamics teaches that things tend to become more disordered over time as energy is expended.) Here is one example of how their solution creates a ridiculous scientific problem. They equate the increase in universal entropy (disorder) with sin. Since the earth was "very good," they believe there was no Second Law of Thermodynamics. But, if that were true, then Adam couldn't have walked, and his heart couldn't have pumped blood. Cells need energy provided by biochemical oxidative-phosphorylation reactions in accordance with the Second Law of Thermodynamics. Without increasing entropy, plants couldn't move water up their roots. Without increasing entropy, plants couldn't make sugar by the process of photosynthesis. In fact, without the Second Law of Thermodynamics, the sun couldn't shine. Yes, God could create a miraculous economy not dependent on the laws of physics, but that was not the condition of the earth in Genesis 1:2. The earth was already in a high entropic condition of great physical disorder. It was, "without form, and void." (During the six days of Genesis 1:3-31, God was decreasing the entropy already existing in the previously created universe.) The Second Law of Thermodynamics wasn't created because of Adam's sin. **The rejection of a scientific law is a strange way to defend a religious belief.** The rejection of common sense is an even stranger way to defend a religious belief.

Who Introduced Sin into the World?

Young-Earth creationists believe death did not exist before Adam sinned. They say Adam introduced sin into the world.

Romans 5:12 "Wherefore, as by one man sin entered into the world, and death by sin; and so death passed upon all men, for that all have sinned:" (KJV)

This is the verse they use, and yes, they are right. But, they are only partially right. There is a difference between sin being committed on the earth and sin entering into the world. Adam didn't commit the first sin on earth. The first sin was committed by Lucifer. The first sin came in the form of a question. Now, asking a question is not a sin unless it is asked with the intent of causing someone else to sin. Leading someone into sin is actually a greater sin. Lucifer twisted God's truth so Eve would question God's command and His character. Lucifer committed the first sin on earth.

First Sin—Genesis 3:1 "Now the serpent was more crafty than any of the wild animals the LORD God had made. He said to the woman, 'Did God really say, "You must not eat from any tree in the garden?"'" (NIV)

Was the universe still very good after Satan did this? The only way the universe could be very good at this point is if Satan's attempt to deceive Eve was very good. If it was a sin to deceive Eve, then sin had already entered creation and the universe was no longer very good.

Next, Lucifer came right out and lied to her. This was sin number two:

Second Sin—Genesis 3:4 "'You will not surely die,' the serpent said to the woman." (NIV)

Since God told Adam and Eve they would die if they ate the fruit, and Satan said they wouldn't die, who lied; God or Satan? If sin didn't enter the world until Adam's sin, then Satan didn't lie. But, this means God lied. If Satan's lie was not a sin, then God must have considered it very good, since the universe was still very good according to anti-gap creationists. Did God consider Satan's lies very good at this point?

Then Lucifer made a statement containing a partial truth. It was a hidden-lie intended to cause Eve to think she could be like God. This was the third sin:

Third Sin—Genesis 3:5 "For God knows that when you eat of it your eyes will be opened, and you will be like God, knowing good and evil." (NIV)

Was Satan's claim the truth, or was it a lie? If it was true, then Adam and Eve would have become like God (or gods) after eating the fruit. Since they didn't become like God (or gods), then Satan told another lie as he tempted Eve to disobey God? If lying and tempting people to sin are not sins, then what are they? According to other creationists, Satan's lies and temptations of Eve must have been very good. If they were sinful, or if they were evil, then how can they say sin hadn't yet been committed? How could they believe the creation was still very good?

The fourth sin was when Eve took the fruit and ate it.

Fourth Sin—Genesis 3:6a "When the woman saw that the fruit of the tree was good for food and pleasing to the eye, and also desirable for gaining wisdom, she took some and ate it" (NIV)

Eve disobeyed God. Is disobeying God a sin or not? If disobeying God is a sin, then Eve sinned before Adam sinned? Since Eve sinned before Adam sinned, how can creationists who hate the Gap Theory insist sin did not enter the world until Adam sinned?

Sin number five was when Eve offered the forbidden fruit to Adam.

Fifth Sin—Genesis 3:6b "She also gave some to her husband, who was with her," (NIV)

Was it very good for Eve to give the fruit to Adam so he would sin? It must have been, because even at this point, sin and evil hadn't entered the very good creation according to anti-Gap Theory creationists. If they are correct, then the words and deeds of Satan and the words and deeds of Eve were not sinful. In fact, they must have been very good. Compare what anti-Gap Theory creationists think about the sins of Satan and the sins of Eve, with what God thought about the sins of Satan and the sins of Eve.

Genesis 3:14-16 "And the LORD God said unto the serpent, Because thou hast done this, thou *art* cursed above all cattle, and above every beast of the field; upon thy belly shalt thou go, and dust shalt thou eat all the days of thy life: *{15}* And I will put enmity between thee and the woman, and between thy seed and her seed; it shall bruise thy head, and thou shalt bruise his heel. *{16}* Unto the woman he said, I will greatly multiply thy sorrow and thy conception; in sorrow thou shalt bring forth children; and thy desire *shall be* to thy husband, and he shall rule over thee." (KJV)

Obviously, God considered the words and deeds of Satan and Eve sinful. He cursed them for what they said and did, and He cursed them even before He placed a curse on Adam. God considered their words and deeds as sin! Since God is immutable, He never changes His attitude about sin. This means He considered their sins as sin, even before Adam sinned. God knew the universe was no longer very good even before Adam disobeyed. The only way the universe could still be very good after these five sins, is to believe lying, maligning God, tempting others to sin, and disobeying God are very good. Otherwise, sin had already entered the universe before Adam sinned.

Sin number six was when Adam ate the fruit. (Some theologians say the Bible associates the number six with sin and with man. This may be the reason.)

Sixth Sin—Genesis 3:6c "and he ate it." (NIV)

Adam actually committed the sixth sin. Five sins had been committed on the earth before Adam sinned. Adam didn't cause sin to enter into the world, but he did cause sin to enter into the "world system." The word used for "world" in Romans 5:12 is *KOSMOS*, (Strong's Number G2889) and it means more than just the physical world; it means the world system, the world of man. God wasn't saying sin entered the physical world by Adam; He was saying Adam's sin was the introduction of sin into man's world. Adam was the one given authority over the world-system; not Eve; not Satan. So, it was because of him that sin entered the world-system. It was because of his sin that death came upon the world of man. Romans 5:12 emphasizes Paul was talking about men when he said, "all have sinned." Animals don't sin; Plants don't sin. Paul was talking about humans.

1 Corinthians 15:21-23 "For since by **man** *came* death, by **man** *came* also the resurrection of the dead. *{22}* For as in Adam all die, even so in Christ shall all be made alive. *{23}* But every **man** in his own order: Christ the firstfruits; afterward **they that are Christ's** at his coming." (KJV)

The key point Young-Earth creationists overlook (sometimes in ignorance and sometimes on purpose) is that these passages are talking about the death of MEN, not about death in general. The statements, "Passed upon all MEN" and "every MAN in his own order," mean we are not talking about the death of animals and plants. Applying this to all living things means all the cockroaches and brussels sprouts that ever lived will someday receive resurrection bodies like Jesus. After all, it says, "in Christ shall **ALL** be made alive." Is this ridiculous? Yes, of course. The Bible does not say there was no death before sin. The Bible says there was no death for **MAN** before sin. God did not intend for man to die. They were the ones made in His image; animals weren't made in His image. This is a big distinction. The Bible doesn't say God was going to kill animals if Adam sinned. God gave no warning to Adam that his sin would lead to the death of all living things.

Genesis 2:17 "but you must not eat from the tree of the knowledge of good and evil, for when you eat of it **YOU** will surely die." (NIV)

God told Adam that he would die, not the animals, if he ate of the Tree of the Knowledge of Good and Evil. Where in the Bible does it say animals would die because of Adam's sin? Where in the Bible does it say animals DIDN'T die before Adam sinned? It's an idyllic picture, but the Bible doesn't teach it. True, Genesis 1:30 says God made birds and land animals vegetarians, but that isn't the same as saying they didn't die. Cows and rabbits are vegetarians, but they still die. Young-Earth creationists assume animals didn't die because animals didn't kill. That's an interpretation, not a declaration. If all the insects were fruitful and multiplying after their kind, and none of their offspring died, then it wouldn't take very long before the earth was knee deep in bugs. Furthermore, this vegetarian diet applied only to animals created during the six-day Restoration. Nothing is said about animals that had lived in the Pre-Adamic world. Science shows there had been millions of years of predation and death before Adam, and it doesn't violate Genesis 1:30. True scientific discoveries do not contradict true Biblical teachings. Still, Young-Earth creationists believe Adam's sin affected the entire universe. They quote Romans 8:22.

Romans 8:22 "For we know that the whole creation groans and suffers the pains of childbirth together until now." (NASB)

This is true, but Romans 8:22 is not Romans 5:12. Romans 5:12 mentions Adam's sin. Romans 8:22 DOES NOT mention Adam's sin. It says all creation is suffering, but it doesn't attribute it to Adam. Can we blame the suffering of the entire universe on Adam's sin? Did Adam's sin cause Jupiter and Saturn to groan? Is Andromeda Galaxy suffering the pains of childbirth because of Adam? To what extent did Adam's sin reach? The Bible tells us.

Genesis 3:17 "Then to Adam He said, 'Because you have listened to the voice of your wife, and have eaten from the tree about which I commanded you, saying, "You shall not eat from it;" Cursed is the **ground** because of you; In toil you shall eat of it All the days of your life.'" (NASB)

"Cursed is the **GROUND** because of you." That's all God says. The ground was cursed because of Adam. It doesn't say God cursed the stars and the galaxies and the quasars because of Adam. Young-Earth creationists are adding to God's Word when they say the entire universe is suffering because of Adam's sin. I want to show you what the Bible actually says, with some emphasis, so there is no uncertainty about what God reveals about His curse on man. Romans 5:12-19 and 1 Corinthians 15:21-22 are dealing with the subject of HUMAN death, not animal death. Animals are not mentioned in these verses. They aren't mentioned in Genesis 2:16-17 either.

Romans 5:12-19 "Wherefore, as by one **man** sin entered into the world, and death by sin; and so death passed upon all **men**, for that **all** have sinned: *{13}* (For until the law sin was in the world: but sin is not imputed when there is no law. *{14}* Nevertheless death reigned from **Adam** to **Moses**, even over **them** that had not sinned after the similitude of **Adam's** transgression, who is the figure of **him** that was to come. *{15}* But not as the offence, so also *is* the free gift. For if through the offence of **one many** be dead, much more the grace of God, and the gift by grace, *which is* by one **man, Jesus Christ**, hath abounded unto **many**. *{16}* And not as *it was* by **one** that sinned, *so is* the gift: for the judgment *was* by **one** to condemnation, but the free gift *is* of many offences unto justification. *{17}* For if by one **man's** offence death reigned by **one**; much more **they** which receive abundance of grace and of the gift of righteousness shall reign in life by **one, Jesus Christ**.) *{18}* Therefore as by the offence of **one** *judgment came* upon all **men** to condemnation; even so by the righteousness of **one** *the free gift came* upon all **men** unto justification of life. *{19}* For as by one **man's** disobedience **many** were made sinners, so by the obedience of **one** shall **many** be made righteous." (KJV)

1 Corinthians 15:21-22 "For since by **man** *came* death, by **man** *came* also the resurrection of the dead. *{22}* For as in **Adam all** die, even so in **Christ** shall **all** be made alive." (KJV)

Genesis 2:16-17 "And the LORD God commanded the **man**, saying, Of every tree of the garden **thou** mayest freely eat: *{17}* But of the tree of the knowledge of good and evil, **thou** shalt not eat of it: for in the day that **thou** eatest thereof **thou** shalt surely die." (KJV)

I have highlighted thirty-nine nouns and pronouns in these three passages of Scripture that refer to human beings. My challenge to you is to go back and highlight all the nouns and pronouns that refer to animals. I'll give you a minute or two to do that…

Couldn't find any? Well, that's because they aren't there.

There is not a single mention of animal death in these passages. Adding animals into these verses is a debater's trick. If God makes thirty-nine references to humans and zero references to animals, then what right does anyone have to hint, much less insist, it includes animals? Again, if "all" includes animals in 1 Corinthians 15 and Romans 5, then Jesus died for all the sins of all animals, and all animals will be resurrected and receive glorified bodies like Christ. This is not what the Bible teaches! "All" refers ONLY to humans throughout the context of these passages. If God tells us something thirty-nine times, how many more times does He have to tell us before we believe it? The death that God is telling us about in these passages is the death of MAN. That is the literal interpretation of these passages. Including animals in these passages is NOT a literal interpretation!

Them Bones, Them Bones, Them Dry Bones

I would now like to toss a few arguments back at the Young-Earthers. I'm not doing this out of meanness. Remember, I was once a Young-Earther myself, so I'm not trying to imply I am somehow superior. I do this out of a desire to let the truth glorify our Lord Jesus Christ. I fear some of what Young-Earth creationists teach may cast doubt on God's character and on the Gospel of Jesus Christ. I can't let this slip by unchallenged. I can excuse a lot of ignorance and misconceptions, since we all have lots of ignorance and misconceptions. However, there are some errors that are without excuse.

A large number of Young-Earth creationists are opposed to the Restoration Theory because it means God built this present world on top of, "a heap of bones." They are appalled at the idea. They despise the Restoration Theory. They hate the idea of God making something living out of something dead; something clean, out of something corrupt. They say God would never do such a horrible thing. They ask, "How could God say the earth was very good on Day Six if it was a restoration of something filled with death and decay?" They imply that such an act would violate His Holy character. (I guess they must believe restoration is a bad thing.)

Friend, if you have this attitude, then you have slapped Jesus Christ in the face. If you believe this, and claim to be a Christian, then you'd better get down on your knees and reevaluate your relationship with the Lord. This is exactly what Jesus did on the Cross. This is exactly what Jesus did for me. So, don't expect me to ignore your insults against His character. I was dead and corrupt and filled with decay. There was nothing good or clean or wholesome in me. Nothing! He went to the Cross to restore me and make something very good of me. How can you hate the idea that God would restore a corrupted earth, without also hating the idea He would restore corrupted man? Do you despise the work of Jesus? Do you hate the fact He restores corrupt things? How can you object to God restoring a corrupt earth in the past when this is precisely what He will do to the earth in the future? (2 Peter 3:13)

There are a number of Young-Earth books, magazines, and websites that insist God would never build something good on top of something dead. They illustrate their opinion with a variety of cartoons where Adam and Eve are looking down in revulsion at the skeletons beneath their feet. They insist God would never create the Garden of Eden on top of dead animals! They are disgusted by the thought of God building something good on top of a, "heap of dead bones." They say a good God would never do this. Well, if they are right, then God is not good.

God had Solomon build the Temple on a foundation of white limestone blocks. In fact, the walls were white limestone as well. Limestone is sedimentary rock composed of the skeletal remains of dead marine organisms; DEAD ANIMALS. God seemed to have no problem building His Holy Temple on a pile of dead things. He had no problem placing the Holy Ark of the Covenant on top of a, "heap of dead bones." And remember, the Ark was so holy that anyone who touched it, other than the High Priest on the one designated day a year, would be struck dead. The very idea of making His dwelling place on a, "heap of dead bones," reveals what a merciful and gracious God He is! God seemed okay with making His Dwelling place, the Holy of Holies, sit on top of millions of long-dead sea creatures. According to the Young-Earth definition of "very good," God did a disgusting thing when He had Solomon build the Temple. That makes God evil.

Do you see what these Young-Earth creationists do? They impose their own standards of good and evil on God. They create their own God. Since they are disgusted by the thought of a wicked, fallen, sinful Pre-Adamic world being restored, they say their God would be disgusted by the thought of a wicked, fallen, sinful Pre-Adamic world being restored. They have created their own God in their own image. They follow in the footsteps of the religious Pharisees. The unbelieving Pharisees rejected what God revealed through the life of Jesus because it didn't agree with their interpretations of the Bible. In the same fashion, these Young-Earth creationists reject what God reveals through science because it doesn't agree with their interpretations of the Bible.

I truly believe most Young-Earth creationists don't realize how grievous the consequences of their beliefs are. They have been deceived into believing something that potentially nullifies the Gospel. Regrettably, there is more at stake than whose view of science is better, and that is why I bring up these points. Recall how I objected to the Day-Age Theory because it means we could interpret Christ's time in the grave as three ages, not three literal days. The Young-Earth Theory presents a false idea that allows this same kind of destruction of the Gospel. Some well-known Young-Earth creationists knowingly say God would never make something good out of something corrupt—a new earth from an old earth. How does this look to unbelievers? How can an unbeliever believe we represent the God who says, "Thou shalt not lie," if we tell lies about God? **If we say God would never restore anything corrupt, how can a sinner believe Christ will restore him to new life?** This lie about God's actions and His character puts an almost impenetrable barrier between sinners and the Gospel. When Christian creationists of any camp teach things that can be used against the message of the Gospel, I become quite concerned.

Apparent Age

Of all the ideas Young-Earth creationists have been deceived into believing, Apparent Age is the most un-Biblical and most un-scientific. The issue of Apparent Age is so important, it must be fully addressed. What is Apparent Age? Apparent Age is the idea God created things in the universe so they appeared old, even though they weren't. Now, there is a certain amount of truth to this. When God created Adam and Eve, they appeared to be adults. One day after they were created, they didn't appear to be one-day-old babies. The same was true for mighty oak trees. Mighty oak trees were mighty oak trees, not saplings. They had tree rings, giving them strength… and the appearance of age. If we could have taken photographs of all the living things in Eden on the day they were created, we would have pictures of plants and animals in all stages of maturity. There would be an appearance of many different ages even though everything was one day old. Baby ducks would be just as old as mama ducks, but they would have had different apparent ages.

The all-important question about Apparent Age is this: Did God create things with apparent age simply for the sake of appearances? Putting it another way, did God create things to appear old just so we would make incorrect conclusions about their age? Believe it or not, this is the line of thinking that has been used by the "church" for centuries. When early geologists began looking at the strata, they began to realize the earth appeared old. The "church" came along and said God merely put the strata there to make the earth appear old, even though it wasn't. When early paleontologists realized the fossils made the rocks appear old, the "church" came along and said God merely created fossils to make the rocks look old. There was no connection between fossils and once-living organisms. Fossils were just strange rock formations created by God. There had never been any plants or animals like those on the earth. When early astronomers began peering out into space, they realized the universe appeared old. The "church" came along and said God only made it appear old, and that telescopes were instruments of the devil. The "church" has earned a bad reputation down through the centuries by its stubborn rejection of scientific observations that disagree with "accepted theology." We do little better today, and Apparent Age is one of those "accepted theologies" that drives more people away from the Gospel than draws them to it.

Church Doctrines Don't Necessarily Equal Bible Doctrines

God has revealed many things about the creation, and while some of what He reveals is written in symbolic language, the Bible is truly accurate. The atheist will be quick to point out that the Bible teaches a number of false ideas. At one time, you could have been burned at the stake for believing the earth was a sphere, orbited the sun, or rotated on its axis. At one time, you could have been beheaded for saying Jupiter had moons, or comets orbited the sun, or the moon wasn't perfectly round. This is what the "church" taught, but it is not what the Bible taught. There is a difference. The "church" failed to understand the Bible. Understanding what the Bible reveals in the area of science can be difficult. (There is a difference between revelation and speculation.) The key is to compare Scripture to Scripture, and to compare it to true observations. Keep in mind the Bible was written in a way it could be understood by ancient nonscientific people, as well as by modern scientific people. One of the biggest misconceptions was the claim the Bible said the earth is stationary while the sun orbits it. Here are the verses used to make that claim:

Psalms 19:1-6 "The heavens declare the glory of God; And the firmament shows His handiwork. *{2}* Day unto day utters speech, And night unto night reveals knowledge. *{3} There is* no speech nor language *Where* their voice is not heard. *{4}* Their line has gone out through all the earth, And their words to the end of the world. In them He has set a tabernacle for the sun, *{5}* Which *is* like a bridegroom coming out of his chamber, *And* rejoices like a strong man to run its race. *{6}* Its rising *is* from one end of heaven, And its circuit to the other end; And there is nothing hidden from its heat." (NKJV)

Ecclesiastes 1:4-5 "*One* generation passeth away, and *another* generation cometh: but the earth abideth for ever. *{5}* The sun also ariseth, and the sun goeth down, and hasteth to his place where he arose." (KJV)

1 Chronicles 16:30 "Fear before him, all the earth: the world also shall be stable, that it be not moved." (KJV)

If you carefully read these and similar passages found in Psalms 93:1 and Psalms 96:10, you'll see how the Bible uses Phenomenological Language. (Phenomenological Language describes something as it appears, as opposed to Ontological Language, which describes something as it is.) Days really don't speak! Nights don't have knowledge. The sun is said to be LIKE a bridegroom and LIKE a strong man running a circular racetrack. It is referred to as "he" and "his." These are key words indicating symbolic imagery. It's not meant to be taken literally. The instant you add a word such as "like" to a description, you make it clear the items being described are not equivalent. They are similar, but they are not the same. You wouldn't hold up an apple and say, "This is LIKE an apple." You wouldn't say that, because it IS an apple. Now, you could hold up an orange and say, "This is LIKE an apple." They are similar because they are both round, they are both fruits, they are both edible, and they both have seeds. They are like each other, but they aren't the same as each other. The instant the Bible said the sun was like a runner running a circular path, the Bible proved the sun did not actually run a circular path. It looked like that, but it didn't actually do that. The ancient Jews would have understood this. God was very careful in describing the sun in such a way that it agreed with the observations of the ancient Hebrews without contradicting the science we modern people know to be true. His Words matched His Works. If ancient, ignorant Jewish goat-herders were the authors of the Bible, they wouldn't have added the word "like" because they would have thought the sun actually traveled in a circular fashion. The true Author of these verses knew it didn't. These verses are simply describing what the sun appears to be doing; not what it is actually doing. We do the same thing ourselves every time we talk about "sunrise" and "sunset." (The sun is not going down; the horizon is going up.)

What about the earth not being moved? Here again we need to compare Scripture with Scripture to see what these words mean. The very same words are used in other parts of the Bible to tell us David will not be moved. (Psalms 21:7) The Bible also says Israel will not be moved. (1 Chronicles 17:9) Furthermore, the righteous will not be moved. (Psalms 55:22) It's obvious that, "not being moved," is a Hebrew idiom meaning established and unending. It does not refer to physical location and mobility. The Jews moved around. David was ambulatory. Righteous people change locations. The Bible doesn't say the earth is fixed in its position. Instead, it says the earth will never have an ending.

In God (Can) We Trust?

I don't think God created things with apparent age merely to trick us or deceive us. I think He created things the way they were because that was the way they best functioned. Oak trees had rings because tree rings give strength to trees. Mama ducks were bigger because baby ducks needed somebody to lead them to the water. The mama duck appeared mature, because the mama duck was mature. Maturity was its function, not its age. Adam and Eve were adults because as adults they could fully enjoy fellowship with God. God gave everything Functional Age; not Apparent Age. Now, trying to ascribe function to things can be difficult. This is especially true when we realize we're talking about how God views functions. **God created things for a purpose; not for appearance.** I cannot find anything in the Bible that indicates God created things with apparent age just so we would be fooled by their appearance. Yet, this is exactly what Young-Earth creationists claim when they say God made the universe look old just to fool atheists and evolutionists into believing the universe is old. The Bible says we can learn things about God by viewing His handiwork, but if His handiwork is skewed, if what we see is not what is, then what does viewing His handiwork tell us about God? I understand perfectly why an unbeliever wonders about God when he is told God miraculously created fossils in the strata just to trick us into thinking the earth was more than 6,000 years old. What function can fossils possibly serve? None, other than to prove God is deceptive. I understand why an unbeliever would question God's character when he is told God changed the laws of physics after the Flood so radioactive dating techniques would produce false ages. We need to be very careful when we stand so near such a dangerous precipice. Let's not push logic and reason over the edge and make God a God of deception and fakery. Let's not defend our interpretations of the Bible when such interpretations run counter to well-proven scientific facts. The effects are devastating. God appears to be untrustworthy if our observations of His universe cannot be trusted. The deadly trap is this:

ONCE WE CONVINCE PEOPLE THEY CAN'T TRUST GOD'S REVELATION OF THE PHYSICAL WORLD, HOW CAN WE ASK THEM TO TRUST HIS REVELATION OF THE SPIRITUAL WORLD?

Astronomy 101½

As we look out into space, we see stars and galaxies thousands, millions, and even billions of light-years away. I look at a star a million light-years away, and say the light I now see actually left that star a million years ago and is just now reaching the earth. I reach this conclusion by using the same logic I use when standing at the train station in New York, watching a train come in from Boston. I know how far away Boston is. I know how fast the train goes. I can calculate when the train left. Young-Earth creationists criticize my logic. I can do that for a train from Boston, but I can't apply that same logic to the light from a distant star. The reason my logic is faulty, they tell me, is because God created the light from that star in transit. The train from Boston wasn't created already in transit. They say the light was. In other words, God not only created the star; He created light waves emanating from that star. God created the star and He created a beam of light all the way to earth on the fourth day of creation so it would APPEAR in the sky on the fourth night of creation. According to Young-Earth creationists, the universe is not billions of years old. They say God created all the stars, all their beams of light, in all directions, to all the farthest reaches of space, all on the same day, six thousand years ago. Therefore, the universe only appears to be populated by stars millions or billions of years old. Thus, God gave the universe Apparent Age. Now, this might explain the stars He created, but it doesn't explain the stars He destroyed.

In 1987 astronomers had the privilege of witnessing a supernova, one of the most awesome displays seen in the heavens. I'm not an astronomer, so I can't describe this in the best astronomical terms, but simply put, a supernova is a star that is so old, and has burned so much of its mass, that its gravity can no longer sustain its size. When this happens, it explodes. The event seen in 1987 was the supernova of a star located in the Large Magellanic Cloud approximately 168,000 light-years from earth. How do we explain what happened? According to astronomers, the star actually exploded 168,000 years ago, and the light of that explosion had just then reached the earth. The star they saw before the explosion had been gone for 168,000 years, but it took that long for the last of its light to reach earth. This is the same explanation a Day-Ager or a Restored-Earther would give. A Young-Earther couldn't accept this. If he did, then he'd have to admit the universe is at least 168,000 years old. If the Young-Earthers are correct, then the farthest away we could see a supernova would be 6,000 light-years. The only answer the Young-Earther can give, is to say God again created an appearance of age. He made it APPEAR as if that star exploded 168,000 years ago. At this point, however, they step over the edge of logic and take the Gospel down with them.

The star is not there now. The star couldn't have been there 168,000 years ago according to the Young-Earth Theory. The universe didn't exist 168,000 years ago. If God created a star in the Large Magellanic Cloud 6,000 years ago, and made it go supernova that very day, it would take another 162,000 more years before we could see it explode. So, what astronomers observed in 1987 couldn't have been the explosion of a star in the Large Magellanic Cloud. It was only an apparent explosion of a star in the Large Magellanic Cloud. Since the star is not there now, it means God merely created a 6,000 light-year-long beam of light, so it appeared as if the star was there. But, if what they saw was only a stream of photons, then what they saw was not a real star, only an apparent star. What astronomers observed in 1987 wasn't the explosion of a star. It was an apparent explosion of an apparent star. It was only the end of a beam of light created in mid-stream, six-thousand years ago. The star never really existed. The explosion never really happened.

In order to make the universe appear old, God created the appearance of a star and the appearance of an explosion, but neither was real. If Young-Earth creationists are correct, then that explosion couldn't have been a real supernova. It had to be an apparent supernova because it was beyond the 6,000 light-year limit for real supernovae to be seen.

168,000 light-years is a long way, but actually that explosion was relatively close to the earth. (It was visible to the naked eyed.) Astronomers have seen supernovae of stars millions of light-years away. According to the Young-Earth Theory, these can't be real supernovae either; they can only be apparent supernovae. God apparently has been creating the appearance of stars that never existed and explosions that never happened. Like a good stage magician, God makes us see things that only appear to be real.

The same can be said of galaxy positions. We can map the movements and locations of the galaxies in the universe, but when we do, we have a map of where they were millions and billions of years ago. Because they are moving, we know they aren't in those same locations today. If the Young-Earth people are correct, then they were never in those locations. So, why does God make it appear as if they were in places they never were? Likewise, astronomers have photographs of two distant galaxies moving toward each other on a collision course. But, that was where they were millions of years ago. If you could instantaneously transport yourself to their location today, you would see they have already merged into one larger galaxy. In fact, they merged millions of years ago. Since the universe didn't exist millions of years ago, according to the Young-Earth Theory, they never existed as two separate galaxies. "They" are one galaxy today and were never two separate galaxies. So, why does God create the appearance of two separate galaxies when "they" never existed as two separate galaxies? If the universe isn't billions of years old, then the heavens reveal that God is a God of deception. **The heavens reveal things that never existed, in places they never were, doing things that never happened.** If I did that to you, you would say I was deceptive. If the Young-Earth Theory is true, then we have to say the same thing about our Creator. We can't trust what we see with our eyes because our Creator has been fooling our eyes.

If the Young-Earth Theory is correct, then we can't trust what God has revealed about the cosmos. The 1987 Large Magellanic Cloud supernova proves we cannot trust our eyes. What APPEARS to have happened, is not what ACTUALLY happened. **This means we can't know if something we see is a real something, or if it's merely an apparent something.** If I can't trust a truly repeatable, truly testable, truly proven scientific observation, then how can I trust anything else my senses tell me? How am I to know if the freight train speeding my way is a real freight train or simply an apparent freight train? How can I know if I should jump off the tracks? The answer is, I can't! Now, I know that interpretations of observations can be argued, but Christians have no right to argue the observations aren't real. If I see a rock on the ground, you can't tell me the rock doesn't exist. This is, in effect, what Young-Earthers are saying about stars and supernovae. They say the stars were never there and the supernovae never happened. It is ironic that some atheists are desperately trying to prove what really happened, happened, while some Christians are desperately trying to prove what really happened, didn't happen. No, it's worse than ironic; it's shameful. If Young-Earth creationists are correct, then God has given us an untrustworthy revelation of His universe. If the heavens declare anything about

God, they declare the works of His hand are a sleight of hand. In short, we can't trust God because one of His invisible attributes would be the attribute of deception.

Now, here's where the Gospel comes in. How do we know Jesus rose from the tomb? We know because there were eyewitnesses. In fact, more than 500 people saw the risen Christ. Regrettably, some people of other religions argue against the Resurrection by saying God merely sent them an illusion of a risen Christ. Jesus was still dead and rotting in the grave, but God sent these 500 people an apparent Christ. How do we respond to such a claim? We reject it because God is not a God of deception or trickery; God would never deceive us. BUT HOW CAN WE SAY THAT, IF WE ALSO INSIST GOD MADE APPARENT EXPLOSIONS THAT NEVER HAPPENED OF APPARENT STARS THAT NEVER EXISTED? If the Young-Earthers are right about the age of the universe, then we can't prove the Resurrection of Christ was real. Eyewitnesses don't mean squat! It may have been an APPARENT RESURRECTION OF AN APPARENT CHRIST. The bottom line is this: If God can deceive us about a star exploding in the heavens, then God can deceive us about Jesus rising from the tomb. If Jesus didn't rise from the grave, then our faith is in vain.

"Hold on," they'll scream. They can prove how light from a star 168,000 light-years away could have gotten here in 6,000 years. Young-Earth creationists have a Plan B. They say the speed of light is slowing down. They say the speed of light was billions of time faster in the past. Therefore, the light of that exploding star would have gotten here much quicker. Well, I'm going to let the physicists and astronomers answer that one. Go read their books. They have mathematical formulas far more complex than my brain can handle. I'm not that smart, so I'll make my argument simple. According to the Laws of Physics, matter and energy cannot be created or destroyed. If the Young-Earth Theory depends on something that violates a proven scientific law, then it ought to be tossed out. It does, and it should! You see, a well-known mathematical formula of physics is Albert Einstein's equation $e=mc^2$. (e is energy, m is mass, and c is the speed of light.) This means matter can be changed to energy, and energy can be changed to matter, and the quantity of matter or energy involved is determined by the speed of light. If I have a rock with a certain mass, I can calculate how much energy would be generated if the rock was completely transformed to energy. I would do this by multiplying its mass (m) by the speed of light squared (c^2). Now, if the speed of light was greater in the past, then my rock would have had more energy in the past. If the speed of light was a billion times greater in the past, then my rock would have had a quintillion (a billion times a billion) times more energy in the past then than it does now. In fact, the total energy of the universe in the past would have been a quintillion times greater. This would mean the universe has lost energy over time. In other words, if the speed of light has slowed down, then energy has been destroyed since the creation. This violates the Laws of Physics. Matter and energy cannot be created or destroyed. This Young-Earth explanation contradicts a proven Law of Physics. It also contradicts the claim that Christ sustains all things (Hebrews 1:3). If Christ really is sustaining all things, then the mass and energy of the universe has been sustained. Nothing could be lost. Of course, if you're good with math, you could rewrite this formula as $e/c^2=m$. Then you could claim the speed of light is slowing down and energy is not being lost. Instead of energy being destroyed, it would mean mass is being created. If this is true, then we have a quintillion times more mass in the universe now than at creation. Sadly, that violates the same Law of Physics. It also invalidates the claim that God finished creating on the seventh day (Genesis 2:3). Combine Genesis 2:3 with Hebrews 1:3 and you'll see the Bible told us how matter and energy cannot be created or destroyed. This is another one of those little scientific clues God gave us. This is how He set up the universe: Matter and energy cannot be created or destroyed. The Young-Earth interpretation says otherwise. **If the speed of light has changed since the beginning, then matter and energy have been created or destroyed since the beginning.** This belief disagrees with both science and the Bible; neither God's Word, nor God's Work are reliable sources of truth. The Gap Theory doesn't make this mistake. The Works of His hands and the Words of His mouth don't contradict. Why are Christians so obstinately defending creation theories contradicting His Work and His Word?

    Okay, okay, we'll go to Plan C. Many Young-Earth creationists now talk about how God warps space so the light from that exploding star could have gotten here faster. It traveled through Riemannian Space. Yeah, try telling that to the traffic cop who pulls you over for speeding. "Honest, officer. I was only doing 35. It's just that my car was going through Riemannian Space so it appeared I was going 85." What is Riemannian Space? Riemannian Geometry deals with the geometry of curved surfaces. We are probably more familiar with Euclidian Geometry, which is Plane Geometry, Solid Geometry and a few other things dealing with the dimensions of space. You probably remember from high school geometry, one of Euclid's axioms said the shortest distance between two points is a straight line. It's true, but what if those two points are on a curved plane? Could there be a shorter distance? Yes, most certainly. If you lived in London, England and wanted to go on a jolly holiday to Sydney, Australia, then the shortest distance would be about 10,000 miles. But, that's the distance along the curved surface of the earth. If you could bore a hole through the earth, you could shave a couple of thousand miles off your trip. Now, even though it would be shorter by going through the center of the earth, I wouldn't recommend it. It would take a frightfully long time and once you broke through the crust and hit all that magma and molten iron, your holiday wouldn't be very jolly. Well, jolly or not, this is what some very well-known Young-Earth creationist use to explain the travel of light from distant stars. The light from all those stars millions and billions of light-years away got here (and is still getting here) via Riemannian Space. It means photons of light are escaping the curved surface of our universe. (Yes, there is evidence space is curved.) Then they travel into a place that is not our universe (not part of the time-space continuum where our Laws of Physics apply), and then reemerge just so we can see them as stars in the night sky. Amazing!

    There are so many problems with this idea, I don't know where to begin. Science demands repeatable, testable observations. Young-Earthers know this because this is the kind of evidence they demand from evolutionists. In spite of that, they can't provide that same kind of evidence for their own theory of creation. They use science fiction to defend their interpretation instead of science fact. For something to escape the confines of the time-space continuum it would have to reach a velocity greater than the speed of light. The photons traveling at the speed of light would have to be traveling faster than themselves to do it. Then, once they got out of the universe, they would have to get back into the universe at just the right spot so they would appear to be coming from just the right place. Amazingly amazing!

There is an even bigger counter-argument that destroys this nonsense: YOU CAN TEST IT YOURSELF. All you need are two very sensitive, highly complex, superbly engineered sensing devices… your eyes. Go outside on a clear night and look up at the stars. Light from those stars is traveling along the surface of our curved universe, Euclidian Space. Supposedly, light is also traveling straight through Riemannian Space. Now, if this is true, then every star less than 6,000 light-years away should be present in the night sky two times. Proxima-Centauri, the nearest star to our sun is about four and a half light-years away. If its light is traveling through both Euclidian Space and Riemannian Space, then we should see two Proxima-Centaurii separated by a space of however far it has moved in four and a half years. We should be able to see a Euclidian Proxima-Centauri and Riemannian Proxima-Centauri in the night sky. Furthermore, new Euclidian Stars should be popping into view every night. Today, we can see Euclidian Stars less than 6,000 light-years away. A thousand years ago, we could have seen only Euclidian Stars less than 5,000 light-years away. At the time of Christ, we could have seen only Euclidian Stars less than 4,000 light-years away. At the time of King David, astronomers could have seen only Euclidian Stars less than 3,000 light-years away. As time passed, the light from farther and farther Euclidian Stars would have finally reached us. When they did, they would appear as duplicates of the Riemannian Stars we already saw. But as far back as history records, no one has reported this. There should be two Stonehenges marking the movement of the stars. One would be the Euclidian Stonehenge and the other would be the Riemannian Stonehenge. Since the sun is a star, and since light passes through Riemannian Space, we should see two suns separated by about eight and a half minutes of earth rotation and revolution. (The sun is about eight and a half light-minutes away.) Go outside and look at your shadow on a sunny day. If light passes through Riemannian Space, then you should have two shadows. One shadow would be caused by the light of the sun that passed through Euclidian Space and the other shadow would be caused by the light that passed through Riemannian Space. Do you expect to see two shadows? You should if you're a Young-Earth creationist who uses Riemannian Space as a way of defending the Young-Earth Theory.

I could go on, but again we have people saying God makes things appear to be doing what they aren't doing. We are told to believe God made the universe appear old, just so He could damn people to hell who think the universe appears old. God again becomes deceptive. Dear Christian, we should think long and hard about what we preach before we preach it. If it impugns God's character, we should do what Job did when God confronted him with his ignorance and arrogance.

Job 40:3-5 "Then Job answered the LORD: {4} 'I am unworthy--how can I reply to you? I put my hand over my mouth. {5} I spoke once, but I have no answer-- twice, but I will say no more.'" (NIV)

Why Not Flood-Geology?

The arguments for and against Flood-Geology are unending. Hundreds of books and thousands of articles have been written attacking and defending Flood-Geology. I cannot possibly cover more than a few basic reasons why I think Traditional-Geology disproves Flood-Geology. What is Traditional-Geology? Traditional-Geology is what accredited, university-trained geologists would accept as scientific. Traditional-Geology is accepted by every geologist who isn't a Flood-Geologist. Traditional-Geologists include more than unbelievers too. There are plenty of Christian geologists who reject Flood-Geology. That's why there has been so much material written against it. If I had to guess, I would say there are many more Christian Traditional-Geologists than Christian Flood-Geologists, but that's just a guess. Anyway, PLEASE note very carefully I did not say Traditional-Geology disproves the Flood. I said it disproves Flood-Geology. Traditional-Geology disproves Flood-Geology, but not the Flood, because Flood-Geology has very little to do with the Flood. Instead, it is a creation by some very fertile minds using very few facts. (Dr. Dill's Gardening Tip #1: It doesn't matter how much fertilizer you add; if you don't have seeds, you won't get a crop.) Flood-Geology has no "seeds" but lots of "fertilizer." It is largely based on false interpretations of Scripture and distortions of science. I won't go into the details because that would fill several books, and those books have been written by others already. I only want to point out a few glaring problems with Flood-Geology.

Specimen Ridge

Specimen Ridge is a large area in Yellowstone National Park. This area has an interesting arrangement of geological strata. There are about fifty layers that alternate between forest material and volcanic ash. Traditional-Geology explains it this way: Yellowstone is a volcanic area. Millions of years ago, a lush forest grew there, but suddenly a volcano erupted. When that happened, the forest was destroyed and was covered in volcanic ash. Over time, a new forest grew. Years passed and another volcanic eruption destroyed and covered the new forest. The forest grew again and later, another volcanic eruption covered the forest. The Traditional-Geologist tells us this section of Yellowstone experienced many, many such volcanic eruptions several million years ago. Layer after layer of forest material and volcanic ash were formed.[7] Today, millions of years later, tourists can visit this area to see the evidence for themselves. Of course, if those tourists were Flood-Geologists, they couldn't accept this interpretation of the evidence. Flood-Geology says this couldn't have happened millions of years ago. It couldn't be the results of new forests growing up after volcanic eruptions. That would take too long. The earth isn't old enough for that to happen. Instead, these layers must have been deposited by the Great Flood. The flood waters rose and brought in vast amounts of forest material from surrounding areas. The Great Flood was so catastrophic it uprooted trees, entire forests in fact, and transported them for miles. The waters then suddenly calmed over the area of Specimen Ridge and the forest material settled out. Then the water gently receded so as not to wash away the newly deposited forest material. Once the water receded, a volcano erupted and blanketed everything in ash. Then the volcano stopped and the tumultuous waters rose again. This brought in a new load of forest material ripped from another location miles away. Now, somehow this cataclysmic flood was strong enough to carry tons and tons and tons of forest material, yet so gentle it didn't disturb the new layer of volcanic ash. The flood became calm again and the new forest material was deposited on top of that new volcanic ash. Then the waters gently receded again. Then a volcano erupted again. Then a new layer of volcanic ash covered the new layer of forest material. Then the flood waters became violent again and swept in a new forest ripped from a new location miles away and deposited that on top of the new layer of ash. Then the water receded again. Then a volcano erupted again, and so on, and so on until fifty layers were deposited. Over the course of about a year, the waters of the Great Flood rose twenty-five times, receded twenty-five times, and twenty-five volcanic eruptions occurred in between those times. This means about every two weeks the waters rose, fell, and a volcano erupted.

Is the Flood-Geology interpretation scientific? I don't think so, but I'm not a geologist. Traditional-Geologists laugh at the "science" of Flood-Geologists. Flood-Geologists laugh back. Personally, I don't see how such powerful waves of water could have deposited new material without ripping out the freshly-deposited material in the layer below it. I find it difficult to believe the volcanic forces in the great depths below Specimen Ridge knew exactly when to become active and when to go dormant so the layers would alternate. I find it hard to believe twenty-five volcanic eruptions would occur in the same area in less than a year. I'm not a vulcanologist either, but it was my impression that once a volcano erupts, the pressure below it lessens and a dormant period follows. Usually this dormant period is quite long. There is a lot of Flood-Geology "science" that doesn't make sense to me, but again let me direct you to your Christian bookstore. Christian Traditional-Geologists and Christian Flood-Geologists have lots to say about it. The science of Traditional-Geologists seems much more reliable to me.

BUT, let's say Flood-Geologists prove their view is right. Let's assume they have the scientific evidence to prove the waters of the Great Flood did exactly what they say it did. Let's let them win the scientific argument! Now that we have the "scientific" evidence the Flood so violently rose and receded twenty-five times, let's compare it with the Biblical evidence. Let's see if the Biblical account matches the Young-Earth "scientific" account. What does the Bible say about the water levels?

Genesis 7:10-24 "And after the seven days the floodwaters came on the earth. {11} In the six hundredth year of Noah's life, on the seventeenth day of the second month--on that day all the springs of the great deep burst forth, and the floodgates of the heavens were opened. {12} And rain fell on the earth forty days and forty nights. {13} On that very day Noah and his sons, Shem, Ham and Japheth, together with his wife and the wives of his three sons, entered the ark. {14} They had with them every wild animal according to its kind, all livestock according to their kinds, every creature that moves along the ground according to its kind and every bird according to its kind, everything with wings. {15} Pairs of all creatures that have the breath of life in them came to Noah and entered the ark. {16} The animals going in were male and female of every living thing, as God had commanded Noah. Then the LORD shut him in. {17} For forty days **the flood kept coming** on the earth, and as the waters **increased** they lifted the ark high above the earth. {18} The waters **rose** and **increased** greatly on the earth, and the ark floated on the surface of the water. {19} They **rose** greatly on the earth, and all the high mountains under the entire heavens were covered. {20} The waters **rose** and covered the mountains to a depth of more than twenty feet. {21} Every living thing that moved on the earth perished--birds, livestock, wild animals, all the creatures that swarm over the earth, and all mankind. {22} Everything on dry land that had the breath of life in its nostrils died. {23} Every living thing on the face of the earth was wiped out; men and animals and the creatures that move along the ground and the birds of the air were wiped from the earth. Only Noah was left, and those with him in the ark. {24} The waters flooded the earth for a hundred and fifty days." (NIV)

For the first hundred and fifty days, the water rose; it kept coming; it increased. It didn't decrease. The Bible doesn't say the water rose and receded, rose and receded, rose and receded. "The flood kept coming on the earth." The waters didn't recede. The Bible doesn't say a thing about the waters going down during the first hundred and fifty days. The Biblical account doesn't match the Young-Earth "scientific" account. Furthermore, Genesis 7:19-20 says the waters covered even the highest mountains to a depth of more than twenty feet. Hmmm? Let's see. Specimen Ridge has an altitude of about 8,500 feet. Mount Everest has an altitude of about 29,000 feet. That means when Mount Everest was covered by twenty feet of water, Specimen Ridge was covered by 20,500 feet of water. For the top of Specimen Ridge to be repeatedly covered by dry volcanic ash, the water had to drop 20,500 feet. Then the water went up 20,500 feet, then dropped 20,500 feet, then went up 20,500 feet, *etc.* for twenty-five times. According to Flood-Geologist, twenty-five 20,500-foot waves flooded over Specimen Ridge without disturbing any of the newly deposited layers of sediment. That's hard to believe. Let's look now at what the Bible says about the water levels dropping.

Genesis 8:1-5 "But God remembered Noah and all the wild animals and the livestock that were with him in the ark, and he sent a wind over the earth, and the waters **receded**. *{2}* Now the springs of the deep and the floodgates of the heavens had been closed, and the rain had stopped falling from the sky. *{3}* The water **receded steadily** from the earth. At the end of the hundred and fifty days the water had **gone down**, *{4}* and on the seventeenth day of the seventh month the ark came to rest on the mountains of Ararat. *{5}* The waters **continued to recede until the tenth month**, and on the first day of the tenth month the tops of the mountains became visible." (NIV)

The Bible is very clear. The water didn't go up and down as it receded. It, "receded steadily." It, "continued to recede," until the mountains were finally uncovered. As you read the chapter, nothing says the water was going up and down, up and down. The tops of the mountains didn't become visible until the first day of the tenth month. If the Bible is true, the mountains had been covered for anywhere between two months to six months. (The Bible doesn't tell us the day the mountains first became covered; it only tells us the day they first became uncovered.) The most straightforward and literal understanding of the Biblical account of the Flood is that even Mount Everest was covered by more than twenty feet of water until the first day of the tenth month. Specimen Ridge, 20,500 feet below this, surely wouldn't have been visible until much later. Flood-Geologists say this isn't true. Specimen Ridge was covered, then uncovered, then covered, then uncovered for twenty-five times. If Flood-Geologists are correct, then the tops of thousands of other mountains would have been visible long before the first day of the tenth month. If the top six inches of Specimen Ridge were uncovered, 20,500 feet of Mount Everest would have been visible. I find it strange how God seemed to overlook Mount Everest being visible so many times before the first day of the tenth month. He also didn't see the other mountains. Every time the water receded enough for Specimen Ridge to be visible, every mountain taller than 8,500 feet would have been visible. Did God not see them? Did He forget to tell Moses what really happened? If what Flood-Geologists say is true, then the Bible gives us a false account of what really happened during the Flood. If what Flood-Geologists say about Specimen Ridge is true, then God didn't tell us the truth about the Flood. What He told us doesn't match with Flood-Geology… and it isn't a matter of Him merely leaving out some details. I'm sure Flood-Geologists will say God simply didn't tell Moses about the water going up and down, but God didn't omit telling Moses what the water was doing. He said the water, "kept coming on the earth." Three times He said it rose, and then He said it kept rising. If the water had risen and fallen, He could not have said what He said. That would not be an omission. That would be a lie. In the same fashion, God couldn't have said the water, "receded steadily," and, "continued to recede," if it was undergoing increases and decreases in depth. Again, that would not be an omission. That would be a lie. **Young-Earth/Flood-Geologists put their time, energy, and emotion into a theory that winds up proving God is a liar if they are right.**

Green River Varves

If you thought the waters of the Great Flood were magic over Specimen Ridge, wait until you learn what they did along the Green River in the western United States. The Green River Basin includes parts of Colorado, Utah, and Wyoming.[8] First, let me tell you about varves. Varves are annual sediment deposits on the bottom of lakes, ponds, or other bodies of still or slow-moving water. Varves are formed when different kinds of waterborne particles settle to the bottom. One of the most common types of varves is the clay/pollen couplet. Rivers and streams carry fine clay particles in suspension. These clay particles settle to the bottom in places where the water becomes still. During spring and summer, the water also carries large amounts of pollen from trees and flowers. This also settles to the bottom where the water becomes still. There are places along the Green River Basin where scientists have examined varves for decades. What they have observed is the bottom of the river basin grows a new varve couplet every year. There is a layer of clay silt and there is a layer of pollen deposited each year. They have been able to prove the varves in the Green River are due to annual sedimentation of clay silt and pollen. Young-Earth creationists agree to a certain point. They accept the annual sedimentation explanation only back to the Great Flood. That means they believe only the top 4,000 or so varve couplets were caused by annual clay/pollen sedimentation. According to Flood-Geologists, the identical clay/pollen varves seen in the river basin strata below that level were caused by the Great Flood. Just as in the case of Specimen Ridge, the waters moved up and down. In this case, instead of bringing in uprooted forests, they brought in alternating deposits of pollen and clay silt. Now, I don't know much about hydraulics, the science of fluids, but I bet it would be difficult to figure out how cataclysmic, raging waters could deposit so many microscopic particles so gently over hundreds of miles of river in less than a year. Where did that much pollen come from? Most plants produce pollen only one time a year. And plants can't even do that if they are under thousands of feet of water. The biggest difficulty appears when you learn how many clay/pollen varves there are in the Green River Basin. There are places that have twenty million clay/pollen varves. Traditional-Geologists say the river has been there for millions of years. Young-Earth/Flood-Geologists disagree. They have three explanations.

The first, I have mentioned already: The Great Flood did it. This time, instead of twenty-five ebbs and flows of the Great Flood like at Specimen Ridge, there had to be twenty million ebbs and flows in one year. Does this make sense? There are about 31 million seconds in a year. Apparently, they believe a wall of water came rushing down the Green River carrying clay silt. This was followed 0.78 seconds later by a wall of water carrying pollen. This was followed 0.78 seconds later by a wall of water carrying clay silt. This was followed 0.78 seconds later by a wall of water carrying pollen. This was followed 0.78 seconds later by a wall of water carrying clay silt. This went on for a year; and remember, it had to be even faster since it was completely underwater most of the time. This doesn't seem very scientific to me, especially when you factor in the astonishing fact the amount of pollen in the layers correlates to both the eleven-year cycle of sunspots and the 21,000-year eccentric orbital cycle of the earth.[9] Both of these cycles affect the climate of the earth and therefore the growth rate of plants and the amount of pollen produced. The pollen in the Green River varves matches both of those cycles; it was not laid down by Noah's Flood.

Their second explanation says God put all those twenty million varves in place, including the eleven-year and 21,000-year cycles, in order to give the Green River the appearance of being millions of years old. We've talked about the concept of Apparent Age. This seems very deceptive to me. Why would unbelievers want to believe a deceptive God?

Their last explanation is that the varves are not due to sedimentation of clay and pollen. Instead, they are due to some chemical process. This is playing the "What-If Game." I'll talk more about the "What-If Game" later. For now, let's examine this explanation. They have no evidence to defend it. There is plenty of evidence these layers were caused by sedimentation of clay particles and pollen particles. Microscopic examination of the layers reveals alternating clay particles and pollen particles. Scientists have observed this for nearly a century. There is no indication they were caused by chemical reactions, and even if the varves were created by chemicals, the explanation defies logic. Now, instead of alternating walls of pollen-water/clay-water every 0.78 seconds, there had to be walls of water with alternating chemicals every 0.78 seconds. Claiming it was a chemical reaction does not prove it was a chemical reaction, but that's the logic of Flood-Geologists. They insist they are right just because we can't prove they are wrong. This "logic" is not scientific, and it is certainly not God-honoring. I could just as easily claim space aliens came to Earth a thousand years ago, dug the entire Green River Basin, deposited twenty million varves of clay silt and pollen, and then zapped the entire human race with a memory-erasing beam so we wouldn't know they did it. You can't disprove that explanation either, but I'm not going to win a Nobel Prize with it. I don't think Flood-Geologist will win Nobel Prizes with their explanations either.

Coral Reefs

The waters of the Great Flood performed acts of magic by depositing all the layers of sediment at Specimen Ridge in between those volcanic eruptions. The waters of the Great Flood performed even greater magic by depositing all those varves along the Green River Basin. Yet, those feats were nothing compared to how the Flood constructed the world's largest coral reefs according to the Young-Earth Theory. Coral is actually a marine animal. Rather than swimming around its whole life looking for food, it likes to settle down, build a little calcium carbonate house, and wait for food to come to it. (Kind of like calling out for pizza.) Coral also likes to stay close to family. New coral will attach itself to older coral. This way, it uses part of the old coral's house as part of its house. This saves energy for the coral. In time, as newer coral builds on previous layers of coral, a coral reef forms. (And, as layers build on layers, the underlying coral units die. If this didn't happen, coral reefs couldn't form. There had to be animal death before Adam sinned, or there would be no coral reefs. Without coral reefs, the animal species that depend on coral reefs couldn't have lived until after the Flood.) Traditional-Geologists tell us it takes thousands and thousands of years to form coral reefs. Traditional-Geologists quote Traditional-Biologists who say the fastest a coral reef can grow is about one-half inch per year.[10] This means a mile-wide coral reef would have needed over 100,000 years to become that large. There are active coral reefs today that appear to be much older. This is the Traditional-Geologist/Biologist opinion. Flood-Geologists tell us these coral reefs didn't grow on site. Instead, they were formed when the Great Flood ripped up smaller coral reefs all across the oceans and deposited them in these locations. Those coral reefs only APPEAR to be 100,000 years old. Flood-Geologists get an F- in biology when they say this because coral is not the same as clay silt or grains of pollen. Those kinds of particles are deposited just willy-nilly by water, but this isn't true of coral. When coral polyps build their houses, they build them in a vertical orientation. They have a top to their house and they have a bottom to their house. They also have a different type of construction if they build their house on the seaward side of the reef as opposed to the landward side of the reef. Since they attach themselves to previously built coral houses, their walls fit the contours of the walls of the corals next to them. This means if you took a chunk of coral and examined it under the microscope, you could tell which way was up, which way was down, which way was in, and which way was out. Then, like a giant three-dimensional jigsaw puzzle, you could fit individual corals together by the contours of their shells. In addition, coral polyps growing in the summer are larger than those growing in the winter. Biologists can see these annual growth "rings" in coral reefs. If Flood-Geologists are telling us the truth, then the Great Flood ripped apart thousands of smaller coral reefs and transported billions of individual coral units over hundreds or even thousands of miles. Then the waters of the Flood matched the coral species (There are over 2,500 species of coral.) so the correct species were connected to each other, then it assembled each coral unit in the correct up/down, in/out orientation, and in their correct summer-winter patterns. The waters also knew exactly how to reshape the three-dimensional contours of each coral shell so its shape would fit perfectly with the contours of the coral units to which it would later be attached. All this would give large coral reefs the APPEARANCE of having developed on site, when they actually came from small coral reefs hundreds or thousands of miles apart. This way, those ungodly scientists who don't believe in the Young-Earth Theory would be fooled into believing coral reefs took hundreds of thousands of years to form.

    This scientific problem doesn't bother the determined Young-Earth/Flood-Geologist. When criticized, his response is, "But what if God had done this?" (The "What-If Game.") "Couldn't God cause the Flood waters to transport billions of individual coral units over thousands of miles, sort them out according to species, reshape them, and reassemble them to make them look like they had grown on site? Would this be too difficult for God?" Some Old-Earth creationists dismiss this question from Young-Earth creationists because such an act of God seems to make no sense. They ask, "Why would God do such a thing?" To which the Young-Earth creationist responds by saying, "We don't know why, but we also don't know why God does a lot of things. We believe on the basis of faith." This answer is intended to make it look as if Old-Earth creationists have no faith. The real answer, of course, is that God most certainly could have done this. God sustains and controls the universe's 10^{80} fundamental particles of matter and 10^{195} units of space, 10^{43} times per second. (These represent the Planck units; the smallest units of matter, space, and time physically possible in the universe... and this is just "finger-work" for Him—Psalms 8:3.) A few trillion coral units wouldn't be a problem. It's not a question of COULD God do this? It's not a question of WOULD God do this? The question is, DID God do this? On what basis do Young-Earth creationists believe God did this to coral reefs? Do they have any scientific evidence for this? NO! Do they have a passage of Scripture that says God did this? NO! They have an unsupported interpretation of the Bible that relies on an unobserved interpretation of nature. Yes, they believe on the basis of faith, but it is not faith in the Bible; it is faith in their own interpretation of the Bible.

My Sentiments on Sediments

The geological record reveals a distinct pattern of appearance of the various fossils. This is the basis for the Fossil Index System. Now, while the evolutionary interpretation of the geological strata is incorrect, the raw data are still valid. Specific fossils and fossil types do appear in a fairly set order. Smaller, simpler things do show up before the larger, more complex things. Why is this? What could have caused this? Day-Age creationists say God created things in that order, but as we have seen, that order doesn't coincide with the Genesis Creation Account. Young-Earth creationists say this was the result of sedimentation during the Great Flood. The main reason fossils appear where they do, they say, is because smaller organisms would have been more easily washed away by flood waters. Larger organisms such as mammals tend to be more buoyant. Size and density are the reasons all the drowned organisms settled out in the sediment the way they did. This explanation fails the scrutiny of logic. Modern snails are the same size and density as ancient snails, but modern snails aren't found in the same layers. Turkey-sized dinosaurs are the same size as turkey-sized turkeys, but turkey fossils are never found alongside dinosaur fossils. If size, density, and buoyancy are the factors that determine where fossils appear in the geological strata, then modern fish should be right next to primordial fish, modern plants ought to be in the same strata as primitive plants, and modern insects should be the fossil neighbors of ancient insects. Young-Earth creationists counter this by saying we need to consider the mobility factor. Larger, more complex organisms are more mobile and could have run to the high mountains when the Flood hit. Young-Earth creationists tell us the organisms we think of as "more modern" were not more modern than the ones we think of as "more primitive." Instead, they were just more mobile—they could move faster. Their fossils would appear later in the strata because they would have reached the high mountains before being washed away by the Flood. This seems reasonable at first glance, but it too is illogical. Many dinosaurs could run faster than many mammals. Modern snails couldn't outrun a Tyrannosaurus. So, why are Tyrannosaurus fossils always deeper than modern snails? Apple trees have the same mobility as ancient Bryophytes. Where are apple tree fossils and ancient Bryophyte fossils found in the same strata? Modern sleek, shiny, scaly fish have no more ability to run to the mountain tops than the primitive squishy, slimy, fishy-things that supposedly swam in the same lakes and same oceans at the same time. Why don't their fossils appear in the same geological strata? A prairie dog in Kansas had less chance of reaching the mountains than a Pterodactyl. So, why don't we find prairie dog fossils in strata deeper than Pterodactyl fossils?

Speaking of running dinosaurs, how do you explain dinosaur nests in-between fossil-bearing strata?[11] Paleontologists have found dinosaur nests containing eggs with fully developed baby dinosaurs inside; some even hatched. Since these nests are on top of fossil-bearing strata, these "fleeing" dinosaurs had to tread water while the Flood deposited thousands of feet of fossil-bearing sediment beneath them. Then, when the water temporarily receded, they took the time to mate, build nests, and lay eggs. They didn't seem in much of a hurry to get to the mountains. There had to be enough time for the eggs to incubate and the babies to develop before being covered by more fossil-bearing sediment when the water rose again. Nothing in the Bible indicates animals mated and reproduced during the Flood. **If all the fossils and all the geologic strata were created by the Flood, how do you explain the geologic evidence of animals living normal lives in-between layers of fossil-bearing strata?** Again, this interpretation is not based on the Words of the Bible or on the facts of science.

Nevertheless, if you are familiar with the arguments for and against Flood-Geology, then you know I would be lying if I said there were no examples of strata that seem out of place. There are many examples of younger fossils found beneath older fossils, and the arguments about how this happened are unending. Regardless of the explanations, these out-of-place fossils are still geological exceptions. The vast majority of fossils fit in very well with Traditional-Geology. They fit so well that almost any geologist can examine a fossil specimen and tell you where it fits in the geological scheme, and be right most of the time. This was why the Fossil Index System seemed like a great defense for evolution. Almost all fossils fit into the Traditional Geological position. When they are out of place, the explanations of the Traditional-Geologists (overthrusts, earthquakes, landslides, sinkholes, local floods, *etc.*) seem to me to be more scientific. It is also possible that "older fossils on top of newer fossils" might be the result of God restoring species that had long been dead, even for millions of years. (Living Fossils) If these restored "older" species were later buried and fossilized, they would be found on top of the fossils of "newer" species. Thus, the geological order would APPEAR out of place. God restoring "older" species during the Creation Week seems a lot easier explanation for out-of-order fossils, than Noah's Flood.

Carbon 14

You have probably heard about Carbon Dating. If you are not familiar with it, let me explain. Normal carbon is carbon 12. This means it has six protons and six neutrons in its nucleus. It is written as ^{12}C. Carbon 14 also has six protons in its nucleus, but it has eight neutrons. It is written as ^{14}C. Most ^{14}C atoms are made from nitrogen atoms in the upper atmosphere. Nitrogen has seven protons and seven neutrons in its nucleus. It is written as ^{14}N. When cosmic rays strike atoms in the upper atmosphere, neutrons can be knocked out of those atoms. Those neutrons are released at high energy levels. If a freed neutron collides with a nearby nitrogen atom, it can knock out one of the nitrogen atom's protons and take its place. The nucleus of the nitrogen atom thereby gains one neutron but loses one proton. When the nucleus loses a proton, it no longer has seven positive charges. This means the atom can no longer maintain seven negatively charged electrons in its orbit. As a result, one electron is lost. From that point on, the atom becomes carbon rather than nitrogen. It has six protons in its nucleus and six electrons in orbit around it. From that point on, it acts exactly like normal carbon in chemical reactions. For instance, it becomes carbon dioxide, CO_2, when oxidized by oxygen, O_2, in the air. The big difference between normal ^{12}C and ^{14}C, is that ^{14}C is radioactively unstable and decays over time. It has a half-life of about 5,700 years. This means every 5,700 years, one-half of the ^{14}C in any substance will have decayed back to nitrogen, ^{14}N. (If you want to impress your friends, tell them it happens when a neutron emits an electron and an anti-neutrino, thereby becoming a proton… they'll think you're smart.)

Most scientists assume the atmospheric ratio of ^{12}C to ^{14}C is relatively constant because the bombardment of cosmic rays is assumed relatively constant. They also assume the atmospheric concentrations of nitrogen, oxygen, and other gases are relatively constant. These two assumptions are what make Young-Earth creationists doubt the validity of Carbon Dating. While I agree there may be some exceptions with these assumptions in certain cases, I still believe in the majority of cases the Carbon Dating System provides reliable "in-the-ball-park" dates.

Plants take in carbon in the form of carbon dioxide in the air. As long as a plant is living, its $^{12}C/^{14}C$ ratio will be the same as the $^{12}C/^{14}C$ ratio in the air. When the plant dies, it no longer takes in carbon. Scientists can calculate how old the plant material is by measuring the $^{12}C/^{14}C$ ratio in the dead plant material. Since animals eat plants directly or indirectly, animals have the same $^{12}C/^{14}C$ ratio as the plants they eat. As long as they are alive, they will have the same $^{12}C/^{14}C$ ratio as what they are eating. When animals die, they no longer take in new carbon and the same radioactive decay process occurs. Carbon Dating is therefore used to measure the age of material that was once living. It can't directly measure the age of rocks and minerals. In addition, after about ten half-lives, the amount of ^{14}C is too small to differentiate from background ^{14}C levels. (There is a small amount of naturally-occurring ^{14}C in just about all environments.) This limits Carbon Dating to 60,000 years or so. Now, there are a lot of assumptions made when using Carbon Dating.

Young-Earth creationists have accused Old-Earth creationists of making wildly incorrect assumptions for Carbon Dating. I don't think they have, but I'm sure you have your own opinion. The real problem for me was when I learned how some Young-Earth creationists "invalidate" the Carbon Dating System by using deceptive information… dirty tricks. (I SAID "SOME," NOT "ALL.") There are some Young-Earth creationists who have taken tissue from living or freshly killed organisms and have had it Carbon Dated as being several thousand years old. They say this proves Carbon Dating is invalid. Many people believe them. I did at one time, but then I discovered what really happened. I also discovered they knew what really happened, but didn't reveal it. They hid the truth.

The $^{12}C/^{14}C$ ratio in any living organism is going to be the same ratio as in what it takes in. Since plants take in carbon dioxide from the air, plants have the same ratio as in the air. Animals will have the same ratio only if they consume **new** plant material. If you took 5,000-year-old organic debris and fed it to organisms that feed on organic debris, then you would have organisms with the same $^{12}C/^{14}C$ ratio as in the 5,000-year-old organic debris. They would look 5,000 years old according to Carbon Dating. In other words, **feed it 5,000-year-old carbon and it will look 5,000 years old by Carbon Dating.** If you took these organisms and fed them to higher organisms, then those higher organisms would also have a Carbon Date of 5,000 years. Any biologic niche contaminated by "old carbon" will produce organisms that appear old according to Carbon Dating.

This is what some Young-Earth creationists do: They find a place contaminated with "old carbon" to collect their samples. For instance, they find a river that has cut a channel or valley down through several geological layers. They go to a layer that is 5,000 years old. They take out living organisms that have been feeding on the 5,000-year-old carbon in that layer. Then they use Carbon Dating to show how these living organisms have been, "dead for 5,000 years." This deceptive technique is used to convince people Carbon Dating is wrong. This is their "proof" the earth is young. Ironically, they verify the Carbon Dating system. They use organisms made of 5,000-year-old carbon, and Carbon Dating shows they are made of 5,000-year-old carbon. The Carbon Dating is right, but their interpretation is wrong. They don't tell us that! Instead, they tell us Carbon Dating is erroneous, and they make it look as if Old-Earth Christians are wrong. They use a deception to defend their theory. Is this something Christians should do? Where does the Bible say we can use deception to defend the truth? If they do this out of ignorance, then it's a little more excusable. However, they should know better. I have no problem questioning some of the assumptions of the Carbon Dating System. But, I have a big problem with using lies to discredit it. If they intentionally lie, they bring shame to Christians and to Christ. Unfortunately, you can find Christian books, Christian magazines, Christian newsletters, Christian newspapers, Christian Internet Websites, Christian videos, Christian radio programs, and Christian churches that still use this dirty trick. Atheistic college professors are aware of this Young-Earth trick. They use it to put a stumbling block between their students and the Gospel. What are students to think about Christ when their professors show them that Christians deliberately lie?

There is another scientific fact concerning ^{14}C that Flood Geologists must contort in order to make the evidence fit the Young-Earth Theory. As I have mentioned, the half-life of ^{14}C is about 5,700 years. This means any plant material less than ten ^{14}C half-lives old (about 60,000 years) would still have detectable ^{14}C. Plant material younger than one half-life would have lots of ^{14}C. Now, here is the tricky part. When did Noah's Flood happen? According to Flood Geologists it was about 4,000-4,500 years ago. Okay, that sounds reasonable to me. But that means any plant material laid down by the Flood would still have plenty of ^{14}C. Does that pose a problem for scientists? No. They have had no problem finding ^{14}C in wood, charcoal, and other plant material as old, and even older than the Flood. Manmade timbers, tools, utensils, and other artifacts made of wood from 4,000 years ago, 5,000 years ago, and even 6,000 years ago have been discovered, historically documented, and accurately carbon dated. There has been no time in the last several thousand years that ^{14}C wasn't present in the atmosphere for plants to assimilate. Here is the problem: If coal comes from plant material buried by the Flood, (as Ellen White and the Young-Earth-Flood Geologists claim) then coal should have enough ^{14}C to prove it is less than 5,000 years old. If coal was created by the Flood, it should have a great deal of ^{14}C.

How much ^{14}C is found in coal? The answer is virtually zero. At most, there are only background traces of ^{14}C in coal. The reason coal has a trace amount of ^{14}C is because coal can be externally contaminated with ^{14}C. In fact, there is a trace level of ^{14}C in just about any substance exposed to air, water, bacteria, fungi, or any organic chemical. It is this background contamination of ^{14}C that limits the carbon-dating technique to about 60,000 years. External contamination is not the only source of ^{14}C in coal. Internal contamination happens when other long-lived radioactive isotopes in the coal decay and create ^{14}C via other radioactive decay products. That means new ^{14}C can be created in coal, but it is not ^{14}C from an organic source. The fact coal has virtually zero ^{14}C, proves it is was not created by the Flood.

How can this be if the Flood-Geologists are right? If the plants that became coal grew 4,000 to 5,000 years ago, they should have the same levels of ^{14}C as found in other plants growing in the same time period. Wooden timbers from 4,500 years ago (as determined by historical records and dendrochronology) have been shown to have a ^{14}C content that dates them to 4,500 years ago. Since those timbers were cut from trees 4,500 years ago, it proves ^{14}C was present in the atmosphere 4,500 years ago. Why did those trees have ^{14}C, but the trees and ferns that ended up in coal seams have no ^{14}C? There shouldn't be a difference in the ^{14}C levels. The Young-Earth explanation is illogical. They say there was no ^{14}C in the atmosphere before the Flood because the Pre-Flood earth was covered by a very thick, very dense canopy of water that prevented cosmic rays from creating ^{14}C in the upper atmosphere. If that was true, then there shouldn't be ^{14}C in any wood or plant material from that same time period. In spite of what Young-Earth creationists claim, there have been numerous artifacts from 4,500 years ago that prove the atmospheric ^{14}C level was what Old-Earth creationists say it was. Since coal has virtually zero ^{14}C, it means it has been around so long that all its ^{14}C has decayed back to ^{14}N. In reality, all the scientific indicators of age, both radiometric and geologic, point to an age for coal of about 200-300 million years.

Undeterred by facts, Young-Earth creationists present a second possibility: God miraculously removed all the ^{14}C from coal to give the earth an apparent age of millions of years. He left the ^{14}C in all the other wood and plant material at the time of the Flood, but not in coal. He took the ^{14}C out of coal. Either that, or He miraculously added ^{14}C to all the manmade timbers and organic artifacts after the Flood, so scientists would foolishly think there was ^{14}C in the atmosphere 4,500 years ago. I've always wondered why Young-Earth creationists criticize Old-Earth creationists for believing the earth is millions of years old, when God has done everything He could do to make it appear millions of years old. (And there are dozens of verified, independent, scientific indicators of an old universe.) It sure seems as if God wants people to think the earth is old. Is God deceptive?

Japanese Plesiosaur

Young-Earth creationists believe dinosaurs and humans were contemporaries 6,000 years ago. Old-Earth creationists disagree. They say there is no evidence for such a claim. Young-Earth creationists say they have proof for their belief. In 1977, fishermen on a Japanese fishing trawler hauled in a gigantic rotting carcass off the coast of New Zealand. The fishermen didn't know what it was and immediately speculated it was a Plesiosaur, a marine dinosaur (reptile) that lived 100 to 200 million years ago. Young-Earth creationists were ecstatic. Here was a dinosaur that wasn't millions of years old. Young-Earth creationists immediately began using this discovery as a way to prove their theory was true. Some used this discovery as a way of ridiculing Old-Earth creationists. Here again, Mr. Deception raised his ugly head. Within a few weeks of the discovery, scientific tests indicated the cartilage in the carcass came from a shark. It wasn't a reptile. Within a few months, amino acid analyses of its proteins proved the carcass was a Basking Shark (*Cetorhinus maximus*). Basking Shark experts looked at the photographs of the rotting carcass and affirmed it was a rotting Basking Shark. Sadly, some Young-Earth creationists still claim this was a Plesiosaur. God is not deceptive, but these Young-Earth creationists are.

Paluxy River Footprints

After I learned the Theory of Evolution was a lie, I began searching for answers about creation. I initially accepted Day-Age creationism, but discovered it contradicted the Bible. I didn't know what to believe. However, as soon as I saw photographs of human footprints in the same geological strata as dinosaur footprints, I became a Young-Earther. This was in 1972 and I was young and easily impressed. I consumed volumes of Young-Earth books and pamphlets to learn more about these footprints in the riverbed of the

Paluxy River near Glen Rose, Texas. These weren't ordinary footprints. These were footprints of dinosaurs and humans in the same limestone. This seemed like absolute proof men and dinosaurs lived together 6,000 years ago. The photographs were clear. It appeared the dinosaur footprints and the human footprints were real. For years, Young-Earth creationists wrote article after article and book after book about how this "proved" they were right. Old-Earth creationists refuted their evidence, but that made the Young-Earth creationists more determined than ever to show the world their "proof."

Then something very bad happened to their "proof." It was shown to be incorrect, and it was shown to be incorrect by some of the same Young-Earth creationists who once believed it. It was eventually shown that the evidence was a combination of wild imaginations, hoaxes, poor data, misunderstandings, ignorance, and just a little bit of longing for fame and fortune. Yes, money could be made from those footprints. The scientific evidence was wrong, and I strongly salute the integrity of the Young-Earthers who have rejected it. However, there are still Young-Earth creationists who peddle this kind of snake oil for personal fortune and fame.

Magnetic Field Decay

The earth has a magnetic field around it. This is good. It helps shield the earth from charged particles emitted from the sun. It allows us to see the Northern and Southern Lights. It also makes compass navigation possible. These things have nothing to do with creation, but there is one aspect of the earth's magnetic field that Young-Earthers use to defend their position. The magnetic field of the earth is decaying; it is getting weaker. Scientists have been able to determine the rate of decay, and it seems to create a problem for Old-Earthers. If you know the rate of decay, then you can calculate the strength of the field in the past. This is what Young-Earthers have done, and initially, I was impressed by their claim. If you extrapolate backward in time, even a few thousand years, you can conclude the earth had a tremendously stronger magnetic field. If you go back millions of years, then the magnetic field of the earth would have been so great it would have melted the crust of the earth. In the same fashion magnetic-induction stovetops heat iron cookware, the magnetic field of the earth would have heated the iron in the crust to a point it would have been molten. Obviously, a molten earth would not be good for life. Even if dinosaurs had compasses they wouldn't be able to navigate very well on a molten surface, and they certainly wouldn't have enjoyed the Northern Lights. Therefore, Young-Earth creationists say the earth cannot be millions of years old. This sounds very scientific and very believable, and it is still being used to convince people the earth is only a few thousand years old. Yet, like so many other Young-Earth scientific claims, there is more to the story than they tell.

Yes, the magnetic field is getting weaker, but it hasn't always done so. There were times when it got stronger. The magnetic field is constantly changing. In fact, scientists have discovered the magnetic field has reversed its polarity numerous times in the past.[12]

It gets weaker, then it changes polarity, then it gets stronger in the opposite direction, then it gets weaker, then it changes polarity. It cycles back and forth in its polarity. The needle on your compass does not point to the geographic North Pole, it points to the magnetic North Pole. The magnetic pole moves around. If you were alive hundreds of thousands of years ago, the needle of your compass would have pointed to the magnetic "north" pole, but it would have been closer to the geographic South Pole. Still, many Young-Earthers use this argument to prove their point. This is as scientific as if I measured the temperature increase during the first few hours of the morning and then used this rate of increase to extrapolate ahead. If the temperature rose ten degrees in the first four hours after sunrise, I could then calculate that within a week, the earth would be over four hundred degrees. Extrapolations don't work for cyclic phenomena.

Mississippi River Delta

I once believed the Young-Earth argument that the Mississippi River was five to seven thousand years old. This was based on another extrapolation. The Mississippi River carries millions of tons of silt into the Gulf of Mexico every year. Therefore, the Mississippi River delta is growing larger every year. Scientists have been able to measure its rate of increase. By looking at the total area of the delta and dividing the area by the rate of increase, it is possible to show it would take only five to seven thousand years to create the delta. This sounds very scientific, but like many Young-Earth arguments, it is based on some incorrect assumptions. First, the delta hasn't always grown at the same rate. In fact, due to compaction, erosion, hurricanes, and tropical storms, the delta can be washed away. It has gotten smaller at times. Extrapolations don't work here because we aren't dealing with a steady rate of growth. Second, as the Mississippi River meanders in its course, the mouth of the Mississippi changes locations. Its current location came about five to seven thousand years ago during the thaw of the last ice-age. The current Mississippi River Delta is only five to seven thousand years old, but not the Mississippi River. It has been there for over two million years.

Now, if anyone has a right to use extrapolations dealing with the Mississippi River Delta, it's Old-Earth Geologists. You see, Young-Earth Geologists weren't telling the whole truth. The delta is not only gaining in area, it's gaining in depth. This is a three-dimensional problem, but Young-Earthers have applied a two-dimensional explanation. So much sediment has been deposited that its weight has pushed the earth's crust downward. How far down has the crust beneath the Mississippi River Delta been pushed? Oh, about seven miles.[13] Young-Earth/Flood-Geologists say Noah's Flood did this. Noah's Flood deposited this seven-mile thick layer of sediment. This creates some problems. First, when you use extrapolations to determine the age of the delta, you discover it would have taken much longer than five to seven thousand years to deposit that much volume (not area) of river sediment. Next, how could a flood five-miles deep (fifteen cubits above Mount Everest) carry a seven-mile thick deposit of sediment? The only way this could happen is if two miles of sediment stood above the surface of the Flood waters. But, if that were so, then the Bible made a mistake when it said the entire earth was covered with water. In addition, geology has shown that the Mississippi River Delta sediment is sitting on top of fossil-laden strata that was there before the river and its delta were even formed. Young-Earthers say the Mississippi River (created by the Flood) deposited that Mississippi River sediment (created by the Flood) on top of layers of non-Mississippi River sediment (created by the Flood). This could happen only if the water that created the delta was seven miles higher than the water that created the strata below it. Water can't do that; water seeks its own level. If seven miles of sediment was dumped on top of the strata created by the Flood, there should be a seven-mile high mountain at the end of the Mississippi River, not a seven-mile layer of sediment below the surface.

Young-Earthers explain what "really" happened. It just so happened that the horrendous earthquakes and tectonic forces accompanying the Flood caused the earth to sink seven miles at the mouth of the Mississippi River. A seven-mile deep hole suddenly formed. Then a seven-mile pile of river sediment quickly fell into that seven-mile deep hole. It was lucky the hole in the ocean floor just happened to be there. Otherwise, a seven-mile high mountain would have been created at the mouth of the Mississippi River. If that had happened, much of North America would be under water today. It was lucky those massive earthquakes were able to create a hole in just the right spot. Even luckier is that other massive earthquakes just happened to create other massive holes in the ocean floor at the mouths of every other major river. The Nile, the Amazon, the Yangtze, and others have deep depressions in the strata at their mouths, and their holes are all filled in with their own river sediment. What a coincidence all those deep depressions were formed in just the right spots in the ocean floor, and then all those right spots were filled with river-borne sediment. Now, let's ask two key questions. First, is this Young-Earth explanation scientific? No. They have no scientific evidence the deltas of the world's rivers were formed in this fashion. Second, is this Young-Earth explanation Biblical? No, and this is going to shock some people. There is no Biblical statement that says earthquakes accompanied Noah's Flood.

No Earthquakes; No Volcanoes

Many Young-Earth creationists now realize the difficultly in explaining how the Flood covered Mt. Everest since there isn't enough water currently on the earth to do that. Where did all the water go? From where did it all come? Besides the rain, they say it came from sub-crustal reservoirs under hundreds of thousands of pounds of pressure. Then, when the earth's crust cracked along the mid-Atlantic seabed (which isn't mentioned in the Bible) and circumnavigated the earth pole-to-pole, (which isn't mentioned in the Bible) a massive-massive-super-super-heated column of water (which isn't mentioned in the Bible) shot up into the ionosphere where it froze in the cold of space. (which isn't mentioned in the Bible) Then, it fell back to earth as ice and snow, (which isn't mentioned in the Bible) thereby creating the ice-age that followed the Flood. (which isn't mentioned in the Bible) After the Flood, the water drained back into those sub-crustal reservoirs, leaving just enough water to form our oceans, lakes, and rivers. Sounds convincing, right? Well, yes, but only if you are a Young-Earth/Flood-Geologist. To the rest of us, it sounds like a cheap science fiction B-movie. This explanation has no scientific evidence supporting it. In fact, it defies physics. (Oh, and did I tell you none of this is mentioned in the Bible?) The only way the water could refill those super-heated high-pressure reservoirs is if the atmospheric pressure forced it back down. (Gravity alone, couldn't do it.) The atmosphere had to be under hundreds of thousands of pounds of pressure to push that water back down again. Noah, his family, and all the animals on the Ark would have been killed by that pressure. Not only that, but the heat released from all that super-super-heated water would have raised the temperature of the lower atmosphere by hundreds of degrees as it ascended. The conditions on the earth during the Flood would have been like a giant pressure-cooker.

In an effort to explain how the Flood could create miles and miles of strata without being miles and miles deep, many Young-Earth creationists no longer believe the Flood was miles and miles deep. Five miles of ocean wasn't needed to cover Mt. Everest because Mt. Everest wasn't formed until after the Flood. Neither were all the other mountains. Some Young-Earth creationists believe the earth was relatively flat before the Flood. They say the mountains mentioned in Genesis 7:20 were actually hills. That way, five miles of water wouldn't have been needed to cover the earth. (Of course, that destroys the argument that faster animals were able to flee to the high mountains before being washed away by the Flood.) Many Flood-Geologists now say the great tectonic and volcanic forces accompanying the Flood caused the formation of all the mountains after the flood ended. They talk about how the continents were split apart and then slammed together. They explain how tremendous Post-Flood earthquakes and volcanic activity formed the great mountains we have today. These are very interesting explanations, but none of it comes from science. None of it comes from the Bible. That's right; none of this is mentioned in the Bible.

Genesis 7:11 "In the six hundredth year of Noah's life, on the seventeenth day of the second month—on that day all the springs of the great deep burst forth, and the floodgates of the heavens were opened." (NIV)

The Bible says the springs of the deep burst forth. Along with the rain, the springs on the ocean floor suddenly released tremendous amounts of water, BUT IT DOESN'T SAY THERE WERE EARTHQUAKES AND VOLCANOES. Adding earthquakes and volcanoes to the formula is a Biblical interpretation, not a Biblical declaration. (What is not a Biblical interpretation, is the revelation there are springs on the ocean floor. This geological fact wasn't known until the 20th century and the invention of submarines, bathyspheres, sonar, and underwater cameras. When the Bible was written, no one knew there were springs on the ocean floor. No one had ever seen them. This is another amazing example of how God's Word matches His work.) The Bible doesn't say earthquakes accompanied the Flood. The Bible doesn't say the earth's crust broke along the mid-Atlantic seabed. The Bible doesn't say the continents were forced apart. The Bible doesn't say the continents were slammed together. The Bible doesn't say there were massive volcanic eruptions during the Flood. The Bible doesn't say an ice-age followed the Flood. The Bible doesn't say great holes formed in the ocean floor at the mouth of where every major river would later flow. The Bible doesn't say Noah's Flood washed mountains into the sea. The Bible doesn't say great tectonic forces created new mountains. The Bible doesn't tell us great forests of trees were ripped out by raging waters and transported for hundreds of miles. In fact, the only tree mentioned in the Biblical Flood account is an olive tree. Noah released a dove from the ark shortly after the tops of the mountains had become visible. The dove returned with a freshly-plucked olive leaf in its beak. The olive tree had not been ripped out. The Flood was so gentle, it didn't even uproot this tree. Even though it had been under water for a year, it was still alive and producing leaves. (I believe God miraculously preserved the life of many, if not all plants. The Flood wasn't designed to kill plants. If God had allowed the Flood to kill all the plants, then all the animals would have died of starvation while waiting for the vegetation to regrow after they departed the ark.) According to the Bible, the Flood wasn't the horrendous earth-destructive force Young-Earth creationists say it was.

Genesis 6:7 "And the LORD said, I will destroy man whom I have created from the face of the earth; both man, and beast, and the creeping thing, and the fowls of the air; for it repenteth me that I have made them." (KJV)

Well, won't you look at that! God never said the Flood would destroy plant life. He makes no mention of great forests being ripped out and carried for hundreds of miles. He doesn't say mountains will be washed away. The purpose of the Flood was to destroy humans and air-breathing animals. It accomplished this quite effectively by steadily increasing and then steadily decreasing in depth without radically reshaping the entire face of the earth. (Just because it covered the entire face of the earth, it doesn't mean it changed the entire face of the earth.) Since God never said the Flood would destroy plants, and since plants survived the Flood, where do Young-Earth creationists get the idea great forests were ripped out and carried for hundreds of miles? God's Word makes no such claim. God's work (the science of geology) reveals no such event. God's Word agrees with His work. It's sad that Young-Earth creationists don't agree with either.

Every indication from the Bible is the Flood wasn't tumultuous. Besides the olive tree not being uprooted, there are other indicators the Flood wasn't what the Young-Earth/Flood-Geologists say it was. We don't know exactly where Noah lived when he built the ark, but it likely wasn't far from Eden. (The people in those days seemed to have no desire to spread out over the earth.) Since we know the general area where the ark rested after the Flood, the Mountains of Ararat, we can measure how far the ark drifted during its approximately one-year voyage. It was probably only two or three hundred miles, at the most. When you see movies of Noah's Flood, they always show the ark being tossed about by tremendous wind and waves. Tremendous wind and waves aren't mentioned in the Bible. Since the ark wasn't a sailing vessel, it had no means of propulsion or navigation. Its movement was caused by whatever wind and waves it experienced during that year. If the wind and waves had been as great as Young-Earth/Flood-Geologists say they were, the ark would have been blown thousands of miles. Since the ark didn't drift very far, the wind and waves must not have been very powerful. In addition, we see from the Bible that the local terrain hadn't changed much.

Genesis 2:10-14 "A river flowed out of Eden to water the garden, and there it divided and became four rivers. {11} The name of the first is the Pishon. It is the one that flowed around the whole land of Havilah, where there is gold. {12} And the gold of that land is good; bdellium and onyx stone are there. {13} The name of the second river is the Gihon. It is the one that flowed around the whole land of Cush. {14} And the name of the third river is the Tigris, which flows east of Assyria. And the fourth river is the Euphrates. (ESV)

In Genesis 2:10-14 Moses gives a description of three lands outside of Eden: Havilah, Cush, and Assyria. He also names four rivers that came out of Eden and flowed into those lands: The Pishon, the Gihon, the Tigris, and the Euphrates. The river that watered the Garden did something unusual; it split into four rivers. Rivers don't normally split into two or more smaller rivers. Generally, two or more smaller rivers combine to form a single, larger river. The river that watered the Garden became four rivers. This may seem like an impossible trick, but there are cases of natural bifurcations where single rivers or creeks split into two separate rivers or creeks. I don't know of any that later divide into four, but the task wouldn't be impossible if the bifurcations split again. It's also possible the river could have gone underground and resurfaced as more than one river later. This happens today with the waters coming off Mount Hermon. Some of the water goes underground and then resurfaces as two rivers that later flow into the Jordan River. Another possibility is the river flowing out of Eden fed into a lake with more than one outlet. It's also possible these were God-engineered bifurcations; He could have created the terrain necessary for this to happen. However the rivers did what they did, they were still present at the time of Moses. The Flood seemed to have changed only their point of origin, not their entire courses. (Assuming it was the Flood that did it.) Young-Earth/Flood-Geologists believe the Tigris and Euphrates Rivers at the time of Moses were different rivers than the Tigris and Euphrates rivers at the time of Adam. They believe the Great Flood would have destroyed the original rivers and changed the entire geography. They say the rivers at the time of Moses were only named after the original rivers that once flowed out of Eden. They point out we do the same thing when we name a city, such as Paris, Kentucky after the original Paris in France. The problem with their claim is Genesis 2:14 tells us the Pre-Flood Tigris ran along the east side of Assyria. That geographical area wouldn't have been named

Assyria during Adam's time; Assyria as a nation didn't yet exist. Moses was describing the Pre-Flood geography of the Land of Eden in terms of the geography in his day. Moses points out how the Pre-Flood Tigris River was located exactly where the Post-Flood Tigris River was located; along the east side of Assyria. That means it was the same river in the same place. The Flood didn't change the geography. He also associates the Pre-Flood Euphrates with the Pre-Flood Tigris in the same area. That association still existed after the Flood. Additionally, Moses referred to Havilah and Cush as geographical areas where those rivers flowed. Havilah and Cush wouldn't have been named Havilah and Cush at the time of Adam, either. (Cush, also spelled Kush, was located in the southern Mesopotamia area. It was named after Cush, the grandson of Noah and was the ancestral home of the Kashites. It was not Cush—Ethiopia located in Africa.) However, as geographical areas, these lands would have been there. Moses spoke of the gold, bdellium, and onyx for which Havilah was noted in his time. He indicated the Pre-Flood Havilah contained the same valuable ore and gems as the Post-Flood Havilah. Whatever these three Pre-Flood geographical lands were called during the time of Adam, they were still present when Moses wrote Genesis. The Flood didn't destroy those three Pre-Flood lands. The Flood didn't destroy those four Pre-Flood rivers. They were still present at Moses' time. Why do I believe this? There are two reasons. First, what would be the use of naming the geographical boundaries of Eden to the Israelites if those boundaries no longer existed? Second, when Moses named the rivers and lands, he expressed it in terms of unchanging conditions. The *King James* translates the Hebrew using *is* in the italics when describing the rivers and the lands. As I mentioned before, the *King James* uses italics to indicate words that weren't in the Hebrew, but were added to the English to make it read better in English. This means "is" was not in the Hebrew. I will later explain the differences between using "*is*" in italics, and using "**is**" not in italics. For now, let me just say Moses wrote it in a way to express the idea the original rivers and lands were still there and relatively unchanged. Noah's Flood didn't radically alter the geology of that region of the earth.

In May 2010, when I published the second edition of this book, I claimed there were no massive volcanic eruptions or globally destructive earthquakes that accompanied Noah's Flood. I had two reasons for believing this. First, they were not mentioned in the Bible. Second, Young-Earth/Flood-Geologists never presented any real scientific evidence FOR those events. (They insisted they did, but it was nothing more than using the assumptions they needed, to reach the conclusions they wanted.) True, I had no scientific evidence AGAINST those events, but I was convinced if they had happened, God would have recorded them in the Bible and/or geology would have recorded them in the strata. In May 2010, another Gap Theory defender published his own book defending the Gap Theory of Creation. The author is Gaines Johnson, and his book is *The Bible, Genesis & Geology*.[14] We were literally half a world apart, but the Holy Spirit was using him to teach me some geology lessons. When I read his book, I was amazed to see how the geologic evidence proved there were no massive volcanic eruptions or globally destructive earthquakes that accompanied Noah's Flood. His book is full of geologic evidence that proves the Gap Theory. He reveals how the geological evidence proves the earth existed long before Adam. He also reveals the evidence Noah's Flood didn't destroy or reshape the entire face of the earth as Young-Earth creationists believe. He explained how the findings of the 1993 Greenland Ice Sheet Project Two (GISP2), the evidence of global dust spikes, and the paleoclimate indicators agree with the true Biblical account of creation... The Ruin-Restoration Theory.

I was pleased to see how Gaines proved God's Work (Geology) fits God's Word (The Bible) when presented with the scientific evidence in light of the Ruin-Restoration Theory. I was more than pleased to see how the Holy Spirit is raising up Christians all over the world to rekindle the teaching of the Gap Theory. I was more than, more than pleased when Gaines published the second edition to his book[15] in September 2013. In his second edition, Gaines documents even more geological evidence in favor of the Gap Theory. If you really want to know the geologic facts, then you really have to read Gaines Johnson's book. Of course, if you are a Young-Earth creationist who really doesn't want to know the facts, then don't.

I could list many more holes in Young-Earth/Flood-Geology. I won't do that because it isn't the ultimate purpose of this book. However, if you want to learn more, then I recommend Alan Hayward's book, *Creation and Evolution*.[16] I have listed ten arguments, but that doesn't even scratch the surface of the surface. He lists hundreds. I have purchased multiple copies of Dr. Hayward's book over the years so I can lend them to friends and not worry about them not being returned. It is a permanent part of my library. It should be part of your library too. Dr. Hayward, a Christian, does an excellent job at debunking Young-Earth/Flood-Geology. For now, I think I have listed enough evidence to make my point clear. Young-Earth Theology is much worse than Day-Age Theology at explaining the geological strata. I was foolish for once believing it.

If we view all this from the perspective of the Restoration Theory, we see how it fits. The geological strata reveal the events of the Pre-Adamic world, the first beginning. The six days of Genesis reveal the events of the restored world, the second beginning. The order of restoration doesn't match the order of creation because they were different events at different times. The order in which things were first created is not mentioned in Genesis 1:1. This means the geological strata shouldn't be expected to agree with the events described during the six days. The geological strata we see today are the results of pre-restoration geological forces, modified to some degree by the Great Flood and current geological forces. If this true, then some aspects of geology would indicate old ages, while other aspects of geology would indicate young ages. This is exactly what geology reveals if Young-Earth and Old-Earth Geologists are telling us the truth about what they discover. Both Young-Earthers and Old-Earthers do seem to have some valid arguments. There are some things that look young and there are some things that look old. When an Old-Earther proves some piece of the puzzle is old, then he is looking at something from the first beginning. When a Young-Earther proves some piece of the puzzle is young, then he is looking at something from the second beginning. The Gap Theory removes the conflict between these two views. Old-Earthers and Young-Earthers don't have to be enemies.

Chapter Six: A Closer Look at the Bible

If I quit right here, it is possible some of you would be convinced the Day-Age Theory and the Young-Earth Theory fail to answer some crucial scientific questions. They lack scientific evidence. On that basis, you might agree the Gap Theory provides a better solution. Most of you, however, would not be convinced. I doubt I have changed the minds of many Day-Age and Young-Earth creationists. To be honest, if I were a diehard Day-Ager or a Young-Earther, I probably wouldn't be convinced either. The reason I wouldn't be convinced is not because the scientific evidence was lacking, but because I would feel a higher obligation to defend the Bible. As long as I believed the Bible truly taught the universe was 6,000 years old, I would continue to defend the Young-Earth Theory. As long as I believed the Bible truly taught the "days" were long ages, I would continue to defend the Day-Age Theory. What I really need to know is this: WHAT DOES THE BIBLE TRULY TEACH?

Is the earth young? Is it old? You'll have to decide for yourself, but I'd like to share my opinion with you. The Gap Theory suggests both ages are valid because the earth had two different beginnings. The Gap Theory suggests the earth had a beginning that may have been billions of years ago, and another beginning that was thousands of years ago. If the Bible reveals the earth had two different beginnings, then the Gap Theory is the most plausible theory. Is this what the Bible reveals? Let's start by looking at how several Hebrew scholars translate the first two verses of Genesis.

Twenty-Seven Correct Translations of Genesis 1:1-2a

1.) "In the beginning God created the heaven and the earth. And the earth was without form, and void; and darkness *was* upon the face of the deep" (KJV)

2.) "In the beginning God created the heavens and the earth. The earth was without form, and void; and darkness *was* on the face of the deep" (NKJV)

3.) "In the beginning God created the heavens and the earth. The earth was unformed and chaotic, and darkness lay upon the face of the deep" (BV)

4.) "In the beginning God created the heavens and the earth. The earth was formless and empty, and darkness lay upon the face of the deep" (NBV)

5.) "In the beginning God created the heavens and the earth. But the earth was empty and void, and darkness was over the face of the abyss" (Martin Luther Translation)[17]

6.) "When God in the beginning formed the heaven and the earth, (then) the earth was waste and void, and darkness was upon the face of the deep" (Von Bohlen Translation)[18]

7.) "In the beginning God **Elohim** created the *heaven* **heavens** and the earth. And the earth *was without form* **became waste**, and void; and darkness was upon the face of the *deep* **abyss**." (ERRB) (emphasis in original)

8.) "When God set about to create the heaven and the earth, the world being then a formless waste, with darkness over the seas" (Speiser Translation)[19] (SPEIS)

9.) "In the beginning when God created the heavens and the earth, the earth was a formless void and darkness covered the face of the deep" (NRSV)

10.) "In the beginning God created the heaven and the earth. But (then) the earth became waste, and darkness was upon the face of the deep" (Dillman Translation)[20]

11.) "In the beginning of God's preparing the heavens and the earth, the earth hath existed waste and void, and darkness is on the face of the deep" (Robert Young Translation)[21]

12.) "When God began to create the heavens and the earth, the earth was a desolate waste, with darkness covering the abyss" (S&G)

13.) "In the beginning God created the sky and the earth. The earth was empty and had no form. Darkness covered the ocean" (NCV)

14.) "In the beginning which was not a beginning, in eternity past, *ELOHIM* (the Son) created out of nothing the entire universe, including Planet Earth. But the earth had become desolate and empty with darkness on the face of the raging waters" (Robert B. Thieme Translation)[22]

15.) "In the beginning God created the heavens and the earth. And now, as far as the earth was concerned, it was waste and void, and darkness was upon the face of the deep" (Leupold Translation)[23]

16.) "In the beginning God created the heavens and the earth. Now the earth was a formless void, there was darkness over the deep" (NJB)

17.) "At the beginning of the creation of the heavens and the earth, the earth it was without form or life, and darkness was upon the face of the deep" (Cassuto Translation)[24]

18.) "In the beginning God created the heaven and the earth. But the earth had become a ruin and desolation; and darkness was upon the face of the deep" (Arthur Custance Translation)[25]

19.) "In the beginning God created the heavens and the earth. Now the earth was formless and empty, darkness was over the surface of the deep" (NIV)

20.) "When God began to form the universe, the world was void and vacant, darkness lay on the abyss." (MB)

21.) "In the beginning God created the heaven and the earth. The earth was unformed and empty; clouds covered the abyss" (English translation of the Crampon Translation)[26]

22.) "In the beginning, God created the heaven and the earth, But the earth was unsightly and unfurnished, and darkness was over the deep" (Septuagint, Bagster Edition)[27]

23.) "In the beginning God created the heavens and the earth. Now the earth had become waste and wild, and darkness was on the face of the roaring deep" (EMP)

24.) "In the beginning Elohim created the heavens and the earth. And the earth came to be (the earth became) formless and empty, and darkness was on the face of the deep." (SCRIP)

25.) "**In a beginning Elohim created the heavens and the earth. As for the earth, it came to be a chaos and vacant, and darkness was over the surface of the abyss.**" (CVOT) (emphasis in original)

26.) "In the beginning God created the heavens and the earth. And the earth was formless and void, and darkness was over the surface of the deep" (NASB)

27.) "In the beginning God created the heavens and the earth. And the earth was waste and void and darkness was upon the face of the deep" (RSV)

28.) "Look, look, look. See God. See God create. See God create the heavens and the earth. Create, God, create! Oh, oh, oh, see the earth. The earth is without form, and void..." (The New Dill Nonstandard Translation)

(Of these twenty-eight translations of the Bible, I'll leave it up to you to decide which twenty-seven are correct translations, and which translation is incorrect.)

Isn't it amazing how many different translations of Genesis 1:1-2 there are? I don't know what it says about mankind, but we can't even finish the first sentence of the first paragraph of the first chapter of the first book of the Bible without creating a controversy. There seems to be about as many translations as there are Hebrew scholars. I suppose it's only human nature for each Hebrew scholar to come out with, "the best translation ever." I've also noticed that nearly all of these scholars are, "the world's foremost authority in ancient Hebrew," but very few totally agree with how the others translate Genesis 1:1-2. They all tend to say things like, "Yes, it can be translated the way Dr. So-And-So puts it, but..." At this point they show you how wrong Dr. So-And-So is and how right they are by translating it the way they believe.

After reading a number of books dealing with the Genesis account of creation, I have made a couple of deductions about the translations of Genesis. Before I mention those deductions, I want to reveal my own authority and expertise in this area: I have none. I cannot read Hebrew. I can, however, read the comments of those who are experts in Hebrew. If you are a Hebrew scholar and wish to criticize my opinion, please feel free to do so. If you aren't a Hebrew scholar and you hear experts criticizing me on the grounds I'm not a scholar, I ask you to remember one thing. My opinion on the translation of the creation accounts is not MY opinion. It comes from a number of Hebrew scholars who are highly qualified and respected in this area. My role in this is similar to the little boy who knew nothing about chess, but challenged the world's top two chess masters to play him simultaneously. He claimed he would beat at least one of them, or at worst, tie them both. His only request was that he be allowed to move second against one of them and move first against the other. To everyone's surprise he played brilliantly. He lost to one of the chess masters, but as he had predicted, he beat the other. When the losing chess master asked him how he could play such superb chess while knowing nothing about the game, he revealed his secret. He merely repeated the moves of the first player against the second, and responded against the first player with how the second player responded to those same moves. In reality, he played one chess master against the other. That's what I'm doing when I enter the area of Hebrew translations. I quote the scholars, and quote their quotes about other scholars' quotes. So, when I tell you my opinion of how the Hebrew is supposed to be translated, it is not my opinion. It is the opinion of Hebrew scholars.

As I said, I've made two deductions about the translations of the Genesis account. My first deduction is that Hebrew must be a "rubber" language. Evidently, its rules of grammar and varied word definitions make it highly flexible. Meanings, seemingly, can be stretched to define almost anything. In truth, every one of the above listed translations (excluding mine, of course) can be defended by the rules of Hebrew grammar. Every one of those translations was made by knowledgeable and fully qualified Hebrew scholars. We non-scholars must tread lightly. We are at the mercy of the scholars, so I ask my readers to be wary. Don't let anyone tell you even one of those twenty-seven translations of Genesis 1:1-2 is without grammatical support. He who makes such a statement is a liar. Every one of those translations has ardent supporters who are noted and well-educated Hebrew scholars. This doesn't mean they reveal the exact same information. While they are all grammatically correct, they cannot all be informationally correct. (I'll explain this later.)

My second deduction is about Hebrew scholars. I'm sure this isn't true of all Hebrew scholars, but it probably describes the majority. I have concluded that each scholar translates the text based on what he believes the Bible says. This may not seem like a startling statement, but if you'll think about it for a minute or two, you'll see the significance. If a translator has a preconceived idea of what the text is supposed to say, then it shouldn't be a big surprise when he translates it the way it's supposed to be. I would venture to guess most Biblical Hebrew scholars studied the Bible during the process of becoming Biblical Hebrew scholars. The question then arises, "How did they get the knowledge it takes to become a Biblical Hebrew scholar?" I suspect they studied Biblical Hebrew in a seminary, a university, a Bible college, or some other establishment of higher education. This being the case, it seems only natural that scholars would tend to know what they've been taught. It wouldn't be strange if the majority of scholars trained in a Southern Baptist seminary, for instance, translated the text in a fashion similar to how Southern Baptist seminaries believe it is supposed to be translated. Likewise, if you were trained in a Presbyterian seminary, you might have a tendency to translate the Hebrew in a fashion similar to what Presbyterian seminaries teach. A young man studying to be a Catholic priest would translate the Hebrew in a way that fell into line with Catholic teachings. If you were taught Hebrew by scholars who believed the *King James Version* was the only valid translation, then it would make sense for you to translate Genesis in a way that compared favorably with the *King James Version*.

You shouldn't be astonished to discover the various Biblical creation theories center on what has been historically believed by different churches, denominations, and other organizations. Many organizations hold strongly to their opinions, and often require members and prospective members to believe and adhere to the very opinions they seek to defend. One would expect their translations and teachings to agree with their translations and teachings. I have not read many accounts of scholars agreeing with translations of the Bible that might disprove their own preconceived theories. (One notable exception was Gleason Archer. I'll tell you more about him in the next chapter.) Now, I'm not accusing Hebrew scholars of being academically dishonest; just of being human. We all tend to think and believe what we were taught to think and believe, and we all tend to defend our thoughts and beliefs. We all have Mental Inertia. We all tend to get upset when others challenge the things we believe. Nobody likes to have his opinions disproved or ridiculed. This is especially true for those of us with academic initials following our names. We don't like to admit we could be wrong. However, if we are Christians, then we should be more than willing to let truth prove or disprove our opinions. If we are wrong, then we should reject our false opinions and willingly accept the truth. Let's begin a detailed search for the truth about the creation as revealed in the Bible.

Seeking Informational Correctness: Genesis 1:1

"IN THE BEGINNING"

Some view this as the absolute beginning of everything, including time and space. There was no period of time prior to this because there was no such thing as time "before" this. Others consider this only the beginning of God's formative acts, but not the absolute beginning of absolutely everything. Ephraim Speiser seems to indicate this in his translation:

Genesis 1:1 "When God set about to create the heaven and the earth, the world being then a formless waste…" (SPEIS)

"When," implies time existed prior to the creation. You could substitute it with the phrase, "Once upon a time," and it would mean the same thing. "Being then a formless waste," implies the earth also existed prior to this. Von Bohlen, Robert Young, Smith and Goodspeed, Moffatt, and *The New Revised Standard* translations seem to have similar opinions. They believe Genesis describes a formation of the universe; not an actual creation.

"GOD CREATED"

At least everybody agrees on who the Creator was. It was God. The opinions vary on whether "created" means out of nothing or merely fashioned out of what was already there, but at least we give God the credit.

"THE HEAVEN"

Several translations say, "heaven," while others say, "heavens." Thieme lumps "heavens and earth" together as, "the entire universe," while *The New Century Version* says, "the sky and the earth." The Hebrew word *SHAMAYIM*, (Strong's Number H8064) translated, "heaven," is a plural word, and should be rendered, "heavens." I think God used a plural word as a clue there is more than one kind of heaven. In the Bible, *SHAMAYIM* is used to define three places.

1.) God uses *SHAMAYIM* to describe the location of the sun, moon, and stars.

Genesis 1:16-17 "And God made two great lights; the greater light to rule the day, and the lesser light to rule the night: *he made* the stars also. {17} And God set them in the firmament of the **heaven** to give light upon the earth," (KJV)

2.) He also uses *SHAMAYIM* to describe the location of where the birds fly. Genesis 1:20 "And God said, Let the waters bring forth abundantly the moving creature that hath life, and fowl *that* may fly above the earth in the open firmament of **heaven**." (KJV)

Today we know there is a difference between the place where the birds fly and the place where the stars exist. Because God used the same word to describe both places, some people think God made a mistake. They say He must have been unaware of the difference between atmosphere and outer space. I disagree. God did make a distinction. One heaven is the place where birds fly. This *SHAMAYIM* is the atmosphere. Another heaven is the place where the sun, moon, and stars exist. This *SHAMAYIM* is outer space. God used the same word for both places because He wasn't interested in revealing atmospheric and cosmological physics to the ancient Hebrews. They would think of *SHAMAYIM* as we think of the word "sky." We see the stars shine in the sky, but we also see birds fly in the sky. There is nothing incorrect about calling it "sky" in either case.

3.) The Bible also uses *SHAMAYIM* to describe the place where God and the angels exist.

Genesis 28:12 "And he dreamed, and behold a ladder set up on the earth, and the top of it reached to **heaven**: and behold the angels of God ascending and descending on it." (KJV)

I believe Genesis 1:1 speaks of the creation of both the physical realm and the spiritual realm. I believe creation exists in two parts because the Hebrew word *SHAMAYIM* is in a special kind of plural known as a Dual. In English, the word "scissors" is a dual. We speak of a pair of scissors. If I told you, "The scissors are on the table," how many scissors are on the table. One pair? A dozen? You wouldn't know, because "scissors" is plural whether we are talking about a single pair of scissors or a box full of scissors. A pair of scissors is single entity, but it has a dual nature. We do the same thing with a pair of pliers. The object may be singular, but it exists and functions in a dual nature. I believe, although I cannot prove it, that a dual-word is used for "heavens" because God created two kinds of heavens in Genesis 1:1. One was physical. It included the atmosphere where the birds fly and outer space where the stars shine. The other was supernatural. It was the spiritual heaven where the angels dwell and where God is worshipped by those angelic beings. Creation has a dual-nature because it is both physical and spiritual.

(Note: God does not "live" in the Spiritual Heaven as a necessity. The Spiritual Heaven is a created-place; therefore, He exists/existed before He created it. He **IS**, in and of Himself, without any need for a "place" to exist. Some people believe the place where God "exists" is called, "The Third Heaven." They believe it is where only God dwells, and it is distinct from "The Second Heaven" where the angels dwell. Having never been there, I cannot speak with authority, but the Biblical descriptions of God in Heaven always include the presence of angelic beings around Him. This makes it difficult for me to believe there is a distinction between a "Second Heaven," and a "Third Heaven." When Paul speaks of the third heaven in 2 Corinthians, I think he was speaking of himself, and I think he wasn't speaking of a place, but of a time. Paul was taken to the future heaven; the new heaven God will create when He creates the New Heavens and the New Earth. The New Heaven will be the third heaven with respect to time; not place.)

2 Corinthians 12:2 "I knew a man in Christ above fourteen years ago, (whether in the body, I cannot tell; or whether out of the body, I cannot tell: God knoweth;) such an one caught up to the **third** heaven." (KJV)

The word Paul uses is *TRITOS*, (Strong's Number G5154) and it is used in two ways. It means one-third of something. "A third-part of the stars," "a third-part of the waters," "a third-part of men," *etc*. It also means the third in a sequence of things or events. "The third day," "the third watch," "the third hour," "the third trumpet," *etc*. I don't think Paul was taken to the "one-third" heaven, but I do think he was taken to the same heaven John was taken in *The Book of The Revelation of Jesus Christ*. John was taken to the future heaven, to see the events of the future.

Revelation 4:1 "After this I looked, and behold, a door standing open in heaven! And the first voice, which I had heard speaking to me like a trumpet, said, 'Come up here, and I will show you what must take place after this.'" (ESV)

In other words, I don't believe the Bible describes one heaven stacked on top of another heaven, stacked on top of another heaven. Instead, I think it describes: 1.) The original and perfect heavens in the past before Lucifer rebelled. 2.) The heavens of the present that suffer from the effects of sin. 3.) The future heavens that will be remade/restored because the first heavens were corrupted/defiled/desecrated. You see, when Satan rebelled, he caused both the physical universe and the spiritual universe to be ruined. ("ALL creation groans.") This is why God will create the New Earth AND the New Heavens (plural) in the future. The Ruin-Restoration Theory reveals more than just the origin and fate of the physical realm. Paul and John were taken to the Third Heaven; the Future Heaven.

So, Genesis 1:1 refers to the creation of both the physical universe and the spiritual universe. Creation exists and functions as a dual, and we exist in both, even though we cannot directly perceive the spiritual realm under normal circumstances. I think it is possible in the original creation that the two parts weren't as separated as they are now. I believe God's judgment on Satan resulted in a disruption of the original creation. Satan's sin caused all creation to groan, not just the physical realm. I think when God creates the New Heavens and Earth, they will be restored to what they were before; maybe even better.

I have no clue from Genesis 1:1 this is true, but the first three words of the Gospel of John intrigue me.

John 1:1 "**In the beginning** was the Word, and the Word was with God, and the Word was God." (KJV)

John begins his Gospel the same way the Book of Genesis began. I don't think it was a coincidence, and I don't think first-century Jewish and Christian readers would have missed the connection. It would be like me giving a speech starting with, "Four score and seven years ago…." No matter what topic followed, you would instantly understand I was connecting my speech to Lincoln's Gettysburg Address. I think John makes this connection because he wants to give us some additional information about the Creation. I believe this allows us to take the additional information John reveals, and apply it to Genesis 1:1. What else does John reveal?

John 1:3 "All things were made by him; and without him was not any thing made that was made." (KJV)

John reveals that everything that was made, was made by Jesus in the beginning. Except for God, everything that exists was created. The physical universe exists; therefore, it was created by Jesus in the beginning. The spiritual universe exists; therefore, it was created by Jesus in the beginning. I think Genesis 1:1 describes the creation of two kinds of heavens, the spiritual and the physical. This is one reason I do not think Genesis 1:1 is a title or a summary of Genesis 1:3-31. Genesis 1:3-31 (the six days of creation) only involve aspects of the physical realm. These verses do not describe the creation of the angels or the creation of the spiritual realm where they abide. John 1:1-3 describe the creation of ALL things. John 1:1-3 includes the angels and the angelic universe. Since John connects his words to Genesis 1:1, but not to Genesis 1:3-31, I believe we have solid evidence Genesis 1:1 and Genesis 1:3-31 are not describing the same creation, the same beginning. They are two different beginnings at two different times.

You probably noticed Genesis doesn't say He set the lights, "in the heavens," or the birds fly, "in the heavens." The text actually talks about the "firmament" of the heavens. The word for "firmament" is *RAQIYA*. (Strong's Number H7549) Again, God uses *RAQIYA* as part of the description for both the place where the stars are and the place where the birds fly. We know there is a difference between the two places, but I don't think God intended to reveal this to the ancient Hebrews. The use of this word implies that both the atmosphere and outer space have some kind of "firmness;" some kind of physical substance. Psalms 19:1 gives a parallelism between the "heavens" and the "firmament." It reveals these are physical aspects of creation because they are things we can see. We can't physically see the spiritual heaven.

Psalms 19:1 "To the chief Musician, a Psalm of David. The **heavens** declare the glory of God; and the **firmament** sheweth his handywork." (KJV)

I think this is another pre-scientific clue about the universe. The atmosphere, although invisible to the ancient Hebrews, is not a nothing. Outer space, as part of the space-time continuum, is not a nothing. *RAQIYA* conveyed the idea of something solid, or at least something solid enough to hold up the waters in the sky, (clouds; the waters above the firmament) yet at the same time it was something of such an open consistency, that birds could fly in it. *RAQIYA* also conveyed the idea of an "expanse," "dome," or, "arch." The word *RAQIYA*, in the sense of being a dome covering the earth, is an indication the description of events in the Genesis Creation Account is given from an earthbound perspective. The sky is seen as a dome above the earth because the viewer is standing on a spherical surface around which the celestial objects appear to move. Go to your local planetarium and you will notice it most likely has a domed-shaped ceiling. A dome is a very good description of outer space if you are looking at it from an earthbound perspective. It is an even more accurate description of the atmosphere. The atmosphere is a spherical ocean of air encircling the earth. It is "solid" enough to suspend water in the form of clouds, yet it is "fluid" enough to let birds fly through it. God is very accurate in His choice of words. *RAQIYA* describes both the atmosphere and outer space. Its specific interpretation depends on whether the context is talking about the atmosphere (the place where birds fly) or outer space (the place where the sun, moon, and stars are).

"AND THE EARTH"

"The earth" pretty much means the earth as far as I can tell from the scholars.

Merism, Merism on the Wall

Do you remember I said some people want to make Genesis 1:1 and Genesis 1:2 a title and a subtitle? I gave my reasons for rejecting the concept, but I left out one of their main arguments until now. I first wanted to develop the specific meanings of "heavens" and "earth." One of the reasons they believe Genesis 1:1-2 doesn't describe WHAT was literally created, is because they believe the term "heavens and earth" is a merism. A merism is a literary device, often used in poetry, where two contrasting words are combined to express the idea of totality, without expressing the specific meanings of the words themselves. An example would be like saying, "I searched high and low for my yellow sneakers." "High" is the opposite of "Low," but when they are put together as a merism, they don't imply I searched literally in high places and low places. It simply means I searched everywhere.

"Title-Subtitle" defenders suggest that if "the heavens and the earth" is a merism, then Genesis 1 is poetry and not a literal description of creation. They say it isn't describing the literal creation of the literal heavens and the literal earth. In defense of their idea, they point out how this resolves the apparent conflict between WHAT was created in Genesis 1:1 and WHAT was created in Genesis 1:16. There is no conflict between God creating "the heavens" in Genesis 1:1 and God creating the sun, moon, and stars in Genesis 1:16 (Day Four). There is no conflict because Genesis 1:1 doesn't describe WHAT God literally created. They assume "the heavens and the earth" means "the universe" in a poetic sense, and then they assume their assumption is correct. This allows them to interpret Genesis 1:1 and Genesis 1:2 as a non-literal title and subtitle. Such an interpretation would be a good defense for the Title-Subtitle Theory if two things are true:

1.) The phrase "the heavens and the earth" is always a merism in the Bible.

2.) Poetry always excludes literal ideas, thoughts, concepts, and descriptions.

Let's look at the first point. The simplest, most straightforward interpretation is, "the heavens and the earth," means the literal heavens and the literal earth. "Heavens" and "earth" are used together in other places in the Bible, and in most places the meaning is just as questionable as in Genesis 1:1. While it appears to be used in a literal sense everywhere else, the non-literalists insist it is actually used as a merism everywhere else. Are they correct?

The Book of 2 Samuel tells us about the time when Absalom, one of David's sons, rebelled against his father and declared himself king. David temporarily had to flee Jerusalem, but he didn't give up. He ordered Joab, his commander, to take the army and capture Absalom. He gave Joab specific orders not to kill Absalom. Absalom fled and Joab pursued. Here is what happened next:

2 Samuel 18:9 "And Absalom met the servants of David. And Absalom rode upon a mule, and the mule went under the thick boughs of a great oak, and his head caught hold of the oak, and he was taken up between **the heaven and the earth**; and the mule that *was* under him went away." (KJV)

When Joab found Absalom hanging between the heavens and the earth (*SHAMAYIM*—Strong's Number H8064 and *ERETS*—Strong's Number H7776, the exact same words as in Genesis 1:1) by his head, he killed him against David's orders. If *SHAMAYIM* and *ERETS* always form a merism, then 2 Samuel 18:9 makes no sense. Was Absalom taken up by the head between "the universe?" No. He was literally suspended between the literal ground and the literal sky. No merism is suggested. There is no basis for insisting *SHAMAYIM* and *ERETS* is always a merism. Now let's look at the second point. Does poetry always exclude literal ideas, thoughts, concepts, and descriptions? We know it doesn't exclude such things in English.

Roses are red.
Violets are blue.
This is a poem,
But still it's true.

Roses are literally red and violets are literally blue. (Of course, there are variations in the colors of both.) This little poem describes the literal colors of literal flowers. But this is English! Can ancient Hebrew poetry describe literal things? Yes, of course it can; it can express both literal and non-literal ideas. I already mentioned one poetic device used in Hebrew, the Parallelism, and we have seen how it can express non-literal ideas.

Isaiah 42:13 "The LORD will go forth like a warrior, He will arouse *His* zeal like a man of war. He will utter a shout, yes, He will raise a war cry. He will prevail against His enemies." (NASB)

The Lord does not literally go forth like a warrior. Warriors have to walk and run into battle. God doesn't have to walk or run anywhere. God doesn't literally shout like warriors. Warriors have to take in a deep breath and then force the air out of their lungs while manipulating their vocal cords, mouth, tongue, and lips in order to raise a war cry. God doesn't have lungs, lips, vocal cords, *etc*. This parallelism is expressing a poetic, non-literal description of God. It expresses a truth about God, but not a literal truth.

Next question: Can a poetic parallelism describe a literal truth?

Genesis 4:23 "And Lamech said unto his wives, Adah and Zillah, Hear my voice; ye wives of Lamech, hearken unto my speech: for I have slain a man to my wounding, and a young man to my hurt." (KJV)

This is Lamech's song in which he boasts of killing a young man. In the Hebrew, it is poetic. Notice the parallelisms:

"Lamech said unto his wives."
"Hear my voice; ye wives of Lamech,"

"a man to my wounding,"
"a young man to my hurt."

While this is poetic parallelism, it describes the two literal wives of Lamech. It describes the literal Lamech literally killing a literal young man. Hebrew poetry does not always describe non-literal things. It can be quite literal. This means "the heavens and the earth" (even if it is a merism) can describe the creation of the literal heavens and the literal earth. There is no justification for insisting Genesis 1:1 doesn't describe the literal creation of the literal heavens and earth.

Seeking Informational Correctness: Genesis 1:2

Okay, now that we can't agree on Genesis 1:1, let's move on to Genesis 1:2 and see if we can continue the confusion. You might be wondering why there is so much concern over the relationship between Genesis 1:1 and Genesis 1:2. Here's where things start getting messy. Is Genesis 1:1 a title? Is it a summary? Is it part of the sequence of events, or is there a break in the action? Does Genesis 1:2 follow immediately after Genesis 1:1, or long after? You might be asking yourself, "How does Genesis 1:1 fit with Genesis 1:2?" Well now, aren't you clever to ask that? That's exactly what I was going to talk about next. You'll love this! This is the stuff controversies are made of, so grab a handful of scathing comments and indignant rebuttals, and let's look at Genesis 1:2 one part at a time.

"AND"

Genesis 1:2 begins with the Hebrew letter *WAW* (ו), but I often call it a word because it expresses the idea, concept, thought of a word in English. Sometimes it is written and pronounced as *VAV*. *WAW* happens to be one of those famous "Hebrew-rubber-words" with a variety of meanings. *WAW* is translated, "and," "but," "now," "then," "now then," "but then," "and then," and other such linking-words. There is no end to the arguments over how *WAW* is supposed to be translated. Scholars tend to agree *WAW* can be translated all these ways, but according to scholars, it is the context that determines how it should be translated; and that's the problem! We have completed only one sentence and there is practically no context. Naturally, scholars translate it a certain way because they have already decided what the context is supposed to be.

Let me give you an example of how context causes *WAW* to be translated different ways. If I said, "The apple was ripe but it was bitter," then you would get the idea that being bitter isn't the normal condition of ripe apples. The word "BUT" sets up a contrast between the two parts of the sentence. If I said, "The apple was ripe and it was sweet," then I would have conveyed to you that sweetness is something ripe apples normally are. In English, we have two separate words "but" and "and." In Hebrew, *WAW* would be used for both "and" and "but." You could say the apple was ripe *WAW* (but) bitter. You could also say the apple was ripe *WAW* (and) sweet. If you came across the Hebrew words *TAPPAWACH* (apple) *BASHAL* (ripe) *WAW* ("and" or "but") *MAR* (bitter), then you wouldn't necessarily know if *WAW* was to be translated, "and" or "but," unless you knew how ripe apples were supposed to taste. If you didn't know what apples were, or if you never tasted a ripe apple, then you might incorrectly translate it as, "The apple was ripe and it was bitter." You might think ripe apples are normally bitter. If you knew ripe apples are normally sweet, then you would translate it as, "The apple was ripe but it was bitter." Even though both ways of translating it are grammatically correct, you'd have to know something about ripe apples before you could translate this sentence in a way that would reveal the correct information. In this example, the "context" is the previously known fact ripe that apples are not supposed to be bitter. With this previous knowledge in mind, you would translate *TAPPAWACH BASHAL WAW MAR* as, "The apple was ripe BUT it was bitter." (Note to Hebrew scholars: Before you e-mail and blast me, please forgive me for being so simplistic. I realize this isn't proper Hebrew. I'm just trying to make a point on how the translation of *WAW* varies with context.)

Do you see how *WAW* can be translated, "and" or "but," and be GRAMMATICALLY correct but INFORMATIONALLY incorrect? **"And" implies Genesis 1:2 is part of the sequence of events, while "but" implies there is a break or a contrast in the action between Genesis 1:1 and Genesis 1:2.** If you believe there is a break or a contrast between Genesis 1:1 and Genesis 1:2, then you are more likely to translate it, "but." If you believe Genesis 1:1 and Genesis 1:2 describe the same creation event, then you are more likely to translate it, "and." If you are a Hebrew scholar, you're not likely to translate it, "but," if you believe Genesis 1:1 and Genesis 1:2 describe the first day of creation. Likewise, if you're a Hebrew scholar who believes there is a gap between Genesis 1:1 and Genesis 1:2, then you probably aren't going to translate it, "and."

We can correctly translate Genesis 1:2 grammatically, but we have to know what happened at the beginning before we can correctly translate it informationally. We have to know whether we need an "and" or a "but" to determine how *WAW* should be translated. The "context" in this situation is the previously known fact of whether or not there was a break in the creative works of God between Genesis 1:1 and Genesis 1:2. This is one of those situations where we need to know the truth before we know what is true.

WAW is also translated, "now," in some of the translations. All three of these translations are grammatically correct, but each carries a little different information. As a conjunction, "and" implies Genesis 1:2 is a continuation of Genesis 1:1. As a disjunction, "but" implies there is some kind of break or contrast between Genesis 1:1 and Genesis 1:2. "Now" merely calls attention to Genesis 1:2 without specifying a particular relationship to Genesis 1:1. *WAW*, when translated, "now," can also imply "now then."

Note that a translation for *WAW* is completely left out in some versions. That too is grammatically correct. However, since it is in the original Hebrew, I don't think *WAW* should be overlooked too lightly. The Holy Spirit inspired Moses to use *WAW*, and I question the motives for ignoring it. Putting a linking-word between Genesis 1:1 and Genesis 1:2 forces the reader to think about what the link between the sentences reveals. The first sentence reveals God's creative acts; the second sentence reveals a desolate earth. There must be some relationship between God's creative acts and earth's desolate condition. By using *WAW*, I think the Holy Spirit wanted to make us wonder about that relationship. It's my opinion *WAW* in this position eliminates the possibility that Genesis 1:1 is a title. If Genesis 1:1 is a title, then the creation starts at Genesis 1:2 with the linking-word, *WAW*. If the creation starts with a linking-word, then to what is it linked? There is no previous Scripture to which we could compare, contrast, or relate the desolate condition of the earth. There was no previous time or space. Why start Genesis 1:2 with a connecting word if nothing existed prior to Genesis 1:2? To what was it connected? If *WAW* is untranslated, then the description of creation begins in Genesis 1:2 with a preexisting, desolate and dead earth. Even more interesting is the fact the *WAW* in Genesis 1:2 is in a disjunctive form rather than a simple conjunctive form. In the Hebrew, it creates a contrast between verse one and verse two, rather than a comparison. The text reads, "BUT the earth…" instead of, "AND the earth." If you leave out the *WAW*, you lose the sense of contrast the Holy Spirit placed between them.

But, *WAW* is correctly translated a number of ways. And, it is grammatically correct to ignore it in translation. Now, if someone tells you it can't be translated, "and," or "but," or "now," or it can't be left out, then you have my permission to laugh in their face. But, in case they don't believe you, have them look up every single "and," "but," and "now" in a concordance and check out the corresponding Hebrew words. And, since there are over 19,000 "ands," "buts," and "nows" in the *King James Version* of the Old Testament, they should stay busy for a while. And, I know it's not quite proper to start an English sentence with a conjunction or a disjunction. But, I wanted you to get a feel for how these words force you to compare the relationships between sentences. Now, back to our study.

"THE EARTH"

Again, this is generally translated, "the earth;" the little speck of dust in the universe inhabited by a race of creatures who inherently love controversy. In fact, if an issue isn't controversial enough, we seem to have a way of making it so. Sadly, there is even a controversy over what *ERETS* means in Genesis 1:2. Everyone believes *ERETS* in Genesis 1:1 is the earth, but some insist *ERETS* in Genesis 1:2 is the Land of Israel. You see, *ERETS* can be translated, "earth," "ground," "field," "dirt," or "land." They say it refers to "The Land," which is Israel. In this view, Genesis 1:3-31 describes God creating life, *etc.* in the land where Israel will someday be. Israel, therefore, is the center of all creation. You can probably guess who might favor this view. This translation stretches an already "rubber" word. The context seems to indicate this is the same *ERETS* (earth) mentioned in Genesis 1:1, and I have yet to see a Hebrew scholar translate Genesis 1:1 as, "In the beginning, God created the heavens and Israel."

"WAS"

Starting with, "was without form, and void," the controversies worsen. At this juncture brotherly love gets laid aside. Kid gloves are replaced by brass knuckles. It's not just the scholars' ability to translate Hebrew that's at stake. Entire churches, denominations, and schools have argued over this sentence. Reputations are on the line. There's too much at stake to let some idiot translate this in a fashion other than the way my church, my denomination, and my organization say it should be. Every knowledgeable scholar agrees with me. If you don't believe it, just ask the knowledgeable scholars who agree with me. God wouldn't dare create the universe in a fashion that would disagree with what I believe. The Bible can't teach something contrary to what I... Oops, please excuse me. Momentarily I started thinking I was a scholar.

The biggest controversy of them all deals with how the Hebrew word *HAYAH* (Strong's Number H1961) should be translated in this context. *HAYAH* is similar, but not equivalent to the English infinitive verb, "to be." In its various forms, it can be translated, "be," "am," "are," "is," "was," "will be," "will become," "had been," "has been," "had become," "has become," "became," "come to pass," "came to pass," and a whole list of others. *HAYAH* is such a "Hebrew rubber-word," if you dropped it on the floor, it would bounce around for a week. In fact, *The New American Standard Bible* has over 120 different translations for *HAYAH*. If you'll look back at the various translations you'll see most of the time it is translated, "was," but there are some exceptions. Custance translates it, "had become." It is also translated, "had become," by Rotherham (*The Emphasized Bible*) and by R. B. Thieme. Jahn (*The Exegeses Ready Research Bible*) translates *HAYAH* as, "became," and Dillman does the same. *The Scriptures* translates it, "came to be." Speiser translates it, "being then," while Robert Young uses the words, "hath existed." In more modern English, we could rephrase Young's translation as, "had existed."

Genesis 1:2 in the *King James Version* of the Bible says:

Genesis 1:2 "And the earth **was** without form, and void; and darkness ***was*** upon the face of the deep. And the Spirit of God moved upon the face of the waters." (KJV)

The word "was" is used twice in this verse. The first time it is used, it is not in italics; it says, "the earth was..." The second time it is used, it is in italics; it says, "and darkness *was*..." This difference is important. As I mentioned previously, italics are used in the *King James Bible* to indicate words that are not in the original Hebrew or Greek, but have been added by the English translators to help the text make more sense to English readers. You might be asking yourself, "If a word is not needed in the Hebrew to make sense, why would it be needed in the English to make sense?" The reason is because ancient Hebrew-speaking people did not think exactly like modern English-speaking people. For that matter, modern Hebrew-speaking people do not think exactly like modern English-speaking people. In fact, modern English-speaking people do not think exactly like modern Spanish-speaking people, who do not think exactly like modern French-speaking people, who do not think exactly like modern Urdu-speaking people, who do not think exactly like modern Swahili-speaking people, who do not think exactly like...

You see, if you ask language experts, they will tell you how language influences not just what we think, but how we think. We think in terms of language. Therefore, our thoughts, ideas, beliefs, and worldviews are affected by our language and our culture. Of course, this doesn't mean it is impossible for the people of one language and culture to effectively communicate with the people of another language and culture, but it isn't as simple as word-to-word substitutions. I remember when I was in college, I took a class called, "Latin Classics in Translation." In this class, we read a number of books the typical First-Century Roman citizen would have read. There was a lot of Greek and Roman mythology, political and historical writings, and even the writings of some of the most famous ancient philosophers. Of course, all these books were translated into English since none of us students knew Latin. We would read chapters in these books and discuss them in class with the professor. The professor was fluent in Latin, and I remember there were many times he would expound on the meaning of the Latin text. The translations were good, but the English couldn't always convey the same thoughts as the Latin. He would explain what the Latin words meant to the ancient Romans, and how they viewed the meanings of those words. It would always reveal more and better concepts than could be found by reading the English alone.

As is true for ancient Latin, so it is true for ancient Hebrew; even more so since English is a lot closer to Latin than it is to Hebrew. **We must not be satisfied with a mere word-to-word substitution if we expect to understand the Bible.** Too many English-speaking Christian creationists think they can understand Genesis 1:2 by substituting a single English word for an entire Hebrew thought. This is often the approach used by those who claim they believe, "the literal interpretation of the Bible." For them, *HAYAH* is always equivalent to "was" as a past, completed, static condition. They never bother to investigate the various meanings and shades of meaning *HAYAH* conveyed to the ancient Hebrew people.

So, why is the first "was" in Genesis 1:2 not in italics, while the second "was" is? There are two main reasons for not using a form of "is," or "was," or "be" in Hebrew. The first reason is Hebrew doesn't always require it to connect or complete a thought. I will talk about this later in more detail than you can probably stand. The second reason is if no form of "is," or "was," or "be" is meant to be in the text. This is the case in Genesis 1:2. A second "was" is not needed because the first "was" describes a series of conditions that are all linked to the first "was." There is no need for a second "was." You don't always need a second verb for a series of conditions or descriptions that are linked. The first verb describes the entire series of conditions or descriptions. For example: I could say, "I was tired, and I was hungry, and I was thirsty." But, I could say, "I was tired, and hungry, and thirsty." I wouldn't need to add two more uses of "was" to convey the same thought. I could also say, "I was tired, hungry, and thirsty," and even exclude an unneeded "and." Genesis 1:2 describes three conditions of the earth: 1.) It was without form. 2.) It was void. 3.) Darkness was on the face of the deep (ocean). The Hebrew didn't have periods, and commas, and semi-colons, *etc.* like the English does. They used the word "and" (which was the single Hebrew letter *WAW*—ו) to connect thoughts and ideas. Even allowing for *HAYAH* to mean "was," it says, "AND the earth WAS without form AND void AND darkness on the face of the deep." So, while there are two "ands" that follow the "was" in the Hebrew, there is only one "was." It sounds better to the English ear to add a second "was," even though the first "was" is all that is needed in the Hebrew.

That is one reason the second "was" in Genesis 1:2 is in italics. There is another reason. Continue reading and you will see numerous cases of "was" and numerous cases of "*was*." Why the difference? Hebrew is one of those languages that doesn't need a form of "to be" in order to complete or connect a thought. In English, I would say, "Linda Dill is my wife." In Hebrew, it isn't necessary to add "is." It would be proper to say, "Linda Dill my wife." The word "is" really adds nothing to the thought. The first "was" in the Hebrew of Genesis 1:2 is there, but the second "*was*" isn't. The second "*was*" is not in the Hebrew because it is not needed in Hebrew. (Or maybe I should say, "It not in the Hebrew because it not needed in the Hebrew.") No *HAYAH* is needed in the second part of this sentence because Hebrew doesn't require it to connect two or more thoughts. So, when *HAYAH* is used, it is often for a reason other than just to complete or connect a thought. *Strong's Dictionary of the Hebrew Language*[28] defines *HAYAH* this way:

"H1961. *HAYAH*, haw-yaw'; a prim. root; to exist, *i.e.* be or become, come to pass (always emphatic, and not a mere copula or auxiliary)..."

Note that Strong says *HAYAH* is not a mere copula; not a mere connecting word.

The New American Standard Exhaustive Concordance of the Bible[29] says this:

"H1961. *HAYAH*; a prim. root; to fall out, come to pass, become, be..."

While there are many correct translations of *HAYAH*, the major point of conflict centers around whether *HAYAH* should be translated as some form of "was" or some form of "became." Some creationists say the passage should be translated, "...the earth WAS without form, and void..." Others say it should be translated, "...the earth BECAME without form, and void..." You would think the grammatical form would decide how to translate it. Unfortunately, as soon as you read one scholar who tells you one thing, you'll find two other scholars who tell you something else. Whether you translate it "was" or "became" seems to depend on two things:

1.) The context
2.) Your preconceived ideas about the context

How you translate *HAYAH* in Genesis 1:2 depends on what you want Genesis 1:2 to say. Of course, this depends a great deal on what you were previously taught about the creation. People have preconceived ideas about what Genesis is supposed to say, and they will often do anything or say anything to defend their opinions. A zealous opinion is a poor substitute for truth. I think you can see now what I meant when I said that while all those different translations may be grammatically correct, they are not all informationally correct. All those translations of Genesis 1:1-2 are grammatically correct. Each translator worded it the way he did because he previously knew (or thought he knew) something about the creation that supplied the context on which he could determine the "best way" to translate it. While each translation is grammatically correct, they don't all carry the same information. Look back at Thieme's translation for instance. He incorporates the concept of the space-time continuum by letting us know the beginning "began" in eternity past, not in time or space. This is a very clever translation, but to translate it this way, Thieme previously had to know space and time did not exist before the creation. Only God existed before the creation. Thieme wasn't an eyewitness to creation, so how could he know time didn't exist "before" the creation? How could he know space didn't exist "before" the creation? He could attain this knowledge only by studying other parts of the Bible. Look at John 1:1-3.

John 1:1-3 "In the beginning was the Word, and the Word was with God, and the Word was God. {2} The same was in the beginning with God. {3} All things were made by him; and without him was not any thing made that was made." (KJV)

John clearly tells us everything that exists was made by Jesus. If Jesus didn't make it, it never came into existence. Time exists; therefore, time had to be made by Jesus. Space exists; therefore, space had to be made by Jesus. John lets us know that God preexisted all things, including time and space. John lets us know that everything, which includes the space-time continuum, was made by God and did not exist eternally. There was no eternal matter and energy before the creation. (Not even the so-called "Quantum Vacuum.") Creation was a real creation, a creation out of nothing, and not merely a formation. With John's information in mind, we can understand why it would be informationally correct to translate Genesis 1:1 in such a way as Thieme did. Even time and space had their beginning at the beginning. It would be informationally wrong to translate Genesis 1:1 in a way that might indicate matter and energy were co-eternal with God. Even though Genesis 1:1 can be translated that way grammatically, it would not harmonize with John 1:1-3 and the rest of the Bible. (Plus, it would not harmonize with science. Science now proves time and space had a real beginning—the Big Bang.) It is important to understand how the key to translating Genesis 1 is found in what the rest of the Bible tells us about the creation. For this reason, I reject all translations of Genesis 1:1 and Genesis 1:2 that are grammatically correct but cause the Bible to contradict itself.

"... WITHOUT FORM, AND VOID; AND DARKNESS *WAS* UPON THE FACE OF THE DEEP."

"... without form, and void; and darkness *was* upon the face of the deep" (KJV)

"... without form, and void; and darkness *was* on the face of the deep" (NKJV)

"… unformed and chaotic, and darkness lay upon the face of the deep" (BV)

"… formless and empty, and darkness lay upon the face of the deep" (NBV)

"… empty and void, and darkness was over the face of the abyss" (Martin Luther Translation)

"… waste and void, and darkness was upon the face of the deep" (Von Bohlen Translation)

"… a ruin and desolation; and darkness was upon the face of the deep" (Arthur Custance Translation)

"… waste and void and darkness was upon the face of the deep" (RSV)

"… unformed and empty; clouds covered the abyss" (English translation of the Crampon Translation (French))

"… formless void and darkness covered the face of the deep" (NRSV)

"… waste, and darkness was upon the face of the deep" (Dillman Translation)

"… waste and void, and darkness is on the face of the deep" (Robert Young Translation)

"… a desolate waste, with darkness covering the abyss" (S&G)

"… empty and had no form. Darkness covered the ocean" (NCV)

"… desolate and empty with darkness on the face of the raging waters" (R. B. Thieme Translation)

"… waste and void, and darkness was upon the face of the deep" (Leupold Translation)

"… a formless waste, with darkness over the seas" (Speiser Translation)

"… formless void, there was darkness over the deep" (NJB)

"… without form or life, and darkness was upon the face of the deep" (Cassuto Translation)

"… formless and empty, darkness was over the surface of the deep" (NIV)

"... without form became waste, and void; and darkness was upon the face of the deep abyss." (ERRB)

"... unsightly and unfurnished, and darkness was over the deep" (Septuagint, Bagster Edition)

"... formless and void, and darkness was over the surface of the deep" (NASB)

"... waste and wild, and darkness was on the face of the roaring deep" (EMP)

"... formless and empty, and darkness was on the face of the deep." (SCRIP)

The words "without form, and void" are the Hebrew words *TOHUW WA-BOHUW*, and "darkness" is *CHOSHEK*. Whatever these words mean, we can certainly tell the earth wasn't a very nice place. *Strong's Dictionary of the Hebrew Language*[30] defines them as:

> *TOHUW* (Strong's Number H8414) "to-hoo; from an unused root mean. to lie waste; a desolation (of surface), *i.e.* desert; fig. a worthless thing; adv. in vain:—confusion, empty place, without form, nothing, (thing of) nought, vain, vanity, waste, wilderness."

> *BOHUW* (Strong's Number H922) "bo-hoo; from an unused root (mean. to be empty); a vacuity, *i.e.* (superficially) an undistinguishable ruin:—emptiness, void."

> *CHOSHEK* (Strong's Number H2822) "kho-shek;... lit. darkness; fig. misery, destruction, death, ignorance, sorrow, wickedness:—dark (-ness), night, obscurity."

I've listed enough different translations for you to get a feeling for what these words mean. However, I'm not going to argue over any of these words, except for one aspect of their meanings. (At least not for now; I'll become quite argumentative concerning these things later in the book.) The one factor we need to consider is whether these words should be translated in a literal sense or translated in a figurative sense? IT IS VERY IMPORTANT TO KNOW WHEN A WORD IS USED LITERALLY AND WHEN IT IS USED FIGURATIVELY. Our interpretations cannot be informationally correct if we don't know the difference between literal and figurative words. (Don't confuse figurative with untrue. If I say something in the Bible is figurative, it does not mean I am saying it is untrue. When God told the Israelites He carried them out of Egypt on "eagles' wings" in Exodus 19:4, He really didn't have millions of eagles swoop down and carry the people out of Egypt. This was figurative language. When Jesus compared Christians to wheat and unbelievers to tares in Matthew 13:30, He was expressing a truth in a figurative fashion. We Christians aren't literal stalks of wheat with kernels of grain growing out of our heads. We do, however, produce spiritual "fruit." When Jesus spoke this truth, He wasn't being literal. If He was being literal, then there are no Christians in the world. No one has grain sprouting from his head. The Bible often uses figurative language, figures of speech, and other non-literal devices to explain truth. When Jesus spoke about plucking out your eye to keep you from sinning, and hating your mother and your father in order to be His disciple, He was using hyperbole. He wasn't literally telling us to do these things. He was merely using the language of His time and culture to express these truths.)

Now, look back at Strong's definitions of *TOHUW* and *CHOSHEK*. He lists both the literal and the figurative meanings of these words. He lists only a literal meaning for *BOHUW* because *BOHUW* is used only in its literal sense in the Bible. I'm going to list all the verses in the Bible that use *TOHUW* and *BOHUW* because I want you to understand how they are used in the Bible.

King James Version Translations of *TOHUW* and *BOHUW*

TOHUW is used twenty times in the Bible. *TOHUW* literally describes a physical condition, but figuratively, it describes a lack of value or purpose. *BOHUW* is used three times. *BOHUW* is always literal in the Bible. The bold words are translations of ***TOHUW***. The bold and underlined words are translations of **<u>BOHUW</u>**. The three references in bold and underlined print in brackets are the verses with both.

{Genesis 1:2} "And the earth was **without form**, and **<u>void</u>**; and darkness *was* upon the face of the deep. And the Spirit of God moved upon the face of the waters." (KJV)

Deuteronomy 32:10 "He found him in a desert land, and in the **waste** howling wilderness; he led him about, he instructed him, he kept him as the apple of his eye." (KJV)

1 Samuel 12:21 "And turn ye not aside: for *then should ye* go after **vain** *things*, which cannot profit nor deliver; for they *are* **vain**." (KJV)

Job 6:18 "The paths of their way are turned aside; they go to **nothing**, and perish." (KJV)

Job 12:24 "He taketh away the heart of the chiefs if the people of the earth, and causeth them to wander in a **wilderness** *where there is* no way." (KJV)

Job 26:7 "He stretcheth out the north over the **empty place**, *and* hangeth the earth upon nothing." (KJV)

Psalms 107:40 "He poureth contempt upon princes, and causeth them to wander in the **wilderness**, *where there is* no way." (KJV)

Isaiah 24:10 "The city of **confusion** is broken down: every house is shut up, that no man may come in." (KJV)

Isaiah 29:21 "That make a man an offender for a word, and lay a snare for him that reproveth in the gate, and turn aside the just for a **thing of nought**." (KJV)

{<u>**Isaiah 34:11**</u>} "But the cormorant and the bittern shall possess it; the owl also and the raven shall dwell in it: and he shall stretch out upon it the line of **confusion**, and the stones of **<u>emptiness</u>**." (KJV)

Isaiah 40:17 "All nations before him *are* as nothing; and they are counted to him less than nothing, and **vanity**." (KJV)

Isaiah 40:23 "That bringeth the princes to nothing; he maketh the judges of the earth as **vanity**." (KJV)

Isaiah 41:29 "Behold, they *are* all vanity; their works *are* nothing: their molten images *are* wind and **confusion**." (KJV)

Isaiah 44:9 "They that make a graven image *are* all of them **vanity**; and their delectable things shall not profit; and they *are* their own witnesses; they see not, nor know; that they may be ashamed." (KJV)

Isaiah 45:18-19 "For thus saith the LORD that created the heavens; God himself that formed the earth and made it; he hath established it, he created it not **in vain**, he formed it to be inhabited: I *am* the LORD; and *there is* none else. *{19}* I have not spoken in secret, in a dark place of the earth: I said not unto the seed of Jacob, Seek ye me **in vain**: I the LORD speak righteousness, I declare things that are right." (KJV)

Isaiah 49:4 "Then I said, I have laboured in vain, I have spent my strength **for nought**, and in vain: *yet* surely my judgment is with the LORD, and my work with my God." (KJV)

Isaiah 59:4 "None calleth for justice, nor *any* pleadeth for truth: they trust **in vanity**, and speak lies; they conceive mischief, and bring forth iniquity." (KJV)

{<u>**Jeremiah 4:23**</u>} "I beheld the earth, and, lo, *it was* **without form**, and **<u>void</u>**; and the heavens, and they *had* no light." (KJV)

BOHUW means void or empty. The Bible always uses the literal meaning of *BOHUW*. *TOHUW*, on the other hand, can be either literal or figurative. In its literal meaning, *TOHUW* describes a desolation, a barren wasteland, or a bleak wilderness. *TOHUW* figuratively describes purposelessness, non-productiveness, worthlessness, meaninglessness, vanity, or uselessness. So, what does *TOHUW* mean in Genesis 1:2? Genesis 1:2 is giving us the physical condition of the earth. We are seeing earth as it literally was. It was a desolation, a wasteland. Some describe it as a chaos, (but such a thing cannot exist) and it was uninhabited. There is nothing figurative in Genesis 1. Genesis 1 is describing the physical creation. There is nothing hinting Genesis 1:2 should be interpreted in a figurative sense. To translate *TOHUW* figuratively here would mean God had no use or purpose or reason for creating earth. It would be saying, "In the beginning God created the heavens and the earth, but the earth had no purpose...." It might be grammatically correct to translate it figuratively, but such a translation would mean God had no purpose for the earth. It would imply earth's existence had no meaning, value, or worth. It would indicate God had no use for the earth, or creating it was something He did in vain. This interpretation makes the Bible disagree with itself.

Jeremiah 51:15 "It is he who made the earth by his power, who established the works by his wisdom, and by his understanding stretched out the heavens." (NRSV)

    Clearly, the Bible indicates God planned His creation carefully; it was no useless, pointless, thoughtless, vain act. Therefore, *TOHUW* must be translated in its literal sense. *TOHUW* describes the physical condition of the earth at the beginning of Genesis 1:2. Not only was it *TOHUW*, a desolation, it was also *BOHUW*, empty. Most likely this is referring to being empty of life. Genesis 1:2 describes earth as dark, desolate, and dead. Genesis 1:3-31 describe what God did to that dark, desolate, and dead planet. It is important to understand how Genesis 1:3-31 describe these events from an earthly perspective. When we read these verses, we are not looking down from heaven. We are looking at things as if we were standing on the earth watching Him work. I now ask the question, "Do these words describe the earth when God first created it, or did the earth become dark, desolate, and dead later?" What we need to decide is whether there is a break, a disconnect, or a difference between the creation of the earth in Genesis 1:1 and the dark, desolate, and dead earth in Genesis 1:2. The only way we can know how to translate Genesis 1:1-2 is to know what the rest of the Bible reveals about the creation.

    Before we go on, I want to look again at the three passages in Scripture where *TOHUW* and *BOHUW* are used together. I'm doing this because critics of the Gap Theory almost always say *TOHUW*, in the physical sense, doesn't imply Divine judgment. Now this may be true of *TOHUW* when used by itself, but when combined with *BOHUW*, the meaning becomes specific. Here again are those three passages:

Genesis 1:2 "And the earth was **without form**, and **void**; and darkness *was* upon the face of the deep. And the Spirit of God moved upon the face of the waters." (KJV)

Isaiah 34:11 "But the cormorant and the bittern shall possess it; the owl also and the raven shall dwell in it: and he shall stretch out upon it the line of **confusion**, and the stones of **emptiness**." (KJV)

Jeremiah 4:23 "I beheld the earth, and, lo, *it was* **without form**, and **void**; and the heavens, and they *had* no light." (KJV)

Isaiah 34:11 has a variety of different translations. Let's look at some of them:

Isaiah 34:11 "The desert owl and screech owl will possess it; the great owl and the raven will nest there. God will stretch out over Edom the measuring line of **chaos** and the plumb line of **desolation**." (NIV)

Isaiah 34:11 "But pelican and hedgehog shall possess it, And owl and raven shall dwell in it; And He shall stretch over it the line of **desolation** And the plumb line of **emptiness**." (NASB)

Isaiah 34:11 "Pelicans and herons will take possession of the land. Owls and crows will live there. He will stretch the measuring line of **chaos** and the plumb line of **destruction** over it." (GW)

Isaiah 34:11 "But the hawk and the porcupine shall possess it, the owl and the raven shall dwell in it. He shall stretch the line of **confusion** over it, and the plumb line of **emptiness**." (ESV)

Isaiah 34:11 "The desert owl and the screech owl will possess it, and the great owl and the raven will dwell there. *The LORD* will stretch out a measuring line and a plumb line over her for *her* **destruction** and **chaos**." (HCSB)

Isaiah 34:11 "And the pelican and the bittern shall possess it, and the great owl and the raven shall dwell in it. And he shall stretch out upon it the line of **waste**, and the plummets of **emptiness**." (DBY)

The most noticeable difference is in the animals that possess the land. It appears there are disagreements over what they are. (Oh, goodie! Let's start a new controversy. All those who think it is hedgehogs will burn in hell.) No, I'm not even going to try to figure out what those Hebrew words mean, but I do want to figure out what *TOHUW* and *BOHUW* mean. These passages use *TOHUW* and *BOHUW* in the sense of being a physical (in space

291

and time) condition. The point I want to make is that *TOHUW* and *BOHUW* in both Isaiah 34 and in Jeremiah 4 describe a physical condition that is the result of Divine judgment. In Isaiah 34, God is describing His judgment of Edom. In Jeremiah 4, God is describing His judgment of the earth. Some say it is not the "earth," but "the land" (Israel) that is judged. Others say this is a prophetic look at earth's future, not its past. We will look at those things in detail later. For now, it doesn't change the meaning of *TOHUW* when combined with *BOHUW*. Whether it is "earth" or "land;" whether it is past or future, the context still reveals the condition of being *TOHUW* and *BOHUW* is the result of God's judgment.

The Context of Isaiah 34:11 and Jeremiah 4:23

One of the most-used techniques of rebuttal is to say your opponent takes his Bible passages out of context. This technique is often used to refute the Gap Theory's claim *BOHUW* refers to judgment in Genesis 1:2. There are some who say *BOHUW* refers only to "emptiness" or "being unfilled" in a static, unchanged state. They say it means life had not yet been created; not that life had been destroyed. They say it carries no sense of destruction or judgment. They say we Gap Theory defenders take our passages out of context in order to reach our preconceived conclusion. Since they believe *BOHUW* doesn't refer to judgment, thy believe we Gap Theory proponents are wrong to connect *BOHUW* with any kind of Divine judgment in Genesis 1:2.

Another one of the most-used techniques of rebuttal is to keep making the same claim, even if it is false, over and over and over again until you convince yourself (and others) your claim is true. It is especially helpful if you can garner a following of supporters who never bother checking your claims or actually reading the Bible. This is the case when people claim *BOHUW* is not connected to Divine judgment. Let's read the only two passages of Scripture, beside Genesis 1:2, where *BOHUW* is used… I will add some emphasis to make the context clear. If you look hard enough, I think you might get a small hint these passages deal with God's wrath, God's judgment, and God's destruction of evil. (**<u>BOHUW</u>** is translated, "emptiness," in Isaiah 34:11 and, "void," in Jeremiah 4:23.)

Isaiah 34:1-11 "Come near, ye nations, to hear; and hearken, ye people: let the earth hear, and all that is therein; the world, and all things that come forth of it. *{2}* For **the indignation of the LORD** *is* upon all nations, and *his* **fury** upon all their armies: **he hath utterly destroyed them, he hath delivered them to the slaughter.** *{3}* **Their slain** also **shall be cast out,** and **their stink** shall come up out of **their carcases**, and the mountains shall be **melted with their blood.** *{4}* And all the host of heaven **shall be dissolved**, and the heavens shall be rolled together as a scroll: and **all their host shall fall down**, as the leaf falleth off from the vine, and as a falling *fig* from the fig tree. *{5}* For **my sword shall be bathed** in heaven: behold, **it shall come down upon Idumea**, and upon **the people of my curse**, to **judgment**. *{6}* **The sword of the LORD is filled with blood**, it is made fat with fatness, *and* with the blood of lambs and goats, with the fat of the kidneys of rams: for the

LORD hath **a sacrifice in Bozrah**, and **a great slaughter in the land of Idumea**. *{7}* And the unicorns shall come down with them, and the bullocks with the bulls; and **their land shall be soaked with blood**, and their dust made fat with fatness. *{8}* For *it is* **the day of the Lord's vengeance**, *and* **the year of recompenses** for the controversy of Zion. *{9}* And **the streams thereof shall be turned into pitch**, and **the dust thereof into brimstone**, and **the land thereof shall become burning pitch**. *{10}* **It shall not be quenched** night nor day; **the smoke thereof shall go up for ever**: from generation to generation **it shall lie waste**; **none shall pass through it for ever and ever**. *{11}* But the cormorant and the bittern shall possess it; the owl also and the raven shall dwell in it: and he shall stretch out upon it the line of **confusion**, and the stones of **<u>EMPTINESS</u>**." (KJV)

Jeremiah 4:1-31 "If thou wilt return, O Israel, saith the LORD, return unto me: and if thou wilt **put away thine abominations** out of my sight, then shalt thou not remove. *{2}* And thou shalt swear, The LORD liveth, in truth, **in judgment**, and in righteousness; and the nations shall bless themselves in him, and in him shall they glory. *{3}* For thus saith the LORD to the men of Judah and Jerusalem, Break up your fallow ground, and sow not among thorns. *{4}* Circumcise yourselves to the LORD, and **take away the foreskins of your heart**, ye men of Judah and inhabitants of Jerusalem: **lest my fury come forth like fire**, and **burn that none can quench** *it,* **because of the evil of your doings**. *{5}* Declare ye in Judah, and publish in Jerusalem; and say, Blow ye the trumpet in the land: cry, gather together, and say, Assemble yourselves, and let us go into the defenced cities. *{6}* Set up the standard toward Zion: retire, stay not: **for I will bring evil from the north**, and **a great destruction**. *{7}* **The lion is come up** from his thicket, and **the destroyer of the Gentiles is on his way**; he is gone forth from his place **to make thy land desolate;** *and* **thy cities shall be laid waste, without an inhabitant**. *{8}* For this **gird you with sackcloth, lament and howl**: for **the fierce anger of the LORD** is not turned back from us. *{9}* And it shall come to pass at that day, saith the LORD, *that* **the heart of the king shall perish**, and **the heart of the princes; and the priests shall be astonished**, and **the prophets shall wonder**. *{10}* Then said I, Ah, Lord GOD! surely thou hast greatly deceived this people and Jerusalem, saying, Ye shall have peace; whereas **the sword reacheth unto the soul**. *{11}* At that time shall it be said to this people and to Jerusalem, A dry wind of the high places in the wilderness toward the daughter of my people, not to fan, nor to cleanse, *{12} Even* a full wind from those *places* shall come unto me: **now also will I give sentence against them**. *{13}* Behold, **he shall come up as clouds**, and **his chariots** *shall be* as a whirlwind: his horses are swifter than eagles. **Woe unto us! for we are spoiled**. *{14}* O Jerusalem, **wash thine heart from wickedness**, that thou mayest be saved. **How long shall thy vain thoughts lodge within thee?** *{15}* For a voice declareth from Dan, and publisheth **affliction** from mount Ephraim. *{16}* Make ye mention to the nations; behold, **publish against Jerusalem**, *that* watchers come from a far country, and **give out their voice against the cities of Judah**. *{17}* As keepers of a field, are they against her round about; because **she hath been rebellious against me**, saith the LORD. *{18}* Thy way and thy doings have procured these *things* unto thee; **this *is* thy wickedness, it is bitter** because, because it reacheth unto thine heart. *{19}* My bowels, my bowels! **I am pained at my very heart;** my heart maketh a noise in me; I cannot hold my peace, because thou hast heard, O my soul, **the sound of the trumpet, the alarm of war.** *{20}* **Destruction upon destruction** is cried; for **the whole land is spoiled**: suddenly are **my tents spoiled**, *and* my curtains in a moment. *{21}* How long shall I see the standard, *and* hear the sound of the trumpet? *{22}* For **my people *is* foolish, they have not known me; they *are* sottish children, and they have none understanding: they *are* wise to do evil, but to do good they have no knowledge.** *{23}* I beheld the earth, and, lo, *it was* **without form, and <u>VOID</u>**; and the heavens, and they *had* **no light.** *{24}* I beheld the mountains, and, lo, **they trembled,** and all **the hills moved lightly.** *{25}* I beheld, and, lo, *there was* **no man**, and all **the birds of the heavens were fled.** *{26}* I beheld, and, lo, **the fruitful place *was* a wilderness,** and **all the cities thereof were broken down at the presence of the LORD,** *and* **by his fierce anger.** *{27}* For thus hath the LORD said, **The whole land shall be desolate**; yet will I not make a full end. *{28}* **For this shall the earth mourn,** and **the heavens above be black**: because I have spoken *it,* I have purposed *it,* and will not repent, neither will I turn back from it. *{29}* **The whole city shall flee for the noise of the horsemen and bowmen**; they shall go into thickets, and climb up upon the rocks: **every city *shall be* forsaken,** and **not a man dwell therein.** *{30}* And *when* **thou *art* spoiled**, what wilt thou do? Though thou clothest thyself with crimson, though thou deckest thee with ornaments of gold, though thou rentest thy face with painting, **in vain shalt thou make thyself fair;** *thy* **lovers will despise thee, they will seek thy life.** *{31}* For I have heard a voice as of **a woman in travail,** *and* **the anguish** as of her that bringeth forth her first child, the voice of the daughter of Zion, *that* **bewaileth herself,** *that* spreadeth her hands, *saying,* **Woe *is* me now!** for my soul is **wearied because of murderers.**" (KJV)

There are Gap Theory haters who will tell you *BOHUW* is not used to describe God's wrath and judgment. They say it has nothing to do with destruction. It must be hard for them to read these passages without realizing the truth. Either they are extremely poor readers, or else they have extremely hardened hearts. In case they have poor reading skills, I will repeat these passages, but print only the words and phrases that speak of wrath, judgment, sin, and destruction. That way they can't possibly miss the context. (If they still miss the context, I cannot help them. It's not their reading skills that need help!)

the indignation of the LORD
his **fury**
he hath utterly destroyed them
he hath delivered them to the slaughter
Their slain
shall be cast out
their stink
their carcases

melted with their blood
shall be dissolved
all their host shall fall down
my sword shall be bathed
it shall come down upon Idumea
the people of my curse
judgment
The sword of the LORD is filled with blood
a sacrifice in Bozrah
a great slaughter in the land of Idumea
their land shall be soaked with blood
it is the day of the Lord's vengeance
the year of recompenses
the streams thereof shall be turned into pitch
the dust thereof into brimstone
the land thereof shall become burning pitch
It shall not be quenched
the smoke thereof shall go up for ever
it shall lie waste
none shall pass through it for ever and ever
confusion
<u>EMPTINESS</u>
put away thine abominations
in judgment
take away the foreskins of your heart
lest my fury come forth like fire
burn that none can quench
because of the evil of your doings
for I will bring evil from the north
and a great destruction
The lion is come up
the destroyer of the Gentiles is on his way
to make thy land desolate
thy cities shall be laid waste, without an inhabitant
gird you with sackcloth
lament and howl
the fierce anger of the LORD
the heart of the king shall perish
the heart of the princes; and the priests shall be astonished
the prophets shall wonder
the sword reacheth unto the soul

now also will I give sentence against them
he shall come up as clouds
his chariots *shall be* **as a whirlwind**
his horses are swifter than eagles
Woe unto us
we are spoiled
wash thine heart from wickedness
How long shall thy vain thoughts lodge within thee
Affliction
publish against Jerusalem
give out their voice against the cities of Judah
she hath been rebellious against me
this *is* **thy wickedness**
it is bitter
I am pained at my very heart
the sound of the trumpet
the alarm of war
Destruction upon destruction
the whole land is spoiled
my tents spoiled
my people *is* **foolish**
they have not known me
they *are* **sottish children**
they have none understanding
they *are* **wise to do evil**
to do good they have no knowledge
without form, and <u>VOID</u>
no light
they trembled
the hills moved lightly
there was **no man**
the birds of the heavens were fled
the fruitful place *was* **a wilderness**
all the cities thereof were broken down at the presence of the LORD
by his fierce anger
The whole land shall be desolate
For this shall the earth mourn
the heavens above be black
The whole city shall flee for the noise of the horsemen and bowmen
every city *shall be* **forsaken**
not a man dwell therein

thou *art* spoiled
in vain shalt thou make thyself fair
***thy* lovers will despise thee**
they will seek thy life
a woman in travail
the anguish
bewaileth herself
Woe *is* me now
wearied because of murderers

So, how do these anti-gap people justify the claim *BOHUW* cannot refer to Divine judgment in Genesis 1:2? They say Isaiah 34:11 and Jeremiah 4:23 refer to future events while Genesis 1:2 refers to a past event. This is a distinction without a difference. Is it possible to use the same word with the same meaning when describing both future and past events? How else can you use words in a language that doesn't have tenses like we have in modern English? Hebrew verb stems don't focus so much on WHEN something happens, as much as they focus on HOW something happens—active, passive, number, voice, gender… that sort of thing. In fact, it is the context that determines the tense. Look at what a Hebrew educational website has to say about this:

> "Tense – Whereas English verbs indicate tense by means of spelling changes or through the use of 'helping verbs' (e.g., I talk, I talk*ed*, I *shall* talk), Hebrew verbs are *not* marked for tense. You cannot tell – just by looking at a verb form without the context – *when* the action occurs."[31]

All the claims *BOHUW* doesn't imply Divine judgment are proved false simply by looking at the context of the passages where it is used. The context of Isaiah 34:11 is Divine judgment. The context of Jeremiah 4:23 is Divine judgment. What is the context of Genesis 1:2? Well, what image comes to mind as you read it? The earth is without form and it is void; it is desolate and dead; there is no life; it is a "chaos." There is no light; the heavens are black and the abyss covers the globe. This kind of ominous, foreboding imagery certainly opens itself up to the possibility we are looking at the aftermath of a world that had suffered Divine judgment. It is cyclic reasoning to conclude *BOHUW* can't refer to Divine judgment in the past. It presupposes the earth was never judged in the past, and then it uses that presupposition to defend its conclusion. It is a clever trick, but it violates a fundamental rule of Biblical interpretation. When you have an unquestionable definition of a word or phrase in one part of the Bible, you have no right to ignore or change that definition in other parts of the Bible without a reason other than personal interpretation.

2 Peter 1:20 "But know this first of all, that no prophecy of Scripture is *a matter* of one's own interpretation," (NASB)

BOHUW unquestionably refers to Divine judgment in Isaiah 34:11. *BOHUW* unquestionably refers to Divine judgment in Jeremiah 4:23. If there were no other arguments for the Gap Theory, I think my interpretation of Genesis 1:2 stands on this evidence: I have God telling me in two other places in Scripture that *TOHUW* and *BOHUW* are physical descriptions of His judgments. I have men telling me my interpretation is wrong because it contradicts their interpretations. Until someone can prove there is a passage in Scripture that uses *TOHUW* and *BOHUW* together in a non-Divine judgmental setting, then I'm going to believe God and not men. The combination of *TOHUW* and *BOHUW* describes a Divine judgment in space and time. In Genesis 1:2, that space is the earth. In Genesis 1:2, that time is before Adam. The Pre-Adamic earth was judged and made desolate and dead by God's judgment. Genesis 1:3-31 describe how God restored the desolate and dead earth He had judged. The earth has had two beginnings.

Chapter Seven: The Restoration Theory

I believe God originally created the universe out of nothing at some distant time in the past. Matter and energy did not coexist with God. At that instant of "timelessness" God created space, time, energy, and matter. I don't think He created the universe with galaxies, stars, and planets intact; I think He created them later. Now, some believe Genesis 1:1 indicates they were created intact and instantaneously. However, "created" doesn't necessarily imply an instantaneous point of time. God has a funny way of describing events that happen over long periods of time as if they happen together. (I guess it's an occupational hazard of being omniscient, omnipresent, and eternal.)

The Hebrew word for "created" in Genesis 1:1 is *BARA*—Strong's Number H1254. It doesn't mean *EX NIHILO* and instantaneous creation in other passages of Scripture. God **created** Jerusalem. (Isaiah 65:18) God **created** Israel. (Isaiah 43:15) God **created** the blacksmith to make the sword and the warrior to use it. (Isaiah 54:16) These were not instantaneous *EX NIHILO* creations. Jerusalem wasn't built in a nanosecond. The nation of Israel didn't pop into existence out of nothing. Blacksmiths and warriors don't suddenly appear in the blink of the eye. Since *BARA* does not mean instantaneous *EX NIHILO* creation in these cases, we can't jump to the conclusion it means instantaneous *EX NIHILO* creation when referring to the heavens and the earth. So, what does Genesis 1:1 say?

I make two claims about what *BARA* means in Genesis 1:1. First, I say it means *EX NIHILO* creation. Second, I say it was a process over time. Having said this, I will be the first to admit my claims can't be verified if I remain in Genesis 1:1. To prove my points, I must go to other passages of Scripture.

We know it means *EX NIHILO* creation. As we have already seen, the first chapter of the Gospel of John reveals how everything that exists (other than God) was created out of nothing by Jesus in the beginning. Matter exists; matter was created *EX NIHILO* by Jesus in the beginning. Energy exists; energy was created *EX NIHILO* by Jesus in the beginning. Space exists; space was created *EX NIHILO* by Jesus in the beginning. Time exists; time was created *EX NIHILO* by Jesus in the beginning. By going to another part of Scripture, we can learn the context that allows us to make an informationally correct interpretation of Genesis 1:1. The universe was created *EX NIHILO*.

What about the meaning of "created" in terms of whether it was instantaneous or a process? Is there a passage of Scripture that can supply us with the context for how we are to interpret Genesis 1:1?. Yes! Grammatically, Genesis 1:1 could describe the instantaneous creation of an intact earth, but there is a passage in the Book of Job that seems to indicate otherwise.

Job 38:4-6 "Where were you when I laid the foundation of the earth? Tell me, if you have understanding. *{5}* Who determined its measurements--surely you know! Or who stretched the line upon it? *{6}* On what were its bases sunk, or who laid its cornerstone..." (NRSV)

Here we have God telling Job something about the creation of the earth. God is revealing information to Job He didn't reveal to Moses. In fact, some scholars believe Job lived before Moses and the Book of Job is older than the Pentateuch. Other scholars believe Moses wrote the Book of Job to tell the Israelites coming out of Egypt about Job's experience living among the pagans, so they could understand, resist, and reject the mythologies, superstitions, religions, and beliefs of the pagan people they would encounter in the Promised Land. That's an issue for others to argue. What I want to focus on is what was revealed. God used imagery, some figurative language, to describe the earth's creation. God mentions a foundation and laying the foundation. He talks about laying a cornerstone. He talks about stretching the line on it and measuring it. He asks Job about the bases that were sunk. All this seems to imply the earth was constructed, as a building would be, over some period of time. Laying a foundation, laying out its measures, stretching a line upon it, laying a cornerstone, and sinking its bases would have been imagery suggesting a building-process to Job, not an instantaneous creation. Job understood what constructing a building involves. It takes raw materials and it takes time. Why would God suggest materials if the earth was made from nothing? Why would God mention a process of time if He had created the earth instantaneously? Now don't go goofy on me and start using this to defend the Flat-Earth Theory. This doesn't mean we're supposed to believe the earth is sitting on a big pile of rocks. These images are figurative. Earth has no foundation; it's floating in space. It has no cornerstone; it's a sphere. We know this from scientific observations. (True science filters out false theology.) If we took these words to be literal descriptions of the earth, then we'd have to believe the earth was made of giant stones built on a foundation. Since these words are figurative, we don't have to defend a doctrine that says the earth is lying on a foundation of stones. Nevertheless, God is revealing something to Job by using imagery. What does He reveal? **Throughout the Bible, when God uses imagery, figurative language, similes, metaphors, parables, hyperbole, or whatever, it is designed to reveal truth.** God doesn't use imagery to convey nothing. In fact, the use of imagery, such as Jesus teaching in parables, teaches far more than stating raw facts alone. Jesus calls us, "sheep." Are we literal sheep? No, but like sheep we are helpless, hopeless, stupid, prone to wander, and from the perspective of God's Holy character, we stink! He used one word, "sheep," to describe a number of human characteristics. While the image of us being sheep may hurt our egos, it is not misleading. It reveals the truth about us, to us. In the Bible, figurative language reveals literal truth.

    The same must be true for the imagery God uses in Job. God is using imagery to teach us something about the creation. If the earth wasn't created by means of a process over time, then this imagery is misleading. God should have asked Job, "Where were you when I created the earth…" and left it at that. He didn't have to suggest a process if there was no process. In fact, He shouldn't have suggested a process if there was no process. There are two reasons why we should worry about God suggesting things that aren't true. First, it means God can add false information and concepts to the Bible. That's not good. Second, it means we can't trust the Bible's teachings about Jesus Christ. If the imagery about laying down the foundation of the earth is misleading, then the imagery about the Good Shepherd laying down His life for His sheep can also be misleading. We can't trust that imagery either. If the imagery in Job doesn't convey the truth about creation, then the imagery of the Good Shepherd may not convey the truth about Jesus. That's worse! **If we can't trust God's figurative language to reveal literal truth, then we might as well throw the Bible into the trash.** As I look at this passage in Job, I can't help but interpret it to be figurative language revealing literal truth about earth's creation. It was a material-consuming, time-consuming process; not instantaneous.

Let me now guess what some will say. They will say this contradicts the doctrine of *EX NIHILO* Creation. It doesn't. As I said before, creation out of nothing does not imply instantaneous creation. If God created matter and energy out of nothing, and then used what He created to create/make/form the universe over time, it would still be *EX NIHILO*. It all came out of nothing. I think this is why the Bible uses three different words to describe God's creative acts: *BARA* ("create;" Strong's Number H1254), *ASAH* ("make;" Strong's Number H6213), and *YATSAR* ("form;" Strong's Number H3335). Using all three of these words together suggests both creation and process.

"Okay, Steve," they'll say, "but why can't that time-consuming process be the creative acts of God during the six days of creation? That was a process over time. What makes you think God wasn't telling Job about those six days?"

The answer is because the two accounts, Job 38:4-6 and Genesis 1:3-31, describe different aspects of earth's creation. They don't describe the same events. In Job, God describes the earth's foundation; He speaks of its bases and its cornerstone. If I had to put this in modern terms, I would suggest God was talking about the earth's core, its mantle, and its crust. The verses in Job describe the creation of the earth from the surface down. Genesis 1:3-31 describe the atmosphere, the oceans, the clouds, the trees, the birds, the animals, and man. These verses describe what God did from the surface up. (Which is again why I think the description is given from the vantage point of someone standing on the surface of the earth; not from a heavenly or from a cosmic viewpoint.) Yes, that was a process over time too, but it was a different process at a different time.

In addition to Job's revelation about the process of the creation of the earth, there is another reason I don't think the heavens and the earth were instantaneously created intact. It is a scientific reason, and it follows the same reasoning as my objection to the Young-Earth concept of Apparent Age—it is contrary to scientific observations. Proponents of the Instantaneous/Intact Creation Theory say God would not create a universe less than perfect. A perfect universe would have a perfect and intact earth, filled with perfect and intact life, orbiting a perfect and intact sun, inside a perfect and intact galaxy the instant it was created. This begs the question: What does "perfect" mean?

I know some creationists believe if the universe wasn't created instantaneously, intact, and perfect, then it somehow besmirches God's perfect character. They repeatedly say, "Since God is perfect, everything He created would be perfect." This is a true statement, but what does "perfect" mean in relationship to created things? Galileo was persecuted by the "Church" because he looked at the moon through a telescope, measured its dimensions, and discovered it was slightly wider than it was high. He didn't know why, but that was what he measured. We know why today. The centrifugal force of any rotating body will cause it to bulge at its center. The moon, the earth, and all other rotating bodies (including galaxies) are shaped by centrifugal force and gravity. Is centrifugal force evil? Is gravity imperfect? As soon as the "Church" learned of Galileo's discovery, they denounced him as a heretic. They believed if the moon wasn't perfectly spherical, then it wouldn't be perfect. Since a perfect God would create only a perfect moon, Galileo was blaspheming God. Their problem was they had a definition of "perfect" that fit their preconceived beliefs. Why is a non-perfectly spherical moon, not a perfect moon? If the moon was perfectly what God wanted it to be, then why wouldn't it be perfect by His standards? Why couldn't God create the moon exactly what it was and give it the exact function He wanted? Where in the Bible does it say God created the moon perfectly spherical?

The problem is with these creationists. They superimpose their idea of perfection over God's idea of perfection. They put their ideas of what the universe should be, above what God's idea of what the universe should be. These creationists say Process-Creation is not God-honoring because it doesn't involve Instantaneous-Creation. But, why would Process-Creation be less God-honoring than Instantaneous-Creation? Do they say this of babies being born? Is the miracle of life less God-honoring because we are fearfully and wonderfully made/formed/knitted (a process) in our mother's womb? Does being created by fertilization, conception, cellular multiplication, blastulation, gastrulation, differentiation, specialization, growth, development, and birth mean the process isn't God-honoring… or that God is less than perfect? When you consider how the entire process of life and reproduction is directed, implemented, and controlled by organic nano-machines operating according to quaternary-base encoded instructions in Deoxyribose Nucleic Acid molecules, why isn't that a miracle that honors God? Is life an imperfect creation of God because living creatures reproduce by means of a process? Does using preexisting DNA molecules to create new life make life less-perfect? According to the Instantaneous/Intact Creation Theory, it must be. New life isn't instantaneous and intact, so it must not be God-honoring. How about the process of creating Adam? Was that less than perfect because it wasn't instantaneous? God first formed man's body from the dirt, and then He breathed into his nostrils the breath of life. Granted, it didn't take nine months, but it was still a process; body first, then life. God also brought land plants and animals into existence from the soil; not *EX NIHILO*.

Genesis 1:11 "And God said, Let the **earth** bring forth grass, the herb yielding seed, *and* the fruit tree yielding fruit after his kind, whose seed *is* in itself, upon the earth: and it was so." (KJV)

Genesis 1:24 "And God said, Let the **earth** bring forth the living creature after his kind, cattle, and creeping thing, and beast of the earth after his kind: and it was so." (KJV)

Genesis 2:9 "And out of the **ground** made the LORD God to grow every tree that is pleasant to the sight, and good for food; the tree of life also in the midst of the garden, and the tree of knowledge of good and evil." (KJV)

Genesis 2:19 "And out of the **ground** the LORD God formed every beast of the field, and every fowl of the air; and brought *them* unto Adam to see what he would call them: and whatsoever Adam called every living creature, that *was* the name thereof." (KJV)

Was this less-perfect than if He had created everything *EX NIHILO*? The Bible reveals how God created/made/formed living organisms by a process. Of course, it wasn't the process of evolution, so we creationists don't need to get worried. Nevertheless, there is no reason to think the stars, galaxies, and planets had to be created instantly and intact. Process-Creation does not negate God's perfection.

According to the Instantaneous/Intact Creation Theory, all the stars, galaxies, nebulae, planets, moons, quasars, and all other celestial bodies were created intact and perfect in the beginning. (Genesis 1:1) That means there weren't clouds of hydrogen that coalesced into stars over millions of years. This means it didn't take billions of years for our planet, our sun, our solar system, and our galaxy to gradually form from the matter and energy that came out of the Big Bang. According to this theory, these things were perfect and intact the instant God created them *EX NIHILO*. Science disagrees. The belief the universe was created instantaneously, regardless of when you think it happened, is scientifically indefensible. As stars age, their sizes, luminosities, densities, and frequencies-of-light-change. As galaxies age, their sizes, shapes, colors, and rotational velocities change. The pertinent scientific fact is that as you look out at the universe, you can see stars and galaxies of many different ages. Some are old, and some are young. It's like looking at people. Some people look like young children; some look like me—old geezers. Why do people appear to be different ages? The reason is because they ARE different ages. I believe the same is true about stars and galaxies. They appear to be different ages, because they ARE different ages. Unlike the Young-Earth creationists, I don't believe God created the stars and galaxies with Apparent Ages. This means a young galaxy looks young because it is young. An old galaxy looks old because it is old. But, for this to be true, it means the universe has been aging since the beginning. Observations show how the stars and galaxies are in various stages of age. Stars and galaxies have changed over time. They are not what they used to be; they have aged.

If the Instantaneous/Intact Creation Theory is true, then the earth could not have been formed by space dust four-billion years ago. It would have been perfect and intact when created. Likewise, the sun had to be perfect and intact four-and-a-half-billion years ago. It could not have been formed by clouds of hydrogen gas. If this theory is true, then no stars were formed from clouds of gas over time; no planets were formed from dust over time; no galaxies were formed from stars coalescing by the force of gravity over time. We shouldn't be able to look out at the universe and see stars and galaxies of different ages. We shouldn't see new stars and galaxies forming, and we shouldn't see old stars and galaxies dying. Nevertheless, astronomers and cosmologists see young and old stars, and young and old galaxies. You can argue, but the evidence from science is strong enough to force anyone who cares an ounce about science to agree with what astronomers and cosmologists say about their observations. (Of course, this doesn't prevent some creationists from denouncing scientists as heretics.)

Let me explain my position. Let's start by assuming the universe is fourteen-billion years old. (I know many will disagree, but I want to start with this assumption in order to test this assumption with the observations made by scientists. If this assumption agrees with the scientific observations, then it is probably correct. If it doesn't, then it is wrong.) Let's also assume the universe came into existence *EX NIHILO* in the Big Bang event. Matter and energy, and time and space, all came out of nothing BY THE COMMAND OF GOD. Scientific observations show how the universe has been expanding since its creation, and these scientific observations agree with what the Bible says. (I'll talk more about this stretching-out in Chapter Eleven.) God has been stretching out the universe since the beginning. Where the galaxies and stars are now are not where they have always been. Their locations have changed. Their qualities and conditions have changed. I believe they changed because God used the process of aging to form the stars, galaxies, and planets to be what He wants them to be today. In other words, God created stars and galaxies by processes, just as He created the earth by a process, if what Job tells us is true.

One-billion years ago the stars and galaxies were not what they are today. One-billion years ago they were what God wanted them to be one-billion years ago. Five-billion years ago they were what God wanted them to be five-billion years ago. Ten-billion years ago they were what God wanted them to be ten-billion years ago. Fourteen-billion years ago they did not exist because God did not want them to exist fourteen-billion years ago. If you accept the scientific evidence, then you know the earth and the sun weren't here five-billion years ago. They weren't here five-billion years ago because God did not want them to be here five-billion years ago. God has a plan for His universe, and in His plan, the universe wasn't ready for our sun, our planet, or life on our planet five-billion years ago. Everything the earth is now has come about by a process of formation. It wasn't created instantaneously and intact at the same time the universe came into existence fourteen-billion years ago. In fact, God didn't want any stars, galaxies, or planets fourteen-billion years ago. If we look back to fourteen-billion-years ago, we don't see any stars and galaxies. The only thing we see is the background microwave radiation left over by the Big Bang. (We can look back in time by looking out to distance. It takes light from a star a million light-years away, a million years to reach us. It takes light from a galaxy ten-billion light-years away, ten-billion years to reach us. The farther out we look, the farther back in time we see.)

Scientists have seen how the universe has been undergoing an aging process. There was a time when there were no stars and galaxies, but as time went on, stars and galaxies began to form. With even more time, some of them began to die. (Supernovae, for instance.) In other words, the universe reveals that matter and energy came out of nothing, and then later formed into stars and galaxies as the universe expanded. In short, the observations of the heavens declare how the universe was created by a process, and not instantaneously. If the heavens declare the glory of God and reveal His handiwork, then the glory of God and the handiwork of God was to create the universe by a process. To believe the Bible teaches an instantaneous and intact creation requires us to believe that what God reveals in Scripture is not what God reveals in space. His Words and His Works don't match. And, I reject this idea for the same reason I reject the Theory of Evolution. Does the expansion of the universe and the formation of stars and galaxies prove God is less-than-perfect? If you think so, then I have four recommendations for you:

1.) Mark this spot in this book, and quit reading it right now.

2.) Go to your favorite Christian bookstore and purchase Hugh Ross' book, *The Improbable Planet*,[32] and read it.

3.) When you finish reading his book, if you still think the Process-Creation of the stars, galaxies, planets, moons, *etc.* doesn't honor God, or it makes God less than perfect, then you have my permission to quit reading my book, and I won't be upset at you. (I will pity you, however.)

4.) Otherwise, resume reading my book.

If you don't want to read Dr. Hugh Ross' book, shame on you, but I will summarize it. First, he is a creationist. He does not believe life was created by any process of evolution. While the conditions needed for life on this planet were created by a process, life was not created by a process; it was created by God. Next, Dr. Ross proves how the universe was fearfully and wonderfully made, knitted, shaped, formed, constructed, and ordered over time with such intricate precision and design, that life could not be here otherwise. This design and construction even included the moon. Its size, composition, density, orbital and rotational qualities, and its distance from the earth are all factors that if they weren't exactly what they were, and if they didn't come about exactly the way they did, and if they didn't happen exactly when they did, then we wouldn't be here. He speaks of the Fine-Tuning of the universe. A lot of creationists like to use Fine-Tuning as evidence that God created the universe. (Fine-Tuning = Divine Tuning) However, creationists who hate the Big Bang Theory don't realize how virtually all the Finely-Tuned characteristics are what they are because of the Big Bang. If you believe the Big Bang and the gradual formation of the universe over time sullies God's character, then you cannot use the Fine-Tuning Arguments to defend the Bible. I'll have more to say about the Fine-Tuning Argument in the next chapter.

I believe Genesis 1:1 describes the original creation of the heavens and earth. I don't know what processes He used to create the earth, but I know those processes didn't end up with a dead and dark submerged waste-planet! He didn't use those processes to create it *TOHUW WA-BOHUW*. He used those Pre-Adamic processes to create/form/make a Pre-Adamic earth that was beautiful and teeming with life. It wasn't until after sin entered the universe, through Lucifer, that something terrible began happening to the earth. Lucifer began corrupting all of creation, both heaven and earth. All of creation "groans" because of his sin. I think he began defiling the earth and the life on it. I believe God intervened and judged the earth, leaving it dead and dark for an unspecified, but probably very short, period of time. I believe Genesis 1:3-31 describe the restoration. I don't think everything was fully restored to what it had been, but it was restored enough for man's needs. According to the Restoration Theory, Pre-Adamic life on earth was destroyed by God's judgment. Following its *TOHUW WA-BOHUW* period, the earth was restored by God during six literal days. According to the Restoration Theory, all living things today are descendants of the living things He created and restored on the earth during those six days; nothing evolved. The Gap Theory does not defend the Theory of Evolution.

So, why do other creationists say the Gap Theory defends evolution when it doesn't? Why do people say and believe things they know aren't true? It brings up the question of motives. (This is why learning WHY someone believes something is just as important as learning WHAT they believe.) Today, both Young-Earth and Day-Age creationists reject the Gap Theory. Their reasons are different, but their motives are identical. Their rejection of the Restoration Theory brings to light a much darker motive for their beliefs.

Young-Earth creationists say the six days were literal days. In their minds, if the days were literal, then the universe cannot be old. The Gap Theory agrees the days were literal days, but Young-Earthers still reject it because it goes contrary to their most cherished belief, the belief the universe is young. Young-Earth creationists are not as concerned with WHAT the days were, as they are with WHEN the days were. Young-Earth creationists care more about the earth being young than they do about the days being literal. This is why they reject the Gap Theory. They spend virtually all their time, talent, and money on trying to prove the universe is only a few thousand years old. Too many doctorates have been earned, too much money has been spent, and too many reputations are on the line to permit them to accept a theory that allows the universe to be old. Allowing that would mean they have put their own prestige above what God wants revealed in His Word. Now, I believe God revealed what He wants us to know. What does He reveal in the very first chapter of the very first book of the Bible? God reveals the six days were literal days, but He doesn't say a thing about when those six days were. God could have told Moses the exact time it happened, but He didn't. God did not tell Moses whether it was a few thousand years before or several billion years before. God's emphasis is on WHAT the days were, not on WHEN the days were. Young-Earth creationists reverse the emphasis. The age of the universe is more important. **If the days being literal was more important, then they wouldn't attack the Gap Theory.**

Day-Age creationists have the same motive for rejecting the Restoration Theory, but their reason is different. In their case, they can't let the days be anything but ages. By their thinking, if the universe is old, then the days must be ages. So, like the Young-Earthers, they reject the Gap Theory. The Gap Theory allows for the universe to be billions of years old just like the Day-Age Theory. Day-Age creationists still reject it because it says the days were literal. The Gap Theory attacks their most cherished belief, the belief the days are ages. **If the age of the universe was more important, then they wouldn't attack the Gap Theory.** Instead, they have put in too much effort, written too many books, and given too many lectures emphasizing the days are ages. If they admit the days were literal, then they would have to admit their efforts were misguided. This is why they must insist, like the Young-Earth creationists, that *HAYAH* cannot be translated, "became." They have the same motive. Personal prestige, reputation, and ego overshadow God's revelation. Ironically, both Day-Age creationists and Young-Earth creationists commit the same error they accuse evolutionists of committing. Namely, they have painted themselves into philosophical corners, and can't escape without admitting they were wrong. No one wants to look foolish, so no one budges from his corner. Their own clever theories become more important than what the evidence shows.

Because of this, both camps say *HAYAH* should not or cannot be translated, "became." What does the Bible say? *HAYAH* is translated, "became," "become," "came," "came to pass," and "come to pass," about 800 times in the *King James Version*. *HAYAH* is translated this way 89 times in Genesis alone.

HAYAH in Genesis (KJV) as Some Form of "Became"

1.) Genesis 2:7 "And the LORD God formed man of the dust of the ground, and breathed into his nostrils the breath of life; and man **became** a living soul." (KJV)

2.) Genesis 2:10 "And a river went out of Eden to water the garden; and from thence it was parted, and **became** into four heads." (KJV)

3.) Genesis 3:22 "And the LORD God said, Behold, the man is **become** as one of us, to know good and evil: and now, lest he put forth his hand, and take also of the tree of life, and eat, and live for ever:" (KJV)

4.) Genesis 4:3 "And in process of time it **came to pass**, that Cain brought of the fruit of the ground an offering unto the LORD. (KJV)"

5.) Genesis 4:8 "And Cain talked with Abel his brother: and it **came to pass**, when they were in the field, that Cain rose up against Abel his brother, and slew him." (KJV)

6.) Genesis 4:14 "Behold, thou hast driven me out this day from the face of the earth; and from thy face shall I be hid; and I shall be a fugitive and a vagabond in the earth; and it shall **come to pass**, that every one that findeth me shall slay me." (KJV)

7.) Genesis 6:1 "And it **came to pass**, when men began to multiply on the face of the earth, and daughters were born unto them," (KJV)

8.) Genesis 7:10 "And it **came to pass** after seven days, that the waters of the flood were upon the earth." (KJV)

9.) Genesis 8:6 "And it **came to pass** at the end of forty days, that Noah opened the window of the ark which he had made:" (KJV)

10.) Genesis 8:13 "And it **came to pass** in the six hundredth and first year, in the first month, the first day of the month, the waters were dried up from off the earth: and Noah removed the covering of the ark, and looked, and, behold, the face of the ground was dry." (KJV)

11.) Genesis 9:14 "And it shall **come to pass**, when I bring a cloud over the earth, that the bow shall be seen in the cloud:" (KJV)

12.) Genesis 9:15 "And I will remember my covenant, which is between me and you and every living creature of all flesh; and the waters shall no more **become** a flood to destroy all flesh." (KJV)

13.) Genesis 11:2 "And it **came to pass**, as they journeyed from the east, that they found a plain in the land of Shinar; and they dwelt there." (KJV)

14.) Genesis 12:11 "And it **came to pass**, when he was come near to enter into Egypt, that he said unto Sarai his wife, Behold now, I know that thou art a fair woman to look upon:" (KJV)

15.) Genesis 12:14 "And it **came to pass**, that, when Abram was come into Egypt, the Egyptians beheld the woman that she was very fair." (KJV)

16.) Genesis 14:1 "And it **came to pass** in the days of Amraphel king of Shinar, Arioch king of Ellasar, Chedorlaomer king of Elam, and Tidal king of nations;" (KJV)

17.) Genesis 15:1 "After these things the word of the LORD **came** unto Abram in a vision, saying, Fear not, Abram: I am thy shield, and thy exceeding great reward." (KJV)

18.) Genesis 15:17 "And it **came to pass**, that, when the sun went down, and it was dark, behold a smoking furnace, and a burning lamp that passed between those pieces." (KJV)

19.) Genesis 18:18 "Seeing that Abraham shall surely **become** a great and mighty nation, and all the nations of the earth shall be blessed in him?" (KJV)

20.) Genesis 19:17 "And it **came to pass**, when they had brought them forth abroad, that he said, Escape for thy life; look not behind thee, neither stay thou in all the plain; escape to the mountain, lest thou be consumed." (KJV)

21.) Genesis 19:26 "But his wife looked back from behind him, and she **became** a pillar of salt." (KJV)

22.) Genesis 19:29 "And it **came to pass**, when God destroyed the cities of the plain, that God remembered Abraham, and sent Lot out of the midst of the overthrow, when he overthrew the cities in the which Lot dwelt." (KJV)

23.) Genesis 19:34 "And it **came to pass** on the morrow, that the firstborn said unto the younger, Behold, I lay yesternight with my father: let us make him drink wine this night also; and go thou in, and lie with him, that we may preserve seed of our father." (KJV)

24.) Genesis 20:12 "And yet indeed *she is* my sister; she *is* the daughter of my father, but not the daughter of my mother; and she **became** my wife." (KJV)

25.) Genesis 20:13 "And it **came to pass**, when God caused me to wander from my father's house, that I said unto her, This is thy kindness which thou shalt show unto me; at every place whither we shall come, say of me, He is my brother." (KJV)

26.) Genesis 21:20 "And God was with the lad; and he grew, and dwelt in the wilderness, and **became** an archer." (KJV)

27.) Genesis 21:22 "And it **came to pass** at that time, that Abimelech and Phichol the chief captain of his host spake unto Abraham, saying, God is with thee in all that thou doest:" (KJV)

28.) Genesis 22:1 "And it **came to pass** after these things, that God did tempt Abraham, and said unto him, Abraham: and he said, Behold, here I am." (KJV)

29.) Genesis 22:20 "And it **came to pass** after these things, that it was told Abraham, saying, Behold, Milcah, she hath also born children unto thy brother Nahor;" (KJV)

30.) Genesis 24:14 "And let it **come to pass**, that the damsel to whom I shall say, Let down thy pitcher, I pray thee, that I may drink; and she shall say, Drink, and I will give thy camels drink also: let the same be she that thou hast appointed for thy servant Isaac; and thereby shall I know that thou hast showed kindness unto my master." (KJV)

31.) Genesis 24:15 "And it **came to pass**, before he had done speaking, that, behold, Rebekah came out, who was born to Bethuel, son of Milcah, the wife of Nahor, Abraham's brother, with her pitcher upon her shoulder." (KJV)

32.) Genesis 24:22 "And it **came to pass**, as the camels had done drinking, that the man took a golden earring of half a shekel weight, and two bracelets for her hands of ten shekels weight of gold;" (KJV)

33.) Genesis 24:30 "And it **came to pass**, when he saw the earring and bracelets upon his sister's hands, and when he heard the words of Rebekah his sister, saying, Thus spake the man unto me; that he came unto the man; and, behold, he stood by the camels at the well." (KJV)

34.) Genesis 24:43 "Behold, I stand by the well of water; and it shall **come to pass**, that when the virgin cometh forth to draw water, and I say to her, Give me, I pray thee, a little water of thy pitcher to drink;" (KJV)

35.) Genesis 24:52 "And it **came to pass**, that, when Abraham's servant heard their words, he worshipped the LORD, bowing himself to the earth." (KJV)

36.) Genesis 24:67 "And Isaac brought her into his mother Sarah's tent, and took Rebekah, and she **became** his wife; and he loved her: and Isaac was comforted after his mother's death." (KJV)

37.) Genesis 25:11 "And it **came to pass** after the death of Abraham, that God blessed his son Isaac; and Isaac dwelt by the well Lahairoi." (KJV)

38.) Genesis 26:8 "And it **came to pass**, when he had been there a long time, that Abimelech king of the Philistines looked out at a window, and saw, and, behold, Isaac was sporting with Rebekah his wife." (KJV)

39.) Genesis 26:32 "And it **came to pass** the same day, that Isaac's servants came, and told him concerning the well which they had digged, and said unto him, We have found water." (KJV)

40.) Genesis 27:1 "And it **came to pass**, that when Isaac was old, and his eyes were dim, so that he could not see, he called Esau his eldest son, and said unto him, My son: and he said unto him, Behold, here am I." (KJV)

41.) Genesis 27:30 "And it **came to pass**, as soon as Isaac had made an end of blessing Jacob, and Jacob was yet scarce gone out from the presence of Isaac his father, that Esau his brother came in from his hunting." (KJV)

42.) Genesis 27:40 "And by thy sword shalt thou live, and shalt serve thy brother; and it shall **come to pass** when thou shalt have the dominion, that thou shalt break his yoke from off thy neck." (KJV)

43.) Genesis 29:10 "And it **came to pass**, when Jacob saw Rachel the daughter of Laban his mother's brother, and the sheep of Laban his mother's brother, that Jacob went near, and rolled the stone from the well's mouth, and watered the flock of Laban his mother's brother." (KJV)

44.) Genesis 29:13 "And it **came to pass**, when Laban heard the tidings of Jacob his sister's son, that he ran to meet him, and embraced him, and kissed him, and brought him to his house. And he told Laban all these things." (KJV)

45.) Genesis 29:23 "And it **came to pass** in the evening, that he took Leah his daughter, and brought her to him; and he went in unto her." (KJV)

46.) Genesis 29:25 "And it **came to pass**, that in the morning, behold, it was Leah: and he said to Laban, What is this thou hast done unto me? did not I serve with thee for Rachel? wherefore then hast thou beguiled me?" (KJV)

47.) Genesis 30:25 "And it **came to pass**, when Rachel had born Joseph, that Jacob said unto Laban, Send me away, that I may go unto mine own place, and to my country." (KJV)

48.) Genesis 30:41 "And it **came to pass**, whensoever the stronger cattle did conceive, that Jacob laid the rods before the eyes of the cattle in the gutters, that they might conceive among the rods." (KJV)

49.) Genesis 31:10 "And it **came to pass** at the time that the cattle conceived, that I lifted up mine eyes, and saw in a dream, and, behold, the rams which leaped upon the cattle were ringstreaked, speckled, and grisled." (KJV)

50.) Genesis 32:10 "I am not worthy of the least of all the mercies, and of all the truth, which thou hast showed unto thy servant; for with my staff I passed over this Jordan; and now I am **become** two bands." (KJV)

51.) Genesis 34:16 "Then will we give our daughters unto you, and we will take your daughters to us, and we will dwell with you, and we will **become** one people." (KJV)

52.) Genesis 34:25 "And it **came to pass** on the third day, when they were sore, that two of the sons of Jacob, Simeon and Levi, Dinah's brethren, took each man his sword, and came upon the city boldly, and slew all the males." (KJV)

53.) Genesis 35:17 "And it **came to pass**, when she was in hard labour, that the midwife said unto her, Fear not; thou shalt have this son also." (KJV)

54.) Genesis 35:18 "And it **came to pass**, as her soul was in departing, (for she died) that she called his name Benoni: but his father called him Benjamin." (KJV)

55.) Genesis 35:22 "And it **came to pass**, when Israel dwelt in that land, that Reuben went and lay with Bilhah his father's concubine: and Israel heard it. Now the sons of Jacob were twelve:" (KJV)

56.) Genesis 37:20 "Come now therefore, and let us slay him, and cast him into some pit, and we will say, Some evil beast hath devoured him: and we shall see what will **become** of his dreams." (KJV)

57.) Genesis 37:23 "And it **came to pass**, when Joseph was come unto his brethren, that they stripped Joseph out of his coat, his coat of many colours that was on him;" (KJV)

58.) Genesis 38:1 "And it **came to pass** at that time, that Judah went down from his brethren, and turned in to a certain Adullamite, whose name was Hirah." (KJV)

59.) Genesis 38:9 "And Onan knew that the seed should not be his; and it **came to pass**, when he went in unto his brother's wife, that he spilled it on the ground, lest that he should give seed to his brother." (KJV)

60.) Genesis 38:24 "And it **came to pass** about three months after, that it was told Judah, saying, Tamar thy daughter in law hath played the harlot; and also, behold, she is with child by whoredom. And Judah said, Bring her forth, and let her be burnt." (KJV)

61.) Genesis 38:27 "And it **came to pass** in the time of her travail, that, behold, twins were in her womb." (KJV)

62.) Genesis 38:28 "And it **came to pass**, when she travailed, that the one put out his hand: and the midwife took and bound upon his hand a scarlet thread, saying, This came out first." (KJV)

63.) Genesis 38:29 "And it **came to pass**, as he drew back his hand, that, behold, his brother came out: and she said, How hast thou broken forth? this breach be upon thee: therefore his name was called Pharez." (KJV)

64.) Genesis 39:5 "And it **came to pass** from the time that he had made him overseer in his house, and over all that he had, that the LORD blessed the Egyptian's house for Joseph's sake; and the blessing of the LORD was upon all that he had in the house, and in the field." (KJV)

65.) Genesis 39:7 "And it **came to pass** after these things, that his master's wife cast her eyes upon Joseph; and she said, Lie with me." (KJV)

66.) Genesis 39:10 "And it **came to pass**, as she spake to Joseph day by day, that he hearkened not unto her, to lie by her, or to be with her." (KJV)

67.) Genesis 39:11 "And it **came to pass** about this time, that Joseph went into the house to do his business; and there was none of the men of the house there within." (KJV)

68.) Genesis 39:13 "And it **came to pass**, when she saw that he had left his garment in her hand, and was fled forth," (KJV)

69.) Genesis 39:15 "And it **came to pass**, when he heard that I lifted up my voice and cried, that he left his garment with me, and fled, and got him out." (KJV)

70.) Genesis 39:18 "And it **came to pass**, as I lifted up my voice and cried, that he left his garment with me, and fled out." (KJV)

71.) Genesis 39:19 "And it **came to pass**, when his master heard the words of his wife, which she spake unto him, saying, After this manner did thy servant to me; that his wrath was kindled." (KJV)

72.) Genesis 40:1 "And it **came to pass** after these things, that the butler of the king of Egypt and his baker had offended their lord the king of Egypt." (KJV)

73.) Genesis 40:20 "And it **came to pass** the third day, which was Pharaoh's birthday, that he made a feast unto all his servants: and he lifted up the head of the chief butler and of the chief baker among his servants." (KJV)

74.) Genesis 41:1 "And it **came to pass** at the end of two full years, that Pharaoh dreamed: and, behold, he stood by the river." (KJV)

75.) Genesis 41:8 "And it **came to pass** in the morning that his spirit was troubled; and he sent and called for all the magicians of Egypt, and all the wise men thereof: and Pharaoh told them his dream; but there was none that could interpret them unto Pharaoh." (KJV)

76.) Genesis 41:13 "And it **came to pass**, as he interpreted to us, so it was; me he restored unto mine office, and him he hanged." (KJV)

77.) Genesis 42:35 "And it **came to pass** as they emptied their sacks, that, behold, every man's bundle of money was in his sack: and when both they and their father saw the bundles of money, they were afraid." (KJV)

78.) Genesis 43:2 "And it **came to pass**, when they had eaten up the corn which they had brought out of Egypt, their father said unto them, Go again, buy us a little food." (KJV)

79.) Genesis 43:21 "And it **came to pass**, when we came to the inn, that we opened our sacks, and, behold, every man's money was in the mouth of his sack, our money in full weight: and we have brought it again in our hand." (KJV)

80.) Genesis 44:24 "And it **came to pass** when we came up unto thy servant my father, we told him the words of my lord." (KJV)

81.) Genesis 44:31 "It shall **come to pass**, when he seeth that the lad is not with us, that he will die: and thy servants shall bring down the gray hairs of thy servant our father with sorrow to the grave." (KJV)

82.) Genesis 46:33 "And it shall **come to pass**, when Pharaoh shall call you, and shall say, What is your occupation?" (KJV)

83.) Genesis 47:20 "And Joseph bought all the land of Egypt for Pharaoh; for the Egyptians sold every man his field, because the famine prevailed over them: so the land **became** Pharaoh's." (KJV)

84.) Genesis 47:24 "And it shall **come to pass** in the increase, that ye shall give the fifth part unto Pharaoh, and four parts shall be your own, for seed of the field, and for your food, and for them of your households, and for food for your little ones." (KJV)

85.) Genesis 47:26 "And Joseph made it a law over the land of Egypt unto this day, that Pharaoh should have the fifth part; except the land of the priests only, which **became** not Pharaoh's." (KJV)

86.) Genesis 48:1 "And it **came to pass** after these things, that one told Joseph, Behold, thy father is sick: and he took with him his two sons, Manasseh and Ephraim." (KJV)

87. and 88.) Genesis 48:19 "And his father refused, and said, I know it, my son, I know it: he also **shall become** a people, and he also shall be great: but truly his younger brother shall be greater than he, and his seed **shall become** a multitude of nations." (KJV)

89.) Genesis 49:15 "And he saw that rest was good, and the land that it was pleasant; and bowed his shoulder to bear, and **became** a servant unto tribute." (KJV)

Note that "came to pass" means "came to happen" or "came to be." Note, also that "come to pass" means "come to happen" or "come to be." All 89 of these verses describe dynamic/changing conditions or events. Not one of them describes a static/unchanging past condition or event. Can *HAYAH* denote "becoming" rather than "being?" Absolutely! Are the Young-Earth and Day-Age statements about *HAYAH* true? No. They are opinions, and very biased ones at that. Using *The Complete Word Study Old Testament King James Version*,[33] I counted 316 *HAYAH*s in Genesis. (See Chapter Twelve for more details about *HAYAH*.) Since *HAYAH* is translated as some form of "became" or "become" nearly one-third of the time in the *King James Version*, I fail to see how anyone can claim *HAYAH* can't be translated as some form of "became" or "become." Personal opinion has a way of becoming "proven fact" given enough time and ignorance. This is why I emphasize we must be careful when people make themselves appear scholarly. I have never objected to personal opinions as long as they are so labeled. However, when opinions are proclaimed as facts and defended by untrue statements, I get angry. I get even angrier if Christians do it. No lie, no matter how eloquently expressed, will ever glorify Jesus Christ. My warning to you is to be very careful what you read and whom you believe, especially if a non-Hebrew or Greek scholar tries to convince you he is one. Once again, I openly admit I am not a scholar in Hebrew or Greek. However, the Restoration Theory is a theory that has been believed and defended by a number of excellent Hebrew and Greek scholars. For me, it is simply the theory that seems to explain all the facts the best.

How My Thinking Evolved

Even before I became a creationist, I was aware of the Restoration Theory. I first read about it in *The New Scofield Reference Bible*.[34] Dr. C. I. Scofield (1843-1921), certainly a qualified Biblical scholar, preferred the Restoration Theory. I was intrigued by the idea of a prior earth and a later restoration, but I remained unconvinced. At the time, I was still a theistic evolutionist.

Later, I purchased a copy of the eye-opening book, *Dispensational Truth*,[35] by Clarence Larkin (1850-1924). He believed in the Restoration Theory, as well. I was entertained by his presentation, especially by his diagrams and drawings, but I wasn't convinced. I clung tightly to theistic evolution.

It wasn't until after I was challenged with some Bible verses about man being created before woman that I began to suspect something was wrong with evolution. I previously believed Adam and Eve were figurative symbols of men and women; not two literal individuals. If what I had believed was true, then the Bible taught that males came before females. That was an evolutionary impossibility. This prompted me to begin looking into the science of evolution.

Once I finished my studies in science and discovered evolution was a lie, I returned to the Bible to see what it truly said about our origin. I tried to use the same logical approach to determine truth in the Bible, as I had used to determine truth from science. I wanted to let the Bible speak for itself. My motive was not to force the Bible to defend or defeat any particular creation theory. I wasn't even trying to force the Bible to defend creationism. That was the very thing I was attempting to discover. This was my goal: I wanted to see if the Bible taught evolution as I had believed, and as I had been told. By that time, I knew if the Bible taught evolution, then the Bible was wrong and Jesus was a hoax. I was so strongly convinced from the scientific evidence that evolution was a lie, that if the Bible did teach evolution, then I was ready to toss Christianity into the waste basket and start searching for my true Creator. After seeing evolution wasn't taught in the Bible, I first opted for the Day-Age Theory, and then for the Young-Earth Theory. I was persuaded by the arguments in the Young-Earth books I read that the Day-Age theory was Biblically wrong. Because of that, I believed the universe, the earth, and life on the earth were originally created only a few thousand years ago during a six-day period.

I originally questioned my Theistic-Evolution belief because I was confronted with some passages of Scripture that couldn't be reconciled with the Theory of Evolution. I later questioned my Day-Age belief because I was confronted with some passages of Scripture that couldn't be reconciled with the Day-Age Theory. (The "days" were literal days.) In the same fashion, I questioned my Young-Earth belief when I was confronted with some passages of Scripture that couldn't be reconciled with the Young-Earth Theory. As I studied the Bible, I found some problem passages that didn't fit. The passage in Job 38 was one of them; I soon found others. Because of this, I began studying the different creation theories. I slowly began to understand how the Restoration Theory explained other problem Biblical statements concerning the creation. It reconciled the Genesis account with the parallel creation accounts mentioned elsewhere in the Bible. Whether or not it made scientific sense wasn't an issue with me at the time. I was trying to discover what the Bible truly said. Once I realized this was what God had revealed, I went back and looked at the science of the Restoration Theory. By that time, I was firmly a creationist, so I certainly wasn't trying to find evidence to defend evolution. Some creationists say if you believe in the Restoration Theory, you are an evolutionist. This is a wrong conclusion. I believe in the Restoration Theory, but I totally reject evolution. I believe there was no evolution happening in the time period between Genesis 1:1 and Genesis 1:3. I believe there was no evolution happening during the time God made the earth *TOHUW WA-BOHUW*. Genesis 1:2 says the earth was dead. There could be no evolution because there was no life. God tells us the earth was a desolate waste, devoid of life, and totally uninhabitable. It was dark and covered with water. Nothing could live. Evolution never happened. Life on the earth was originally created by God. Life on earth was destroyed sometime later. Life on earth was again created by God during the six twenty-four-hour days described in the Book of Genesis. The Restoration Theory cannot be used to blend evolution with the Bible. Life did not evolve during the gap. Nothing could evolve because everything was dead. Even evolutionists agree dead things don't evolve very well. Theistic evolutionists who try to blend evolution with the Bible by using the Gap Theory are wrong. If evolution ever occurred, the geological strata would have recorded it. Rather than proving evolution, the fossils in the geological strata prove evolution never happened. True science filters out false theology. If you are a Young-Earth creationist or a Day-Age creationist, and have rejected the Gap Theory because you were told it defends evolution, then you can discard that argument. The Gap Theory (at least, the Gap Theory I believe and defend) does NOT defend evolution.

The Scholars Speak

Before I continue, let me say one thing. If you don't like my opinion, that's fine. But don't criticize it on the basis it has no grammatical support or that scholars don't accept it. If anyone tells you this, they are wrong. I absolutely, positively guarantee there have been many scholars down through the ages who have defended the Restoration Theory. The idea of a Pre-Adamic global catastrophe is thousands of years old. In spite of that, many Christian creationists claim Thomas Chalmers invented the Gap Theory in 1814 to make the Bible fit Darwin's Theory of Evolution. This claim is not true for two reasons. First, it was in 1803 when Chalmers began lecturing on this view, not 1814. Second, this was six years before Charles Darwin was born. It was also three years before the London Geological Society (the oldest geological society in the world) was formed. Chalmers' views preceded some of the works of the, "Fathers of Geology." William Buckland wrote *Vindiciæ Geologiæ; or the Connexion of Geology with Religion Explained* in 1820; Georges Cuvier presented his *Discourse on the Upheavals of the Surface of the Globe* in 1826; Charles Lyell presented his *Principles of Geology* in 1830. It seems more likely the science of geology was influenced by the Gap Theory, than the Gap Theory was influenced by the science of geology. **The Gap Theory had been around for centuries; the scientific study of Geology hadn't.** It disturbs me how Christians who know the truth still say things they know aren't true. If it was Chalmers' motive to make the Bible fit Darwin's theory, then he was a prophet because he made his claims before Darwin was born. He certainly wasn't the only Pre-Darwinian Gap Theory advocate.

Rabbi Simeon (Simeon ben Jochai—also spelled Simeon bar Yochai, Simeon ben Yohai, and Simon Jochaides) lived in the late 1st century to the mid-2nd century A.D. This put him 1,700 years before Darwin. Was Rabbi Simeon trying to harmonize the Bible with The Theory of Evolution when he wrote his *Sefer Hazzohar* (*The Book of Light*) in the early 2nd century? Here is a comment (made two years before Darwin published his book) by The Reverend Joseph Baylee concerning Rabbi Simeon's interpretation of the Genesis Creation Account:

> "*The Zohar* is one of the most ancient of the Jewish expositions of scripture. It is commonly ascribed to Simon Jochaides, who is said to have written it at or before the Christian era. The following extract is from Capillus's *Exercitatio ad locum Zoharis*, fol. 24, 6, *ad locum* Gen. ii. 4,5,6:—'These are the generations of heaven and earth, &c. Wherever it is written '*aille*' (these), *e.g.*, 'with *toledoth*' (generations), the former words are to be separated (*profanantur priora*). And these are the generations of the '*thohu*' (without form), which are signified in verse 2. The earth was '*thohu ve bohu*' (without form and void). Those are they of which it is said that **the blessed God created the worlds, and destroyed them**, and therefore the earth was '*thohu ve bohu*,' desolate and empty.'—Here then, the most ancient Jewish expositor, and one whose authority has been reverenced by the Jews, and by many Christians in all subsequent ages, declares that **the words 'without form and void' mean the destruction of a previous creation**."[36]

In 1818 John Bird Sumner, the Archbishop of Canterbury, the head of the Church of England, defended the notion our world was the restoration of a previously ruined world:

> "According to that history, we are bound to admit that only one general destruction or revolution of the globe has taken place, since the period of that creation which Moses records, and of which Adam and Eve were the first inhabitants. The certainty of one event of that kind would appear from the discoveries of geologers, even if it were not declared by the sacred historian. **But we are not called upon to deny the possible existence of previous worlds, from the wreck of which our globe was organized, and the ruins of which are now furnishing matter to our curiosity**. The belief of their existence is indeed consistent with rational probability, and somewhat confirmed by the discoveries of astronomy, as to the plurality of worlds."[37]

William Daniel Conybeare (1787-1857) and William Phillips (1775-1828) in *Outlines of the Geology of England and Wales*[38] (1822) listed three possible interpretations of the Genesis Creation Account that could agree with what geology had revealed. The first possibility was the days were literal twenty-four-hour days that happened only a few thousand years ago. This interpretation meant all the geologic strata and fossils were created between the Fall of Adam and the Flood of Noah. (The Young-Earth Theory at that time did not teach that Noah's Flood created all the geologic strata and fossils, as does the Modern Young-Earth Theory.) They marginally allowed for the Young-Earth Theory, but personally rejected it because it was contrary to their belief there was another world before this present world.

> "1st. If we adhere to the common interpretation of the periods of creation as having been literally days of twenty-four-hours, **and refuse to admit the existence of another order of things previous to that recorded by the inspired writer**, we might still perhaps find a sufficient space of time for the purposes required in the interval between the creation as thus limited, and the deluge."

Their second suggestion was the days were not literal twenty-four-hour days. Instead, they were long periods of time. (Day-Age)

> "Or secondly, We may perhaps without real violence to the inspired writer, regard the periods of the creation recorded by Moses and expressed under the term of days, not to have designated ordinary days of twenty-four-hours, but periods of definite but considerable length; such a mode of extending the signification of this term being not unexampled in other parts of the sacred writings. Those who embrace this opinion will of course assign the formation of the secondary strata, in great part at least to these *Days of Creation*; and we have the authority of several divines in favor of such an interpretation."

Day-Age was more palatable, but they still didn't prefer it. Their final, and preferred, interpretation was the Bible simply didn't record the events that had transpired during the intermediate period between the original creation in Genesis 1:1 and what follows in Genesis 1:2. Simply put, there was a gap of time the Holy Spirit didn't reveal to Moses.

> "Or thirdly, It does not seem inconsistent with the authority of the sacred historian to suppose that after recording in the first sentence of Genesis the fundamental fact of the original formation of all things by the will of an intelligent Creator, he may pass, sub silentio, some intermediate state **whose**

ruins formed the chaotic mass he proceeds to describe, and out of which, according to his farther narrative, the present order of our portion of the universe was educed; upon this supposition **the former world whose remains we explore may have belonged to this intermediate era.**"

William Mullinger Higgins' 1832 explanation of the Genesis Creation Account was most certainly in line with the then commonly accepted Gap Theory. He believed the fossils came before the six days of creation:

> "The first chapter of Genesis, which contains all that God has revealed concerning the creation, may be divided into three periods: first, there is a statement that the heavens and earth were formed by God. **There is then a description of the earth previous to the days of creation**, and afterwards a somewhat detailed account of the order in which the Almighty furnished the world during the six days."[39]

> "But, whatever may have been the application of this assertion to the Israelites, there is a direct statement that God created the heavens and the earth. **This was done before the six days; how long, we are not informed, and are, consequently, at liberty to attempt to determine it by the assistance of science**. The sacred historian then describes the state of the earth at the time which immediately preceded the days of creation. The passage should be thus rendered: But the earth was invisible and unfurnished."[40]

> "It is evident then, both from Genesis and Geology, that **after the creation of the earth and before the days, all or nearly all the fossiliferous rocks which compose the crust of our globe, were formed.**"[41]

Higgins believed the fossils came before the six days. He believed all these plants and animals died before the six days. This means he believed there was Pre-Adamic death. According to Higgins, the creation of plants and animals during the six days was not the original creation of plants and animals.

In the following year, 1833, English historian and Gap Theory defender Sharon Turner said:

> "The Mosaic chronology begins with the formation of Adam, and with the six preceding days or periods, which commenced with the production of light. **What interval occurred between the first creation of the material substance of our globe, and the mandate for light to descend upon it; whether months, years, or ages, is not in the slightest degree noticed.**

Geology may shorten or extend its duration as it may find proper; there is no restriction on this part of the subject."[42]

Another Pre-Darwinian Gap Theory defender was Edward Hitchcock (1793-1864), President of Amherst College, and Professor of Natural Theology and Geology. He said:

"The theory of interpretation which is now the most extensively adopted among geologists, supposes that Moses merely states that God created the world in the beginning, without fixing the date of that beginning; and that **passing in silence an unknown period of its history, during which the extinct animals and plants found in the rocks might have lived and died**, he describes only the present creation which took place in six literal days, less than 6,000 years ago."[43]

Note Hitchcock said the Gap Theory was "THE MOST EXTENSIVELY ADOPTED" theory. He wrote this four years before Darwin published his book. Was the Gap Theory really that well-known in 1855? In 1995, Paul Keith Conkin, who has written over twenty books on various aspects of American history, made this comment about Edward Hitchcock and the prevalence of the Gap Theory:

"Hitchcock rejected the day-age theory so popular among British scientists and liberal churchmen. By it, the word *day* in the two somewhat variant Genesis accounts of creation meant a vast age. Thus, roughly, the days of creation corresponded with past geological ages, with humans originating in the present age. This theory had all types of problems, including an unjustified attribution of preternatural insights to the author or authors of Genesis.

In place of the day-age solution, **Hitchcock preferred another rather widespread theory (today called the 'gap theory'), which had circulated in some form for centuries.** He believed that eons of time elapsed between the creation of the world and the six days detailed in Genesis. He thus crammed all the vast geological history of the earth into this long interim, including the creation of life at the beginning of each age."[44]

Conkin points out that even at the time of Edward Hitchcock, the Gap Theory had been around for centuries. He doesn't say how many centuries, but taking a minimum of two centuries, it means the Gap Theory was known in the 1600's. It was known long before that, but this alone proves the Gap Theory was NOT created as a compromise to fit the Bible with Darwin. People who tell you the Gap Theory was created to accommodate evolution are either deceived or deceivers; or both. It was the most, or one of the most, accepted theories before Darwin's time.

Albert Barnes[45] (1798-1870) noted the significance of the use of *HAYAH* in Genesis 1:2. He made this comment in 1834, twenty-five years before Darwin published his Theory of Evolution.

> "Passing now from the subject to the verb in this sentence, we observe it is in the perfect state, and therefore denotes that the condition of confusion and emptiness was not in progress, but had run its course and **become** a settled thing, at least at the time of the next recorded event. If the verb had been absent in Hebrew, the sentence would have been still complete, and the meaning as follows: 'And the land was waste and void.' **With the verb present, therefore, it must denote something more. The verb** היה *hāyáh* **'be' has here, we conceive, the meaning 'become;'** and the import of the sentence is this: '**And the land had become waste and void.**' This affords the presumption that the part at least of the surface of our globe which fell within the cognizance of primeval man, and first received the name of land, may not have been always a scene of desolation or a sea of turbid waters, but may have met with some catastrophe by which its order and fruitfulness had been marred or prevented.
>
> **This sentence, therefore, does not necessarily describe the state of the land when first created, but merely intimates a change that may have taken place since it was called into existence.** What its previous condition was, or what interval of time elapsed, between the absolute creation and the present state of things, is not revealed. How many transformations it may have undergone, and what purpose it may have heretofore served, are questions that did not essentially concern the moral well-being of man, and are therefore to be asked of some other interpreter of nature than the written word."

On June 17, 1855 Charles Haddon Spurgeon (1834-1892) delivered a sermon at New Park Street Chapel in Southwark, London. He made this comment about the history of the earth:

> "In the 2d verse of the first chapter of Genesis, we read, 'And the earth was without form, and void; and darkness was upon the face of the deep. And the Spirit of God moved upon the face of the waters.' We know not how remote the period of the creation of this globe may be—**certainly many millions of years before the time of Adam**. Our planet has passed through various stages of existence, and different kinds of creatures have lived on its surface, all of which have been fashioned by God. But before that era

came, wherein man should be its principal tenant and monarch, the Creator gave up the world to confusion."[46]

Thirty-five years later, in 1889, Spurgeon revealed more information in another sermon:

"Observe the work of creation. God took care that even in the material universe there should be a grand foundation for His noble edifice. We have the story of the fitting up of the world, during the seven days, for the habitation of man. But we have not the history of the creation of the earth before that time. To prepare for the seven days' rapid furnishing of the earth for man, **millions of years may have elapsed.** The foundation was laid with great care. No limit can be set to the period preceding the making of man, if you only follow the Word of God in Genesis."[47]

In 1896 (four years after his death) Spurgeon's book, *The Teachings of Nature in the Kingdom of Grace*, was published. It revealed this comment Spurgeon made about creation:

"I will not venture upon any dogmatic theory of geology, but there seems to be every probability that this world has been: fitted up and destroyed, re-fitted and then destroyed again, many times before the last arranging of it for the habitation of men. 'In the beginning God created the heaven and the earth;' **then came a long interval**, and at length, at the appointed time, during seven days, the Lord prepared the earth for the human race."[48]

Spurgeon believed the earth existed for millions of years before Adam. Spurgeon believed the earth had been destroyed by God in the time between Genesis 1:1 and Genesis 1:2. Spurgeon believed the six days were literal days. Spurgeon believed in the Gap Theory. Since we know he began preaching this at least four years before Charles Darwin published his book, I don't think you can accuse Spurgeon of trying to make the Bible fit the Theory of Evolution. I also don't think you can accuse Spurgeon of being ignorant of what the Bible says.

This doesn't prove the Gap Theory is true, but it does prove one thing. There were Hebrew scholars who believed the Gap Theory long before Darwin's great-great-great grandpappy was born. The Gap Theory was not created by Thomas Chalmers in the 19th century as Young-Earth creationists still claim in the 21st century. As I continued my research, I discovered more scholars who defended the Gap Theory.

Edward Bouverie Pusey (1800-1882) was the Regius (Royal) Professor of Hebrew at Oxford for fifty-four years. (1828-1882) As you can guess, no one was appointed to this preeminent position by merely taking an introductory course in Hebrew; this was the top position. As you can also guess, no one except a brilliant Hebrew scholar could hold that position for fifty-four years. As you can further guess, Pusey was an extremely gifted Hebrew scholar as seen by the fact he attained that high position at the young age of 28. What did this gifted, brilliant, top Hebrew scholar believe about the Gap Theory? Pusey believed in the Gap Theory. Pusey also pointed out that both St. Basil (A.D. 330-379) and St. Jerome (A.D. 347-420) believed there was a long gap of time between Genesis 1:1 and Genesis 1:3. Here is what Pusey said:[49]

> "The claims of geology do not even touch upon theology. **The belief that creation, at least, dated backward for countless ages, was current in the Church some 1400 years before Geology**. 'Six thousand years of our world,' says St. Jerome,[o] 'are not yet fulfilled; and **what eternities, what times, what originals of ages, must we not think there were before**, in which Angels, Thrones, Dominions, and the other Powers served God, and, apart from the vicissitudes and measures of times, subsisted, at the command of God!' **'Almost all the teachers of the Church throughout the world,'** says a later Greek writer,[p] **'teach that the whole spiritual and angelic being existed before this world out of nothing.'** Holy Scripture expressly speaks of the stellar system, as existing before the foundation of the earth.[q] 'Where wast thou, when I founded the earth? declare, if thou knowest understanding. Who laid the measures thereof, for thou knowest! or Who stretched out the line upon it? Whereon are the foundations thereof sunken? or who laid the cornerstone thereof? When all the morning stars jubilated together, and all the sons of God shouted for joy?' And this agrees with the remarkable parenthetic mention of 'the stars' in Genesis, when, in the detailed account of the creation of the sun and moon and of their offices for our earth, there are appended the simple words, 'and the stars,' as though it was intended only to guard against the error, that they might otherwise be thought to be uncreated. Then, there is nothing to connect the time spoken of in Gen. i. 2. with that of the first great declaration of the creation of all things in the beginning.
>
> [o] in Tit. c. i. quoted by Petav. de Angel. i. 15. opp. iii. 38.
> [p] Graec. Script. MS. ib. n. 22. See S. Basil in Hexaem. Hom. i., S. Greg. Naz., S. Chrys. and others, *ibid*.
> [q] Job xxxviii. 4-7"

John Nelson Darby (1800-1882) wrote:[50]

"The passage in Isaiah 45:18, 'he created it not in vain (chaotic)', is conclusive that **the earth was not created chaotic at first. The earth got into the state of chaos**–it may be what destroyed the animals; but we know nothing about it: what I do know by faith is that God created everything."

Darby believed the earth was not created a chaos. Something caused the earth to become one. He also believed all the animals on earth were destroyed during that time. Was Darby a scholar? Did he know Hebrew? Yes, and yes! He was a qualified theologian and Hebrew scholar, and he believed something bad happened between Genesis 1:1 and Genesis 1:2.

In 1861, Anglican Theologian John William Burgon (1813-1888) published *Inspiration and Interpretation Seven Sermons Preached Before the University of Oxford*[51] in response to a book (*Essays and Reviews*[52]) written by seven Church of England theologians whom he considered part of the liberalism and heresy movement infiltrating the Church of England. Burgon was known as a fervent defender of the truth and inerrancy of the Bible. In 1863, he was made vicar of the University Church of St. Mary the Virgin (This church goes back to Anglo-Saxon times and became the center from which Oxford University was established.) In 1867, he was appointed Gresham Professor of Divinity (Gresham University was established in 1596). He was the Dean of Chichester Cathedral from 1876 to 1888. (Chichester Cathedral was founded in 1075.)

Burgon said their book, *Essays and Reviews*, "embodies the infidel spirit of the present day." Indeed it did. It attacked the historicity of the Book of Genesis, the authorship of Moses, the reality of miracles, the authenticity of prophecy, and it even refuted special creation. The book proudly announced that "creation" was just another name for ignorance of how life began. It also praised Charles Darwin for *The Origin of Species* published four months earlier in 1859. It claimed that Darwin provided final proof, "in favour of the grand principle of the self-evolving powers of nature."

Burgon immediately responded to all their false claims. Concerning the issue of creation, he appealed to the long-held view by the Church of England that the new discoveries of geology did nothing to negate the creation account in Genesis.

"For really, since the fossil Flora, and the various races of animated creatures which Geologists have classified with so much industry and skill, confessedly belong to a period of immemorial antiquity; and, with very rare exceptions indeed, represent extinct species,—I, as an interpreter of Scripture, am not at all concerned with them. Moses asserts nothing at all about them, one way or the other. **What Revelation says, is, that nearly 6000 years ago, after a mighty catastrophe,—unexplained alike in its**

cause, its nature, and its duration,—the Creator of the Universe instituted upon the surface of this earth of ours that order of things which has continued ever since; and which is observed at this instant to prevail: that He was pleased to parcel out His transcendent operations, and to spread them over six days; and that He ceased from the work of creation on the seventh day. All extant species, whether of the vegetable or the animal Kingdom, including Man himself, belong to the week in question. And this statement, as it has never yet been found untrue, so am I unable to anticipate by what possible evidence it can ever be set aside as false."

Burgon revealed how the Gap Theory was considered to be both Biblically orthodox and a doctrine that refuted the Theory of Evolution. It was not something created by man in order to harmonize evolution with the Bible.

Jamieson, Fausset, and Brown echo the thought in their commentary (1871) on Genesis 1:2.[53]

"… the earth was without form and void-- or in 'confusion and emptiness,' as the words are rendered in Isaiah 34:11. This globe, at some undescribed period, **having been convulsed and broken up**, was a dark and watery waste for ages perhaps, till out of this chaotic state, the present fabric of the world was made to arise."

Alfred Edersheim[54] (1825-1889) made this comment about Genesis 1:1 and Genesis 1:2.

"The first verse in the book of Genesis simply states the general fact, that 'In the beginning'– whenever that may have been–'God created the heaven and the earth.' Then, in the second verse, we find earth described as it was at the close of the last great revolution, preceding the present state of things: 'And the earth was without form and void; and darkness was upon the face of the deep.' **An almost indefinite space of time, and many changes, may therefore have intervened** between the creation of heaven and earth, as mentioned in ver. 1, and the chaotic state of our earth, as described in ver. 2."

R. A. Torrey[55] (1856-1958) was a graduate of Yale University and Yale Divinity School who became a world-renowned evangelist and Bible teacher. Torrey wrote over forty books dealing with the doctrines and teachings of the Bible. He was Dean of The Bible Institute of Los Angeles (Now Biola University) from 1912 to 1924. When faced with the "problem" of reconciling "science" with the teachings of the Bible concerning the creation, he wrote:

> "It must be said, however, that men of science are constantly changing their views of what was the exact order of creation. Very recently discoveries have been made that have overthrown theories of the order of creation held by many men of science, which did not seem to some to harmonize with the order as given in the first chapter of Genesis; but these recent discoveries have brought the order into harmony with the order as given in that chapter. There is no need of going in detail into this order of creation as taught by modern science and Genesis 1. For there is grave reason to doubt if anything in Genesis 1 after verse 1 relates to the original creation of the universe. **All the verses after the first seem rather to refer to a refitting of the world that had been created and had afterward been plunged into chaos by the sin of some Pre-Adamic race, to be the abode of the present race that inhabits it, the Adamic race.**
>
> The reasons for so thinking are, first, that the words translated 'without form and void' ('waste and void,' RV) are used everywhere else in the Bible of the state of affairs that God brought upon persons and places as a punishment for sin. For example, in Isaiah 34:11 we read of the judgment that God shall bring upon Idumea as a punishment for their sins in these words: 'He shall stretch over it a line of confusion, and the plummet of emptiness' (RV). The Hebrew words translated 'confusion' and 'emptiness' are the same that are translated 'without form and void' in Genesis 1:2. We read again in Jeremiah 4:23-27: 'I beheld the earth, and, lo, it was waste and void.' In both instances the words 'waste and void' refer to a ruin which God had sent as a punishment for sin, and the assumption is very strong that they have a similar significance in Genesis 1.
>
> The second reason for this interpretation is stronger yet, namely, that the Bible expressly declares that God did not create the earth 'in vain' (Isaiah 45:18). But the word translated 'in vain' in this passage is precisely the one translated 'without form' in Genesis 1:2. In the Revised Version of Genesis 1:2 and Isaiah 45:18 the word is translated in both instances 'waste.' Here then is a plain and specific declaration in the Bible that God did not create the earth 'without form' (or rather 'waste,' RV), so it is clear that Genesis 1:2 cannot refer to the original creation. The word translated 'was' in Genesis 1:2 can with perfect propriety be translated 'became.' Then Genesis 1:2 would read: 'And the earth became waste and void.' In that case in Genesis 1:1 we have the actual account of creation. It is very brief but

wonderfully expressive, instructive and suggestive. **In Genesis 1:2 we have a brief but suggestive account of how the earth became involved in desolation and emptiness, presumably through the sin of some Pre-Adamic race. Then all after verse 2 does not describe the original creation of the earth, but its fitting up anew for the new race God is to bring upon the earth— the Adamic race.** Even if we allow the word 'was' to stand in Genesis 1:2, and do not substitute the word 'became,' it does not materially affect the interpretation. If this is the true interpretation of the chapter **(and the argument for this interpretation seems conclusive)**, then of course this record cannot by any possibility come into conflict with any discoveries of geology as yet made or to be made, for the geological strata lie back of the period here described."

British evangelist and preacher G. Campbell Morgan (1863-1945) wrote and spoke in defense of the Gap Theory. Dr. Morgan was known for studying the Bible very thoroughly. His practice was to read a portion of Scripture fifty times before writing a sermon or commentary on it. This is his comment on the Genesis Creation Account in *Exposition on the Whole Bible*.[56]

"The opening sentence of the Book of Genesis is an interpretation of the fact 'that what is seen hath not been made out of things which do appear' (Hebrews 11:3), and accounts for the things which are seen. The whole chapter, and, indeed, all subsequent Scripture, must be read in the light of this statement as to origins. **This sentence is followed immediately by a declaration, without detail, of a cataclysm which overtook the earth. It then proceeds to show how the God who created, restored the earth to fruitfulness and order."** (emphasis mine)

He also made this comment about the Gap Theory in a sermon entitled, *In the Beginning, God*.[57]

"Between the first and second verses of this chapter there is a great gap, so great that we cannot bridge it, a mystery so dark that we cannot explain it. 'The earth was waste and void, and darkness was upon the face of the deep.' That is not how God made it. That is not the suggestion of the first verse. The suggestion of the first verse is that of perfection, harmony, a cosmic order.... **The first verse of the Bible declares that God did originally create, and from the third verse to the end of the chapter we have the account, not of original creation, but of the restoration of a lost order, the bringing of cosmos out of chaos.**"

A. W. Pink[58] (1886-1952), another scholar who believed the Gap Theory, wrote:

> "What is found in the remainder of Genesis 1 refers not to the primitive creation but to the *restoration* of that which had fallen into ruins. Genesis 1:1 speaks of the original creation; Genesis 1:2 describes the then condition of the earth six days before Adam was called into existence. To what remote point in time Genesis 1:1 conducts us, or as to how long an interval passed before the earth '*became*' a ruin, we have no means of knowing; but if the surmises of geologists could be conclusively established there would be no conflict at all between the findings of science and the teaching of Scripture. **The unknown interval between the first two verses of Genesis 1 is wide enough to embrace all the prehistoric ages** which may have elapsed; but all that took place from Genesis 1:3 onwards transpired less than six thousand years ago." (emphasis his)

Lewis Sperry Chafer[59] (1871-1952), the founder and first president of Dallas Theological Seminary, believed in the Gap Theory. I find it difficult to understand how those who hate the Gap Theory can continue to say qualified Biblical scholars don't support it. Chafer was qualified enough to establish and preside over a very prestigious theological seminary. Here is his comment on Ezekiel 28:11-19, a passage that deals with Lucifer's origin and fall:

> "Ezekiel 28:11-19. A considerable portion of this immediate context is to be taken up verse by verse, but in preparation for that understanding it may be observed that revelation concerning Satan begins with the dateless period between the creation of the heavens and the earth in that perfect form in which they first appeared (Genesis 1:1) and **the desolating judgments which ended that period, when the earth became waste and empty** (Genesis 1:2; Isaiah 24:10; Jeremiah 4:23-26)."

Donald Grey Barnhouse, Th.D. (1895-1960) was the pastor of the Tenth Presbyterian Church in Philadelphia, Pennsylvania for thirty-three years. He was the founder of the Evangelical Foundation in Philadelphia, author of over thirty Christian books, Bible commentaries, and study-aids. He was also noted for his radio program, *The Bible Study Hour*. In 1965, he wrote *The Invisible War*,[60] a book that described the origin and history of sin and evil in the universe. The origin, of course, was Lucifer. Barnhouse taught that evil and sin began with the rebellion of Lucifer during the gap of time between the original creation of the heavens and the earth in Genesis 1:1 and the desolation of the earth in Genesis 1:2. This Pre-Adamic desolation was the result of God's judgment on Lucifer. Barnhouse described how, starting in Genesis 1:3, God began the process of restoring the earth for the purpose of creating a new creature to replace Lucifer; man. Barnhouse was a firm believer and defender of the Ruin-Restoration Theory.

> "Probably one of the commonest errors in Biblical interpretation is the thought that the first verse of Genesis and the second verse are closely connected in time. This error leads many readers to believe that God had originally created the earth in chaotic form. Their minds are driven to the rim of the first verse, 'In the beginning God created the heavens and the earth,' and they too readily suppose it possible to go right on into the next verse, 'And the earth was without form and void, and darkness covered the face of the deep.'
>
> **Yet there is no doubt that between the two there is a great gulf fixed**. I say 'no doubt,' for the matter is amply demonstrated by the Scriptures themselves. Following the close of the passage, the punctuation after the first verse of the Bible is a mighty period, or, even better, what the English grammarians call a 'full stop.' In the beginning God created the heavens and the earth. Period. There is divine prelude to the symphony of Scriptures. That verse takes us back, back, back, into the edges of a past eternity in which God, the Father, Son, and Spirit, lived in that entirely sufficient majesty of being which encompasses Deity. If this had been recorded in the book of Psalms, there might well have been written here the word *Selah*—pause. Stop and consider. You are on the edge of an abyss. **Something happened to the heavens and the earth which God had created.** Millions of years may have run their course during that first creation, and other millions may have elapsed in the interval between the two verses. We do not know. But there was an interval, and we can be absolutely certain that it was a great one."

Gleason Archer[61] (1916-2004), a well-known and highly respected Hebrew scholar, also recognized the possibility of a gap between Genesis 1:1 and Genesis 1:2. This is significant because Archer believed in the Day-Age Theory instead of the Gap Theory. Although he didn't believe the Ruin-Restoration Theory, he certainly knew it was possible, and he wasn't afraid to express a truth that might be contrary to his own ideas.

> "It should be noted in this connection that the verb 'was' in Genesis 1:2 may quite possibly be rendered '**became**' and be construed to mean: 'And the earth became formless and void.' Only a cosmic catastrophe could account for the introduction of chaotic confusion into the original perfection of God's creation. **This interpretation certainly seems to be exegetically tenable**…"

Archer also revealed a very important fact about the meaning of *HAYAH*.

"Properly speaking, this verb *hayah* **never has the meaning of static being like the copular verb 'to be.' Its basic notion is that of becoming or emerging as such and such, or of coming into being**... Sometimes a distinction is attempted along the following lines: *hayah* means 'become' only when it is followed by the preposition *le*; otherwise there is no explicit idea of becoming. But this distinction will not stand up under analysis. In Genesis 3:20 the proper rendering is: 'And Adam called the name of his wife Eve, because she **became** the mother of all living.' No *le* follows the verb in this case. So also in Genesis 4:20: 'Jabal **became** the father of tent dwellers.' **Therefore there can be no grammatical objection raised to translating Genesis 1:2: 'And the earth became a wasteness and desolation.'**"

Wait! Here is a man who received degrees at both Harvard and Princeton, graduated with honors, was a professor of Biblical languages for forty years, was chosen to be one of the translators for *The New American Standard* Bible AND one of the translators for *The New International Version* Bible, who wrote who-knows-how-many textbooks on the ancient Hebrew language, and what did he say?

"THEREFORE THERE CAN BE NO GRAMMATICAL OBJECTION RAISED TO TRANSLATING GENESIS 1:2: 'AND THE EARTH BECAME A WASTENESS AND DESOLATION.'"

Excuse me if I laugh at those anti-Gap Theory "experts" who say it is impossible to translate Genesis 1:2, "And the earth became a wasteness and desolation." I'll say more about the preposition *le* and its relation to the meaning of *HAYAH* in Chapter Twelve. For now, let me ask you this question: "Do you really want to say Dr. Archer didn't know how to translate Hebrew?" Many Young-Earth and Day-Age creationists say he didn't. They continue preaching the tired claim *HAYAH* cannot be translated, "became." They obviously believe Archer was unscholarly. Was Gleason Archer unscholarly when he co-authored the *Theological Wordbook of the Old Testament*? He and fellow Hebrew scholars R. Laird Harris and Bruce K. Waltke, who as far as I know are Old-Earth, but not Gap Theory, proponents, said this about *HAYAH*:

"**Very seldom in the OT is hayâ used to denote either simple existence or the identification of a thing or person.** This can be illustrated by a quick glance at almost any page of the KJV on which one will find numerous examples of words such as 'is, are, was, were,' in italics, indicating that these are additions by the translators for the sake of smoothness, but not in the Hebrew itself. In such cases the Hebrew employs what is known grammatically as a nominal sentence, which we may define most simply as a sentence lacking verb or a copula, for example: I (am) the Lord your God; the Lord (is) a sun and shield; the land (is) good; and in the NT, blessed (are) the poor. **This almost total lack of hayâ as a copula or existential particle has led some to use this phenomenon as confirming evidence that 'static' thought was alien to the Hebrews, the latter thinking only in 'dynamic' categories.**"[62]

In other words, here are three world-renown Hebrew scholars who prove *HAYAH* almost never means what anti-Gap Theory creationists say it means. If it is very seldomly used to denote the simple existence of something, then it is very unlikely it denotes the simple existence of the earth being without form and void in Genesis 1:2. Such thought was, "alien to the Hebrews." The earth becoming without form and void, is a much more accurate translation. It is how an ancient Hebrew would have understood it. "Was" in the sense of simple existence is not the usual meaning of *HAYAH*. Whether these three scholars accepted or rejected the Gap Theory is not the issue. Some Hebrew scholars who allow for a Gap linguistically, still reject the Gap Theory scientifically. (This is because there are versions of the Gap Theory that contradict science.) Still, Young-Earth creationists believe these three men were unscholarly. They believe the same thing about Hebrew scholar Martin Anstey when he expressed his scholarly opinion in his book, *The Romance of Bible Chronology*[63] (1913).

> "The opening verse of Genesis speaks of the creation of the heavens, and the earth, in the undefined beginning. From this point we may date the origin of the world, but not the origin of man. For **the second verse tells of a catastrophe–the earth became a ruin, and a desolation**. The Hebrew verb *hayah* (*hayah* = to be) here translated was, signifies not only 'to be' but also 'to become,' 'to take place,' 'to come to pass.' When a Hebrew writer makes a simple affirmation, or merely predicates the existence of anything, the verb *hayah* is **never expressed**. Where it is expressed **it must always be translated by our verb to become**, never by the verb to be, if we desire to convey the exact shade of the meaning of the Original. The words *tohu va-bohu*, translated in the A.V. 'without form and void' and in the R.V. 'waste and void' should be rendered *tohu*, a ruin, and *bohu*, a desolation. They do not represent the state of the heavens and the earth as they were created by God. They represent only the state of the earth as it afterwards became–'a ruin and a desolation.' This interpretation is confirmed by the words of Isaiah 45:18, 'He created it not *tohu* (a ruin): He formed it to be inhabited (habitable, not desolate).'

This excludes the rendering of Genesis 1:2 in the A.V. and the R.V. as decisively as the Hebrew of Genesis 1:2 requires the rendering of *hayah* by the word '**became**' instead of the word 'was,' or better still 'had become,' **the separation of the Vav from the verb being the Hebrew method of indicating the pluperfect tense.**"

The *WAW* (*VAV*) is separated from the *HAYAH* in Genesis 1:2. This means it is in the pluperfect tense. The pluperfect tense designates an action completed over a period of time, before a specific point of past time. Examples are: I had flown to New York before flying to London. Billy had eaten three cupcakes when his mother caught him. The pluperfect is the "had" form of a past action where the action is completed before the action that follows the verb. It shows how one action is completed before another action. You can't combine "had" with "was" as a form of a past descriptive condition. Such a translation would read, "And the earth had was without form, and void." It makes no sense in Hebrew. It makes no sense in English. The *HAYAH* of Genesis 1:2 is not merely describing a condition; it is describing a past completed ACTION completed before the events that follow. "Was" in a static descriptive sense doesn't fit!

Warren Baker and Eugene Carpenter[64] are two more highly qualified and knowledgeable Hebrew scholars who affirmed (in 2003) *HAYAH* means "to become."

> "*hāyāh*: A verb meaning to exist, to be, to become, to happen, to come to pass, to be done. It is used over 3,500 times in the Old Testament. In the simple stem, the verb often means to become, to take place, to happen. It indicates that something has occurred or come about, such as events that have turned out a certain way (1 Samuel 4:16); something has happened to someone, such as Moses (Exodus 32:1,23; 2 Kings 7:20); or something has occurred just as God said it would (Genesis 1:7,9). Often a special Hebrew construction using the imperfect form of the verb asserts that something came to pass (cf. Genesis 1:7,9). Less often, the construction is used with the perfect form of the verb to refer to something coming to pass in the future (Isaiah 7:18,21; Hosea 2:16).
>
> **The verb is used to describe something that comes into being or arises.** For instance, a great cry arose in Egypt when the firstborn were killed in the tenth plague (Exodus 12:30; cf. Genesis 9:16; Micah 7:4); and when God commanded light to appear, and it did (Genesis 1:3)."

Gap Theory opponents say Baker and Carpenter are not Hebrew scholars. What do Gap Theory opponents say about two other Hebrew scholars, Merrill F. Unger and William

White, Jr., who edited *Nelson's Expository Dictionary of the Old Testament*? They gave this definition for *HAYAH*:

> "*hāyāh* (הָיָה), 'to become, occur, come to pass, be.' This verb occurs only in the Hebrew and Aramaic. The Old Testament attests *hāyāh* about 3,560 times, in both Hebrew and Aramaic.
>
> Often this verb indicates more than simple existence or identity (this may be indicated by omitting the verb altogether.) Rather, the verb makes a strong statement about the being or presence of a person or thing. Yet the simple meaning 'become' or 'come to pass' appears often in the English versions."[65]

Unger and White go on to give an example of how *HAYAH* is correctly translated, "became," in Genesis 19:26:

> "In miracle accounts, *hāyāh* often appears at the climax of the story to confirm the occurrence of the event itself. Lot's wife looked back and 'became' a pillar of salt (Gen. 19:26); the use of *hāyāh* emphasizes that the event really occurred. This is also the force of the verb in Gen. 1:3, in which God said, 'Let there *be* light.' He accomplished His word so that there *was* light."[66]

Were Unger and White unqualified to define *HAYAH*? If *HAYAH* is used to describe how Lot's wife became a pillar of salt, why is it wrong to use the same word in Genesis 1:2 to describe how the earth became without form and void? If the use of *HAYAH* indicates the reality of an event, then wouldn't it indicate the earth becoming without form and void was just as real an event as Lot's wife becoming a pillar of salt?

I know that you know that I know very little about the Hebrew Language. I know that you know that I am not a Hebrew scholar. But, I want you to know something I do know. I know that any Hebrew scholar who knows the Hebrew language well enough to write a Hebrew dictionary, knows the meaning of *HAYAH*. *HAYAH* is such a basic Hebrew word, and it is used so often in the Bible, I can't imagine a Hebrew scholar who writes a Hebrew dictionary doesn't know what *HAYAH* means. It would be the equivalent of me saying Noah Webster didn't understand the meaning of the English word "be" when he wrote his English dictionary in 1828. Here is something else I know, that you should know:

William Wilson wrote a Hebrew dictionary. Actually, it was more than a dictionary; it was a Hebrew word study. It goes into much more depth and explanation than a mere dictionary. How did William Wilson define and explain the meaning of *HAYAH*?

"היה to come to pass, to happen; to be; to begin to be, *i.e.* to become, especially with ל to be made or done;..."[67]

So, while I can't imagine anyone claiming a scholar like William Wilson doesn't know the meaning of *HAYAH*, there are people who defy my imagination and say *HAYAH* can never be translated, "became." If what they say is true, there should be no scholars who defend the Gap Theory. Are there such scholars?

Charles Andrew Coates[68] (1862-1945) defended the Gap Theory.

"'In the beginning God created the heavens and the earth.' That is all we get about the original creation. Then in the second verse we find things **fallen into a state of ruin**. 'And the earth was waste and empty, and darkness was on the face of the deep.' This was certainly not as it was created..."

William Kelly[69] (1820-1906) also believed the earth had two beginnings.

"...the first verse speaks of an original condition which God was pleased to bring into being; the second, of **a desolation afterwards brought in**; but how long the first lasted, what changes may have intervened, when or by what means the ruin came to pass, is not the subject-matter of the inspired record..."

Arno Clement Gaebelein[70] (1861-1945) wrote about the earth becoming waste and void.

"The original earth passed through a great upheaval. A judgment swept over it, which in all probability must have occurred on account of the fall of that mighty creature, Lucifer, who fell by pride and became the devil. The original earth, no doubt, was his habitation and he had authority over it which he still claims as the prince of this world. Luke 4:5-6 shows us this. **The earth had become waste and void**; chaos and darkness reigned. What that original earth was we do not know, but we know that animal and vegetable life was in existence long before God began to restore the earth."

Frederick William Grant[71] (1834-1902) spoke of the fall of the original earth.

"For plainly the work of the six days begins with this: 'God said, "Let there be light;" and there was light.' But as plainly the earth, although waste and desolate, was there before that, not created then. Moreover the words 'without form and void,' for which 'waste and desolate' would be preferable as a reading, imply distinctly a state of ruin, and not of development;... **There was, then, a primary creation, afterward a fall;**"

Frank Binford Hole[72] (1874-1964) taught the earth suffered a catastrophe long after its original creation.

"In verse 2 we move from that remote epoch to a time much nearer our own, and we descend, as regards this earth, to a state of very great imperfection. It is found 'without form;' that is, a ruin, a waste: it is also 'void:' that is, empty. Isaiah 45:18 plainly says, 'He created it not in vain, He formed it to be inhabited.' This is very striking, for here again the proper word for creation is used, as in our first verse, and 'in vain' is a translation of the same word as 'without form' in our verse. So we have a definite confirmation of the thought that the state of the earth as in verse 2, was one that supervened, long after the original creation, as **the result of some catastrophic event** which is not revealed to us."

Louis Ginzberg[73] (1873-1953), noted professor and Jewish historian, wrote about how the ancient Jews traditionally believed there had been more than one world before our present world.

"Nor is this world inhabited by man the first of things earthly created by God. **He made several worlds before ours**, but He destroyed them all, because He was pleased with none until He created ours."

Another theologian who defended the Restoration Theory was Robert B. Thieme, Jr. (1918-2009). He was an excellent Hebrew and Greek scholar, and he believed in the Theory of Restoration. I would not want to be the man who claimed Thieme wasn't a Hebrew scholar or that he was ignorant of what the Bible taught. Thieme was one of the great theologians of our time, and I have tremendous respect for his opinions and his scholarly viewpoints. In his book, *Creation, Chaos, and Restoration*,[74] Thieme explained the Hebrew of Genesis 1. He showed how Genesis describes the restoration of earth after a period of Divine judgment.

Next, I read the writings of Finis Jennings Dake (1902-1987). His notes and comments in *Dake's Annotated Reference Bible*[75] made it very clear the Restoration Theory was not only permissible, but it was the only theory that explained some troublesome passages in Isaiah, Ezekiel, and Jeremiah. Again, I would not want to accuse Dake of being uneducated or of being an evolutionist.

There were other scholars who defended the Restoration Theory as well. Erich Sauer (1898-1959) wrote *The King Of The Earth*[76] and George H. Pember (1837-1910) wrote *Earth's Earliest Ages*.[77] They both believed the earth had been destroyed and later restored.

James Montgomery Boice (1938-2000) was a well-known and much respected Biblical theologian. He was Chairman of the International Council of Biblical Inerrancy and founder of the Alliance of Confessing Evangelicals. Now, it seems to me if you were the chairman of a council of hundreds of top evangelical theologians who believed in Biblical inerrancy, then you wouldn't likely defend a Biblical interpretation of creation if you thought it was in error. So, why did Dr. Boice defend the Gap Theory? It was because he didn't think it was in error. I want you to read a partial transcript of a message[78] he gave on *The Bible Study Hour Radio Broadcast* concerning the Gap Theory. In the first part of his message, Dr. Boice describes the Gap Theory, and mentions several Biblical Scholars who defended it. They included Thomas Chalmers, G. H. Pember, Harry Rimmer, Arthur W. Pink, Arthur Custance, C. S. Lewis, Donald Grey Barnhouse, and Francis Schaeffer. Then he goes on to say:

> "So here we have a very, very interesting theory. How are we to look at it? Is this perhaps the truly Christian view of creation? Well, we have to say that today this theory is in disrepute among many conservative evangelicals and among many Biblical and believing scientists. I'd like to say, as we begin to look at it in some detail, that in my judgment those modern evangelicals who are critical of the theory really have not done it justice. Which is to say they haven't really taken the Biblical evidence that's been presented by the Gap theorists seriously enough. Let me suggest what some of that evidence is. **The exegetical base is really the strength of the theory**. Whether or not this solves all the geological problems is another question. Exegetically, these men were certainly Biblical scholars, and they made a very, very good case for what their theory holds."

Dr. Boice went on to list five arguments for the Gap Theory. Four of those are exegetical arguments and one is theological:

1.) Genesis 1:1 and Genesis 1:2 are separated by a disjunction, thereby suggesting they are two different accounts of two different creations.

2.) The Hebrew word structure shows how the first day of creation (re-creation) began at verse three, not at verse one. This means Genesis 1:1 was not the same creation as Genesis 1:3-31.

3.) The Hebrew word *HAYAH* is translated, "become" or "had become," in numerous places in Scripture.

4.) The phrase *TOHUW WA-BOHUW* may imply a destruction of something that was previously orderly.

5.) The Fall of Satan and the introduction of death seems to have been in the Pre-Adamic age in which the geological strata and fossils were formed.

When someone tells you there are no scholars who believe the Gap Theory, what does that tell you? They think John Nelson Darby, Charles Spurgeon, G. Campbell Morgan, Donald Barnhouse, A. W. Pink, James Montgomery Boice, Albert Barnes, R. A. Torrey, and all these others weren't scholars. I think you don't need to be a scholar to know they are wrong.

Of course, this doesn't mean I accept all the various teachings of all these men in all doctrinal issues, but at least their motive for believing the Gap Theory wasn't because they felt a need to defend evolution. Many people dismiss the Restoration Theory as a modern attempt to blend the Bible with Darwin's Theory of Evolution. Those who say this have never really studied the Gap Theory in depth. They don't know its true history.

Bernard Ramm (1916-1992) studied it in depth, and while not agreeing with it himself, he showed it wasn't a 19th century invention. In his book, *The Christian View of Science and Scripture*, he listed several pre-Darwinian scholars who believed in the Gap Theory. These include Edgar, King of England (A.D. 943-975), Simon Episcopius (1583-1643), J. G. Rosenmuller (1736-1815), William Buckland (1784-1856), J. Pye Smith (1774-1851), and others. Since Darwin's *Origin of Species* wasn't yet written, it's hard to imagine these Restored-Earth scholars were trying to blend the Bible with Darwin. In fact, he revealed how the Gap Theory was the most widely accepted view among serious Biblical creationists who reject evolution.

> **"The gap theory has become the standard interpretation throughout hyper-orthodoxy**, appearing in an endless stream of books, booklets, Bible studies, and periodical articles. In fact, it has become so sacrosanct with some that to question it is equivalent to tampering with Sacred Scripture or to manifest modernistic leanings."[79]

If you remember, Edward Hitchcock said the Gap Theory was the most extensively adopted theory of creation in 1855. Bernard Ramm said it was the standard interpretation in 1954. If it was so widely believed during that one-hundred-year period, why are we to believe there were no scholars who ever believed it? Contrary to what some creationists say, there were many scholars who believed it, and those scholars didn't hide their works. This information is readily available to anyone who seeks truth. In spite of this, I can go to any Christian bookstore and purchase books written by Christians who say *HAYAH* cannot be translated, "became." Right now, I can go to dozens of Internet websites (created and maintained by Christians) that vehemently proclaim the Gap Theory is without merit because there is no justification for translating *HAYAH* as "became." Today, I can go to any of the Christian bookstores in town and find books written by Christian creationists who say there are few scholars who defend the Gap Theory. Some say there are none. My main concern for such untrue proclamations is that unbelievers are offended by Christians who knowingly lie. Why would they believe our claims about Christ if we prove ourselves to be liars? Would you believe the claims of liars?

Without Form, and Void

When I purchased the book, *Without Form and Void*,[80] by Arthur C. Custance (1910-1985), I found what I consider to be the best source available for determining the meaning of Genesis 1:1-2. More than any other book, his book convinced me of the truth underlying the Restoration Theory. If you want to know what *HAYAH* means in Genesis 1:2, then you need to read *Without Form and Void*. Don't let someone convince you to reject the Restoration Theory if you haven't read this very scholarly work. If someone criticizes the Restoration Theory, ask them, "Have you read Arthur Custance?" I can't encourage you enough to purchase and read it. In fact, if you could afford no other book on the subject, (Including mine if you haven't bought it already.) this is the book to buy. Custance was most certainly a Hebrew scholar, and his book explains in detail why the grammar of Genesis 1:2 is best translated, "but the earth had become…" Furthermore, he shows the Restoration Theory was believed long before Darwin. In fact, it predates the Christian Church. Custance explains how the Targum of Onkelos, the earliest Aramaic Old Testament (c. A.D. 110) spoke of the earth being "laid waste" (destroyed) in Genesis 1:2. Custance also reveals many of the early Church fathers, including Justin Martyr (A.D. 100-165), St. Gregory Nazianzen (A.D. 330-390), Origen (A.D. 182-254), Theodoret (A.D. 393-457), and Augustine (A.D. 354-430) believed there was a long gap of time between the creation of the earth and the creation of Adam. (Although, not all of them described it as a period of Ruin-Restoration.) He also includes the names of several well-known scholars who wrote and defended some form of the Ruin-Restoration Theory before Darwin wrote about his Theory of Evolution in 1859. These include Simeon ben Jochai (2nd century A.D.), Caedmon (A.D. 650), Alcuin of York (A.D. 735-804), Hugo St. Victor (A.D. 1097-1141), Thomas Aquinas (A.D. 1226-1274), Benedict Pererius (16th century A.D.), Dionysius Petavius (A.D. 1583-1652), Johann August Dathe (A.D. 1731-1791), Thomas Chalmers (A.D. 1780-1847), John Harris (A.D. 1802-1856), J. H. Kurtz (A.D. 1809-1890), and others. In all, he mentions directly or indirectly about eighty scholars who have expressed their belief in some form of a gap of time between Genesis 1:1 and Genesis 1:3. I highly encourage you to purchase and study this book. I warn you, however; it is a very scholarly book, written for scholars. A working knowledge of Hebrew, Greek, and

Latin is necessary if you want to understand Custance fully. (His arguments are based on a thorough knowledge of these ancient languages.) He reveals how ancient scholars revealed the truth about the Gap Theory. I absolutely insist you purchase and read his book if you are a scholar who rejects this theory. Having said that, don't let that deter you from getting his book if you aren't a scholar. I am not a scholar; therefore, you don't need to be a scholar to understand his conclusion. His book can be ordered at:

Doorway Publications
38 Eldora Drive Unit 41
Hamilton, Ontario, Canada L9C 7L6

It is also available on the Internet at http://www.custance.org

It becomes apparent it is possible to translate Genesis 1:2, "but the earth had become without form, and void." How you translate it depends on more than just the rules of grammar; it depends on what you think the sequence of events was. This in turn depends on what you think God did at the beginning. We find ourselves stuck in a loop. What we think happened in the beginning depends on how we translate this passage. How we translate this passage depends on what we think happened in the beginning. To translate this passage with the information God intended to reveal requires that we know something about the events and details of the beginning. We need to know the truth in order to know the truth. Since none of us was present at the beginning, our knowledge of the beginning is dependent on God's revelation. The more truth God reveals to us, the more truth we can know. The more truth we know, the better we can translate Genesis 1:1-2. This is why we must not remain fixed in Genesis 1. We must see what God has revealed about the creation in other parts of the Bible.

Another Creation Account

My belief in Theistic Evolution was shaken when I was challenged with Scriptures that said Adam came before Eve. I knew enough about science to know men couldn't have evolved without women. (It didn't take a lot of science to figure that out.) The Bible said Adam was alone, but that would be evolutionarily impossible. I knew something was wrong with my belief in evolution. The same thing happened to my Day-Age beliefs; they were shattered by the teachings of Scripture that proved the "days" were days. Likewise, my Young-Earth beliefs about creation were shaken when I was challenged with Scriptures that indicated God did not originally create the earth a dead and dark desolate waste. It is important for you to realize my change in creation theories did not come about because some scientific theory said the universe was old. I did not change my mind because I felt compelled to compromise the Bible with evolution. My change of theories came about because I firmly believe Scripture cannot contradict Scripture. If God originally created earth a desolate waste, then the Bible contradicts the Bible. The earth was a desolate waste at the beginning of the six days of creation, but it was not created that way.

Isaiah 45:18 "For thus saith the LORD that created the heavens; God himself that formed the earth and made it; he hath established it, he created it not in vain, he formed it to be inhabited: I *am* the LORD; and *there is* none else." (KJV)

Isaiah 45:18 "For thus says the Lord, who created the heavens (he is God!), who formed the earth and made it (he established it; he did not create a chaos, he formed it to be inhabited!):" (RSV)

Isaiah 45:18 "For thus says the Lord, who created the heavens, (He is the God who formed the earth and made it, He established it and did not create it a waste place, But formed it to be inhabited.)" (NASB)

Isaiah 45:18 "For thus says the Lord who created the heavens— He is the true God— Who formed the earth and made it— He established it— He created it not a chaos, He formed it for a dwelling place." (S&G)

Isaiah 45:18 "For thus says the Lord, who created the heavens (he is God!), who formed the earth and made it (he established it; he did not create a chaos, he formed it to be inhabited!):" (NRSV)

Isaiah 45:18 "**For thus says Yahweh, Creator of the heavens; He is the One, Elohim, the Former of the earth and its Maker, He Himself established it; He did not create it a chaos; He formed it to be indwelt: I am Yahweh, and there is no other**;" (CVOT) (emphasis in original)

Guess what Hebrew word God used when He said He did not create the earth a chaos? He used *TOHUW*, the same word He used to describe the earth in Genesis 1:2! God is giving us another account of earth's creation. As we have seen, God gave Job some additional details about the creation of the earth. He does the same for Isaiah. He's giving Isaiah a physical description of the earth at the time He created it. God is telling Isaiah He did not create it *TOHUW*. God did not create earth a desolate waste.

There are those who would like you to believe *TOHUW* is used in the figurative sense here in Isaiah 45:18 but in the literal sense in Genesis 1:2. This isn't so. There is nothing in Isaiah 45 indicating God is speaking figuratively when He describes the creation of the earth. In this chapter, God describes literal things about Cyrus, Jacob, the heavens, the stars, the sun, Egypt, Israel, the merchants of Ethiopia, the Sabeans, carved images, and other physical things. None of these is figurative. God is literal in his descriptions of events, people, and places. God is literal in his description of earth. It would be very strange to shift from giving literal descriptions to giving figurative symbols without any clues. God describes literal things before verse 18 and literal things after verse 18. What makes anyone believe He's not being literal in verse 18? The answer is this: If *TOHUW* in Isaiah 45:18 is a literal description of earth, then the earth was not created a literal desolation, and that throws a monkey wrench into the theology of all the other creation theories.

The Meaning of *TOHUW* in Isaiah 45:18

I believe Isaiah has given us a description of what the earth was like before Genesis 1:2. Anti-Gap Theory creationists don't agree. They say there can be a different interpretation of this passage. Yes, they agree *TOHUW* can be translated as an OBJECT of the verb; "a chaos," "a waste," or "a desolation." However, they say *TOHUW* can also be translated as a MODIFIER of the verb; "in vain" or "for naught." Is their claim valid? Again, I think we have a situation where both interpretations may be grammatically correct according to the rules of Hebrew grammar, but only one interpretation conveys the information God wants us to know. Why is this important to the Gap Theory? Because if *TOHUW* in Isaiah 45:18 describes an object (a desolate waste), then the earth was not created that way. This would mean at the end of Genesis 1:1, the earth was not a desolate waste. It would imply the earth was created in a beautiful, well-ordered condition. This would further imply that for it to be *TOHUW* in Genesis 1:2, it must have BECOME a desolate waste. On the other hand, if *TOHUW* in Isaiah 45:18 describes a purpose, then this passage has no bearing on the Gap Theory. It would simply be telling us God had a purpose for earth regardless of its physical condition when created.

TOHUW can be translated, "a desolate waste," or it can be translated, "in vain." The scholars have debated for centuries over which translation of *TOHUW* should be used in Isaiah 45:18. Since they can't agree, and since I'm not a Hebrew scholar, my opinion will not be authoritative. However, I think God has given us His opinion. (And His opinion is authoritative.) As long as we don't look at the context, I think we can translate it either way. If we isolate the word *TOHUW* by itself, I don't think we can determine the correct interpretation. But, if we look at the context, I think we can discern the correct meaning of *TOHUW*. In the context of Isaiah 45:18, *TOHUW* is the object of the verb *BARA*. When used in regard to God's activities, *BARA* means "to create." *BARA* is also used to describe shaping, making, producing, cutting, clearing, and other such ideas when used of man's activities. (But when used of man's activities, the verb is in a different form.) I want to focus on how *BARA* is used in connection with God's activities. That's the context of Isaiah 45:18. Here are the uses of *BARA* in the *King James Version* that describe God's actions. I will leave Isaiah 45:18 out of the list so we can look at it last. The words in bold print are translations of the verb **BARA**. The underlined and bold words are the **objects** of *BARA*. Notice *BARA* always refers to a WHAT, never to a WHY or a HOW. **The object of *BARA* is always a noun or pronoun**. It is a person, place, or thing. It is never an adverb, adjective, or other modifier. Now, I'm not saying such a use is impossible in Hebrew, but it is never used that way in the Bible when God does the creating. I think this is God's clue to us. It would seem to me the best translation of *TOHUW* when used with *BARA* is to translate it as the noun object "a desolate waste," not as the adverb modifier "in vain."

The Uses of *BARA* for God's Creations
(Other than in Isaiah 45:18)

1.) Genesis 1:1 "In the beginning God **created** the <u>**heaven**</u> and the <u>**earth**</u>." (KJV)

2.) Genesis 1:21 "And God **created** <u>**great whales**</u>, and every <u>**living creature**</u> that moveth, which the waters brought forth abundantly, after their kind, and every <u>**winged fowl**</u> after his kind: and God saw that *it was* good." (KJV)

3. and 4. and 5.) Genesis 1:27 "So God **created** <u>**man**</u> in his *own* image, in the image of God **created** he <u>**him**</u>; male and female **created** he <u>**them**</u>." (KJV)

6.) Genesis 2:3 "And God blessed the seventh day, and sanctified it: because that in it he had rested from all his <u>**work**</u> which God **created** and made." (KJV)

7.) Genesis 2:4 "These *are* the generations of the <u>**heavens**</u> and of the <u>**earth**</u> when they were **created**, in the day that the LORD God made the earth and the heavens," (KJV)

8.) Genesis 5:1 "This *is* the book of the generations of Adam. In the day that God **created** <u>**man**</u>, in the likeness of God made he him;" (KJV)

9. and 10.) Genesis 5:2 "Male and female **created** he <u>**them**</u>; and blessed them, and called their name Adam, in the day when <u>**they**</u> were **created**." (KJV)

11.) Genesis 6:7 "And the LORD said, I will destroy <u>**man**</u> whom I have **created** from the face of the earth; both man, and beast, and the creeping thing, and the fowls of the air; for it repenteth me that I have made them." (KJV)

12.) Exodus 34:10 "And he said, Behold, I make a covenant: before all thy people I will do <u>**marvels**</u>, such as have not been **done** in all the earth, nor in any nation: and all the people among which thou *art* shall see the work of the LORD: for it *is* a terrible thing that I will do with thee." (KJV)

13.) Numbers 16:30 "But if the LORD **make** <u>**a new thing**</u>, and the earth open her mouth, and swallow them up, with all that *appertain* unto them, and they go down quick into the pit; then ye shall understand that these men have provoked the LORD." (KJV)

14.) Deuteronomy 4:32 "For ask now of the days that are past, which were before thee, since the day that God **created** **man** upon the earth, and *ask* from the one side of heaven unto the other, whether there hath been *any such thing* as this great thing *is,* or hath been heard like it?" (KJV)

15.) Psalms 51:10 "**Create** in me **a clean heart**, O God; and renew a right spirit within me." (KJV)

16.) Psalms 89:12 "The **north** and the **south** thou hast **created** **them**: Tabor and Hermon shall rejoice in thy name." (KJV)

17.) Psalms 89:47 "Remember how short my time is: wherefore hast thou **made** all **men** in vain?" (KJV)

18.) Psalms 102:18 "This shall be written for the generation to come: and the **people** which shall be **created** shall praise the LORD." (KJV)

19.) Psalms 104:30 "Thou sendest forth thy spirit, **they** are **created**: and thou renewest the face of the earth." (KJV)

20.) Psalms 148:5 "Let them praise the name of the LORD: for he commanded, and **they** were **created**." (KJV)

21.) Ecclesiastes 12:1 "Remember now **thy Creator** in the days of thy youth, while the evil days come not, nor the years draw nigh, when thou shalt say, I have no pleasure in them;" (KJV)

22.) Isaiah 4:5 "And the LORD will **create** upon every dwelling place of mount Zion, and upon her assemblies, a **cloud** and **smoke** by day, and the **shining of a flaming fire** by night: for upon all the glory *shall be* a defence." (KJV)

23.) Isaiah 40:26 "Lift up your eyes on high, and behold who hath **created these** *things*, that bringeth out their host by number: he calleth them all by names by the greatness of his might, for that *he is* strong in power; not one faileth." (KJV)

24.) Isaiah 40:28 "Hast thou not known? hast thou not heard, *that* the everlasting God, the LORD, the **Creator** of **the ends of the earth**, fainteth not, neither is weary? *there is* no searching of his understanding." (KJV)

25.) Isaiah 41:20 "That they may see, and know, and consider, and understand together, that the hand of the LORD hath done this, and the Holy One of Israel hath **created <u>it</u>**." (KJV)

26.) Isaiah 42:5 "Thus saith God the LORD, he that **created** the **<u>heavens</u>**, and stretched them out; he that spread forth the earth, and that which cometh out of it; he that giveth breath unto the people upon it, and spirit to them that walk therein:" (KJV)

27.) Isaiah 43:1 "But now thus saith the LORD that **created <u>thee</u>**, O Jacob, and he that formed thee, O Israel, Fear not: for I have redeemed thee, I have called *thee* by thy name; thou *art* mine." (KJV)

28.) Isaiah 43:7 "*Even* every one that is called by my name: for I have **created <u>him</u>** for my glory, I have formed him; yea, I have made him." (KJV)

29.) Isaiah 43:15 "I *am* the LORD, your Holy One, the **creator** of **<u>Israel</u>**, your King." (KJV)

30. and 31.) Isaiah 45:7 "I form the light, and **create <u>darkness</u>**: I make peace, and **create <u>evil</u>**: I the LORD do all these *things*." (KJV)

(Note: Many people laugh at this verse. They say it proves the Scriptures were written by primitive, ignorant men who knew nothing about light. They point out that darkness is the absence of light, therefore, it does not need to be created. In the next chapter, I'll try to explain what it means for God to create darkness.)

32.) Isaiah 45:8 "Drop down, ye heavens, from above, and let the skies pour down righteousness: let the earth open, and let them bring forth salvation, and let righteousness spring up together; I the LORD have **created <u>it</u>**." (KJV)

33.) Isaiah 45:12 "I have made the earth, and **created <u>man</u>** upon it: I, *even* my hands, have stretched out the heavens, and all their host have I commanded." (KJV)

34.) Isaiah 48:7 "**<u>They</u>** are **created** now, and not from the beginning; even before the day when thou heardest them not; lest thou shouldest say, Behold, I knew them." (KJV)

35.) Isaiah 54:16 "Behold, I have **created <u>the smith</u>** that bloweth the coals in the fire, and that bringeth forth an instrument for his work; and I have **created <u>the waster</u>** to destroy." (KJV)

36.) Isaiah 57:19 "I **create** **the fruit of the lips**; Peace, peace to *him that is* far off, and to *him that is* near, saith the LORD; and I will heal him." (KJV)

37.) Isaiah 65:17 "For, behold, I **create** **new heavens** and a **new earth**: and the former shall not be remembered, nor come into mind." (KJV)

38.) Isaiah 65:18 "But be ye glad and rejoice for ever *in **that*** which I **create**: for, behold, I **create Jerusalem** a rejoicing, and her people a joy." (KJV)

39.) Jeremiah 31:22 "How long wilt thou go about, O thou backsliding daughter? for the LORD hath **created** **a new thing** in the earth, A woman shall compass a man." (KJV)

40.) Ezekiel 21:30 "Shall I cause *it* to return into his sheath? I will judge thee in the place where **thou** wast **created**, in the land of thy nativity." (KJV)

41.) Ezekiel 28:13 "Thou hast been in Eden the garden of God; every precious stone *was* thy covering, the sardius, topaz, and the diamond, the beryl, the onyx, and the jasper, the sapphire, the emerald, and the carbuncle, and gold: the workmanship of thy tabrets and of thy pipes was prepared in thee in the day that **thou** wast **created**." (KJV)

42.) Ezekiel 28:15 "Thou *wast* perfect in thy ways from the day that **thou** wast **created**, till iniquity was found in thee." (KJV)

43.) Amos 4:13 "For, lo, he that formeth the mountains, and **createth** the **wind**, and declareth unto man what *is* his thought, that maketh the morning darkness, and treadeth upon the high places of the earth, The LORD, The God of hosts, *is* his name." (KJV)

44.) Malachi 2:10 "Have we not all one father? hath not one God **created us**? why do we deal treacherously every man against his brother, by profaning the covenant of our fathers?" (KJV)

Every time *BARA* is used in the Bible for God creating, it refers to some THING being created, some object. Great whales are created. Winged fowls are created. Man is created. The universe is created. Jerusalem is created. A new heavens and a new earth are created. A new heart is created. These are objects of *BARA* and not modifiers of *BARA* when used of God's creations. Let me clarify what this means by using an example in English.

1.) Jim built the house.
2.) Jim built skillfully.

In the first sentence, "house" (a noun) describes WHAT Jim built. In the second sentence, "skillfully" (an adverb) describes HOW Jim built. The first sentence contains an OBJECT of the verb, while the second sentence contains a MODIFIER of the verb. We could describe other modifiers of Jim's work. We could say, "Jim built joyfully," or "Jim built quickly," or "Jim built in vain," or any number of other things that describe how, or why, or when Jim built. But these things are never WHAT Jim built. Only an OBJECT of the verb will tell us WHAT Jim built. The subject and the verb are identical, but the information gleaned from the sentences is different. One has an object; the other has a modifier. Now let's look at Isaiah 45:18 again. We have two choices.

Isaiah 45:18 "For thus saith the LORD that created the heavens; God himself that formed the earth and made it; he hath established it, he **created** it not in vain, he formed it to be inhabited: I *am* the LORD; and *there is* none else." (KJV)

Isaiah 45:18 "For thus says the LORD, who created the heavens (he is God!), who formed the earth and made it (he established it; he did not **create** it a chaos, he formed it to be inhabited!): I am the LORD, and there is no other." (NRSV)

Throughout the entire Bible, when *BARA* is used to describe God's creations; it describes God creating an object or objects—nouns or pronouns. It never describes how, why, or when—adverbs or adjectives. The logical choice for Isaiah 45:18 is to accept *TOHUW* as a physical object, the object of *BARA*. This is the way all the other words are used with *BARA* when God creates. This is the way *BARA* is translated even in the first part of Isaiah 45:18, "the LORD, who **created** the heavens." This first usage should set the context. Isaiah is talking about the creation of the heavens and the earth. He is giving us another account of creation. Isaiah's contemporaries would have thought of Genesis when they read his words. That seems to be Isaiah's intent. Isaiah is telling us God did not create a *TOHUW*, a desolate waste, when He created the earth. Now, it is true that Isaiah includes a purpose statement (a modifier of the verb) later in the sentence. He says, "He formed it to be inhabited," but this purpose statement does not include *BARA*. Instead of *BARA*, Isaiah says, "He formed (*YATSAR*) it to be inhabited." *YATSAR* is not the same as *BARA*. Neither is the word *ASAH* when he says, "… and made (*ASAH*) it." All three words are used in this verse. Although these words are sometimes used interchangeably, God is making a distinction between *BARA*, *YATSAR*, and *ASAH* in Isaiah 45:18. The first *BARA* in this verse tells us WHAT God created—the heavens. The second *BARA* in this verse also tells us WHAT God created—the earth. Isaiah tells us God created an earth that wasn't a desolate waste.

We need to establish whether *TOHUW* in Isaiah 45:18 is a noun or an adverb. We need to know what part of speech it is in the Hebrew. Since I am not a Hebrew scholar, (I'm not even a Hebrew neophyte.) I can't supply the answer. But, I can supply a scholarly work that does supply the answer. That scholarly work is *The Complete Word Study Old*

Testament King James Version.[81] This is an important work because it shows the forms, tenses, stems, moods, voices, parts of speech, *etc.* of all the Hebrew and Greek words in the context of where they are used. This book answers the question about how *TOHUW* is used in Isaiah 45:18 by showing you what part of speech it is in the Hebrew.

Isaiah 45:18 "For [3588 cj] thus [3541 ad] saith [559 qpf] the Lord [3068 nn] that created [1254 qpta] the heavens; [8064 df,du,nn] God [430 df,pl,nn] himself [1931 pnp] that formed [3335 qpta] the earth [776 df,nn] and made [6213 wcj,qpta,pnx] it; he [1931 pnp] hath established [3559 pipx,pnx] it, he created [1254 qpf,pnx] it not [3808 ptn] **in vain,** **8414 nn** he formed [3335 qpf,pnx] it to be inhabited: [3427 pp,qnc] I [589 pnp] *am* the Lord; [3068 nn] and *there is* none [369 wcj,ptn] else. [5750 ad]" (KJV)

(Keys to word usages in *The Complete Word Study Old Testament King James Version*: ad—Adverb; cj—Conjunction; cs—Construct; df—Definite Article; dfp—Definite Article with a Prefixed Preposition; du—Dual; **nn—Noun**; hipt—Hiphil Participle; pimv—Piel Imperative; pipf—Piel Perfect; pl—Plural; pnp—Personal Pronoun; pnx—Pronominal Suffix; pp—Prefixed Preposition; ptn—Particle of Negation; qnc—Qal Infinitive Construct; qpf—Qal Perfect; qpta—Qal Participle Active; wcj—Waw Conjunctive)

Note *TOHUW* is a noun. The [nn] superscript following the word means "noun." It is not an adverb. This is enough proof for me that *TOHUW* is a noun in Isaiah 45:18. It describes WHAT God created, not WHY He created it. It is the same in Genesis 1:2.

Genesis 1:2 "And the earth [776 wcj, df, nn] was [1961 qpf] **without form,** **8414 nn** and void; [922 wcj, nn] and darkness [2822 wcj, nn] *was* upon [5921 pr] the face [6440 pl, cs, nn] of the deep. [8415 nn] And the Spirit [7307 wcj, cs, nn] of God [430 pl, nn] moved [7363 pipt] upon [5921 pr] the face [6440 pl, cs, nn] of the waters. [4325 df, pl, nn]" (KJV)

Isaiah 45:18 and Genesis 1:2 both describe the creation. Both passages use the noun *TOHUW*. They both show WHAT God created. All these things are literal. The creation isn't figurative. The heavens and earth aren't figurative. God isn't figurative. Isaiah and Moses both talk about the same creation. You can't let one of these passages be figurative without both passages being figurative. If one is literal, the other is literal. They both describe the same God, the same creation, the same earth. They both use *BARA* and they both use *TOHUW*. Both passages describe the creation of the earth. In Genesis, God tells us the earth either "was" or "became" *TOHUW*, a desolate waste. In Isaiah, God tells us He did not create earth *TOHUW*, a desolate waste. According to Isaiah 45:18, the earth was not a desolate waste at its creation. But, by Genesis 1:2 it was a desolate waste. Genesis 1:2 must therefore describe what the earth had become sometime after its original, non-*TOHUW* creation in Genesis 1:1. The only way I can see how both passages could be true is if Genesis 1:2 reads: "… but the earth had become without form, and void."

Objecting in Vain

At this point, opponents of the Ruin-Restoration Theory object to interpreting *TOHUW* in Isaiah 45:18 as a physical condition by calling attention to the very next verse:

Isaiah 45:19 "I have not spoken in secret, in a dark place of the earth: I said not unto the seed of Jacob, Seek ye me **in vain**: I the LORD speak righteousness, I declare things that are right." (KJV)

Their argument is this: The very same word, *TOHUW*, is translated, "in vain," not in "a ruin," or "a destruction," or a "chaos." They argue that since *TOHUW* in Isaiah 45:19 seems to be used as an adverb, why would *TOHUW* in Isaiah 45:18 be any different? The answer is twofold. First, *TOHUW* is not used in connection with *BARA* or with God's activity in Isaiah 45:19. It describes what men are doing. It is totally unrelated to Genesis 1:2. Second, the context shows Isaiah didn't use this word as an adverb here, either. He used it as a noun. Isaiah 45:19 creates a parallelism. "I have not spoken," in the first part of the sentence, is parallel to, "I said not," in the second part of the sentence. Since this is a parallelism, the objects that follow the verbs are also parallel.

I have not spoken—in a dark place
I said not—in vain

Therefore, "in a dark place," in the first part of the sentence is parallel to, "in vain" (*TOHUW*) in the second part of the sentence. In other words, God has not spoken to His people in secret, dark places, and so He tells them not to seek Him in such places. God does not promote some kind of nefarious cult. He is a God of openness, honesty, truth, and light, and He calls His people into that same kind of openness, honesty, truth, and light. (Just look at how Jesus conducted His life and ministry.) If you are in a religion that has secret meetings, secret rituals, secret doctrines, secret revelations, secret knowledge, secret passwords, and secret uniforms or clothing, then you are not following the God of the Bible; you are in a cult. Those things are *TOHUW*. *TOHUW* in verse 19 is a NOUN object; it is not an ADVERBIAL modifier! Let me repeat that:

TOHUW in verse 19 is a NOUN object; it is not an ADVERBIAL modifier!

TOHUW is a WHAT, not a WHY or HOW.

Isaiah 45:19 "I have not spoken in secret, In some dark land; I did not say to the offspring of Jacob, 'Seek Me in **a waste place**'; I, the LORD, speak righteousness. Declaring things that are upright." (NASB)

Isaiah 45:19 "I did not speak in secret, in a land of darkness; I did not say to the offspring of Jacob, 'Seek me in **chaos**.' I the LORD speak the truth, I declare what is right." (NRSV)

Isaiah 45:19 "I did not speak in secret or hide my words in some dark place. I did not tell the family of Jacob to look for me in **empty places**. I am the LORD, and I speak the truth; I say what is right." (NCV)

Isaiah 45:19 "I have not spoken in secret, somewhere in a land of darkness. I did not say to the descendants of Jacob: Seek Me in **a wasteland**. I, the LORD, speak truthfully; I say what is right." (HCSB)

Isaiah 45:19 "I have not ptn spoken pipf in secret, dfp,nn in a dark nn place pp,cs,nn of the earth: cs,nn I said qpf not ptn unto the seed pp,cs,nn of Jacob, nn Seek pimv,pnx ye me **in vain:** nn I pnp the LORD nn speak qpta righteousness, nn I declare hipt things that are right. pl,nn" (*The Complete Word Study Bible, King James Version*)

    I could just as easily turn their own objection against them. Since *TOHUW* in verse 19 is a noun used to describe a physical condition, why would *TOHUW* in verse 18 be any different? The *TOHUW*s in both Isaiah 45:18 and Isaiah 45:19 are noun objects, not adverbial modifiers. This fact absolutely proves Isaiah 45:18 tells us the earth was not a wasteland when God created it. Yet, by the time we get to Genesis 1:2, it is a wasteland. So, if the earth wasn't a wasteland when God created it in Genesis 1:1, but it was a wasteland in Genesis 1:2, then how must we translate Genesis 1:2?

Genesis 1:2 "But the earth **had become** a wasteland and empty, and darkness was over the face of the deep…"

Let There Be Logic

    "Yes, Yes, Yes," my opponents will say. "You are right that some Hebrew scholars translate *TOHUW* in Isaiah 45:18 as a noun object, but there are other scholars who translate it as an adverbial purpose clause. What makes you so sure your scholars are better than our scholars?"

    To be honest, I dare not set myself up as the Grand Decider of which Hebrew scholars are better than others. However, I don't need a fancy degree in Hebrew to recognize a logical contradiction when I see one. If *TOHUW* is meant to define a purpose clause in Isaiah 45:18, then it creates a logical contradiction with Genesis 1:2. According to the anti-gap creationists, Isaiah 45:18 means God created the earth for the purpose of being inhabited. They say Isaiah 45:18 contains a purpose clause. What was that purpose? It was to be inhabited! This creates a contradiction. You see, **if God created the earth without form, and void, and in darkness, and completely submerged under water in**

Genesis 1:2, then it was in a condition that couldn't be inhabited; at least not by 99.99999+% of the life that inhabits the earth. If He created the earth without form, and void, and dark, and completely under water for the purpose of being inhabited, then what kind of organisms was He planning to inhabit those conditions? Think of it this way:

Suppose I told you I was going to build an enclosure for the purpose of being inhabited by some animals. Then, when I completed my building project, I showed you the enclosure. You look at the enclosure and immediately notice it is an aquarium; it's filled with water. Since it is a water-filled aquarium, what types of animals do you think I intended to put in my enclosure? Wouldn't it be obvious my purpose for building a water-filled aquarium was for it to be the habitation of fish and/or other aquatic life? I think it would be obvious what my purpose was. If I meant to build an enclosure to house gerbils, then I made a mistake in what I built. If I wanted to build an enclosure for gerbils, then I should have put in dry ground. A water-filled aquarium would not provide the conditions for the purpose of housing gerbils. You could look at the conditions of what I built, and you would know my purpose for building it. The conditions of my enclosure reveal the types of animals I purposed to inhabit it.

So, all we need to do is look at the conditions of the earth in Genesis 1:2, and we will be able to see what kinds of organisms God purposed to put on the earth. According to the anti-gap creationists, Genesis 1:2 is the description of how God created the earth in Genesis 1:1. (It WAS that way; it didn't BECOME that way.) According to anti-gap creationists, the purpose of that creation was for the earth to be inhabited. But, what was its condition? It was completely covered in water, there was no dry land, and there was no light. Now, what kind of organisms can live in those conditions? Certainly not land animals. Birds couldn't live there either. In fact, not even plants could live there because there would be no sunlight. Without sunlight, the only possible lifeforms that could survive would be the thermophilic chemosynthetic bacteria and archaea that live on the ocean floor in hydrothermal vents. If God created the earth *TOHUW WA-BOHUW* and *CHOSHEK* for the purpose of being inhabited, then God's purpose for the earth was for it to be inhabited by thermophilic chemosynthetic bacteria and archaea; nothing else could inhabit a dark and submerged *TOHUW WA-BOHUW* earth. Anti-Gap Theory creationists can't say God created a desolate, dead, dark, and submerged earth for the purpose of being inhabited. At best, they must say God created a desolate, dead, dark, and submerged earth **for the purpose of being recreated** for the purpose of being inhabited. So:

1.) God did not create the earth *TOHUW WA-BOHUW* and *CHOSHEK* for the purpose of inhabiting it with plants. Plants cannot inhabit those conditions.

2.) God did not create the earth *TOHUW WA-BOHUW* and *CHOSHEK* for the purpose of inhabiting it with fish. Fish cannot inhabit those conditions.

3.) God did not create the earth *TOHUW WA-BOHUW* and *CHOSHEK* for the purpose of inhabiting it with birds. Birds cannot inhabit those conditions.

4.) God did not create the earth *TOHUW WA-BOHUW* and *CHOSHEK* for the purpose of inhabiting it with land animals. Land animals cannot inhabit those conditions.

5.) God did not create the earth *TOHUW WA-BOHUW* and *CHOSHEK* for the purpose of inhabiting it with man. Man cannot inhabit those conditions.

It is painfully obvious *TOHUW WA-BOHUW* and *CHOSHEK* describe the earth's condition; not its purpose. That's why Isaiah used a noun object instead of an adverbial modifier to describe the earth. Since Isaiah said God did not create the earth in that condition, *TOHUW WA-BOHUW* and *CHOSHEK* describe what the earth had become after its original non-*TOHUW*, non-*BOHUW*, and non-*CHOSHEK* creation.

I love the claims made by anti-Gap Theory creationists. They say they don't believe the Gap Theory because they believe in, "the literal interpretation of the Bible." I don't think they fully understand what "literal" means, but I want to focus on their statement. If you believe the Bible is literal, then you have to believe the Bible's words are used in their literal sense according to the rules of Hebrew grammar and syntax. That means you have to believe a word is a noun when the noun form of the word is used. You have to believe a word is a verb when the verb form of the word is used. You have to believe a word is an adverb when the adverb form of the word is used. That's the only way you can believe in a literal interpretation of the Bible. If you take a noun and translate it as a verb, an adverb, an adjective, or any other part of speech, then you cannot claim to be taking the Bible literally. So, if you believe the Bible is literal, then you have to believe two things about Isaiah 45:18. You have to believe *BARA* is a verb (because it is) and you have to believe *TOHUW* is a noun (because it is). But since *TOHUW* is a noun, then it is not an adverb and cannot be used to describe HOW or WHY God created. It is a noun and describes WHAT He created. **Isaiah 45:18 tells us God did not create the earth a literal, physical wasteland. Any other interpretation is not a literal interpretation of the Bible.** Go ahead and say you believe in, "the literal interpretation of the Bible," but don't say it and then insist on a non-literal interpretation of Isaiah 45:18. God literally tells us He did not create the earth without form, and void. This verse proves the Gap Theory.

BARA vs. *ASAH*

Before I leave the subject of *BARA*, let me clarify something. Some Young-Earth scholars insist *BARA* ("create") and *ASAH* ("make") are always synonymous. They say there are no distinctions between these two words. They say these two words are always interchangeable throughout Scripture. They say this because they use Exodus 20:11 as "proof" God created the universe only a few thousand years ago.

Exodus 20:11 "For *in* six days the LORD **made** heaven and earth, the sea, and all that in them *is,* and rested the seventh day: wherefore the LORD blessed the Sabbath day, and hallowed it." (KJV)

The Hebrew word translated, "made," in Exodus 20:11 is *ASAH*. The Lord made (*ASAH*) the heavens and the earth and the sea. So, they argue there is no difference between God making (*ASAH*) the heavens and the earth in Exodus 20:11 and God creating (*BARA*) the heavens and the earth in Genesis 1:1. In their way of thinking, this eliminates the possibility that God created anything before the six days. This would disprove the Gap Theory, but I think their argument fails. Exodus 20:11 describes what God did during the six days of Genesis 1:3-31, not what He did in Genesis 1:1. How do I know that? I know it because God did not make ALL the things in the heavens, in the earth, and in the sea in Genesis 1:1. Genesis 1:1 mentions only the heavens and the earth; it does not mention ALL the things in them. "All that is in them," would include ALL the things created and made and formed during the six days. (Fish, trees, plants, animals, birds, Adam and Eve, the Garden of Eden, the Tree of the Knowledge of Good and Evil, the Tree of Life, *etc.*) These things aren't mentioned in Genesis 1:1 because they ALL weren't created in Genesis 1:1. This means Exodus 20:11 is a summary of the six days during which ALL these things were made and created and formed. It is not a summary of Genesis 1:1. It says nothing about what He had created before the six days. As a summary of the six days, *ASAH* is a better word than *BARA*. Their argument doesn't prove there was no gap of time between Genesis 1:1 and Genesis 1:2 unless you first assume there was no gap of time between Genesis 1:1 and Genesis 1:2. You can't prove the age of the earth unless you first assume there was no period of time before Day One. No age is mentioned in Exodus 20:11. It is silent on the issue. Young-Earth creationists make an interpretation for an age of the earth, but there is no declaration for an age of the earth in Exodus 20:11. In Genesis 1:1 *BARA* is used. In Exodus 20:11 *ASAH* is used. Why the difference? *ASAH* is a better word than *BARA* to describe God's different kinds of works over the entire six days because it is more inclusive than *BARA*. In fact, God Himself used *ASAH* to summarize what He did during the six days.

Genesis 1:31 "And God saw every thing that he had **made**, and, behold, *it was* very good. And the evening and the morning were the sixth day." (KJV)

Since God used *ASAH* in Genesis 1:31 as a summary of the six days, how can Young-Earth creationists say we Gap Theory believers are wrong to say *ASAH* in Exodus 20:11 is a summary of the six days? *ASAH* is not used in Genesis 1:1; *ASAH* does not describe the initial creation of the heavens and the earth. That means Exodus 20:11 does not describe the initial creation of the heavens and the earth. It describes the restoration.

ASAH can include "creating," "making," and "forming" because God did all three of those things during the six days. The purpose of both Genesis 1:31 and Exodus 20:11 is to summarize what God did during the six days, not what He did before Day One. During the six days, God created (*BARA*) some things. He also made (*ASAH*) and formed (*YATSAR*) other things out of what He had created. It doesn't say God "created" all that is in the heavens and the earth and the sea in six days. It says God "made" ALL these things in six days. "Making" would be a better word to describe His actions. Over those six days He created some things, made other things, and formed yet other things. Since the six days describe "creating," "making," and "forming," I believe we are looking at something other than the original *EX NIHILO* creation in Genesis 1:1. Genesis 1:1 doesn't mention "making" or "forming." I believe Genesis 1:3-31 and Exodus 20:11 describe what God did after (long after) the original *EX NIHILO* creation. The creative acts of God during the six days included *EX NIHILO* creations, but they were not the same *EX NIHILO* creations as Genesis 1:1. I believe the six days were a restoration, or at least a partial restoration, of whatever it was Lucifer and his angels corrupted. I think it included the heavens and the earth and the sea because ALL of creation had been corrupted prior to this. All three words, *BARA*, *ASAH*, and *YATSAR* are used in Isaiah 45:18, but this doesn't mean the words are equivalent. There are slight differences of meanings in these words. If they can't mean different things, then Isaiah 43:7 makes no sense.

Isaiah 43:7 "Everyone who is called by My name, And whom I have **created** for My glory, Whom I have **formed**, even whom I have **made**." (NASB)

Everyone called by God has been created (*BARA*), formed (*YATSAR*), and made (*ASAH*) by God. (I find it fascinating how God uses the same three words for creating man that He uses for creating the earth. There seems to be a parallel between the creation of the earth and the creation of man.) If all these words mean the exact same thing, then we were all created *EX NIHILO*—out of nothing. No one came from previously existing matter. No one was ever made or formed. This would mean no one was physically conceived, physically developed *en utero*, and then physically born. If all these words mean the same thing, then all of us were created *EX NIHILO*. That's what *BARA* means in Genesis 1:1. If *ASAH* and *YATSAR* are always equivalent to *BARA*, then you were created *EX NIHILO*. Now, if you think you were created *EX NIHILO*, go ask your mother. She'll tell you otherwise!

In spite of what their mothers say, many Young-Earth creationists still believe these words always mean the same thing. While I have no doubt these words CAN be used interchangeably in certain places in Scripture, I don't believe they are interchangeable throughout Scripture. In fact, this Young-Earth view is a dangerous idea. If *ASAH* always means the exact same thing as *BARA*, then *BARA* always means the exact same thing as *ASAH*. If they are completely interchangeable, then we can determine HOW God created (*BARA*) the universe simply by looking at the meaning of *ASAH*. (They supposedly mean the same thing.)

Genesis 1:11 "And God said, Let the earth bring forth grass, the herb yielding seed, *and* the fruit tree **yielding** fruit after his kind, whose seed *is* in itself, upon the earth: and it was so." (KJV)

ASAH is used to describe fruit trees making fruit. We know how this happens. Fruit trees take in preexisting water, preexisting nutrients, and preexisting minerals from the soil. They take in preexisting carbon dioxide from the air. They harness preexisting energy from sunlight. Then, from all this preexisting matter and energy, they make (*ASAH*) new fruit in accordance to the preexisting laws of physics that govern the actions of preexisting matter and energy within the realm of preexisting time and space. Now, if *ASAH* is always equivalent to *BARA*, then *BARA* is always equivalent to *ASAH*, and we would have to agree that God used preexisting matter and energy, and preexisting time and space, to create (*BARA*) the universe. After all, that is what *ASAH* means in Genesis 1:11, and if *ASAH* and *BARA* are always equivalent, then that's what *BARA* means in Genesis 1:1. This argument by Young-Earth creationists winds up disproving the very method of creation (*EX NIHILO*) they seek to defend. Their interpretation creates a bigger Biblical problem than it solves. *ASAH* in Exodus 20:11 is not identical to *BARA* in Genesis 1:1. Exodus 20:11 is not describing the same period of time as Genesis 1:1; it is a summary of Genesis 1:3-31.

Anti-gap creationists create Biblical problems when they say *BARA* is always equivalent to *ASAH*. Look at Genesis 3:7.

Genesis 3:7 "And the eyes of them both were opened, and they knew that they *were* naked; and they sewed fig leaves together, and **made** themselves aprons." (KJV)

In Genesis 3:7 we learn Adam and Eve **made** (*ASAH*) aprons for themselves. Since *BARA* means *EX NIHILO* creation, then *ASAH* must mean *EX NIHILO* creation if these anti-Gap Theory creationists are telling us the truth that *ASAH* and *BARA* always mean the same thing. If they are telling us the truth, then Adam and Eve created their aprons out of nothing. Simple logic tells us these people aren't telling us the truth. *ASAH* and *BARA* are not always interchangeable.

Likewise, when God told Noah to **make** the Ark, in Genesis 6:14, did God tell Noah to **create** the Ark *EX NIHILO* by Noah's spoken word alone? He did, if *ASAH* means the same thing as *BARA*.

Genesis 6:14 "**Make** thee an ark of gopher wood; rooms shalt thou make in the ark, and shalt pitch it within and without with pitch." (KJV)

In Genesis 18:6, when the Lord and two angels came to visit Abraham before the destruction of Sodom and Gomorrah, Abraham told Sarah to **make** cakes for them to eat.

Genesis 18:6 "And Abraham went quickly into the tent to Sarah and said, "Quick! Three seahs of fine flour! Knead it, and **make** cakes." (ESV)

Abraham obviously knew Sarah could **make** cakes, but not **create** cakes from nothing, because he told her to get three seahs of fine flour. If *ASAH* meant create, then Sarah would not have needed the flour. She could have created the cakes from nothing by simply saying, "Let there be cakes."

ASAH is also use in Genesis 1:7 when it says, "And God **made** the firmament..." Now if "made" means "create," and "firmament" means "atmosphere," then God didn't create the atmosphere until Day Two. This is what some Young-Earth creationists believe. But if that were true, then it means the earth had no atmosphere on Day One, and it would have been in a complete vacuum. This creates a scientific impossibility. If the earth had no atmosphere, then the ocean would have boiled off instantly. There could be no ocean if the earth had no atmosphere. Without an atmosphere, the earth would be as dry and barren as the moon. Obviously, the earth had some kind of atmosphere on Day One because it was covered by water. This means God didn't **create** the atmosphere on Day Two. He did, however, **make** the atmosphere on Day Two. He made it in the sense of fashioning it, crafting it, formulating it, composing it, *etc*. It doesn't imply an *EX NIHILO* creation. He **made** the atmosphere so it would be suitable for the living things He was about to create. To me, this implies something terrible had happened to the Pre-Adamic atmosphere. It is clear that *ASAH* in Genesis 1:7 is not identical to *BARA* in Genesis 1:1.

The Gap Theory proposes a much better solution. "Made the firmament" means God "produced the firmament." It doesn't mean He created the atmosphere *EX NIHILO* in Genesis 1:7. I think Genesis 1:7 is telling us God fashioned/produced/formed the atmosphere by restoring the atmosphere to what it had been before. It seems likely something had happened to the air that made life on earth impossible. Whether it was poisonous fumes and ash from volcanic activity or choking dust and debris from asteroid and meteor impacts, I can't say. Scientists tell us the earth has suffered more than one massive "kill-off" caused by such deadly atmospheric conditions. Whether or not they are correct, I don't know. I also don't know what kind of corruption, destruction, and pollution Satan may have caused in the Pre-Adamic world. Whatever it was, the Bible seems to imply the atmosphere had to be restored/remade because it "groaned" from the corruption that filled the universe. The Gap Theory provides an interpretation that creates no Biblical or scientific contradictions. The only way the Young-Earth Theory can prevent these contradictions is if it allows *ASAH* to mean something different than *BARA*. But if Young-Earth creationists allow that, then they can't insist Exodus 20:11 refers to the same creation as Genesis 1:1.

Fifty Ways to Leave Your Theory

Young-Earth creationists claim Exodus 20:11 says God **CREATED** the heavens and the earth in six days. However, Exodus 20:11 does not say God **CREATED** the heavens and the earth in six days! It says, "**MADE.**" They have replaced the word "**MADE**" with the word "**CREATED**," and that changes the meaning of Exodus 20:11. God warns us about changing the meaning of His Word, but Young-Earth creationists readily ignore His warning. There is a difference between the Hebrew word *ASAH* and the Hebrew word *BARA*. They have the exact same distinction between the English word "made" and the English word "created." If they were the same in Hebrew, they would be translated the same in English. Here are 50 English translations of Exodus 20:11, and NONE of them says, "created!" NONE of them translates *ASAH* equivalent to *BARA*!

Exodus 20:11

1.) Exodus 20:11 "For in six days *the* LORD **made** the heaven, and the earth, and the sea, and all the *things* in them. And he rested on the [^{2}day ^{1}seventh]. Because of this *the* LORD blessed the [^{2}day ^{1}seventh], and sanctified it." (ABP)

2.) Exodus 20:11 "For in six days the LORD **made** heaven and earth, the sea, and all that in them is, and rested the seventh day: why the LORD blessed the sabbath day, and hallowed it. (AKJV)

3.) Exodus 20:11 "For in six days the Lord **made** the heavens and the earth, the sea and everything that is in them, and He rested (ceased) on the seventh day. That is why the Lord blessed the Sabbath day and made it holy [that is, set it apart for His purposes]." (AMP)

4.) Exodus 20:11 "For in six days Jehovah **made** heaven and earth, the sea, and all that in them is, and rested the seventh day: wherefore Jehovah blessed the sabbath day, and hallowed it." (ASV)

5.) Exodus 20:11 "For in six days the Lord **made** heaven and earth, and the sea, and everything in them, and he took his rest on the seventh day: for this reason the Lord has given his blessing to the seventh day and made it holy." (BBE)

6.) Exodus 20:11 "For in sixe dayes the Lorde **made** heauen and earth, the sea, and all that in them is, and rested the seuenth day: wherfore the Lorde blessed the seuenth day, and halowed it." (BISHOPS)

7.) Exodus 20:11 "For in six days the Lord **made** the heaven and the earth, and the sea and all things in them, and rested on the seventh day; therefore the Lord blessed the seventh day, and hallowed it." (BRENTON)

8.) Exodus 20:11 "Because the LORD **made** the heavens and the earth, the sea, and everything that is in them in six days, but rested on the seventh day. That is why the LORD blessed the Sabbath day and made it holy." (CEB)

9.) Exodus 20:11 "In six days I **made** the sky, the earth, the oceans, and everything in them, but on the seventh day I rested. That's why I made the Sabbath a special day that belongs to me." (CEV)

10.) Exodus 20:11 "For in six days, *ADONAI* **made** heaven and earth, the sea and everything in them; but on the seventh day he rested. This is why *ADONAI* blessed the day, *Shabbat*, and separated it for himself." (CJB)

11.) Exodus 20:11 "For in six days Jehovah **made** the heavens and the earth, the sea, and all that is in them, and rested on the seventh day; therefore Jehovah blessed the sabbath day, and hallowed it." (DBY)

12.) Exodus 20:11 "For in six days the Lord **made** heaven and earth, and the sea, and all things that are in them, and rested on the seventh day: therefore the Lord blessed the seventh day, and sanctified it." (DRB)

13.) Exodus 20:11 "For, in six days, did Yahweh **make** the heavens and the earth, and the sea—and all that in them is, and rested on the seventh day, -for this cause, Yahweh blessed the sabbath day and hallowed it." (EMP)

14.) Exodus 20:11 "That is because the LORD worked six days and **made** the sky, the earth, the sea, and everything in them. And on the seventh day, he rested. In this way the LORD blessed the Sabbath—the day of rest. He made that a very special day." (ERV)

15.) Exodus 20:11 "For in six days the LORD **made** heaven and earth, the sea, and all that is in them, and rested on the seventh day. Therefore the LORD blessed the Sabbath day and made it holy." (ESV)

16.) Exodus 20:11 "The reason is that in six days the LORD **made** everything—the sky [heavens], the earth, the sea, and everything in them. On the seventh day he rested. So the LORD blessed the Sabbath day and ·made it holy [consecrated/sanctified it]." (EXB)

17.) Exodus 20:11 "In six days I, the LORD, **made** the earth, the sky, the seas, and everything in them, but on the seventh day I rested. That is why I, the LORD, blessed the Sabbath and made it holy." (GN-TEV)

18.) Exodus 20:11 "For in sixe dayes the Lord **made** the heauen and the earth, the sea, and all that in them is, and rested the seuenth day: therefore the Lorde blessed the Sabbath day, and hallowed it." (GNV)

19.) Exodus 20:11 "In six days the LORD **made** heaven, earth, and the sea, along with everything in them. He didn't work on the seventh day. That's why the LORD blessed the day he stopped his work and set this day apart as holy." (GW)

20.) Exodus 20:11 "For the LORD **made** the heavens and the earth, the sea, and everything in them in six days; then He rested on the seventh day. Therefore the LORD blessed the Sabbath day and declared it holy." (HCSB)

21.) Exodus 20:11 "because the LORD **made** the heavens and the earth and the sea, and all that is in them, in six days, then he rested on the seventh day. Therefore, the LORD blessed the Sabbath day and made it holy." (ISV)

22.) Exodus 20:11 "for in six days the LORD **made** heaven and earth, the sea, and all that in them is, and rested on the seventh day; wherefore the LORD blessed the sabbath day, and hallowed it." (JPSB)

23.) Exodus 20:11 "for *in* six days the LORD **made** the heavens and earth, the sea, and all that *is* in them and rested the seventh day; therefore, the LORD blessed the sabbath day and sanctified it." (JUB)

24.) Exodus 20:11 "For *in* six days the LORD **made** heaven and earth, the sea, and all that in them *is,* and rested the seventh day: wherefore the LORD blessed the sabbath day, and hallowed it." (KJV)

25.) Exodus 20:11 "For in sixe dayes the Lord **made** heauen and earth, the sea, and all that in them is, and rested the seuenth day: wherefore the Lord blessed the Sabbath day, and halowed it." (KJV—1611)

26.) Exodus 20:11 "For in six days the LORD **made** heaven and earth, the sea, and all that in them is, and rested the seventh day. Therefore the LORD blessed the Sabbath day and hallowed it." (KJ21)

27.) Exodus 20:11 "For in six days the Lord **made** the heavens and the earth, the sea, and all that is in them, and rested on the seventh day; therefore the Lord blessed the sabbath day, and hallowed it." (LEESER)

28.) Exodus 20:11 "because *in* six days Yahweh **made** the heavens and the earth, the sea and all that *is* in them, and on the seventh day he rested. Therefore Yahweh blessed the seventh day and consecrated it." (LEX)

29.) Exodus 20:11 "For *in* six days Jehovah **made** the heavens and the earth, the sea, and all which *is* in them, and He rested on the seventh day; on account of this Jehovah blessed the sabbath day and sanctified it." (LTV)

30.) Exodus 20:11 "For *in* six days Jehovah **made** the heavens and the earth, the sea, and all that *is* in them, and rested the seventh day. Therefore Jehovah blessed the Sabbath day, and sanctified it." (MKJV)

31.) Exodus 20:11 "For in six days the LORD **made** the heavens and the earth, the sea and all that is in them, and rested on the seventh day; therefore the LORD blessed the sabbath day and made it holy." (NASB)

32.) Exodus 20:11 "The reason is that in six days the LORD **made** everything—the sky, the earth, the sea, and everything in them. On the seventh day he rested. So the LORD blessed the Sabbath day and made it holy." (NCV)

33.) Exodus 20:11 "For in six days the LORD **made** the heavens and the earth and the sea and all that is in them, and he rested on the seventh day; therefore the LORD blessed the Sabbath day and set it apart as holy." (NET)

34.) Exodus 20:11 "for in six days the LORD **made** heaven and earth, the sea, and all that is in them, and rested the seventh day; therefore the LORD blessed the seventh day, and made it holy." (NHEB)

35.) Exodus 20:11 "In six days the Lord **made** the heavens, the earth, the sea and everything in th5m. But he rested on the seventh day. So the Lord blessed the Sabbath day and made it holy." (NIRV)

36.) Exodus 20:11 "For in six days the Lord **made** the heavens, the earth, the sea, and everything in them; but on the seventh day he rested. That is why the Lord blessed the Sabbath day and set it apart as holy." (NLT)

37.) Exodus 20:11 "For in six days the Lord **made** the heavens, the earth, the sea and all that is in them. And He rested on the seventh day. So the Lord gave honor to the Day of Rest and made it holy." (NLV)

38.) Exodus 20:11 "In six days *Yahweh* **made** heaven, earth, and the sea, along with everything in them. He didn't work on the seventh day. That's why *Yahweh* blessed the day he stopped his work and set this day apart as holy." (NOG)

39.) Exodus 20:11 "For in six days the Lord **made** heaven and earth, the sea, and all that is in them, but rested the seventh day; therefore the Lord blessed the sabbath day and consecrated it." (NRSV)

40.) Exodus 20:11 "For in sheshet yamim Hashem **made** Shomayim and Ha'Aretz, the yam, and all that in them is, and rested Yom HaShevi'i; for this reason Hashem blessed Yom HaShabbos, and set it apart as kodesh." (OJB)

41.) Exodus 20:11 "For in six days the LORD **made** heaven and earth, the sea, and all that in them is, and rested the seventh day; therefore the LORD blessed the sabbath day, and hallowed it." (RSV)

42.) Exodus 20:11 "For in six days יהוה **made** the heavens and the earth, the sea, and all that is in them, and rested the seventh day. Therefore יהוה blessed the Sabbath day and set it apart." (SCRIP)

43.) Exodus 20:11 "For in six days the Lord **made** the heaven, earth, and sea, and everything in them, and rested the seventh day; so he blessed the Sabbath day and set it aside for rest." (TLB)

44.) Exodus 20:11 "For in six days Adonai **made** heaven and earth, the sea, and all that is in them, and rested on the seventh day. Thus Adonai blessed Yom Shabbat, and made it holy." (TLV)

45.) Exodus 20:11 "For in sixe dayes the Lorde **made** both heauen and erth and the see and all that in them is and rested the seuenth daye: wherfore the Lorde blessed the Sabbath daye and halowed it." (TYN)

46.) Exodus 20:11 "For the Eternal **made** the heavens *above,* the earth *below,* the seas, and all the creatures in them in six days. Then, on the seventh day, He rested. That is why He blessed the Sabbath Day and made it sacred." (VOICE)

47.) Exodus 20:11 "for in six days Yahweh **made** heaven and earth, the sea, and all that is in them, and rested the seventh day; therefore Yahweh blessed the Sabbath day, and made it holy." (WEB)

48.) Exodus 20:11 "For in six days the LORD **made** heaven and earth, the sea, and all that is in them, and rested the seventh day: wherefore the LORD blessed the sabbath-day, and hallowed it." (WEBSTER)

49.) Exodus 20:11 "for in sixe dayes God **made** heuene and erthe, the see, and alle thingis that ben in tho, and restide in the seuenthe dai; herfor the Lord blesside the dai of the sabat, and halewide it." (WYC)

50.) Exodus 20:11 "for six days hath Jehovah **made** the heavens and the earth, the sea, and all that *is* in them, and resteth in the seventh day; therefore hath Jehovah blessed the Sabbath-day, and doth sanctify it." (YLT)

In my 40+ years of study of this issue, I have not discovered a single reputable English translation that agrees with what the Young-Earth creationists claim about Exodus 20:11. Oh, there are plenty of Young-Earth creationists' books, videos, literature, and websites that say Exodus 20:11 proves God CREATED the universe in six days, six to eight thousand years ago. Yet, they provide no linguistic evidence for their claim. Why not? They can't. There is no evidence for it. For over six hundred years, English translators have consistently translated Exodus 20:11 using the word "MADE," and never the word "CREATED." Young-Earth creationists like to brag about accepting "the literal translation" of the Bible. If that were true, why don't they accept the literal translation of every English translation since John Wycliffe in 1395? I suspect they will tell us these English translators don't understand English.

Chapter Eight: A Closer Look at the Six Days

Don't you love those quizzes that give you a pattern to complete like, "What's the next number in this series: 2… 4… 8… 16… 32… ___?" Well, we're going to do the same thing with the first chapter in Genesis. Each of the six days begins with a Divine decree of, "And God said, Let…" Each day ends with, "and the evening and the morning were…" The Bible reveals when the days began and when the days ended. God makes the beginning and ending of each day very obvious. God also tells us what He created on each particular day. He tells us WHAT was created WHEN. So, let's take a little quiz to see if we know WHAT was created WHEN. We will start at Day Six and work back to Day One using the *King James Version*.

The Six Days of Creation

DAY 6

ENDED: Verse 31
"And the evening and the morning were the sixth day."

BEGAN: Verse 24
"And God said, Let the earth bring forth the living creature after his kind, cattle, and creeping thing, and beast of the earth after his kind: and it was so."

DAY 5

ENDED: Verse 23
"And the evening and the morning were the fifth day."

BEGAN: Verse 20
"And God said, Let the waters bring forth abundantly the moving creature that hath life, and the fowl *that* may fly above the earth in the open firmament of heaven."

DAY 4

ENDED: Verse 19
"And the evening and the morning were the fourth day."

BEGAN: Verse 14
"And God said, Let there be lights in the firmament of the heaven to divide the day from the night; and let them be for signs, and for seasons, and for days, and years:"

DAY 3

ENDED: Verse 13
"And the evening and the morning were the third day."

BEGAN: Verse 9
"And God said, Let the waters under the heaven be gathered together unto one place, and let the dry *land* appear: and it was so."

DAY 2

ENDED: Verse 8
"And the evening and the morning were the second day."

BEGAN: Verse 6
"And God said, Let there be a firmament in the midst of the waters, and let it divide the waters from the waters."

DAY 1

ENDED: Verse 5
"And the evening and the morning
??????????????????????????

BEGAN: Verse ?

Now answer this question: When did the first day of creation begin?

Do you need a clue? Okay, look for the verse BEFORE VERSE FIVE that says, "And God said, Let..." Look closely; don't be fooled by any preconceived ideas!

The answer is verse three. Verse three says, "**And God said, 'Let** there be light'..."

The first day of the six-day creation begins at Genesis 1:3, not at Genesis 1:1. God set up a pattern for us to see how He separated the days.

The Beginning of Each Day

Day One—Verse 3: "And God said, let..."
Day Two—Verse 6: "And God said, let..."
Day Three—Verse 9: "And God said, let..."
Day Four—Verse 14: "And God said, let..."
Day Five—Verse 20: "And God said, let..."
Day Six—Verse 24: "And God said, let..."

The End of Each Day

Day One—Verse 5: "And the evening and the morning were the first day."
Day Two—Verse 8: "And the evening and the morning were the second day."
Day Three—Verse 13: "And the evening and the morning were the third day."
Day Four—Verse 19: "And the evening and the morning were the fourth day."
Day Five—Verse 23: "And the evening and the morning were the fifth day."
Day Six—Verse 31: "And the evening and the morning were the sixth day."

The twelve points of this pattern are apparent and consistent, but Young-Earth creationists and Day-Age creationists reject this pattern. They say Day One begins at Genesis 1:1. Personally, when I see a pattern in the Bible created by the Holy Spirit, I'm going to interpret His Word according to His pattern. Genesis 1:1-2 is not part of Day One. Genesis 1:1-2 describe events BEFORE the first day of creation. Therefore, Genesis 1:1-2 must have occurred before the events of Genesis 1:3-31.

This pattern is why others want to make Genesis 1:1-2 a summary or title instead of an act of creation. They recognize Genesis 1:1-2 doesn't fit the pattern, but they can't let them describe any creation before Day One. Therefore, it must be a title or summary of the following verses. This interpretation creates a contradiction. If Genesis 1:1-2 is a title/summary of what God does during the six days, then the title/summary is erroneous. The creative acts of Genesis 1:1 begin with an *EX NIHILO* creation. The heavens and the earth are created out of nothing. The creative acts of Genesis 1:3-31 begin with preexisting matter and energy. If Genesis 1:3-31 is a parallel account of Genesis 1:1-2, then God's creative acts in Genesis 1:1 ought to be the same as His creative acts in Genesis 1:3-31. They aren't! Genesis 1:1 says God created (*BARA*) the earth (*ERETS*), but Genesis 1:3-31 never tells us that. It uses *BARA* for the creation of things ON THE EARTH, but it never uses *BARA* for the creation OF THE EARTH. The same is true for the heavens. The heavens, the earth, and the ocean are already there. The initial states of these creative acts don't match. The first is from nothing; the second is from pre-existing matter.

Not only don't their initial states match, their final states don't match. At the end of the six days, the earth is inhabited by life according to Genesis 1:31. Yet, Genesis 1:2 ends with the earth desolate and dead. At the end of Genesis 1:31, there is light. At the end of Genesis 1:2, the earth is in darkness. At the end of Genesis 1:31, the earth is "very good." At the end of Genesis 1:2, the earth is "without form, and void." The conditions don't match. This is why I reject the idea Genesis 1:1-2 is a title or summary that describes the same period of time as Genesis 1:3-31. It would be hard to imagine Genesis 1:1-2 describes the creation week when the description makes such big mistakes. Did God fail to realize this when He inspired Moses to write? Genesis 1:1-2 can't be a title or summary of Genesis 1:3-31 because they start and end with different conditions They also describe different acts of creation. The things created in Genesis 1:1 (the heavens, earth, and ocean) are not created in Genesis 1:3-31. The things created in Genesis 1:3-31 (modern-day plants, fish, birds, animals, Adam and Eve, *etc*.) are not created in Genesis 1:1. If Genesis 1:1-2 is a title/summary of Genesis 1:3-31, they would describe the same acts of creation. They don't. Therefore, Genesis 1:1-2 must have occurred before the events of Genesis 1:3-31.

There is another reason Genesis 1:1-2 cannot describe the same conditions and events as Genesis 1:3-31. God describes them differently. As He restores the heavens and the earth, He gives us His opinion. During the six days, He contrasts the conditions and events of the restoration with the conditions and events in Genesis 1:2. God said the light was good in Genesis 1:4. He never said the darkness was good in Genesis 1:2. God said the appearance of dry land was good in Genesis 1:10. He never said the water-covered earth was good in Genesis 1:2. God said the earth with plant life in Genesis 1:12 was good. He never said the earth without plant life was good in Genesis 1:2. God said the sun, moon, and stars shining in the night sky in Genesis 1:18 was good. He never said the darkened sky in Genesis 1:2 was good? God said the creation of aquatic life and birds in Genesis 1:21 was good. He never said the lifeless oceans and sky in Genesis 1:2 were good? Finally, God said the creation of animals and man on Day Six was very good. He never said the dead, desolate, and dark earth in Genesis 1:2 was very good. Every mention of "good" in Genesis 1:3-31 describes the opposite condition of the things described in Genesis 1:2. Wouldn't this imply God considered the earth in Genesis 1:2 as the opposite of good? (This is why God doesn't call the restoration of the atmosphere on Day Two, "good." The condition of the atmosphere is not mentioned in Genesis 1:1-2.) By revealing His evaluations of the days, God tells us He did not consider Genesis 1:1-2 and Genesis 1:3-31 equivalent. The restoration was declared, "good." The original creation wasn't. The original creation came before the six days. Genesis 1:1 is a creative act all by itself. Since Genesis 1:1 is a creative act, then God created the heavens and the earth before Day One of the creation week. God reveals two separate acts of creation. The first is Genesis 1:1 and the second is Genesis 1:3-31. There were two beginnings: DUO-GENESIS.

Let's look at this in more detail. If there was only one creation, (one beginning) then there is a problem. When God created the "heavens and the earth" in Genesis 1:1, what did He create? The most ancient belief from the Hebrews themselves is God created time, space, matter, and energy in the beginning. (This agrees with the modern belief from science that time, space, matter, and energy came into being at the Big Bang.) Genesis 1:1 speaks of the creation of the physical universe, but it doesn't give us the details. It doesn't tell us how long ago it was, or how long it took. When God created the "heavens" in Genesis 1:1, did He create the galaxies, the quasars, the nebulae, the sun, the moon, and the stars, or did He just create the raw matter and energy He would use later to create the galaxies, the quasars, the nebulae, the sun, the moon, and the stars? Either way, Genesis 1:1 proves God created something before Genesis 1:3. If He didn't create matter and energy in the beginning, then did He create the physical time-space continuum with nothing physical in it? That interpretation contradicts Genesis 1:1 because it says He also created the earth. (It also contradicts science. Science proves time, space, matter, and energy all came into existence at the Big Bang.) Now, it is grammatically possible to believe Genesis

1:1-2 means God created the time-space continuum with nothing but the desolate and dead earth in it. If you believe that, however, you can't turn around and say Genesis 1:1-2 is a summary of the six days of creation. The six days don't end with an empty universe filled only by a desolate and dead earth. The two creations don't match according to their details. So, if you believe God created the time-space continuum with just the earth in it, then logically Genesis 1:1-2 was an act (or acts) of creation that came before the six days of creation. (Genesis 1:3-31) On the other hand, if you interpret the "heavens" to mean more than empty space, (It included the galaxies, the quasars, the nebulae, the sun, the moon, and the stars.) then you have to agree the sun, moon, and stars existed before Genesis 1:3-31, the six days of creation. Either way you interpret the "heavens," the context demands a creative act (or acts) before the six days.

What does it mean when God created (*BARA*) the heavens in Genesis 1:1? What does it mean when God made (*ASAH*) the sun, moon, and stars in Genesis 1:16? It's obvious that "made" does not mean the same thing as "create" in this context. The six days chronologically came after Genesis 1:1. Genesis 1:1 and Genesis 1:16 can't be referring to the same events. God couldn't have created the sun and the stars and the moon on Day Four if He had created them before the first day. Nevertheless, the Bible says He made them on Day Four. "Made" in Genesis 1:16 must mean something different than "create" in Genesis 1:1. Contrary to what some people think, creation did not begin with, "Let there be light." Something physical had been created before God said, "Let there be light." The heavens had been created (*BARA*) and the earth had been created. (*BARA*) This immediately raises the question, "What was the physical source of that light?" If there were three days and three nights before Day Four, from where/what did that light come?

Some Young-Earth creationists believe there was a glowing ball of matter somewhere out in space, but it wasn't the sun. Where they find that in the Bible is beyond me. It doesn't fit with any known scientific discoveries either. Other Young-Earth creationists say God Himself was the source. "God is light," they quote. (1 John 1:5) While it is true God is light, Genesis 1:3 doesn't say God was the source of that light. That is an assumption, not a revelation. Yes, God is light, but God is not the same as natural/physical light. God is not photons. God is not a particle and/or a wave of electromagnetic energy depending on how you measure Him. God's Light is a supernatural light that cannot be blocked, impeded, modified, or altered by physical matter the way physical light can be. There can be no shadows of God's Light; it penetrates all things. His Light penetrates the body, the soul, and the spirit. That's why it is so unbearable for fallen man to stand in His Glory. His Light is a terrible thing for fallen man to experience. Throughout Scripture, when God reveals even the tiniest, faintest glimpse of His Light, people fall down in terror and awe. Moreover, they would die if He did not supernaturally preserve them. No; God's Light is not the same as natural light. The light we see in the natural realm is a dim foreshadow (excuse the pun) of God's Light. The light God commanded into being in Genesis 1:3 cannot be the Light of God Himself. You see, the literal translation of Genesis 1:3 is, "Then God said, 'Light: come to be,' and light came to be." It is our old friend

HAYAH, the word used for a dynamic "coming to be." He commanded this light to, "come into being." We will look at *HAYAH* in much greater detail later; for now, let me quickly say *HAYAH* is not a word that can be used of any of God's eternal attributes. God could not command one of His eternal attributes to "come into being." He has always been Light. His Light is eternal and cannot be created. Furthermore, the context of Genesis 1 is the physical realm. All the other things He commands to "come into being" (*HAYAH*) are physical things. When He says, "Let the waters…," He is talking about physical water. When He says, "Let the dry land…," He is talking about physical land. When He says, "Let the firmament (atmosphere) divide the waters," He is talking about the physical atmosphere. When He says, "Let the earth bring forth grass, fruit trees, *etc*.," He is talking about physical vegetation. When He says, "Let the waters bring forth moving creatures and fowl that fly in the heavens, and let the earth bring forth living creatures," He is talking about physical fish, birds, and animals. The light He commanded to come into being in Genesis 1:3 was also a physical thing. It was physical light; not His own supernatural Light. If it was His own inherent, supernatural Light, it already existed eternally. He could not command His eternal, supernatural Light to, "come into being." He couldn't use *HAYAH* for this command since *HAYAH* is used in connection with "becoming" or "coming to be." There is no grammatical, historical, Biblical, or scientific justification for stepping outside the context of the natural realm when looking for the source of the light in Genesis 1:3. God provides the context for all He called into being in Genesis 1:3-31. That context is the physical realm. Besides, if God was the source of light during the day, what happened to God during the night? Did He quit being light? Did His attributes change? Did He quit being God?

Detour into Darkness

Since we're talking about God's Light, let me take a detour here and go back to what I said about God creating darkness.

Isaiah 45:7 "I form the light, and create darkness: I make peace, and create evil: I the LORD do all these *things*." (KJV)

Two thoughts come to mind as I read this verse. The first thought is a fact. The second thought is a speculation. First the fact: Since God's Light is eternal and cannot be created or uncreated, and since God is omnipresent, it would be impossible for the universe to experience darkness if God's presence was visible. (Remember, we aren't talking about physical, photonic light.)

1 John 1:5 "This then is the message which we have heard of him, and declare unto you, that God is light, and in him is no darkness at all." (KJV)

God is light and God is omnipresent in His universe. Therefore, His Light would be omnipresent in the universe unless He did "something" to make it possible for His Light not to be seen. That "something" was to create darkness. God created darkness as a way by which His Light would not be seen in the physical universe. "Darkness" in this sense is the hiding of the experience of God's Light, not the non-existence of His Light. His Light is eternal and can never become non-existent; it is as universally present as He is. His light is all around us; we just don't see it. God created some system, method, or process by which His Light would be invisible and undetectable. He called it, "darkness," and from time to time during the course of history, He would draw back the curtain of darkness a little and let a few select people have small glimpses of His Light. It was always a terrifying experience for mortal men. (We love the darkness.) Darkness must be created or else the universe would be completely filled with God's Light. (Which is what its future-eternal state will be, praise the Lord!)

Now, let's look at my speculation. If God can hide His Eternal, Glorious, Supernatural, Spiritual Light in the physical realm, then I believe He could do the same thing to physical, photonic light. The Gap Theory is often rejected on the belief it would be impossible for the earth to be dark if the sun existed before Day One. If the sun existed before the earth was created, then the earth could have never been in darkness as described in Genesis 1:2. But I believe God hid physical light in the physical realm just as He hides His Own Spiritual Light in the physical realm. He simply made the photons go dark. I don't know how He did it, but it seems to me Isaiah 45:7 (creating darkness) makes the Gap Theory a viable explanation for why the Pre-Adamic earth was dark even though the sun already existed. God created darkness to be the "garment" in which He wrapped the earth. (Job 38:9) Darkness wasn't an eternal condition; it had to be created. Light had to be hidden in order for darkness to cover the face of the deep. The earth was in light at one time, but then God wrapped it in darkness at a later time. Since God can hide His Own Supernatural Light, I don't think it would be any problem for Him to hide the physical light of the sun, the moon, and the stars.

If you ask people what God's first act of creation was, many will tell you it was light. They quote Genesis 1:3, "And God said let there be light," as their proof. Other people will tell you the creation of the heavens and the earth in Genesis 1:1 came before light was created in Genesis 1:3. So, when was light created? Whether light was created in Genesis 1:1 or Genesis 1:3 depends on the creation theory. The problem with explaining WHEN light was created, is connected to WHY the earth was dark in Genesis 1:2. Day-Age believers believe light was created in Genesis 1:1, but then they have to rely on some form of the Canopy Theory to explain why the earth was dark in Genesis 1:2. (I would take a detour to explain the Canopy Theory here, but since I am already in a detour, I don't want to take a detour from my detour. I'll explain the Canopy Theory later.) Young-Earth believers say light was created in Genesis 1:3, but then they have to come up with an explanation for the physical source of that light, since the sun, moon, and stars weren't created until Genesis 1:16. Gap Theory believers believe Genesis 1:3 was the restoration, not the creation, of the light that had once been. The earth was dark in Genesis 1:2 because God had extinguished the light. However, the Gap Theory doesn't say when light was FIRST created. The Gap Theory allows for light to have been formed/fashioned by a process; not *EX NIHILO* and not instantaneously. The Gap Theory recognizes the Bible does not use *BARA* in connection with light. The Bible doesn't say God created (*BARA*) light in Genesis 1:1. The Bible doesn't say God created (*BARA*) light in Genesis 1:3. The Bible doesn't say God created (*BARA*) light in Genesis 1:16. Read Isaiah 45:7 again very carefully:

Isaiah 45:7 "I form the light, and create darkness: I make peace, and create evil: I the LORD do all these *things.*" (KJV)

Notice Isaiah says God FORMED light. The word Isaiah used is *YATSAR*. I have mentioned *YATSAR* before, and briefly said it means, "to form." And yes, it means, "to form," but it also means "to fashion," "to mold," "to shape," "to craft," "to forge," and things like that. It never means "to create" in the sense of creating something from nothing, and it never means "to create" instantaneously. It is not equivalent to *BARA*. It always means to cause something to come into being by a process that requires forming, molding, carving, shaping, crafting, *etc*. Isaiah doesn't say God CREATED light, and neither does anyone one else in the Bible; not in the Old Testament and not in the New Testament. The Bible never says God CREATED light. (Except in the general sense He created all things.) It never directly connects *BARA* with *OWR*. The only two words the Bible uses in explaining the origin of light are *HAYAH* and *YATSAR*. Light came to be, and light was formed. *ASAH* (made) is used in connection with *OWR* only in Psalms 136:7 where it says God made the great "lights." (In the plural, not the singular.) In this case *OWR* is used for the bodies of light; the sun, moon, and stars, but not light itself. This means the Bible speaks only of light coming to be, and light being formed. The Bible never speaks of light being created.

I know what you're thinking: "Well, this is interesting, and possibly even strange, but what does it prove?" I think it proves God's Word agrees with God's Work. The Bible says light was formed, not created *EX NIHILO*. What does science reveal about the origin of light? It was formed, not created *EX NIHILO*. Time, space, matter, and energy were created *EX NIHILO* instantaneously at the Big Bang, but visible light wasn't created at that time. Light formed much later.

You've probably seen videos or movies depicting the Big Bang. They always show a tremendous blast of light accompanied by the deafening sound of a huge explosion. The truth is it wasn't an explosion. In reality, it was an extremely rapid expansion of nothing into timespacematterenergy… and then into timespace and matterenergy… and then into time-space and matter-energy… and then into time and space and matter and energy. There was no explosion and there was no sound. In fact, there was no light. At the instant of the Big Bang, there were no neutrons, or protons, or electrons, or photons, or mesons, or leptons, or leprechauns, or anything like that. There was no light because it took time for light to form. Light came into being because the universe had to be fashioned into a consistency that allowed for light. That process took about 400,000 years. Prior to that, the universe was too hot and dense for light. It wasn't until the universe was stretched-out and cooled that light came into being. Prior to that, the universe was photon-opaque. Once the universe was fashioned into the proper conditions, it became photon-transparent. Science proves light CAME INTO BEING (*HAYAH*) and was FORMED (*YATSAR*) 400,000 years after the universe was created. Science never describes light as being created from nothing. Science describes the origin of physical light the same way God does in the Bible.

How did Isaiah, who lived 2,800 years ago, know light was formed but never created? How did all the human authors of the Books of the Bible know they should never say light was created? It seems to me if the Bible was written by a bunch of primitive, ignorant shepherds and fishermen bent on glorifying a God of their imaginations, then at least one of them would have said God created light. Creating light would seem to be a glorious, miraculous, awe-inspiring thing for God to do. Why not give Him that glory? Why not? Because while a bunch of primitive, ignorant shepherds and fishermen were given the blessings of writing the Bible, they were not the authors of the Bible; the Holy Spirit was. That is why the Words of God perfectly match the Works of God.

Back Into the Light

Okay, the detour is over. Let's get back to talking about the light. The light described in Genesis 1:3-13 (from the beginning of Day One to the end of Day Three) is photonic light/physical light. We know this because Genesis defines each time period as an evening/dusk/sunset and a morning/dawn/sunrise. Dusk is the time of the solar day at which the sun has "set" below the horizon, but due to atmospheric refraction, its light is still present. The same is true of dawn. It is the time of day when the sun's light is visible because of refraction, even though the sun itself has not yet "risen" above the horizon. In both cases, the sun is not visible, but its light is. Dusk and dawn are caused by air molecules (physical particles) refracting/bending/distorting waves of physical (photonic) light. If the light from Day One to Day Three was God's Light, then we would have to admit that something physical has power over one of God's attributes. We would have to admit that God's Light can't penetrate physical particles. The only reason it was dark on one side of the earth for nights one through three was because the earth blocked the light. If that was God's Light, then we must believe physical particles can somehow block, bend, distort, impede, or degrade God's Light so as to cause dawn, dusk, and night. If physical particles can do that to one of God's attributes, then we might also speculate that mass, or gravity, or electromagnetic energy, or aluminum foil wrapped around our heads could somehow distort or degrade God's Righteousness and Justice. I think I'll start a new religion: As long as we wear aluminum foil on our heads, God's Omniscience can't penetrate our thoughts and we can go around lusting and hating and coveting all we want. (But watch out for a sudden increase in lightning strikes on people wearing aluminum foil on their heads.)

As you carefully read the text, you will see there are no distinctions made between the source of light for the first three days and the source of the light for the last three days. God doesn't say He was that light for three days and then the sun became that light after that. That's what Young-Earthers want you to believe, but no Bible verse states that. There is no Biblical indication the source of light for days one through three differs from the source of light for days four through six. Both of these light sources divided the day from the night in the exact same way for the exact same duration. Both of these lights were natural lights that produced natural shadows and partial shadows of identical nature and duration (night, dusk, dawn). Both of these lights were coming from the exact same position in space, or else there would be a shift in the measurement of day and night when God shifted the sources of light. (A twelve-hour day wouldn't follow the previous twelve-hour night, or a twelve-hour night wouldn't follow the previous twelve-hour day; there would be some change in the pattern.) All six days had the same kind of light and the same source of light, the sun. The sun was created before Day Four. That agrees with Genesis 1:1, but it appears to contradict Genesis 1:14-18.

Genesis 1:14-19 "And God said, Let there be lights in the firmament of the heaven to divide the day from the night; and let them be for signs, and for seasons, and for days, and years: *{15}* And let them be for lights in the firmament of the heaven to give light upon the earth: and it was so. *{16}* And God made two great lights; the greater light to rule the day, and the lesser light to rule the night: *he made* the stars also. *{17}* And God set them in the firmament of the heaven to give light upon the earth, *{18}* And to rule over the day and over the night, and to divide the light from the darkness: and God saw that *it was* good. *{19}* And the evening and the morning were the fourth day." (KJV)

Those who adhere to the Day-Age Theory can't explain this. The sun couldn't have been created millions of years after grass and trees and seed-bearing plants. Something seems wrong; something is in the wrong order. The Young-Earth Theory has a different explanation: The sun, moon, and stars weren't created until four days after the creation of the earth. But, as we have seen, this raises the question about what it means when it says the "heavens" were created in Genesis 1:1. If the sun, moon, and stars weren't created, then the heavens were empty, and that raises another question. How could the heavens declare the Glory of God, if the heavens were empty? If the heavens of Genesis 1:1 contained nothing, they declared nothing. Nothing reveals nothing. It also raises a question about the purpose or FUNCTION of the light. Genesis 1:14 says the light of Day Four was, "to divide the day from the night," but the light called into existence on Day One (Genesis 1:3) ALREADY had been dividing the day from the night. This wasn't a new function because it wasn't a new light. Days one through three had experienced this same division. The earth already had three days and three nights; three evenings and three mornings. The division of day and night on Day Four was not a new division. It was not a new function. It was already happening. The light of Day One was already dividing the day from the night. The light of Day Four was not a new creation. If you were standing on the earth during the first three days, you would have seen three periods of dark and three periods of light. Light and dark were already divided. The light and dark periods of days one through three were literal twenty-four-hour days. The light and dark periods of days four through six were literal twenty-four-hour days. The light of days one through three produced identical twenty-four-hour days as the light of days four through six. Genesis 1:14 doesn't hint of a change in the source of light. Genesis 1:14 doesn't say the light on Day Four had a different duration. Genesis 1:14 doesn't say the light on Day Four had a different function. Rather, it was a continuation of the same source with the same duration and the same function. The light of days one through three produced the same duration of day and night the sun produced in days four through six. The Bible gives no indication there was a switch in the source of the light that divided the days from the nights. The Bible doesn't change the function of the light in Genesis 1:14. That's why I think it was the sun. The sun was given the function of dividing the day and the night in Genesis 1:3, and it continued that same function in Genesis 1:14. What is different is this: If you look carefully at the passage, you will see there are some new functions added to the LIGHTS on Day Four. The LIGHT of Genesis 1:3 divided the day from the night. The LIGHTS of Genesis 1:14 were going to be for "signs," for "seasons," for "days," and for "years." Note how it has shifted from "LIGHT" (singular) to "LIGHTS" (plural). We now include the moon and the stars and we now have four new functions: signs, seasons, days, and years. What are these new functions?

What-If?

Before I talk about these new functions, I want to talk about the "What-If Game." The reason I'm doing this is because I am going to play the "What-If Game" too. I'm going to propose some explanations for what God was doing with the LIGHT, and what God was doing with the LIGHTS. The things I will propose are not things the Bible directly says happened. They are things I think fit best with what the Bible does directly say happened. There seems to be some confusion, so everybody proposes "What-If" scenarios. The Young-Earth creationists have two "What-If" proposals. First, "What if God was that source of light?" Second, "What if there was a glowing ball of matter in space?" The Day-Age creationists have only one "What-If" proposal. "What if the days were ages?" Actually, the Day-Age proposal doesn't help at all. How could there be plant life on earth for millions of years, but no sun? Anyway, everyone else makes "What-If" proposals, so I feel I should be allowed to do it as well. However, my "What-If" proposals will not be like their "What-If" proposals. Mine will be scientifically and/or Biblically plausible. I won't resort to things such as the speed of light being changed. Young-Earthers propose things that are highly improbable, and certainly not observable. Their "What-If" list is quite illogical. What if there were no Laws of Thermodynamics? What if light traveled through

Riemannian Space? What if tremendous earthquakes caused the earth's crust to create deep depressions at the exact spots where the mouth of every major river would be? What if gigantic, cataclysmic waves of water, moving hundreds of miles per hour, were powerful enough to rip out forests, but so calm at the same time and in the same place, as to allow pollen to settle gently to the bottom undisturbed? My "What-If" proposals, on the other hand, are things God has done elsewhere in the Bible or else things that are scientifically observable and probable. Mine are at least believable. That doesn't mean these things are what God DID, but it certainly means these things are things God WOULD DO, COULD DO, or HAS DONE. The things I propose will have scientific or Scriptural precedents.

What Was the Condition of the Earth Just Before the Restoration?

God mentions the heavens and the earth in Genesis 1:1. God mentions the earth and the deep in Genesis 1:2. An interesting thing to ask is, "Why did He mention the earth if it was completely under water and in total darkness, as other creationists suggest?" After all, if we were looking at this from a time-space perspective, you wouldn't even see the earth. Why mention the earth if there was no earth to see? God mentions the earth even though the earth had never been visible according to the creationists who reject the Ruin-Restoration Theory. What is God's purpose for giving us the Genesis Creation Account? What if Genesis 1 is the historic description of what you would see God creating in the beginnings if you were there? After all, why would the Genesis Creation Account describe things you couldn't see? When God created the plants, could they be seen? When God created fish and birds, could they be seen? When God created the animals, could they be seen? When God created Adam and Eve, could they be seen? Yes. You could see everything He created. This means you could see the heavens and the earth when He created them in Genesis 1:1. But, how could you see the heavens if there was no light? How could you see the earth if it was completely under water and in complete darkness? Everything else God created and made in the Genesis Creation Account were things that could be seen. Why would the creation of the heavens and the earth be different? God is describing the things we would see if we were in time/space watching Him create. That means you would have seen the heavens and the earth in Genesis 1:1 when He created them. That means the earth wasn't under water when it was created. (If it was, you couldn't see it.) That means it came to be under water at a later point in time. That also means there was something in the heavens that could be seen. If God created the time-space continuum with nothing in it except the dead, desolate, and darkened earth, then there would nothing else in the universe. So, why does God mention the heavens if there was nothing to see? Logic tells us the things in the heavens were visible before God turned out the lights. Logic also tells us the earth could be seen before God covered it in water. Logic tells us the Gap Theory is true.

Phony Photons

God said, "Let there be light," on Day One (Genesis 1:3). God also said, "Let there be lights," on Day Four (Genesis 1:14). In neither place does He use *BARA*, the word for "create." He uses *HAYAH* in both places. Since He didn't use *BARA* in either place, we must not jump to the conclusion these were new creations. Young-Earth creationists jump to that conclusion. But, what if light wasn't a new creation? What if light existed prior to Genesis 1:3? Gap Theory proponents believe the sun, the moon, and the stars were created long before Genesis 1:14. The heavens were dark only because the light from these luminaries was hidden during the time God judged the earth. On Day Four, He simply called them back into appearance. On Day Four, God made the heavenly luminaries REAPPEAR in the sky. According to the Gap Theory, Genesis 1:14-16 speaks of the lights coming into view (experience), not of them coming into being (existence). *HAYAH* is used here to describe the experiential, not the existential. (It is imperative to know the difference when interpreting the meaning of *HAYAH* in its various usages. This often provides the key to whether an interpretation is just grammatically correct, or if it is informationally correct.)

The Gap Theory teaches this was the reappearance of the sun, moon and stars that had been there for billions of years. The light had existed all along; it's just that God prevented the earth from experiencing it. The earth could now experience their light again. Young-Earth creationists don't like this interpretation. Young-Earth creationists positively go crazy at this interpretation. They insist God actually created the heavenly luminaries on Day Four, even though the word *BARA* is not used for anything on Day Four. They object to the Gap Theory's idea that on Day Four, God made the stars REAPPEAR in the night sky. I find this a strange objection when you recall how they believe God created beams of light in mid-stream on Day Four to make the "stars" APPEAR in the night sky. According to Young-Earth creationists, those weren't actual stars Adam saw in the night sky; they only APPEARED to be stars. Young-Earth creationists have no problem believing God would cause the APPEARANCE of stars, but they have a problem believing God would cause the REAPPEARANCE of stars. They have no problem with believing the light appeared to come from the stars, but they have a problem believing the light actually came from the stars. They believe God CREATED (*BARA*) beams of light in mid-stream, but that requires some fancy interpretation skills. It disagrees with what the Bible says about light. We have seen how the Bible never says God CREATED (*BARA*) light; anywhere, at any time. The Bible says God formed (*YATSAR*) light, and light came to be (*HAYAH*) at God's command, but the Bible never says God created (*BARA*) light. Isaiah never says God created (*BARA*) light. Moses never says God created (*BARA*) light. Job never says God created (*BARA*) light. The Old Testament never says God created (*BARA*) light. The New Testament never says God created (*KTIZO* Strong's Number G2936—the Greek equivalent of the Hebrew *BARA*.) light. The only people who say that are Young-Earth creationists.

Let's go back and reexamine the supernova in the Large Magellanic Cloud seen in 1987. If the Young-Earth creationists are correct, the star never existed. God CREATED (*BARA*) a stream of photons so a star would APPEAR to be there. The photons that appeared to be coming from that star never actually came from a star. In fact, not a single photon, from a single "star" seen in the night sky of Day Four actually originated from a star according to the Young-Earth Theory. All the "stars" seen on Day Four only APPEARED to be coming from stars. They were merely beams of photons that never really came from stars. They were all APPARENT stars; none of them was real. The nearest star, other than the sun, is about four light-years away. If God originally CREATED (*BARA*) all the luminaries in the sky on Day Four, then it would have taken about eight minutes before the sun would be seen at the surface of the earth. The moon would have been seen less than two seconds later. However, it would have taken four years for the first star to be seen. If you could see "stars" in the night sky on Day Four, it was only because God CREATED (*BARA*) photons in mid-stream so they would APPEAR to be coming from stars. This is their rationale for defending Apparent Age: **Young-Earth creationists believe all the photons seen in the night sky on Day Four never actually came from stars.** This was light God CREATED (*BARA)* in mid-stream. (Even though the Bible never uses *BARA* in connection with light.)

So, here is what I think is strange: They accept the interpretation that God CREATED (*BARA*) photons to appear, as long as those photons had no real historic connection to the stars. But they reject the interpretation that God LET (*HAYAH*) the photons appear, if those photons had a real historic connection to the stars. They don't mind believing God CREATED (*BARA*) light in the night sky, if it defends Apparent Age. They object to the idea God MADE (*ASAH*) light in the night sky, if it defends Actual Age. They want you to believe Genesis uses *BARA* when describing the light of the sun, moon, and stars. A quick look at the Hebrew of Genesis 1:14 and Genesis 1:16 will show you how un-Biblical their belief is:

Genesis 1:14 "And God said, '**Let** (*HAYAH*) there be lights in the expanse of the heavens to separate the day from the night. And let them be for signs and for seasons, and for days and years,'" (ESV)

Genesis 1:16 "And God **made** (*ASAH*) the two great lights—the greater light to rule the day and the lesser light to rule the night—and the stars." (ESV)

The Bible uses *HAYAH* and *ASAH* to describe the bodies of light and their beams of light seen on Day Four. Young-Earth creationists say God CREATED (*BARA*) the bodies of light and their beams of light on Day Four. They reject what the Bible says. They reject the notion that what you saw in the night sky on Day Four was ACTUAL. They accept the notion that what you saw in the night sky on Day Four was only APPARENT. What God made visible was not what God actually made. I define that as deception.

Here is a challenge for Non-Gap Theory creationists: Give me the list of things God created, made, and formed during the creation week that were not ACTUAL, but only APPARENT? Were the fish only apparent? Were the fruit trees only apparent? Was the dry ground only apparent? Were the animals only apparent? Did He make it look like trees, and birds, and fish, and animals were there when they actually weren't? No. They were ACTUAL. Since nothing else created by God was APPARENT, what gives the Young-Earth creationists the right to say the stars seen in the night sky on Day Four were APPARENT stars? (Those photons didn't ACTUALLY come from those stars.) Don't you find it strange that God would use phony photons as a way of revealing His handiwork?

God used *HAYAH* in Genesis 1:14 when He said, "Let there be lights in the firmament." He didn't use *BARA*. Likewise, God used *ASAH*, not *BARA*, when He described what He did with the lights in Genesis 1:16. Instead of "create" two great lights, the Bible says He "made" or "produced" (*ASAH*) two great lights.

Genesis 1:14-18 "And God said, **Let there be** lights in the firmament of the heaven to divide the day from the night; and let them be for signs, and for seasons, and for days, and years: *{15}* And let them be for lights in the firmament of the heaven to give light upon the earth: and it was so. *{16}* And God **made** two great lights; the greater light to rule the day, and the lesser light to rule the night: *he made* the stars also. *{17}* And God set them in the firmament of the heaven to give light upon the earth, *{18}* And to rule over the day and over the night, and to divide the light from the darkness: and God saw that *it was* good." (KJV)

It seems to me if God created (*BARA*) any of these things on Day Four, He would have used *BARA* somewhere in Genesis 1:14-18. He seems to pick His words carefully so we won't accidentally think these things were new creations. (They already existed.) He does not use the word "create" for any of His works on Day Four, so I think we need to be careful if we try to use the word "create" for any of His works on Day Four.

Now, there have been as many disputes over what *BARA* and *ASAH* mean as there have been over what *YOM* means. *BARA* and *ASAH* sometimes can be used to mean the same thing. Usually there is a distinction, even though this distinction is often overlooked. One thing is certain; *BARA* and *ASAH* are not absolutely synonymous. It seems to me quite logical to expect the use of different words if there were different beginnings. God created (*BARA*) the heavens and the earth in Genesis 1:1. This absolutely means to create. I believe this included the sun, moon, and stars. Genesis 1:3 and Genesis 1:14 are not new creations, but a command to let (*HAYAH*) their light come into being. In other words, God caused these lights to shine where they previously had been hidden.

Whoa, you may immediately ask the question, "If the sun was already in existence, how could its light be hidden; how could the earth be dark?" Well, the Gap Theory proposes some "What-If" explanations too. What if the darkness that enveloped the earth was a special kind of darkness? The Gap Theory says the sun had been created, yet the earth was dark before Day One. How do I explain this? I don't believe the earth was dark because the sun hadn't yet been created. I believe the earth was dark because it was being judged. A supernatural darkness accompanied God's judgment. Is there a Biblical example of this? Yes. Do you remember what happened between the sixth hour and the ninth hour of Christ's crucifixion? Darkness covered the land (Matthew 27:45). Why did darkness cover the land? Jesus was being judged for our sins. This wasn't an eclipse. The Passover generally falls on the first full moon after the Spring Equinox, and it's impossible for a solar eclipse to happen during a full moon. This was a special kind of darkness. God caused light to cease being. Light no longer was. God made a supernatural darkness on the day Christ was judged for our sins. Darkness is a picture of judgment. Over and over again in Scripture, darkness is connected with God's judgment.

(Note: Darkness itself is not evil, but it often represents a separation from God.)

What was the ninth plague on Egypt? God brought about a supernatural darkness through Moses because of Egypt's sin.

Exodus 10:22 "And Moses stretched forth his hand toward heaven; and there was a thick darkness in all the land of Egypt three days:" (KJV)

This wasn't an eclipse either. Eclipses don't last three days. This was darkness so thick it could be felt. This was a supernatural darkness. It was dark in Egypt, but it was still light in Goshen where the Jews lived. Why wasn't it dark where the Jews lived? They weren't being judged. Darkness fell on Egypt because Egypt was being judged. The Gap Theory proposes the earth was dark before Day One because it was being judged. Is this impossible? Do you think God would never darken the earth in judgment?

Isaiah 13:9-11 "Behold, the day of the LORD cometh, cruel both with wrath and fierce anger, to lay the land desolate: and he shall destroy the sinners thereof out of it. *{10}* For the stars of heaven and the constellations thereof shall not give their light: the sun shall be darkened in his going forth, and the moon shall not cause her light to shine. *{11}* And I will punish the world for *their* evil, and the wicked for their iniquity; and I will cause the arrogancy of the proud to cease, and will lay low the haughtiness of the terrible." (KJV)

The sun will be darkened and the moon and stars will no longer give light. The earth will be dark at the final judgment. Therefore, the idea that God's judgment can cause the earth to be dark is not without Scriptural support. It isn't a Biblical impossibility. Yes, this is a "What-If" proposal, but it is a "What-If" proposal that has Biblical credibility.

The Gap Theory proposes that the sun, moon, and stars were created before Genesis 1:3. The Gap Theory proposes that the earth was dark because God was judging it. Since Adam wasn't created yet, the most likely explanation is God was judging the earth for the sins of Lucifer and his fallen angels. God judged the earth and made it desolate, dead, and dark because of Lucifer's sin. God then called the light of the sun to come back into view on Day One of the Restoration. He didn't create a new source of light. The sun was already there, only now He allowed its light to "come to be" once again. That light began dividing the days from the nights. Once again there were evenings and mornings, light and dark; but things weren't completely back to normal. The sun still wasn't directly visible and the stars and the moon could not be seen. How could this be? Here is another "What-If" proposal of the Gap Theory. What if it was so cloudy the sun, moon, and stars couldn't be seen?

Genesis 1:6-8 "And God said, Let there be a firmament in the midst of the waters, and let it divide the waters from the waters. {7} And God made the firmament, and divided the waters which *were* under the firmament from the waters which *were* above the firmament: and it was so. {8} And God called the firmament Heaven. And the evening and the morning were the second day." (KJV)

The firmament is the atmosphere, the sky; the place where the birds fly. The water under the sky was the ocean. The waters above the sky were the clouds. What if by the end of the second day, the clouds were so thick the sun, moon, and stars were not visible, even though their light was still present? Is this "What-If" proposal credible? Of course it is. How many times have you gone outside at night to look at the stars and the moon only to discover it was too cloudy to see them? How many dreary, gray, overcast days have you experienced when you couldn't see the sun, but its light was still present? This is no magical "What-If" proposal. The Gap Theory doesn't require the Laws of Physics to be altered or suspended. According to the Gap Theory, it was so cloudy during the first three days that the sun, moon, and stars weren't visible. This happens all the time. There are many days and nights in which the heavenly bodies can't be seen. This "What-If" doesn't require changes to the Laws of Physics or a twisted interpretation of the Bible.

The Canopy Theory

If you are familiar with the different theories and sub-theories of creation, you may think I am now supporting the Canopy Theory. I am... but I am not. It depends on which Canopy Theory we are examining. You see, there are different versions of the Canopy Theory. There are Young-Earth, Day-Age, and Gap versions of the Canopy Theory. Generally, the Canopy Theory is the idea that at some time in the past, all (or almost all) of the water now in our oceans was locked up in a great, watery canopy high above the earth. There are three versions of when the canopy was created:

1.) The canopy was created on Day One: This is the version accepted by those Young-Earth and Day-Age creationists who believe the Canopy Theory. Of course, how long the canopy covered the earth depends on whether you believe the Young-Earth Theory or the Day-Age Theory.

2.) The canopy was created before Day One: Some Gap Theorists believe a super-thick, super-dense canopy covered the earth as a result of God's judgment of the Pre-Adamic (Luciferian) civilization. They say the canopy caused the darkness that was on the face of the deep.

    I can't disprove these views, but I think they create two problems.

    a.) If ALL the water on earth was locked up in a great atmospheric canopy, there would be no deep. There would be no ocean.

    b.) If there was an ocean on the earth, and a great water canopy above the earth, then water was already beneath the firmament and above the firmament on Day One. God's command for the waters to divide above and beneath the firmament on Day Two would make no sense; they were already divided as ocean and canopy. How much of the earth's water was in the canopy and how much was in the ocean? How much water was where? If there were oceans and clouds, then the waters were already divided above and below the firmament. If the waters were already separated as oceans and clouds in Genesis 1:2, then God's command for the waters to separate above and below the firmament in Genesis 1:6 would have been a meaningless command.

    The problem centers around how you define "canopy." How thick or dense would it have to be? Would a thick cloud cover be sufficient or would it take the whole ocean? I can find no Bible passages that give us answers to these questions. As such, I find this theory troublesome. I admire my fellow Gap Theory supporters for trying to find an explanation for why the earth was dark before God restored the light, but I don't think this solution works. If a physical water-canopy was the cause of the physical darkness, then there had to be more water in the canopy than even the darkest, cloudiest day ever seen. I've seen some very cloudy days, but never one that was completely devoid of light. How much water in the atmosphere would be required to do that? Science can give us the answer. Sunlight penetrates the ocean to a depth of about 500 feet. To block all light, the gaseous canopy had to have a thickness/density equivalent of at least 500 feet of liquid water. Anything less, and the sun's light would still be seen; it wouldn't be dark. Now, that's a lot of water. If there was that much water in the atmosphere, then water was already above and below the firmament before Day Two. The oceans and clouds already existed and were already divided before God divided them. This Biblical "solution" creates a Biblical problem. The problem most Canopy Theory creationists have with the darkness is they seem to believe it was a natural event. They believe the PHYSICAL water blocked the PHYSICAL light. I don't think that was the situation. I think it was a supernatural darkness that had nothing to do with atmospheric conditions.

3.) The canopy was created on Day Two: The Bible tells us God separated the waters beneath the firmament from the waters above the firmament on Day Two. This view is divided into two sub-views. Which firmament is this—the one in which the birds fly or the one in which the sun, moon, and stars shine?

    a.) One sub-view says the water above the firmament was the clouds in the atmosphere.
    b.) The other sub-view says the water above the firmament was at the edge of outer space just beneath heaven.

According to the second sub-view, there is a layer of water (or ice) enclosing the entire universe. It separates the physical universe from the spiritual heaven. I don't accept this second sub-view because if it was in outer space it could not exist as a canopy of water. It would instantaneously evaporate (or sublimate) in the vacuum of outer space. It wouldn't be much of a canopy if it had zero atmospheric pressure. I also don't accept this second sub-view because there is no physical edge of the universe. The universe is curved, so everything that physically exists, exists inside of space that touches only space. It is like walking on the surface of the curved earth. No matter how far you walk, you will never bump into the moon. There is no physical boundary between the universe and heaven; therefore, water could not exist at this "boundary."

Regardless of when you believe the canopy was created, (Day Two, Day One, or before Day One) you now have to decide when you believe the canopy was removed. There are three versions of that, as well.

1.) The canopy was removed or partially removed on Day One. ("Let there be light.")

2.) The canopy was removed on Day Four: If the darkness was caused by the canopy, then the canopy was partially removed on Day One, ("Let there be light.") and then completely removed on Day Four. ("Let there be lights in the firmament.") Day-Age and Gap Theorists believe the sun, moon, and stars were created billions of years before Day Four. However, the sun, moon, and stars weren't visible in the sky until Day Four. Their light could be seen through the partially removed canopy on days one, two, and three, but the bodies of light could not be seen until the canopy was completely removed on Day Four. Whether I accept this version of the Canopy Theory depends on how thick and dense the canopy was. You see, the atmosphere can hold a great deal of water, but there is a limit to how much it can hold. The amount of water it can hold depends on its temperature. Air can hold only so much water at any given temperature. Very cold air can hold very little water. The air at the North and South Poles is actually very dry. To hold enough gaseous water to be equivalent to 500 feet of liquid water, the temperature of the atmosphere would need to be at or near the boiling point. If the canopy was that thick and dense, then the atmosphere would have been too hot for plants on Day Three. This wouldn't be "good." If we are talking about a cloud cover just thick and dense enough to hide the sun, moon, and stars from view, but not dense enough to harm life, then I could agree with this version of the Canopy Theory.

3.) The canopy remained until the time of Noah: Some think this canopy was the source of the water for the Flood. This idea is unworkable. If the atmosphere contained an equivalent of 500 feet of water, then the atmospheric pressure on the surface of the earth would be increased to a point where life would be impossible. Again, science can provide us with answers. That much water would increase the air pressure to approximately 260 pounds per square inch. This much pressure would make it impossible for man to live more than a few seconds. (Normal air pressure is 14.7 pounds per square inch at sea-level.) At 260 pounds per square inch, the oxygen/carbon dioxide exchange in the capillaries of the lungs would be adversely affected. Plus, the hemoglobin in the red blood cells would spontaneously oxidize, causing instant death by hyperoxygenemia. Few organisms could live at such pressure. In addition to this scientific problem, there is a Biblical problem. If the canopy was that dense/thick, then the sun, and moon, and stars would not have been visible until after the Flood. To the contrary, the Bible says those celestial bodies were visible in the sky even before Adam was created. This means the canopy would contain only enough water to create a thin, partly cloudy sky; not even thick enough to hide the stars. It wouldn't have been much of a canopy in that case. Certainly not enough to rain for forty days and forty nights.

We find ourselves asking again, "How thick and dense was the canopy?" If the canopy was too thick/dense, then men couldn't live. Neither could they have seen the sun, moon, and stars until after the Flood. If the canopy was so thin that the sun, moon, and stars were visible, then why call it a canopy? It wouldn't even be as thick and dense as a partly cloudy day. I admire Gap Theory creationists for trying to find ways to defend the Global Flood in Noah's day. They believe the physical water had to come from some physical place, so why not from a super-canopy? But, defending the Global Flood by relying on a Global Canopy seems to leave God out of the picture. These "Global-Flood-Caused-By-A-Global-Canopy" believers seem to limit themselves to natural explanations. They seem to forget they don't have to explain the Flood by natural explanations alone. As far as I am concerned, Noah's Flood was a miraculous event, start-to-finish. God didn't have to get the water from anywhere. God can create water out of nothing, and when done with it, He can make it cease to exist. I believe most of the water that came upon the earth during

Noah's Flood was created by God just for that event. God created water to fall from the sky, and God created water to burst forth from the ocean floor. Then, when it was all over, God un-created as much of the water as He wanted. Many things about the Flood can be attributed to natural processes, but that doesn't mean it was entirely a natural event. To what extend God wanted to use nature or miracles, was up to Him.

Here is what I think happened. In judgment, God covered the Pre-Adamic earth in a thick cloud. The cloud wasn't sufficiently thick or dense to make the earth dark and cold enough to kill all life. He created a swaddling band of darkness to do that. Job 38:9 says God made both a cloud cover AND a swaddling band of darkness for the earth. I think the swaddling band was supernatural.

Job 38:9 "When I made the cloud the garment thereof, and thick darkness a swaddlingband for it," (KJV)

At some point in time, God caused light to cease on the Pre-Adamic earth. I don't know if it was restricted to the earth or if it was universal. I suspect it was just the earth because Genesis 1:2 mentions, "the surface of the deep," but nothing else. Plus, only the earth is mentioned in Job 38:9 when it speaks of a garment of cloud and a swaddling band of thick darkness. Whether this was universal or not, it was a period of supernatural darkness and extreme cold on the earth. (Maybe colder than the earth had ever been.) I believe it came on very suddenly. As soon as God removed the light of the sun, the temperature began to plummet. I don't know how quickly the temperature of the earth would fall without any sun, but if all sunlight stopped all over the world and it remained completely dark, then I believe the earth would experience a very rapid temperature drop. Without any source of heat, I imagine the temperature would fall far below zero in a very rapid time.

I believe the earth became so cold that the atmosphere could no longer hold the water it previously held. As the air got colder and colder, its water vapor and cloud cover condensed into water droplets, and then froze into ice crystals and snow. Normally, water droplets, ice crystals, and snow can remain airborne because of the movement of the air molecules. Moving air molecules buoy up water droplets, ice crystals, snow, and even hail. However, if it was as cold as I think it was, then even the movement of the air molecules was restricted. It takes heat to create wind, and since there was so little heat, there would be very little wind. The air would become deathly still. This blanket of super-cold air slowed the movement of the suspended water droplets, ice crystals and snow. With their motion stopped, these suspended particles were no longer buoyed up, and they fell to the ground. The land quickly became covered by ice and snow. (Maybe more snow and ice than the earth had ever experienced.) At that point, all the water (liquid and solid) settled to the surface. There were no clouds in the upper atmosphere. (No water above the firmament.) Just prior to the six days of restoration, the earth was experiencing a super ice-age. (Maybe worse than any ice-age before it.) The entire earth was covered by water and by ice and snow, and no land could be seen. There was water below the firmament, but there was no water above the firmament because the super-cold air caused all the water in the atmosphere to condense and freeze and fall to the ground… at least all the visible water. Again, Genesis describes what you would see if you were standing on the earth watching God work. At this point, you wouldn't see any water (clouds) above the firmament. Later, when God separated the waters above and below the firmament, it was water in its visible forms—oceans and clouds. Now, before you accuse me of playing the "What-If Game," let me tell you I am playing the "What-If Game." But, as I said before, my "What-If's" are plausible. Such a global ice-age isn't scientifically impossible. Scientists have discovered the earth has experienced many ice-ages in the past. Some of them covered the earth so completely, even land at the equator was under ice.

In Genesis 1:2, (still before Day One) the Spirit of God "hovered" over the face of the waters. The word used in Genesis 1:2 for "hovered" is *RACHAPH*, (Strong's Number H7363) and it is also used for an eagle brooding her eggs. The Holy Spirit began warming the earth like an eagle incubating her eggs to bring them to life. The warmth began evaporating the water, but the air was still so cold, a thick fog instantly covered the ground. Then on Day One, (Genesis 1:3) God commanded the light of the sun to be restored. (The supernatural swaddling band was removed.) The sun's light was good, and it created the division of light and dark, day and night. Once the swaddling band of supernatural darkness was removed and the light of the sun shone on the earth on Day One, the process of cloud formation began. The sky became cloudy as God separated the waters below the firmament (the oceans and other surface water) from the waters above the firmament (the clouds) on Day Two. At this point, the sun, moon, and stars weren't directly visible in the sky because of the fog and cloud cover. On Day Two, the earth was so foggy and cloudy that you could see light, but you couldn't see the sun, moon, and stars as you looked up. (Which is the perspective from which Genesis 1:3-31 is viewed.) By Day Two there was water above the firmament as well as water below it.

Genesis 1:7 "And God made the firmament, and divided the waters which *were* under the firmament from the waters which *were* above the firmament: and it was so." (KJV)

I think the Bible tells us the clouds were so thick on Day Two, that the sun, moon, and stars weren't directly visible in the sky. The clouds weren't so thick that they created unlivable temperatures or pressures, but they were thick enough to hide the celestial bodies of light. Then by Day Three, the natural warmth of the sun and the supernatural warmth created by the Holy Spirit caused a great thaw and the melting water flowed into the ocean basins. The ice and snow that once had hidden the dry land melted enough for dry land to appear.

Dry Land

After calling light back into existence (Day One) and separating the waters above the firmament from the waters below the firmament, (Day Two) God then caused the dry land to appear. (Day Three)

Genesis 1:9 "And God said, Let the waters under the heaven be gathered together unto one place, and let the dry *land* appear: and it was so." (KJV)

Genesis 1:9 does not say God "created" dry land on Day Three. Genesis 1:9 says God commanded it "to appear." The word "appear" is the Hebrew word *RAAH* (Strong's Number H7200) and it means to see, to appear, to become visible, to expose, to display, to behold, *etc*. It is the very same word translated, "saw," in all the places in Genesis 1 that say, "and God saw...." In the context of creation, it means either "to see," or "to make something seen." This is important because it shows how God's work in Genesis 1:3-31 doesn't always mean He brings something new into being. It can also mean He brings something preexisting into view. He now made it possible for dry land to be seen. Dry land wasn't a new creation. It already existed, but it couldn't be seen. (I think this very same principle applies to the appearance of the sun, moon, and stars the next day. They existed before Day Four, but were not visible from the surface of the earth until God made it possible for them to be seen.) The Bible doesn't say there was no land before Genesis 1:9. The Bible simply says it could not be seen. So, how could land exist but not be seen?

The Young-Earth Theory says the earth was completely under water when it was created. There were no mountains above the water, no continents, no islands; everything was under water. But, does Genesis 1:2 say there was no land above the water? No. Genesis 1:2 says darkness covered the face of the ocean, but it doesn't say the ocean covered the face of the earth. It does not say the earth was completely covered by liquid water. The only thing the Bible reveals about the land is that it was hidden from view. Is there another way land could be hidden from view without being completely covered by liquid water? Yes. If the earth was experiencing the ice-age I suspect it was, then the earth was partially covered by liquid water (oceans, seas, and lakes) and the rest was completely covered by ice and snow. Is this "What-If" possible? Yes; even today, virtually all of Antarctica is under ice and snow. Its land is there, but it cannot be seen.

The Gap Theory proposes that God didn't create the dry land in Genesis 1:9, He only let it appear/be seen/be revealed/be exposed. (Which is what *RAAH* means.) Part of the earth was below sea-level, and that part was covered by water. Part of the earth was above sea-level, and that part was covered by ice and snow. Part of the earth was below the waters; part of the earth was above the waters. The earth was standing in the water and out of the water.

2 Peter 3:5 "For this they willingly are ignorant of, that by the word of God the heavens were of old, and the earth **standing out of the water and in the water**:" (KJV)

This doesn't describe Noah's Flood. During Noah's Flood, the entire earth was covered by water, even Mt. Everest. 2 Peter 3:5 describes a world destroyed by a flood, but that flood doesn't match the conditions of Noah's Flood.

2 Peter 3:5-6 "For this they willingly are ignorant of, that by the word of God the heavens were of old, and the earth standing out of the water and in the water: {6} Whereby the world that then was, being overflowed with water, perished:" (KJV)

The Gap Theory proposes exactly what Genesis 1:9 and 2 Peter 3:5 literally say.

Old Lights—New Functions

At this point there was dry land and light, but it was still too cloudy to see the sun, the moon, and the stars. By Day Four, the upper atmosphere warmed enough to cause the water droplets and ice crystals to evaporate and sublimate into water vapor. Water vapor is transparent; water droplets and ice crystals are not. On Day Four, God **made** the heavenly bodies appear in the sky when He **made** the atmosphere transparent again. The atmosphere was now clear enough for them to be seen. These bodies of light weren't created (*BARA*) on Day Four, but they were made (*ASAH*) on Day Four. They were made in the sense that God produced these lights in the sky. *ASAH* conveys the idea of making, doing, establishing, preparing, providing, producing, bringing forth, or causing. It doesn't necessarily imply creating. The same word is used when Adam and Eve **made** coverings for themselves when they sewed fig leaves together. (Genesis 3:7) They didn't create anything. They **made** a covering so their nakedness couldn't be seen. In this case, God removed a covering (the thick clouds) so the lights in the sky could be seen. All it means is by Day Four, the upper atmosphere had warmed to the point that much or most of the opaque water (suspended liquid droplets and solid ice crystals) changed into its transparent (gaseous water vapor) form. There is nothing unscientific or physically impossible about this. From an earthbound perspective, God **made** the sky appear. God **made** the sun, the moon, and the stars appear. God **made** these lights in the sky visible. They needed to be visible because God was going to give them some new functions. Besides dividing the day from the night, these functions were for "signs," for "seasons," for "days," and for "years." God intended for man to understand the significance of these new functions. If the sun, moon, and stars were not visible, these new functions wouldn't be understood. Let's look at these functions.

Years

There are actually two types of years. There is the solar year and the lunar year. The solar year is the time it takes the earth to make one revolution around the sun. From the perspective of the earth, due to its angle of tilt, this is seen as the sun moving in its relative position in the sky with respect to the horizon. During the summer, the sun appears higher in the sky; and in the winter, it is lower. The lunar year is a little more difficult, and can consist of twelve or thirteen cycles of the phases of the moon. Many cultures used lunar calendars. Israel used a combined lunar/solar calendar. On the fourth day, God assigned the function of measuring the years by the newly visible heavenly bodies. God wanted man to be able to measure the passing of years.

Seasons

The beginning and ending of each of the four seasons can be determined by position of the sun and the stars. The position of the stars is important because the earth's revolution around the sun is not exactly 365 days. It's a little under 365 ¼ days. If we relied on the sun alone, we would soon find the seasons no longer matched the calendar. This could be confusing in an agricultural society. That's why we add a leap day in February every four years. Even this is not perfectly accurate, so from time to time there are additional corrections made to the calendar. It is the visibility of the stars that allowed man to calculate these corrections. Nowadays, scientists use atomic clocks, but historically astronomers used the position of the stars to do this.

Days

This is not the same as dividing the day from the night. Instead, this was the function of being able to determine when special days, holy days, feast days, *etc.* were to occur each year. As I mentioned, the Passover came on a full moon after the Spring Equinox. If the moon was not visible, it would have been impossible for primitive man (man without modern time-keeping equipment) to determine the day of the Passover.

Signs

The subject of heavenly signs in the Bible stirs up a great deal of speculation. Unfortunately, much of that speculation is focused on astrology. This is a subtle deception the devil uses to get people to look to the creation for truth, instead of to the Creator. Even more unfortunately, some Christians have fallen for this deception. It saddens me that born-again Christians sometimes fall into his trap. Some think the cyclical movements and positions of the stars influence, or are connected with the events of the Bible. For instance, some Christians think the Star of Bethlehem that announced the birth of Christ was a comet, or a supernova, or Venus aligning with Jupiter in the constellation Virgo. Those kinds of interpretations always seem to come from people who want to deny miracles. It may seem hard to believe, but there are people who call themselves Christians, yet in the same breath, deny God has performed miracles during the course of history. The Red Sea didn't miraculously part at the command of God. Instead, a very low tide happened just as the Jews needed to flee Egypt. Manna wasn't a miraculous food God created for the Jews. No, it was the dried, sugary secretions of some kind of ground-dwelling insect. 185,000 Assyrian soldiers weren't killed by an angel outside the walls of Jerusalem in one night. Instead, they all died of some highly contagious disease. Jesus really didn't die on the Cross; He merely fainted and was revived by the cool of the tomb. These kinds of interpretations of Scripture always come from people who want to deny God the Glory He rightly deserves. They want to limit God's ability to interact with the world to strictly naturalistic interactions. He has to wait for the proper alignment of the stars before He can act. Using astrology to interpret Scripture is an attempt to convince people God's interaction with history is limited. Thus, it is an attempt to deceive people that God's control of history is limited. I can assure you Genesis 1:14 has nothing to do with astrology, fortune telling, magic, or mysticism.

Genesis 1:14 "And God said, Let there be lights in the firmament of the heaven to divide the day from the night; and let them be for signs, and for seasons, and for days, and years:" (KJV)

God gave the celestial bodies specific functions. The sun, moon, and stars reveal days and nights, days, seasons, and years. There is nothing mystical or magical about those functions. God simply made it possible for us to tell time and to create accurate calendars by observing the heavenly bodies. We needed to be able to do that, so God gave us a way to do it. But, what does it mean by "signs?" What are signs? The Hebrew word is *OTH* (Strong's Number H226) and it means a sign, a mark, a signal, or a miracle. The mark on Cain in Genesis 4:15 was an *OTH*. After Noah's Flood, the rainbow became an *OTH* in Genesis 9:13-17. Each of the miracles God gave Moses and Aaron to perform in Egypt was an *OTH*. Circumcision was an *OTH*. The blood on the doorpost of the Hebrew homes before the Exodus was an *OTH*. Sometimes an *OTH* was a miracle, such as the water of the Nile turning to blood. Sometimes an *OTH* was natural, such as putting the blood of a slain lamb on the doorposts. An *OTH* was a way to reveal something about God in a non-verbal (not spoken or written) way. The Jews didn't have to take the lamb's blood and literally write on their doorposts, "Hey, God. This is a Jewish house, so pass over it and don't kill anybody here." All they had to do was paint the doorposts and the lintels with the lamb's blood, and the message was clear. Of course, the Lord didn't need the blood on the doorposts to tell Himself which homes were Jewish. The sign wasn't there for God's benefit; it was a message to the Jews and to the Egyptians. It was a non-verbal message that revealed something about God: God was both a God of Wrath, and a God of Mercy. He was going to kill Egyptians, but spare the Jews.

Throughout the Bible, signs (both miraculous signs and non-miraculous signs) were meant to reveal something about God. Of course, the revelations weren't always in plain sight. Sometimes, the information was hidden so unbelievers couldn't see it. The enlightening power of the Holy Spirit was required to understand the spiritual truth revealed in the physical sign. (They had to know the truth in order to know the truth.) When Jesus healed the man born blind in John 9:7, the physical aspect of the miracle revealed nothing about Jesus until the Holy Spirit revealed the spiritual aspect of the miracle. Being able to see Jesus physically didn't tell the man who Jesus was. He could see Jesus with his physical eyes, but he still didn't see Jesus spiritually. It wasn't until after being challenged by the Pharisees that he began to realize Jesus was at least a prophet of God. Then, after speaking with Jesus again, his spiritual eyes were opened, and he realized Jesus was God. Only God could have given him sight. This miracle (sign) revealed that Jesus was God.

So, if we interpret Genesis 1:14 as telling us the heavenly bodies are designed by God to reveal information about Himself, then we suddenly discover the scientific observation of the heavens is a far-more powerful tool to understanding God, God's character, God's work, and God's plan, than what astrology, horoscopes, and eschatological speculations might reveal. For one thing, astrology, horoscopes, and eschatological speculations can never be trusted. Sometimes they are right; most of the time they are wrong. For another thing, they are forbidden by God.

Deuteronomy 18:10-14 "No one among you is to make his son or daughter pass through the fire, practice divination, tell fortunes, interpret omens, practice sorcery, *{11}* cast spells, consult a medium or a familiar spirit, or inquire of the dead. *{12}* Everyone who does these things is detestable to the LORD, and the LORD your God is driving out the nations before you because of these detestable things. *{13}* You must be blameless before the LORD your God. *{14}* Though these nations you are about to drive out listen to fortune-tellers and diviners, the LORD your God has not permitted you to do this." (HCSB)

If we interpret Genesis 1:14 the way God intended it to be interpreted, then what we learn will never be wrong. Genesis 1:14 tells us the same thing other Scripture passages tell us.

Psalms 19:1-3 "For the director of music. A Psalms of David. The heavens declare the glory of God; the skies proclaim the work of his hands. *{2}* Day after day they pour forth speech; night after night they display knowledge. *{3}* There is no speech or language where their voice is not heard." (NIV)

Romans 1:20 "For since the creation of the world His invisible attributes, His eternal power and divine nature, have been clearly seen, being understood through what has been made, so that they are without excuse." (NASB)

The Scriptures reveal that observing the heavenly bodies was meant to tell us something about God. This is what signs were meant to do. Throughout the Bible when God used signs and miracles, it was a way of revealing something about Himself to fallen men. The heavens were meant to reveal God. In other words, if we study the heavens, we can learn things about God. What I find most fascinating about this is that here in the 21st century, we have learned far more about God by studying the cosmos, than what the ancient Hebrews could have learned by studying the cosmos. No one in Old or New Testament times had to ability to study the universe like we can today; therefore, they couldn't learn what we have learned about God today.

Set in the Firmament of the Heavens

God set these lights in the firmament of the heavens according to Genesis 1:17. The word "set" is *NATHAN*. (Strong's Number H5414) The image that comes to mind is that God creates the stars and then hangs them in space somewhat like children hanging ornaments on a Christmas tree. This is very picturesque, but it isn't what *NATHAN* means. It doesn't mean "to create," or even "to make." Instead, it conveys the idea of giving, presenting, or bestowing. It is used to appoint, to assign, or to delegate. If a king were to appoint an ambassador to a foreign nation, this is the word that would be used. The king doesn't create the ambassador, but he does set him up with a special mission or purpose. Genesis 1:17 doesn't say God created (*BARA*) the lights, but it does say He assigned the lights a special purpose. What is this purpose?

The Invisible Attributes of God

What does the visibility of the heavenly bodies have to do with revealing the invisible attributes of God? To be honest, I don't know if I have the answer, but since God gave (*NATHAN*) the heavenly bodies these functions, I'm sure He had a good reason. I'll play the "What-If" Game again.

What if God wanted to reveal something about Himself when we look at the sky?

Romans 1:20 "For since the creation of the world His invisible attributes, His eternal power and divine nature, have been clearly seen, being understood through what has been made, so that they are without excuse." (NASB)

The visible reveals the invisible. The visible heavenly bodies reveal God's invisible attributes. What do they reveal? For starters, the precision of the movements of the heavenly bodies reveals a God of supreme power and control. These are two of His invisible attributes—omnipotence and sovereignty. Gazing at the stars makes us wonder about the intricacies and complexity of the universe; how it began and how life came to be. They cry out for an eternal, intelligent, and supernatural Creator and Life-Giver. These are five more invisible things revealed by the visible. The sun is always where it should be. The moon never fails to be on time. The stars are so constant in their movements, that mariners and travelers can determine their latitude and longitude by measuring the position of the stars in the night sky. The celestial bodies show God is dependable; another invisible attribute. God declared how the days and seasons and years would continue as long as the earth exists, (Genesis 8:22) and to this day, the heavenly bodies remain a testimony to God's veracity. God keeps His promises; He is a God of truth. So far, I have listed ten of God's invisible attributes revealed by the visible sky: He is powerful, He is sovereign, He is eternal, He is intelligent, He is supernatural, He is the Creator, He is the Giver of life, He is dependable, He keeps His promises, and He is a God of truth. So far, these are things the ancient Hebrews and Christians could have learned about God by observing the heavens. Lest ye think God wrote the Scriptures with only them in mind, let me tell you what the heavens declare about God in the light of 21st century astronomy and cosmology. (As I said before, God wrote the Scriptures to reveal truth to both primitive man and modern man.)

The Fine Tuning of the Universe

Earlier, I mentioned Dr. Hugh Ross and his book, *The Improbable Planet*.[82] Dr. Ross is one of many Christian astronomers and cosmologists who have discovered some amazing truths about God by observing His handiwork. What scientists have learned about God by observing the universe in the last fifty years dwarfs what scientists learned about God by observing the universe in all previous human history. As modern scientists studied the observable events following the Big Bang, they discovered some remarkable facts no one could have imagined. The creation of the universe left scientific, observable, measurable evidence it had been created by a supernatural Being of such power and intelligence that we cannot even begin to imagine what He is. Real scientists didn't have to resort to claims God made things "appear" certain ways in order to make Him look Glorious. (Such as: Apparent Age, Apparent Stars, Apparent Supernova, Apparent Movement of Galaxies, Riemannian Space, *etc*.) No; what really happened with the Big Bang reveals a far more Glorious God than anything the Young-Earth creationists could dream up. The real events of the creation left evidence that God is so far beyond what we can think or imagine, that we ought to put our hands over our mouths before we say stupid things about God and make fools of ourselves.

With better and better instrumentation, scientists of today can observe God's handiwork in ways the ancients couldn't. The invention of the telescope in the early 1600's opened new widows to the heavens, but even that gave us a limited view of what God created. Today, we have much stronger and clearer optical telescopes, radio telescopes, infrared telescopes, ultraviolet telescopes, x-ray telescopes, gamma-ray telescopes, telescopes mounted on platforms hundreds of miles above the earth's atmosphere, and even some that have traveled millions of miles away from the earth. All this improved technology has given us the ability to study God's handiwork in finer and finer detail, and with more and more precision. All this improved technology has given us "eyes" to see the very fabric of the universe. We now have the ability to measure the values of the very parameters that cause the universe to be what it is today, and those values have stunned scientists. It has been discovered that the values of those parameters are so precisely tuned, that any variation in the slightest, and there would be no stars, no galaxies, no planets, and no life. Without looking for design in the universe, and without intending to find evidence for an intelligent and powerful Creator, today's astronomers and cosmologists (even those who are atheists) have stumbled onto God's greatest sign in the heavens: The universe reveals God.

1. The Strength of Gravity

It has now been discovered the strength of the Gravitational Force (created by the Big Bang) is exactly what it had to be in order for the universe to become what it is.

> "A change in gravity's strength by one part in 10^{60} of its current value would mean that the universe would have either exploded too quickly for galaxies and stars to form, or collapsed back in on itself too quickly for life to evolve."[83]

(Note: This speaks of the evolution of life. This statement and this discovery were not made by Christian creationists seeking to manipulate the data to prove God's existence.)

If gravity varied by so much as:

± 0.000,000,000,000,000,000,000,000,000,000,000,000,000,000,000,000,000,000,001%

Then the earth, moon, and stars would have never come into existence.

2. The Rate of Inflation

As matter and space expanded after the Big Bang, the rate of expansion was exactly what it had to be.

> "Its value just one second after the big bang had to be exactly one to precision of about fourteen decimal places."[84]

If the velocity of Inflation varied by:

$$\pm\ 0.000,000,000,000,1\%$$

Then stars couldn't have formed, the sun wouldn't be here, and there would be no life.

3. Strong Nuclear Force

The Strong Nuclear Force is what holds the nuclei of the atoms together. The strength of that force is what allows the elements to be what they are. The value of the strength of the Strong Nuclear Force was determined at the Big Bang. Any variation in the slightest, and you wouldn't be reading this book.

> "If the strong nuclear force were very slightly weaker by just one part in 10,000 billion, billion then protons and neutrons would not stick together, and the only element possible in the universe, would be hydrogen only. There would be no stars, and no planets, or life in the universe. However, if the strong nuclear force were slightly too strong by the same fraction amount, the protons and neutrons would tend to stick together so much that there would basically only be heavy elements, but no hydrogen at all—If this were the case, then life would also not be possible, because hydrogen is a key element in water and in all life-chemistry."[85]

If the strength of the Strong Nuclear Force varied by:

$$\pm\ 0.000,000,000,000,000,000,000,000,000,000,000,000,1\%$$

Then we wouldn't be here.

4. Weak Nuclear Force

The Weak Nuclear Force is one of the Four Fundamental Forces of Nature, and it is involved in radioactive decay and creating elements. It is an essential force for making the universe what it is today, and the strength of that force was also determined by the Big Bang.

> "The nuclear weak force is one of the four fundamental forces in the universe and operates inside the nucleus of an atom. It is so finely tuned that an alteration in its value by even one part of 10 to the power of 100 (1 with a hundred zeros) would have prohibited a life permitting universe."[86]

If the strength of the Weak Nuclear Force varied by:

± 1 in 10^{100} (I'm not going to type all those zeroes.)

Then life could have never existed.

5. The Ratio of Strong Nuclear to Electromagnetic

Not only are the Fundamental Forces of Nature exactly what they have to be, they are precisely balanced with each other so the universe can be what it is.

> "Increase it by only 1 part in 10^{40} and only small stars can exist, decrease it by the same amount and there will only be large stars. You must have both large and small stars in the universe. The large ones produce elements in their thermonuclear furnaces and it is only the small ones that burn long enough to sustain a planet with life."[87]

If the Ratio of the Strong Nuclear Force to the Electromagnetic Force varied by:

$\pm$ 0.000,000,000,000,000,000,000,000,000.000,000,001%

Then there would be no life on earth.

6. The Ratio of Electrons to Protons

Just as the strengths of the forces have to be in balance with each other, the number of subatomic particles have to be in balance with each other.

> "Unless the number of electrons is equivalent to the number of protons to an accuracy of one part in 10^{37}, or better, electromagnetic forces in the

universe would have so overcome gravitational forces that galaxies, stars, and planets never would have formed."[88]

If the Ratio of Electrons to Protons varied by:

± 0.000,000,000,000,000,000,000,000,000,000,000,01%

Then the stars, the galaxies, and the earth could have never been formed.

7. Quarks and Anti-Quarks

The exact numbers of particles that make up matter have to be exactly what they are, or the universe wouldn't exist. Quarks are the fundamental particles that make up the protons and neutrons in the atoms. Quarks and Anti-Quarks were created by the Big Bang, and within a fraction of a second after the Big Bang, the Quarks and Anti-Quarks annihilated each other on contact. The number of Quarks slightly outnumbered the Anti-Quarks. (Scientists say they can't explain why the numbers were different.) It was the "extra" Quarks that later combined with each other to make protons and neutrons. The total mass of the universe was determined within one nanosecond of the Big Bang. The amount of mass created by the Big Bang was exactly what it had to be in order for the universe to form. If the mass was any greater, the universe would have collapsed back on itself before stars could form. If the mass was any less, the universe would have expanded so quickly the particles could never coalesce into stars and galaxies. How precisely balanced was the Quark/Anti-Quark Ratio?

Scientists now know the density of that mass could have varied by no more than 1 part in 10^{62} one nanosecond after the Big Bang. The density of the universe one nanosecond after the Big Bang was 447,225,917,218,507,401,285,016.0 grams/cm^3. If the density of the universe one nanosecond after the Big Bang was 447,225,917,218,507,401,285,016.2 grams/cm^3, then the universe would have collapsed back on itself before stars could form. If the density of the universe one nanosecond after the Big Bang was 447,225,917,218,507,401,285,015.8 grams/cm^3, then the universe would have expanded too quickly for stars to form.[89]

If the density of the universe one nanosecond after the Big Bang varied by:

± 0.000,000,000,000,000,000,000,000,000,000,000,000,000,000,000,000,000,001%

Then stars, galaxies, planets, moons, and life would have never come into existence.

A nanosecond after the Big Bang, if the amount of matter created varied by one-hundred thousandth, of one-billionth, of one-billionth, of one-billionth, of one-billionth, of one-billionth, of one-billionth percent, the universe would not be here.

Now, I don't know about you, but I think all this screams, "We were created by God!" (And these are only seven of the over 150 finely-tuned parameters known today.[90]) Only a Being of unimaginable power and intelligence could have done this. This is what is revealed by observing the heavenly bodies. This is the sign (*OTH*) God designed when He set (*NATHAN*) the sun, moon, and stars in place. This is what God was telling us in Genesis 1:14; only He didn't make it known until we able to learn more. Why did He give us a sign we couldn't fully understand until we invented the instruments that gave us better and more precise observations of the heavens? Just when mankind began to think our scientific discoveries made God obsolete, God revealed scientific facts that destroyed our rebellious thoughts. When man attempted to use science to discredit God, God used science to destroy those vain attempts. In fact, the scientific evidence we now have for God's existence is greater than any time in the past. Rather than disproving God, science proves God. Modern man has less of an excuse for rejecting God than the "primitive, superstitious, ignorant goat-herders" whom atheists think authored the Bible. So, how does this fit with the Gap Theory? What does Genesis 1:14 have to do with WHICH creation theory is true? I don't know if I have all the answers, but I have two answers.

First, the vast majority of the Fine-Tuning Arguments are based on what observations of the Big Bang have revealed. If you are a Young-Earth creationist, you can't use these Fine-Tuning Arguments. You don't believe the Big Bang Model. You can't insist the Strength of Gravity was finely tuned by the Big Bang. You can't believe the Rate of Inflation was exactly what it needed to be. (You don't even believe there was an Inflation.) You can't insist the Strong Nuclear Force and the Weak Nuclear Force are exactly what they are because the Big Bang created them exactly that way. You must reject the idea the Big Bang created the perfect ratio of Strong Nuclear Force to Electromagnetic Force necessary for life. Likewise, you can't believe the ratio of the Number of Electrons to the Number of Protons had anything to do with the creation of the universe. You can't use the ratio of the Number of Quarks and Anti-Quarks that came out of the Big Bang as evidence a super-powerful, super-intelligent Creator created the universe. You must reject all these arguments. You have to insist they are not indicators of Design; you have to insist they are indicators of Apparent Design. You take the same view atheists take. Atheists think all the "Design" that came from the Big Bang is only Apparent Design, because they don't believe in a Designer. Young-Earth creationists think all the "Design" that came from the Big Bang is only Apparent Design, because they don't believe in the Big Bang. They don't think the values of these parameters were the result of God creating the universe by Process Creation. Young-Earth creationists think the values of these parameters are the result of God trying to make unbelievers (and heretics, like me) falsely believe He created the universe by a process of creation that resulted in these values. It's all one big cosmic deception. Young-

Earth creationists wind up rejecting a great deal of the scientific *OTH* God reveals about Himself. I don't agree with the Day-Ager's interpretation that the "days" were long ages, but I certainly can't criticize them for ignoring and rejecting what the Fine-Tuning Arguments reveal about God. At least they aren't anti-science.

But, there is a second thing I believe the *OTH* of Genesis 1:14 was meant to reveal about God. The Fine-Tuning Arguments reveal His invisible attributes of intelligence and power, but I believe there is something even more important revealed by the heavens. **I believe God wanted to reveal His invisible attribute that was MOST important to fallen man!** God is powerful, God is intelligent, God is eternal, *etc.*, and these things are seen in the sky regardless of which theory of creation is correct. But, if the Gap Theory is true, then the skies reveal something about God that the Day-Age and Young-Earth Theories don't reveal: **God is a God of Restoration**. If the Gap Theory is true, then when we look at the heavens, we see God as a God of Judgment AND as a God of Forgiveness. The earth was destroyed by His judgment, but He is a Merciful God and a Compassionate God. He is a God whose plans cannot be thwarted. His purpose for the earth will be accomplished. Sin can't defeat Him. Sin didn't take Him by surprise. Lucifer and his fallen angels didn't destroy God's plan for creation. These attributes were revealed by the heavenly bodies when God lifted His judgment and caused light to shine into the darkness caused by sin. If you didn't know the earth was ruined and restored, then you wouldn't see these invisible attributes of God in the visible heavens. You might see His power, but you wouldn't see His forgiveness. You might see His intelligence, but you wouldn't see His mercy. None of His merciful and compassionate and forgiving attributes is visible in the sky if the earth had only one beginning. But, if there were two beginnings, then the heavens declare these additional attributes of God. They declare that the God who judges is also the God who restores.

Yes, this is a "What-If" proposal, but how does it compare to the "What-If" proposals of the other theories? What do the heavens declare if the Young-Earthers are correct? They declare we can't trust what we see. He's not trustworthy. Stars that were never there and never exploded were made to look as if they were there and had exploded. Because His handiwork is deceptive, the stars reveal that God is deceptive. What do the heavens reveal if the Day-Agers are correct? They reveal how God's Word and His Works don't agree. According to His WORKS, He created the sun before the plants and trees, but according to His WORD He got it mixed up and told us the sun didn't appear (Day Four) until millions of years after the creation of the plants and trees. (Day Three) The sky of the Day-Age Theory reveals God as a God of confusion. Unlike those theories, the Gap Theory has "What-Ifs" that give God glory.

I believe Adam knew he was made from the earth. I believe Adam knew the earth had been judged and restored. Adam looked at his own fallen nature and at the judgment God had pronounced upon him. He was now *TOHUW WA-BOHUW* in God's eyes. (*TOHUW WA-BOHUW* is the condition of fallen man's soul—it is desolate and dead.) He looked at the earth, then he looked at the sky, and he suddenly understood: God was a God of Restoration, Redemption, Compassion, Mercy, and Forgiveness. I believe Adam, the man made from the dirt of the earth, knew he would ultimately share in the destiny of the earth. I believe Adam knew that someday he would be restored just like the earth had been. I think God sovereignly planned the Ruin and Restoration of the earth so we would be able to look at the heavens and see Him as Our Savior, Redeemer, and Restorer from sin and death. These are the invisible attributes God revealed in the visible heavens ONLY IF THE GAP THEORY IS TRUE. This is the special mission, the assignment, the *NATHAN*, He bestowed on the sun and the moon and the stars when He "set" them in the heavens. They are "ambassadors" telling us God restored light and life to earth. He could have left earth dark and dead forever, but He didn't. In His love and mercy and forgiveness, He brought the earth out of the bondage of sin and death and into the light of new life. **If the other creation theories are true, then you can't see God's attributes of redemption and forgiveness in the heavens**.

Look at the stars. If the Gap Theory is true, then the only reason you see them is because God restored their light. Look at the moon. If the Gap Theory is correct, then you can see it only because God redeemed our planet from the sin and death Lucifer brought upon it. Look at the sun. (But don't look too long.) If the Gap Theory is true, then you can understand it was God's grace that caused its light to shine where the darkness of sin had ruled. If the Gap Theory is not true, you can't see God's forgiveness in the visible sky. You can't see any of His redemptive attributes. The Young-Earth Theory doesn't reveal God as a God of forgiveness. (Remember, they are the ones who are appalled at the thought of God creating something good out of something bad.) The Day-Age Theory doesn't reveal God as a God of Restoration. (Genesis 1:3-31 does not speak of God restoring order to the universe, but of creating things in the wrong order.) The Gap Theory gives testimony to the most important thing we sinners need to know about God. God is a God of mercy, compassion, grace, forgiveness, redemption, and most of all, restoration. We know He is the God who restores because we see in Genesis 1:3-31 that He restored creation. God is the God who redeems and restores that which was corrupted. God can restore life to what once was dead. Rather than being angry at the idea God created a very good world on top of, "a heap of bones," we ought to rejoice that He is the kind of God who would do that very thing. God is the God who restores! God is the God who forgives! If the Gap Theory is true, sinners can have hope in the God of Genesis 1:3-31. **Instead of creating conflicts with the Gospel of Jesus Christ, the Gap Theory demonstrates the Gospel of Jesus Christ**.

I believe God is smart enough and powerful enough and sovereign enough to make His Works and His Words agree. God's Word reveals His redemptive attributes. Why shouldn't His Work reveal His redemptive attributes? Why would God reveal His power, sovereignty, and intelligence in the heavenly bodies but not His mercy, grace, and forgiveness? If the Gap Theory is not true, then God doesn't reveal these attributes in the heavens. If the Gap Theory is not true, then God's Work doesn't reveal what His Word reveals. His Works don't match His Words. We need to see all of God's attributes, but the attributes we sinners need to see most are His attributes that cause us to see Him as our Savior. Even the fallen angels know God is a God of omnipotence, omniscience, and omnipresence, but they don't see Him as a God of forgiveness and mercy and grace. All people in all cultures and in all times need to see these attributes. God reveals them in the heavens for all to see. There is no place on earth where people cannot understand that God is a God of Restoration. All they have to do is look at the sky and realize the celestial bodies are visible only because God restored them. Unfortunately, the Gap Theory has been rejected and forgotten for so long, the world has been blinded to everything the heavens fully reveal about God. I believe this is the work of Satan. Above all else, Satan does not want us to see God as a forgiving God. When other creationists speak out against the Restoration Theory, I believe they are unintentionally helping Satan blind the world to the fact God is our Restorer and Redeemer. They diminish the glory of God.

Which creation theory gives God the greatest glory and honor and praise and majesty? Cosmogony recapitulates soteriology. That's the theory I believe!

400

Chapter Nine: The Original Earth

Isaiah 45:18 provides us with the knowledge that God did not create the earth a desolate waste. This should be enough to convince us that God did not create the earth a desolate waste, but some theologians still disagree. So, let's look at another account of the early earth. God has provided us with another glimpse of earth prior to Genesis 1:3. This glimpse is found in Jeremiah 4:23-26. The context of Jeremiah 4 is a warning to Israel. God is warning the Jews about their idolatry and their sin. They have rebelled against Him. From verse one to verse twenty-two, He reminds them of their wickedness and calls for their repentance. If they don't repent, they risk His wrath and judgment. Suddenly, starting at verse twenty-three, Jeremiah begins a series of four "I beheld…" statements followed by physical descriptions of the earth. The first of these descriptive statements reads as follows according to the various translators:

Jeremiah 4:23 "I beheld the earth, and, lo, *it was* without form, and void; and the heavens, and they *had* no light." (KJV)

Jeremiah 4:23 "I beheld the earth, and indeed *it was* without form, and void; And the heavens, they *had* no light." (NKJV)

Jeremiah 4:23 "I looked at the earth, and it was formless and empty; and at the heavens, and their light was gone." (NIV)

Jeremiah 4:23 "I looked on the earth, and lo, it was waste and void; and to the heavens, and they had no light." (RSV)

Jeremiah 4:23 "I looked on the earth, and lo, it was waste and void; and to the heavens, and they had no light." (NRSV)

Jeremiah 4:23 "I looked at the earth. It was empty and had no shape! I looked at the sky. And its light was gone." (NCV)

Jeremiah 4:23 "I beheld the earth, and see, it was formless and empty, and the heavens had no light." (NBV)

Jeremiah 4:23 "I looked to the earth—it was a formless waste; to the heavens, and their light had gone." (NJB)

Jeremiah 4:23 "I see the earth. It's formless and empty. I see the sky. Its lights are gone." (GW)

Jeremiah 4:23 "I looked at the earth, and lo! it was chaos; At the heavens, and their light was gone." (S&G)

Jeremiah 4:23 "I looked on the earth, and behold, it was formless and void; and to the heavens, and they had no light." (NASB)

Jeremiah 4:23 "I looked at the earth, and saw it was formless and empty. And the heavens, they had no light." (SCRIP)

Jeremiah 4:23 "I saw the earth, and behold it was a chaos and vacant, And the heavens, and they had no light." (CVOT) (emphasis in original)

Jeremiah describes what God revealed to him about the earth. It is *TOHUW WA-BOHUW* and dark. Jeremiah describes the earth in the very same condition it was in Genesis 1:2. He uses the very same words. He is seeing the earth in a formless, void, and dark condition. This is important because **THERE IS ONLY ONE TIME IN HISTORY WHEN THE EARTH WAS *TOHUW WA-BOHUW* AND DARK**. It was *TOHUW WA-BOHUW* and dark only during the time before the six days of Genesis, before Genesis 1:3. Search the Scriptures: Since the creation of Adam, the earth has never been a desolate waste, devoid of life, and dark. More importantly, it will never be in such a condition in the future. The heavens and the earth will pass away as described in 2 Peter 3:10, but they will pass away only in the sense of being remade. They will not be unmade. The earth will be remade with a great, fervent heat, but it will not become a desolate waste. In fact, it will be made perfect. Jeremiah is not seeing the future earth. The earth will not become without form, and void at the Final Judgment. God will not destroy all life on it; it will not be dead. Jeremiah is seeing the earth during the time prior to Genesis 1:3, the only time in its history when it was *TOHUW WA-BOHUW* and dark. It will never again be *TOHUW WA-BOHUW* and dark.

Now, just so I'll know that you know what I know, I'm going to repeat this. The earth has never been *TOHUW WA-BOHUW* and dark since Adam. The earth will never be *TOHUW WA-BOHUW* and dark in the future. The earth was *TOHUW WA-BOHUW* and dark only once. So, if God reveals a glimpse of earth in its *TOHUW WA-BOHUW* and dark condition, then it must be a glimpse of earth during the only time it was *TOHUW WA-BOHUW* and dark. Jeremiah is looking at the past, at the Pre-Adamic earth.

The question must be asked. What does the early earth in a state of darkness and desolation have to do with Israel being judged by God's wrath? Why does Jeremiah insert a description of the Pre-Adamic earth among his other warnings to Israel? I purposely left off the rest of Jeremiah's description of the earth so you could first see how similar Jeremiah 4:23 is with Genesis 1:2. I did this because Jeremiah goes on to reveal things about the Pre-Adamic earth the Book of Genesis doesn't reveal. Remember, it's okay for God to do this. Very few topics in the Bible are exhaustively covered in only one portion of Scripture. The creation account is no different. Jeremiah tells us something more about the early earth. It's important to understand Jeremiah doesn't contradict what Moses told us in Genesis. Jeremiah simply gives us additional information about the earth prior to the six days of restoration. God tells us something through Jeremiah that shakes up the whole picture of earth's history. Jeremiah is about to say something you may have not known before: **There was life on earth before the six days of Genesis.** Jeremiah 4:23-26 is the key to understanding the relationship between Genesis 1:1 and Genesis 1:2. This key allows us to translate Genesis informationally, not just grammatically.

Jeremiah 4:23-26 "I beheld the earth, and, lo, *it was* without form, and void; and the heavens, and they *had* no light. {24} I beheld the mountains, and, lo, they trembled, and all the hills moved lightly. {25} I beheld, and, lo, *there was* no man, and all the birds of the heavens were fled. {26} I beheld, and, lo, the fruitful place *was* a wilderness, and all the cities thereof were broken down at the presence of the LORD, *and* by his fierce anger." (KJV)

Jeremiah 4:23-26 "I beheld the earth, and indeed *it was* without form, and void; And the heavens, they *had* no light. {24} I beheld the mountains, and indeed they trembled, And all the hills moved back and forth. {25} I beheld, and indeed *there was* no man, And all the birds of the heavens had fled. {26} I beheld, and indeed the fruitful land *was* a wilderness, And all its cities were broken down At the presence of the LORD, By His fierce anger." (NKJV)

Jeremiah 4:23-26 "I looked at the earth, and it was formless and empty; and at the heavens, and their light was gone. {24} I looked at the mountains, and they were quaking; all the hills were swaying. {25} I looked, and there were no people; every bird in the sky had flown away. {26} I looked, and the fruitful land was a desert; all its towns lay in ruins before the LORD, before his fierce anger." (NIV)

Jeremiah 4:23-26 "I looked on the earth, and lo, it was waste and void; and to the heavens, and they had no light. {24} I looked on the mountains, and lo, they were quaking, and all the hills moved to and fro. {25} I looked, and lo, there was no man, and all the birds of the air had fled. {26} I looked, and lo, the fruitful land was a desert, and all its cities were laid in ruins before the LORD, before his fierce anger." (RSV)

Jeremiah 4:23-26 "I looked on the earth, and lo, it was waste and void; and to the heavens, and they had no light. {24} I looked on the mountains, and lo, they were quaking, and all the hills moved to and fro. {25} I looked, and lo, there was no one at all, and all the birds of the air had fled. {26} I looked, and lo, the fruitful land was a desert, and all its cities were laid in ruins before the LORD, before his fierce anger." (NRSV)

Jeremiah 4:23-26 "I looked at the earth, and it was empty and had no shape. I looked at the sky, and its light was gone. {24} I looked at the mountains, and they were shaking. All the hills were trembling. {25} I looked, and there were no people. Every bird in the sky had flown away. {26} I looked, and the good, rich land had become a desert. All its towns had been destroyed by the Lord and his great anger." (NCV)

Jeremiah 4:23-26 "I beheld the earth, and see, it was formless and empty, and the heavens had no light. {24} I beheld the mountains, and look! They trembled, and all the hills were in commotion. {25} I looked, and see! There was no man, and all the birds of heaven had fled. {26} I looked, and behold! The garden land was a desert, and all the cities were broken down before the Lord in the presence of His fierce anger." (NBV)

Jeremiah 4:23-26 "I looked to the earth—it was a formless waste; to the heavens, and their light had gone. {24} I looked to the mountains—they were quaking and all the hills were rocking to and fro. {25} I looked—there was no one at all, the very birds of heaven had all fled. {26} I looked—the fruitful land was a desert, all its towns in ruins before Yahweh, before his burning anger." (NJB)

Jeremiah 4:23-26 "I see the earth. It's formless and empty. I see the sky. Its lights are gone. {24} I see the mountains. They are shaking, and the hills are swaying. {25} I see that there are no people, and every bird has flown away. {26} I see that the fertile land has become a desert, and all its cities are torn down because of the LORD and his burning anger." (GW)

Jeremiah 4:23-26 "I looked at the earth, and lo! it was chaos; At the heavens, and their light was gone. {24} I looked at the mountains, and lo! they were quaking; and all the hills swayed to and fro. {25} I looked, and lo! there was no man, and all the birds of the air had flown. {26} I looked, and lo! the garden land was desert, and all its cities were ravaged before the Lord, before his glowing anger." (S&G)

Jeremiah 4:23-26 "I looked on the earth, and behold, it was formless and void; and to the heavens, and they had no light. {24} I looked on the mountains, and behold, they were quaking, and all the hills moved to and fro. {25} I looked, and behold, there was no man, and all the birds of the heavens had fled. {26} I looked, and behold, the fruitful land was a wilderness, and all its cities were pulled down before the Lord, before His fierce anger." (NASB)

Jeremiah 4:23-26 "**I saw the earth, and behold,** it was **a chaos and vacant, And the heavens, and they had no light. {24} I saw the mountains, and behold,** they were **quaking, and all the hills, they rocked. {25} I saw, and behold** there **was no humanity, And every flier of the heavens, they had bolted** away. {26} **I saw, and behold, the crop** land was a **wilderness And all it cities, they were broken down because** of **Yahweh's presence, Because of the heat of His anger.**" (CVOT) (emphasis in original)

What is God telling the Jews? Before we answer that, we have to ask another question: What would the Jews of Jeremiah's time think when they read a description of the earth in a *TOHUW WA-BOHUW* and dark condition? The only other place in the Bible where the phrase *TOHUW WA-BOHUW* is mentioned is in Genesis 1:2. The Book of Genesis was written about 800 years before, so they were quite familiar with Genesis. Clearly, they would have made an instant connection to the creation account in Genesis. (Remember, the Bible was written by ancient Hebrews to ancient Hebrews, so we must always take into account how the ancient Hebrews would have interpreted Scripture.)

It seems impossible to think these words in Jeremiah wouldn't have created a mental connection to the same words in Genesis. It seems obvious God wanted the people of Jeremiah's time to make this connection. So, what was God telling them? He's warning them about His judgment and wrath by calling to mind a historical fact they understood about the early earth. They knew God had judged the earth before Adam. Jeremiah 4:23-26 is a parenthetical description of that judgment. Jeremiah stops in mid-thought to describe to the Jews what God's anger had once caused. As you read from verse 1 to 22, you see how God is declaring what SHALL/WILL happen to Israel in the future if they don't repent. Here are some of those future SHALL/WILL events in verses 1-22:

vs. 6   I **WILL** bring evil (a future event)
vs. 7   thy cities **SHALL** be laid waste (a future event)
vs. 9   it **SHALL** come to pass at that day (a future event)
vs. 9   the heart of the king **SHALL** perish (a future event)
vs. 9   the priests **SHALL** be astonished (a future event)
vs. 9   the prophets **SHALL** wonder (a future event)
vs. 12   now also **WILL** I give sentence (a future event)
vs. 13   Behold, he **SHALL** come up as clouds (a future event)
vs. 13   his chariots **SHALL** be as a whirlwind (a future event)
vs. 21   How long **SHALL** I see standard, and hear the sound of the trumpet (a future event)

Now temporarily remove verses 23-26 (Jeremiah's Parenthesis) and go right to verses 27-30. The text continues a smooth flow of what SHALL/WILL happen in the future. Here are some more of those future SHALL/WILL events in verses 27-30.

vs. 27   the whole land **SHALL** be desolate (a future event)
vs. 27   yet **WILL** I not make a full end (a future event)
vs. 28   For this **SHALL** the earth mourn, and the heavens above be black (a future event)
vs. 29   The whole city **SHALL** flee (a future event)
vs. 29   they **SHALL** go into thickets (a future event)
vs. 30   and when thou art spoiled, what **SHALL** thou do? (a future event)
vs. 30   your lovers **WILL** despise you, they **WILL** seek your life (a future event)

Verb tenses (stems) in Hebrew are not quite the same as verb tenses in English, but the English translations do an excellent job at capturing the intent of Jeremiah's parenthetical vision. Verses 23-26 don't describe what **SHALL** be in the future; they describe what **WAS** in the past. The tense changes from the future to the past. Here are the descriptions of the past as seen in the verses 23-26 parenthesis:

vs. 23 it **WAS** without form, and void (a past event)
vs. 23 their light **WAS** gone (a past event)
vs. 24 the mountains **WERE** quaking (a past event)
vs. 24 the hills **WERE** swaying (a past event)
vs. 25 there **WAS** no man (a past event)
vs. 25 the birds of the heavens **WERE** fled (a past event)
vs. 26 the fruitful place **WAS** a wilderness (a past event)
vs. 26 all the cities thereof **WERE** broken down (a past event)

It is very important to recognize this temporary shift to the past tense. Jeremiah is looking at the past in verses 23-26! If you miss this, you miss the meaning of his warning. Jeremiah is warning Israel with a vision of the past. God reminded them, that in His judgment and fierce anger, He made the earth a desolate waste, devoid of life, and dark in the past. That means at some time in the past, before Jeremiah's day, the earth was without form and void, dark, its mountains and hills were shaken, there were no people, the vegetation had been ruined, and all it cities were destroyed… and all this was done by the anger of God. The only time the earth could have been in that condition was before the six days of restoration. Jeremiah is looking at the Pre-Adamic earth.

Some people still object. They don't think God would warn Israel about a future judgment by looking back at a past judgment. They ignore the shift in tense because they don't want to believe God would warn Israel with a vision about the past. They cling tightly to their interpretation that Jeremiah's vision is entirely future and has nothing to do with the past. If they admitted it was a vision of the past, before Jeremiah's time, then they would have to explain WHEN, before Jeremiah's time, God had judged the earth and made it *TOHUW WA-BOHUW* and dark. The easiest way to get around this little obstacle is to pretend God doesn't warn people about future judgments by referring to past judgments. A quick look at Psalms 95 shows how God did that very thing in David's time.

Psalms 95:8-11 "Do not harden your hearts, as at Meribah, As in the day of Massah in the wilderness, *{9}* When your fathers tested Me, They tried Me, though they had seen My work. *{10}* For forty years I loathed *that* generation, And said they are a people who err in their heart, And they do not know My ways. *{11}* Therefore I swore in My anger, Truly they shall not enter into My rest." (NASB)

God warned the Jews of David's time not to harden their hearts as their forefathers had done in Moses' time. God refers back to a past judgment to warn Israel about a future judgment. Those who think God wouldn't use a past judgment as a warning for a future judgment don't understand God very well; or prophecy. Just as God made a connection between David's time and Moses' time, God made a connection between Jeremiah's time and the time before Adam. This is that connection: God is warning the people of Jeremiah's time, that unless they repent and forsake their evil ways, He will do the same thing to them He did to the Pre-Adamic earth. If they do not cease their rebellion, He will make Israel desolate just like He had made the early earth desolate, but unlike the early earth, He will not make a full end of them (vs. 27)

Jeremiah 4:27 "For thus hath the LORD said, The whole land shall be desolate; yet will I not make a full end." (KJV)

Jeremiah 4:27 "**For thus says Yahweh: A desolation shall the entire earth become, (Though I shall not make** a full **end** to it)." (CVOT) (emphasis in original)

Jeremiah 4:27 "This is what the LORD says: The whole earth will be ruined, although I will not destroy it completely." (GW)

Question: When did God have a great, fierce, burning, glowing anger at the earth? When did He make the earth *TOHUW WA-BOHUW*? When did He make a full end of the earth? When has the earth had no man and no light?

Answer: This can only be describing earth prior to Adam. Jeremiah is using *TOHUW WA-BOHUW*, the same words God used to describe the Pre-Adamic earth in Genesis 1:2. In both passages earth is desolate and lifeless. Both passages say the earth is without light. Jeremiah must be looking at the Pre-Adamic world because from the time of Adam until all eternity, the earth will be populated by man. **Earth will never be without man.** Man became a permanent fixture on the earth the day God created Adam from its dust. If earth ever becomes devoid of people, then God's promise to the Jews will be broken.

Jeremiah 31:35-36 "This is what the LORD says, he who appoints the sun to shine by day, who decrees the moon and stars to shine by night, who stirs up the sea so that its waves roar-- the LORD Almighty is his name: *{36}* '**Only if these decrees vanish from my sight,' declares the LORD, 'will the descendants of Israel ever cease to be a nation before me.'**" (NIV)

God's promise will never be broken. The Jews will never cease as long as the earth exists. Since God's promises cannot be broken, the earth will never be without the Jews. At no time in the future will the earth be without Jews. This means earth will never be without man. During the time of the final judgment, the holy things will remain; only the evil things will be destroyed. The saved will remain on the earth, but the damned will be removed. Jeremiah is looking at the earth with "NO MAN." That does not describe the future judgment of the earth.

Joel 2:31-32 "The sun will be turned into darkness, And the moon into blood, Before the great and awesome day of the LORD comes. {32} And it will come about that **whoever calls on the name of the LORD Will be delivered; For on Mount Zion and in Jerusalem There will be those who escape**, As the LORD has said, Even among the **survivors** whom the LORD calls." (NASB)

Mount Zion, Jerusalem, and people will still be on the earth during this future judgment. The heavens will be darkened, but the earth will not be in the state of having all its cities destroyed and having no man. There will be survivors! Jeremiah 4:23-26 is not describing the future; it is describing the Pre-Adamic past.

2 Peter 3:7 "But the present heavens and earth by His word are being reserved for fire, kept for the day of judgment and destruction **of ungodly men**." (NASB)

This will not be a day of judgment and destruction of all men, only ungodly men. At that time, the earth will not be in the state of having NO MAN. Again, there will be survivors; righteous men and women who still dwell upon the earth.

Matthew 13:41-43 "The Son of man shall send forth his angels, and they shall gather out of his kingdom all things that offend, and them which do iniquity; {42} And shall cast them into a furnace of fire: there shall be wailing and gnashing of teeth. {43} Then shall **the righteous shine forth as the sun in the kingdom** of their Father. Who hath ears to hear, let him hear." (KJV)

We really need to hear what our ears hear. Only the ungodly will be judged and destroyed on that day; the righteous will remain. Earth will still be populated by men! Jeremiah can only be describing the Pre-Adamic earth. Earth was *TOHUW WA-BOHUW* and without man before Adam, but it will never be that way again. Genesis 1:2 describes the only time earth was a desolate waste with no man and no light. Jeremiah 4:23 is a glimpse of Genesis 1:2. Jeremiah was looking at the earth's past, not its future.

What else did Jeremiah see in this earth-before-Adam? He saw the earth's gardens, or fruitful places, had become a desolate wilderness. "Fruitful places," "garden land," "crop land," and "rich land" describe such things as gardens, fields of grain, orchards, and vineyards. This is land that had been cultivated. Jeremiah reminded the Jews that God in His anger turned these fruitful places into wasteland. But, that means there was plant life on earth before it became *TOHUW WA-BOHUW*. It was not *TOHUW WA-BOHUW* because God hadn't yet created fruitful places; it became *TOHUW WA-BOHUW* because God destroyed the fruitful places already there. This means the creation of plants on Day Three (Genesis 1:11-13) was actually a restoration of plants. Jeremiah also saw that birds had lived on the earth before it became *TOHUW WA-BOHUW*. The creation of birds on Day Five (Genesis 1:20-23) was a restoration of birds. Now, I wonder what kind of plants and birds these were, but what really grabs my attention is the mention of cities. Jeremiah looked and saw that ALL of earth's cities had been pulled down and destroyed by God's wrath.

When have all of earth's cities been destroyed? Was this the Great Flood of Noah's time? Some say so, but there are two major differences between the earth Jeremiah sees and the earth at the time of Noah's Flood. The earth wasn't dark during Noah's Flood. (I'll develop that thought in more detail later.) In addition, the earth wasn't without people during Noah's Flood. There were eight souls who did not perish. It would be wrong for Jeremiah to say there was, "no man," because there were four men and four women still on the earth. Jeremiah mentions nothing about a flood in Jeremiah 4:23-26. Jeremiah is not looking at a flooded earth. He is looking at mountains shaking, hills swaying, and gardens made into deserts. If Jeremiah is seeing deserts, he is not seeing a global flood. Jeremiah isn't warning them about a future global flood. Instead, Jeremiah is warning them with a description of God making the earth *TOHUW WA-BOHUW*, "without form and void." When did God do this? Some say this *TOHUW WA-BOHUW* condition is a vision of the future "end-times" judgment. They interpret the final judgment as a time when God will come and destroy the earth and all life on it. Is this a description of earth's future? No. If this applies to the future, then all the cities, including Jerusalem, will be destroyed. If this applies to the future, than all men, including the righteous, will be destroyed. This will never happen according to the Bible. It cannot be a look at the end-times. When God comes to make His final judgment on the earth, He will come to restore Jerusalem, not destroy it. He will come to rescue His people on the earth, not remove them from the earth.

If all the cities on earth were destroyed and there were no men on earth in Jeremiah's vision, then Jeremiah was looking at the Pre-Adamic earth. He was not looking at the future. There will never be a time in the future when all men on earth are dead. If Jeremiah saw the fruitful places (fields, gardens, orchards, *etc*.) of the earth as barren wilderness, then he wasn't looking at the earth of the future. God promised that as long as the earth exists, it would be fruitful.

Genesis 8:22 "While the earth remaineth, **seedtime and harvest**, and cold and heat, and summer and winter, and day and night shall not cease." (KJV)

Plant life will remain on the earth forever. This means the earth without plants (Jeremiah 4:23) is a description of the Pre-Adamic past. The Jews of Jeremiah's time knew God had judged and destroyed the Pre-Adamic earth. They understood Jeremiah wasn't looking at the future earth. I wish more people of our day knew this.

To *HAYAH* or not to *HAYAH*: That is the Question

There is one aspect of Jeremiah's vision of the early earth that may seem troublesome for the Gap Theory. Jeremiah doesn't use *HAYAH* ("*was*" is in italics) when he describes what he SEES, whereas Moses uses *HAYAH* when he describes what God is DOING.

Jeremiah 4:23-24 "I beheld the earth, and, lo, *it **was*** without form, and void; and the heavens, and they *had* no light. {24} I beheld the mountains, and, lo, they trembled, and all the hills moved lightly." (KJV)

Genesis 1:2 "And the earth **was** without form, and void; and darkness *was* upon the face of the deep. And the Spirit of God moved upon the face of the waters." (KJV)

Some opponents of the Ruin-Restoration Theory have tried to use this difference as a way of proving Genesis 1:2 describes a static condition. Jeremiah explains it in terms of a static condition, therefore the earth in Genesis 1:2 must have been in a static condition of "was," not a dynamic condition of "became."

Arthur Custance did an excellent job of refuting their argument. He showed what the ancient Hebrew people thought when *HAYAH* was used, and what they thought when *HAYAH* wasn't used.[91] Custance reminds us that Jeremiah is seeing a point in time. God is showing Jeremiah a "snapshot" of the Pre-Adamic earth, not a "video" of the Pre-Adamic earth. Jeremiah is not seeing a replay of how the earth came to be in Genesis 1:2; he is seeing an image of what the earth was in Genesis 1:2. When used to describe what that condition **was** in his vision, Jeremiah would not have used *HAYAH*. He was merely describing the image God showed him. On the other hand, in Genesis 1, Moses is not describing an image of what God is SEEING; he is describing what God is DOING. Genesis is not a static description of just what you would see if you were present at the creation. Genesis is a dynamic description of what you would see God DOING. It's dynamic. This is obvious since Genesis says, "God created," "God said," "God moved," "God called," "God made," "God formed," *etc*. The emphasis is on God's actions. Quite to the contrary of what anti-gap people say, Jeremiah's account shows how the Hebrew of Genesis 1:2 would have been written if God had intended to describe the earth as a static description of WAS instead of a dynamic description of BECAME. Jeremiah's account clarifies how the ancient Hebrews didn't use *HAYAH* when they thought of "being" in a static sense, but used it when they thought of "being" in a dynamic/changing sense. Custance explained this over forty years ago.

> "Indeed, this is precisely what Jeremiah 4.23 does. Jeremiah's vision was a vision of a moment. He saw the earth as a Chaos. More than this, he saw a Cosmos as a Chaos, for he actually says that the evidence of civilization lay in ruins...., men and cities had been overwhelmed. He was not concerned in reverting to the past in order to say that this scene of devastation had come about over a period of time by such-and-such a process. He merely says that when he saw it, it presented to his mind's eye a scene of devastation. It is almost as though the Author of Scripture had given us this passage in order to assist us in our understanding of Genesis 1.2 which so nearly parallels it while at the same time differing from it in such an important detail - the introduction of היה."[92]

Once again I want to make this clear. Jeremiah sees the earth in its history before man. He sees the earth as a desolate waste, devoid of life and light. Furthermore, this desolate condition was not the result of God not yet creating life and light. Instead, it was the result of God's judgment. Jeremiah is telling the Jews about God's judgment. He's warning them about God's judgment. That's the context of this passage. If the *TOHUW WA-BOHUW* condition of the earth was not the result of God's judgment, then it makes no sense for Jeremiah to mention it in a passage dealing with God's judgment. Jeremiah connects it to God's judgment because there had been life, but it was destroyed. There had been light, but God took away that light. God judged the earth. Earth's life was destroyed and its cities were thrown down. These passages do not describe the earth at any time in its history since Adam, or anytime in its future.

There are some who say this vision of death, destruction, and darkness is a vision of Israel, not the earth. Remember *ERETS* means "land" as well as "earth." Because of this, some people say Jeremiah is looking at the Land of Israel in the end-times. But this idea doesn't work either. Remember, God promised the Jews they will never be destroyed. There never has been a time in the past, and there never will be a time in the future when Israel fits the description in this vision. True, Israel will be judged in the future when Christ returns, but it will be a remaking of Israel; a restoration. In fact, it will be the long-awaited restoration. The wicked will be removed, but the righteous will remain. Christ is not going to make Israel a dead and dark desolation when He returns. Israel never has been and never will be *TOHUW WA-BOHUW* and dark. Jeremiah's vision does not describe Israel (*ERETS*) at any time in its history; past, present, or future. Jeremiah's vision does not describe the earth (*ERETS*) at any time in the present or the future. Therefore, Jeremiah must be seeing the earth in the past, prior to the restoration. Jeremiah must be seeing the earth destroyed by God's judgment before Adam. The best interpretation of Genesis 1 is to let Scripture interpret Scripture and realize the six days of creation were six literal days in which God restored the earth and the life on it.

Is Jeremiah 4:23-26 Literal or Figurative?

There are those who insist Jeremiah is being figurative, *i.e.* the "world system" was useless, vain, corrupt, *etc.*, and was in "spiritual darkness." Once again I disagree. There was no "world system." There could be no "world system" because there was "no man." Men weren't created yet. The word "earth" in verse twenty-three is not symbolic of the "world system." Jeremiah is describing the literal earth. Jeremiah is being literal when he tells us about the literal sin and the literal rebellion of the literal Jews. He's being literal when he tells us the literal God is literally angry with the literal Jews and that He is literally going to bring literal judgment and literal destruction down of them if they don't literally repent and literally turn back to Him. I have read commentaries stating that since Jeremiah is writing poetry here, this portion of Scripture can't be taken literally; it must be a metaphor or allegory. What a ridiculous comment. Are we to believe in all of human literature there has never been poetry that expressed literal ideas, literal words, literal thoughts, literal truths, or spoke about literal events or conditions?

Some will say we can't take Jeremiah's description of earth as literal. Some will say he was using spiritual symbolism as a way to convince the Jews to repent of their wicked ways and return to the Lord. Some will say references to worldwide darkness, worldwide destruction of plant life, and worldwide destruction of cities are merely poetic tools used to express God's wrath. Again, as in Isaiah 45, there is nothing in context to indicate these things are anything but literal. Jeremiah lists God's literal warnings to Israel before Jeremiah 4:23-27. Jeremiah lists God's literal warnings to Israel after Jeremiah 4:23-27. What clue is there that Jeremiah 4:23-27 is not a literal warning to Israel? The only reason for not accepting these verses as literal is because if they are literal, then the Young-Earth and Day-Age interpretations of Genesis have to be discarded. I cannot accept these God-inspired words of Jeremiah to be figurative symbols of a nonexistent reality. Look at all the other warnings God gave Israel. God ALWAYS WARNED THEM ABOUT LITERAL JUDGMENTS. When God warned Moses about Israel wandering around in the wilderness for forty years, that is literally what happened. When God warned Israel their idolatry would lead to their destruction by foreign nations, they were literally destroyed by foreign nations. When God warned the Jews about being taken into captivity to Babylon for seventy years, they were taken into literal captivity to Babylon for literally seventy years. When Jesus wept over Jerusalem and warned His people of impending judgment and destruction, that is exactly what Rome did. **God's warnings to Israel have never described non-literal judgments.** Judgment means literal judgment; destruction means literal destruction. God's warnings never describe non-literal conditions, even if He uses poetry to reveal them. Poetic words can describe literal meanings. If a young man uses poetry to express his love for a young woman, would she be justified in thinking he doesn't literally love her because he used poetry? When Jeremiah warned Israel of how utterly it might be destroyed by God's wrath, he refers to a time when the earth was literally made *TOHUW WA-BOHUW* by God's wrath. Why would this warning refer to a non-literal condition? God never did that! I can only interpret this to mean there was a literal time in earth's history when God made it literally *TOHUW WA-BOHUW*. To interpret *TOHUW WA-BOHUW* in a figurative sense here would be ridiculous. God never refers to figurative judgment. Instead, He warns us with true, physical destruction, and in this instance, He referred to the Pre-Adamic earth as His example. Divine judgment fell on the Pre-Adamic earth and God made it literally *TOHUW WA-BOHUW*.

The original earth was not a desolation. Isaiah said the earth wasn't created that way. Jeremiah said it was made that way after God, in His wrath, destroyed the life and the cities already there. Genesis 1:1 and Genesis 1:2 cannot be translated in such a way as to imply the earth was originally created without form, and void. Even if the grammar allows it, such a translation must be laid aside in favor of an equally valid translation that doesn't introduce a contradiction into the Bible. If God originally created earth *TOHUW*, then Isaiah lied to us. If there were no plants and birds and cities in the Pre-*TOHUW WA-BOHUW* earth, then Jeremiah lied to us. If these men lied, then God lied. I can't allow God's character to be smeared by those who make Him out to be a liar simply because they wish to cling to their own preconceived ideas. God is not a liar; men are!

Does God Speak Hebrew?

Can we be sure *TOHUW* and *BOHUW* imply Divine judgment in Genesis 1:2? According to Jeremiah 4:23, these words refer to Divine judgment. Jeremiah warns Israel they will be made *TOHUW WA-BOHUW* if they don't repent. Are *TOHUW* and *BOHUW* used elsewhere? Yes. They are also found in Isaiah 34:11. (*TOHUW* in bold; *BOHUW* in underlined and bold.)

Isaiah 34:8-11 "For the LORD has a day of vengeance, a year of retribution, to uphold Zion's cause. {9} Edom's streams will be turned into pitch, her dust into burning sulfur; her land will become blazing pitch! {10} It will not be quenched night and day; its smoke will rise forever. From generation to generation it will lie desolate; no one will ever pass through it again. {11} The desert owl and screech owl will possess it; the great owl and the raven will nest there. God will stretch out over Edom the measuring line of **chaos** and the plumb line of **desolation**." (NIV)

In Isaiah 34, God speaks of His judgment of all the nations and especially of Edom. Isaiah 34:11 tells us what God will do to Edom when He judges it. God uses the words *TOHUW* (chaos) and *BOHUW* (desolation). Theologians and Hebrew scholars have been arguing for years over what these words mean in Genesis 1:2. How many times have you heard Biblical scholars say we need to let Scripture interpret Scripture? You've probably been bombarded with that phrase a gazillion times. Everybody claims they want to let Scripture interpret Scripture, but what they really mean is to let THEIR interpretation of Scripture interpret Scripture. What they're really saying is, "If your interpretation of Scripture looks like it's going to disprove my interpretation of Scripture, then you must be taking it out of context."

When we don't know the meaning of a word or phrase in the Bible, the first and best way of learning its meaning is to go elsewhere in the Bible to see what it means. If we do that with *TOHUW* and *BOHUW*, then we discover it means Divine judgment. *TOHUW* and *BOHUW* mean Divine judgment in Jeremiah! *TOHUW* and *BOHUW* mean Divine judgment in Isaiah! What would make me think *TOHUW* and *BOHUW* have a different meaning in Genesis? What rule of Biblical interpretation allows us to ignore the clear meanings of words and phrases found elsewhere in the Bible, just so we can interpret those words and phrases the way we want? Dear friends, a lot of people hate the Gap Theory. A lot of scholars believe interpreting Genesis 1:2 as the result of Divine judgment is a stretched interpretation. They say it is weak and without merit. They say there is no Biblical basis for believing it. I disagree. As far as I'm concerned, the burden of proof ought to be to show Genesis 1:2 doesn't refer to Divine judgment. We have two passages of Scripture that use these words to describe Divine judgment. Jeremiah 4:23 and Isaiah 34:11 are the only verses besides Genesis 1:2 that use *TOHUW* and *BOHUW* together. In both of those verses *TOHUW* and *BOHUW* refer to God's judgment. We ought to let Scripture really interpret Scripture. We ought to let words mean what they mean! We ought to let God say what He wants to say. God knew what He was going to say in the Book of Isaiah. He knew what the words would convey to Jeremiah. He knew all their meanings, shades of meanings, connotations, denotations, implications, and whatever. Hey, God speaks Hebrew! God chose two words to describe the Pre-Adamic earth, and He picked the same two words that describe conditions of Divine judgment. Did God blunder in the selection of these two words? Didn't He know what He would imply by using them? I think God knew which Hebrew words expressed what He wanted us to know. God wanted us to know Genesis 1:2 describes a Divine judgment.

A Look at Satan's World

I believe it was Lucifer and the fallen angels who caused earth to be made desolate and the universe to groan under the power of sin. I believe this because the Bible tells us about a judgment prior to Adam, but it says nothing directly about humans. It indirectly mentions Pre-Adamic humans only if you presuppose, as I do, that these Pre-Adamic cities were built by Pre-Adamic humans. However, I don't think they were humans like us. I don't think they would have been made in the image and likeness of God. They may have been very intelligent creatures capable of making tools and building cities, but I don't think they would have been responsible for the sin that caused God to judge the earth. If they existed, they were probably victims of Lucifer's sin and the sin of his angels. The Bible tells us about the sin and rebellion of Lucifer. The Bible says one-third of the angelic hosts were pulled into that rebellion. (Revelation 12:4) God doesn't want us to be ignorant about those rebellious angels. That's why I think they were the ones who brought about the judgment mentioned in Jeremiah 4:23-26. If they weren't, then God gives us no clues for understanding Jeremiah's revelation. If the Bible tells us about sin and rebellion prior to the six days of Genesis, then it must be referring to the only creatures mentioned in the Bible who sinned and rebelled prior to those six days. It must be referring to Lucifer and his fallen angels.

Now, where do I get the notion Lucifer and the angels sinned and rebelled before the six days? The Bible says, "God saw every thing He had made, and behold, it was very good. And the morning and the evening were the sixth day." If Lucifer had sinned and rebelled before the sixth day, how could God say everything He made was very good? Young-Earth creationists insist the Gap Theory creates a contradiction here. Let's examine their argument.

The simplest interpretation of Genesis 1, they say, is that everything, including angels, was created during those six days. The easiest interpretation is that Genesis 1:1 is the first creative step in a series of creative steps taking place over a six-day period in which absolutely everything was created. This would be the most logical and straightforward interpretation of the Bible if there was only one beginning. This would be the case if the original creation described in Genesis 1:1 was the same creation as the creation described in Genesis 1:3-31. This would be the only explanation if there was only one creation. If the Bible revealed only one beginning, then I'd have to agree that Lucifer and the rest of the angels were created during that beginning. If "made" (*ASAH*) was always equivalent to "create" (*BARA*), then we could conclude that since everything God had MADE was very good, then everything God had CREATED was also very good. But if the six days of creation (restoration) were not the same as the original creation, then "very good" would be referring to the things God made during the six days. It wouldn't necessarily refer to everything He had created in Genesis 1:1. If the earth was restored by God during those six days, then "every thing He had made" refers to His works of restoration. If there were two different beginnings, then Genesis 1:31 refers to the second beginning, the restoration, but not to the first beginning, the original creation.

Go back and carefully read Genesis 1. The chapter ends at verse thirty-one where God saw everything He made was very good. During the creation week He declared the things He created and made as, "good." He spoke light into existence and said light was good. He separated the water from the land so dry land appeared, and He said that was good. He commanded plants to grow and they grew; He said that was good. When He set the sun and moon and stars in place, He said that was good. Sea creatures came into being by His command, and He said that was good. The same was true for land creatures; He said they were good. Finally, after the creation of man and woman, God looked at all He had done during the six days, and said it was very good. Do you see a difference between how the week started and how it ended? Genesis 1:2 was not good. The words He used bring to mind the exact opposite condition; the earth wasn't good. It was desolate and dead. There was no light. Even without knowing the exact meanings of *TOHUW*, *BOHUW*, and *CHOSHEK*, I think we'd get the idea the condition of the earth WASN'T GOOD. Genesis 1:1-2 do not fit into the six days. That's the whole point of revealing earth's dead condition. Satan's world was NOT good. God wants us to know the earth needed to be reborn, and He wants us to know the Holy Spirit was the One who provided its rebirth. The earth had to be born again. It needed a new beginning, and that's exactly what happened. The Holy Spirit brooded over the surface of the abyss and the restoration began. The earth was reborn; it had a new beginning. God's proclamation of "very good" was referring to the restored earth and the restored life on it. It wasn't referring to the fallen angels. They were not restored. The restoration of the physical realm did not include a restoration of the angelic realm. God was preparing a place for man.

Whose Cities Were These?

If there were Pre-Adamic cities on the earth, then there was life on the Pre-Adamic earth. Whose cities were they? Why did God destroy them in His wrath? Why is God reminding the Jews of what He did to the Pre-Adamic earth? He's warning them they face the same destructive wrath. God is telling them that just as He destroyed the Pre-Adamic cities, He will destroy them, with the exception He won't make a full end to them.

Who built these cities that were destroyed before Adam was created? Two sub-theories have emerged. The first is that some type of human-like creatures (but not true humans created in the image and likeness of God) existed before Adam. If this is true, then it certainly explains the extremely ancient fossils and artifacts geologists, paleontologists, and archaeologists have discovered. The second sub-theory says angels dwelt on the Pre-Adamic earth and built cities.

I'll deal with the second sub-theory first. I have no proof for what I am about to say, but I find it very strange to think angelic creatures built the Pre-Adamic cities. The reason I think they weren't angels is because the evidence proves they were limited to stone-age technology. I can't imagine angels would be limited to stone tools. I can't imagine angels could build only mud huts with thatched roofs, or live in caves. It seems impossible to believe angels had to use stone-tipped spears to kill animals so they could eat. The Bible seems to indicate angels are very powerful and intelligent creatures, so I wonder why they would have planted gardens using sharp sticks to plow furrows for their seeds. No. The evidence indicates these creatures were very primitive. I may be wrong, but I don't think the cities God destroyed in the Pre-Adamic earth were built by angels. Some kind of prehistoric "men" lived on the Pre-Adamic earth.

The only logical conclusion is that these cities were built by Pre-Adamic, human-like creatures… unless, of course, you are a Young-Earth creationist who believes they were built by Adam's descendants. If that is true, then I am wrong about them being Pre-

Adamic. Does the Bible give any indication these cities were built and destroyed before true men existed? Yes it does; Jeremiah 4:25 says there was, "no man."

Jeremiah 4:25 "I looked, and behold, there was no man, And all the birds of the heavens had fled." (NASB)

If all the cities on earth were destroyed and there were no men on the earth, then either these cities were:

1.) Built by Pre-Adamic "men," who were later all killed.

Or:

2.) Built by the descendants of Adam, who were later all killed.

Since you're reading this book, you know all the descendants of Adam were not killed. These cities were not built by the descendants of Adam. True man had not yet been created. They must have been built by human-like creatures who had the intelligence and skill to build cities, use tools, plant gardens, *etc*. Jeremiah is viewing the earth when there was, "no man." He describes the earth before Adam. Now, there is another place in Scripture that gives us a view of the earth before Adam and Eve were created. That place is Genesis 1:26-27.

Genesis 1:26-27 "And God said, Let us make man in our image, after our likeness: and let them have dominion over the fish of the sea, and over the fowl of the air, and over the cattle, and over all the earth, and over every creeping thing that creepeth upon the earth. *{27}* So God created man in his *own* image, in the image of God created he him; male and female created he them." (KJV)

There are two ways you can interpret the phrase, "in our image." One way is that God was going to create humans as a new, never-before-seen creature, and He would make them in His image. The other way to interpret this is that He was going to create men who would now be made in His image. This second interpretation opens itself up to the idea that humans, or at least human-like creatures, existed in the Pre-Adamic world, but these men were not made in the image of God. They had been there, but Lucifer probably destroyed them. As part of God's plan and work of restoration, He was going to restore men just like He restored other lifeforms, but now this man was going to be a new creature; he was now going to be made in the image of God. In the Pre-Adamic world, God created men not in His image. In the restored world, God created men in His image. In this sense, "in His image," becomes a qualifying phrase that distinguishes the "old man" from the "new man." The "old man" was carnal, nothing more than a very intelligent and skillful animal. He had no ability to have an intimate relationship with his Creator. He had no ability to understand spiritual truths. He didn't know good from evil. He could walk, talk, build cities, use tools, *etc.*, but he was not made in the image and likeness of God. Therefore, he could not be part of God's family. Lucifer had dominion over the "old men," and probably enslaved them, used them, brutalized them, and murdered them. And I think this explains the judgment and destruction of the Pre-Adamic earth. It wasn't judged and destroyed because of any sin the Pre-Adamic human/human-like beings committed. I don't think they had the capacity to sin. They were like intelligent animals that had no knowledge of good and evil. I believe the earth had "no man" because Lucifer murdered them. I think he murdered them because they wouldn't worship and serve him like he wanted. I think their murder was the reason God brought about the complete end to Lucifer's kingdom. God destroyed the old world a few to several thousand years ago, and then created/recreated a new world with a new man over a six-day period. The new man was different. By being in the image and likeness of God, he could commune with God, worship God, walk with God, understand spiritual truths, and be a true child of God. This new man was now going to have dominion over Lucifer. Satan had brought "man" down, but God now raised man up. God gave Adam dominion over the earth.

The Gap Theory proposes THERE WAS INTELLIGENT LIFE ON EARTH BEFORE THE SIX DAYS OF GENESIS. There was a Pre-Adamic civilization. This means Genesis 1:3-31 was not part of the original creation of the earth. Earth had an earlier beginning. I strongly believe the six days of Genesis 1:3-31 were six twenty-four-hour days. I am convinced all life now on earth originated from those living things God restored/created during those six days. However, I am equally convinced there was life on earth prior to those six days, and all Pre-Adamic life was destroyed by God's judgment. I am also convinced no living thing, including those things alive before Adam, got here by any process of evolution.

Let's Look at "Let"

In the first chapter of Genesis, The Bible uses the word "let" to describe God's creative acts. Here is a list of the "let" passages in the *King James Bible*:

Genesis 1:3 "… Let there be light:"

Genesis 1:6a "… Let there be a firmament in the midst of the waters,"

Genesis 1:6b "… let it divide the waters from the waters."

Genesis 1:9a "… Let the waters under the heaven be gathered together unto one place,"

Genesis 1:9b "… let the dry *land* appear:"

Genesis 1:11 "… Let the earth bring forth grass, the herb yielding seed, *and* the fruit tree yielding fruit after his kind,"

Genesis 1:14a "… Let there be lights in the firmament of the heaven…"

Genesis 1:14b "… let them be for signs, and for seasons, and for days, and years:"

Genesis 1:15 "… let them be for lights in the firmament of the heaven to give light upon the earth:"

Genesis 1:20 "… Let the waters bring forth abundantly the moving creature that hath life, and fowl *that* may fly above the earth in the open firmament of heaven."

Genesis 1:22 "… let fowl multiply in the earth."

Genesis 1:24 "… Let the earth bring forth the living creature after his kind, cattle, and creeping thing, and beast of the earth after his kind: and it was so."

Genesis 1:26a "… Let us make man in our image, after our likeness:"

Genesis 1:26b "… let them have dominion over the fish of the sea, and over the fowl of the air, and over the cattle, and over all the earth, and over every creeping thing that creepeth upon the earth."

In English, we often need a word like "let" in order to make it sound correct. In Hebrew, the word "let" is not there. In most cases it is a rendering of the verb *HAYAH*. (God said, "Light BE, and light CAME TO BE.") However, it's not always *HAYAH*. Other verbs are used depending on what is brought into existence. For instance, in Genesis 1:11, God commands: "Earth, bring forth grass, the herb yielding fruit, the fruit tree yielding fruit." In Genesis 1:22 God commands: "Fowl, multiply in the earth." In Genesis 1:20 God commands: "Waters, bring forth abundantly the moving creature…" Regardless of the verb, we still add "let" in English to make it sound better to us. We translate it, "Let birds multiply on the earth," because it sounds better than saying, "Birds, multiply on the earth." So, the presence or absence of the word "let" is not all that important. What is important is how (and why) God sets up a pattern:

1.) First there is a certain condition.
2.) Then He gives a "let" command.
3.) Then the condition changes to something it wasn't before.

The conditions AFTER the "let" commands are not the same conditions as BEFORE the "let" commands. In Genesis 1:3 we see, "Let there be light, and light came to be." There was no light before the command, but there was light after the command. As we go through all these commands we see how they reveal the same thing. First, the waters were not divided by the firmament. Then God commanded the waters to be divided. After the command there was water above and below the firmament. There was no grass or herbs or trees until God commanded them to come into being. Then there was grass and herbs and trees. In each case we see the condition AFTER the "let" command is the opposite of the condition BEFORE the "let" command.

Now, I know you're saying, "Yes, that's obvious. That's the whole point of the passage. It proves God created all these things." Of course, you are right, and I'm not trying to be condescending, but I think this pattern reveals the condition of the earth just before God restored it. Let's look at verse nine more closely.

Genesis 1:9 "And God said, 'Let the waters under the heaven be gathered together unto one place, and let the dry *land* appear: and it was so.'" (KJV)

We all agree (I hope) no dry land was visible before this command. Dry land would not have been visible if either of two sets of conditions were present. The first is if the earth was completely under liquid water as the Young-Earth and Day-Age creationists say. The second is if the earth was partially under water, (oceans, seas, and lakes) and the parts that weren't under water were under a thick layer of ice and snow (An Ice-Age) as the Gap Theory suggests. Both theories agree that dry land did not appear until after the "let" command.

So much for the dry land; we all agree. Where we differ is the answer to this question: What was the condition of the waters before and after the "let" command? After the "let" command, the waters were gathered together and they were in one place. Now, if the pattern holds true, then it means before the "let" command, the waters were NOT gathered together (they were separated) and they were NOT in one place (they were in multiple places). Again, throughout all the rest of the creation account, the conditions that followed the "let" commands are the opposite of the conditions that preceded the "let" commands. This means before the waters were commanded to gather together, they were scattered apart. This means before the waters were commanded to be in one place, they were in multiple places. So, how do you get scattered waters, in multiple places if the whole earth is completely under liquid water? You can't.

Here is an experiment you can do at home. Take two bowls of equal size. Fill the first bowl with a cup of water. Now look at the water. Is it gathered together? Yes! Is it in one place? Yes, of course it is. Now, go to the freezer and get a cup of ice cubes. Put the ice cubes in the second bowl so none of them touch each other. Arrange them so the ice cubes are spaced over the bottom of the bowl. Put some of them on the right and some of them on the left. Put some at the front and some at the back. Now look at the ice cubes. The ice cubes are made of water, but in this case the water is not gathered together. All the water in the bowl is not in one place. We have equal amounts of water in both bowls, but the water is divided/separated/scattered in the second bowl. Now, put the bowl of ice cubes in a warm, sunny window, and after an hour or two look at it. What happened? The water (ice cubes) that was in multiple places is now in one place. The water that was separated is now gathered together. This simple experiment duplicates what happened when God commanded the waters to be gathered together unto one place. At His command, great ice sheets began to melt and flow into the oceans so dry land would appear. This interpretation agrees with pattern of all the other "let" commands. The conditions before the "let" command are the opposite of the conditions after the "let" command. The Gap Theory is the only creation theory that maintains the integrity of God's revealed pattern in Genesis 1.

If the earth was completely under liquid water, then the waters were already gathered together and they were already in one place. **Why would God command the waters to gather together into one place if they were already gathered together in one place?** That "gathering place" would have been the worldwide ocean. There would have been only one ocean, and all the waters would have been gathered together into it before God commanded them to do this. The anti-Gap Theories have God commanding the waters to do something that had been accomplished before He commanded it. Nowhere in Scripture does God give commands for something to become what it already is. This means the pattern of the "let" commands is very important in determining the condition of the earth in Genesis 1:2. The conditions before the commands were not the same as after the commands. The only way to "gather the waters together" is if they were not "gathered together" before the command. Do you see the picture? If you were there, you would have seen some water over here, some water over there, and even more water over there. (oceans, seas, and lakes) But you wouldn't have seen any dry land because it was completely covered by ice and snow.

If the other creationists are correct about the earth being completely submerged under liquid water in Genesis 1:2, then the water of the earth was already gathered together and it was already in one place. This makes God's command unnecessary. This also makes God's command ineffective. The waters didn't have to do anything to be gathered together into one place if they were already gathered there. Plus, this gathering together happened only after the Holy Spirit began brooding (warming) the surface of the deep and the surface of the ice. It was also after God commanded light to come back into existence. I think this is significant. Heat and light would have begun the melting process (supernaturally hastened, I believe) so the newly melted ice and snow would flow downward into the already existing liquid water (the deep). Thus, the waters would gather together into one place, and dry land would appear. This is how God "let" the dry land appear. The earth was not completely under liquid water when it was originally created. Instead, I think Genesis reveals that just prior to the restoration, the earth was experiencing an ice-age. I believe it was very intense, and it came on very suddenly, but it wasn't of long duration. I believe the earth was suddenly plunged into darkness and suddenly became a desolate, dead, and frozen wasteland sometime within the last several thousand years. Now, if science could find evidence of animals suddenly dying in an ice-age sometime in the last several thousand years, then I think we might be looking at the geological evidence the earth was *TOHUW WA-BOHUW* prior to Adam. Oh, wait… they've already found that.

Chapter Ten: Earth's Two Beginnings (Duo-Genesis)

Does "The Beginning" = "The Creation?"

I believe the earth had two different beginnings at two different times. Both Young-Earth and Day-Age creationists laugh at that belief. They use Matthew 19:4 to prove there was only one beginning. They insist Jesus believed in only one beginning because He used the word "beginning" (in the singular) to define the period of time during which He created man. Of course, they disagree on when and how long that period of time was. Young-Earth creationists say it was on the sixth twenty-four-hour day of the creation of the heavens and the earth, about six to eight thousand years ago. (The Beginning was a short period of time.) Day-Age creationists say it was billions of years after the creation of the heavens and the earth. (The Beginning was a long period of time.) Whichever it was, they say if Jesus believed there was only one beginning, then there was only one beginning; not two as the Gap Theory proposes.

Matthew 19:4 "And he answered and said unto them, Have ye not read, that he which made *them* **at the beginning** made them male and female," (KJV)

On the surface, Matthew 19:4 seems to support the assumption there was only one beginning. Jesus doesn't say God made us male and female at the beginnings; He said God made us male and female at the beginning. Because He uses "beginning," it appears they have a good argument. It appears as if Jesus is telling us there was only one beginning. Since Jesus described only one beginning, anti-Gap Theory creationists assume the creation of Adam and Eve was during that one beginning; "In the beginning."

The question shouldn't be: Why did Jesus use "beginning" (singular) here? The question should be: To which beginning was He referring? Other creationists automatically assume He was speaking about, "In the beginning, God created the heavens and the earth." I believe He was talking about a new kind of beginning; the beginning of Adam and Eve as husband and wife. That's the subject of His talk with these Pharisees who were questioning Him about marriage and divorce. God did something different with humans that He didn't do with the animals. He took flesh and bone from the male to make the female. He did this as a way of showing how husbands and wives were MADE to be one. So, when were Adam and Eve created? Adam and Eve did not begin, "in the beginning." (Genesis 1:1) They came later, during the Restoration. I'm not sure why other creationists think using "beginning" (singular) for man's creation proves their point. Of course, Jesus used the singular. They had only one beginning. Jesus' use of "beginning" in the singular proves humans had only one beginning. We didn't evolve over millions of years.

Notice Jesus doesn't say, "**IN** the beginning." He says, "**AT** the beginning." There is a difference between "in" (*EN*—Strong's Number G1711) and "at" (*APO*—Strong's Number G575). *EN* is a preposition denoting a resting position in time, space, or condition. *EN* is used in John 1:1 when it says, "IN the beginning was the Word." The use of *EN* makes sense in John 1:1 because it is referring to God in eternity, before time and space began. God doesn't move into or out of eternity. Jesus does not use *EN* here for Adam and Eve; they did not exist "in the beginning." Instead, He uses *APO*. *APO* means "from," "out from," or "proceeding from." Here, it means "from" the beginning. (It was not the beginning; it followed the beginning.) I think Jesus' use of a different preposition ought to make anti-Gap Theory creationists realize He was not speaking about, "**In** the beginning." He was not referring to Genesis 1:1.

Let's put the Anti-Gap assumption to the Biblical test. Does Matthew 19:4 = Genesis 1:1? Do they describe the same beginning? If we are to be good students of the Bible, we must listen carefully to what Jesus actually said, and not be led astray by what people say Jesus said. Let's analyze Matthew 19:4 in detail. Jesus said God made us male and female from the beginning. What does "made" mean? "Made" is the Greek word *POIEO* (Strong's Number G4160) and it means "accomplish," "act," "cause," "do," "establish," "made," "make," and many other such words. It is used 576 times in the New Testament, but it is never translated, "create," in the *King James Bible*, and only one time in the *New American Standard Bible*.

Hebrews 12:27 "And this *word,* Yet once more, signifieth the removing of those things that are shaken, as of things that are **made**, that those things which cannot be shaken may remain." (KJV)

Hebrews 12:27 "This *expression,* 'Yet once more,' denotes the removing of those things which can be shaken, as of **created** things, so that those things which cannot be shaken may remain." (NASB)

Since it is translated, "created," only once in over 500 uses, it is plain to see that "made" is not identical to "created." So, why did Jesus use "made" instead of "created" when He spoke about the beginning of man? It seems apparent to me that Jesus knew "made" and "created" didn't always mean the exact same thing. I think He made the same distinction between "create" and "make" that is made in the first chapter of Genesis:

1.) Genesis 1:1, where only *BARA* (create) is used. This is the first beginning.

2.) Genesis 1:3-31, where *ASAH* (made) is added. This is the second beginning.

As we have seen, *BARA* and *ASAH* don't always mean the exact same thing. Even in Exodus 20:11, which Young-Earthers always quote, *ASAH* is used to summarize the events of Genesis 1:3-31, the six days of restoration, not the events of the original creation in Genesis 1:1.

Exodus 20:11 "For *in* six days the LORD **made** (*ASAH*) heaven and earth, the sea, and all that in them *is,* and rested the seventh day: wherefore the LORD blessed the sabbath day, and hallowed it." (KJV) (emphasis mine)

It is true; *BARA* (create), *ASAH* (make), and *YATSAR* (form) are used in various places of Scripture to describe both the creation of the earth and the creation of man, but they are not always synonymous. In Isaiah 45:18, for example, the Holy Spirit makes a distinction.

Isaiah 45:18 "For thus says the LORD, who **created**" (*BARA*) "the heavens (He is the God who **formed**" (*YATSAR*) "the earth and **made**" (*ASAH*) "it, He established it *and* did not **create**" (*BARA*) "it a waste place, *but* **formed**" (*YATSAR*) "it to be inhabited), 'I am the LORD, and there is none else.'" (NASB)

In Isaiah 45:18, three words (*BARA, YATSAR,* and *ASAH*) are used for the earth, but only *BARA* is used for the heavens. *YATSAR* and *ASAH* are not used for the heavens. Now, go back and look at Genesis 1:1. Genesis 1:1 uses only *BARA*. Genesis 1:3-31 uses *BARA* and *ASAH* to describe the six days of creation. *YATSAR* (formed) is used later in Genesis 2:7 to give the details of Adam's creation on the sixth day.

Genesis 2:7 "And the LORD God **formed** man *of* the dust of the ground, and breathed into his nostrils the breath of life; and man became a living soul." (KJV)

Isaiah uses these three words to describe different components of the creation. This means we should be careful we don't substitute one word for another when it comes to discovering what the Bible truly teaches about the Creation. We should not substitute "created" for "made" as we try to determine the meaning of the text. Doing so distorts the meaning. Jesus did not use "created" when He said God "made" them male and female from the beginning. The only way to fully understand what Jesus meant, is by reading what He fully said. If you search the Scriptures, you will see Jesus didn't use just one word to describe the period of time in which He created Adam and Eve; He used two words. Matthew did not quote every word Jesus spoke. Now, Matthew is not wrong; he makes no error. He just does not give every detail. The Holy Spirit inspired the writers of Scripture to do this many, many times. I can't think of any major doctrine or truth in which the entire doctrine or truth is taught is a single passage of Scripture. The Bible splits things up ("here a little, and there a little"—Isaiah 28:10,13) so we have to search all the Scriptures to arrive at all the truth He wants us to know. Mark quotes the same words of Jesus, but he adds more information.

Mark 10:6 "But **from** the beginning **of the creation** God made them male and female." (KJV)

     Mark records the full words of Jesus. Jesus said God MADE them male and female FROM (*APO*) THE BEGINNING OF THE CREATION. He doesn't just say, "from the beginning." He adds a prepositional phrase, "of the creation," to clarify a point about the MAKING of men and women. Jesus is telling us Adam and Eve were MADE from the beginning of the creation. He uses two words, not one, to describe the period of time in which Adam and Eve were MADE.

     Why use both words? Rather than being an indication of a single period, I think He used both words to divide the creation into two parts. He used "beginning" as a modifier of "creation." The beginning of the creation is not the same as the creation itself. It's the same as if I said, "I'm traveling to New York at the beginning of the month." The beginning of the month is not the same as the month itself. It is only a portion of the month; it is the first part of the month. I think Jesus used two words so we wouldn't think the words "beginning" and "creation" defined the exact same period of time. I think He reveals Adam and Eve were created at the beginning of some time period He called, "the creation." But, therein lies the problem. Adam and Eve were not created at the beginning of the creation of the universe; they were the last things created. Adam and Eve were not created at the beginning of the six days; they were created on the last day. Jesus contradicts Scripture unless He is using the word "creation" in reference to the creation of man, and not to the creation of the heavens and the earth. Jesus used two words, *ARCHE* (Strong's Number G746) for "beginning," and *KTISIS* (Strong's Number G2937) for "creation." By using both words, Jesus tells us the creation had a beginning. (Otherwise, Jesus wouldn't have said it.) Well, if the creation had a beginning, then it seems logical to assume the creation had an ending.

     There I go making another assumption. Let's see if Scripture confirms my assumption. Was there an end of creation?

Genesis 2:1-3 "Thus the heavens and the earth **were finished**, and all the host of them. *{2}* And on the seventh day God **ended** his work which he had made; and he rested on the seventh day from all his work which he had made. *{3}* And God blessed the seventh day, and sanctified it: because that in it he had rested from all his work which God created and made." (KJV)

     Scripture confirms my assumption. The creation had an ending; it ended on Day Seven.... But wait a minute! Is the creation mentioned in Genesis 1:3-2:3 the exact same thing as the creation mentioned in Mark 10:6? The reason I ask this is because something appears wrong. If *ARCHE* designates the beginning of the *KTISIS*, then *ARCHE* and *KTISIS* do not define the exact same period of time. Jesus said God made us male and female at the BEGINNING of the CREATION. Again. that doesn't seem to fit with the creation account in Genesis 1. They weren't created at the beginning of that creation.

Here's where Young-Earthers and Day-Agers can agree on something. No matter whether you believe the days of creation were literal twenty-four-hour days or figurative billion-year "days," the statement made by Jesus seems wrong. God didn't make Adam and Eve at the BEGINNING of the creation. According to the Young-Earth interpretation, it was on the sixth day—at the END of the creation. According to the Day-Age interpretation, it was 14 billion years after the Big Bang—again, Adam and Eve were created at the end of the creation. In neither scenario did God make Adam and Eve AT THE BEGINNING of creation. Adam and Eve came AT THE END of the creation regardless of which creation scenario you choose. They were the last acts of creation. Being created at the END of the creation doesn't match with what Jesus said about them being made at the BEGINNING of the creation.

So, what do we do? Since Jesus knows everything and Jesus never lies, then we must believe God created Adam and Eve from the BEGINNING (*ARCHE*) of some time period Jesus called, "the creation" (*KTISIS*). In order to reconcile Jesus' words with Genesis, we must realize Jesus is using "creation" in a different way than how the Young-Earth and Day-Age Theories use it. The solution is simple. He isn't talking about the creation of the heavens and the earth, the sun, the moon, the stars, the fish, the birds, and the creeping things. Adam and Eve were not created at the beginning of those things. He is talking about the creation of MAN. From the beginning of the creation of MAN, God made us male and female.

Was the creation of man at the same beginning of creation as everything else? The answer is no. And the answer is no whether you are a Day-Ager or a Young-Earther. The Day-Age Theory is wrong if God created Adam and Eve at the beginning of the creation of the heavens and the earth. Adam and Eve were created billions of years later, at the END of the creation. The Young-Earth Theory is wrong if God created Adam and Eve at the beginning of the six days, He created them at the END of the six days. God did not create Adam and Eve from the beginning of either period of creation. Only the Gap Theory includes the concept of another beginning; another creation. The beginning Jesus is referring to is the creation of mankind, not the creation of the heavens and the earth. From the beginning of the creation of mankind, He made them male and female. This eliminates the possibility of man and woman slowly evolving from some lower asexual organism over millions of years. From the beginning, (*APO ARCHE*) of the creation of humans, they were made male and female. If this is not so, then Jesus was in error when He said Adam and Eve were made male and female from the beginning of creation.

Yes, the creation of man was part of the six literal twenty-four-hour days of creation in Genesis, but it wasn't at the beginning of that creation; it was at the end. When Jesus was speaking here, He wasn't teaching about the creation of the universe. That had no relevance to the subject at hand. He was teaching about the sanctity of male-female marriage by pointing out that God made us male and female from our beginning. That was the context of His discourse with these Pharisees who wanted a cheap excuse for easy divorce. Jesus was talking about the beginning of the creation of the human race. The creation of the sun, moon, stars, fish, birds, cattle, and creeping things has nothing to do with the sanctity of marriage. The creation of the human race was special because it marked the beginning of a new creation. Even though this was at the end of the six days of creation, it was the beginning of the creation of the human race. Up until this point, God had merely created/restored plants and animals. Now, He was going to create something new. The creation of man marked a new beginning. It was this beginning of the creation that Jesus was explaining in Mark 10:6.

Two Creation Accounts = One Creation

Many scholars and theologians believe the Book of Genesis gives two different accounts of two different creations. They say Genesis 1:3-2:3 is one account of creation and Genesis 2:5-25 is another account of an entirely different creation. In other words, they try to say there is a discrepancy in the Bible concerning creation. They base their opinion on the fact the details of Genesis 1:3-2:3 don't seem to agree with the details of Genesis 2:5-25. One difference is in the names used for God. Genesis 1:3-2:3 uses only the name *ELOHIM* (Strong's Number H430) for God. Genesis 2:5-25 adds the name *YAHWEH*. (also, spelled *YEHOVAH, YAHVEH, JEHOVAH,* or *YHVH*—The Tetragrammaton.) (Strong's Number H3068). Likewise, in Genesis 1, man is just called, "man," but in Genesis 2, he is called, "Adam." Other so-called contradictions are given. In Genesis 1:3-2:3, animals are created before humans, but in Genesis 2:5-25, Adam is created before animals. In Genesis 1:3-2:3, trees were created before man, while in Genesis 2:5-25, trees were created after man. These scholars use these "discrepancies" to make it look like these creation accounts were stolen from two different pagan mythologies that had two different "gods." They believe the writers of Genesis (They refuse to believe it was Moses.) merged them into one imperfect creation story. (By the way. If you are wondering where Genesis 2:4 fits into the equation, I'll explain it later. Some say it refers to what came before it; some say it refers to what comes after it.)

Trust me; there are no contradictions between Genesis 1:3-2:3 and Genesis 2:5-25. The reason they don't seem to agree is because they are complementary accounts. They both give an account of creation. Genesis 1:3-2:3 gives the general account. Genesis 2:5-25 gives a detailed account of Day 6. The events in Genesis 2 do not describe a different creation, in a different Garden, with a different man and woman, at a different time. If you read Genesis carefully, you will see Genesis 2:5-25 is focused on the events happening IN the Garden in Eden, not on the events of the oceans, the dry land, the sun, the moon, the stars, *etc*. Genesis 2:5-25 is the detailed account of the beginning of the human race. (The beginning which Jesus referred to when speaking to the Pharisees.) The account in Genesis 2 reveals that God first created man, then planted a Garden in Eden, and then placed Adam in the Garden.

Genesis 2:7-9 "And the LORD God formed man *of* the dust of the ground, and breathed into his nostrils the breath of life; and man became a living soul. *{8}* And the LORD God planted a garden eastward in Eden; and there he put the man whom he had formed. *{9}* And out of the ground made the LORD God to grow every tree that is pleasant to the sight, and good for food; the tree of life also in the midst of the garden, and the tree of knowledge of good and evil." (KJV)

It doesn't say God created all the trees in the entire world after Adam. It mentions only trees that were pleasant to the sight, and good for food. It is speaking of just the trees He created in the Garden. The same is true of the animals He created in the Garden. Genesis 2 does not describe the creation of every animal in the world; just every animal He created in the Garden. Genesis 2 describes the livestock, the beasts of the field, and the birds of the air that inhabited the Garden. God created them from the ground after He had created Adam. It was these creatures that God brought to Adam to name and to cause him to realize he was alone. (He had no female counterpart.) God wanted Adam to know he needed a wife to fulfill his existence. Adam was meant to be in a relationship with Eve. Together, they were meant to be in a relationship with *YAHWEH*.

These scholars are correct to point out how different names are used for God, but they reach the wrong conclusion. They think the Bible is a conglomerate of stories from other cultures that used two different names for God. The real reason for the two different names of God is because God wanted to reveal a difference in how He interacted with man in the two accounts. *ELOHIM* is a more generic, impersonal name for "God." In fact, it is the same word for "gods" when speaking about the "gods" of the pagan nations. Genesis 1:3-2:3 does not convey the intimate relationship between God and man. That's why man is called, "man." However, in Genesis 2:5-25, God reveals His personal relationship with man by calling man, "Adam," and by adding *YAHWEH* as His personal name. *YAHWEH* is often described as meaning, "The One Who Exists," or "The Self-Existent One," or "The Eternal One." It is a much more personal word than *ELOHIM*. It is considered the proper name for the God of Israel, and it reveals God's relationship to us, and how He interacts with us. **Our caused-existence is personally related to God's self-existence.** In other words, Genesis 2:5-25 causes us to understand that we were not created to be like the animals. We were created to be like God. We are special; we have a personal relationship with the Creator. Only people could understand that. Animals have no idea, no concept, no awareness of being created by God. This addition of *YAHWEH* points out how our relationship with God is something very special. We aren't just smart animals. The emphasis of Genesis 2:5-25 is to highlight the personal relationship God has with humans. *YAHWEH*, the Personal God, has a purpose for Adam and Eve.

Matthew 19 and Mark 10

In Matthew 19 and Mark 10, Jesus' opponents were not asking Him questions about the creation of the heavens and the earth. They were asking Him about the relationship between husbands and wives. They were trying to trick Him into contradicting the Scriptures concerning marriage and divorce. It seems reasonable for Jesus to go back to the beginning of marriage to explain God's purpose for marriage. He would not need to go back to the creation of the heavens and the earth to explain that. His answers to their questions would begin at the beginning of the creation of Adam and Eve. He would explain what God intended for men and women in order to show them how twisted and perverted their "rules" concerning divorce had become. Jesus simple went back to the details of the creation of Adam and Eve (Genesis 2:5-25) to do this. He did not need to go back to the overall account of the six days of creation (Genesis 1:3-Genesis 2:3) to make His points. He would start at the beginning of the creation of man and woman in order to answer their questions concerning men and women; marriage and divorce. So, when Jesus spoke about making us male and female from the beginning of creation, He wasn't focusing on WHEN we were created male and female, He was revealing WHY we were created male and female. The WHY of the creation of marriage is found in Genesis 2:5-25. (It was not good for man to be alone.) It was from THAT beginning of THAT creation, that Jesus used to denounce the beliefs of the Pharisees.

Does this prove the Ruin-Restoration Theory? No; at least not by itself. But, it proves the words "beginning" and "creation" don't necessarily define one specific single period of time throughout the entire Bible. This is what other creationists want you to believe. Jesus used the word "beginning" in Mark 10:6 in reference to a period of time He called, "the creation;" but, this wasn't the same period of time as the creation of the sun, moon, earth, stars, galaxies, *etc.* Jesus made a distinction between the creation of the heavens and the earth, and the creation of the human race. One of the claims of the Young-Earth and Day-Age Theories is there was only one beginning/one creation. They say Genesis 1:1 through Genesis 2:3 is the one and only creation. Jesus revealed this isn't true. The words "beginning" and "creation" have different meanings based on their context. What these creationists have done is make the assumption there was only one creation, and then they define the words "beginning" and "creation" to fit their assumption. Jesus' definition of the words "beginning" and "creation" doesn't fit their assumption.

The Beginning of the Beginning

Now, can I prove my original assumption? Can I prove the earth had two beginnings? I think I can. Let's approach this problem first from the assumption there was only one beginning. I'll assume the six-day period of creation was the one and only beginning, the one and only creation of everything, including the angels. I will assume there was no other beginning. In other words, "In the beginning God created the heavens and the earth," is the same thing as the six days of Genesis. I now have to check this assumption with Biblical facts to test its validity. If the Bible gives no clues of two different beginnings, then this assumption is probably true. If the Bible gives clues there were two separate and distinct beginnings, then this assumption is most definitely false. As it turns out, God has given us clues of two different beginnings. My first clue is found in Job 38. I already mentioned part of what God told Job, but now I want to show you some more.

Job 38:4-7 "Where wast thou when I laid the foundations of the earth? declare, if thou hast understanding. {5} Who hath laid the measures thereof, if thou knowest? or who hath stretched the line upon it? {6} Whereupon are the foundations thereof fastened? or who laid the corner stone thereof; {7} When the morning stars sang together, and all the sons of God shouted for joy?" (KJV)

"The morning stars" and "the sons of God" are terms used in the Old Testament for angelic beings. God tells Job the angels were eyewitnesses to the creation of the earth. They sang when God laid its foundation. This means they came before the earth was created. If "laying the foundation of the earth," "measuring it," "stretching the line upon it," "fastening the foundations," and "laying the corner stone" all refer to the creation of the earth, then Lucifer and the angels were in existence before the creation of the earth. They couldn't have witnessed any of those things if they weren't already there. If the earth was created on the first day of Genesis, as anti-Gap Theory creationists say, then the angels had their beginning before the first day. The beginning of the angels came before the beginning of the earth. This means there was more than one beginning. Now, let me add a side note here that helps support the Restoration Theory. I can't imagine the angels, Lucifer included, shouting for joy just because a dead, desolate, and water-submerged speck of dust was created. I could see them getting excited about the creation of the sun, the stars, and the quasars. They are spectacular in their power and beauty, but the creation of a desolate and dead waste planet is hardly worth singing about. Because the creation of the earth caused the angels to sing and shout with joy, it must have been created in some condition other than *TOHUW WA-BOHUW*. The angels' joy over the creation of the earth confirms Isaiah's statement the earth was not created a desolate waste. We know then, to be eyewitnesses of earth's creation, the angels were created before the earth, before the six days of Genesis. We also know that to be eyewitnesses the earth, they had to be able to see the earth. This wouldn't have been possible if there was no light. It would be hard to argue the universe had no light before the earth, because the angels themselves are creatures of light. That's why they are figuratively referred to as "morning stars." The word "Lucifer," is the Latin translation of the Hebrew *HEYLEL* (Strong's Number H1966) and it means "shining," or "the shining one." That's why he is called the "son of the morning."

Isaiah 14:12 "How art thou fallen from heaven, O Lucifer, son of the morning! *how* art thou cut down to the ground, which didst weaken the nations!" (KJV)

Joaozinho Martins, a fellow Gap Theory defender and author, presented another Biblical fact that proves light existed when the angels were created. As I have pointed out, the angels were created before the earth. They were eyewitnesses of earth's creation. My friend Joaozinho agrees with this fact in his book, *Pre-Historic Pre-Adamic Theology*,[93] but he added another fact about Lucifer's creation I had missed. He explains Ezekiel 28:13.

Ezekiel 28:13 "Thou hast been in Eden the garden of God; every precious stone *was* thy covering, the sardius, topaz, and the diamond, the beryl, the onyx, and the jasper, the sapphire, the emerald, and the carbuncle, and gold: the workmanship of thy tabrets and of thy pipes was prepared in thee in the **DAY** that thou wast created." (KJV) (my emphasis)

Joaozinho pointed out that Lucifer was created during the DAY. Young-Earth creationists have a hard task before them if they try to defend their belief that light never existed before Day One of the Creation Week. Lucifer was created before the earth, but he was created during a period of light. The Hebrew word "day" in Ezekiel 28:13 is *YOM*, and yes, it is the same word, with the same meaning we studied earlier. Joaozinho did an excellent job in his book proving how *YOM* (in the singular) always describes the presence of light in the Bible. (That was why God called the light, "day.") Even "mornings" and "evenings" contain some light, and as such, they technically cannot be considered parts of the "night." (That was why God called the darkness, "night.") Since Lucifer was created in a period of time God called, "day," we must agree that days were present when Lucifer was created. That means light existed before the earth existed. The darkness that covered the earth in Genesis 1:2 was not the original condition of the earth. I encourage you the get Joaozinho's book and study it thoroughly—it contains facts that prove the Young-Earth and Day-Age Theories are false.

Light existed before the creation of the earth. This means "darkness over the face of the deep" was not the condition of the earth when it was created. Since the angels could see the earth at its creation, light existed before the earth was created. (When God said, "Let there be light," in Genesis 1:3, it wasn't the original creation of light. It was light restored.) Job 4:7 also indicates all the angels were together and joyous. Most theologians agree the period described by, "When the morning stars sang together, and all the sons of God shouted for joy," indicates the time before Lucifer sinned. Therefore, Job teaches us two things. The angels had their own creation, their own separate and distinct beginning before the earth was created, and Lucifer didn't sin until after the earth was created. (By the way, if you are a Young-Earth creationist who hates the idea the angels were created before the creation of the earth, then you must reject the notion that the words, "the morning stars," refer to angels. You must be a literalist and insist they refer to literal stars. That's fine, but in that case, you have to believe the literal stars were created before the creation of the literal earth. After all, the stars "sang" when they "saw" the foundation of the earth being created. Of course, that means you would have to reject your belief the stars weren't created until Day Four, after the creation of the earth.)

Okay, one clue isn't very convincing, especially if it deals with the creation of angels. I may have proved there were two beginnings, but so far I've shown only that the first beginning was the creation of angels. Most creationists probably don't care if the angels were created before the six days of Genesis. Angels are a separate type of being and live in a separate type of existence. Let's look at the next clue.

Ezekiel 28:12-15 "Son of man, take up a lament concerning the king of Tyre and say to him: 'This is what the Sovereign LORD says: "You were the model of perfection, full of wisdom and perfect in beauty. *{13}* You were in Eden, the garden of God; every precious stone adorned you: ruby, topaz and emerald, chrysolite, onyx and jasper, sapphire, turquoise and beryl. Your settings and mountings were made of pure gold; on the day you were created they were prepared *{14}* You were anointed as a guardian cherub, for so I ordained you. You were on the holy mount of God; you walked among the fiery stones. *{15}* You were blameless in your ways from the day you were created till wickedness was found in you."'" (NIV)

The title, "King of Tyre," is a mysterious title for Lucifer, and so we see he wasn't a sinner when he was created. God didn't create him that way. He didn't begin that way. He existed in a perfect condition for an unspecified period of time before he sinned. In fact, he even walked around in Eden before his rebellion. (I believe this was a Pre-Adamic Eden that was destroyed and later restored like the other fruitful places.) This means Lucifer didn't sin until after the earth was created. This agrees with Job. Now, if there was only one period of creation, one beginning, then Lucifer was still perfect when God finished creating the heavens and the earth. Lucifer did not fall during the time God was creating. Lucifer did not sin during the time period the Bible refers to as the beginning. Fine, that's no problem. Young-Earth creationists, Day-Age creationists, and just about every other creationist agree. Almost everybody puts Lucifer's Rebellion sometime after Day Six. This is because God declared all His works very good on Day Six, and everybody but Gap Theory creationists says this includes Lucifer and the angels. Only Gap Theory creationists believe Lucifer had fallen before Day Six, and the words "very good" described only the restorative works of the six days. Other creationists believe "very good" can only apply to the initial creation, and not to a "repair-job" creation. Why not? If the automotive body repairman fixed my dented fender so it was as good as new, why couldn't I tell him he did a "very good" job? The "very good" at the end of the six days refers to what God restored over the six days. Let's move to our third clue. This is something Jesus said about Lucifer. John 8:44 "Ye are of *your* father the devil, and the lusts of your father ye will do. He was a murderer **from the beginning**, and abode not in the truth, because there is no truth in him. When he speaketh a lie, he speaketh of his own: for he is a liar, and the father of it." (KJV)

"He was a murderer **from** the beginning." Note that Jesus does not say, "**in** the beginning." Jesus is using the exact same words He used in Mark 10:6 when referring to the creation of Adam and Eve. He uses *APO ARCHE*. What beginning is He talking about? Is "the beginning" in John 8:44 the same as "the beginning" in Mark 10:6? If it was the same beginning, then Lucifer was a murderer from Day Six. (The day God made Adam and Eve.) If not, then the Bible clearly reveals two separate beginnings. If "from the beginning" equals "from the creation," as other creationists claim, then Lucifer was a murderer "from the creation." Jesus said Lucifer was a murderer from the beginning, but Ezekiel says Lucifer had no iniquity when he was created. Jesus can't be saying Lucifer was a murderer from his own creation unless the Bible contradicts itself. Lucifer did not begin as a fallen angel! He was not created that way. Lucifer began perfect. Was Jesus saying Lucifer was a murderer from the beginning of the universe? Well, if there was only one beginning, then yes! If the six days of Genesis was the time everything began, then Lucifer was a murderer from the time everything began. Yet we know this can't be true. Job and Ezekiel have shown us that Lucifer didn't fall until after the creation of the earth. Lucifer was not a sinner from THAT beginning, but Jesus still said he was a sinner from SOME beginning. The assumption there was only one beginning starts to break down. Could Jesus be referring to some other beginning? According to Jesus, Lucifer was a murderer from the beginning. The Apostle John understood his Master's teaching, and taught this as well.

1 John 3:8 "He who sins is of the devil, for the devil has sinned **from the beginning**. For this purpose the Son of God was manifested, that He might destroy the works of the devil." (NKJV)

The Greek word used for "beginning" by both Jesus and John is *ARCHE*. (Strong's Number G746) This word is used many times in reference to the creation.

Matthew 19:4 "And he answered and said, 'Have ye not read, that He who created *them* from the **beginning** MADE THEM MALE AND FEMALE.'" (NIV)

John 1:1-2 "In the **beginning** was the Word, and the Word was with God, and the Word was God. {2} The same was in the **beginning** with God." (KJV)

Hebrews 1:10 "And, Thou Lord, in the **beginning** hast laid the foundation of the earth; and the heavens are the works of thine hands." (KJV)

2 Peter 3:4 "And saying, Where is the promise of his coming? For since the fathers fell asleep, all things continue as *they were* from the **beginning** of creation." (KJV)

Since Ezekiel reveals Lucifer wasn't created a sinner, Jesus and John can't be referring to Lucifer's creation. Since Job reveals Lucifer hadn't yet sinned when the earth was created, then Jesus and John can't be referring to the creation of the earth. Lucifer must have fallen into sin after the earth was created but before the "beginning" Jesus and John mention. Now, if this isn't the beginning of the earth, and it isn't the beginning of Lucifer, then what "beginning" is it? What beginning are Jesus and John talking about?

If "the beginning" equals "the creation," as anti-Gap Theory creationists claim, then Lucifer was a murderer and a sinner and a liar from "the creation." That means he was created that way. Since this can't be true, Anti-Gap Theory creationists attempt to alter the definition of "the beginning" by saying it doesn't mean the absolute beginning; it means more or less around the time of the beginning. They believe Lucifer fell after the six days; therefore, being a murderer and a liar from "the beginning" would be from a time period literally **AFTER** the six days. By this non-literal definition, Lucifer could have fallen any time **AFTER** the creation, and God would still call it "the beginning." But, if you allow that non-literal definition of "the beginning" to stand, then you can't insist God made us male and female from the literal beginning. He could have made us sometime after the beginning. This doesn't fit with what Jesus said. "The beginning" is either "the beginning" or it's not! (Assuming there is only one beginning.) Here's the funny part: Anti-Gap Theory creationists say "the beginning" **EQUALS** the six days, but they also say "the beginning" was **AFTER** the six days. (Lucifer, who was a sinner from the beginning, didn't become a sinner until **AFTER** the six days.) They don't mind defining "the beginning" as a period of time **AFTER** the six days because it helps fit the fall of Satan into their scenario. Yet, they object to Gap Theory creationists defining "the beginning" as a period of time **BEFORE** the six days because it helps fit the fall of Satan into our scenario. In other words, "the beginning" means the same thing as the six days; but "the beginning" doesn't mean the same thing as the six days. It's a direct contradiction. Anti-Gap Theory creationists can't have it both ways. If "the beginning" always equals "the creation," then "the creation" always equals "the beginning," and someone has lied to us. Lucifer was either perfect in all his ways from the beginning, or else he was a murderer and a liar from the beginning. (Again, assuming there was only one beginning.) This assumption creates a discrepancy.

Let's look at Lucifer a little closer. Ezekiel mentions one beginning, the creation of Lucifer, a point of time when Lucifer was perfect. Jesus and John mention another beginning, a point of time when Lucifer was already a sinner. These can't be referring to the same beginning. If they are, then one part of the Bible contradicts another part of the Bible. This would have Jesus and John say Lucifer was a sinner from the time he was created, while Job and Ezekiel say Lucifer wasn't a sinner until later. But where does that leave us? Jesus and John must not be referring to the same beginning Job and Ezekiel mention. The beginning Jesus and John mention had to be after that beginning, after Genesis 1:1. So, what beginning is Jesus talking about that was after Genesis 1:1? Jesus must know there was more than one beginning.

Let me repeat this. I want you to see what I'm getting at, and I know it's a difficult concept. Jesus and John said Lucifer was a sinner from the beginning. Was it the beginning of Lucifer? No. Lucifer was perfect in all his ways from the day he was created. Were Jesus and John talking about the beginning of the heavens and the earth? No. Lucifer was one of the angels shouting and singing for joy when the earth was created. We also see him later walking around on earth while still perfect. Since iniquity wasn't found in Lucifer until after some time had passed, we know time was already in existence. Time can't pass if time doesn't exist. In addition, time can't exist if space doesn't exist; they are a continuum. Since time and space were created together in the beginning, then the universe already had begun before Lucifer fell. He was a sinner from the beginning, but this beginning couldn't be the beginning of the universe. If Genesis 1:1-31 describes the one and only beginning of the universe, then there is a problem with somebody's Biblical testimony. If Lucifer was a sinner from the beginning, then Ezekiel and Job were wrong. If Lucifer wasn't a sinner from the beginning, then Jesus and John were wrong.

The End of the Beginning

If the Gap Theory is false, then we have a Biblical contradiction. Jesus and John said something about Lucifer that contradicts what Job and Ezekiel said. If we look closely at what Jesus and John said, we will discover something else. Even if Job and Ezekiel had said nothing about Lucifer, there is yet another discrepancy. It is a related discrepancy, but it is distinct. This second discrepancy is about the chronology of Lucifer's fall. How does the timing play out? Jesus and John said Lucifer was a sinner from the beginning. Okay, when did Lucifer first sin? It had to be after the creation of the earth but before the time he deceived Eve. Let's see if we can do some more investigating.

If we assume the Gap Theory is wrong, then we must assume Lucifer didn't fall until after the six days. Again, this is what other creationists claim. They say God's declaration on Day Six that everything was "very good" included Lucifer and the angels. On the other hand, we Gap Theory creationists say this declaration included only the things He restored during those six days. We say the six-day period of restoration was the second beginning. We say Lucifer was a sinner from the second beginning, but not from the first beginning. His rebellion occurred between the two beginnings. Now, if the Gap Theory is wrong, then Lucifer couldn't have sinned until after the six days were finished. In fact, it couldn't have been on the seventh day either. The text says God was pleased with all His work and He blessed the seventh day and declared it holy. I don't think Young-Earth creationists would consider the seventh day blessed and holy if it was the day Lucifer rebelled and introduced sin into the universe.

According to Gap Theory creationists, Lucifer became a sinner before Day One. According to other creationists, Lucifer couldn't have become a sinner until day eight at the earliest. I hope you see the problem with their logic. If Lucifer was a sinner from the beginning, as Jesus and John said he was, then Jesus and John made a mistake. The beginning was already over by day eight. Genesis 2:4 says Genesis 1 is the account of how the heavens and earth WERE CREATED. It's in the past tense. The creation week was finished.

"The beginning" ended on Day Seven. ANY TIME AFTER DAY SEVEN WAS NOT PART OF THE BEGINNING. If "the beginning" was the time period in which God created everything, then the beginning was over. If Lucifer didn't sin until after the beginning was over, then Jesus and John couldn't have said he was a sinner from the beginning. The chronology is all messed up. If the original creation of the universe is the same creation as the six days of Genesis, then there is no other beginning, and we have a contradiction in God's Word. This can't be possible. The original creation of the heavens and the earth (Genesis 1:1) and the six days of creation (Genesis 1:3-31) must be two separate beginnings occurring at two different times. Lucifer wasn't fallen at the first beginning, the original creation of the earth, but he had fallen before the second beginning, the six days of Genesis. The Gap Theory explains this.

If Lucifer was a murderer from the beginning, as Jesus said, then the Young-Earth Theory is false. The first murder wasn't until Cain murdered Abel. If we assume Lucifer was the agent who prompted Cain to kill Abel (thereby making Lucifer a murderer from the beginning), we need to figure out when that happened. We can't determine an exact date, because the Bible doesn't give us all the dates. We don't know how old Adam and Eve were when they sinned and were expelled from the Garden. The Bible doesn't tell us how old Adam and Eve were when Cain and Able were born. The Bible doesn't tell us how old Cain and Able were when Cain murdered Able, but we know they were old enough to farm and to tend sheep. We know Adam was one-hundred and thirty years old when he fathered Seth, and we know Seth was born to replace Abel. Seth was born after the first murder. So, while we can't know the exact time, I feel comfortable in thinking the first murder was about 120-130 years after the beginning. If the creation week was the one and only beginning, then Lucifer wasn't a murderer from the beginning. He wasn't a murderer until about 120-130 years after the beginning. That means, "a murderer from the beginning," cannot refer to Cain murdering Abel. Lucifer was a murderer before that. Job and Ezekiel were right when they told us Lucifer wasn't a sinner from the (first) beginning. Jesus and John were right when they told us Lucifer was a sinner from the (second) beginning. Jesus was right when He said Lucifer was a murderer from the (second) beginning. The earth had two beginnings. The chronology seems obvious; Lucifer had murdered someone before the Six Days. Since there is no indication angels can die, Lucifer must have murdered "men" who lived on the Pre-Adamic earth.

Lucifer's Rebellion

The Bible presents several clues the earth had two beginnings. Like a jigsaw puzzle, we can fit these pieces together to get a picture of what happened in the beginnings. This next piece of the puzzle concerns the timing of Lucifer's fall. When did Lucifer first rebel against God? When was iniquity first found in him? When did he become Satan, the devil? Was it before Adam was created or after? Gap Theory creationists say Lucifer fell before God created Adam. Other creationists believe Lucifer fell after Adam was created. They don't believe God would say everything was very good, if sin and rebellion had been present. They believe there was no sin, no death, and no judgment until after the creation week. They believe the declaration of, "very good," applied to all of creation, including the angels. All of creation did not groan at this point. At the end of the seventh day, Lucifer and all the angels were still perfect, still shouting for joy, and still worshipping God. We need to ask a question. When did Lucifer sin? In order to answer that question we need to ask another question. When did God judge him, strip him of his authority, and cast him out of Eden? Let's look again at his original commission from God.

Ezekiel 28:13-16 "You were in Eden, the garden of God; every precious stone adorned you: ruby, topaz and emerald, chrysolite, onyx and jasper, sapphire, turquoise and beryl. Your settings and mountings were made of gold; on the day you were created they were prepared. *{14}* **You were anointed** as a guardian cherub, for so **I ordained you**. You were on the holy mount of God; you walked among the fiery stones. *{15}* You were blameless in your ways from the day you were created till wickedness was found in you. *{16}* Through your widespread trade you were filled with violence, and you sinned. So I drove you in disgrace from the mount of God, and I expelled you, O guardian cherub, from among the fiery stones." (NIV)

  The text goes on to say other things about God's judgment on Lucifer, the King of Tyre. It becomes difficult to understand fully what God is saying. Some of this appears to have happened already; some of it appears to be future. God goes on to say how Lucifer became proud because of his beauty and corrupt because of his splendor. It also talks about God casting him to the earth and turning him to ashes by a consuming fire that comes out from within him. We know this hasn't happened yet. Some of the confusion is probably because God is speaking about two different entities, in two different realms, at two different times. Two different experiences (one in the natural realm and one in the spiritual realm) seem to be blended into one. In Ezekiel 28:12, the Lord is speaking about the "KING of Tyre," but back in Ezekiel 28:2 the Lord was speaking about the "PRINCE of Tyre." I'm not sure I understand this, but it seems as if Lucifer is the King of Tyre while some man is the Prince of Tyre over whom Lucifer had control. Ezekiel 28:1-10 and Ezekiel 28:11-19 are descriptions of two different judgments. Ezekiel 28:1-10 speaks of a judgment of a human king while Ezekiel 28:11-19 speaks of a judgment over Lucifer. We know Ezekiel 28:11-19 does not refer to a human being because no man has been the Anointed Guardian Cherub. No man has been on the Holy Mount of God. No man has walked among the Fiery Stones.

Lucifer appears to have been put in charge of Eden. We don't know how long he exercised that authority, but he eventually sinned because of his pride. (Which means he wasn't a sinner from the beginning.) He was then judged by God and stripped of his title. An important point in my argument is the chronology. God didn't strip him of his authority until after he rebelled. As long as Lucifer remained perfect in all his ways, there was no need (or basis) for God to judge him or to cast him out of Eden. So, when did this happen? I believe the Bible teaches that Lucifer sinned, was judged, and was stripped of his position of authority before Adam was created. If this happened before Day Six, then it would mean Satan rebelled in the Pre-Adamic world. This in turn would mean "very good" applied only to the six days of restoration, not to the previous creation. All I need to do now is to prove Lucifer sinned before Adam was created. I think I can do that, but we need some more clues. Like good detectives, we need to examine all the clues before we make our final accusation. (I say, "Lucifer did it; in the garden; with the forbidden fruit.")

Satan: Prince of this World

What do we know about Lucifer? God reveals many things about him, but He has chosen not to reveal everything about him. That's fine; God doesn't have to reveal any more than He wishes. There are things about the devil that God doesn't tell us in the Bible. Naturally, this has led many to make speculations about him. That's fine too. I think it is okay to try to fill in the missing pieces of the puzzle as long as we fully understand we are only making guesses. Making guesses about things that AREN'T in the Bible is allowable, but we have to remember to see how they fit with the things that ARE in the Bible. I could speculate that Lucifer has red skin, horns, a pointed tail, and he carries a pitchfork. That's a very common image of Satan, but it's not from the Bible. It's wild, human speculation. The more we rely on what the Bible truly reveals about Lucifer, the less wild our speculations about him will be. Gap Theory creationists make some speculations about Lucifer. We speculate Lucifer sinned and was judged before Adam was created. Other creationists also make speculations about Satan. They speculate Lucifer didn't sin until after Day Seven. Let's see whose speculations fit with what the Bible tells us. Let's first look at some of the things we know about Lucifer.

He was created by God; he is a created being. Lucifer is not eternal. Lucifer is not omnipotent. Lucifer is not omniscient. Lucifer is not omnipresent. Simply put, Lucifer is not God. Now, he wants to be like God. He wants glory like God, but he is not and never will be God.

Isaiah 14:13-15 "For thou hast said in thine heart, I will ascend into heaven, I will exalt my throne above the stars of God: I will sit also upon the mount of the congregation, in the sides of the north: *{14}* I will ascend above the heights of the clouds; **I will be like the most High.** *{15}* Yet thou shalt be brought down to hell, to the sides of the pit." (KJV)

We know Lucifer rebelled against God and has been judged, but we also know the final judgment hasn't been fully implemented yet. Lucifer is still free to roam the earth. He is even allowed to enter into God's presence in heaven at times.

Job 1:6-7 "One day the angels came to present themselves before the LORD, and Satan also came with them. {7} The LORD said to Satan, 'Where have you come from?' Satan answered the LORD, 'From roaming through the earth and going back and forth in it.'" (NIV)

We know his freedom is temporary. Someday he will be bound for a thousand years. After that, he will be set free to bring about one last battle against God. He will then be defeated by Christ, and he and all his followers, both angelic and human, will be cast into the Lake of Fire. There, they will be in eternal, unending torment for their eternal, unending hatred of God.

Matthew 13:41-42 "The Son of man shall send forth his angels, and they shall gather out of his kingdom all things that offend, and them which do iniquity; {42} And shall cast them into a furnace of fire: there shall be wailing and gnashing of teeth." (KJV)

"Gnashing of teeth" refers to anger and hatred. (The Pharisees gnashed their teeth at Stephen when he gave them the Gospel Message.—Acts 7:54) Now, the problem we need to address concerns Satan's authority over the earth. The Bible says Lucifer is the Prince of this world. This puzzle-piece needs to be put into place.

1 John 5:19 "We know that we are children of God, and that the whole world is under the control of the evil one." (NIV)

2 Corinthians 4:4 "In whom the god of this world hath blinded the minds of them which believe not, lest the light of the glorious gospel of Christ, who is the image of God, should shine unto them." (KJV)

John 12:31 "Now is the judgment of this world: now shall the prince of this world be cast out." (KJV)

John 14:30 "I will not speak with you much longer, for the prince of this world is coming. He has no hold on me," (NIV)

Ephesians 2:2 "Wherein in time past ye walked according to the course of this world, according to the prince of the power of the air, the spirit that now worketh in the children of disobedience:" (KJV)

John 16:8-11 "And He, when He comes, will convict the world concerning sin, and righteousness, and judgment; {9} concerning sin, because they do not believe in Me; {10} and concerning righteousness, because I go to the Father, and you no longer behold Me; {11} and concerning judgment, because the ruler of this world has been judged." (NASB)

I don't fully understand what this means or why God allows it, but it is a clear declaration of God's Truth. Satan has authority over the earth. This played a central part in Satan's temptation of Christ.

Matthew 4:8-10 "Again, the devil took him to a very high mountain and showed him all the kingdoms of the world and their splendor. {9} 'All this I will give you,' he said, 'if you will bow down and worship me.' {10} Jesus said to him, 'Away from me, Satan! For it is written: "Worship the Lord your God, and serve him only."'" (NIV)

What was Satan offering Christ? Satan offered Jesus, the Son of David and legal heir to David's throne, the opportunity to set up His earthly Kingdom without having to go to the cross. Jesus chose to reject his offer. Instead, He chose to establish His earthly kingdom at the proper time and in the proper way. This Kingdom is what we refer to as the Millennial Reign of Christ. This is what Christ will set up when Satan is bound for a thousand years. I don't fully understand what it will be like. I know it will be wonderful and Christ Himself will be physically present as King, but it will be a physical kingdom. It will be an earthly kingdom. It is not the final state of all things. The final perfection of the universe will not happen until after the final judgment. Once Satan is released, there will be one final rebellion, one final battle, and one final judgment. This is followed by the final Restoration: the New Heavens and the New Earth; a perfect, eternal Kingdom, which I understand even less, but eagerly await all the more.

Satan offered Christ the chance to set up His earthly kingdom without opposition. Lucifer would freely surrender his authority over the earth. Satan would give up his earthly kingdom in exchange for one, itty-bitty, little thing: Jesus would have to be willing to bow down before him. All Jesus had to do was acknowledge that Lucifer was worthy of worship, and then Jesus could be King of the earth. He wouldn't have to go to the cross. Satan seemed fine with losing his earthly kingdom. Why? Why would he make this offer? It seems ridiculous that Lucifer would willingly give up his authority over earth in exchange for something so simple, even pointless. It seems even more ridiculous that Jesus wouldn't be willing to accept his offer. Here was a chance for Jesus to establish His earthly kingdom without having to be crucified. Why not accept Lucifer's surrender?

There must be more at stake than meets the eye. Something very important must have been happening in this confrontation. There was something going on that transcended the sins of men. This wasn't just about who had authority over the earth. There was something much deeper, and much older. ("A Deeper Magic from Before the Dawn of Time," as C. S. Lewis described the power of Aslan's death.)[94] Satan knew something very,

very critical. Satan knew he could get something in exchange. Satan knew God couldn't execute final judgment on him if Christ accepted his offer. If Jesus had bowed down to Lucifer, Jesus would have acknowledged that Lucifer was worthy of worship. **How could the Father condemn someone whom the Son had acknowledged as being worthy of worship?** Satan knew he could escape eternal damnation, and he was willing to give up his authority over the earth in exchange for that freedom. Jesus could get His earthly kingdom, but it would be the kingdom Lucifer offered, not the Kingdom God had planned. The earthly kingdom Lucifer offered, although full of splendor and wonder, would never be what God intended. It would be inhabited by fallen men whose sins could never be forgiven. This kingdom would be a glorious kingdom, but it would be a kingdom of the unrestored. If Jesus had bowed down, He would have given Lucifer worship equal to the worship of God. (**I will be like the most High.**) If Jesus had bowed down before him, He would have exalted Lucifer above all the angels. (**I will exalt my throne above the stars of God.**) Yes, Lucifer would leave the earth, but he would **ascend into heaven, above the heights of the clouds, to the mount of the congregation, in the sides of the north**. Yes, Satan would lose an earthly kingdom, but he would win a heavenly kingdom. His rebellious "I Wills" would have come to fruition. Jesus rejected Lucifer's offer. Instead, He chose the Cross. You see, the Cross wasn't just the focal point of human history; it was the focal point of angelic history as well.

1 John 3:8 "He who sins is of the devil, for the devil has sinned from the beginning. For this purpose the Son of God was manifested, that He might destroy the works of the devil." (NKJV)

Christ came to restore that which was lost. The five "I wills" of the cherub Lucifer were defeated by one "thy will" when the man Jesus surrendered His will to the will of the Father.

Who Had Authority Over the Earth When?

My next question is this: How could Lucifer have authority over the earth? How could Lucifer, a created being, offer Christ the Creator, authority over His own earth? We discover our puzzle pieces are made of smaller puzzle pieces. We have the piece of the puzzle that says Lucifer has authority over the earth. He claimed to have that authority and Jesus didn't dispute it. This seems odd considering how Jesus was very quick to put Pontius Pilate in his proper place when he claimed to have authority over Jesus.

John 19:10-11 "Pilate therefore said to Him, 'You do not speak to me? Do You not know that I have authority to release You, and I have authority to crucify You?' {11} Jesus answered, 'You would have no authority over Me, unless it had been given you from above...'" (NASB)

If Satan did not have the authority he claimed to have, I think Jesus would have said so immediately. Jesus' lack of rebuttal to Lucifer's claim, along with the other Bible verses we have seen, leaves us with no interpretation but that Lucifer has real authority over the earth. He is its prince. He is its ruler. So, let me ask, "When did he get that authority?" Let me rephrase that question into three questions. The first question is, "When did he FIRST get that authority?" Once we answer the first question, we will discover there is a second question. "When did he LOSE that authority?" Once we answer that, a third question pops up: "When did he REGAIN that authority?" Look back at our previous puzzle piece.

Ezekiel 28:13-14 "You were **in Eden**, the garden of God; every precious stone adorned you: ruby, topaz and emerald, chrysolite, onyx and jasper, sapphire, turquoise and beryl. Your settings and mountings were made of gold; on the day you were created they were prepared. *{14}* You were **anointed** as a guardian cherub, for so **I ordained you**. You were on the holy mount of God; you walked among the fiery stones." (NIV)

The answer to the first question is easy. God gave Lucifer his position of authority. This was before Lucifer's fall. The Bible doesn't explain all that was involved with this position of authority, but this is the passage of Scripture that describes it. He got this authority before he fell. He got this authority directly from God; God ordained him. This makes sense. He had to get this authority from God. All authority ultimately comes from God. This is God's universe.

1 Chronicles 29:11 "Yours, O LORD, is the greatness and the power and the glory and the majesty and the splendor, for everything in heaven and earth is yours. Yours, O LORD, is the kingdom; you are exalted as head over all." (NIV)

Just as God gave authority to Pilate, God gave Lucifer authority. It was a much bigger authority than Pilate's. Pilate had authority over a very small piece of real estate for a very short time. Lucifer was given authority over the whole earth for a much longer time. God gave Lucifer authority over the earth, and this authority was given when Lucifer was still perfect in all his ways. But how does this fit with God giving Adam authority over the earth? We know God gave Adam authority over the earth on Day Six.
Genesis 1:26 "And God said, Let us make man in our image, after our likeness: and let them have dominion over the fish of the sea, and over the fowl of the air, and over the cattle, and over all the earth, and over every creeping thing that creepeth upon the earth." (KJV)

Who had authority over the earth on Day Six? There seems to be a problem with the chronology. Since Lucifer got his authority before he fell, it was obviously given to him before Adam fell. Lucifer was given this authority while he was still perfect in all his ways. This means it was given to him before he led Adam and Eve into sin. (Gap Theory creationists say they weren't even created yet.) This ordination happened when the universe was still perfect. This authority was given before sin was introduced. Now the problem with the chronology arises. Creationists who reject the Gap Theory say sin wasn't introduced until after Day Seven. Unfortunately for their theory, by Day Six, God had already stripped Lucifer of his authority over the earth and had given it to Adam. On DAY SIX, God gave authority over the earth to Adam not to Lucifer.

Genesis 1:27-31 "So God created man in his *own* image, in the image of God created he him; male and female created he them. *{28}* And God blessed them, and God said unto them, Be fruitful, and multiply, and replenish the earth, and subdue it: and **have dominion over the fish of the sea, and over the fowl of the air, and over every living thing that moveth upon the earth.** *{29}* And God said, Behold, I have given you every herb bearing seed, which *is* upon the face of all the earth, and every tree, in the which *is* the fruit of a tree yielding seed; to you it shall be for meat. *{30}* And to every beast of the earth, and to every fowl of the air, and to every thing that creepeth upon the earth, wherein *there is* life, *I have given* every green herb for meat: and it was so. *{31}* And God saw every thing that he had made, and, behold, *it was* very good. And the evening and the morning were **the sixth day**." (KJV)

Psalms 8:4-8 "What is man, that thou art mindful of him? and the son of man, that thou visitest him? *{5}* For thou hast made him a little lower than the angels, and hast crowned him with glory and honour. *{6}* **Thou madest him to have dominion over the works of thy hands; thou hast put all things under his feet:** *{7}* All sheep and oxen, yea, and the beasts of the field; *{8}* The fowl of the air, and the fish of the sea, *and whatsoever* passeth through the paths of the seas." (KJV)

Adam was given authority over the earth on Day Six. Adam was given authority over the earth on the very day he was created. Who was the ruler over the earth on Day Six? It was Adam, not Lucifer. Do you see the problem? If Lucifer had been given authority over the earth and had not yet sinned, then God stripped Lucifer of his authority before he rebelled. According to other creationists, Lucifer had not yet sinned by Day Six. Yet, here we see God already stripped him of his authority and gave it to Adam. So, we have to ask the second question about Lucifer, "When did he LOSE his authority?" The answer is he lost it after he had sinned. If Lucifer had not yet sinned before Day Six, then God was wrong to strip Lucifer of his authority and cast him out of Eden. It would have been wrong for God to give Adam that authority on Day Six.

Ezekiel 28:13-17 "You were in Eden, the garden of God; Every precious stone was your covering: The ruby, the topaz, and the diamond; The beryl, the onyx, and the jasper; The lapis lazuli, the turquoise, and the emerald; And the gold, the workmanship of your settings and sockets, Was in you. On the day that you were created They were prepared. *{14}* You were the anointed cherub who covers, And I placed you *there*. You were on the holy mountain of God; You walked in the midst of the stones of fire. *{15}* You were blameless in your ways From the day you were created, Until unrighteousness was found in you. *{16}* By the abundance of your trade You were internally filled with violence, And you sinned; **Therefore** I have cast you as profane From the mountain of God. And I have destroyed you, O covering cherub, From the midst of the stones of fire. *{17}* Your heart was lifted up because of your beauty; You corrupted your wisdom by reason of your splendor. I cast you to the ground; I put you before kings, That they may see you." (NASB)

God says, "Therefore I have cast you...." The "therefore" refers back to the fact Lucifer had sinned. This judgment was the RESULT of his sin. God didn't judge Lucifer until after iniquity was found in him. Lucifer had been walking around in Eden, and he had been given authority over the earth. By the time we get to Day Six, we see Adam is walking around in Eden and is given authority over the earth. Lucifer no longer had that authority. Lucifer had been stripped of his authority BEFORE Day Six. God's pronouncement on Day Six, that everything was very good, did not include Lucifer. He had been stripped of his authority over Eden because he had rebelled before Adam was created. If there was only one beginning and one Garden of Eden, the chronology doesn't fit.

If God gave Adam authority over the Garden on Day Six, how could He give Lucifer the same authority over the same Garden on the same day? It would seem odd for God to give Lucifer authority over the Garden if He had given that authority to Adam already. Either God was lying to Lucifer when He told him he had authority over the Garden, or else God was lying to Adam when He told him he had authority over the Garden. They both can't have the same authority over the same Garden at the same time. Obviously, Lucifer had been stripped of his authority before Day Six. The only explanation is that the earth had two Gardens of Eden. The first Garden of Eden was a Pre-Adamic garden where Lucifer walked around in and was given rule. The second Garden of Eden was a garden planted after Adam was created. The restored Garden of Eden was given to Adam to walk around in and to rule. We now have the answer to my second question, "When did Lucifer lose his authority?" He lost it before Adam was created. Lucifer sinned, was judged, and lost his authority over the earth in the Pre-Adamic world.

Opponents to the Gap Theory will protest. "Where does the Bible say Lucifer sinned before Day Six? The Bible says everything was 'very good' at the end of Day Six." They will accuse us Gap Theory proponents of reaching our conclusion without any Scriptural evidence. Actually, there is a verse of Scripture that indicates the presence of sin and evil by Day Six.

Genesis 2:15 "And the LORD God took the man, and put him into the garden of Eden to dress it and to **keep** it." (KJV)

We need to look at the Hebrew words for "dress" and "keep." We need to understand what they mean. The first word, "dress," is *ABAD* (Strong's Number H5647) and it means to work, serve, labor, cultivate, and other such ideas. Certainly, Adam was given the task of cultivating, working, serving, and taking care of the Garden. That idea presents no controversy. But what does "keep" mean. The Hebrew word is *SHAMAR* (Strong's Number H8104) and it means to guard, to protect, beware of, keep watch over, *etc.* It also means to "take care of" but not in the same sense of merely tending something. It seems to carry the idea of taking care of something in the sense of not letting something bad happen. It was used of Noah keeping animals in the ark so they wouldn't perish.

Genesis 6:20 "Of fowls after their kind, and of cattle after their kind, of every creeping thing of the earth after his kind, two of every *sort* shall come unto thee, to **keep** *them* alive." (KJV)

God used it to tell Jacob He would keep him (protect him) from danger wherever he went.

Genesis 28:15 "And, behold, I *am* with thee, and will **keep** thee in all *places* whither thou goest, and will bring thee again into this land; for I will not leave thee, until I have done *that* which I have spoken to thee of." (KJV)

It was used of keeping sheep. Certainly, shepherds had to feed and water the flocks, but they also had to protect them from lions, bears, wolves, and thieves.

Genesis 30:31 "And he said, What shall I give thee? And Jacob said, Thou shalt not give me any thing: if thou wilt do this thing for me, I will again feed *and* **keep** thy flock." (KJV)

The Levites had to protect and serve in the tabernacle/temple to keep evil people from entering them.

Numbers 1:53 "But the Levites shall pitch round about the tabernacle of testimony, that there be no wrath upon the congregation of the children of Israel: and the Levites shall **keep** the charge of the tabernacle of testimony." (KJV)

Numbers 3:32 "And Eleazar the son of Aaron the priest *shall be* chief over the chief of the Levites, *and have* the oversight of them that **keep** the charge of the sanctuary." (KJV)

Jeremiah 35:4 "And I brought them into the house of the LORD, into the chamber of the sons of Hanan, the son of Igdaliah, a man of God, which *was* by the chamber of the princes, which *was* above the chamber of Maaseiah the son of Shallum, the **keeper** of the door:" (KJV)

Of all the verses where *SHAMAR* is used, I think the most interesting is Genesis 3:24.

Genesis 3:24 "So he drove out the man; and he placed at the east of the garden of Eden Cherubims, and a flaming sword which turned every way, to **keep** the way of the tree of life." (KJV)

Once Adam sinned and was expelled from the Garden of Eden, not only did he lose his job as KEEPER of the Garden, he was KEPT from the Garden by Cherubim and a Flaming Sword. Talk about a role reversal. Here was the man who had been given the authority to be the Guardian of the Garden, but now was guarded from the Garden. It's the same word. Adam was now a sinner like Lucifer. He was defiled. He was corrupt. The Cherubim and Flaming Sword were given the task of protecting the Garden from the evil, sin, and corruption Adam would have brought into it if he were allowed to enter it again.

So, here's my question. If Adam was made Guardian of the Garden, from what or from whom was the Garden in need of protection? If *SHAMAR* implies protecting something from sin, evil, corruption, defilement, death, *etc.*, why was Adam given the task of being the *SHAMAR* of the Garden on Day Six? If there was no sin, evil, corruption, defilement, or death, then why post a guard? If there was no sin before Day Six, from what was the Garden being protected? From whom was Adam supposed to guard the Garden? Certainly, if God had made Lucifer the Overseer of the Garden, then God didn't intend for Adam to keep Lucifer out of the Garden... unless, of course, Lucifer had rebelled before Day Six. Obviously, Lucifer was corrupt, defiled, evil, and sinful by Day Six. By Day Six, Lucifer was already a potential source of sin, evil, corruption, defilement, and death. Lucifer had fallen already. God's command to Adam to guard the Garden seems to imply there was a very real danger of it being defiled. The Garden needed protection. The Garden needed protection from Lucifer. By giving Adam the job of being the Guardian in the Garden, the text seems to hint that evil existed outside the Garden. This idea is supported by the Hebrew word used for "garden." That word is *GAN* (Strong's Number H1588) and it is derived from the word *GANAN* (Strong's Number H1589). *GANAN* means to surround, to protect, or to defend. A *GAN* was an area with an enclosure meant to surround and protect it. In the ancient world (and even today) people built fences, walls, or hedges around their gardens. This wasn't to keep the plants from escaping; it was meant to keep intruders (both animal and human) out. Walls are mentioned in connection with gardens in 2 Kings 25:4, Nehemiah 3:5, Jeremiah 39:4, and Jeremiah 52:7. Jesus gave a parable about a man who planted a vineyard and built a wall around it. (Matthew 21:33 and Mark 12:1 speak of building a tower and a wall around a garden—both of these were built for the protection of the garden.) The primary root word for "garden" means "to defend" or "to protect." This seems to indicate God built some kind of protective enclosure around the Garden of Eden. Whether it was an actual wall or not, I don't know. Whatever it was, it was meant to help Adam keep Satan out. It's very likely Satan indwelt the serpent because he knew a direct, personal assault on the Garden would have been thwarted by Adam. Rather than an open attack, Lucifer decided to use a much more subtle approach: Sneak in through the serpent, confront the woman rather than the man, use doubt and deception rather than force, and let sin be introduced surreptitiously. His plan worked. He was indeed the most subtle of all creatures.

None of this fits together if there was only one creation, one beginning, and one Garden of Eden. Earth had to have two beginnings. The only way to fit all these puzzle pieces together is to understand the Bible tells us there was an original creation, an original Garden of Eden, a rebellion by Satan, a judgment and destruction of the earth, and then a second creation. The Garden of Eden Adam lived in was the restoration of the Garden of Eden Lucifer had lived in. It had been destroyed by God's wrath due to Satan's rebellion, but it was restored along with all the other fruitful places during the six days of restoration. My assumption about the phrase "from the beginning" was true. Jesus made that statement about Lucifer in reference to the second beginning, but not to the first beginning. He was referring to the beginning that took place over the six days of Genesis; the restoration. Lucifer was a murderer from this beginning because he had previously murdered Pre-Adamic "men" in the original earth. The Gap Theory explains this apparent contradiction.

Lucifer Caused the Original Earth to Become *TOHUW WA-BOHUW*

Lucifer walked around on the earth before he fell. It was not yet *TOHUW WA-BOHUW*. The earth was beautiful and Lucifer walked around in the Pre-Adamic Garden of Eden. How long he remained unfallen and how long the original earth remained beautiful is not revealed, but by the time we get to Genesis 1:2, we see earth was no longer beautiful. Lucifer's sin falls in the gap between Genesis 1:1 and Genesis 1:3. The *TOHUW WA-BOHUW* condition of the earth falls in that gap as well. In other words, Lucifer sinned during the same Pre-Adamic period in which the earth received a judgment for sin. This is why I think the condition of the earth was the result of God's judgment on the sins of Lucifer and the fallen angels. I hope you're beginning to see how all this fits together. Is there anything else? Is there another clue that might tie Lucifer's fall to the destruction and judgment of the earth between Genesis 1:1 and Genesis 1:3? Look at Isaiah 14.

Isaiah 14:12-17 "How art thou fallen from heaven, O Lucifer, son of the morning! *how* art thou cut down to the ground, which didst weaken the nations! *{13}* For thou hast said in thine heart, I will ascend into heaven, I will exalt my throne above the stars of God: I will sit also upon the mount of the congregation, in the sides of the north: *{14}* I will ascend above the heights of the clouds; I will be like the most High. *{15}* Yet thou shalt be brought down to hell, to the sides of the pit. *{16}* They that see thee shall narrowly look upon thee, and consider thee, *saying*, Is this the man that **made the earth to tremble**, that did shake kingdoms; *{17} That* **made the world as a wilderness**, and **destroyed the cities** thereof; *that* opened not the house of his prisoners?" (KJV)

Now this is earth-shaking! Look what Isaiah says Lucifer did to the earth. Lucifer made **the earth tremble**. He made **the world a wilderness**. He **destroyed its cities**. Does this sound familiar? Look back at what Jeremiah saw in the Pre-Adamic earth.

Jeremiah 4:24 "I beheld the mountains, and, lo, they **trembled**, and all the hills moved lightly..." (KJV)

Jeremiah 4:26 "I beheld, and, lo, the fruitful place *was* a **wilderness**, and all the **cities thereof were broken down** at the presence of the LORD, *and* by his fierce anger." (KJV)

It seems too great a coincidence for Isaiah and Jeremiah to have such similar visions of the earth if each vision describes the earth at different times. They both are looking at the Pre-Adamic earth. Both Isaiah and Jeremiah see **the earth trembling**. Both prophets see **the world made into a wilderness**. Both see **earth's cities broken down and destroyed**.

Isaiah's and Jeremiah's Views of the Pre-Adamic Earth

Isaiah	Jeremiah
Earth Shaken	Earth Shaken
Land Made into a Wilderness	Land Made into a Wilderness
Cities Destroyed	Cities Destroyed
Lucifer Caused it	God Did it in Judgment

Jeremiah tells us God did this out of judgment for sin. Isaiah tells us Lucifer caused this. The obvious implication is that God did it in judgment of Lucifer's sins. When did this happen? When did Lucifer cause this? When did God shake the earth? When did God make the earth a wasteland or wilderness? When did He destroy all the cities? He hasn't done it since Adam was created, and he won't do it in the future if His promises mean anything. The world is not going to be destroyed when Christ returns to set up His earthly kingdom. The earth won't be destroyed when Satan is bound for a thousand years. The earth won't be made into a wilderness, and all its cities won't be destroyed when Satan is released and engages in one last battle. Christ is the victor, not Lucifer. Christ's kingdom will remain.

Matthew 13:41-43 "The Son of man shall send forth his angels, and they shall gather **out of his kingdom** all things that offend, and them which do iniquity; *{42}* And shall cast them into a furnace of fire: there shall be wailing and gnashing of teeth. *{43}* Then shall the righteous shine forth as the sun **in the kingdom** of their Father. Who hath ears to hear, let him hear." (KJV)

Satan, all fallen angels, and all unsaved people will be removed from the Kingdom at that time. The Kingdom remains, but Satan is removed. The End of Time won't be the end of the earth. Satan will not be able to destroy the earth in the future. The only time he could have done this is in the past. THE ONLY TIME LUCIFER COULD HAVE DESTROYED ALL THE CITIES AND MADE THE WORLD A WILDERNESS WAS BEFORE ADAM WAS CREATED. Again, the Restoration Theory fits these Biblical facts better than the other theories.

What Did Lucifer Do?

I think angels inhabited the earth long before man. I think it was covered with beautiful gardens and it teemed with life. When the earth was created, it was so wonderful they all rejoiced. Earth must have been very beautiful. In fact, I think it's possible the entire universe was much different from what it is now. At that time, the whole of creation did not groan and was not in travail. At that time, the heavens and earth had not yet been shaken by God's judgment.

Suddenly, sin was introduced! Lucifer rebelled against God and pulled a third of the angels into his rebellion. I think he tried to create an empire of his own where he could have mastery. I think he wanted servants and slaves to worship him. It was his sin, not Adam's, that caused the whole universe to groan and be shaken. Lucifer began destroying the earth and the universe by starting a civil war among the angels. Most angels remained faithful to God, but the process of corruption had begun. Lucifer began corrupting and desolating the earth while using his power to twist things to his own purposes. He slowly turned earth into a cesspool of sin. I don't know how long this took, but he and his fallen angels continued to defile creation. Over time, their acts resulted in the death and extinction of many species of plants and animals. God may have created new species in response to the things that became extinct. Layer by layer, the growing geologic strata recorded those events. Eventually God intervened, and in His anger destroyed the kingdom of the angels. He put an end to their civilization. God judged the earth and made it *TOHUW WA-BOHUW*. The earth became without form, and void. He may have changed the angels so they could no longer freely inhabit the physical cosmos like before. Or, He could have changed the physical cosmos itself. The universe now groaned, and the earth was desolate, dead, and dark.

Even in his defeat, Lucifer gloated over what he had done. He felt he had ruined God's universe and thwarted God's sovereign plan. I'm sure such thoughts gave him some kind of sick pleasure. If he couldn't be the god of this world, he at least made it so God couldn't be God of this world. Lucifer couldn't have his way, but at least he had the pleasure of humiliating God by corrupting His creation. Oh, how beautifully ugly was sin's stain now smeared across the face of God's no-longer-perfect universe. At least he did something outside of God's plan... or so he thought. Little did he realize God knew all along he was going to rebel and corrupt all of creation. God knew this would happen, but

He had a plan for earth. God was going to redeem the earth. The earth was going to be born again, and God was going to resurrect the life that inhabited it. This time, however, there was going to be something different. This time there was going to be a new creature, a creature who would be no brute beast. This one was going to be made in the image of God, and be given dominion over the earth. (Just as the Christian is made into the image of Christ and becomes a co-heir with Christ.) I'm sure this galled Lucifer. He desired to have mastery over the earth, but he couldn't have it. Now, this puny creature, this man made from dirt, was going to have that authority. This creature was to be made lower than the angels, but God was going to make him ruler over the earth. God was going to make man, not Lucifer, a king. God was also going to show Lucifer these lowly creatures would do what he and his rebellious angels wouldn't do. They would worship God, and by doing so, would acknowledge that only God was worthy of worship. They would choose to obey God and love God rather than rebel against Him. Although man was far inferior to the angels in power, knowledge, intelligence, and abilities, man would recognize that God alone is worthy of worship. The Dirt-Man would prove Lucifer was not justified in seeking worship for himself.

God began restoring the earth. How fitting it was that His first act of restoration was to send light into the world. Darkness is often a symbol of sin and judgment, and the first thing God did was to separate the light from the darkness. Years later, God would send another light into the world: Jesus, the Light of the world. He would separate the light from the darkness as well. It was equally fitting that God's last act of restoration was the creation of a new creature with whom He could have intimate fellowship. In a similar fashion, Jesus' last act was to go to the cross so we could become new creatures and have intimate fellowship with Him.

When Did Satan Regain Authority Over the Earth?

Lucifer lost his dominion over the earth when he was judged for his sin. How did he regain that dominion? Did God give it back to him as a reward for causing Adam and Eve to sin? That wouldn't make sense. That would be like a judge rewarding a car thief with the title to your car because he tricked you into leaving the doors unlocked and the key in the ignition. If Adam lost his dominion because of sin, surely the one who committed the greater sin would not be given that dominion by God. So, how could he claim to have authority over the earth? The answer is someone gave him authority over the earth. How do I know someone gave Lucifer authority over the earth? By now I hope you guess I will say, "The Bible tells me so."

Luke 4:5-8 "The devil led him up to a high place and showed him in an instant all the kingdoms of the world. {6} And he said to him, 'I will give you all their authority and splendor, for **it has been given to me**, and I can give it to anyone I want to. {7} So if you worship me, it will all be yours.'" (NIV)

Someone gave the devil authority over the earth after he had been stripped of it. Who could have given him that authority? Surely God wouldn't reward Lucifer for causing Adam to sin! God had stripped Lucifer of his authority because of his own sin. Leading Adam and Eve into sin would not be a cause for reward. God didn't give Lucifer his authority back to him. But, if God didn't give him that authority, who did? Here is the answer the Gap Theory proposes: Lucifer regained that authority when Adam gave it to him. (Which means Adam had authority over the earth at that time, but Lucifer didn't—Lucifer had already lost it.) The Gap Theory says God restored the earth, and on the sixth day put it under Adam's dominion. Satan couldn't stand it. I'm sure he hated Adam from the instant God announced He was going to create man in His own image. Lucifer began thinking of ways to destroy this new creature. He began plotting ways to cause man's death. I'm sure he watched Adam and Eve very closely, ever looking for a way to ruin God's plan again. How delighted Satan must have been when he deceived Eve. How much more delighted he must have been when Adam knowingly rebelled against God. Adam's sin brought death to all his descendants. Better still, from Lucifer's point of view, Adam's sin caused him to lose dominion over the earth. Lucifer had been able to conquer man, and in so doing, he seized control of the world over man. Satan gained authority over Adam when Adam willingly joined Satan's rebellion. Lucifer started the rebellion, one-third of the angels submitted themselves to his rebellion, and then Adam and Eve joined his rebellion when they chose to believe Lucifer rather than God. Adam knowingly sided with the devil when he ate the forbidden fruit. In doing so, Adam handed his authority over to Lucifer. **Adam gave his authority to Lucifer by surrendering himself to Lucifer.** By obeying Lucifer rather than God, Adam made himself a slave to Lucifer. Paul tells us what happens when we obey Satan.

Romans 6:16 "Don't you know that when you offer yourselves to someone to obey him as slaves, you are slaves to the one whom you obey—whether you are slaves to sin, which leads to death, or to obedience, which leads to righteousness?" (NIV)

John also warned us about this very thing when he put the ultimate effect of sin in its proper relationship with the events of the creation. Once again, here are John's words.

1 John 3:8 "**He who sins is of the devil**, for the devil has sinned from the beginning. For this purpose the Son of God was manifested, that He might destroy the works of the devil." (NKJV)

Adam made Lucifer his master by making himself his slave. He gave up his authority over the earth. Lucifer seized authority over the earth by deceit. The Greek word for "given" in Luke 4:6 is *PARADIDOMI*, (Strong's Number G3860) and it means, "betrayed," "taken by betrayal," or "seized." It is the word used when Jesus was betrayed by Judas (Matthew 10:4) and when John the Baptist was taken prisoner by Herod.

(Matthew 4:12) Satan betrayed Adam and seized the earth. Lucifer was again the prince of the world, and he set out to enslave men by the power of sin and death. It pleased Satan that Adam's sin led to a change in the earth. Thorns and thistles would plague mankind, and beasts would pose a threat. Man would have to live by the sweat of his brow, and suffer disease, pain, and death. Best of all, this precious little pet of God's was now going to be judged and cast into the Lake of Fire. Again, even though Lucifer knew he couldn't defeat God, he got pleasure out of knowing he could ruin God's plans.

But God knew about this too. He knew Adam would sin. He didn't want Adam to sin, but He knew he would. So, God expelled Adam from the Garden and let death reign over man… but God had a plan for man. God was going to do something even the angels couldn't comprehend. **God had made man in His image and likeness, knowing someday He would come in the image and likeness of man.** He was going to become one of these puny creatures, one of these Dirt-Men. How strange it must have seemed to the angels; they could have never envisioned such a thing. God had never taken on the nature of angels. God was now going to take on the nature of humans and live their miserable life and die their miserable death. More than that, the Son was going to bear their sins and die in their place. He was going to let the wrath of the Father be poured out on Himself for all the sins they had committed. Jesus would let the judgment fall on Himself rather than on His beloved children. This seemed impossible to imagine. God would bear the judgment of man's sin? Not even the angels could grasp what God had in store for man. What Lucifer couldn't understand was that through the Son's death, God would utterly defeat sin and destroy Satan's enslavement of man forever.

Hebrews 2:14-16 "Forasmuch then as the children are partakers of flesh and blood, he also himself likewise took part of the same; that through death he might destroy him that had the power of death, that is, the devil; *{15}* And deliver them who through fear of death were all their lifetime subject to bondage. *{16}* For verily he took not on *him the nature of* angels; but he took on *him* the seed of Abraham." (KJV)

Through all this, God would raise up creatures who would someday be more than mere servants of God, they would be the sons and daughters of God. They would be more than just subjects to the King; they would reign with the King. They would become kings in God's Kingdom. No angel ever held that honor. Though men were made lower than angels, they would be raised up to a greater glory if, and only if, they accepted what God the Son did for them on Calvary's Cross. Those who are saved (those who have claimed the Blood of Christ as their only hope) will be appointed by God as judges over the fallen angels. Satan planted the seeds of his own destruction on the day he first held iniquity in his heart, and he inadvertently selected his judges when he led Adam and Eve into sin.

1 Corinthians 6:3a "Know ye not that **WE** shall judge angels?" (KJV)

Was Lucifer's murder and destruction of Pre-Adamic "men" the last straw? Is this why God destroyed his kingdom and his world? Could this be why God created a new man, like the old "men," but now made in His own image and likeness? Is this why the Bible says Lucifer was a murderer **from** the beginning, but not **in** the beginning? I think the Gap Theory answers a lot of questions that go unanswered by the other theories. If the Restoration Theory is true, then the earth's history typifies the history of the man made from its soil. The earth was created perfect. Sin destroyed its original condition. This was followed by judgment and death. Next, there was a rebirth. Although reborn, the earth was still subject to sin and decay. It was very good, but not yet perfect. (Note that God declared the works of the six days to be "very good," not "perfect." If there had been no sin prior to this, Lucifer still would have been perfect, all creation still would have been perfect, and God would have declared all His works to be perfect.) The earth on Day Six was not perfect. The earth awaits a future perfection. This is what happened to earth, and this is what happened to man. Man was created perfect, but man fell into sin and judgment; he experienced death. The rebirth of the Christian is like the restoration of the earth. The restoration of the Christian is also very good, but not yet perfect. We too are still subject to sin and decay and are awaiting a future perfection. Both the earth and saved men wait for the day when they will be made perfect again. Someday there will be a new heavens and a new earth, and saved men will receive new and perfect bodies. Someday both we and the earth will no longer be subject to sin and decay. At that time the whole of creation will no longer groan under the bondage of sin. If the Restoration Theory is true, then the history of earth is a foreshadow (prophecy) of the history of the believer in Jesus Christ. The earth had two beginnings and the Christian has two beginnings. Are there other writers of Scripture who suggest there were two beginnings?

Let Light Shine

Saved man, the man who accepts Jesus Christ as his Savior, has two beginnings. He has a first beginning when he is born and he has a second beginning when he is born again. This second birth involves both a washing and a renewing. (Titus 3:5) Something old is cleansed (sin is removed) and something new (spiritual life) is created. The old creature passes away and the new creature comes to life. (2 Corinthians 5:17) More than any other apostle, Paul constantly taught that sinful man must be restored by God's grace. (Ephesians 2:8) He repeatedly returned to this truth of the Scriptures: Fallen man must be restored. Looking at his own background as the great persecutor of Christians, it is no wonder he felt so burdened with this doctrine. It is his recurrent theme, and he explained it in many ways and in many places in the New Testament. He often referred back to the Old Testament to show how this idea had been demonstrated in Scripture. One such instance was 2 Corinthians 4:6.

2 Corinthians 4:6 "For God, who said, 'Let light shine out of darkness,' made his light shine in our hearts to give us the light of the knowledge of the glory of God in the face of Christ." (NIV)

Paul explains the restoration of fallen man by going back to the Genesis account of creation. Paul reminds us how God commanded light to shine on the darkened earth. **The parallel he makes is between the darkened state of man and the darkened state of the earth.** This parallel is an extremely poor example if the darkness that covered the earth was not the result of sin. If the earth was originally created in darkness, as many anti-Gap Theory people say, then this would mean Paul is teaching that man's darkened state was not the result of sin either. Paul would be teaching that God created Adam that way. Instead of teaching that man had become sinful, he would be teaching that man was sinful when God first created him. Paul does not teach that! He understands man was created perfect, but later became bad. He understands the earth was created perfect, but later became bad. This is the only way this comparison makes any sense. **He uses God's restoration of the earth as a way of explaining God's restoration of man.** Paul understands Genesis 1:3 was the revelation of light; not the creation of light. How do I know Paul understands this? Paul tells me so. Paul does not say, "For God who CREATED light to shine..." Paul says, "For God, who SAID, 'let light shine...'" The Greek word he uses is *EPO*, (Strong's Number G2036) and it doesn't mean to create. It means to speak or call or command. Paul says God commanded the light to shine. ("And God said, 'light come to be,' and light came to be.") **Paul uses the physical light on the earth as a parallel of the spiritual light God shines into our hearts when He saves us.** Paul understands God must first shine His Light into fallen man BEFORE he can be restored. His Light comes BEFORE our restoration. His Light is not created AFTER we believe. Instead, His Light existed BEFORE our belief. Although His Light exists before we are saved, we cannot see it. It is supernaturally hidden from our fallen hearts just as the light of the sun was supernaturally hidden from the fallen earth. It is not until after God commands His Light to shine into our hearts that we can see, "The light of the knowledge of the glory of God in the face of Jesus Christ." In other words, God has to enlighten us before we can know that when we look at Jesus Christ, we are looking at God Himself. His Light must first shine in our hearts before we can attain that knowledge. The light of the Gospel has to be shone into us before we can see the truth of the Gospel. The light of the Gospel is faith. God must give us the faith to believe the Gospel before we can believe the Gospel. (We must know the truth before we can know the truth.) It's not possible for natural man, fallen man, unrestored man, spiritually blind man to understand the things of God. (1 Corinthians 2:14) That's why faith is a gift. (Ephesians 2:8) God causes His Light to shine into our darkened souls. Paul understands this, so he uses the example of God causing light to shine into the darkened earth. Why does Paul use this example? Because it is a perfect parallel. The first thing God does when He begins the process of restoring us is to shine His Light into our hearts. We can't understand, or comprehend, or accept the truth of the Gospel without that light. HE HAS TO CAUSE HIS

LIGHT TO SHINE INTO US FIRST. We are spiritually dead. Our souls are darkened because we are a fallen race. We are sinners by virtue of The Fall, and light is not in us. We cannot cause His Light to shine in us any more than the earth could have caused the light of the sun to shine on it. The earth was powerless to create physical light. It could only receive it. We are powerless to create spiritual light. That's why it must be a gift. We can only receive what God reveals. Paul uses this example because this is exactly what God did to the fallen earth. He began the restoration process by first causing physical light to shine where sin had caused darkness. The earth was dark because of sin. We were dark because of sin. The earth was in physical darkness and we were in spiritual darkness. Both kinds of darkness were the result of sin. Both kinds of darkness came to an end when God commanded light to shine into the darkness. There could be no physical life on earth without physical light. There can be no spiritual life in man without spiritual light. In both cases, it is the revelation of light, not the creation of light. Physical light preexisted the physical darkness of the earth. Spiritual light preexisted the spiritual darkness of our hearts. Paul believed man had become dark because of sin. Paul believed the earth had become dark because of sin. Paul makes this comparison because he understands the symbolic connection between man and the earth. Both darkened man and the darkened earth needed light from God to be restored.

Born of Water and The Spirit

Paul wasn't the only one in the New Testament to speak about the connection between the restoration of the earth and the restoration of man. Jesus alluded to this in His discussion with Nicodemus.

John 3:1-12 "There was a man from the Pharisees named Nicodemus, a ruler of the Jews. *{2}* This man came to Him at night and said, 'Rabbi, we know that You have come from God as a teacher, for no one could perform these signs You do unless God were with him.' *{3}* Jesus replied, 'I assure you: Unless someone is born again, he cannot see the kingdom of God.' *{4}* 'But how can anyone be born when he is old?' Nicodemus asked Him. 'Can he enter his mother's womb a second time and be born?' *{5}* Jesus answered, 'I assure you: Unless someone is born of water and the Spirit, he cannot enter the kingdom of God. *{6}* Whatever is born of the flesh is flesh, and whatever is born of the Spirit is spirit. *{7}* Do not be amazed that I told you that you must be born again. *{8}* The wind blows where it pleases, and you hear its sound, but you don't know where it comes from or where it is going. So it is with everyone born of the Spirit.' *{9}* 'How can these things be?' asked Nicodemus. *{10}* 'Are you a teacher of Israel and don't know these things?' Jesus replied. *{11}* 'I assure you: We speak what We know and We testify to what We have seen, but you do not accept Our testimony. *{12}* If I have told you about things that happen on earth and you don't believe, how will you believe if I tell you about things of heaven?'" (HCSB)

This is one of the most well-known passages in the New Testament that speaks about the necessity of being born of water and the Spirit. Jesus clearly teaches the need for a rebirth that is the work of the Holy Spirit. Now, it is easy for us in the 21st century, with all our commentaries and Bible study tools, to understand what Jesus was telling Nicodemus. But, I want you to put yourself in the place of Nicodemus. Yes, he was a Pharisee and a member of the Sanhedrin. This meant he really was a teacher of Israel. He was like a professor of professors. He really did know the Scriptures (The Old Testament) backward and forward. Still, with all that knowledge, he didn't understand what Jesus was talking about when Jesus told him that he needed to be born again. This shouldn't surprise you when you realize the phrase "born again" is never found in the Old Testament. "Born again" was a new phrase, but it wasn't a new teaching. Jesus expected Nicodemus to understand this idea from his understanding of the Old Testament.

We know Jesus was not speaking literally. What we don't know is why Nicodemus took his message literally. In fact, we really don't know IF Nicodemus took Jesus' words literally. It's possible Nicodemus was so intent on believing Jesus that he simply gravitated to a literal meaning before giving it much thought. It's also possible Nicodemus knew fully well Jesus was speaking in symbols, but wanted to be argumentative, and he saw this as an opportunity to dispute something Jesus taught. We don't know what thoughts about Jesus were going through his mind, or what attitude he had of Jesus when he came to Jesus that night. Some commentators think Nicodemus came in secret because he wanted no one to know about it. Other commentators say Nicodemus may have been listening to Jesus all day, and just wanted to learn so much more that he couldn't wait until the next day. Others think he initially came to refute Jesus privately. We don't know Nicodemus' heart at that moment, but we know Jesus knew his heart.

Jesus told Nicodemus he must be born again. **Nicodemus** either had no clue what this meant, or else he acted like he had no clue what this meant. In response, Jesus asked **Nicodemus** why he didn't understand what "born again" meant, since he was a teacher of Israel? Jesus made two connections in His message for **Nicodemus to consider**.

1.) Jesus connected water with a process of "rebirth."

2.) Jesus connected the Holy Spirit with a process of "rebirth."

We know Jesus wasn't being literal when He spoke of a "rebirth." No one can literally enter into his mother's uterus again and be expelled through the birth canal. We also know Jesus wasn't being literal because He spoke of this "rebirth" as an activity of the wind. He was figuratively speaking about the Spirit. (The word "wind" and the word "Spirit" are the same word in the Greek—*PNEUMA*; Strong's Number G4151.) The physical wind is not a factor in the birthing process. Women can have babies in calm weather and women can have babies in storms. The wind has nothing to do with literal birth. Nevertheless, Jesus expected **Nicodemus** to mentally connect something in the Old Testament about water and the Holy Spirit to a process of rebirth.

Now, there are many passages in the Old Testament that talk about the Spirit removing the heart of stone and replacing it with a heart of flesh. There are passages about the Spirit regenerating our spirits. However, none of these passages connect this idea with being born again. The imagery of the birthing process is never given in the Old Testament. Jesus' imagery connected physical rebirth to the process of being saved. That imagery is never used in the Old Testament to describe salvation. That's why **Nicodemus** was confused. If Jesus had said, "Unless someone is regenerated by the Spirit, he cannot see the kingdom of God," then I don't think **Nicodemus** would have missed the point. The problem is Jesus said, "Unless someone is born again, he cannot see the kingdom of God." Those words are not in the Old Testament. There are three resurrections of men mentioned in the Old Testament, but being resurrected is not the same as being born again. The imagery of water, wind, and birth is not connected to these resurrections because they were resurrections of the old physical life, not the new spiritual life. These resurrected men were not born again; they were not new creations. They all physically died later.

1 Kings 17:17-24—Elijah raises the widow's son.

2 Kings 4:18-37—Elisha raises the son of the Shunammite woman.

2 Kings 13:21—A dead man's body touched the bones of Elisha and was raised.

Nicodemus certainly could have connected the work of the Holy Spirit to the resurrection of these men, but not to the rebirth of these men. Rebirth is not mentioned in these accounts. Water is not mentioned in these accounts. So, how could **Nicodemus** make a connection between water, the Spirit, and rebirth? Jesus certainly expected him to make that connection based on his knowledge of the Old Testament. This means the Old Testament must somewhere reveal something that connects the work of the Holy Spirit with the concept of rebirth, and it must have something to do with water. But where is that mentioned in the Old Testament? It never mentions it in reference to the resurrection of people. The Old Testament never mentions anyone being born again. If the Old Testament does not connect water and the work of the Holy Spirit to the rebirth of SOMEONE, then it must connect water and the work of the Holy Spirit to the rebirth of SOMETHING. Where are water and the Spirit connected to the rebirth of something in the Old Testament? That connection is found only in the first chapter of Genesis.

This is exactly what the Spirit did to bring about the rebirth of the dead earth covered in water. The earth was dead because of sin. Nicodemus was dead because of sin. The earth needed to be born again. Nicodemus needed to be born again. The earth was born of water (the deep) and the Spirit. (The Spirit moved upon the face of the waters.) That is the connection Nicodemus should have understood from the first chapter of Genesis. The earth needed to be born again of water (cleansing) and the Spirit. (regeneration) People need to be born again of water (cleansing) and the Spirit. (regeneration) The earth was restored by a process of washing and renewal. We are restored by a process of washing and renewal.

Titus 3:5 "He saved us, not because of works done by us in righteousness, but according to His own mercy, by the **washing** of regeneration and **renewal** of the Holy Spirit," (ESV)

We must be washed and we must be renewed. Salvation has two parts; cleansing and renewal. Both parts are necessary for salvation, and both parts are the work of God. Both parts were foreshadowed by the cleansing and restoration of the Pre-Adamic earth.

<u>Rebirth</u> = <u>Removal of Sin</u> + <u>Renewal of Life</u>.

That's why we are new creations. God causes us to be born again the same way He caused the earth to be born again. That's the only place in the Old Testament where water and the Spirit are connected with the idea of a rebirth. The earth, made dead by **Lucifer**'s sin, was washed by the flood of the deep and renewed by the work of the Holy Spirit. Jesus connected the Ruin-Restoration of the earth to the Ruin-Restoration of the believer. Jesus expected **Nicodemus** to have known that. I suspect Jesus expects us to know that too.

All Shook Up

There is another Biblical clue that shakes up the various creation theories. As we have seen in Jeremiah 4:24, the earth was shaken by God's wrath sometime in the past. The word used is *RAASH*, (Strong's Number H7493) and it means to shake, to make tremble, or to make afraid. It is an interesting word! It is often used in connection with Divine judgment. Isaiah 13:13, Ezekiel 38:20, Joel 2:10 and Joel 3:16 use *RAASH* to describe what God will do at the final judgment.

Isaiah 13:9-13 "Behold, the day of the LORD is coming, Cruel, with fury and burning anger, To make the land a desolation; And He will exterminate its sinners from it. *{10}* For the stars of heaven and their constellations Will not flash forth their light; The sun will be dark when it rises, And the moon will not shed its light. *{11}* Thus I will punish the world for its evil, And the wicked for their iniquity; I will also put an end to the arrogance of the proud, And abase the haughtiness of the ruthless. *{12}* I will make mortal man scarcer than pure gold, And mankind than the gold of Ophir. *{13}* Therefore I shall make the heavens tremble, And the earth **will be shaken** from its place At the fury of the LORD of hosts In the day of His burning anger." (NASB)

Ezekiel 38:18-20 "And it shall come to pass at the same time when Gog shall come against the land of Israel, saith the Lord GOD, that my fury shall come up in my face. *{19}* For in my jealousy and in the fire of my wrath have I spoken, Surely in that day there shall be a great **shaking** in the land of Israel; *{20}* So that the fishes of the sea, and the fowls of the heaven, and the beasts of the field, and all creeping things that creep upon the earth, and all the men that are upon the face of the earth, **shall shake** at my presence, and the mountains shall be thrown down, and the steep places shall fall, and every wall shall fall to the ground." (KJV)

Joel 2:10 "The earth shall quake before them; the heavens **shall tremble**: the sun and the moon shall be dark, and the stars shall withdraw their shining:" (KJV)

Joel 3:13-17 "Put ye in the sickle, for the harvest is ripe: come, get you down; for the press is full, the vats overflow; for their wickedness is great. *{14}* Multitudes, multitudes in the valley of decision: for the day of the LORD is near in the valley of decision. *{15}* The sun and the moon shall be darkened, and the stars shall withdraw their shining. *{16}* The LORD also shall roar out of Zion, and utter his voice from Jerusalem; and the heavens and the earth **shall shake**: but the LORD will be the hope of his people, and the strength of the children of Israel. *{17}* So shall ye know that I am the LORD your God dwelling in Zion, my holy mountain: then shall Jerusalem be holy, and there shall no strangers pass through her any more." (KJV)

RAASH isn't always used to describe judgment at the end time. It is also used to describe the earth shaking at other times. For instance, *RAASH* is used to describe the shaking of Mt. Sinai in the presence of God. (Psalms 68:8) The earth shook, but it wasn't the end of the world. One distinction in the case of Mt. Sinai is that while several passages indicate there was a tremendous thunderstorm, they don't use *RAASH* in connection with the heavens. (The sun, moon, and stars.) At Mt. Sinai, only the earth shook. There are other words for "shake" and "tremble" used in connection with the earth shaking. (earthquakes) However, those words are not used to describe the shaking of both the heavens and the earth; *RAASH* is. We've seen *RAASH* in Joel 3:16 used for the shaking (judgment) of the heavens and the earth. (All of creation) It is also used in that way in Haggai 2:6 and Haggai 2:21. Let's examine Haggai 2:6 first.

Haggai 2:6 "This is what the LORD Almighty says: 'In a little while I will once more **shake** the heavens and the earth, the sea and the dry land.'" (NIV)

The Prophet Haggai is looking at the future, and he says something that really captures my attention. Haggai 2:6 uses *RAASH* in reference to shaking the heavens and the earth at the final judgment, but it adds one comment easily missed if not read carefully. Haggai tells us the Lord Almighty says He will, "ONCE MORE shake the heavens and the earth." Do you see what God is telling us? To do this once more means He's done it before. The same Hebrew words, "once" and "more," used in Haggai 2:6 (*ECHAD*—Strong's Number H259 and *OWD*—Strong's Number H5750) are used in Exodus 11:1 where God tells Moses He will once more bring a plague on Egypt.

Exodus 11:1 "Now the LORD said to Moses, '**One more** plague I will bring on Pharaoh and on Egypt; after that he will let you go from here. When he lets you go, he will surely drive you out from here completely.'" (NASB)

God used "one more" because He had sent plagues on Egypt before this.

When Ahab, King of Israel coaxed Jehoshaphat, King of Judah, to make an alliance with him to go to war against the King of Syria, Jehoshaphat wanted to enquire of the Lord. Ahab brought forth four hundred prophets (false prophets) who all said the Lord would give them the victory. Jehoshaphat wasn't convinced, so he asked Ahab if he had a prophet of the Lord, (a true prophet) to tell him what the Lord would say. (This event is recorded in both 1 Kings 22:8 and 2 Chronicles 18:7) Ahab's reply included the phrase *ECHAD OWD*:

1 Kings 22:8 "And the king of Israel said unto Jehoshaphat, *There is* **yet one** man, Micaiah the son of Imlah, by whom we may enquire of the LORD: but I hate him; for he doth not prophesy good concerning me, but evil. And Jehoshaphat said, Let not the king say so." (KJV)

2 Chronicles 18:7 "And the king of Israel said unto Jehoshaphat, *There is* **yet one** man, by whom we may enquire of the LORD: but I hate him; for he never prophesied good unto me, but always evil: the same *is* Micaiah the son of Imla. And Jehoshaphat said, Let not the king say so." (KJV)

As you can see, after presenting all four hundred false prophets, Ahab admitted he had one more prophet he could call forward. It could be translated, "There is one yet prophet," or "There is one more prophet." No matter how you translate it, it means there weren't just four hundred prophets, there was one more prophet, Micaiah the son of Imlah.

The "once more" in Haggai 2:6 means God had shaken (judged) the heavens and the earth before this. Yet, if you search the Scriptures, you'll see no such event after Genesis 1:2. While it is true the Great Flood of Noah's time was a judgment of the earth, the Great Flood didn't shake the heavens. The Flood went only twenty feet higher than the tallest mountain. The heavens weren't affected. The heavens weren't shaken by Noah's Flood. God firmly established the heavens, the sun, the moon and the stars to mark the seasons and days and years in Genesis 1:14-18. He set them in place and fixed them in position BEFORE Adam was created. God established their movements with such precision that we can still mark years and seasons and days by their motion. We can still see His invisible attributes in them. The Great Flood of Noah's time was a judgment of the earth, not of the heavens and the earth. God has not shaken (judged) the Post-Adamic heavens and earth. The heavens and earth will not be shaken until the final judgment. "I will once more shake the heavens and the earth," can only mean the Pre-Adamic heavens and earth were shaken by God's judgment. Only the Restoration Theory incorporates a Pre-Adamic judgment of the heavens and the earth.

Now, I know what the Gap Theory doubters will say. Not every translation says, "once more." That's true, but many do. Why do some say, "once more," and others don't? I don't know. I suspect it is grammatically possible to translate it either way. I suspect the translators who left out the "once more" omitted it because they didn't see a need for it. I suppose they thought it might be confusing to say, "once more," if they didn't realize God had shaken the heavens and the earth once before. Many Gap Theory doubters quote the *King James Version* to prove it doesn't say, "once more."

Haggai 2:6 "For thus saith the LORD of hosts; **Yet once**, it *is* a little while, and I will shake the heavens, and the earth, and the sea, and the dry *land;*" (KJV)

It would be easy to refute their argument simply by listing other translations that render it as, "once more" or "once again."

Haggai 2:6 "For thus says the LORD of hosts, '**Once more** in a little while, I am going to shake the heavens and the earth, the sea also and the dry land.'" (NASB)

Haggai 2:6 "For thus says the LORD of hosts: **Once again**, in a little while, I will shake the heavens and the earth and the sea and the dry land;" (NRSV)

Haggai 2:6 "This is what the LORD All-Powerful says: 'In a short time I will **once again** shake the heavens and the earth, the sea and the dry land.'" (NCV)

Haggai 2:6 "For thus says the LORD of hosts: Yet **once more**, in a little while, I will shake the heavens and the earth and the sea and the dry land." (ESV)

Haggai 2:6 "For thus said יהוה of hosts, '**Once more**, in a little while, and I am shaking the heavens and earth, the sea and dry land.'" (SCRIP)

Haggai 2:6 "For thus says Yahweh of hosts: Still **once more**, it is a little while, and I shall make the heavens and the earth and the sea and the drained land quake;" (CVOT)

Haggai 2:6 "For thus said Jehovah of Hosts: Yet **once more** -- it *is* a little, And I am shaking the heavens and the earth, And the sea, and the dry land," (YLT)

Haggai 2:6 "Moreover, the Lord who rules over all says: 'In just a little while I will **once again** shake the sky and the earth, the sea and the dry ground.'" (NET)

Haggai 2:6 "This is what the LORD of Armies says: **Once again**, in a little while, I am going to shake the sky and the earth, the sea and the dry land." (GW)

Haggai 2:6 "For the Lord of Hosts says this: '**Once more**, in a little while, I am going to shake the heavens and the earth, the sea and the dry land.'" (HCSB)

Haggai 2:6 "For this is what the LORD Almighty says: In just a little while I **will again** shake the heavens and the earth. I will shake the oceans and the dry land, too." (NLB)

Haggai 2:6 "For this is what ADONAI-Tzva'ot says: 'It won't be long before **one more time** I will shake the heavens and the earth, the sea and the dry land;'" (CJB)

Haggai 2:6 "For thus says the Lord of hosts: '**Once more** (it is a little while) I will shake heaven and earth, the sea and dry land;'" (NKJV)

Since these other qualified Hebrew scholars translated it, "once more" or "once again," then I believe I have a valid argument. Nevertheless, I want to show those who quote the *King James*, that this was exactly what the KJV translators were thinking when they said, "yet once."

The Hebrew word for "once" is *ECHAD*, and there is no disagreement over what this word means. We have seen it before in Genesis 1:5 as *YOM ECHAD* where they are translated, "one day," "first day," or "day one." *ECHAD* is the word for "one," "once," "first," and other such words that derive their meaning from the number one. Now, we must determine what *OWD* means. Does it mean "yet?" Does it mean "again?" Does it mean "more?" Actually, it means all of those because they have a common meaning. Look at how the *King James* translators translated *OWD* in other parts of Genesis.

Genesis 4:25 "And Adam knew his wife **again**; and she bare a son, and called his name Seth: For God, said she, hath appointed me another seed instead of Abel, whom Cain slew." (KJV)

Genesis 8:12 "And he stayed **yet** other seven days; and sent forth the dove; which returned not again unto him any more." (KJV)

Genesis 9:15 "And I will remember my covenant, which is between me and you and every living creature of all flesh; and the waters shall no **more** become a flood to destroy all flesh." (KJV)

Genesis 24:20 "And she hasted, and emptied her pitcher into the trough, and ran **again** unto the well to draw water, and drew for all his camels." (KJV)

Genesis 31:14 "And Rachel and Leah answered and said unto him, Is there **yet** any portion or inheritance for us in our father's house?" (KJV)

The word "yet" means the same thing as "again" or "more" in this context. If I said, "I haven't YET finished writing my book," it means I have MORE of my book to write. The translators of the *King James Bible* were correct to translate it, "yet," because they apparently believed there will be one yet (one more) judgment of the heavens and the earth. I'm not sure how you can interpret the words *ECHAD* (one or once) and *OWD* (more or again) except as, "one more" or "once again." I'm sure Hebrew scholars will argue about this from now until the heavens and the earth are shaken on the last day. I wish them luck! For me, the best translation of God's Word is when God Himself interprets what He has written. God does just that. Haggai's words are echoed in the Book of Hebrews.

Hebrews 12:25-27 "See to it that you do not refuse Him who is speaking. For if those did not escape when they refused him who warned them on earth, much less shall we escape who turn away from Him who warns from heaven. *{26}* And His voice shook the earth then, but now He has promised, saying, 'YET ONCE MORE I WILL SHAKE NOT ONLY THE EARTH, BUT ALSO THE HEAVEN.' *{27}* And this expression, 'Yet once more,' denotes the removing of those things which can be shaken, as of created things, in order that those things which cannot be shaken may remain." (NASB) (emphasis NASB)

The context of this portion of the Book of Hebrews is a warning about the Last Judgment. At the Last Judgment both heaven and earth will be shaken. God uses this warning about the Last Judgment as a way to warn us that our present-day disobedience will lead to present-day judgment. (In this case He is using a future judgment rather than a past judgment to warn us.) Chapter Twelve explains how God disciplines us in order to perfect us. If we don't heed the warnings of His discipline, we will not escape the judgment of His wrath. The writer of Hebrews reminds us we must be perfect and holy if we are to come to Mount Zion, the heavenly Jerusalem, and dwell in God's presence. Those things which are imperfect and unholy cannot stand before God, and they will be removed from His Kingdom. Two examples of God's judgment are given. The writer of Hebrews reviews what happened to Esau. He sold his birthright, (rejected God) and for that he was rejected by God. The writer also refers to a time when Israel rejected God. God brought the Israelites to Mt. Sinai (Exodus 19) to give Moses the Ten Commandments. God made His presence known; He gave ample proof it was He who came down to the mountain. At that time, the earth shook and it terrified the Israelites. It terrified Moses too, but he was allowed to approach God. While Moses was away, even though the people knew it was God on the mountain, they rebelled and engaged in pagan orgies and calf worship. They rejected God.

They did not heed His warnings, and so they were judged. The writer of Hebrews is urging us not to make the same mistake, because God will do something even greater than Sinai when He comes for the final judgment. This won't be just another Sinai. At Sinai, He shook only the earth, but now God tells us, "Yet once more I will shake not only the earth, but also the heaven." The writer of the Book of Hebrews refers back to the words of Haggai. The Holy Spirit inspired both writers to make it clear He is not talking about a judgment of the earth alone. **The writer of Hebrews verifies that "once more" should be included in the translation of Haggai 2:6.** Scripture clarifies Scripture! Haggai 2:6 should be translated, "In a little while I will once more shake the heavens and the earth." The "once more" refers to God shaking "created things," the creation, the physical universe. This is not a shaking of just the earth; this is a shaking of all creation. "Once more" God will judge the heavens and the earth. The heavens and the earth were judged before, and they will be judged again at the final judgment. The writer of the Book of Hebrews confirms what Haggai told us. God has ONCE BEFORE shaken not only the earth, but also the heavens. The heavens and the earth are the physical realm, the "created things," "those things that can be shaken." God has ONCE BEFORE shaken the physical realm. God has ONCE BEFORE judged creation. The Bible tells us the final judgment of the heavens and the earth is not the first judgment of the heavens and the earth; they have been judged before. Now, if they have been judged before, for whose rebellion were they judged? Not Adam's; he wasn't created yet. Whose sin resulted in God shaking the heavens and the earth the first time? It was not man. Remember, according to Genesis 3:17, only the ground was judged because of Adam's sin.

Genesis 3:17 "Then to Adam He said, 'Because you have listened to the voice of your wife, and have eaten from the tree about which I commanded you, saying, "You shall not eat from it;" Cursed is the **ground** because of you; In toil you shall eat of it All the days of your life.'" (NASB)

Only the angelic rebellion led by Lucifer could have caused the heavens to be judged too.

Before we leave *RAASH* behind, we need to look at Haggai 2:20-23. This is the third passage of Scripture that uses *RAASH* to describe the shaking of both the heavens and the earth. Now, at first reading it seems as if this portion of Scripture is not describing the end times. Instead, it is talking about Zerubbabel, who was the governor of Judah at that time.

Haggai 2:20-23 "And again the word of the LORD came unto Haggai in the four and twentieth day of the month, saying, *{21}* Speak to Zerubbabel, governor of Judah, saying, **I will shake the heavens and the earth**; *{22}* And I will overthrow the throne of kingdoms, and I will destroy the strength of the kingdoms of the heathen; and I will overthrow the chariots, and those that ride in them; and the horses and their riders shall come down, every one by the sword of his brother. {23} In that day, saith the LORD of hosts, will I take thee, O Zerubbabel, my servant, the son of Shealtiel, saith the LORD, and will make thee as a signet: for I have chosen thee, saith the LORD of hosts." (KJV)

Zerubbabel was the son of Shealtiel, the son of Jehoiachin, the last legal king of Judah before Babylon destroyed Jerusalem. Zerubbabel was heir to the throne and he should have been Judah's king. Here we see he is only its governor. Why wasn't he the king? We need to see what happened to dear Grandpa Jehoiachin. King Jehoiachin was the last of King David's royal line to sit on the throne legally. I say, "legally," because Jehoiachin was carried off to Babylon, and Babylon put Jehoiachin's uncle Zedekiah on the throne. Jehoiachin's son Shealtiel had the legal claim to the throne, but Babylon chose Zedekiah to rule in Jerusalem instead. It may have been Shealtiel wasn't old enough, but for whatever reason, it was Babylon, not God, who made Zedekiah king. Zedekiah had no legal claim to David's throne in God's eyes. (Zedekiah later rebelled against Babylon and was carried off there to die.) Jehoiachin, therefore, was Israel's last legally reigning king before the Babylonian conquest. Now, Jehoiachin had two other names in the Bible. He was called Jeconiah, and he was also called Coniah. He was an evil king, and the Lord brought judgment on him when Babylon captured Judah and replaced him with Zedekiah. Coniah never returned from Babylon. Coniah was so evil God cursed him and declared that none of his offspring would ever be king.

Jeremiah 22:24-30 "As I live, saith Jehovah, though Coniah the son of Jehoiakim king of Judah were the signet upon my right hand, yet would I pluck thee thence; {25} and I will give thee into the hand of them that seek thy life, and into the hand of them of whom thou art afraid, even into the hand of Nebuchadrezzar king of Babylon, and into the hand of the Chaldeans. {26} And I will cast thee out, and thy mother that bare thee, into another country, where ye were not born; and there shall ye die. {27} But to the land whereunto their soul longeth to return, thither shall they not return. {28} Is this man Coniah a despised broken vessel? is he a vessel wherein none delighteth? wherefore are they cast out, he and his seed, and are cast into the land which they know not? {29} O earth, earth, earth, hear the word of Jehovah. {30} Thus saith Jehovah, Write ye this man childless, a man that shall not prosper in his days; for no more shall a man of his seed prosper, sitting upon the throne of David, and ruling in Judah." (KJV)

Several years after Babylon conquered Israel, Babylon itself was conquered by the Persians. King Cyrus of Persia made a decree to have Jerusalem rebuilt, and he sent Zerubbabel to be its governor. Was Haggai looking at that event? Was he anticipating God would restore Zerubbabel to the throne? No. Haggai was not looking for Zerubbabel to take the throne. Haggai was looking much further into Zerubbabel's future. Haggai 2:21 indicates he was looking to the time when God was going to shake the heavens and the earth, the final judgment. How do I know Haggai wasn't looking at Zerubbabel? The answer is because this never happened in Zerubbabel's time. The heavens and the earth weren't shaken in Zerubbabel's time. Zerubbabel was never made king. Zerubbabel was not Messiah. He wasn't restored to David's Throne. All of the events Haggai predicted haven't yet come to pass. Did God break His promise? No. This passage does not say God would make Zerubbabel the king. Instead, it says He would make him a "signet ring." What did this mean?

Look back at what God said about Coniah. If Coniah was a signet ring on God's right hand, God would pluck him off. A signet ring was a symbol of legal authority. In other words, God removed Coniah's legal claim to the throne. Now look at what God said about Zerubbabel, the grandson of Coniah. God said He would make Zerubbabel a signet ring. This means God gave the legal claim to the throne back to Zerubbabel. That was great, but the curse of Coniah remained; Zerubbabel never became king. Haggai wasn't looking at Zerubbabel. He wasn't looking at Zerubbabel's son. He didn't become king either. Nor was he looking at Zerubbabel's grandson, great-grandson, great-great-grandson, or great-great-great-grandson. Even though they all held the legal claim to David's Throne, none of Zerubbabel's offspring became King because they were of Coniah's bloodline. They were the Kings in Exile.

Ten generations later (Matthew 1:13-16) the last King in Exile was born. His name was Joseph, and he was a carpenter who lived in Nazareth. He was betrothed to a young virgin named Mary. By the power of the Holy Spirit, Mary conceived a son named Jesus. Joseph was not the biologic father of Jesus, but by marriage and adoption, Joseph was the legal father of Jesus. Joseph made Jesus his legal heir. That meant Jesus held the legal claim to the throne of David. At the same time, Jesus was not of Coniah's bloodline. The curse of Coniah did not apply to Him. He had the right to claim the Throne of David and establish Himself as King of Israel because He was the legal heir of David through Joseph and the biological heir of David through Mary. Still, He didn't do it. Oh, the crowds wanted Him to. His disciples wanted Him to. Even Satan tried to get Him to take the throne, but Jesus refused. He refused because He knew He was not to set up His Kingdom until Satan's authority over the earth was removed.

The promise God made to Zerubbabel was fulfilled. Zerubbabel wasn't made King, but the "signet," the authority of the Royal Line, was continued through him. In the end, his greatest Son, Jesus, would become the King. Haggai 2:21 is referring to a future judgment of the heavens and the earth. Haggai looked forward to the time when the heavens and the earth will be shaken when Jesus Messiah, the rightful King, sits on David's throne. But as Haggai looked toward the future, he also looked back at the time when the heavens and the earth had been shaken before. That's why Haggai said, "In a little while I will once more shake the heavens and the earth, the sea and the dry land." Haggai knew the earth had two beginnings.

Two Creation Accounts = Two Beginnings

Back in Chapter Two, I mentioned there has been an attempt to make the first chapter of Genesis read as if it was a series of "accounts" God related to Moses over a six-day period. This idea says there weren't six days of creation, only six days of storytelling. Now, while this idea fails the test when comparing Scripture to Scripture, there is something very interesting revealed by using the plural of *TOWLEDAH*.

Genesis 2:4 "These *are* the **generations** of the heavens and of the earth when they were created, in the day that the LORD God made the earth and the heavens," (KJV)

This same word is used when listing the genealogies (plural) of families in the Bible. Here are some examples:

Genesis 5:1 "This *is* the book of the **generations** of Adam. In the day that God created man, in the likeness of God made he him;" (KJV)

Genesis 10:1 "Now these *are* the **generations** of the sons of Noah, Shem, Ham, and Japheth: and unto them were sons born after the flood." (KJV)

Genesis 11:10 "These *are* the **generations** of Shem: Shem *was* an hundred years old, and begat Arphaxad two years after the flood:" (KJV)

Genesis 11:27 "Now these *are* the **generations** of Terah: Terah begat Abram, Nahor, and Haran; and Haran begat Lot." (KJV)

You can substitute "accounts" or "historical records" for the word "generations" in these passages and it gives you a better idea of what is being revealed. Because the plural is used in each of these cases, we know each text points to more than one father-to-son generation. The word describes multiple generations in a family's lineage over a period of time.

The same is true for Genesis 2:4. By using the plural of *TOWLEDAH*, God is telling us there is more than one account of creation. Genesis 2:4 says "THESE" (plural) are the "ACCOUNTS" (plural) of the creation of the heavens and the earth. Genesis 2:4 says there is more than one creation account in the text. Now here's the question that needs an answer: Does Genesis 2:4 point back to what had been revealed prior to this, or does Genesis 2:4 point forward to what is about to be revealed? Or does it point to both? You see, many people have recognized Genesis 2:4 uses *TOWLEDAH* in the plural, and so they believe one creation account is found in Genesis 1 and another creation account is found in Genesis 2. Now, you would think that as a person who believes there were two beginnings—two creations, I would agree with this interpretation. I don't. This interpretation gives atheists a reason for claiming there is a contradiction in the Bible. In Genesis 1, trees are created before man; in Genesis 2, man is created before trees. (Adam before the Garden) This interpretation creates a contradiction, and I reject any interpretation of the Bible that creates contradictions. Therefore, I don't think *TOWLEDAH* points to one creation account in Genesis 1 and a second creation account in Genesis 2.

So, where is Genesis 2:4 pointing? The answer is simple. Genesis 2:4 is pointing to Genesis 1:1-2:3 because it says these are the accounts of the creation (*BARA*) of the heavens (*SHAMAYIM*) and the earth (*ERETS*). Where are *BARA*, *SHAMAYIM*, and *ERETS* used together in this portion of Scripture? They are used in Genesis 1:1-2:3. They are not used in Genesis 2:5-25. Genesis 2:4 speaks of the heavens and the earth created in Genesis 1:1-2:3. Genesis 2:4 looks back at what happened before. It is not looking ahead to what follows. Genesis 2:5-25 speaks only of the earth. Those verses don't use *BARA* and they don't mention *SHAMAYIM*. Genesis 2:5-25 doesn't give an account of the creation of the heavens and the earth; only the details of the things made or formed on Day Six. Genesis 2:5-25 is not a different creation account. Rather than being a different creation, these verses provide additional details about the same creation. They reveal more about Adam, about the planting of the Garden of Eden, about the naming of the animals, and about the creation of Eve, but it is the same creation. There is no contradiction about Adam being created before and after trees being created. Adam was created after trees were created on Day Three, but he was created before God planted the Garden of Eden on Day Six. The Scriptures make no error. The confusion over which way Genesis 2:4 points is a result of how human translators punctuated the sentences and how they split the verses. Let's look at how the *King James Version* lists Genesis 2:4

Genesis 2:4 "These *are* the generations of the heavens and of the earth when they were created, in the day that the LORD God made the earth and the heavens," (KJV)

Note the comma following the word "created." ("…when they were created, in the day…") There was no punctuation in the original Hebrew text, so the commas, periods, semi-colons, *etc.* were inserted by men. The translators of the KJV recognized there was some kind of break or pause after the word "created." So, they put in a comma and kept it as one sentence. I think a mistake was made in the punctuation. I believe a period should follow the word "created," and the sentence should end at Genesis 2:4a.

Genesis 2:4a "These *are* the generations of the heavens and of the earth when they were created."

A new sentence should start at Genesis 2:4b.

Genesis 2:4b "In the day the LORD God made the earth and the heavens."

There are some translations that use this same punctuation. They put a period after verse 4a.

Genesis 2:4 "These are the generations of the heavens and the earth when they were created. In the day that the LORD God made the earth and the heavens," (NRSV)

Genesis 2:4 "This is the account of the creation of the heavens and the earth. When the LORD God made the heavens and the earth," (NLT)

Genesis 2:4 "This is the story of the creation of the sky and the earth. When the LORD God first made the earth and the sky," (NCV)

Genesis 2:4 "This is the account of the heavens and the earth when they were created. On the day the LORD God made earth and sky—" (CEB)

Genesis 2:4 "Here is the history of the heavens and the earth when they were created. On the day when *ADONAI*, God, made earth and heaven," (CJB)

    Genesis 2:4 does not point to what follows because it mentions the creation of the heavens. Nothing is mentioned about the creation of the heavens in the rest of the second chapter. Now, here is the important point: How can verse 4 say, "THESE are the ACCOUNTS," if there has been only one creation? If there has been only one creation, then Genesis 1:1-2:3 is that one account of that one creation. Genesis 1:1 starts with God creating the heavens and the earth, and Genesis 2:3 ends with God resting from all His work. If this was one creation, then *TOWLEDAH* should be in the singular. God should say, "THIS is the ACCOUNT," but God says, "THESE are the ACCOUNTS." **This means there is more than one creation account in the first chapter of Genesis.** Instead of containing one account of creation, Genesis 1 contains two accounts of creation. So, what are these two accounts of creation in Genesis 1?
    As I mentioned, the translators of the *King James Bible* recognized some kind of break after the word "created," but I think they made another mistake in not stopping to analyze what that break signified. The break signified there was a distinction made between what was "created," and what was "made." If they had recognized that, they would have recognized how it fits with the plural of *TOWLEDAH*. The Bible mentions two accounts. One was, "when they were **created**." The other was, "in the day that the LORD God **made** the earth and the heavens." I think the text should read like this:

Genesis 2:4 These *are* the accounts of the heavens and of the earth when: 1.) they were created. 2.) in the day that the LORD God made the earth and the heavens.

The first account is Genesis 1:1. This verse tells us God created (*BARA*) the heavens and the earth. Genesis 2:4 also tells us of the *BARA* of the heavens and the earth. Notice the order of mention: ***SHAMAYIM — ERETS.*** The heavens are mentioned first and then the earth. This is the same order as in Genesis 1:1. This means Genesis 1:1 is the first account of creation.

What is the second account? The second part of Genesis 2:4 uses *ASAH* for the second account. God **made** the earth and the heavens. Again, notice the order of mention: ***ERETS— SHAMAYIM.*** The earth is mentioned first and then the heavens. This is the same order as seen in Genesis 1:3-31. The earth is already in existence before God makes the things in the sky. Where do we find *ASAH* used during the making of the heavens and the earth in Genesis 1? We find it in Genesis 1:7, "God **MADE** the firmament." We see it in Genesis 1:16, "God **MADE** two great lights." *ASAH* is used when God **MADE** the animals in Genesis 1:25. It is also used when God **MADE** man in Genesis 1:26. *ASAH* is used in the account of creation that describes the six days of creation. This is clearly God's intent because He uses *ASAH* in Genesis 1:31 when He makes His pronouncement on the sixth day.

Genesis 1:31 "And God saw every thing that he had **made**, and, behold, *it was* very good. And the evening and the morning were the sixth day." (KJV)

The Bible gives two accounts of creation. The first is in Genesis 1:1. The second is in Genesis 1:3-2:3. Since the details of these accounts don't match, (The two accounts begin and end with different physical conditions of the heavens and the earth.) and since the words are not identical, (Only *BARA* is used to describe the first creation while *ASAH* is added to describe the second creation.) then these accounts are not describing the same creation event. "THESE" verses are the "ACCOUNTS" of two different creations. Genesis 2:4 indicates there have been two different creations, two different beginnings. Genesis 1:1 was the first beginning and the seven days of Genesis 1:3-2:3 were the second beginning. Two separate beginnings are described in Genesis 1.

Two Global Floods

According to creationists who reject the Gap Theory, there was only one beginning. They don't believe the earth had an original creation, a destruction, and a later restoration. They don't believe the earth had two beginnings. So, many interpret Genesis 1:1-2 as being the first part of Day One. This means God created the earth in the condition Genesis 1:2 describes. What was that condition? It was dark and covered by water. Young-Earth creationists believe God initially created the earth that way. They think Genesis 1:1-2 was a very short period of the first twenty-four-hour day. They believe God created the earth already dark and already covered by water. Being dark and covered by water was not something the earth came to be; it was something the earth was when it was created. This is their interpretation of *HAYAH*. The earth was dark and the earth was covered by water when God first created it. Light and dry land had not yet been created according to Young-Earth creationists. Day-Agers, on the other hand, realize the earth couldn't have been created that way. Day-Age creationists know the scientific evidence doesn't support the idea the earth was covered by water for millions of years before the surface was seen. They also know the scientific evidence doesn't support the idea the earth was present for millions of years before the sun and the stars came into existence. Day-Age creationists know the sun and the stars were already shining when the earth was created. The earth did not begin in darkness. They know the universe and the earth are billions of years old, so they interpret the "days" of Genesis as being long ages. Day-Age creationists think the first "day" was billions of years. But, as we have seen, this creates a problem with the order of appearance of things. If the days are long ages, and if they are in the correct order, then the earth was dark and covered by water for billions of years before the sun, moon, and stars were visible. Day One has to come before Day Four, or else God made a mistake in His account of creation in Genesis. Day-Agers reject our interpretation of *HAYAH*, but they can't reconcile the order of creation unless our interpretation of *HAYAH* is correct. Day-Agers have a real problem if you ask them, "When was Genesis 1:2? When was the earth completely covered by water and in complete darkness?" They know there was light before the earth was created. It didn't begin in darkness. Somehow, it must have become dark after its original beginning. They know the earth's hot crust was present long before surface water formed. The earth did not begin under water. Somehow, it must have become covered by water after its original beginning. They know the earth had to become dark and become covered by water, but they still insist we Gap Theory creationists are wrong to say *HAYAH* means "had become." We Gap Theory creationists believe the earth became covered by water. We believe there was light before the earth became dark. We believe the earth became dark and covered by water sometime after its original creation. We believe God judged the original earth. We believe He covered it in darkness and destroyed the life on it with a worldwide flood. In other words, the earth has experienced two global floods. One was at the time of Noah and the other was before Adam's creation. **The fact the earth has been subjected to two global floods is a foundational component of the Gap Theory.** Both Young-Earth and Day-Age creationists reject the idea the earth was flooded twice. That's unfortunate, because God apparently believes the world was flooded twice. Look again at what He told Job.

Job 38:1-11 "Then the LORD answered Job out of the whirlwind and said, *{2}* 'Who is this that darkens counsel By words without knowledge? *{3}* 'Now gird up your loins like a man, And I will ask you, and you instruct Me! *{4}* 'Where were you when I laid the foundation of the earth? Tell *Me*, if you have understanding, *{5}* Who set its measurements, since you know? Or who stretched the line on it? *{6}* 'On what were its bases sunk? Or who laid its cornerstone, *{7}* When the morning stars sang together, And all the sons of God shouted for joy? *{8}* '**Or *who* enclosed the sea with doors, When, bursting forth, it**

went out from the womb; *{9}* When I made a cloud its garment, And thick darkness its swaddling band, *{10}* And I placed boundaries on it, And I set a bolt and doors, *{11}* And I said, 'Thus far you shall come, but no farther; And here shall your proud waves stop'?" (NASB)

Look very closely at what God reveals to Job about this global flood. God tells Job there was a time when the sea burst forth like a pregnant woman's "water" breaking just before she gives birth. The imagery of a pregnant woman's "water" breaking is an imagery of birth; it begins the birth. This birthing imagery indicates God is telling Job something about the earth's beginning. (Actually, the earth's second beginning.) Gap Theory creationists believe Job 38:1-7 refers to earth's first beginning, while Job 38:8-11 refers to an event long after earth's initial creation. These two accounts in Job are separated by the word "or" in verse eight. The first part describes the sons of God shouting for joy at the initial creation. The second part describes a global flood. Was this the Great Flood of Noah's time? No. The Great Flood at Noah's time wasn't at the beginning. It was about 1,650 years after the beginning. God is giving Job details about the earth being covered by water at its beginning. Note how the waters burst forth. This means the earth didn't begin under water. The water burst forth from the earth (not from rain) and covered the earth. At its beginning, the earth wasn't covered by water. This means the water that covered the earth in Genesis 1:2 had to burst forth from the earth. The earth became covered by water. It wasn't created under water. Note also, how the earth wasn't created in darkness. Just as a baby is born before it can be wrapped in a swaddling band, the earth was created before it was covered in a garment of clouds and wrapped in a swaddling band of darkness. The earth became dark after its creation. Again, this doesn't fit the description of Noah's Flood.

But, didn't the waters burst forth at the time of Noah's flood? Yes. Both Job 38:8 and Genesis 7:11 describe the waters bursting forth, but they describe different global floods. These aren't the same flood because the details don't match. In Job, God says the earth was covered by water and thick darkness. The earth was dark during this flood, but the earth wasn't dark during Noah's Flood. In Noah's time, the waters came upon the earth for forty days and forty nights. There were days and nights. There was light during Noah's Flood; the earth wasn't dark. In addition, God tells Job these waters didn't completely cover the earth. God tells Job He, "enclosed the sea with doors." He placed boundaries on it. He stopped its proud waves. They reached a certain point and He let them go no farther. This wasn't true at Noah's time. God did not stop the waves from covering the entire earth during Noah's Flood. All the earth was covered, even the tallest mountains. God is telling Job about a different global flood. God is describing the earth at a different time. In Noah's Flood, the entire earth was covered by water. In Noah's Flood there was light. In this other global flood, the entire earth wasn't covered by liquid water. In this other global flood, there was no light. These are two different global floods. The earth has been flooded twice!

I've always believed if we seek truth from the Bible, then we need to go to the One who wrote the Bible. We must honestly and humbly go before the Holy Spirit and ask Him to enlighten us before we start making claims about what the Bible says. You see, the Bible reveals much more than any of us can know, and many truths are hidden. The Holy Spirit reveals those truths to us IF, WHEN, and HOW He decides. Sometimes He honors our diligent work and dedication to His Word after we spend hours and hours buried deeply in Bible commentaries, Bible studies, Bible dictionaries, systematic theologies, historical texts, topical studies, cross-reference guides, *etc.* Then again, sometimes He bypasses all that and has one of our friends simply tell us what it is we seek to know. Such was the case of my study of Psalms 104:1- 9.

Psalms 104:1-9 "Bless the LORD, O my soul! O LORD my God, Thou art very great; Thou art clothed with splendor and majesty, *{2}* Covering Thyself with light as with a cloak, Stretching out heaven like a *tent* curtain. *{3}* He lays the beams of His upper chambers in the waters; He makes the clouds His chariot; He walks upon the wings of the wind; *{4}* He makes the winds His messengers, Flaming fire His ministers. *{5}* He established the earth upon its foundations, So that it will not totter forever and ever. *{6}* Thou didst cover it with the deep as with a garment; The waters were standing above the mountains. *{7}* At Thy rebuke they fled; At the sound of Thy thunder they hurried away. *{8}* The mountains rose; the valleys sank down to the place which Thou didst establish for them. *{9}* Thou didst set a boundary that they may not pass over; That they may not return to cover the earth." (NASB)

I can't tell you how many years I looked at this passage and wondered what flood it was describing. This passage looks very similar to the flood described in Job 38, but I just couldn't find the key that would unlock the truth for me. As much as I wanted it to be the Pre-Adamic Flood, I couldn't prove it wasn't Noah's Flood. Now, it seems to place this flood around the same time He established the earth's foundations, and that would be a positive indicator it was much earlier than Noah's Flood. Still, it's difficult to put time constraints on how God views historical events. I'm not too eager to tell God how He should or shouldn't reveal historical facts to us. The fact it ends with the statement that the waters will not cover the earth again, seemed to make it Noah's Flood. This is made even more apparent in some of the various translations.

Psalms 104:9 "You set a boundary they cannot cross; **never again** will they cover the earth." (NIV)

Psalms 104:9 "You set borders for the seas that they cannot cross, so water **will never** cover the earth again." (NCV)

Psalms 104:9 "You set a boundary they cannot cross; they **will never** cover the earth again." (HCSB)

If the water will never, never, never cover the earth again, as some translations seem to imply, then Psalms 104 must be telling us about Noah's Flood. I didn't see any other clues in the text that might indicate otherwise. Even after exhaustive studies, I couldn't convince myself to believe it said want I wanted it to say. With that, I decided Psalms 104 had no connection to the Pre-Adamic Flood and I forgot about it. I was wrong.

While reading a book by friend and fellow Genesis Gap Theory defender, James Lowrance,[95] and after communicating with him via e-mail, he pointed out the key I had missed for so long. The Holy Spirit had revealed a difference in the recession rates of the waters of these two floods. The water of Noah's Flood gradually and steadily receded over a period of about six months (Genesis 8:1-5). We looked at that back in Chapter Five. The water of Noah's Flood seemed to be in no rush, no hurry, and no urgency to abate. If you were an observer at the time, you would have seen the water gradually, slowly, and steadily recede over six months. Now look what it says about the waters mentioned in Psalms 104.

Psalms 104:7 "At Thy rebuke they fled; At the sound of Thy thunder they hurried away." (NASB)

Psalms 104:7 "But at your rebuke the waters fled, at the sound of your thunder they took to flight;" (NIV)

Psalms 104:7 "At thy rebuke they fled; at the voice of thy thunder they hasted away." (KJV)

Some of the translations even say things like the waters, "fled in terror," or the waters "ran away in fear," and other such colorful ways of describing how rapidly the waters receded. This is anthropomorphic, phenomenological language of course, but you get the idea. To an observer, it would have looked as if the water was running in terror. The water of this flood wasn't gradually going down. This water was in a hurry. This water wasn't gradually receding. If all the earth was covered by water, and God commanded the water to recede in one twenty-four-hour day, what would it have looked like? The water would have looked as if it was fleeing in terror. It would have rushed away at an extremely fast rate. It wasn't moving by the force of gravity alone; God's supernatural command caused it to recede in one day. That water was "fleeing" from God. Psalms 104:7 describes what the water would have looked like on Day Three of the Restoration. This does not describe what the water would have looked like after Noah's Flood. Psalms 104 describes the Pre-Adamic Flood. The Holy Spirit used my friend James to unlock Psalms 104 for me.

This prompted me to go back and look at the wording of Psalms 104:9 in the Hebrew. I discovered the words, "never," "never again," or "not ever," are interpretations of the Hebrew word *BAL*. (Strong's Number H1077). *BAL* can be translated, "never," but it is usually translated, "not." There is a difference between "not" and "never" that is determined by the context. Saying I will NOT eat dessert is not the same as saying I will NEVER eat dessert. When describing the plagues God brought down of Egypt when He delivered the Jews from slavery, the Bible says:

Psalms 78:44 "And had turned their rivers into blood; and their floods, that they could **not** drink." (KJV)

We know that *BAL* here did not mean people would never, ever drink the waters of the Nile again. It means "not;" not "never." People drink water from the Nile today. Turning the waters of the Nile into blood was for an immediate situation; a judgment. In Psalms 104:9, the waters covered the earth for an immediate situation; also a judgment. It doesn't mean they would NEVER cover the earth again. The reason I could not understand Psalms 104 was because I was reading men's interpretations, rather than God's declarations. My friend Jim opened my eyes to this.

Psalms 104:9 simply tells us that God placed a boundary on how far the waters could rise; it did not cover the entire face of the earth like Noah's Flood. Then after His command to recede (His rebuke) they didn't come back. God provides a purpose clause at the end of verse 9: "So that they may not return to cover the earth." This purpose clause is aimed at the immediate situation; not forever. The waters of the Pre-Adamic Flood were not permitted to return because God was preparing a new habitation for His new creation, Man. That was the immediate purpose. That's why they were not permitted to return and cover the earth. On Day Three, God commanded the waters to recede, and it became so! There is nothing said about the waters never, ever covering the earth again. What I think happened in the minds of some translators is they superimposed their knowledge of Genesis 9:11 (where God DID tell Noah He would never, ever, ever flood the entire earth again) into Psalms 104. They apparently didn't realize Psalms 104 doesn't describe Noah's Flood. Instead, it is proof the earth has been flooded twice. Let's compare and contrast Job 38, Psalms 104, and Genesis 7 to see what information they reveal about the Floods.

Job 38:
1.) God mentions the creation. ("Where were you when I laid the foundations of the earth?")
2.) There is no mention of rain.
3.) God spoke to the waters.

Psalms 104:
1.) God mentions the creation. ("Who laid the foundations of the earth?")
2.) There is no mention of rain.
3.) God spoke to the waters.

Genesis 7:
1.) God does not mention the creation.
2.) Rain is mentioned.
3.) God did not speak to the waters.

As you can see, Job 38 and Psalms 104 do not describe the same global flood as Noah's Flood in Genesis 7. Young-Earth/Flood-Geologists have two objections to the idea of a Pre-Adamic Global Flood. (Often called, "Lucifer's Flood.") First, they say there is no scientific evidence a Pre-Adamic Global Flood laid down all the geologic layers and created all the fossils.

When I first heard this objection, I almost choked. Young-Earth creationists insist they have proof all the geological layers and all the fossils were created by a global flood. Non-Flood Geologists disagree, but even if the Young-Earth creationists are right, how do they know it was Noah's Flood and not Lucifer's Flood? The real scientific evidence is that the geologic layers and fossils were created millions of years before Noah's Flood. The Gap Theory doesn't say all the geologic layers and fossils were created by Lucifer's Flood a few to several thousand years ago. The geologic layers and fossils were deposited over millions of years before Lucifer's Flood; before God finally turned out the lights and flushed the earthly angelic kingdom down the toilet. I believe that global flood was for a very short period of time. (I suspect it was only a few days.)

Their second objection to a Pre-Adamic Flood is it means Noah's Flood was a "tranquil flood." They hate that idea. If the Gap Theory is correct, then Noah's Flood didn't create all the geologic layers and fossils. Since they already "know" Noah's Flood split continents apart, slammed continents together, created mountain chains, washed away mountain chains, uprooted great forests, as well as all the other horrendously destructive events the Bible never describes, they say we are wrong. Of course, if Noah's Flood was as globally destructive as they say, then it would have wiped out all traces of the Pre-Adamic Flood. In order for Noah's Flood to deposit sedimentary layers that were miles and miles deep, it would have first needed to churn up miles and miles of soil from the Pre-Noahic Flood earth. If what they believe is true, then the lack of geological evidence for a Pre-Adamic Flood could not be used as evidence against a Pre-Adamic Flood. If they believe the Pre-Adamic Flood should have left geological evidence, then they have to admit Noah's Flood wasn't globally destructive. They would have to admit Noah's Flood didn't create all the geologic layers and fossils. It's exactly what they say they believe, but it's exactly what they say they don't believe. Their thoughts are confusing.

When was this other global flood? God told Job He flooded the earth during the time He, "made a cloud its garment, and thick darkness its swaddling band." In other words, God flooded the earth during a period of worldwide darkness. This wasn't done at the time of Noah. God didn't wrap the earth in darkness during Noah's Flood. It couldn't be any time after Noah's Flood; God promised He would never flood the earth again. It couldn't have been between the time of Adam and the time of Noah because the earth was neither flooded nor dark during that period. The sun, moon, and stars were shining and set in the firmament of heaven. God declared they would mark the days, the years, and the seasons even before Adam was created. There was never a time between Adam and Noah when the earth was dark and covered by water. God is telling Job about a global flood that happened before Adam was created. God is telling Job about a Pre-Adamic global flood. God says the waters burst forth. The earth became covered by water only after the waters burst forth. There is no mention of rain. The water that covered the earth in Job 38 burst forth from the earth that was already there. The earth became covered by water; it didn't begin that way. There was dry land before the earth was flooded. It was only after the waters burst forth that the earth became covered by water. The earth was created before becoming covered by water. (This agrees with the scientific history of the earth. Again, the Word of God agrees with the Work of God.) It wasn't created under water. The submerged condition of the earth in Genesis 1:2 was not its original condition.

I continued searching for parallel Scripture accounts that mentioned water covering the earth. I hoped the Bible would give me more information concerning this Pre-Adamic Flood. I found just such a passage in Proverbs 8. The subject of this Proverb is wisdom, more specifically, God's wisdom, and it personifies this wisdom as someone who existed eternally (before time and space) with God, and in whom God delights. I have read commentaries saying "Wisdom" is an allusion to the Second Person of the Godhead, Jesus Christ. This sounds reasonable, but whoever, or whatever this "Wisdom" is, God reveals something about the creation of the earth.

Proverbs 8:22-29 "The LORD brought me forth as the first of his works, before his deeds of old; {23} I was appointed from eternity, from the beginning, before the world began. {24} When there were no oceans, I was given birth, when there were no springs abounding with water; {25} before the mountains were settled in place, before the hills, I was given birth, {26} before he made the earth or its fields or any of the dust of the world. {27} I was there when he set the heavens in place, when he marked out the horizon on the face of the deep, {28} when he established the clouds above and fixed securely the fountains of the deep, {29} **when he gave the sea its boundary so the waters would not overstep his command**, and when he marked out the foundations of the earth." (NIV)

There is no question this passage is talking about the creation and not about Noah's Flood. Note when He created the sea, He set boundaries on it. This is the exact same thing Psalms 104:9 said. Psalms 104:9 said God set a boundary on the deep so it could not pass over it. This is the same thing God revealed in Job 38:10-11. He placed a boundary on the sea, a bolt and doors, and told it, "Thus far you shall come, but no farther." So, we have three passages of Scripture: Job 38, Psalms 104, and Proverbs 8 that prove the original ocean DID NOT entirely cover the original earth. The original earth was not entirely covered by water. Dry land was present before God flooded it. When God gathered the waters together and let dry land appear in Genesis 1:9-10, this was not the first time dry land had been present. This was a restoration of the dry land. Young-Earth creationists are wrong to assume the earth was originally created under water. It became covered by water.

As I have already mentioned, God covered the earth in darkness. When did that happen? It wasn't created that way. Again, just as a baby is born before it is wrapped in swaddling bands, the earth was created before it was wrapped in darkness. (Job 38:9) God uses the imagery of birth to help us determine when this was. The earth was not "born" in thick darkness. God wrapped it in thick darkness (judgment) sometime after it was created. The earth was created in light; then it later became dark. Job's description of the flooded earth becoming dark doesn't match the Genesis 1:2 description of the flooded earth being dark if the *HAYAH* in Genesis 1:2 means what Young-Earth creationists say it means. This means the *HAYAH* in Genesis 1:2 doesn't mean "was;" it means "became." Furthermore, Job's description of the early earth doesn't match Jeremiah's description of the early earth. Job describes a dark and water-covered earth. Jeremiah describes the earth as dark, but not water-covered.

Jeremiah 4:23-26 "I beheld the earth, and, lo, *it was* without form, and void; and the heavens, and they *had* no light. *{24}* I beheld the mountains, and, lo, they trembled, and all the hills moved lightly. *{25}* I beheld, and, lo, *there was* no man, and all the birds of the heavens were fled. *{26}* I beheld, and, lo, the fruitful place *was* a wilderness, and all the cities thereof were broken down at the presence of the LORD, *and* by his fierce anger." (KJV)

Jeremiah beheld mountains, hills, fruitful places, wilderness, *etc.*, but the heavens had no light. Jeremiah's description of the earth does not match the description of the earth in Genesis 1. **Genesis 1:3-8 has LIGHT but no LAND; Jeremiah 4:23-26 has LAND but no LIGHT.** The conditions aren't the same. Jeremiah and Moses could not both be describing earth at the same time unless the Bible contradicts itself.

Multiple Descriptions of the Pre-Adamic Earth

Genesis 1:2	NO DRY LAND	NO LIGHT	NO MAN
Genesis 1:3	NO DRY LAND	LIGHT	NO MAN
Genesis 1:10	DRY LAND	LIGHT	NO MAN
Jeremiah 4:23-26	DRY LAND	NO LIGHT	NO MAN

God has given us different descriptions of earth's condition in the past. We know all four of these describe the Pre-Adamic earth because there were no humans present. On this aspect, they all agree. However, these accounts don't agree concerning the appearance of light and dry land. Now, it's easy to explain the first three descriptions as a revelation of the process of creation. At one time, the earth was covered by water and in darkness. (But remember, Job 38 tells us the earth became dark and covered by water after its initial creation.) Then God commanded light to appear, and light became present, but the earth was still covered by water. Next, God caused the waters to separate and the dry land to appear. The problem becomes apparent when you try to fit Jeremiah 4:23-26 into this chain of events. It doesn't fit anywhere. Genesis 1:2-31 never describes the Pre-Adamic earth as having dry land but no light. The Bible contradicts itself if there was just one beginning. The Bible contradicts itself if there has been only one creation. God made a mistake when revealing the condition of the Pre-Adamic earth if either the Young-Earth or the Day-Age Theories are correct. My friends, God makes no mistakes. He has given us the accounts of different time periods in the Pre-Adamic earth. Jeremiah, Job, and Haggai reveal that God brought darkness upon the earth, judged (shook) the earth, and caused water to burst forth and cover it before Adam. It was during that Pre-Adamic period when the earth became formless and void, dark, and covered by water. It wasn't that way before God judged it. He did not create the earth that way. God tells us what the earth HAD BECOME after its original creation. Why don't we believe Him?

Psalms 104 wasn't the only passage of Scripture I thought (but couldn't convince myself) referred to Lucifer's Flood. The other passage was 2 Peter 3. I'll highlight the parts that seem to defend the Gap Theory.

2 Peter 3:1-18 "This second epistle, beloved, I now write unto you; in *both* which I stir up your pure minds by way of remembrance: *{2}* That ye may be mindful of the words which were spoken before by the holy prophets, and of the commandment of us the apostles of the Lord and Saviour: *{3}* Knowing this first, that there shall come in the last days scoffers, walking after their own lusts, *{4}* And saying, Where is the promise of his coming? for since the fathers fell asleep, all things continue as *they were* from the beginning of the creation. *{5}* For this they willingly are ignorant of, that by the word of God **the heavens were of old**, and **the earth standing out of the water and in the water**: *{6}* Whereby **the world that then was, being overflowed with water, perished**: *{7}* But **the heavens and the earth, which are now**, by the same word are kept in store, reserved unto fire against the day of judgment and perdition of ungodly men. *{8}* But, beloved, be not ignorant of this one thing, that one day *is* with the Lord as a thousand years, and a thousand years as one day. *{9}* The Lord is not slack concerning his promise, as some men count slackness; but is longsuffering to us-ward, not willing that any should perish, but that all should come to repentance. *{10}* But the day of the Lord will come as a thief in the night; in the which the heavens shall pass away with a great noise, and the elements shall melt with fervent

heat, the earth also and the works that are therein shall be burned up. *{11} Seeing* then *that* all these things shall be dissolved, what manner *of persons* ought ye to be in *all* holy conversation and godliness, *{12}* Looking for and hasting unto the coming of the day of God, wherein the heavens being on fire shall be dissolved, and the elements shall melt with fervent heat? *{13}* Nevertheless we, according to his promise, look for new heavens and a new earth, wherein dwelleth righteousness. *{14}* Wherefore, beloved, seeing that ye look for such things, be diligent that ye may be found of him in peace, without spot, and blameless. *{15}* And account *that* the longsuffering of our Lord *is* salvation; even as our beloved brother Paul also according to the wisdom given unto him hath written unto you; *{16}* As also in all *his* epistles, speaking in them of these things; in which are some things hard to be understood, which they that are unlearned and unstable wrest, as *they do* also the other scriptures, unto their own destruction. *{17}* Ye therefore, beloved, seeing ye know *these things* before, beware lest ye also, being led away with the error of the wicked, fall from your own stedfastness. *{18}* But grow in grace, and *in* the knowledge of our Lord and Saviour Jesus Christ. To him *be* glory both now and for ever. Amen." (KJV)

Peter is telling us about the heavens and earth being in a different condition than they were during Noah's Flood. Peter describes a time when the earth was both in the water and out of the water. This doesn't describe the earth during Noah's Flood; the entire earth was covered by water during Noah's Flood. This doesn't describe Noah's Flood because the world didn't perish. Animals and humans were still alive on the ark. This doesn't describe the present earth. Even though the earth is currently standing in the water and out of the water (continents and islands), it has not perished. It doesn't describe the future earth because we know God will never flood it again, and life on earth will never perish. Peter can only be describing a flood that happened before the creation of Adam. Gap Theory proponents have used this passage as a way of defending the idea the earth experienced a Pre-Adamic Flood. I wanted to agree, but there were some problems I couldn't overcome. When Peter said the former earth was "standing in the water and out of the water," I knew this did not fit with Noah's Flood. The problem was that not all translations said it was, "standing in the water and out of the water." Some translations describe it in a different way.

2 Peter 3:5 "They deliberately ignore this fact, that by the word of God heavens existed long ago and an earth was formed out of water and by means of water," (NRSV)

2 Peter 3:5 "But they deliberately forget that long ago by God's word the heavens existed and the earth was formed out of water and by water." (NIV)

2 Peter 3:5 "For when they maintain this, it escapes their notice that by the word of God *the* heavens existed long ago and *the earth* was formed out of water and by water," (NASB)

These translations say the waters of this Flood formed or shaped the face of the earth. The *King James* translation didn't say the waters shaped the earth. It only said some land was below water and some land was above water. As I searched for reasons why it was translated in two entirely different ways, I became less and less certain it didn't refer to Noah's Flood. Even though I believed Noah's Flood didn't form or shape the face of the earth to any great extent, I didn't feel I could prove what I believed. At that time, I couldn't prove Noah's Flood didn't reshape the surface of the earth. I didn't have any evidence the waters of Noah's Flood didn't carve massive valleys and canyons and wash away mountains as it receded. (Other than the fact the Biblical Flood account makes no mention of such massive geological changes.) Because of that, I decided not to use this argument. As you can see, many other Gap Theory defenders were way ahead of me on this point. Once my friend James showed me the difference in the recession rates of the two global floods, I realized he had Biblical proof for two global floods. One Flood receded very gradually. That was Noah's Flood. It was so gradual it didn't even disturb the plant life that God preserved. (The olive tree wasn't destroyed.) That Flood would not have shaped or formed the face of the earth to any great degree. There wouldn't have been much erosion because the recession was so gradual. The other Flood was not so placid. Its waters receded in one day. Such a recession rate would have altered the surface of the earth. Such hydraulic forces could have shaped and formed many of the features we see today.

In the end, it didn't matter which translation of 2 Peter 3:5 was more correct. (Apparently both translations are grammatically correct.) Neither translation fit with Noah's Flood. (These waters didn't recede gradually; Noah's Flood did.) Both translations fit with the Gap Theory. The Pre-Adamic earth was "in the water and out of the water." The land "standing out" of the water was covered by ice and snow and not visible. In addition, the face of the Pre-Adamic earth was formed and shaped by the violent water as it receded on Day Three. Once I knew Peter was describing the Pre-Adamic Flood, I went back and looked at what had happened to the Pre-Adamic earth. That world was destroyed by God's judgment. That world perished. That means all life on earth had died. This adds one more difference between the two Global Floods. During the First Global Flood, all life perished on the land and in the sea. The "deep" described in Genesis 1:2 had no fish or sea creatures. That was why God recreated them on Day Five. (Genesis 1:20-22) Contrast that with Noah's Flood. God didn't need to create fish and sea creatures; they survived the Flood. Here are the differences between the two Global Floods:

<u>Global Flood 1 (Lucifer's Flood)</u>

1.) Earth covered in darkness
2.) Earth not completely covered by liquid water
3.) No man
4.) Water receded in twenty-four-hours
5.) No sea creatures; they had to be created
6.) Earth repopulated by Divine creation of plants and animals

Global Flood 2 (Noah's Flood)
1.) Earth not covered in darkness
2.) Earth completely covered by liquid water
3.) Eight people on the ark
4.) Water receded over about six months
5.) Sea creatures lived through the Flood; they didn't need to be created
6.) Earth repopulated by animals that came off the ark and plants that survived the Flood

Only the Gap Theory agrees with what God revealed through Peter. I thank God for revealing these things to us through Peter. I thank God for revealing these things to me through my friend James Lowrance.

The Past Age

Hebrews 11:3 "Through faith we understand that the worlds were framed by the word of God, so that things which are seen were not made of things which do appear." (KJV)

Hebrews 11:3 has been a verse used to defend the Gap Theory for many years. This is because the word for "framed" has a variety of meanings. Some of those meanings can be taken as evidence the earth was destroyed and then restored. The word is *KATARTIDZO*. (Strong's Number G2675) Its meanings include "to prepare," "to adjust," "to fit," "to frame," "to perfect," "to repair," "to restore," "to mend," and similar things. Let me give you an example of how it is used in the sense of "to repair."

Matthew 4:21 "And going on from thence, he saw other two brethren, James *the son* of Zebedee, and John his brother, in a ship with Zebedee their father, **mending** their nets; and he called to them." (KJV)

The fact they were mending their nets indicated their nets were damaged and needed repair. By applying this idea to the creation of the world, it could be argued the world was "repaired" by the Word of God. ("And God said...") I can't argue this isn't possible, and it may be what God is telling us, but I have to agree with those who disagree. *KATARTIDZO* doesn't always mean to repair something that is broken or in ruin. That is one of its most common meanings, but to insist it must mean "repair" is too close to the edge of blasphemy for me.

Hebrews 10:5 "Wherefore when he cometh into the world, he saith, Sacrifice and offering thou wouldest not, but a body hast thou **prepared** me." (KJV)

I don't think I want to defend an interpretation saying Christ's body was fallen, damaged, in ruin, or in need of repair. He was the perfect, spotless Lamb, without blemish or fault. The fact the Old Testament sacrificial Passover lambs had to be without spot or blemish, was a foreshadow of the fact Jesus was without any defects; physical or spiritual. If He had any kind of defect, He could not have offered Himself as the perfect Sacrifice who atoned for our sins. Hebrews 10:5 probably means, "… a body thou has perfected for me," in the sense God prepared a perfect body for Christ, as opposed to our imperfect bodies. So, while this definition of *KATARTIDZO* may or may not defend the Gap Theory, I don't necessarily want to use it. Instead, I want to focus your attention on something else. Read Hebrews 11:3 again. What was framed? "The worlds" were framed. It's in the plural. How many worlds have we had? We can't answer that until we know what "worlds" means. Some interpret Hebrews 11:3 to mean all the planets and galaxies, and so translate it, "the universe."

Hebrews 11:3 "By faith we understand that the **universe** was formed at God's command, so that what is seen was not made out of what was visible." (NIV)

The word is *AION*, (Strong's Number G165) from which we get "eon." It means "a period of time" or "an age."

Hebrews 11:3 "By faith we understand the **ages** to have been prepared by a saying of God, in regard to the things seen not having come out of things appearing;" (YLT)

If I were a Day-Ager, I would insist this was proof for the Day-Age Theory, and I would jump up and down in excitement. But I'm not, and it isn't, so I won't. Being a Gap Theory creationist, this verse excites me too, but for a different reason. These "ages" were "framed" in the past. According to *A Parsing Guide to the New Testament*,[96] the verb *KATARTIDZO* ("framed") in Hebrews 11:3 is in the perfect, passive, infinitive form. I'm not any better with Koine Greek than I am with ancient Hebrew, but according to Greek scholars, this means it is a verbal noun where the action on *AION* was completed in the past, but with finished results that remain into the present. In other words, these "ages" were completed in the past. Let's look at what this means.

AION means an age, but it means more than just a measure of time like "century" or "millennia." It incorporates not only a passage of time; it incorporates the events and the conditions that occur during that passage of time. That's why we can talk about such things as "The Stone Age," "The Iron Age," "The Industrial Age," "The Age of Enlightenment." These designations don't define specific periods of time such as "The Fifth Century B. C." or our present "Twenty-First Century." Incorporated into *AION* is the concept of specific periods of time-space events. There was a specific period of time, a long time ago, when stone tools and weapons were the height of man's technology. This was the time-space period of "The Stone Age." If I was talking about "The Computer Age," even though I didn't give you specific dates, you would know I wasn't talking about the time-space period of the Egyptian Pharaohs. *AION* combines some aspects of time with some aspects of space. (Since time and space are a continuum, I think the Holy Spirit did a smashing good job at picking a word that incorporates aspects of both concepts.) Because it incorporates both concepts, it is often translated, "world."

Matthew 13:22 "And the one on whom seed was sown among the thorns, this is the man who hears the word, and the worry of the **world**, and the deceitfulness of riches choke the word, and it becomes unfruitful." (NASB)

But you can see how this means the worry of the age. Here are some more verses that translate *AION* (in bold print) as "age."

Matthew 12:32 "And whoever shall speak a word against the Son of Man, it shall be forgiven him; but whoever shall speak against the Holy Spirit, it shall not be forgiven him, either in this **age**, or in the *age* to come." (NASB)

Matthew 13:39 "and the enemy who sowed them is the devil, and the harvest is the end of the **age**; and the reapers are angels." (NASB)

Matthew 13:40 "Therefore just as the tares are gathered up and burned with fire, so shall it be at the end of the **age**." (NASB)

Matthew 13:49 "So it will be at the end of the **age**; the angels shall come forth, and take out the wicked from among the righteous," (NASB)

Matthew 24:3 "And as He was sitting on the Mount of Olives, the disciples came to Him privately, saying, 'Tell us, when will these things be, and what *will be* the sign of Your coming, and of the end of the **age**?'" (NASB)

Ephesians 1:18-21 "*I pray that* the eyes of your heart may be enlightened, so that you may know what is the hope of His calling, what are the riches of the glory of His inheritance in the saints, *{19}* and what is the surpassing greatness of His power toward us who believe. *These are* in accordance with the working of the strength of His might *{20}* which He brought about in Christ, when He raised Him from the dead, and seated Him at His right hand in the heavenly *places, {21}* far above all rule and authority and power and dominion, and every name that is named, not only in this **age**, but also in the one to come." (NASB)

From these passages, we see there are two ages mentioned; there is a present age and there is an age to come. The "age to come" is after "this age." The "age to come" is still future. It hasn't been prepared yet. That future age is not included in the ages (plural) mentioned in Hebrews 11:3 because those ages were prepared in the past. The verb form indicates those ages were completed in the past, but still have results that remain in the present. The age to come has not been completed and its results are not yet present. I'm sure you see where I'm going with this. If there were ages (plural) prepared in the past, and if we are in the present age now, then the Bible reveals there was at least one age prepared before this age. There was an age before this age.

      I'd like to end my argument right here, but I see its own weakness. There could be another way of looking at this. What if we divided earth's history into ages, such as "the Age of Innocence," "the Antediluvian Age," "the Age of the Patriarchs," "the Jewish Age," and "the Church Age?" If these were the ages that were framed, then this is not a defense for the Gap Theory. There wouldn't need to be a past age before the present age to satisfy the grammatical qualities of Hebrews 11:3. (But by now, I hope we are all seeking translations that provide more than correct grammar; I hope we want translations that provide correct information.) If we can learn what period of time the Bible describes as "**this age**," then we can see if Hebrews 11:3 reveals anything significant. We need to seek a Biblical definition for "this age"… Seek and ye shall find.

Luke 20:34-35 "And Jesus said to them, 'The sons of **this age** marry and are given in marriage, {35} but those who are considered worthy to attain to **that age** and the resurrection from the dead, neither marry, nor are given in marriage;'" (NASB)

      Jesus talks about two ages: "THIS AGE" and "THAT AGE." Just like the above verses, Jesus mentions this age and the age that is to come. Jesus tells us when THIS AGE started and when it will end. Jesus tells us when THAT AGE will begin. Now, here is the key to understanding what "this age" means: Jesus defines "THIS AGE" as the age when people marry. When did marriage start? It started with Adam and Eve. This means Adam and Eve were part of THIS AGE. In fact, they were the beginning of this age. (They marked, "the beginning of the creation."—Mark 10:6) When will people no longer marry? It will be after this age has ended. It will be in the age to come. Jesus defines the present age as the time from the creation of Adam and Eve (the beginning of marriage) until the time of the resurrection of the dead. **Jesus reveals there has been only one age since the creation of Adam and Eve: THIS AGE.** Hebrews 11:3 refers to a past age (or ages) before this age. Hebrews 11:3 is telling us there was at least one age before the creation of Adam and Eve. That previous *AION* was a period of time before this present *AION*. There was an age before this age. How long was that age? I don't know, but I certainly wouldn't feel comfortable in calling five days an age. Day One through Day Five of Genesis is the only measurable period of time before Adam that Young-Earth creationists allow. Calling five days "an age" doesn't make much sense. There must have been a long measurable period of time prior to Adam. That's not intended to mean it was just a measurable period of time before this period of time. Remember the word *AION* includes more than just the passage of time; it includes the events during that passage of time. *AION* in Hebrews 11:3 seems to indicate there were events happening in the age before the events of this age. Earth has experienced two different age-events. The earth has had two beginnings.

Stop the Clock

Young-Earth creationists accuse Gap Theory creationists of adding to God's word when we say there was a gap of time between Genesis 1:1 and Genesis 1:2. They say God would have revealed it in the text if there had been a gap. They say we are twisting God's Word to fit our theory. They say there is no evidence in the text such a gap was possible. Actually, there is textual evidence for a gap, such as the use of a parenthetical Disjunctive *WAW* at the beginning of Genesis 1:2, the use of the pluperfect form of *HAYAH* in Genesis 1:2, and the use of the *Rebhia* after Genesis 1:1 in the Masoretic Text. Putting those things aside, a gap of time between Genesis 1:1 and Genesis 1:2 could still exist if God revealed it in other parts of Scripture. God doesn't have to reveal it in Genesis to make it so.

Two questions instantly arise. First, "Does God count time the way we count time?" The answer is obvious; the Creator of time is not restricted by time. His "time" is not our time. He can measure it and describe it anyway He pleases, because He "experiences" it anyway He wants. The second question is, "Where is there evidence that gaps of time exist in Biblical historical narratives when no such gaps are revealed in the immediate context?" The answer is less obvious, but that's exactly what God reveals in 1 Kings 6:1.

1 Kings 6:1 "And it came to pass in the four hundred and eightieth year after the children of Israel were come out of the land of Egypt, in the fourth year of Solomon's reign over Israel, in the month Zif, which *is* the second month, that he began to build the house of the LORD." (KJV)

How many years passed from the time the Jews came out of Egypt until Solomon began building the Temple? The answer seems simple; it was 480 years. Now, what if I told you it wasn't 480 years? What if I told you there were five gaps of time hidden in that verse, and the actual time was 573 years? If you think like a Young-Earth creationist thinks, you would accuse me of being a heretic. You would insist there is no evidence of a hidden gap in this historical narrative, and you would be right. (About the hidden gap; not about me being a heretic.) There is no textual, contextual, or grammatical evidence in this passage that reveals any extra gap(s) of time. That evidence is found in two other parts of Scripture.

Acts 13:17-21 "The God of this people of Israel chose our fathers, and exalted the people when they dwelt as strangers in the land of Egypt, and with an high arm brought he them out of it. *{18}* And about the time of **forty years** suffered he their manners in the wilderness. *{19}* And when he had destroyed seven nations in the land of Chanaan, he divided their land to them by lot. *{20}* And after that he gave *unto them* judges about the space of **four hundred and fifty years**, until Samuel the prophet. *{21}* And afterward they desired a king: and God gave unto them Saul the son of Cis, a man of the tribe of Benjamin, by the space of **forty years**." (KJV)

1 Kings 2:11 "And the days that David reigned over Israel *were* **forty years**: seven years reigned he in Hebron, and thirty and three years reigned he in Jerusalem." (KJV)

   According to Acts 13:17-21 and 1 Kings 2:11, David's reign ended (he died) five-hundred and seventy years after the Jews came out of Egypt. (40 + 450 + 40 + 40 = 570 years) That's already ninety years longer than the four hundred and eighty years mentioned in 1 Kings 6:1. Looking at 1 Kings 6:1 again, we see how Solomon began the work in his fourth year. That means three more years had passed before he began the work on the Temple.

   So, according to Biblical revelation and calculation, the construction of the Temple began 573 years after the Children of Israel came out of Egypt. (570 + 3 = 573 years) This does not agree with 1 Kings 6:1, which says it was 480 years. There is a difference of 93 years. The numbers do not match, and there is no indication in any known text this is due to a scribal error or other human mistake. The evidence from the historic texts is that the Bible reveals two different passages of time from the Exodus to the building of Solomon's Temple. Uh-Oh, is there a contradiction in the Bible? There is if God counts time the same way man counts time. The solution is elegant. While 573 years of physical time actually passed, God counted only 480 of those years as, "Israel Time." Those "hidden" 93 years were not considered by God to count as time in Israel's history; as part of the Dispensation of Israel. In other words, there was a 93-year gap in Israel's history during this "480 year" time period.

   Double Uh-Oh! Where is my evidence? This problem and its solution were revealed in *The Coming Prince*,[97] by Sir Robert Anderson (1841-1918). My good friend Dr. Richard Fee, a professor of Health Sciences at the University of Louisville, introduced me to this excellent book. Sir Robert Anderson was an Assistant Commissioner of Crime in Scotland Yard, as well as a devout Christian theologian and a believer in the Gap Theory. As only a brilliant detective could discover, the clues were found in other parts of Scripture. This 93-year gap of time was composed of five separate gaps in Israel's history. (Again, as God counts Israel's history.) These gaps occurred during the time of the Judges. They were:

1.) An Eight-Year Gap:

Judges 3:7-8 "And the children of Israel did evil in the sight of the LORD, and forgat the LORD their God, and served Baalim and the groves. *{8}* Therefore the anger of the LORD was hot against Israel, and he sold them into the hand of Chushanrishathaim king of Mesopotamia: and the children of Israel served Chushanrishathaim **eight years**." (KJV)

2.) An Eighteen-Year Gap:

Judges 3:12-14 "And the children of Israel did evil again in the sight of the LORD: and the LORD strengthened Eglon the king of Moab against Israel, because they had done evil in the sight of the LORD. *{13}* And he gathered unto him the children of Ammon and Amalek, and went and smote Israel, and possessed the city of palm trees. *{14}* So the children of Israel served Eglon the king of Moab **eighteen years**." (KJV)

3.) A Twenty-Year Gap:

Judges 4:1-3 "And the children of Israel again did evil in the sight of the LORD, when Ehud was dead. *{2}* And the LORD sold them into the hand of Jabin king of Canaan, that reigned in Hazor; the captain of whose host *was* Sisera, which dwelt in Harosheth of the Gentiles. *{3}* And the children of Israel cried unto the LORD: for he had nine hundred chariots of iron; and **twenty years** he mightily oppressed the children of Israel." (KJV)

4.) A Seven-Year Gap:

Judges 6:1 "And the children of Israel did evil in the sight of the LORD: and the LORD delivered them into the hand of Midian **seven years**." (KJV)

5.) A Forty-Year Gap:

Judges 13:1 "And the children of Israel did evil again in the sight of the LORD; and the LORD delivered them into the hand of the Philistines **forty years**." (KJV)

Adding these gaps together, we see the total is 93 years. (8 + 18 + 20 + 7 + 40 = 93) This is exactly the difference between the statement of 1 Kings 6:1 and the calculations based on Acts 13:17-21 and 1 Kings 2:11. In other words, God did not count the Children of Israel, in Israel, as Israel during the five times they were being judged during this whole period. **Judgment times were gaps of time.** During those periods of time, God raised up foreign powers to rule over them. Those periods of judgment were gaps in the history of Israel. God "Stopped-the-Clock" for Israel during those gaps of time. (Or, as Dr. Fee told me, "God put Israel in time-out.")

God's Word makes no mistakes. There are no contradictions, even if one passage seemingly contradicts another. God made no mention of time-gaps in 1 Kings 6:1, yet those gaps were there. The fact God did not reveal the gaps in 1 Kings 6:1 does not mean there were no gaps. It seems reasonable to me, if God can hide five gaps of time within one sentence, (1 Kings 6:1) then He has every right to hide one gap of time between two sentences (Genesis 1:1 and Genesis 1:2). When you further consider how God inserted these five gaps of time during periods of judgment, it makes it even more clear the gap between Genesis 1:1 and Genesis 1:2 was a period of judgment… a period of Pre-Adamic judgment! You can accuse me of playing the "What-If Game" when I put a gap of time between Genesis 1:1 and Genesis 1:2, but you can't accuse me of resorting to something God hasn't done elsewhere in Scripture. The insertion of "silent" gaps of time is the only way to resolve the apparent contradiction between the 480 years and the 573 years. The insertion of a gap of time between Genesis 1:1 and Genesis 1:2 is Biblically sound.

The Gap Theory Under The Electron Microscope

I want you to read the following passages of Scripture because I'm going to give you a quiz. Pay close attention to the word "foundation." Here is the quiz: After reading these passages from God's Word, what do you think the Greek word *THEMELIOS* (Strong's Number G2310) (shown in bold print below) means?

1.) Luke 6:48-49 "He is like a man which built an house, and digged deep, and laid the **foundation** on a rock: and when the flood arose, the stream beat vehemently upon that house, and could not shake it: for it was founded upon a rock. *{49}* But he that heareth, and doeth not, is like a man that without a **foundation** built an house upon the earth; against which the stream did beat vehemently, and immediately it fell; and the ruin of that house was great." (KJV)

2.) Luke 14:29 "Lest haply, after he hath laid the **foundation**, and is not able to finish *it*, all that behold *it* begin to mock him," (KJV)

3.) Acts 16:26 "And suddenly there was a great earthquake, so that the **foundations** of the prison were shaken: and immediately all the doors were opened, and every one's bands were loosed." (KJV)

4.) Romans 15:20 "Yea, so have I strived to preach the gospel, not where Christ was named, lest I should build upon another man's **foundation**:" (KJV)

5.) 1 Corinthians 3:10-12 "According to the grace of God which is given unto me, as a wise masterbuilder, I have laid the **foundation**, and another buildeth thereon. But let every man take heed how he buildeth thereupon. *{11}* For other **foundation** can no man lay than that is laid, which is Jesus Christ. *{12}* Now if any man build upon this **foundation** gold, silver, precious stones, wood, hay, stubble;" (KJV)

6.) Ephesians 2:20 "And are built upon the **foundation** of the apostles and prophets, Jesus Christ himself being the chief corner *stone;*" (KJV)

7.) 1 Timothy 6:19 "Laying up in store for themselves a good **foundation** against the time to come, that they may lay hold on eternal life." (KJV)

8.) 2 Timothy 2:19 "Nevertheless the **foundation** of God standeth sure, having this seal, The Lord knoweth them that are his. And, Let every one that nameth the name of Christ depart from iniquity." (KJV)

9.) Hebrews 6:1 "Therefore leaving the principles of the doctrine of Christ, let us go on unto perfection; not laying again the **foundation** of repentance from dead works, and of faith toward God," (KJV)

10.) Hebrews 11:10 "For he looked for a city which hath **foundations**, whose builder and maker *is* God." (KJV)

11.) Revelation 21:14 "And the wall of the city had twelve **foundations**, and in them the names of the twelve apostles of the Lamb." (KJV)

12.) Revelation 21:19 "And the **foundations** of the wall of the city *were* garnished with all manner of precious stones. The first **foundation** *was* jasper; the second, sapphire; the third, a chalcedony; the fourth, an emerald;" (KJV)

Do you have an answer to my quiz? Of course, you do! It means "foundation." A foundation is something you start with when you want to build something. If we're talking about a building, a foundation is a solid structure you lay down, upon which you erect the rest of the building. If we're talking about an idea, a philosophy, or a theology, then a foundation is a basic concept (or concepts) upon which the rest of its teachings are established. If that was your answer, then you get an A+. That is exactly what *THEMELIOS* means.

Now, let me give you another quiz. Again, look at the word "foundation" (in bold print) and tell me what you think the Greek word means in these passages of Scripture.

1.) Matthew 13:35 "That it might be fulfilled which was spoken by the prophet, saying, I will open my mouth in parables; I will utter things which have been kept secret from the **foundation** of the world." (KJV)

2.) Matthew 25:34 "Then shall the King say unto them on his right hand, Come, ye blessed of my Father, inherit the kingdom prepared for you from the **foundation** of the world:" (KJV)

3.) Luke 11:50 "That the blood of all the prophets, which was shed from the **foundation** of the world, may be required of this generation;" (KJV)

4.) John 17:24 "Father, I will that they also, whom thou hast given me, be with me where I am; that they may behold my glory, which thou hast given me: for thou lovedst me before the **foundation** of the world." (KJV)

5.) Ephesians 1:4 "According as he hath chosen us in him before the **foundation** of the world, that we should be holy and without blame before him in love:" (KJV)

6.) Hebrews 4:3 "For we which have believed do enter into rest, as he said, As I have sworn in my wrath, if they shall enter into my rest: although the works were finished from the **foundation** of the world." (KJV)

7.) Hebrews 9:26 "For then must he often have suffered since the **foundation** of the world: but now once in the end of the world hath he appeared to put away sin by the sacrifice of himself." (KJV)

8.) 1 Peter 1:20 "Who verily was foreordained before the **foundation** of the world, but was manifest in these last times for you," (KJV)

9.) Revelation 13:8 "And all that dwell upon the earth shall worship him, whose names are not written in the book of life of the Lamb slain from the **foundation** of the world." (KJV)

10.) Revelation 17:8 "The beast that thou sawest was, and is not; and shall ascend out of the bottomless pit, and go into perdition: and they that dwell on the earth shall wonder, whose names were not written in the book of life from the **foundation** of the world, when they behold the beast that was, and is not, and yet is." (KJV)

Okay, if you have an answer similar to the answer in the first quiz, then I have some good news for you and some bad news for you. The good news is you answered it the same way virtually every Greek Bible scholar would answer it. The bad news is you all get an F- for giving that answer.

Oh boy, I'm in trouble now. I can just hear the scholars criticizing me for my ignorance and my arrogance. Before I tell you what the Greek word is, I must tell you I have decided to translate it in a way very few scholars would accept. Even the scholar I most admire, Arthur Custance,[98] explained how he had once translated it this way, and felt satisfied with it, but then came to feel he didn't quite have the linguistic support to defend it. I think Custance would have stuck to his original inclination if he had gone to a biologist and asked for the electron microscope version of, "the birds and the bees."

I'm sure you're confused by now, or else you think I am. Here is how this all comes together. The Greek word used in this second set of passages is not *THEMELIOS*. *THEMELIOS* is the usual word for "foundation." The word used in these passages is *KATABOLE*. (Strong's Number G2602) *KATABOLE* is the word from which we get "catabolic," "catabolism," and "catabolize." Any high school biology student would instantly recognize the significance of this word. It means to break down, tear apart, or destroy. Biologically, it defines the portion of metabolism in which large or complex structures are broken down to be used for energy and/or for building new structures via anabolism. Old proteins are catabolized into amino acids so they can be anabolized into new proteins. Carbohydrates and fats undergo similar "destruction" so their components can be used for any number of biological purposes. Since *KATABOLE* is combined with "world" (*KOSMOS*) in these verses, one immediately wonders what and when was the *KATABOLE KOSMOS*, the catabolism of the world? When was the world broken down, destroyed, or torn apart? The context seems to be the period of time elsewhere described as the beginning (*ARCHE*) of the earth. **I believe if I can prove *KATABOLE* means "destruction" when used in connection to the beginning of the earth, then I think I prove the Gap Theory.** As you probably suspect, this isn't as clear cut as it may seem. How do you get "foundation" out of a word that seems to mean a destructive process?

As I mentioned, Arthur Custance once favored this translation as a defense of the Gap Theory. He suggested it should be translated, "disruption," but he pulled back a little when he couldn't find good linguistic support for it from the other scholars. He didn't reject it, but he declined to push the point. The problem was that *KATABOLE* was never translated as a destructive process by Bible scholars. (At least, I've never found a translation or version of the Bible rendering it that way.) The reason they didn't translate it that way was because… well… because Bible scholars never translated it that way. Custance saw the cyclic reasoning in the way scholars translated it. They always translated it the way did because that was how it was always translated. But, Custance also saw the cyclic reasoning in translating it as "disruption." Without some other evidence, he knew he couldn't prove *KATABOLE* meant a destructive process. Certainly, Bible scholars were aware it COULD define a destructive process, but it seemingly wasn't used that way in the Bible. Nobody was willing to champion that definition. Scholars don't like championing unique definitions. Unique definitions are difficult to defend when other scholars attack them. Since I'm not a scholar, I'm not worried about their attacks. I'm only a little boy playing chess.

Sometimes, you have to make a unique definition. When a word is used only once, or when it is used in only one way, then there is no other choice but to make a unique definition. This was the situation surrounding the definition of *KATABOLE*. The only apparent clue was that *KATABOLE* was a noun derived from the verb *KATABALLO*. (Strong's Number G2598) The verb *KATABALLO* was easy to define from Greek literature. It meant to throw down, cast down, break down, destroy, tear down, *etc*. It also meant to lay down, like laying down a foundation. A foundation was built by casting down or laying down or depositing solid material so something could be built on it. (They didn't have concrete.) The material used for a foundation was often stones and rubble torn down (catabolized) from older structures. So, *KATABALLO* expressed two distinct, but related, concepts. One was to tear something down, the other was to lay something down or to deposit something. It is used only three times in the Bible.

2 Corinthians 4:9 "Persecuted, but not forsaken; **cast down**, but not destroyed;" (KJV)

Hebrews 6:1 "Therefore leaving the principles of the doctrine of Christ, let us go on unto perfection; not **laying** again the foundation of repentance from dead works, and of faith toward God," (KJV)

Revelation 12:10 "And I heard a loud voice saying in heaven, Now is come salvation, and strength, and the kingdom of our God, and the power of his Christ: for the accuser of our brethren is **cast down**, which accused them before our God day and night." (KJV)

In 2 Corinthians 4:9, "cast down" (*KATABALLO*) is not the same thing as "destroyed." *APOLLUMI* (Strong's Number G622) is the word used for "destroyed." *KATABALLO* means to tear down or break down, but it doesn't necessarily imply an absolute destruction. Rubble wasn't absolutely destroyed when it was used to lay foundations for new buildings. I think this implies the *KATABOLE KOSMOS* wasn't a total destruction of the earth, but a tearing down or breaking down with the intent of rebuilding something new on it.

Now, look at Hebrews 6:1. Some people argue it should say, "Let us go on unto perfection; not **tearing down** again the foundation of repentance..." If this is true, then *KATABALLO* is used only in a destructive sense in the Bible. Still, the evidence wasn't clear enough to insist on either meaning. *KATABALLO* could mean "tearing down" or it could mean "laying down." But, look again at Hebrews 6:1. Whether it is used for laying down or tearing down, it isn't the foundation itself. *THEMELIOS* is still the foundation. *KATABALLO* may be the verb for laying down or tearing down a *THEMELIOS*, but it is not the *THEMELIOS*. This makes me think we need to be careful if we try to translate the noun *KATABOLE* as "foundation" in the Bible. Anyway, here's where things start becoming strange. Somewhere along the way (and I don't even want to know how this came about) the verb *KATABALLO* developed a sexual association. When a man deposited semen into a woman, he was "throwing down," "casting down," or "laying down" his seed into her. In essence, he was laying down a "foundation" for a new life. The specific definition of *KATABALLO* was determined by its context. Throughout Greek literature it was probably obvious when a writer was writing about tearing down walls and building foundations, and when he was writing about men and women doing you know what.

That was the verb *KATABALLO*. What about the noun *KATABOLE*? It was a little harder to define, especially when used in the Bible. Custance noted three problems. The first problem was nouns don't always mean the exact same thing their related verbs mean. Usually they do, but without linguistic support, no one can use that as an unquestionable argument. The second problem with *KATABOLE* in the Bible was in all of its uses, the context never made it clear which definition was intended. The third problem with *KATABOLE* in the Bible was it was always used in the same way, with one exception. In every verse but one, it was connected with *KOSMOS*... but what did that mean? What was *KATABOLE KOSMOS*? Whatever definition was used, it would be a unique definition by virtue of the fact it wasn't used any other way. So, they always translated it the way it always had been translated. *KATABOLE* was used in eleven verses and in ten of them, it was connected with *KOSMOS*. In all ten of those verses, the Holy Spirit just didn't seem to supply enough context to provide a good definition. So, it was the eleventh verse scholars looked to in order to find its meaning.

11.) Hebrews 11:11 "Through faith also Sara herself received strength to **conceive** seed, and was delivered of a child when she was past age, because she judged him faithful who had promised." (KJV)

The *King James Bible* scholars translated *KATABOLE* as, "conceive," as did many other scholars. **It was translated as a verb, but actually, it is a noun.** In fact, two nouns were used: *KATABOLE* and *SPERMA* (seed—Strong's Number G4690). Translating a noun as a verb was no problem; all the scholars agreed. But, there was a problem! The problem with defining *KATABOLE* as "conceive" is it isn't the normal Greek word used for "conceive" in the Bible. The Bible used the word *SULLAMBANO*. (Strong's Number G4815) It was used when Elizabeth conceived John, when Mary conceived Jesus, and when Rebecca conceived Esau and Jacob. (Luke 1:24, Luke 1:31, and Romans 9:10) If this was what the Holy Spirit meant to say, then why did He pick *KATABOLE SPERMA* and not *SULLAMBANO SPERMA*? What did *KATABOLE SPERMA* mean?

The idea of the noun *KATABOLE* carrying any meaning of destruction didn't seem very likely. Sarah was already barren, and if God gave her, "power unto the destruction of seed," then she wouldn't have become pregnant with Isaac. Destroying seed didn't seem like a good translation. Depositing seed or laying down seed seemed better. By translating it this way, it was possible to define *KATABOLE KOSMOS* as the "foundation of the world" rather than as the "destruction of the world." This was a linguistic clue: Since Hebrews 11:11 explained how Sarah was able to become pregnant, "destruction" didn't seem right. If "destruction" didn't make sense in Sarah's case, then "destruction of the world" didn't make sense either. If *KATABOLE* really did mean destruction in reference to the earth, then it would also seem to mean Sarah became able to destroy seed. The only logical option was to translate *KATABOLE* in the sense of laying down seed. But, that option wasn't without difficulties. If *KATABOLE* meant "deposit" or "lay down," then a new problem arose. What did it mean for Sarah to be given the power to lay down seed?

This brought up all kinds of opinions about what happens during conception. At that time, no one knew what really happened during the conception event. Some speculated the man produced the "seed" and the woman was just the "garden" in which the "seed" grew. Others believed the woman produced the "seed" and the man just provided the "fertilizer" that stimulated the "seed" to grow. Still others believed "seed" was a figurative term, and it was the commingling of the man's fluids with the woman's fluids that started the process. The fluids congealed, and a baby would develop from that little blob of jelly. There were others who were more correct, who believed both the man and the woman produced "seed." These two "seeds" would combine to make one new "seed." After all, the Bible did talk about the "seed of the woman" and "the seed of the man." (Another pre-scientific revelation of a scientific truth.) But, if the text meant Sarah deposited *SPERMA* in order to become pregnant, then it could be interpreted to mean Sarah received the power to impregnate herself. That couldn't be right; that would mean Isaac wouldn't have been Abraham's offspring. So, rather than using such words as "deposit," seed or "lay down" seed, the word "conceive" seed seem more reasonable. It wasn't accurate, but it was better than "destroy" seed. No matter what the process of conception was, the destruction of seed (either hers or Abraham's or the combination) didn't fit with their knowledge of conception. This made it possible to think of *KATABOLE KOSMOS* as "the conception of the world," (*i.e.*, "the foundation of the world") rather than the "destruction of the world." So, the scholars agreed the noun *KATABOLE* could be translated as a verb meaning "conceive" in Sarah's case, rather than as a noun meaning "destruction." They changed a noun to a verb. They altered God's Word.

Not everyone was happy with that translation. There were scholars who knew *KATABOLE SPERMA* didn't mean "conceive seed." Instead, it meant either "the deposition of seed" or "the destruction of seed." They knew it couldn't mean Sarah was able to destroy seed, and they didn't like the idea of Sarah depositing seed. So, they chose another translation. What did these scholars do when faced with the dilemma of Sarah either becoming empowered to destroy seed or becoming empowered to deposit seed? Neither translation made any sense, so they decided God must have meant Abraham was given the power to deposit seed.

Hebrews 11:11 "By trusting, **he** received potency to father a child, even when **he** was past the age for it, as was Sarah herself; because **he** regarded the One who had made the promise as trustworthy. (CJB)

Hebrews 11:11 "**He** was too old to have children, and Sarah [*or* Sarah was too old and] could not have children [was barren/sterile]. It was by faith that **Abraham** was made able to become a father, because **he** [*or* Sarah was made able to bear children, because she] trusted God [considered God faithful/trustworthy] to do what he had promised." (EXB)

Hebrews 11:11 "It was faith that made **Abraham** able to become a father, even though **he** was too old and Sarah herself could not have children. **He** trusted God to keep his promise." (GN-TEV)

Hebrews 11:11 "Faith enabled **Abraham** to become a father, even though **he** was old and Sarah had never been able to have children. **Abraham** trusted that God would keep his promise." (GW)

Hebrews 11:11 "By faith **he** received power of procreation, even though **he** was too old--and Sarah herself was barren--because **he** considered him faithful who had promised." (NRSV)

Other translations also have "Sarah" replaced by "Abraham," even though Abraham is not mentioned in this verse. It doesn't say, "HE was too old." It says, "SHE was too old." It doesn't say, "HE trusted God." It says, "SHE trusted God." Now, I have to make a confession. At first I was critical of these translations. I thought it showed contempt for God's Word. The audacity of changing "Sarah" to "Abraham" and "she" to "he" seemed enormous. Not only was it linguistically incorrect to imply Abraham was given the power/ability to procreate, it was contrary to what the Bible said about Abraham. He wasn't infertile; Sarah was. Abraham already had one son, Ishmael, by Hagar, and then six sons by Keturah, after Sarah died. He wasn't too old even after Sarah died.

Genesis 16:15 "And Hagar bare Abram a son: and Abram called his son's name, which Hagar bare, Ishmael." (KJV)

Genesis 25:1-2 "Then again Abraham took a wife, and her name *was* Keturah. {2} And she bare him Zimran, and Jokshan, and Medan, and Midian, and Ishbak, and Shuah." (KJV)

It was apparent Abraham had the power to procreate. These translators had to distort God's Word to make it say what they wanted it to say. Like I said, I had contempt for these men. However, as I thought more about it, I realized these translators were doing the most honorable thing they could. They knew *KATABOLE SPERMA* did not mean "conceive seed." They were in the same situation as Arthur Custance. I think they knew it meant either the "deposition of seed" or the "destruction of seed," but it made no sense that Sarah would receive the power to do either one. So, they did the best they could with their knowledge of conception. They translated *KATABOLE SPERMA* in a way that wouldn't create a contradiction with science and make the Holy Spirit look stupid. They made up a translation that fit their knowledge of conception. Ahhhhhh, but their knowledge of conception was limited.

I think the Holy Spirit did something no one expected. His knowledge of conception is perfect, and I think He revealed a scientific clue, not just a linguistic clue. I think the Holy Spirit picked the word He wanted, because it defined exactly what happened inside of Sarah. Fast forward from the 1st century, when no one knew the details of conception, to the 20th century and the invention of the electron microscope. We discover something very interesting about *KATABOLE SPERMA*. Catabolism of sperm is exactly what must take place in order for new life to develop. The egg is surrounded by a thick covering called the *Zona Pellucida*. The *Zona Pellucida* does some important things:

1.) It protects the egg.
2.) It produces biochemical signals that attract sperm to it.
3.) It provides specific binding sites for sperm attachment.
4.) It prevents further sperm attachment once a sperm attaches. (It undergoes a rapid electrical discharge, via the cell's sodium pumps, that instantly closes the other binding sites.)
5.) It releases chemical "triggers" that initiate the process of sperm catabolism.

The sperm's DNA is inside its nucleus and must get into the egg's cytoplasm. The chromosomes inside the sperm have to become linked with the chromosomes inside the egg. Even when attached to the *Zona Pellucida*, the sperm can't do that. The sperm's DNA is biologically "miles" away from the egg's DNA. So, the egg produces biological signals in response to the attachment of the sperm. These signals trigger the release of enzymes that start catabolizing the sperm. (*KATABOLE SPERMA*) The sperm has to be broken down into smaller parts because only certain components are allowed into the egg. In addition, the outer membranes of the sperm and the egg have to be catabolized. A portal must be created for the transfer of the sperm's nucleus. This portal is made by catabolizing the membranes of both the egg and the sperm. This portal into the egg has to be just the right size too. The entire sperm isn't allowed into the egg because such an event would trigger a fatal reaction. Only the nucleus, the centrioles, and the flagellum are allowed to enter. The nucleus is needed because it contains the chromosomes. The centrioles are needed because they help position the chromosomes into their proper positions. The flagellum is needed to move the nucleus into place. The rest of the sperm is no longer needed. The rest of the sperm has to be catabolized. The only way to separate the needed parts of the sperm from the unneeded parts of the sperm is by the process of sperm catabolism. (*KATABOLE SPERMA*) If the woman's reproductive system doesn't have the ability to catabolize sperm, she will not be able to become pregnant. If the sperm can't be catabolized, its nucleus can't get inside the egg's cytoplasm. Only after the sperm cell is catabolized is it possible for the sperm's nucleus to be deposited into the egg. Once the sperm's nucleus is laid down (deposited) inside the egg's cytoplasm, its chromosomes line up in their proper place. Once the father's chromosomes are deposited in their proper place, they link with the chromosomes of the mother. Once the chromosomes link together, their DNA combines and conception takes place. Only if this breaking down/laying down process occurs can conception come about. Only after *KATABOLE SPERMA* do we witness the miraculous creation of a new… income tax deduction.

I believe the Holy Spirit picked *KATABOLE SPERMA* because those words define with scientific precision, a biological process that had to take place in order for Sarah to become pregnant. *KATABOLE SPERMA* is not some vague, mystical, symbolic figure of speech. It describes exactly what we learned about conception once we viewed it under the electron microscope. I believe the Holy Spirit was giving us another pre-scientific revelation. I believe He revealed the "breaking down/laying down" of sperm is necessary for conception. I also believe He didn't allow that revelation to be understood until the electron microscope was invented. You see, I think the Holy Spirit likes electron microscopes. I think He thinks they're neat. I think He thinks they're neat because they allow us humans to observe things about His handiwork we couldn't see otherwise. I think He thinks the same thing about the Hubble Space Telescope. I think the Holy Spirit rejoices when scientists reveal new truths about creation. I think God likes scientific discoveries. I think God likes scientists. Every time they discover a new truth about God's handiwork, it allows us to see something about Him. As a Christian, I think we should rejoice when scientists, even those who are atheists, discover new truths about nature. I don't think we should go around bashing scientists. It certainly doesn't help them see their discoveries as insights into the character of God. If you are a scientist and an atheist, then let me ask you to look a little closer at what you see in the universe around you. I think you will begin to see His beauty and His power and His Love if you look more closely at His work. I think you will see the same thing if you look more closely at His Word. It saddens me to see you miss God's miracles when you observe the universe. It saddens me even more that you don't feel the joy of your Creator when you discover a new truth about the universe. It saddens me most to know you won't be able to spend eternity with your Creator learning more about Him and His universe. None of your questions about the universe will be answered in Hell.

Some will accuse me of playing the "What-If Game." Some will accuse me of trying to stretch the meanings of words to make the Bible say what I want it to say. Well, I think they would be right if there was no catabolism of sperm during physical conception. Many creationists have no problem with believing things contrary to scientific observations. They have no difficulty with Biblical interpretations that say things like the speed of light has changed. It's perfectly okay to say light travels through Riemannian Space. They aren't bothered by translations that require fruit-bearing trees to have existed billions of years before the sun was created. With no Biblical or scientific evidence to support their views, some scholars see nothing wrong with interpreting Genesis as saying there was a glowing ball of matter somewhere in space that gave light to the earth for three days before the sun was created. Some scholars believe it is perfectly okay to replace Sarah with Abraham when the Bible says something they don't want to believe. Some creationists see no problem with believing in the "amalgamation" of humans and animals, or that coal can be made from petrified wood. All these things are scholarly and noble and justified, BUT let someone imply the Holy Spirit may have used a scientifically observable process to give us a clue that defends the Gap Theory, and suddenly that idea is denounced as unscholarly. Why do I think *KATABOLE SPERMA* is a pre-scientific revelation of a scientific fact? It's because I don't believe in coincidences. It seems too coincidental for the Holy Spirit's choice of words about Sarah's conception, to accidentally describe a real scientific phenomenon involving Sarah's conception.

Imagine you discovered your dog was dead, and you brought it to me for a necropsy, (a post-mortem examination) and I gave you this report: "Upon examination of the dog's thoracic cavity, I discovered a .22 caliber bullet had penetrated the chest on the right side between the 5th and 6th intercostal space and severed the pulmonary artery. Death was caused by massive internal hemorrhage and hypovolemic shock." With that report in hand, would you think I was using words that described an actual medical event, or words that were symbolic of some mystical, magical, poetic, indefinable phenomenon? I hope my use of precise medical terms would clue you into the fact I wasn't being mystical. I know what those terms mean, and if I had intended to give you some vague report, I wouldn't have used them. I think the Holy Spirit wouldn't have used a precise biological term if He had meant to convey anything else but a precise biological process. I think this is why He said *KATABOLE SPERMA* instead of *SULLAMBANO SPERMA*. I think this is His clue to the meaning of *KATABOLE* in the Bible. I think He is telling us *KATABOLE* means catabolism. *KATABOLE SPERMA* means the catabolism of sperm. If I were a first century Greek scientist, and I knew what happened during conception, I would use the words *KATABOLE SPERMA* to describe the catabolism of sperm that takes place inside the woman. *KATABOLE* means catabolism. *SPERMA* means sperm. *KATABOLE SPERMA* means the catabolism of sperm. It defines a true biological event. Likewise, *KATABOLE KOSMOS* means the catabolism of the world. It defines a true historical event. Once again, God's words match His work.

End of the AGES

The writer of Hebrews reveals another interesting fact about *KATABOLE KOSMOS* that defends the Gap Theory.

Hebrews 9:19-26 "For when every commandment of the law had been declared by Moses to all the people, he took the blood of calves and goats, with water and scarlet wool and hyssop, and sprinkled both the book itself and all the people, *{20}* saying, 'This is the blood of the covenant that God commanded for you.' *{21}* And in the same way he sprinkled with the blood both the tent and all the vessels used in worship. *{22}* Indeed, under the law almost everything is purified with blood, and without the shedding of blood there is no forgiveness of sins. *{23}* Thus it was necessary for the copies of the heavenly things to be purified with these rites, but the heavenly things themselves with better sacrifices than these. *{24}* For Christ has entered, not into holy places made with hands, which are copies of the true things, but into heaven itself, now to appear in the presence of God on our behalf. *{25}* Nor was it to offer himself repeatedly, as the high priest enters the holy places every year with blood not his own, *{26}* for then he would have had to suffer repeatedly since the **foundation of the world**. But as it is, he has appeared once for all at the end of the ages to put away sin by the sacrifice of himself." (ESV)

The writer of Hebrews is explaining the better sacrifice Christ offered with His own blood. Under the Mosaic Covenant, the blood of animals was required to purify the Tabernacle, the vessels in the Tabernacle, the priests, the people, and just about everything else involved in the worship of God. Only blood could atone for sins. Note how these physical things on earth are copies of the true things in heaven. This means there is some kind of spiritual Tabernacle/Temple and some kind of spiritual vessels in heaven. Not much is revealed about these heavenly things, but it is revealed that they needed to be purified too. In fact, they needed to be purified since the "foundation of the world." If the "foundation of the world" (*KATABOLE KOSMOS)* was the same as the "creation of the world," then Jesus would have had to suffer even before sin entered the universe. Obviously, the "catabolism of the world" is not the same thing as the "creation of the world." At the creation of the world (Genesis 1:1), nothing in heaven or earth needed purification. *KATABOLE KOSMOS* does not mean, "the foundation of the world."

This brings up four questions. First, WHY did they need to be purified? Answer: Only something that has been corrupted/defiled by sin needs to be purified. Second, WHO defiled/corrupted these heavenly things so that they needed to be purified? It wasn't Adam. Remember, God cursed only the ground and the man made from it because of Adam's sin.

Genesis 3:17-19 "And unto Adam he said, Because thou hast hearkened unto the voice of thy wife, and hast eaten of the tree, of which I commanded thee, saying, Thou shalt not eat of it: cursed *is* the ground for thy sake; in sorrow shalt thou eat *of* it all the days of thy life; {18} Thorns also and thistles shall it bring forth to thee; and thou shalt eat the herb of the field; {19} In the sweat of thy face shalt thou eat bread, till thou return unto the ground; for out of it wast thou taken: for dust thou *art,* and unto dust shalt thou return." (KJV)

God didn't curse the physical heaven and God didn't curse the spiritual heaven because of Adam's sin. Adam's sin didn't cause the Angelic Realm to become corrupt. It was Lucifer's sin that did that. It seems very likely that Lucifer was the angelic being overseeing the worship of God in heaven. His sin and rebellion against God was most likely the source of corruption and defilement, and the blood of bulls and goats couldn't purify the heavenly things he corrupted. The blood of Jesus was the only sacrifice that could. Christ's death on the Cross did much more than undo the corruption caused by man. It undid the corruption caused by Satan and his angels.

1 John 3:8 "He who sins is of the devil, for the devil has sinned from the beginning. For this purpose the Son of God was manifested, that He might destroy the works of the devil." (NKJV)

Now for the third question. WHEN did the heavenly things become defiled/corrupted? It could not have been at Creation because that would mean God created them defiled/corrupted. God didn't do that! It had to be after the Creation. Creation did not begin corrupt. In the beginning, the spiritual realm and the physical realm were free of sin and corruption. Lucifer was not created a sinner. I believe the corruption Lucifer caused in heaven came after the Creation, but before Adam was created. I believe it was Pre-Adamic. I believe it was in a previous Angelic Age before this present Age of Man.

Finally, the fourth question. HOW did the heavenly things get purified? That corruption could not be purified by human priests. That corruption could not be purified by the blood of bulls and goats. Only Christ's blood could do that. Christ entered the Heavenly Holy Place after His death on the cross. His blood was the only way the heavenly things could be purified. That means they weren't purified until about two thousand years ago. The corruption in the heavenly realm happened before the First Adam, but wasn't purified until the Last Adam. Christ shed His blood on the Cross and then entered into the Heavenly Holy Place to purify it. Now, one of the big differences between the earthly Holy Place and the Heavenly Holy Place was that the priests had to offer their sacrifices year after year. The Heavenly Holy Place was purified only once. Jesus did not need to offer His blood year after year. His blood was the perfect sacrifice. The blood of bulls and goats was only an image, a likeness, a foreshadow of what Christ's blood would accomplish. The blood of bulls and goats was unable to pay for a single sin, while Christ's blood paid for all sins. If Christ's blood was no different than the blood of animals, "then he would have had to suffer repeatedly."

But, note how the writer of Hebrews says it was at the end of the AGES. He uses the plural of *AION*. The writer of Hebrews places Christ's birth, life, death, burial, and resurrection at the end of the AGES. Since Christ came in the present age, then there was at least one age before the present age. The Gap Theory is the only creation theory that says there was an age before the present age. **If Genesis 1:1-2 does not describe an age before Genesis 1:3-31 and following, then there has been only one age, and it would make no sense for the writer of Hebrews to say Christ came at the end of the AGES.** The writer of Hebrews clearly reveals there was at least one age before this age. There was a Pre-Adamic Age before the present Adamic Age. The writer of Hebrews clearly defends the Gap Theory.

KATABALLO in the Septuagint

There is another clue *KATABALLO* and *KATABOLE* have a destructive meaning in the Bible and not a constructive one. This clue takes us back to the 3rd century B.C. when the Septuagint was translated. In the Septuagint, the seventy Hebrew-Greek scholars used the word *KATABALLO* thirty-two times in thirty-one verses. Here is the list of Old Testament passages in which they used *KATABALLO* (words in bold print):

1.) 2 Samuel 20:15 "And they came and besieged him in Abel of Bethmaachah, and they cast up a bank against the city, and it stood in the trench: and all the people that *were* with Joab battered the wall, to **throw it down**." (KJV)

2.) 2 Kings 3:19 "And ye shall smite every fenced city, and every choice city, and shall **fell** every good tree, and stop all wells of water, and mar every good piece of land with stones." (KJV)

3.) 2 Kings 3:25 "And they beat down the cities, and on every good piece of land cast every man his stone, and filled it; and they stopped all the wells of water, and **felled** all the good trees: only in Kirharaseth left they the stones thereof; howbeit the slingers went about *it*, and smote it." (KJV)

4.) 2 Kings 6:5 "But as one was **felling** a beam, the ax head fell into the water: and he cried, and said, Alas, master! for it was borrowed." (KJV)

5.) 2 Kings 19:7 "Behold, I will send a blast upon him, and he shall hear a rumour, and shall return to his own land; and I will cause him to **fall** by the sword in his own land." (KJV)

6.) 2 Chronicles 32:21 "And the LORD sent an angel, which cut off all the mighty men of valour, and the leaders and captains in the camp of the king of Assyria. So he returned with shame of face to his own land. And when he was come into the house of his god, they that came forth of his own bowels **slew** him there with the sword." (KJV)

7.) Job 12:14 "Behold, he **breaketh down**, and it cannot be built again: he shutteth up a man, and there can be no opening." (KJV)

8.) Job 16:9 "He **teareth** *me* in his wrath, who hateth me: he gnasheth upon me with his teeth; mine enemy sharpeneth his eyes upon me." (KJV)

9.) Job 16:14 "He **breaketh** me with breach upon breach, he runneth upon me like a giant." (KJV)

10.) Psalms 37:14 "The wicked have drawn out the sword, and have bent their bow, to **cast down** the poor and needy, *and* to slay such as be of upright conversation." (KJV)

11.) Psalms 73:18 "Surely thou didst set them in slippery places: thou **castedst** them **down** into destruction." (KJV)

12.) Psalms 106:26 "Therefore he lifted up his hand against them, to **overthrow** them in the wilderness:" (KJV)

13.) Psalms 106:27 "To **overthrow** their seed also among the nations, and to scatter them in the lands." (KJV)

14.) Psalms 140:10 "Let burning coals fall upon them: let them be **cast** into the fire; into deep pits, that they rise not up again." (KJV)

15.) Proverbs 7:26 "For she hath **cast down** many wounded: yea, many strong *men* have been slain by her." (KJV)

16.) Proverbs 18:8 "The words of a talebearer *are* as wounds, and they **go down** into the innermost parts of the belly." (KJV)

17.) Proverbs 25:28 "He that *hath* no rule over his own spirit *is like* a city *that is* **broken down**, *and* without walls." (KJV)

18.) Isaiah 16:9 "Therefore I will bewail with the weeping of Jazer the vine of Sibmah: I will water thee with my tears, O Heshbon, and Elealeh: for the shouting for thy summer fruits and for thy harvest is **fallen**." (KJV)

19.) Isaiah 26:5 "For he bringeth down them that dwell on high; the lofty city, he **layeth it low**; he layeth it low, *even* to the ground; he bringeth it *even* to the dust." (KJV)

20.) Jeremiah 19:7 "And I will make void the counsel of Judah and Jerusalem in this place; and I will cause them to **fall** by the sword before their enemies, and by the hands of them that seek their lives: and their carcases will I give to be meat for the fowls of the heaven, and for the beasts of the earth." (KJV)

21.) Ezekiel 6:4 "And your altars shall be desolate, and your images shall be broken: and I will **cast down** your slain *men* before your idols." (KJV)

22.) Ezekiel 23:25 "And I will set my jealousy against thee, and they shall deal furiously with thee: they shall take away thy nose and thine ears; and thy remnant shall **fall** by the sword: they shall take thy sons and thy daughters; and thy residue shall be devoured by the fire." (KJV)

23. and 24.) Ezekiel 26:4 "And they shall **destroy** the walls of Tyrus, and **break down** her towers: I will also scrape her dust from her, and make her like the top of a rock." (KJV)

25.) Ezekiel 26:9 "And he shall set engines of war against thy walls, and with his axes he shall **break down** thy towers." (KJV)

26.) Ezekiel 26:12 "And they shall make a spoil of thy riches, and make a prey of thy merchandise: and they shall **break down** thy walls, and destroy thy pleasant houses: and they shall lay thy stones and thy timber and thy dust in the midst of the water." (KJV)

27.) Ezekiel 29:5 "And I will leave thee *thrown* into the wilderness, thee and all the fish of thy rivers: thou shalt **fall** upon the open fields; thou shalt not be brought together, nor gathered: I have given thee for meat to the beasts of the field and to the fowls of the heaven." (KJV)

28.) Ezekiel 30:22 "Therefore thus saith the Lord GOD; Behold, I *am* against Pharaoh king of Egypt, and will break his arms, the strong, and that which was broken; and I will cause the sword to **fall** out of his hand." (KJV)

29.) Ezekiel 31:12 "And strangers, the terrible of the nations, have **cut** him **off**, and have left him: upon the mountains and in all the valleys his branches are fallen, and his boughs are broken by all the rivers of the land; and all the people of the earth are gone down from his shadow, and have left him." (KJV)

30.) Ezekiel 32:12 "By the swords of the mighty will I cause thy multitude to **fall**, the terrible of the nations, all of them: and they shall spoil the pomp of Egypt, and all the multitude thereof shall be destroyed." (KJV)

31.) Ezekiel 39:3 "And I will smite thy bow out of thy left hand, and will cause thine arrows to **fall** out of thy right hand." (KJV)

32.) Daniel 11:12 "*And* when he hath taken away the multitude, his heart shall be lifted up; and he shall **cast down** *many* ten thousands: but he shall not be strengthened *by it*." (KJV)

As you can see, these prominent Hebrew-Greek scholars used *KATABALLO* to define a destructive process. They never used it in the sense of "laying a foundation," "building a foundation," "conception," or any kind of constructive act. It always described a destructive, tearing down, breaking down, or catabolizing event.

Yes, but that was the verb *KATABALLO*. What about the noun *KATABOLE*? Well, the Hebrew Old Testament has several nouns that can be translated, "foundation," but the Septuagint scholars never used the Greek word *KATABOLE* as a translation for those words. Those seventy ancient Hebrew-Greek scholars gave no indication they thought of *KATABALLO* and *KATABOLE* in any sense other than in a destructive sense. Of course, you can argue they weren't Divinely inspired by the Holy Spirit to be infallible in their translation. However, you can't argue they didn't have knowledge of what *KATABALLO* and *KATABOLE* meant. You can't argue they didn't know the difference between destruction and construction. The linguistic evidence shows *KATABOLE* means "catabolism" in the Bible. *KATABOLE KOSMOS* means "catabolism of the world." *KATABOLE KOSMOS* means there was a time in the past when the world was destroyed so it could be rebuilt into a new and different world. This was not the world of man; this was the Pre-Adamic world of the angelic realm. The world of Lucifer and his angels was destroyed so the world of man could be built. *KATABOLE* describes the destruction of something old so something new can be constructed. That's what happened to the Pre-Adamic earth. There is no better word than *KATABOLE* to describe "Ruin-Restoration." (Breaking Down-Laying Down) I think *KATABOLE KOSMOS* means, "The Ruin-Restoration of the world." Modern scholars can attack my translation if they want. They can respond however they please. My only response is to respond to their response with the response the Holy Spirit makes: The Holy Spirit defines *KATABOLE KOSMOS* as the catabolism of the world… checkmate!

Chapter Eleven: Science and the Restoration Theory

So, how old is the universe? The Restoration Theory makes no statements concerning the exact age of the universe. The Restoration Theory is based on Biblical statements and the Bible doesn't give an age for the universe. A Biblical age for the universe can only be stated as a Biblical interpretation, not a Biblical declaration. It would have been nice if Moses had told us the universe was created four thousand years before he was born, or ten million years before, or ten billion years before, or something. If Paul told us the universe was 13,254,487,219 years old, then we wouldn't need to debate this. The Bible doesn't reveal when the universe and the earth were originally created, when the earth was made *TOHUW WA-BOHUW* and *CHOSHEK*, or how long it remained in that condition. As it is, the Restoration Theory cannot be used to prove any dates. No Biblical creation theory can do that! Remember, the genealogies of men give no clues for the age of the Pre-Adamic earth.

The Bible doesn't tell us the age of the universe. This means we have to turn to science for answers. **The age of the universe is a scientific matter, not a Biblical one.** No matter how great a Hebrew and Greek scholar you are, no matter how many theology degrees you have, you aren't going to find an age for the earth by studying the Bible. If you want to know the age of the universe, then sooner or later, you must enter the realm of science. When you do that, the very first thing you'll notice is the discrepancy between the science of the Young-Earth creationists and the science of the Old-Earth creationists. The problem is not one of Biblical interpretation alone. It is a problem of scientific interpretation as well. (Of course, I'd be naive to believe people's interpretation of science wasn't influenced by their interpretation of the Bible, and *vice versa*.)

Young-Earthers use scientific dating techniques to prove the earth has celebrated only a few thousand birthdays. Old-Earthers use scientific dating techniques to prove we should be putting billions of candles on earth's birthday cake. Which is correct? The answer depends on your assumptions. All dating techniques require faith in basic assumptions. Before you put your faith in a dating technique, you need to understand its assumptions. Is it correct to assume rocks originally contained no radioactive decay products at creation? Are all radioactive decay rates constant? Has cosmic ray bombardment always been the same? Does the $^{14}C/^{12}C$ ratio in the atmosphere vary over time? Has the earth's spin always been slowing at the same rate? Has space dust been accumulating on the earth and moon at constant rates? Whose rates do you believe? Is it valid to assume the earth's magnetic field has always been decaying the way it is today? Can you always use a present-day change to extrapolate backward through time to achieve an absolute age? Did God create the universe with an Apparent Age, and if so, what Apparent Age? In all honesty, I've looked at the various dating techniques, thought about their assumptions, and have come away scratching my head. Now, it is true both sides often use dating techniques so assumption-dependent and biased, they're easy to discount. Unfortunately, it's also true both sides use known false data to persuade the unsuspecting. Still, both sides have more than a few dating techniques that seem valid, at least to me. Each side seems to be able to prove its point to a certain degree.

The Young-Earthers will shake their heads in disbelief. How could I even think the Old-Earth dating techniques might be valid? I'm sure I'll be accused of trying to make the Bible fit the Theory of Evolution. They'll point to a dozen books, written by Young-Earth creationists, that prove the Old-Earth dating techniques are invalid. The Day-Agers will do the same thing. They'll accuse me of being unscientific. They'll point to another dozen books, written by Day-Age creationists, that prove the Young-Earth dating techniques are invalid.

How are we going to resolve this? Who's right? Whose assumptions are we going to believe? Both sides can't be right... or can they? Personally, I think both sides are partially right. Generally, and I mean very generally, I think both sides are making correct observations, but incorrect interpretations. This problem can be approached in three different ways.

1.) We can assume the heavens and the earth were created a few to several thousand years ago. With that assumption as a foundation we can begin searching for the evidence that supports this view.

2.) We can assume the universe is billions of years old, and from there set out in search for supporting evidence.

Both ways of approaching the problem are scientifically valid. This is the scientific method. Make the hypothesis, test the hypothesis, and then accept or reject the hypothesis in light of the evidence. (Of course, in the real world, scientists, including creation-scientists, don't like to reject their own cleverly devised hypotheses.) Both ways are equally Biblical as well. The Bible gives no specific dates. Dates can be assumed, but no verse in the Bible states an age for the universe. Unfortunately, some creationists act as if the Bible does. They confuse their interpretation of a date with an actual Biblical declaration of a date. They make their assumed date the criterion for judging both the scientific and the Biblical evidence. If the evidence doesn't fit their assumption, then they say the evidence is wrong.

3.) A third way to approach this is not to assume any age for the heavens and the earth and let the scientific evidence say what the scientific evidence says.

As you can guess, I prefer this third approach. I prefer it because it doesn't have a built-in bias toward rejecting evidence that doesn't fit a preconceived belief. If I were a Young-Earth creationist, I'd have a tendency to assume all the Old-Earth dates were wrong. If I were a Day-Age creationist, I'd have a tendency to assume all the Young-Earth dates were wrong. But, I'm a Restored-Earth creationist, so that puts no limits of time on me. The heavens and the earth can be just as young or just as old as science finally proves them to be. Now, let me ask you something. What could we conclude if science really could prove some of the Old-Earth dates AND some of the Young-Earth dates? How would such proof affect the Restoration Theory? Finding proof for both ages of the earth would help verify it. If the Restoration Theory is true, then one would expect to find just such evidence. Because the earth had two different beginnings, there would be both old and young dates for things. Conflicting dates wouldn't have to generate conflict. Suddenly, everything seems to fall in line with the Restoration Theory. If the Bible said the earth had only one beginning billions of years ago, then all the Young-Earth dating techniques would be wrong. If the Bible said the earth had only one beginning six thousand years ago, then all the Old-Earth dating techniques would be wrong. But, if the Bible said the earth had two beginnings, then it might be possible for neither side to be completely wrong. Old-Earth is not the true antithesis of Young-Earth. They don't have to conflict. The problem is not with what the Bible and science teach. The problem is with what people WANT the Bible and science to teach. The problem is with motives. What motivates someone to believe a particular view? WHY do people believe what they believe?

When you ask a Young-Earth creationist why he or she believes Genesis should be translated in a Young-Earth fashion, the typical answer is that it's the most clear and straightforward interpretation. Young-Earth creationists argue that God wouldn't write something a dear, sweet, innocent, uneducated little-old-grandmother sitting in her rocking chair, reading her Bible, couldn't understand. Day-Age creationists do the same thing except it isn't Granny sitting in a rocking chair; it's a laboratory full of test tubes, telescopes, and microscopes that wind up being the interpreters of Genesis. God surely wouldn't write something contradictory to observable science.

Wrong on both cases! Consider the Old Testament prophecies of Christ and how many people (dear, sweet grandmothers included) couldn't understand them. Likewise, God has written things that contradicted observable science. In 2 Peter 3:10, Peter revealed atoms could be split.

2 Peter 3:10 "But the day of the Lord will come as a thief in the night; in the which the heavens shall pass away with a great noise, and the elements shall melt with fervent heat, the earth also and the works that are therein shall be burned up." (KJV)

The word for "melt" is the Greek word *LUO*, (Strong's Number G3089) and it means to "loosen," "untie," or "break." It is the same word used when someone unties a donkey from a hitching post. In other words, Peter tells us when the Day of the Lord comes, the elements, the *STOICHEION*, (Strong's Number G4747) the rudimentary particles of matter, the atoms—will be "untied" or "broken" resulting in a fervent heat. It will be this kind of destruction that removes all the evil works of man and Satan. This idea contradicted observable science until 1945 when the first atomic bomb was exploded.

No, we must not insist a particular interpretation is false simply because it disagrees with our conclusions. Regrettably, this is what many Christians from all camps do… even some Gap Theorists. If the Scriptures destroy our interpretations and assumptions, then our interpretations and assumptions are wrong. If science destroys our interpretations and assumptions, then our interpretations and assumptions are wrong.

I know both Day-Age and Young-Earth creationists will object, but is the Restoration Theory really so objectionable? For me, a Restored-Earth is not only not objectionable, it is the only thing that makes sense. I don't see anything wrong with assuming the Restored-Earth scenario, and then testing it against the dating techniques of the Young-Earth and Day-Age creationists. If you'll do this, you'll see how the Restoration Theory seems to fit both sets of data. I think many of the discrepancies in age arise because the two groups are observing two different events/two different ages. The dating techniques may be correct but the conclusions are incorrect.

Living Fossils

The Restoration Theory explains many apparently contradictory observations. If God recreated lifeforms that had become extinct during the Pre-Adamic earth, then one could expect to find evidence of those lifeforms in both Old-Earth and Young-Earth settings. With this in mind, we see how the Restoration Theory explains Living Fossils such as the Coelacanth fish. Coelacanth apparently lived for a long time, but then died out seventy million years ago. Geology records a seventy-million-year absence of Coelacanth, yet living Coelacanth swim the ocean today. This is no problem for the Restoration Theory. What probably happened was Lucifer's destructive acts brought about the extinction of Coelacanth seventy million years ago. Then on Day Five, a few to several thousand years ago, God recreated Coelacanth so fishermen could catch them off the coast of South Africa in 1938. Scientific observation supports the Restoration Theory. The evidence is in favor of a recent creation of lifeforms that had died out ages ago. There were Coelacanth fish on this earth a long time ago. Then they died out. The fossil evidence shows no Coelacanth fish for millions of years. Yet, here they are today. How can that have happened? They had to be recreated! The same can be said of Tuatara lizards, Ginkgo trees, Metasequoia trees, *Neopilinia*, and *Lepidocaris*. The Gap Theory fits this scientific observation. These Living Fossils died out millions of years ago. The geological column faithfully recorded their absence. They were dead and gone! The geologists and paleontologists weren't wrong about their extinction. Then, they were recreated sometime in the last few to several thousand years. The Young-Earthers aren't wrong about their recent creation. Restoration creationists don't have to reject any proven data, Biblical or scientific. In fact, if the Restoration Theory is true, then the Bible has given us a pre-scientific clue into the science of geology. If Satan brought death and devastation to the Pre-Adamic earth, then one could expect to discover geological evidence of death and devastation before man's existence.

This is precisely what geology reveals. Geology is not only a valid scientific discipline, it is a vital key to interpreting the Biblical Creation Account informationally.

Does The Gap Theory Allow for Evolution?

If the earth could be billions of years old, does it mean evolution could have occurred during the gap? No. There was no evolution during the gap (everything was dead) and no evolution after the gap. All life was created/recreated during days 3-6, a period of 96 hours. How about evolution before the gap? Could God have "created" life on the original earth by the process of evolution? I would love to point to the Bible verse that says, "Knowest thou not that God didst not use evolution to create life in the Pre-Adamic earth?" Unfortunately, I can't find that verse. The Bible is silent on how God created life on the original earth. If I claimed the Bible prohibited evolution in the Pre-Adamic world, I would be guilty of confusing a Biblical interpretation with a Biblical declaration. The only thing the Bible prohibits is evolution during and after the *TOHUW WA-BOHUW* and *CHOSHEK* gap. Am I capitulating to the evolutionists? No! We must sift our Biblical theories through the filter of science. I am convinced by SCIENCE that evolution never happened. I believe the scientific facts prove evolution never occurred. It would be foolish to think the Bible taught something contrary to true science.

Was There A Big Bang?

If the universe is old, does it mean there was a Big Bang? Personally, I believe there was. The scientific evidence seems solid, and the Bible may give us a hint in the affirmative. There are some verses that talk about how God "stretched" (in the past tense) and is "stretching out" (in the present tense) the heavens.

Psalms 104:1-2 "Bless the LORD, O my soul! O LORD my God, you are very great! You are clothed with splendor and majesty, {2} covering yourself with light as with a garment, **stretching** out the heavens like a tent." (ESV)

Isaiah 40:22 "It is he who sits above the circle of the earth, and its inhabitants are like grasshoppers; who **stretches** out the heavens like a curtain, and spreads them like a tent to dwell in;" (ESV)

Isaiah 42:5 "Thus says God, the LORD, who created the heavens and **stretched** them out, who spread out the earth and what comes from it, who gives breath to the people on it and spirit to those who walk in it:" (ESV)

Jeremiah 10:12 "It is he who made the earth by his power, who established the world by his wisdom, and by his understanding **stretched** out the heavens." (ESV)

Zechariah 12:1 "The oracle of the word of the LORD concerning Israel: Thus declares the LORD, who **stretched** out the heavens and founded the earth and formed the spirit of man within him:" (ESV)

Some people, including me, interpret this as saying the universe has been expanding from an original point of creation, and is still expanding. It seems to make sense, but I will be the first to admit it is an interpretation. I also admit there are a lot of problems with the Big Bang Theory, but they are scientific problems, not Biblical. Most of the problems with the Big Bang Theory are based on what astronomers and astrophysicists are discovering with further scientific observations and studies. The Restoration Theory doesn't say if the universe began with a Big Bang or not. Whether or not there was a Big Bang is something only science can discover. The Bible does not reveal the mechanics of how God created the universe in Genesis 1:1. A Big Bang, followed by a formation of the universe over billions of years could have been exactly how God created the heavens and earth in the beginning. Such an event would explain why God uses *BARA* (create) and *ASAH* (make) and *YATSAR* (form) to describe the creation in various passages of the Bible. However, the Big Bang was not how He restored the earth and not how He created the life now on it. The details of the Big Bang can be learned only by continued scientific studies, not by theological arguments.

Well, let me qualify what I just said. The details of the Big Bang are not found in the Bible. But, the big picture of the Big Bang seems to have been revealed in the Bible thousands of years ago. Let's compare the details of the Big Bang as revealed by science, with the details of creation as revealed by the Bible. Let's see if God's Word matches His work. First, the science.

In January 1994, an article about the Big Bang was published in *National Geographic Magazine*. It was entitled, *A Short History of the Universe*,[99] and it was written by William R. Newcott. It was an excellent article describing what science knows (and doesn't know) about the beginning of the universe. He described how at the beginning, time did not exist; neither did space, nor matter, nor energy. Somehow the universe exploded into existence. It began as a Singularity, which is a dimensionless point in which time, space, matter, and energy are all one undifferentiated singular thing. And even though it happened billions of years ago, scientists were still able to determine what happened during the first 0.00001 second.

The first event that followed the beginning was the formation of the Gravitational Force. It came into existence at Planck Time 1. (Planck Time is the smallest possible quantum of time. It has a duration of 1×10^{-43} seconds. That's a decimal point followed by 42 zeros, and then a 1.) Gravity was the first Fundamental Physical Force to exist, and even though matter had not yet come into existence, the force that would hold matter together came into being.

The next event was the separation of the Strong Nuclear Force from the Singularity at Time 10^{-36} seconds. The Strong Nuclear Force is the force that holds the protons and neutrons together inside the nuclei of the atoms. There were no atoms at that time, nor could there be if the Strong Nuclear Force hadn't first come into being.

Now, I want you to think about that for a little longer than a Planck Unit of time. If matter came into existence before these first two forces came into existence, the universe would have instantaneously expanded to an infinite size and there would be no atoms, no stars, no planets, no life. We wouldn't be here.

The separation of the Force of Gravity and the Strong Nuclear Force from the Singularity triggered another event necessary for the existence of the universe: Space came into existence. Space started as a dimensionless point and expanded to billions of light years in size. This was called the Inflation Period, and it was finished by Time 10^{-32} seconds. Again, we discover a necessary event happened at just the right time. If matter came into existence before there was space to expand into, the "universe" would have instantly collapsed back onto itself, and nothing would exist.

There was another reason space had to expand so quickly. During the Inflation Period, matter began to come into existence, but it wasn't matter as we think of it. It had no substance. It "existed" only as Quarks, Antiquarks, and the other fundamental particles. The Quarks and Antiquarks annihilated each other on contact, releasing tremendous amounts of energy. For some unknown reason there were more Quarks than Antiquarks. This "excess" of Quarks would later combine into particles of substantive matter. This could not have happened at the extremely high temperature the universe was experiencing at that time. It had to cool first, and the only way it could cool is if its energy could spread out. The heat had to have some place to go, or matter could not come into being. It was the rapid Inflation that allowed the universe to cool enough for substantive matter to come into being. With the Inflation Period coming to an end, the Quarks were cooled enough to combine into triplets and form substantive matter: protons and neutrons. (Quarks cannot exist as singular entities, but must combine with each other to obtain substance.) By Time 10^{-5} seconds, the universe had cooled to one trillion° Kelvin (1,800,000,000,000° Fahrenheit) and protons and neutrons formed. In short, the Big Bang was the process of nothingness becoming everythingness.

What does this have to do with the Bible? If you remember, way back in Chapter One, I mentioned Jewish philosopher and theologian Nahmanides. (A.D. 1194-1270) He, being Jewish, defended the Bible's teaching how the universe (time, space, matter, and energy) was created out of nothing, simply by the spoken Word of God. That meant space had a beginning. That meant time had a beginning. Now, this wasn't a new thought of Nahmanides; this was what the Bible had been teaching since the time of Moses. It was what the Jews historically believed. It was one of the teachings of the Bible that distinguished it from all the pagan cosmogonies. What exactly did the Bible reveal to those who, like Nahmanides, understood the ancient Hebrew language and the ancient Hebrew way of thinking? It revealed a lot more than we English readers can glean from the text. The following description of the creation comes from a book written by Dr. Gerald Schroeder in 1990. In his book, Dr. Schroeder presents what Nahmanides believed to be the correct Jewish interpretation of Genesis 1:1. Dr. Schroeder is a Jewish theologian, but he is also an Applied Physicist. He summarized Nahmanides *Commentary on the Torah*, concerning the creation. Here is what Nahmanides said:

From *Genesis and the Big Bang*[100]

"At the briefest instant following creation all the matter of the universe was concentrated in a very small space, no larger than a grain of mustard. The matter at this time was so thin, so intangible, that it did not have real substance. It did have, however, a potential to gain substance and form to become tangible matter. From the initial concentration of this intangible substance in its minute location, the substance expanded, expanding the universe as it did so. As the expansion progressed, a change in the substance occurred. This initially thin noncorporeal substance took on the tangible aspects of matter as we know it. From this initial act of creation, from this ethereally thin pseudosubstance, everything that has existed, or will ever exist, was, is, and will be formed."

Nahmanides spoke of what happened at the "briefest instant" of time following creation. Scientists today call that "briefest instant," Planck Time. It is the smallest possible unit of time. Nahmanides spoke about space expanding from a tiny point. Scientists today call that, "The Point Singularity." Nahmanides said the universe began stretching out after the creation. Scientists today speak of the Inflationary Period following the initial expansion. Nahmanides revealed how "matter" initially had no substance, but gained substance as the universe expanded. Scientists today know there was a period of time following the Big Bang when matter didn't exist as matter. It wasn't until the universe began expanding, that quarks were able to come into existence and form protons and neutrons. Before that, matter was a thin, noncorporeal pseudosubstance. As you can see, Nahmanides' account of creation parallels the modern science account. Where did he get his knowledge? The Bible! He knew the ancient Hebrew language. He understood the ancient Hebrew way of thinking, and most of all, he knew what the Bible revealed about the creation. According to Nahmanides, the Bible said Genesis 1:1 was a process over time. The universe started from nothing, and then became an infinitesimally small point which expanded over time. Stars, and galaxies, and planets, and the earth came after the initial creation. There was a gap of time between Genesis 1:1 and Genesis 1:2. According to Nahmanides, the historic Jewish view does not match the view of Young-Earth creationists. The earth didn't start out *TOHUW WA-BOHUW*, in darkness, and submerged under water.

It became that way sometime after the initial creation in Genesis 1:1 I'm sure someone will say Nahmanides was trying to make the Bible fit Darwin's Theory of Evolution.

How Long Was the Earth *TOHUW WA-BOHUW*

One of the Day-Age arguments against the Gap Theory is there is no geological evidence the earth has ever been *TOHUW WA-BOHUW* and *CHOSHEK* for millions of years. Day-Agers argue there is no Biblical evidence that God judged the earth for millions of years. Therefore, the Gap Theory's belief the earth was desolate and dead and dark for millions of years is wrong.

What is my response to this argument? I agree with it! There is no geological evidence the earth has ever been *TOHUW WA-BOHUW* and *CHOSHEK* for millions of years. There is no Biblical evidence that God judged the earth for millions of years. Although I agree with their argument, I disagree with their conclusion. The Gap Theory doesn't say the earth was desolate and dead and dark for millions of years. This is a classic Straw-Man argument. They make a claim similar to what the Gap Theory says. Then, they knock down the Straw-Man, making it look like they win the argument. But, who said the *TOHUW WA-BOHUW* and *CHOSHEK* period had to be millions of years long? Why would God need millions of years to destroy life on earth? He created it in three days. (Day Three—plants; Day Five—birds and fish; Day Six—land animals and man) Why couldn't He destroy it in three days? Their argument doesn't prove anything because it presupposes the desolate, dead, and dark period was millions of years long. If the desolate, dead, and dark period was short, just a few days for example, then their argument fails. So, how long was the earth desolate, dead, and dark?

If the gap between Genesis 1:1 and Genesis 1:3 was billions of years, as I believe it was, did the earth have to be *TOHUW WA-BOHUW* and *CHOSHEK* for billions of years? No. The Bible doesn't say this, and there is nothing in the geological record indicating the earth lay desolate, dead, and dark for millions or billions of years. I would be foolish to let my Biblical theory go unfiltered by scientific fact. Does the Bible tell us how long this dead and desolate period was? No, but I think it might give us a clue. Let's see what the Bible does (and doesn't) tell us about this.

The Bible doesn't tell us how long Lucifer and his fallen angels lived on the earth BEFORE they rebelled against God. The Bible doesn't tell us how long Lucifer and his fallen angels lived on the earth AFTER they rebelled against God. The Bible tells us Lucifer rebelled and was judged, but it doesn't tell us when it was. The Bible tells us he was judged and condemned, but it also tells us his condemnation hasn't been fully imposed yet. (To this day he rules the earth, roams the earth, and has access to heaven from time to time.) With such little information, we can only speculate on the age of the earth and the length of time it was desolate, dead, and dark. We need more information. Now, there is one very important thing the Bible tells us about God that might be a factor in how old the universe is: God has a Plan for His universe.

It shouldn't be hard to believe God allowed Lucifer to remain on the earth for a very long time. (Or, was it that God ordained Lucifer to remain on the earth for a very long time? There really is no difference from God's perspective. Maybe in heaven there will be a word defining how God simultaneously ordained/allowed the things He simultaneously caused/experienced in space-time.) Yes, Lucifer rebelled. Yes, Lucifer was judged. Yes, Lucifer was stripped of his authority. But, that wouldn't necessitate his immediate removal from the earth. God's Plan was for him to remain on the earth in his fallen state, awaiting the fulfillment of his future and final judgment. After all, this is what happened to man. Adam rebelled. Adam was judged. Adam was stripped of his authority. Yet, man remains on the earth awaiting his future and final judgment. This is all part of God's Plan. Since fallen man has been alive and active in the Post-Adamic earth for thousands of years, would it be impossible for Lucifer to remain and be active in the Pre-Adamic earth for millions of years? No. I don't think it would be impossible at all. God is a God of patience, and He works His Plan according to His own desire. Since I don't know God's Plan, I dare not say Lucifer couldn't have lived on the earth for a long time. Lucifer and his fallen angels may have lived on the earth for millions of years bringing corruption, death, disease, and violence until God finally stepped in and destroyed their world. I think God destroyed Lucifer's world with a Pre-Adamic Flood and with a darkness and cold so intense the entire surface of the dry land was covered in ice and snow. Such destruction did not need to be millions of years long to kill all life; a few days would suffice.

    I suspect there were many millions of years of life and death (the source of the fossils) on earth before it was finally made *TOHUW WA-BOHUW*. The geologic history of the earth, with all its strata, geologic periods, and its variety of life, including dinosaurs, probably took place over that period of time. The Bible does not reveal how long life existed on the earth before Adam. Nor does the Bible reveal how long the *TOHUW WA-BOHUW* and *CHOSHEK* period was. It doesn't tell us directly, but I think we can estimate its length if we combine some science with some Bible. Let's look at the word "deep" (*TEHOM*—Strong's Number H8415) in Genesis 1:2.

Genesis 1:2 "And the earth was without form, and void; and darkness *was* upon the face of the **deep**. And the Spirit of God moved upon the face of the waters." (KJV)

    If you recall the twenty-seven correct translations of Genesis 1:2 I listed back in Chapter Six, you will remember that some translated *TEHOM* as, "the abyss." What is "the abyss?" The English word "abyss" is derived from *ABYSSUS*, which is the Latin form of the Greek *ABYSSOS*. *ABYSSOS* means, "no bottom." In some pagan cosmologies, they believed the ocean had no bottom. The Bible, on the other hand, spoke of features on the bottom of the ocean… features no human eye ever observed until the 20th century. It spoke of canyons or valleys on the ocean floor. It spoke of springs of water coming up from the ocean floor. It spoke of underwater mountains rising up from the ocean floor.

2 Samuel 22:16 "The valleys of the sea were exposed and the foundations of the earth laid bare at the rebuke of the LORD, at the blast of breath from his nostrils." (NIV)

Job 38:16 "Have you journeyed to the springs of the sea or walked in the recesses of the deep?" (NIV)

Jonah 2:5-6 "The waters compassed me about, *even* to the soul: the depth closed me round about, the weeds were wrapped about my head. *{6}* I went down to the bottoms of the mountains; the earth with her bars *was* about me for ever: yet hast thou brought up my life from corruption, O LORD my God." (KJV)

    Thousands of years before man could possibly have known the truth, the Bible revealed the truth about the ocean floor. When the Bible reveals scientific truth, it is true, even if man can't confirm it… even if man denies it. The Bible revealed truth about the ocean floor. Those revelations are true. The Bible revealed truth about the origin of the universe and the origin of life. Those revelations are true too.
    To the Greeks, Romans, and especially the Hebrews, the abyss conjured up more than just thoughts of something deep. It conjured up all kinds of terror, horror, and evil. Even today, our English word "abysmal" means dreadful, terrible, horrible, frightful, and appalling. If the Greeks and the Romans thought of the abyss with such evil connotations, the ancient Hebrews, who were not a seafaring people like the Greeks and Romans, had even worse thoughts about the abyss. The Hebrews did not think of the ocean as bright blue waters with sunny beaches and warm breezes. The abyss was full of sea monsters… real or imagined. They didn't think of the abyss as a peaceful place with the somnolent sounds of waves and seagulls crying overhead. With its storms, waves, and craggy rocks, certain death awaited anyone who sailed on it. The Hebrews did not think of *TEHOM* as a peaceful, placid body of water. The *TEHOM* was full of fury. It roared. It was tumultuous. It was dangerous.
    With this in mind, we realize *TEHOM* in Genesis 1:2 did not describe a calm, quiet, peaceful ocean to the ancient Hebrews. It was roaring and raging. That's what the ancient Hebrews would have pictured in their minds as they read the second sentence in Genesis. To them, Genesis 1:2 described a violent, turbulent ocean. This gives us a scientific clue as to how long the earth was *TOHUW WA-BOHUW* and *CHOSHEK*; desolate, dead, and dark.
    I think the earth became *TOHUW WA-BOHUW* and *CHOSHEK* very quickly. As soon as God stopped the light, the earth began to freeze. It happened fast, but I don't think it lasted long. More than likely the earth was *TOHUW WA-BOHUW* and *CHOSHEK* for a very short period of time. Various translations of Genesis 1:2 seem to indicate the *TEHOM*, the abyss, was raging or roaring. If this was so, then it was still liquid. If the earth had been without the heat and light of the sun for very long, the surface of the deep would freeze. It wouldn't be raging and roaring. I don't know how long it would take for the surface of the

ocean to freeze if all heat and light from the sun were removed. I'm sure an oceanographer could give us a definite answer to that question, but I don't think it would take many days. I believe the surface of the deep didn't freeze because it didn't stay dark and cold long enough. This was not an ice-age. I believe these were ice-days. It lasted just long enough to cover the dry land with ice and snow, but not long enough for the surface of the deep to freeze. I believe it was long enough to destroy all life, but not long enough to change the geologic features of the earth. I believe the *TOHUW WA-BOHUW* and *CHOSHEK* period was so short, and the Restoration so very good, it did not leave a geologic footprint. Personally, I think God judged the earth and let it lay dead for three days and three nights, and then He began restoring it on a Sunday morning, the first day of the week. Such a scenario would have tremendous parallels with the restorative work of Christ's death, burial, and resurrection.

Pre-Adamic "Men"

It's virtually impossible to discuss life's origin without the subject of "ape-men" popping up. Paleontologists have discovered fossils of ancient creatures that seem to be neither human nor ape. Evolutionists assume they're evolutionary links between apes and man. Young-Earth and Day-Age creationists disagree. So do Restored-Earth creationists. (If they were Pre-Adamic, then they can't be man's ancestors because everything died when God judged the earth.) So, what or who were these "ape-like/man-like" creatures? I see only four possibilities.

1.) The first is they were descendants of Adam, and not Pre-Adamic. This requires you to reject many dating techniques and their basic assumptions. Some people believe, in spite of the morphological differences in their skeletons, these creatures were truly human. Such bone deformities might be due to trauma, malnutrition, disease, arthritis, the environment, selective inbreeding, and a number of other factors. This has been the favorite answer among many creationists; especially in the case of Neanderthal man. Many creationists believe Neanderthal men were truly human because of their use of tools and their custom of burying their dead. Many say if you gave a Neanderthal man a bath, a haircut and shave, and dressed him in a nice business suit, he would blend in if he walked across a typical college campus. That is ridiculous! Anyone bathed, shaved, well-groomed, and in a nice business suit wouldn't blend in on a typical college campus. Some evolutionists said Neanderthal man wasn't human. Then some evolutionists said he was. Then some evolutionists said he wasn't. Then some evolutionists said he was. Then some evolutionists said… Well, I shouldn't criticize evolutionists on this because some creationists have been just as ambivalent. I've been there myself. Recent DNA studies have shown Neanderthal man didn't have human DNA.[101][102] Neanderthal man doesn't appear to have been human. Now, that doesn't automatically make him a link between ape and man, as evolutionists suggest, but it does mean he was not a descendant of Adam.

2.) These "ape-men" could have been nothing more than unknown species of apes. There is a great deal of truth in this theory. Virtually all of the "ape-men" of the past have since been proved to be nothing more than apes, or even less. It's easy to place *Australopithecus* and others in this group, but Neanderthal man poses a problem. If he was an ape, then he was a very sophisticated ape. The tools he made included knives, scrapers, chisels, and cleavers. He made clothing from animal skins and constructed tent-like shelters. He even made calendars by notching grooves into bones so he could keep track of lunar cycles. There is at least one case where a Neanderthal amputated a diseased arm from one of his fellow Neanderthals. I find it difficult to believe Neanderthal was an ordinary hairy ape.

3.) These "ape-men" could have been a variety of man-like animals created by God. God created them; they lived; then they died. Even though they may have had physical characteristics similar to apes and men, they were no relation to either. Neanderthal seems to fit this category best. They were simply highly intelligent creatures God placed on this earth, but subsequently became extinct. Of course, some people think they may not be extinct. You only need to mention the words "Sasquatch" and "Yeti" and hundreds of Bigfoot Believers will inundate you with tons of evidence for the present-day existence of these creatures.

4.) My belief (speculation) is these were Pre-Adamic humans, or at least something very close to humans, whom God once created. They could have been the ones who planted the gardens and fruitful places, and built the cities mentioned in Jeremiah 4:23-26. The Bible gives no description of the creatures who built and lived in those Pre-Adamic cities. It's possible they were human in virtually every way, but lacked the character of being made in God's image. In that aspect, they could have been very much like us physically and mentally, but without the capacity to know moral good and evil. Without a concept of good and evil, these "men" could not have sinned. (Which means the Pre-Adamic judgment of the earth was due to Lucifer's sins.) Without a concept of moral good and evil, these Pre-Adamites would have been helpless against Lucifer's evil. The new man, Adam and Eve, would need to know about good and evil from God's perspective. I think God planted the Tree of the Knowledge of Good and Evil in the Garden as a way of teaching Adam and Eve His perspective of good and evil.

Pre-Adamic Evil and Death

I think Lucifer was given dominion over the earth, including dominion over these creatures for the purpose of glorifying God. I believe Lucifer started out obedient, but eventually his beauty and splendor, and his superiority over these creatures, led to his downfall. In his pride, he wanted these creatures to worship and serve him rather than God. I believe Lucifer wanted to be the ruler of this world. If such Pre-Adamic "people" existed, they may have become the unfortunate victims of Lucifer's attempts to rule the earth in

God's place. If he was unsuccessful in complete domination of them, and if they resisted him, he may have waged war against them, enslaved them, imprisoned them, and murdered them. This could explain the comment in Isaiah 14:17 that Lucifer, "opened not the house of his prisoners." Jesus could have been alluding to this when He said Lucifer was, "a murderer from the beginning." The imprisonment, enslavement, and murder of these innocent "people" could have been the final sin that caused God to destroy Satan's kingdom.

If these "men" were murdered by Lucifer, I think God was justified in re-creating man to bring judgment upon Lucifer. If Lucifer murdered "men," it was only right that men would be his judge. God was going to let man judge the angels. Unlike the "old man," however, the "new man" would be able to understand moral good and evil, so he could rightly judge Lucifer. The new man had to have the capacity to understand good and evil. Otherwise, man's judgment of Satan might be revenge instead of justice.

Now, I don't think Adam and Eve started out with a full understanding of the knowledge of good and evil, but I think they had the capacity to learn it. They were much like toddlers who don't fully understand right and wrong, but have the capacity to learn it as they grow. Don't misunderstand me. Both Adam and Eve were extremely intelligent; far more intelligent than we are. They were not childlike in any other aspect of their personalities. They just didn't start with a full understanding of the knowledge of good and evil.

Why didn't God create them with a full understanding of the knowledge of good and evil? He could have, but if He had, it might have created an epistemological problem with believing the knowledge, facts, and beliefs He automatically placed in them. God knew what good and evil were even before there was evil. But, how would Adam and Eve really know if those things were true, or merely something God made them think was true? I suspect the angels faced this same question. They were created with the knowledge God placed into them. They didn't have to learn it. But, how could they know if it was true or not? It would depend on whether or not God could lie. If God could not lie, then what He placed into their minds would be true. If He could lie, then they wouldn't know for certain if what they believed was really true. They wouldn't know if their created-knowledge of good and evil was true, unless they first knew it was true. Even if God gave them the knowledge that He cannot lie, how would they know even that was true until they could figure out it was true? They would have to know the truth before they knew the truth. I think the reason God didn't automatically create the knowledge of good and evil in Adam and Eve was so they would learn the truth for themselves, and in the process, learn WHY it was true.

Rather than create them with the knowledge of good and evil, God was going to teach them the knowledge of good and evil. To do that, He had to give them two things. 1.) He had to create them in His image and likeness so they would have true volition. Without true volition, they could make no true decisions concerning right and wrong. God didn't want creatures with a set of conditioned responses. He wanted them to be able to make true choices. 2.) God had to give them language (words/ideas) they could understand, as He taught them the truth about the knowledge of good and evil. This second point is very important because if they could not understand what God was telling them, they could not learn what God was teaching them. (This still applies to God's Word today.) They had to understand the meanings of God's words, or else God was embarking on a futile endeavor. (Try giving commands in Cantonese to a classroom of six-year-olds who speak only English.) Adam and Eve had to understand the words God used in His command to them. Otherwise, how could they obey His command? This is why Satan's attack on Eve came in the form of distorting the meaning of God's command. I'll expand on the implications of this in a moment.

I think God intended for Adam and Eve to learn WHY He is good; not just THAT He is good. Here is a funny thing about humans: Knowing THAT something is right or wrong is never as powerful as knowing WHY it is right or wrong. Knowing the WHY, in addition to knowing the WHAT, has a far greater impact on our beliefs, motives, and actions. God wanted them to learn about good and evil from His perspective rather than from Satan's. That was the only way they would come to believe the truth, and know why it was true. So, while they did not start with that much understanding of God, I believe they were created with enough understanding of God to know He should be obeyed. They knew they should try to please God, even if they didn't fully know why. (Toddlers try to please their parents even if they don't fully understand why they should try to please them.) Although they didn't start out with a full understanding of the knowledge of good and evil, I think Adam and Eve eventually would have learned it from God if Satan had not meddled in their lives. If they had waited and learned it from God's words rather than from Satan's words, they would have had an undistorted understanding of right and wrong. If they had undistorted knowledge, they would have known WHY they should love good and WHY they should hate evil. They would share God's perspective of good and evil, not just His knowledge of good and evil. You can see how deceptive Satan was when he told Eve they could possess God's knowledge of good from evil if they ate the fruit. It was a lie with a sliver of truth. They would share God's knowledge of good and evil, but they wouldn't share His perspective of good and evil. If they had learned that, they would have never been tempted to do evil. If they had waited and attained the knowledge of good and evil God wanted them to have, they would have been in the position to declare Lucifer guilty of cosmic treason, and condemn him to eternal death in the Lake of Fire prepared for him… and, it would have been a just condemnation.

I believe God created man to judge Lucifer and the fallen angels. If Adam and Eve remained obedient, they would eventually be able to do that. I think this was why God put the Tree of the Knowledge of Good and Evil in the Garden. The Tree was the test of their obedience, and the testimony to Lucifer that Adam and Eve would do what he and his fallen angels wouldn't do. The Tree was both the Test and the Testimony. Every day Adam and Eve didn't eat its fruit, they were giving testimony that they desired to obey God. Even if they didn't (yet) fully understand good and evil, or why God commanded them not to eat it, their obedience condemned Lucifer. (After all, if a six-year-old knows you are supposed to stop at a red light, how can a sixty-year-old claim innocence when he runs a red light?) By planting the Tree of the Knowledge of Good and Evil in the midst of the Garden, God made it plain that the Tree was the object lesson around which His teachings of good and evil would be based. God was going to use the Tree, and their obedience, as a way of teaching Adam and Eve the truth about good and evil. Every day of not eating from the Tree was a day of positive reinforcement. (Educators and learning experts will tell you positive reinforcement is a much stronger means of learning than negative reinforcement.) Every day they didn't eat of the Tree they were blessed with the privilege of eating from all the other trees, of living in the perfect environment of that beautiful Garden, and with the glorious presence of God. Their faith in God was being strengthened every day by their obedience to God. (The same is true for us today if we would do it.) This daily positive reinforcement was moving them from the point of having little understanding of the knowledge of good and evil, to the point of having God's understanding of the knowledge of good and evil.

Naturally, Satan didn't want them to learn the knowledge of good and evil from God. He didn't want them to know the truth about good and evil. He knew he had to do something to corrupt their understanding. Corrupting man's knowledge of good and evil was his only way of escaping the Lake of Fire. Corrupting his judges' judgment, would have made their judgment invalid. It all centered around the Tree; therefore, Lucifer had to find some way to distort their understanding of the Tree. In order to distort their understanding of the Tree, he had to distort what God was teaching them about the Tree. Satan had to twist, distort, and alter God's words, and lie about God's intentions. He had to get them to accept his teachings about good and evil instead of God's teachings about good and evil. To do this, subtlety was a necessity.

Let me go back and explain the implications of Adam and Eve needing to understand God's words. Adam and Eve were meant to obey God's command concerning the fruit of the Tree of the Knowledge of Good and Evil. This meant they had to understand the words/ideas God used concerning the Tree. If God gave them words/ideas they couldn't understand, they would not know what to do and what not to do concerning the fruit. He used the word "eat" to define WHAT they were not to do with that fruit. (Of course, it wasn't the English word "eat;" it was the word "eat" in whatever language He created in them.) If they didn't understand what "eat" meant, they wouldn't have understood God's command. If they didn't understand God's command, then they couldn't have exercised true volition concerning the fruit of the Tree. Now, I'm sure no one believes they didn't know what "eat" meant. However, there were two other words/ideas God used in His command to them. They had to understand the meanings of those two other words/ideas, or else they wouldn't fully understand His command. Those words/ideas were: "EVIL" (The Tree of the Knowledge of Good and EVIL) and "DIE" (You will surely DIE). If they didn't know what evil meant and they didn't know what dying meant, they could not have understood His command. Think about it. If they had no concept of what evil meant, why warn them about evil? If they had no concept of what dying meant, why warn them about dying? To me, this implies they understood what evil and death were. But, how could they understand the concepts of evil and death if evil and death had never existed?

Young-Earth creationists say there had never been any death in the universe until after Adam sinned. If what they say is true, then it would have been impossible for Adam and Eve to know what death truly meant. How do you explain the color blue to a person born blind? How do you explain the taste of chocolate to someone who has never tasted chocolate, or at least something similar to chocolate? You truly won't know what blue is, until you see it. You truly won't know what chocolate tastes like, until you taste it. If they didn't know what death meant, how could they exercise true volition concerning God's command? Death would be a meaningless concept if Adam and Eve had never observed death. (Of course, God could have created them with that knowledge intact, but again they wouldn't have known it was true unless they first knew the truth. Created-knowledge bypasses the volition; therefore, it would have had no bearing on their obedience, and no part in rightly confirming the guilt of Lucifer in his disobedience.) The only way to know what death meant, would be for Adam and Eve to have observed death. Death had to exist in the universe, or else God was foolish for giving them a command they couldn't understand, with consequences they couldn't understand. I think Adam and Eve knew what death was because they had seen it. The Bible doesn't say there was no plant and animal death before Adam sinned. I believe they witnessed the births, the lives, and the deaths of many animals around them. I think they knew what death meant. I think they knew what evil meant. I think God had taught them about Lucifer and the civilization that existed in the Pre-Adamic world. (God may even have shown them some of the remnants of the previous civilization outside of the Garden: Destroyed cities, fruitful places laid bare, scattered hominid bones, fossils—the things archaeologists and paleontologists dig up even to this day.) I think they knew Lucifer was evil, and I think they understood the Garden had to be protected from Lucifer. Why would Lucifer come disguised as a serpent if they didn't know Lucifer was evil? He was a creature of surpassing beauty and splendor. There was nothing about his outward appearance that displayed evil. Why hide himself from them if they knew nothing about evil? I think Adam and Eve knew Satan had murdered the Pre-Adamites. They knew what evil was, and they knew what death was. I think they had seen the results of both.

Speaking of Pre-Adamic "men," there is a raging debate of whether or not Neanderthals interbred with humans. Some scientists say they did; some scientists say they didn't. The controversy centers on how you interpret DNA similarities between humans and Neanderthals. Yes, there are some Neanderthal gene sequences similar to the ones in humans. By using statistical analysis on the PRESUPPOSED rates of mutations and genetic drift, some scientists claim to be able to pinpoint when we crossbred with Neanderthals. Supposedly, it was hundreds of thousands of years ago. Lest you get too excited (if you're an evolutionist) or too depressed (if you're a creationist) about this idea, let me explain how this has no bearing on the Ruin-Restoration Theory. On one hand, if the Neanderthals were Pre-Adamic and got wiped out by Lucifer, it doesn't mean God couldn't have recreated Neanderthals just as He recreated other Pre-Adamic creatures. There could have been restored Neanderthals in the restored earth. They even could have been on Noah's Ark. If Neanderthals were capable of interbreeding with humans, it could have happened after the Flood. If that was the case, there is the possibility some Neanderthal gene sequences became incorporated into the human gene pool. Although possible, I reject this idea. I believe God merely re-created some of the same gene sequences in humans He previously created in Neanderthals. He has every right to recreate identical gene sequences that perform identical functions in different species. Such genetic similarities are not proof for evolution. **DNA similarities don't prove physical relationship if the similarities are the result of re-creation rather than procreation.**

Whatever was going on in the Pre-Adamic world, we must include Lucifer. If these creatures were Pre-Adamic, they came under the domination of Lucifer. In his desire to have servants and slaves to worship him, it's possible he engaged in selective breeding and genetic alteration programs in order to develop creatures suited to his desires. He may have taken whatever kinds of apes, hominids, or "men" God created and manipulated them for his own purpose. It's not as impossible as it seems. Look at the variety of dog breeds we have "created" during our short history. They range from tiny things scarcely weighing three pounds, on up to huge two-hundred-pound giants. Dogs have a tremendous variety of bones sizes and conformations. Some of their skulls are long and narrow; others are flat in the front and wide. Some have large cranial cavities and others have small ones. Some have very thick pelvises with flattened hip joints while others have nicely rounded ball-and-socket joints. This is what enables some to walk and run better than others. Greyhounds have long, thin, graceful hips and limbs, while Bassets waddle along on short, stubby, "twisted" appendages. They are all dogs, and all of their physical characteristics have been developed by selectively breeding according to our desires.

The variety of physical features seen in the hominid fossils could be explained in a similar fashion. It doesn't seem impossible to think Lucifer may have monkeyed around with the most intelligent creatures God created in the Pre-Adamic world. God may have given these creatures enough intelligence and skill to make and use tools, plant gardens, build cities, and develop a social order. (Even ants have a social order.) Lucifer may have taken advantage of their intelligence and abilities by teaching them (or forcing them) to do the things he wanted them to do, such as build cities where he could be served and worshipped. Is that farfetched? Well, we've taught gorillas to speak sign language. We've taught dogs to guide the blind and to sniff out drugs and bombs. It doesn't take much imagination to believe Satan may have spent millennia experimenting with these creatures until he developed some with hips, knees, pelvises, backs, and hands more suitable to serve him. Could Donald Johanson's "Lucy" (A 3.5 million-year-old *Australopithecus afarensis* skeleton found in Ethiopia in 1974) have been some poor, tortured creature Lucifer bred into existence? What a tremendous discovery Johanson made if such is the case. If this is so, then paleontologists are digging up things far more spectacular than even they realize. I think they are unearthing proof the Bible is historically accurate when it hints of intelligent life before Adam. (Cities that were destroyed and cultivated land that was laid waste.) What a testimony to the truth of the Bible if those fossils are the remains of intelligent Pre-Adamic life. Let's praise the paleontologists for their discoveries, not condemn them.

Chapter Twelve: The Meaning of *HAYAH*

The evidence from qualified Hebrew scholars is that *HAYAH* could be translated, "became" or "had become," in Genesis 1:2. I believe *HAYAH* should be, not just could be, translated that way. If we are seeking an informationally correct translation rather than merely a grammatically correct translation, then we must be willing to look afresh at God's choice of this word/idea in this passage. WE MUST NOT LET OUR PRECONCEIVED IDEAS OVERSHADOW WHAT GOD REVEALS. What information has God communicated to us? Genesis was written in ancient Hebrew, to ancient Hebrews, for ancient Hebrews, by an ancient Hebrew. It seems to me the only way to understand this Divine communiqué is by fully appreciating the mindset of the ancient Hebrews. I'm not sure that is possible. However, the more we think like ancient Hebrews, the better we will be able to translate Genesis 1:2 informationally. This task goes far beyond finding seven verses where *HAYAH* is used one way, thirteen verses where it is used another way, and another sixteen verses where it is used in a third way. We need to dig much deeper. We need to understand what thought process went through the minds of the ancient Hebrews when *HAYAH* was employed. What did the word mean to them? Look again at what *Strong's Dictionary of the Hebrew Language*[103] said about *HAYAH*.

> "H1961. *hayah*, haw-yaw'; a prim. root; to exist, *i.e.* be or become, come to pass (always emphatic, and not a mere copula or auxiliary)…"

James Strong said *HAYAH* is not a mere copula. This is important. A copula is a word, usually a verb, that connects or links a subject to a predicate. I gave the example of how in the Hebrew thought process I would say, "Linda Dill my wife," rather than, "Linda Dill is my wife." This may sound strange to us modern English speakers, but ancient Hebrew people didn't think like we think. They didn't think in terms of *HAYAH* being a mere connecting word. This means we should be cautious in translating *HAYAH* in the sense of a mere connecting word. Remember what Martin Anstey expressed in *The Romance of Bible Chronology*.[104]

> **"When a Hebrew writer makes a simple affirmation, or merely predicates the existence of anything, the verb *hayah* is never expressed. Where it is expressed it must always be translated by our verb to become, never by the verb to be, if we desire to convey the exact shade of the meaning of the original."**

I want to point out something about the English word "was." "Was" has numerous meanings. Look it up in a dictionary and you can easily find several definitions. Even if I translated Genesis 1:2 as, "and the earth WAS without form, and void," it could still describe a dynamic condition. Examine this sentence: "I broke my wife's favorite flower vase, and she was mad." What does "was" mean in this sentence? It obviously means she got mad. She became angry. She wasn't in a constant, unchanging state of anger. Because I broke her favorite vase, she changed from a condition of not being mad, to a condition of being mad. We understand the meaning of "was" because we understand the context of the sentence. We understand the true meaning of my sentence because we automatically determine the exact shade of meaning of "was." You would get the wrong idea about my wife if you failed to understand the various meanings of "was." If you translated my sentence into another language, you could produce a grammatically correct translation that failed to convey the informational truth. If you didn't understand the many nuances of "was" in English, you could make people think she was always mad. The only way to translate my sentence correctly is if you understood the English-speaking mind. If you didn't think like an English speaker, you wouldn't necessarily be able to translate it in a way that captured the correct information. The same is true of ancient Hebrew. We can't fully understand ancient Hebrew if we don't fully understand the ancient Hebrew mind. So, let's delve into the ancient Hebrew mind. I think this comment from *The Complete Word Study Old Testament, King James Version*[105] will help clarify the ancient Hebrew thinking process concerning the idea of being or existence when the verb *HAYAH* was used.

> "1961. *Hāyāh*; probably related to *hāwāh* (1933), 'to breathe.' This verb means to exist, to be, to become, to come to pass, to be done, to happen, to be finished. It is notable that **this verb was not used in a copulative construction in Hebrew**. Bowman (*sic*) maintains that the Hebrews thought only in dynamic categories, not static ones."

THIS WORD WAS NOT USED AS A MERE CONNECTING WORD. That means the "was" in, "the earth was without form, and void," was not used to connect a static description of the earth to its creation. The *HAYAH* in Genesis 1:2 was used to connect the earth's dynamic/changed condition to its creation. Anti-Gap Theory creationists say it describes a static relation, but that is not what it would mean to an ancient Hebrew. To an ancient Hebrew it meant the earth in Genesis 1:2 was different than the earth in Genesis 1:1. According to Hebrew and Greek scholar Thorleif Boman, (1894-1978) *HAYAH* expressed a dynamic existence (coming to be), not a static existence (being). What does it mean they thought only in dynamic categories, not static ones? It means they used *HAYAH* when they wanted to express the idea of dynamic existence. Generally, they didn't use it when the thought of static existence was to be expressed. Let me show how English thought differs from Hebrew thought. Consider these two statements:

1.) I am Steven Dill.
2.) I am president of the Jefferson County Veterinary Medical Association.

Does the "am" in statement one mean the exact same thing as the "am" in statement two? No. The first "am" conveys an idea of static existence. The second "am" conveys an idea of dynamic experience. I haven't always been the president of my local veterinary medical association. I am not its president now. (When I first wrote this, I was its president.) President or not, I remain Steven Dill. These represent two different categories of "being;" two different kinds of "am." In the minds of the ancient Hebrews, the concept of me "being" president of my local association would be expressed using *HAYAH*. It's a dynamic condition. However, *HAYAH* would not be used for the idea of me "being" Steven Dill. That's a static condition. Hebrew distinguishes between these two ideas, as do other languages. Spanish for instance, uses two verbs for "to be." The first is *SER* and the second is *ESTAR*. In Spanish I would say, "*Soy un hombre.*" "I **am** a man." Being a man is a permanent characteristic of me. Therefore, *Soy* (first person, singular of the verb *SER*—"to be.") is the verb of choice. In contrast, I would say, "*Estoy infermo.*" "I **am** sick." Since my present condition of health is not so permanent, *Estoy* (first person, singular of the verb *ESTAR*—to be.") is the verb of choice. It is interesting to look at the Spanish translations of Genesis 1:2. They all use *estar* rather than *ser* to describe the earth's formless and void condition. The Spanish "*estar*" agrees with the Hebrew *HAYAH* more than the English "was." Spanish goes a step further by expressing some characteristics in terms of "having" rather than in terms of "being." In English, I would say, "I am hungry." In Spanish, I would say, "*Yo tengo hambre,*" which literally means, "I have hunger." I am not the same thing as hunger; hunger and I are not equivalent. Spanish does not express my experiential hunger as the equivalent to my existential being. In a similar fashion, *HAYAH* sometimes expresses the idea of "having" rather than the idea of "being" or "becoming." I'm sure many other languages make these same distinctions in various ways. In English, we use the same word for both the existential and the experiential concepts of "being." I am not a Hebrew scholar, (neither existentially nor experientially) but since Hebrew scholars have said it, I can say it too: Generally, *HAYAH* is used for dynamic categories or conditions, and not as a static linking word. What kinds of conditions were considered dynamic? The answer is simple. Any condition that is not static, any condition that has changed, is changing, or will change, was thought of as being dynamic.

HAYAH Used for Dynamic Conditions of Being

Geographical Location

Genesis 38:5 "And she yet again conceived, and bare a son; and called his name Shelah: and he **was** at Chezib, when she bare him." (KJV)

HAYAH is used here because this Canaanite woman (Shuah's daughter) was at Chezib when she gave birth to Shelah, Judah's son. A person's geographical location was not thought of as a permanent condition or state. It was dynamic because our locations change. The third *HAYAH* in Genesis 39:2 is another example of how location was thought of as a dynamic condition.

Genesis 39:2 "And the LORD was with Joseph, and he was a prosperous man; and he **was** in the house of his master the Egyptian." (KJV)

Joseph was in his master's house, but his location was not static. Again, location is dynamic. This is why *HAYAH* is used. If I wanted to tell you my current location in English, I would say, "I am upstairs." If I wanted to say it in Hebrew, I would use *HAYAH*. Without it, I could be misunderstood as saying I AM (I exist as) a hallway, three bedrooms, two bathrooms, and an office. *HAYAH* would indicate that upstairs is my dynamic experiential position and not my static existential being.

So, while a person's location was considered dynamic, the location of more permanent objects was expressed in a more permanent way.

Daniel 5:3 "Then they brought the golden vessels that were taken out of the temple of the house of God which *was* at Jerusalem; and the king, and his princes, his wives, and his concubines, drank in them." (KJV)

The "*was*" in this verse is in italics. No *HAYAH* is used in the Hebrew because this kind of location is thought of as a more permanent condition. The Temple of the House of God didn't move around. Its location didn't change. Therefore, no *HAYAH* was needed to express its location.

Now, if you recall from the end of Chapter Five, I mentioned how Moses described the locations of the rivers coming out of Eden and the lands they flowed into. (Genesis 2:11-14) When describing the locations of the rivers and the lands, he didn't use *HAYAH*. ("*IS*" is in italics.)

Genesis 2:11-14 "The name of the first *is* Pison: that *is* it which compasseth the whole land of Havilah, where *there is* gold; {12} And the gold of that land *is* good: there *is* bdellium and the onyx stone. {13} And the name of the second river *is* Gihon: the same *is* it that compasseth the whole land of Ethiopia. {14} And the name of the third river *is* Hiddekel: that *is* it which goeth toward the east of Assyria. And the fourth river *is* Euphrates." (KJV)

Notice the difference when expressing location. The Canaanite woman **was** at Chezib. Joseph **was** in his master's house. *HAYAH* is used because those kinds of locations change; they are dynamic. When describing the rivers that came out of Eden in relation to Havilah, Cush, and Assyria, their locations hadn't changed; they were static. *HAYAH* is not used. In addition, the conditions of the lands hadn't changed. *HAYAH* is not used for that either. Moses reveals the same rivers were in the same lands. The Flood did not change their locations. The Flood did not change their conditions. That's why he didn't use *HAYAH*. This means Noah's Flood was relatively tranquil; it didn't radically reshape the face of the earth as the Young-Earth/Flood-Geologists claim. The locations of the rivers and the lands hadn't changed. It seems strange that Young-Earth/Flood-Geologists insist Genesis 1:2 describes a formless and void earth that hadn't changed, even though *HAYAH* indicates it was dynamic. But, they say Genesis 2:11-14 describes a change in the lands and rivers around Eden, even though *HAYAH* is not used, indicating they were static. It seems to me, they have their Hebrew backwards.

Temporal Conditions

While we're looking at Genesis 39:2, note the first two *HAYAH*s. Having the Lord's presence was a dynamic condition. The ancient Hebrews considered the Lord's presence as an indicator of His blessing and approval. They didn't think of God's presence with them as an absolute permanent, static condition. God was always with them in one sense, He is omnipresent, but He wasn't "with" them when they were outside His will. God's presence in their lives was dynamic. The second *HAYAH* in Genesis 39:2 was also a dynamic condition. Joseph's condition of prosperity was not permanent either. He would soon be cast into prison.

Age

Genesis 17:1 "And when Abram **was** ninety years old and nine, the LORD appeared to Abram, and said unto him, I *am* the Almighty God; walk before me, and **be** thou perfect." (KJV)

Apparently, the ancient Hebrews viewed a person's age as a dynamic condition. I am 67, but my age is dynamic. Again, since I am a little more familiar with Spanish, I can understand why the Hebrews would think in this fashion. Spanish-speaking people don't express age the same way English-speaking people do. If I gave my age in Spanish, I would say, "*Tengo sesenta y siete años*;" which literally means, "I have sixty and seven years." To an ancient Hebrew, my age would be dynamic. I have become 67. I haven't always been 67, and Lord willing, I won't always be 67. We could translate Genesis 17:1 as, "And when Abram became ninety-nine years old..." (Note *HAYAH* is NOT used in, "I *am* the Almighty God;"—it is in italics. Whereas, it is used in, "be thou perfect." There is a distinction between God's being and our being that I'll explain shortly.)

Occupation or Activity

Age wasn't the only thing they viewed as dynamic. A person's occupation, job, or activity could also be considered dynamic. I am a veterinarian, but I haven't always been one. *HAYAH* would be used if I said, "I am a veterinarian." The tricky part in some of these conditions is trying to determine what it means to be something. There could be a difference in what is meant by saying I am a veterinarian. In one sense, I could say I will always be a veterinarian even if I retire and no longer actively practice veterinary medicine. Yet, in another sense, if I am not actually being a veterinarian, I am not a veterinarian. Here is an example:

Genesis 40:13 "Yet within three days shall Pharaoh lift up thine head, and restore thee unto thy place: and thou shalt deliver Pharaoh's cup into his hand, after the former manner when thou **wast** his butler." (KJV)

Being Pharaoh's butler wasn't a permanent state for this poor fellow. He had been Pharaoh's butler, but now found himself in jail along with Joseph and the Pharaoh's former baker. He was no longer Pharaoh's butler. His occupation was a dynamic condition. *HAYAH* is used to express this idea. Fortunately for him, being in jail was also a dynamic condition. He was going to become Pharaoh's butler once again. (Unfortunately for the baker, he was going to be executed.) This dynamic concept isn't too difficult for us to understand. He WAS a butler one day and he WAS not a butler the next. His condition changed. There are other examples that aren't as easily understood.

Some Physical Characteristics

Genesis 29:17 "Leah *was* tender eyed; but Rachel **was** beautiful and well favoured." (KJV)

Note the first "*was*" is italicized. There is no "was" here; *HAYAH* is not used. Some commentators describe Leah's condition as being one of poor eyesight. The ancient Hebrews apparently thought poor eyesight was a permanent condition. *HAYAH* wasn't required to describe it because it wasn't a changing quality. They might think differently today in our world of eyeglasses, contacts, and laser surgery.

Speculation Alert #1—I've always wondered if this wasn't an ancient Hebrew idiom somewhat akin to our English word "eyesore." When something is ugly or repulsive, we often say it is an, "eyesore." It doesn't literally make our eyes sore, but it does express the idea of being extremely ugly. I think "tender eyed" could be an ancient Hebrew way of saying Leah was so ugly it made your eyes tender just to look at her. This seems to make sense because the text immediately contrasts Rachel's beauty with Leah's condition. Being beautiful is not a contrast to poor eyesight. Why create a contrast in the text if no contrast was intended? It could be why poor old Papa Laban had been unable to marry off Leah before Rachel. It may also explain why Jacob wanted to marry Rachel so strongly, and why he was so upset when he discovered he had been tricked into marrying Leah instead. Still, this is only a guess, but if this was so, then the lack of the *HAYAH* seems to indicate Leah had always been ugly and it wasn't going to change. We mustn't feel too sorry for Leah, however. She gave birth to Judah. This means she was chosen by God to be the maternal ancestor of Jesus Christ; Rachel wasn't. A common theme in the Bible is: "Those whom men reject are often those whom God selects."

Speculation Alert #2—Some of the translations speak of Rachel's "form" and "face." There could be another thought. This verse could be telling us what Rachel grew to become.

Genesis 29:17 "And Leah's eyes were weak, but Rachel was beautiful of form and face." (NASB)

Genesis 29:17 "Leah had weak eyes, but Rachel was lovely in form, and beautiful." (NIV)

Genesis 29:17 "and the eyes of Leah *are* tender, and Rachel hath been fair of form and fair of appearance." (YLT)

The emphasis of the dynamic *HAYAH* could be what Rachel became as she grew to young womanhood. It seems to me, the reference to her form, without trying to be crude, refers to her bodily form, her figure. She had a great figure and she was beautiful. Little girls are cute, they may even be beautiful, but having a beautiful figure is something that comes to be.

In contrast to Leah's condition, whatever it was, Rachel was beautiful and well favored. Outward beauty is a fading quality. I'm sure the ancient Hebrews understood that. Our culture certainly believes it. We spend billions of dollars every year trying to retain the appearance of youth and beauty. Rachel was beautiful, but outward beauty is not a permanent, unchanging condition.

Moral, Spiritual, or Behavioral Characteristics

Genesis 6:9 "These *are* the generations of Noah: Noah **was** a just man *and* perfect in his generations, *and* Noah walked with God." (KJV)

Noah was a just man, but since he was born of Adam's line, we know he was also a sinner. He was born a sinner. He wasn't always a just man, but he did become one. We also know he wouldn't always remain in that state. He would sin again. *HAYAH* is used to express this kind of dynamic "was." God was pleased with Noah's goodness, but see how God contrasts man's being with His own being. Look at these different forms of being.

Leviticus 11:44-45 "For I *am* the LORD your God: ye shall therefore sanctify yourselves, and ye **shall be** holy; for I *am* holy: neither shall ye defile yourselves with any manner of creeping thing that creepeth upon the earth. *{45}* For I ***am*** the LORD that bringeth you up out of the land of Egypt, to be your God: ye **shall therefore be** holy, for I ***am*** holy." (KJV)

HAYAH is necessary to describe man being holy because being holy isn't something we are. It is something we can become. This passage could be translated, "ye shall therefore become holy." Now, look at the "*am*" when it describes God. It is in italics: "for I *am* holy." No *HAYAH* is used because God's state of Holiness is static, unchanging, and permanent. God doesn't "become" Holy. God is not dynamically Holy. God IS statically Holy. He always has been and He always will be. We are not holy in the same sense God is Holy. Do you begin to see what *HAYAH* meant to the ancient Hebrews? This is why I said back in Chapter Eight that the light God spoke into existence (*HAYAH*) could not be the light of God Himself. God is eternally light; His light cannot "become" to exist. *HAYAH* is not used to describe any of God's eternal attributes. This doesn't mean *HAYAH* should always be translated, "became." Other translations are equally valid, but they are still not used to imply conditions of static being. **Genesis 1:2 does not describe a static condition of the earth.** It describes a dynamic condition, a condition that had changed. The earth had changed from a condition of not being "without form, and void," to a condition of being "without form, and void." This is what *HAYAH* conveys. This is what the ancient Hebrews would have thought.

Let's examine this in more detail. I have searched the Book of Genesis to find all the instances of *HAYAH*. If you read these verses, I think you will see why *HAYAH* should be translated, "became" or "had become," in Genesis 1:2. What follows is a list of the English translations (KJV) of *HAYAH* from the Book of Genesis. The list is in alphabetical order, and I included in brackets [ ] the number of times *HAYAH* is translated the way it is. I have marked the first listing with an asterisk. These nine instances are cases where *HAYAH* is in the Hebrew text, but no form of the verb is translated directly in the *King James Bible*. In these cases the *HAYAH* is indirectly expressed in the context of the translation. I'm not going to worry about how *HAYAH* cannot be translated; I have enough problems with how it can be translated.

HAYAH in Genesis (KJV)

* [9] 1:5, 1:8, 1:13, 1:19, 1:23, 1:31, 4:17, 15:12, 32:8
are [3] 42:11, 42:31, 42:36
be [3] 17:1, 24:60, 38:23
became [9] 2:7, 2:10, 19:26, 20:12, 21:20, 24:67 47:20, 47:26, 49:15
become [9] 3:22, 9:15, 18:18, 18:18, 32:10, 34:16, 37:20, 48:19, 48:19
been [1] 47:9
came [1] 15:1
came to pass [63] 4:3, 4:8, 6:1, 7:10, 8:6, 8:13, 11:2, 12:11, 12:14, 14:1, 15:17, 19:17, 19:29, 19:34, 20:13, 21:22, 22:1, 22:20, 24:15, 24:22, 24:30, 24:52, 25:11, 26:8, 26:32,

27:1, 27:30, 29:10, 29:13, 29:23, 29:25, 30:25, 30:41, 31:10, 34:25, 35:17, 35:18, 35:22, 37:23, 38:1, 38:9, 38:24, 38:27, 38:28, 38:29, 39:5, 39:7, 39:10, 39:11, 39:13, 39:15, 39:18, 39:19, 40:1, 40:20, 41:1, 41:8, 41:13, 42:35, 43:2, 43:21, 44:24, 48:1
come to pass [9] 4:14, 9:14, 12:12, 24:14, 24:43, 27:40, 44:31, 46:33, 47:24
continually [1] 8:5
continued [1] 40:4
had [6] 11:3, 11:3, 12:16, 13:5, 26:14, 30:43
had been [2] 13:3, 31:42
hadst [1] 30:30
hath been [3] 31:5, 46:32, 46:34
have [1] 32:5
keep [1] 33:9
let [1] 1:6
let be [10] 1:3, 1:6, 1:14, 1:14, 1:15, 13:8, 24:51, 26:28, 31:44, 37:27
may be [1] 21:30
mayest be [1] 28:3
might be [1] 30:34
seemed [2] 19:14, 29:20
shall be [45] 1:29, 2:24, 3:5, 4:14, 6:3, 6:19, 6:21, 9:2, 9:3, 9:11, 9:13, 9:16, 9:25, 9:26, 9:27, 15:5, 15:13, 17:5, 17:11, 17:13, 17:16, 17:16, 27:33, 27:39, 28:14, 28:21, 28:22, 30:32, 31:8, 31:8, 34:10, 35:10, 35:11, 41:27, 41:36, 41:36, 44:10, 44:10, 44:17, 47:24, 48:5, 48:6, 48:21, 49:17, 49:26
shall have [1] 18:12
shalt be [6] 4:12, 12:2, 17:4, 24:41, 41:40, 45:10
shall seem [1] 27:12
should be [3] 2:18, 18:25, 38:9
to be [5] 10:8, 17:7, 18:11, 34:22, 39:10
was [68] 1:2, 1:3, 1:7, 1:9, 1:11, 1:15, 1:24, 1:30, 2:5, 3:1, 3:20, 4:2, 4:2, 4:20, 4:21, 5:32, 6:9, 7:6, 7:12, 7:17, 10:9, 10:10, 10:19, 10:30, 11:1, 11:30, 12:10, 13:6, 13:7, 15:17, 17:1, 21:20, 23:1, 25:20, 25:27, 26:1, 26:1, 26:28, 26:34, 27:30, 29:17, 30:29, 31:40, 35:3, 35:5, 35:16, 36:12, 37:2, 38:5, 38:7, 38:21, 38:22, 39:2, 39:2, 39:2, 39:5, 39:6, 39:20, 39:21, 39:22, 41:13, 41:53, 41:54, 41:54, 41:56, 42:5, 47:28, 50:9
wast [1] 40:13
were [38] 1:5, 1:8, 1:13, 1:19, 1:23, 1:31, 2:25, 4:8, 5:4, 5:5, 5:8, 5:11, 5:14, 5:17, 5:20, 5:23, 5:27, 5:31, 6:4, 7:10, 9:18, 9:29, 11:32, 25:3, 26:35, 27:23, 30:42, 34:5, 34:25, 35:22, 35:28, 36:7, 36:11, 36:13, 36:14, 36:22, 41:48, 46:12
will be [9] 16:12, 17:8, 26:3, 28:20, 31:3, 34:15, 44:9, 47:19, 47:25

HAYAH is translated, "became" or "become," 18 times while it is translated, "was" or "wast," 69 times. At this point, some creationists will say there are 69 votes for "was" and only 18 votes for "became." From this, they conclude "was" is the winner. Using this conclusion, they insist *HAYAH* in Genesis 1:2 must be translated, "was."

It's not that simple. Word-meanings are not determined by majority use. (Otherwise every word would have only one meaning.) Context, not statistics, determines the various meanings of words, especially in the ancient Hebrew. In this case, however, using statistics is fine with me. If you include the phrases "came," "came to pass," and "come to pass," which mean the same thing as "became" or "become," then you add 73 translations in favor of "became." Adding the phrases "shall be," "shalt be," and "will be," (All of which denote a future dynamic "becoming," rather than a past static "being.") adds 60 more uses of *HAYAH* that denote some form of "becoming." This makes a total of 151 times *HAYAH* is used to mean a dynamic being and not a static being. So, how can anyone say *HAYAH* can't be translated as, "became?"

If I say, "The earth was without form, and void," what does "was" mean? Is "was" always "was" as some say it was, or was "was" something else God said it was? (I've been sitting at this keyboard too long!) The *HAYAH* of Genesis 1:2 is translated, "was." Some say this is the only way it can be translated. Is that true? Is this "was" the same kind of "was" as all the other translations of "was?" The only way to answer this is to look at all the *HAYAH*s in Genesis translated, "was." We can then see if they always express the meaning Young-Earth creationists say it does.

(Note: I am only going to look at the Book of Genesis. I know this puts an artificial limit on how much we can learn about *HAYAH*, but a complete Old Testament study of *HAYAH* is far, far beyond my abilities. Hebrew scholars have written numerous books on the use of *HAYAH*, so if you want to know more, you can easily continue your research. My purpose in writing this section about *HAYAH* is to prove three things.)

1.) Most of the "was" translations actually express the idea of "become" or "come to pass."
2.) Most of the "was" translations are a different form of the verb than in Genesis 1:2.
3.) The exact same form of *HAYAH* is elsewhere translated, "become" or "became."

HAYAH Translated as, "Was" or "Wast," in the *King James Version*

WAS

Genesis 1:2 "And the earth **was** without form, and void; and darkness *was* upon the face of the deep. And the Spirit of God moved upon the face of the waters." (KJV)

Since the *HAYAH* in Genesis 1:2 is the one in question, let's leave it until last. Let's skip ahead to *HAYAH* in Genesis 1:3.

1.) Genesis 1:3 "And God said, Let there **be** light: and there **was** light." (KJV)

HAYAH is used twice. "BE" and "WAS" are both translations of *HAYAH*. What it literally says is, "God said, 'light BE,' and light CAME TO BE." He spoke light into being. Light's existence was a dynamic condition. It came into being. We could substitute, "and it became light," and it would actually make more sense. The same can be said of the other things God created/restored during the Six Days. They all CAME TO BE.

2.) Genesis 1:7 "And God made the firmament, and divided the waters which *were* under the firmament from the waters which *were* above the firmament: and it **was** so." (KJV)

3.) Genesis 1:9 "And God said, Let the waters under the heaven be gathered together unto one place, and let the dry *land* appear: and it **was** so." (KJV)

4.) Genesis 1:11 "And God said, Let the earth bring forth grass, the herb yielding seed, *and* the fruit tree yielding fruit after his kind, whose seed *is* in itself, upon the earth: and it **was** so." (KJV)

5.) Genesis 1:15 "And let them **be** for lights in the firmament of the heaven to give light upon the earth: and it **was** so." (KJV)

6.) Genesis 1:24 "And God said, Let the earth bring forth the living creature after his kind, cattle, and creeping thing, and beast of the earth after his kind: and it **was** so." (KJV)

7.) Genesis 1:30 "And to every beast of the earth, and to every fowl of the air, and to every thing that creepeth upon the earth, wherein *there is* life, *I have given* every green herb for meat: and it **was** so." (KJV)

All these things became so. They weren't always so. "Was" is a good word but not "was" in the past-static sense. These things were dynamic in their being. They came to be; they weren't previously so. The Hebrews thought in dynamic categories. This is why they used *HAYAH*.

8.) Genesis 2:5 "And every plant of the field before it **was** in the earth, and every herb of the field before it grew: for the LORD God had not caused it to rain upon the earth, and *there was* not a man to till the ground." (KJV)

In Genesis 2:5 we see *HAYAH* indicates a dynamic condition. The word "before" shows it is dynamic with respect to time. Before plants were created on Day Three, before they came to be, there WERE no plants on the earth. *HAYAH* is used to describe their dynamic state of nonexistence. Very, very carefully now, contrast this with the last part of the sentence: "*there was* not a man to till the ground." The "*was*" is in italics. No *HAYAH* is used here. Man was not on the earth either, but there is a difference. Earth **was** (dynamic) without plants and earth *was* (static) without man. *HAYAH* is not used to describe man's absence. Man's nonexistence was a static condition. Man had never been! These two different uses of "was" in the same sentence and in the same context indicate the difference between earth dynamically being without plants and earth statically being without man. Whatever the ancient Hebrews thought about this, they made a distinction between plants "not being" and man "not being." They thought of these "not beings" in two different ways. The plants' "not being" was dynamic; it had changed. Man's "not being" was static; man had never existed. This, I believe, is an indication plant life had been there before, but wasn't there now, while man had never been there. (At least not true humans; men made in the image of God.)

This verse takes us back to what I said about Jeremiah 4:25, where Jeremiah described the cities that had been destroyed. He included the fact there was "no man" on the earth. Genesis 2:5 and Jeremiah 4:25 are the only two verses in the Bible that talk about the earth having "no man." These two passages of Scripture indicate there was no man, because man had not yet been created. Such word usage helps support the Restoration Theory.

9.) Genesis 3:1 "Now the serpent **was** more subtil than any beast of the field which the LORD God had made. And he said unto the woman, Yea, hath God said, Ye shall not eat of every tree of the garden?" (KJV)

Was the serpent more subtle, or had the serpent become more subtle? This presents the very same problem as the earth being or becoming without form, and void in Genesis 1:2. There is very little context to give us the clues we need. What does subtle mean? The Hebrew word *ARUWM* (Strong's Number H6175) has two connotations, one is good and the other is bad. It can mean "prudent" or it can mean "crafty." In the context of deceiving Eve, I can't see how we can interpret this word except in its bad sense. Lucifer dynamically possessed or indwelt the serpent. I think he did this because if he had come in his own beautiful, powerful, angelic form, Adam would have recognized him and called out to God for help. (Remember, Adam was meant to guard the Garden.) I do not think the physical animal was subtle in and of itself. It became subtle only by the power of Lucifer. How can an animal be subtle, especially a reptile? While I am not a specialist in reptile medicine, I can say this with authority: Reptiles don't have the neural capacity to be prudent, shrewd, subtle, or crafty. That's not what they are. That's not their static, permanent, ongoing condition or state. God did not create it shrewd or crafty in an evil sense. It wasn't originally that way; it became that way. Lucifer did not possess, indwell, or control this reptile from the beginning of creation. I don't think this animal's relationship with Lucifer was static. I think it was dynamic. I think this reptile became subtle only when Lucifer acted upon it. The serpent, therefore, became subtle. This is what *HAYAH* expresses. I think *HAYAH* expresses the same thing about the earth becoming without form, and void. It wasn't its original condition.

10.) Genesis 3:20 "And Adam called his wife's name Eve; because she **was** the mother of all living." (KJV)

Now here's an interesting *HAYAH*. It is translated, "was," but what does it really mean? Eve wasn't the mother of all living at this point in time. In fact, she wasn't yet the mother of anyone. However, she became the mother of all living. When we modern English speakers see "was" we tend to think in terms of the past. "I was in Scotland." "I was a sailor." "I was sleepy." Many creationists opposed to the Gap Theory say this is the way *HAYAH* must be translated; it must refer to a past, static condition. This verse shows they are wrong. It would be poor English to say, "I was in Chicago next year." It wouldn't make sense to use "was" for a future condition, yet here we have *HAYAH* used for a future condition. It's obvious *HAYAH* doesn't always mean what some people want it to mean. Eve became the mother of all living.

11. and 12.) Genesis 4:2 "And she again bare his brother Abel. And Abel **was** a keeper of sheep, but Cain **was** a tiller of the ground." (KJV)

As was true for Eve, so it was for Cain and Abel. At his birth, Abel was not a keeper of sheep. He became a keeper of sheep. Neither was Cain a tiller of the ground when he was born. Cain became a tiller of the ground. "Became" is a much better translation; it expresses the information more accurately. This same concept of "was" as a future "becoming" is seen in the next two passages as well.

13.) Genesis 4:20 "And Adah bare Jabal: he **was** the father of such as dwell in tents, and *of such as have* cattle." (KJV)

14.) Genesis 4:21 "And his brother's name *was* Jubal: he **was** the father of all such as handle the harp and organ." (KJV)

Jabal and Jubal were apparently inventors. Jabal invented tents and Jubal invented musical instruments. At least this is what I have been told being the "father of" something meant. They became inventors; they became the "fathers" of nomads (tent-dwellers with livestock) and musicians. There had been no nomads or musicians before this, but now there were. Whatever it meant, it didn't mean "was" in the sense of it being a static, past event. "Was" in these two verse means "became."

15.) Genesis 5:32 "And Noah **was** five hundred years old: and Noah begat Shem, Ham, and Japheth." (KJV)

This *HAYAH* expresses the dynamic concept of a person's age. I've mentioned this already. From now on, I'll skip over the instances of *HAYAH* that have been explained. I'll still list them, but unless I see some significant difference, I'll not bother re-explaining my thoughts.

16.) Genesis 6:9 "These *are* the generations of Noah: Noah **was** a just man *and* perfect in his generations, *and* Noah walked with God." (KJV)

17.) Genesis 7:6 "And Noah *was* six hundred years old when the flood of waters **was** upon the earth." (KJV)

18.) Genesis 7:12 "And the rain **was** upon the earth forty days and forty nights." (KJV)

19.) Genesis 7:17 "And the flood **was** forty days upon the earth; and the waters increased, and bare up the ark, and it was lift up above the earth." (KJV)

The Flood was not always upon the earth. It came upon the earth. The rain was not always on the earth. The rain came upon the earth for forty days and forty nights.

20.) Genesis 10:9 "He **was** a mighty hunter before the LORD: wherefore it is said, Even as Nimrod the mighty hunter before the LORD." (KJV)

As we have seen, expressing a person's occupation and activities are dynamic expressions in Hebrew. Nimrod wasn't always a mighty hunter; he became one.

21.) Genesis 10:10 "And the beginning of his kingdom **was** Babel, and Erech, and Accad, and Calneh, in the land of Shinar." (KJV)

This *HAYAH* is dynamic; Nimrod didn't always have a kingdom. These cities were the beginning of his kingdom. The Bible is telling us how his kingdom came to be.

22.) Genesis 10:19 "And the border of the Canaanites **was** from Sidon, as thou comest to Gerar, unto Gaza; as thou goest, unto Sodom, and Gomorrah, and Admah, and Zeboim, even unto Lasha." (KJV)

23.) Genesis 10:30 "And their dwelling **was** from Mesha, as thou goest unto Sephar a mount of the east." (KJV)

These two verses indicate geographical locations. A person's geographical location or position was a dynamic condition in Hebrew thinking. Locations and boundaries change.

24.) Genesis 11:1 "And the whole earth **was** of one language, and of one speech." (KJV)

At first glance, it may seem like we have found *HAYAH* used in a static sense. This isn't a situation where the population of the world became of one language. It was already one language. God confounded their speech at the Tower of Babel. This means it would be wrong to translate this, "And the whole earth became of one language..." Therefore, wouldn't it be equally wrong to translate Genesis 1:2 as "became?" No. This *HAYAH* has an altogether different meaning here. The key to interpreting this verse correctly is to remember *HAYAH* has multiple meanings. It doesn't always translate as some form of "to be." It can also be translated as a form of "to have." Go back and look at the list of different translations of *HAYAH* used in the *King James Bible*. Don't let these other meanings of *HAYAH* throw you off track. Words that are spelled the same and sound the same don't always mean the same. We see this in English. "Tire" means to become exhausted, but a "tire" is something you put on your car. "Fire" means something is burning up, but "fire" also is what a boss does to an incompetent employee. The *HAYAH* in this verse is different than the *HAYAH* in Genesis 1:2. It does not mean the people and the language were identical. It does not mean they became a language. It means they had one language. Now this may seem strange to our English way of thinking. I am not saying *HAYAH* had two entirely unrelated meanings. The meaning of "having" and the meaning of "being" can be related in certain situations. Sometimes it is difficult to distinguish between the experiential and the existential. Examine this sentence:

"The woman is beautiful."

What am I saying? Is she beautiful? Or does she have beauty? (And guys, if your wife asks you, "Sweetie, do you think I am existentially beautiful, or experientially beautiful?"... you'd better have the right answer.) You can see how difficult it could be to distinguish between the two thoughts. How would the ancient Hebrews have thought of this? They would have thought of *HAYAH* in this case as "having" one language rather than "being" one language.

Genesis 11:1 "Now the whole world **had** one language and a common speech." (NIV)

Genesis 11:1 "Now the whole earth **had** one language and the same words." (NRSV)

Genesis 11:1 "Now the whole earth **had** one language and one speech." (NKJV)

Genesis 11:1 "Now the whole earth **had** one language and the same words." (ESV)

Genesis 11:1 "Now the whole earth **had** one language, and the same words." (DBY)

I think I would be on safe ground saying this passage is best understood as "the whole earth HAD one language," rather than "the whole earth WAS one language." These Hebrew scholars say so. You may disagree. That's your choice, but I have yet one more Hebrew scholar who interpreted it in this fashion. I would be careful about disagreeing with Him.

Genesis 11:6 "And the LORD said, Behold, the people *is* one, and they **HAVE** all one language; and this they begin to do: and now nothing will be restrained from them, which they have imagined to do." (KJV)

I'm sure that He who created the Hebrew language understood the Hebrew language. God offers His own interpretation of Genesis 11:1 in Genesis 11:6. He uses different words to make it clear they "HAVE" one language. Genesis 11:6 gives us God's interpretation of Genesis 11:1. The *HAYAH* in Genesis 11:1 doesn't have the same meaning as the *HAYAH* in Genesis 1:2. It's spelled the same, it sounds the same, but it's not the same. It doesn't mean "to be;" it means "to have." Therefore, no one can use Genesis 11:1 as evidence against the Gap Theory. Some have tried this, but the only way they can do it is to interpret the *HAYAH* in Genesis 11:1 in a way God doesn't. I'll stick with God's interpretation!

25.) Genesis 11:30 "But Sarai **was** barren; she *had* no child." (KJV)

It's true Sarah didn't become barren. She already was barren. Being barren, however, is a medical condition and such conditions were often thought of in terms of being dynamic. Now, I'm not sure how the ancient Hebrews viewed all the different medical conditions. We have seen evidence how they viewed Leah's poor vision as a static, non-changing condition. Whatever their thinking was about other medical maladies, I know barrenness was viewed as curse from God. To them it indicated, rightly or wrongly, God's disapproval of them or of something in their lives. This mindset pervaded their culture. It was a shame for a woman to be barren. Having children was, in their thought process, an indicator of God's presence in their lives. Being barren was an indicator God was not with them. As we have seen before, the Hebrews didn't think of God's approval as a static condition. The same was true of God's disapproval. They didn't think it was impossible to appease God and regain His presence and approval. They prayed, they obeyed the Law, they performed the rituals and offered the sacrifices, hoping for this very thing. I cannot be certain, but it seems to me when a woman was barren, she prayed and hoped for it to be a dynamic state, not a static one. This appears to be the thought process of the women mentioned in the Bible who were barren. However they thought about it, in Sarah's case we know it was a dynamic condition. She was barren at this point but she wouldn't always be barren. One day she would give birth to Isaac. Because of this, the *HAYAH* in Genesis 11:30 is also a dynamic "was."

I will skip over the next several verses because we have discussed similar uses of *HAYAH*. I want you to look at them again so you can see for yourself how "came," "came to be," or "became" can often be a better translation.

26.) Genesis 12:10 "And there **was** a famine in the land: and Abram went down into Egypt to sojourn there; for the famine *was* grievous in the land." (KJV)

27.) Genesis 13:6 "And the land was not able to bear them, that they might dwell together: for their substance **was** great, so that they could not dwell together." (KJV)

28.) Genesis 13:7 "And there **was** a strife between the herdmen of Abram's cattle and the herdmen of Lot's cattle: and the Canaanite and the Perizzite dwelled then in the land." (KJV)

29.) Genesis 15:17 "And it came to pass, that, when the sun went down, and it **was** dark, behold a smoking furnace, and a burning lamp that passed between those pieces." (KJV)

30.) Genesis 17:1 "And when Abram **was** ninety years old and nine, the LORD appeared to Abram, and said unto him, I *am* the Almighty God; walk before me, and be thou perfect." (KJV)

31.) Genesis 21:20 "And God **was** with the lad; and he grew, and dwelt in the wilderness, and became an archer." (KJV)

32.) Genesis 23:1 "And Sarah **was** an hundred and seven and twenty years old: *these were* the years of the life of Sarah." (KJV)

33.) Genesis 25:20 "And Isaac **was** forty years old when he took Rebekah to wife, the daughter of Bethuel the Syrian of Padanaram, the sister to Laban the Syrian." (KJV)

34.) Genesis 25:27 "And the boys grew: and Esau **was** a cunning hunter, a man of the field; and Jacob *was* a plain man, dwelling in tents." (KJV)

Note the difference between how Esau was described in the Hebrew and how Jacob was described in the Hebrew. *HAYAH* is used with Esau because he came to be a cunning hunter. He wasn't always a cunning hunter. He had to train and practice and work at it as he grew. His condition was dynamic. Jacob, on the other hand, didn't "become" plain as he grew; he was already plain. *HAYAH* was not used to describe Jacob's condition. He didn't need to do anything to become plain. All he had to do to be plain was to remain what he already was—plain. His condition was static. When *HAYAH* was used, it described a dynamic condition. When *HAYAH* wasn't used, it described a static condition. *HAYAH* was used in Genesis 1:2. What kind of condition did it describe? You're right… it described the dynamic, changing condition of the earth. It became without form and void. It wasn't always without form, and void. In the same way Esau came to be a cunning hunter, the earth came to be without form, and void. That's what the Hebrew says.

35. and 36.) Genesis 26:1 "And there **was** a famine in the land, beside the first famine that **was** in the days of Abraham. And Isaac went unto Abimelech king of the Philistines unto Gerar." (KJV)

37.) Genesis 26:28 "And they said, We saw certainly that the LORD **was** with thee: and we said, Let there be now an oath betwixt us, *even* betwixt us and thee, and let us make a covenant with thee;" (KJV)

38.) Genesis 26:34 "And Esau **was** forty years old when he took to wife Judith the daughter of Beeri the Hittite, and Bashemath the daughter of Elon the Hittite:" (KJV)

39.) Genesis 27:30 "And it came to pass, as soon as Isaac had made an end of blessing Jacob, and Jacob **was** yet scarce gone out from the presence of Isaac his father, that Esau his brother came in from his hunting." (KJV)

40.) Genesis 29:17 "Leah *was* tender eyed; but Rachel **was** beautiful and well favoured." (KJV)

41.) Genesis 30:29 "And he said unto him, Thou knowest how I have served thee, and how thy cattle **was** with me." (KJV)

    At first I thought this *HAYAH* might be expressing the location of the cattle. The cattle were with Jacob. But as I looked at the context, it became apparent Jacob was not telling Laban about his cattle's location. There was more to it than that. Instead of reminding Laban of **where** his cattle had been, Jacob was reminding Laban of **how** his cattle had been. He was reminding Laban of how his cattle had prospered. He is emphasizing what had **become** of Laban's cattle while under his care. Let's see how other versions translate this *HAYAH*.

Genesis 30:29 "But he said to him, 'You yourself know how I have served you and how your cattle have **fared** with me.'" (NASB)

Genesis 30:29 "Jacob said to him, 'You yourself know how I have served you, and how your cattle have **fared** with me.'" (NRSV)

Genesis 30:29 "Jacob said to him, 'You know how I have worked for you and how your livestock has **fared** under my care.'" (NIV)

Genesis 30:29 "And he said to him, Thou knowest how I have served thee, and what thy cattle has **become** with me." (DBY)

Once again we see *HAYAH* as a dynamic condition best translated as, "become."

42.) Genesis 31:40 *"Thus* I **was**; in the day the drought consumed me, and the frost by night; and my sleep departed from mine eyes." (KJV)

Jacob is describing his physical sufferings during the days and nights of taking care of Laban's livestock. He is describing what had become of him during that time. He is describing the dynamics of his situation. He is saying, "This is what became of me." It wasn't "was" in the sense of this is what he always was.

43.) Genesis 35:3 "And let us arise, and go up to Bethel; and I will make there an altar unto God, who answered me in the day of my distress, and **was** with me in the way which I went." (KJV)

44.) Genesis 35:5 "And they journeyed: and the terror of God **was** upon the cities that *were* round about them, and they did not pursue after the sons of Jacob." (KJV)

45.) Genesis 35:16 "And they journeyed from Bethel; and there **was** but a little way to come to Ephrath: and Rachel travailed, and she had hard labour." (KJV)

46.) Genesis 36:12 "And Timna **was** concubine to Eliphaz Esau's son; and she bare to Eliphaz Amalek: these *were* the sons of Adah Esau's wife." (KJV)

47.) Genesis 37:2 "These *are* the generations of Jacob. Joseph, *being* seventeen years old, **was** feeding the flock with his brethren; and the lad *was* with the sons of Bilhah, and with the sons of Zilpah, his father's wives: and Joseph brought unto his father their evil report." (KJV)

48.) Genesis 38:5 "And she yet again conceived, and bare a son; and called his name Shelah: and he **was** at Chezib, when she bare him." (KJV)

49.) Genesis 38:7 "And Er, Judah's firstborn, **was** wicked in the sight of the LORD; and the LORD slew him." (KJV)

As the Hebrew considered goodness or uprightness, so they did with wickedness. It is a dynamic condition of the heart. If it were not so, no one could be saved.

50.) Genesis 38:21 "Then he asked the men of that place, saying, Where *is* the harlot, that *was* openly by the way side? And they said, There **was** no harlot in this *place*." (KJV)

51.) Genesis 38:22 "And he returned to Judah, and said, I cannot find her; and also the men of the place said, *that* there **was** no harlot in this *place*." (KJV)

52. and 53. and 54.) Genesis 39:2 "And the LORD **was** with Joseph, and he **was** a prosperous man; and he **was** in the house of his master the Egyptian." (KJV)

55.) Genesis 39:5 "And it came to pass from the time *that* he had made him overseer in his house, and over all that he had, that the LORD blessed the Egyptian's house for Joseph's sake; and the blessing of the LORD **was** upon all that he had in the house, and in the field." (KJV)

56.) Genesis 39:6 "And he left all that he had in Joseph's hand; and he knew not ought he had, save the bread which he did eat. And Joseph **was** *a* goodly *person,* and well favoured." (KJV)

57.) Genesis 39:20 "And Joseph's master took him, and put him into the prison, a place where the king's prisoners *were* bound: and he **was** there in the prison." (KJV)

58.) Genesis 39:21 "But the LORD **was** with Joseph, and showed him mercy, and gave him favour in the sight of the keeper of the prison." (KJV)

59.) Genesis 39:22 "And the keeper of the prison committed to Joseph's hand all the prisoners that *were* in the prison; and whatsoever they did there, he **was** the doer *of it*." (KJV)

60.) Genesis 41:13 "And it came to pass, as he interpreted to us, so it **was**; me he restored unto mine office, and him he hanged." (KJV)

This is a very important verse in helping us understand *HAYAH*. If you recall the situation, Pharaoh had a troubling dream and wanted someone to interpret it. No one could. Then Pharaoh's butler remembered Joseph in prison, and how he correctly interpreted his and the baker's dreams. He tells Pharaoh that just as Joseph interpreted the dreams, so it became. What Joseph interpreted was what came to be. It wasn't "was" because it hadn't happened at the time Joseph interpreted the dreams. It wasn't until three days later that what he had interpreted came to pass. This *HAYAH* would better be translated, "became" or "came to be."

61.) Genesis 41:53 "And the seven years of plenteousness, that **was** in the land of Egypt, were ended." (KJV)

62. and 63.) Genesis 41:54 "And the seven years of dearth began to come, according as Joseph had said: and the dearth **was** in all lands; but in all the land of Egypt there **was** bread." (KJV)

64.) Genesis 41:56 "And the famine **was** over all the face of the earth: And Joseph opened all the storehouses, and sold unto the Egyptians; and the famine waxed sore in the land of Egypt." (KJV)

65.) Genesis 42:5 "And the sons of Israel came to buy *corn* among those that came: for the famine **was** in the land of Canaan." (KJV)

66.) Genesis 47:28 "And Jacob lived in the land of Egypt seventeen years: so the whole age of Jacob **was** an hundred forty and seven years." (KJV)

67.) Genesis 50:9 "And there went up with him both chariots and horsemen: and it **was** a very great company." (KJV)

This *HAYAH* is used in connection with describing the size of the army that accompanied Joseph when he took Jacob's body back to the land of Canaan to be buried. As a way of describing the size of something, I can see why the ancient Hebrews would think in dynamic terms rather than static ones. The size of something is not equivalent to the thing itself. Armies aren't always the same size. Any particular army could increase or decrease in size over time, yet even with such dynamic change, it would still be an army.

WAST

68.) Genesis 40:13 "Yet within three days shall Pharaoh lift up thine head, and restore thee unto thy place: and thou shalt deliver Pharaoh's cup into his hand, after the former manner when thou **wast** his butler." (KJV)

There you have it! We have finished looking at the 68 instances of *HAYAH* in Genesis (other than Genesis 1:2) translated "was" or "wast" in the *King James Bible*. These are the very verses anti-Gap Theory creationists use to prove "was" in Genesis 1:2 must mean a past, static condition. As you can see, virtually all of them express the idea of "becoming," "came," "came to pass," or "coming to be." If nearly every *HAYAH* translated "was" in Genesis actually expresses the idea of "became," then how can anyone say

HAYAH cannot be translated "became?" Add these to the 151 times *HAYAH* is already translated as some form of "became" in the *King James Bible* and we see how *HAYAH* conveys "became" at least 219 times out of its 316 uses in Genesis. I think "became" becomes a viable translation. **The only way Gap Theory opponents can justify their definition of "was" in Genesis 1:2 is to point to the thousands of instances of *"was"* (in italics) in the *King James Bible*, and pretend it means the same thing as "was" (not in italics).** They don't want you to recognize the difference in meaning when the Hebrews used (and didn't use) the word *HAYAH*. They don't want you to think like the ancient Hebrews.

HAYAH in Genesis 1:2

Unfortunately, we aren't finished. We can't quit here. There is another aspect of *HAYAH* we must study. We need to look at the form of the verb in Genesis 1:2 and compare how that same verb form is translated elsewhere. Since different forms of a verb can express different ideas, we must concentrate our study on the verb form in Genesis 1:2. Some argue that other forms of *HAYAH* may be translated, "became," but the verb form in Genesis 1:2 can't mean "became." We need to see if that is true. The *HAYAH* in Genesis 1:2 is in the *QAL* Perfect form of the verb. So, what does that mean? If you're like me, it doesn't mean much. Since I'm not a Hebrew scholar, we need to see what Hebrew scholars say.

The *QAL* stem

"The *Qal* stem is the basic verbal stem in Hebrew language. Approximately two-thirds of the verbal forms in the Old Testament are in this stem. The *Qal* stem can be divided into two main classes: verbs that represent **action**… and verbs that describe **a state of being**…"[106]

There! Now we are Hebrew scholars! (But, I didn't say we were great Hebrew scholars.) We can now say the *QAL* stem is the basic verbal stem in the Hebrew language, and there is a division between *QAL* verbs of action and *QAL* verbs of being. This gives us another clue to help us determine the meaning of *HAYAH* in Genesis 1:2. Is it in the form that represents ACTION or in the form that describes a STATE OF BEING? If it describes a state of being, then it is more likely the earth was (existentially in a state of being) without form, and void. If it describes action, then it is more likely the earth became (experientially came to be) without form, and void. As you can probably guess, it is in a form that describes action. But what kind of action, you ask?

Hebrew is one of those languages where verbs aren't only concerned about WHEN things happen with respect to time, but HOW things happen with respect to time. In English, our verbs focus predominantly on whether an action is past, present, or future.

Hebrew verbs are also concerned with whether the action is complete or ongoing. As a result, there are two sub-groups of *QAL* verbs that represent action. These are the *QAL* Imperfect and the *QAL* Perfect. Let's look at what they mean.

The *QAL* Imperfect

"The *Qal* Imperfect (qmf) indicates, in the active voice, simple imperfective **action**, viewed as part of a whole event or situation. 'If the priest that is anointed <u>do sin</u>...' (Leviticus 4:3); 'And Moab <u>was sore afraid</u> of the people...' (Numbers 22:3)."[107]

The *QAL* Imperfect form of a verb describes an action as continuous or incomplete with respect to time. The *QAL* Imperfect of *HAYAH* would describe a continuous or incomplete action with respect to time rather than a completed being with respect to time. Therefore, *HAYAH* in the *QAL* Imperfect should not be translated, "was," in the sense of static being. In fact, that's exactly what we see when we look at its translations. We will first look at the *QAL* Imperfect in its basic form and then we will look at a sub-category of the *QAL* Imperfect. Genesis 44:17 is a good example of what the *QAL* Imperfect of *HAYAH* meant to the ancient Hebrews.

Genesis 44:17 "But he said, 'Far be it from me that I should do so! Only the man in whose hand the cup was found **shall be** my servant. But as for you, go up in peace to your father.'" (KJV)

If you remember the story, Joseph set his brothers up for a test. He had his own royal cup placed into Benjamin's sack of grain before they set out from Egypt to return to their father Jacob. When the cup was found, it would look as if Benjamin had stolen it. Joseph said the one who had "stolen" the cup would BECOME his slave. The *QAL* Imperfect of *HAYAH* is used because it describes what Benjamin was to BECOME, not what Benjamin WAS. The *QAL* Imperfect indicates this would be more than a future action. Yes, it was going to be a future action, but it was going to become an on-going, continuous action. The one who "stole" Joseph's cup was going to be Joseph's slave for the rest of his life, or at least, a very long time. It would be ongoing and continuous. You can see how the *QAL* Imperfect reveals more than WHEN the action would be, it reveals WHAT KIND of action it will be. English verbs in the future tense don't always do that. For example, if I said, "I'm going to Mexico," you wouldn't know if I meant I was going to Mexico for a short vacation, or if I was going to Mexico to live the rest of my life. In Hebrew, this sentence would be written with a different form of the verb stem, depending on WHAT KIND of action was involved. Hebrew verb stems reveal more information about the action than English tenses.

Now, you may be wondering why I am mentioning the *QAL* Imperfect of *HAYAH* when the *HAYAH* in Genesis 1:2 is in the *QAL* Perfect. There are two reasons. First, I want you to see how the Hebrews thought when they used *HAYAH*. Even though the form of the verb is different, the verb itself has the same basic underlying concept. That concept was of something dynamic. Secondly, I don't want to skip any "was" translation in Genesis. I don't want you to think I am picking and choosing the verses I want you to see. I don't want you to think I am misleading you. We need to look at the *QAL* Imperfect of *HAYAH*, because it will help us better understand the *QAL* Perfect of *HAYAH*. Let me give you an example of a *QAL* Imperfect "was" translation in the *King James Bible* that doesn't mean "was" in the sense the anti-gap creationists say it means. We need to see if this "was" expresses a dynamic or a static state of being.

Genesis 2:5 "And every plant of the field before it **was** in the earth, and every herb of the field before it grew: for the LORD God had not caused it to rain upon the earth, and *there was* not a man to till the ground." (KJV)

We already looked at this verse and saw how it describes a dynamic action. Note the parallelism between "before—every plant—was" and "before—every herb—grew." The word "grew" is a verb describing action. That means the verb "was" in this case is also a verb describing action. It is the parallel in this parallelism. This verse describes the earth before plants "came to be." Look at how the *New International Version* translates it.

Genesis 2:5 "and no shrub of the field **had yet appeared** on the earth and no plant of the field had yet sprung up, for the LORD God had not sent rain on the earth and there was no man to work the ground," (NIV)

HAYAH is a verb of action here. No shrub had yet appeared. No plant had yet sprung up. No plant had yet grown. No plant had yet come to be. As I mentioned before, God describes the earth without plants as a dynamic condition, but He describes the earth without man as a static condition. No *HAYAH* is used in the phrase about man. Can you begin to get a feel for God's view of earth's condition before man's creation? These are God's words. He picked the way the Pre-Adamic earth should be described. He describes earth without man in a different way than He describes earth without plants. Earth had always been without man, but earth came to be without plants. One condition was static; the other condition was dynamic. The English "was" doesn't convey that same information. Are we willing to listen to God?

So you won't feel cheated, I will list all the *QAL* Imperfect uses of *HAYAH* in Genesis and show how they are translated in the *King James Version*. Again, I'm doing this so you can get a better feel for what went through the minds of the ancient Hebrews.

The *QAL* Imperfect of *HAYAH* in Genesis (KJV)

are [1]: 42:31
be [1]: 38:23
became [8]: 2:7, 2:10, 19:26, 20:12, 21:20, 24:67, 47:20, 49:15
built [1]: 4:17
came [1]: 15:1
came to pass [65]: 4:3, 4:8, 6:1, 7:10, 8:6, 8:13, 11:2, 12:11, 12:12, 12:14, 14:1, 15:17, 19:17, 19:29, 19:34, 20:13, 21:22, 22:1, 22:20, 24:15, 24:22, 24:30, 24:52, 25:11, 26:8, 26:32, 27:1, 27:30, 29:10, 29:13, 29:23, 29:25, 30:25, 30:41, 31:10, 34:25, 35:17, 35:18, 35:22, 37:23, 38:1, 38:9, 38:24, 38:27, 38:28, 38:29, 39:5, 39:7, 39:10, 39:11, 39:13, 39:15, 39:18, 39:19, 40:1, 40:20, 41:1, 41:8, 41:13, 42:35, 43:1, 43:21, 44:24, 44:31, 48:1
continually [1]: 8:5
continued [1]: 40:4
had [4]: 11:3, 12:16, 26:14, 30:43
have [1]: 32:5
hath been [1]: 46:34
keep [1]: 33:9
may be [1]: 21:30
mayest be [1]: 28:3
seemed [2]: 19:14, 29:20
shall be [35]: 1:29, 2:24, 3:5, 6:3, 6:19, 9:2, 9:3, 9:11, 9:25, 15:5, 15:13, 17:16, 27:33, 27:39, 28:14, 28:21, 28:22. 30:32, 31:8. 31:8, 34:10, 35:10, 35:11, 41:27, 41:36, 41:36, 44:10, 44:10, 44:17, 47:24, 48:5, 48:6, 48:21, 49:17, 49:26
shall become [3]: 9:15, 48:19, 48:19
shall seem [1]: 27:12
shalt be [4]: 4:12, 12:2, 41:40, 45:10
should be [1]: 38:9
was [45]: 1:7, 1:9, 1:11, 1:15, 1:24, 1:30, 2:5, 4:2, 4:2, 7:12, 7:17, 10:9, 10:10, 10:19, 10:30, 11:1, 11:30, 12:10, 13:7, 15:12, 17:1, 21:20, 23:1, 25:20 25:27, 26:1, 26:8, 26:34, 31:40, 35:3, 35:5, 35:16, 38:7, 38:21, 38:22, 39:2, 39:2, 39:2, 39:5, 39:6, 39:20, 39:21, 41:54, 47:27, 50:9
were [22]: 2:25, 5:4, 5:5, 5:8, 5:11, 5:14, 5:17, 5:20, 5:23, 5:27, 5:31, 5:32, 9:18, 9:29, 11:32, 26:35, 34:5, 35:22, 35:28, 36:11, 36:22, 46:12
will be [8]: 16:12, 26:3, 28:20, 31:3, 34:15, 44:9, 47:19, 47:25
will become [2]: 34:16, 37:20

Anti-Gap creationists say *HAYAH* must be translated as a form of "was" (being) and not as a form of "became" (action). A quick look at the *QAL* Imperfect form of *HAYAH* in Genesis shows how deeply twisted this claim is. If you look at the context of these verses you will easily see how "came to pass" means "came to be," which has the exact same meaning as "became." The same can be said of "shall be," "shalt be," "will be," and other future-looking phrases. They all mean "shall become" or "will become." They all describe dynamic conditions; not static ones. All the passages where the *QAL* Imperfect of *HAYAH* is translated as, "was," in the *King James Bible* describe dynamic conditions. (Except when *HAYAH* is used in the sense of "having" rather than "being.")

Let's look at a few examples to get a feel for what this meant:

Genesis 1:6-7 "And God said, Let there be a firmament in the midst of the waters, and let it divide the waters from the waters. {7} And God made the firmament, and divided the waters which *were* under the firmament from the waters which *were* above the firmament: and it **was** so." (KJV)

The meaning is apparent. God commanded the firmament to divide the waters, and it became so. It wasn't that way before the command. Notice that *"were"* is used twice in verse seven. Notice they are in italics. This means the *King James* Translators added them in the English to help English-Readers understand the meaning. Hebrew-Readers would see no need for adding *"were."* You could just as easily capture the Hebrew thought-process without adding *"were"* by translating it this way:

Genesis 1:6-7 "And God said, Let there be a firmament in the midst of the waters, and let it divide the waters from the waters. {7} And God made the firmament, and divided the waters under the firmament from the waters above the firmament, and it **became** so."

So, while the ancient Hebrews saw no need for *HAYAH* to describe what the waters **were**, they did see a need for *HAYAH* to describe what the waters **became**. The same thing can be said for the *QAL* Imperfect of *HAYAH* in Genesis 1:9:

Genesis 1:9 "And God said, Let the waters under the heaven be gathered together unto one place, and let the dry *land* appear: and it **was** so." (KJV)

God commanded the waters to gather together into one place and the dry land to appear. After His command, it became so. It wasn't that way before the command. This was a dynamic action, not a static condition.
"Was" is an okay translation for *HAYAH*, but "became" is more accurate. Of the 203 times the *QAL* Imperfect Form of *HAYAH* is used in the sense of "being" in Genesis, virtually all of them describe dynamic conditions. We need to stop and take a very close look at what *HAYAH* meant to the ancient Hebrews before we listen to the claims of modern English-speaking "experts" who say *HAYAH* can't be translated as a form of "became." Moses would laugh at such a claim.

The second biggest problem with understanding what *HAYAH* means is this: We modern English-speakers want it to be equivalent to our modern English verb "to be," and it isn't!

The biggest problem with understanding what *HAYAH* means is this: We want it to mean what WE want it to mean regardless of what it means.

Let's look at a few more *QAL* Imperfect of *HAYAH* verses:

Genesis 9:3 "Every moving thing that liveth shall **be** meat for you; even as the green herb have I given you all things." (KJV)

God is telling Noah that from now on, living creatures will become food for man.

Genesis 15:5 "And he brought him forth abroad, and said, Look now toward heaven, and tell the stars, if thou be able to number them: and he said unto him, So shall thy seed **be**." (KJV)

God is telling Abraham what shall become of his offspring. The *King James* translators knew this hadn't happened yet to Abraham. They knew Abraham did not have countless descendants at the time God was speaking to him. This was God's promise concerning Abraham's descendants. They translated it, "so shall thy seed be" because in their minds, they understood "be" to convey the idea of, "so shall thy seed become."

Genesis 16:11-12 "And the angel of the LORD said unto her, Behold, thou *art* with child, and shalt bear a son, and shalt call his name Ishmael; because the LORD hath heard thy affliction. *{12}* And he will **be** a wild man; his hand *will be* against every man, and every man's hand against him; and he shall dwell in the presence of all his brethren." (KJV)

Ishmael will be a wild man. What does this mean? Was he a wild man at that time? No. He wasn't even born yet. "He will be" a wild man means "He will become" a wild man." Again, the *King James* translators saw nothing wrong with using "be" because they thought of it in the sense of "become." That's why they had no problem translating *HAYAH* with the various forms of "to be." The *King James* translators also knew the ancient Hebrew verbs didn't use tenses in the way English verbs do. English verb tenses are focused more on WHEN things happen, while Hebrew verb "tenses" (stems) focus more on HOW things happen. (Complete, Incomplete, Reflexive, Causal, Potential, *etc.*) The "timing" of conditions and actions was usually expressed in other ways. The exact form of *HAYAH*, and of course the context, was used as a way of expressing the "timing." "Was," "will be," "had been," "coming to be," are all valid translations of *HAYAH* that give a sense of "timing" when used to express "being." However, *HAYAH* had other meanings that didn't directly convey the idea of "being." Look at Genesis 33:9.

Genesis 33:9 "And Esau said, I have enough, my brother; **keep** that thou hast unto thyself." (KJV)

This verse is easy to explain. As I have pointed out, *HAYAH* also has a meaning of "to have" or "to possess." Esau told Jacob to keep possessing, keep having his own flocks and herds because he was wealthy enough without them. The *HAYAH* in Genesis 33:9 is not used in either a static "being" or a dynamic "becoming" sense; it's another thought altogether. Rather than "being," it expresses "having." Sometimes it's difficult to differentiate between "being" and "having." As I mentioned, in Spanish I would say, "I have hunger" rather than "I am hungry." I suppose all languages have this kind of difficulty and they resolve them in different ways. The ancient Hebrews resolved it for the most part by using *HAYAH* as a way of expressing a dynamic "coming to be" rather than a static "condition of being."

Almost all of the *King James* "was" translations of the *QAL* imperfect form of *HAYAH* belong to a sub-category of the *QAL* Imperfect. This sub-category is the *WAW* Consecutive. What is the *WAW* Consecutive? In the next chapter, I will discuss the different forms of *WAW* and how they help determine the proper translation of Genesis 1:1-2. For now, let me tell you the *WAW* Consecutive is a form of *WAW* ("and," "but," "or," "now," *etc.*) used to connect items in such a way as to impart the idea of consecutive actions or conditions. It was one of the ways the Hebrews used to express the "timing" of action and events. A *WAW* Consecutive would be added at the beginning of a new sentence to indicate it followed after (consecutive to) the previous sentence. In English, we put a period at the end of sentences to show where the thoughts and ideas stop. In Hebrew, the *WAW* Consecutive serves a very similar purpose. I mention this because I don't want you to think I am avoiding some forms of the *HAYAH* translated, "was," in the *King James Version*. In one sense this has little direct part in the translation of Genesis 1:2 because the *WAW* in Genesis 1:2 is not a *WAW* Consecutive and the *HAYAH* is not a *QAL* Imperfect. The *WAW* in Genesis 1:2 is a *WAW* Disjunctive and the *HAYAH* is a *QAL* Perfect. However, if you see how *WAW* and *HAYAH* are used in other situations, you can get a feel for what they meant to the ancient Hebrews.

The *WAW* Consecutive

"The *Waw* Consecutive (wcs) If two verbs are referring to the past in one continuous narration, only the first verb is in the Perfect, while any following verb is in the Imperfect with a prefixed *waw*. 'And Judah said unto Simeon… I likewise will go with thee into the lot. So Simeon went with him' (Judges 1:3); '… Yet ye say, Wherein hast thou loved us? … yet

I love Jacob' (Malachi 1:2). Conversely, in a continuous narration referring to the future only the first verb is in the Imperfect, while any following verb is in the Perfect with a prefixed *waw*. '… Let there be sought for my lord the king a young virgin: <u>and</u> let her stand before the king…' (1 Kings 1:2); '… bring *it* into me, <u>and</u> I will hear it' (Deuteronomy 1:7)."[108]

Below are the instances of the *QAL* Imperfect *HAYAH* with the *WAW* Consecutive in Genesis translated, "was," in the *King James Bible*. The **<u>WAW</u>** is in underlined and bold print, and the ***QAL*** **Imperfect** ***HAYAH*** is in bold print.

1.) Genesis 1:3 "And God said, Let there be light: **<u>and</u>** there **was** light." (KJV)

2.) Genesis 1:7 "And God made the firmament, and divided the waters which *were* under the firmament from the waters which *were* above the firmament: **<u>and</u>** it **was** so." (KJV)

3.) Genesis 1:9 "And God said, Let the waters under the heaven be gathered together unto one place, and let the dry *land* appear: **<u>and</u>** it **was** so." (KJV)

4.) Genesis 1:11 "And God said, Let the earth bring forth grass, the herb yielding seed, *and* the fruit tree yielding fruit after his kind, whose seed *is* in itself, upon the earth: **<u>and</u>** it **was** so." (KJV)

5.) Genesis 1:15 "And let them be for lights in the firmament of the heaven to give light upon the earth: **<u>and</u>** it **was** so." (KJV)

6.) Genesis 1:24 "And God said, Let the earth bring forth the living creature after his kind, cattle, and creeping thing, and beast of the earth after his kind: **<u>and</u>** it **was** so." (KJV)

7.) Genesis 1:30 "And to every beast of the earth, and to every fowl of the air, and to every thing that creepeth upon the earth, wherein *there is* life, *I have given* every green herb for meat: **<u>and</u>** it **was** so." (KJV)

8.) Genesis 4:2 "And she again bare his brother Abel. **<u>And</u>** Abel **was** a keeper of sheep, but Cain was a tiller of the ground." (KJV)

The first *HAYAH* in Genesis 4:2 is in the *WAW* Consecutive, *QAL* Imperfect form—"And Abel was." The second *HAYAH* is in the *WAW* Consecutive, *QAL* Perfect form—"but Cain was." As mentioned above, this was the way the Hebrews expressed the future tense in a continuous narrative. Remember, you can't tell the tense of a verb merely by its form; you need to see the context. This means Genesis 4:2 refers to a future event. The context proves "was" does not refer to a past, static condition in Genesis 4:2. Cain and Abel would later become these things.

9.) Genesis 5:32 "**And** Noah **was** five hundred years old: and Noah begat Shem, Ham, and Japheth." (KJV)

10.) Genesis 7:12 "**And** the rain **was** upon the earth forty days and forty nights." (KJV)

11.) Genesis 7:17 "**And** the flood **was** forty days upon the earth; and the waters increased, and bare up the ark, and it was lift up above the earth." (KJV)

12.) Genesis 10:10 "**And** the beginning of his kingdom **was** Babel, and Erech, and Accad, and Calneh, in the land of Shinar." (KJV)

13.) Genesis 10:19 "**And** the border of the Canaanites **was** from Sidon, as thou comest to Gerar, unto Gaza; as thou goest, unto Sodom, and Gomorrah, and Admah, and Zeboim, even unto Lasha." (KJV)

14.) Genesis 10:30 "**And** their dwelling **was** from Mesha, as thou goest unto Sephar a mount of the east." (KJV)

15.) Genesis 11:1 "**And** the whole earth **was** of one language, and of one speech." (KJV)

16.) Genesis 11:30 "**But** Sarai **was** barren; she *had* no child." (KJV)

17.) Genesis 12:10 "**And** there **was** a famine in the land: and Abram went down into Egypt to sojourn there; for the famine *was* grievous in the land." (KJV)

18.) Genesis 13:7 "**And** there **was** a strife between the herdmen of Abram's cattle and the herdmen of Lot's cattle: and the Canaanite and the Perizzite dwelled then in the land." (KJV)

19.) Genesis 17:1 "**And** when Abram **was** ninety years old and nine, the LORD appeared to Abram, and said unto him, I *am* the Almighty God; walk before me, and be thou perfect." (KJV)

20.) Genesis 21:20 "**And** God **was** with the lad; and he grew, and dwelt in the wilderness, and became an archer." (KJV)

21.) Genesis 23:1 "**And** Sarah **was** an hundred and seven and twenty years old: *these were* the years of the life of Sarah." (KJV)

22.) Genesis 25:20 "**And** Isaac **was** forty years old when he took Rebekah to wife, the daughter of Bethuel the Syrian of Padanaram, the sister to Laban the Syrian." (KJV)

23.) Genesis 25:27 "And the boys grew: **and** Esau **was** a cunning hunter, a man of the field; and Jacob *was* a plain man, dwelling in tents." (KJV)

24.) Genesis 26:1 "**And** there **was** a famine in the land, beside the first famine that was in the days of Abraham. And Isaac went unto Abimelech king of the Philistines unto Gerar." (KJV)

25.) Genesis 26:34 "**And** Esau **was** forty years old when he took to wife Judith the daughter of Beeri the Hittite, and Bashemath the daughter of Elon the Hittite:" (KJV)

26.) Genesis 27:30 "And it came to pass, as soon as Isaac had made an end of blessing Jacob, **and** Jacob **was** yet scarce gone out from the presence of Isaac his father, that Esau his brother came in from his hunting." (KJV)

27.) Genesis 35:3 "And let us arise, and go up to Bethel; and I will make there an altar unto God, who answered me in the day of my distress, **and was** with me in the way which I went." (KJV)

28.) Genesis 35:5 "And they journeyed: **and** the terror of God **was** upon the cities that *were* round about them, and they did not pursue after the sons of Jacob." (KJV)

29.) Genesis 35:16 "And they journeyed from Bethel; **and** there **was** but a little way to come to Ephrath: and Rachel travailed, and she had hard labour." (KJV)

30.) Genesis 38:7 "**And** Er, Judah's firstborn, **was** wicked in the sight of the LORD; and the LORD slew him." (KJV)

31. and 32. and 33.) Genesis 39:2 "**And** the LORD **was** with Joseph, **and** he **was** a prosperous man; **and** he **was** in the house of his master the Egyptian." (KJV)

34.) Genesis 39:5 "And it came to pass from the time *that* he had made him overseer in his house, and over all that he had, that the LORD blessed the Egyptian's house for Joseph's sake; **and** the blessing of the LORD **was** upon all that he had in the house, and in the field." (KJV)

35.) Genesis 39:6 "And he left all that he had in Joseph's hand; and he knew not ought he had, save the bread which he did eat. **And** Joseph **was** *a* goodly *person,* and well favoured." (KJV)

36.) Genesis 39:20 "And Joseph's master took him, and put him into the prison, a place where the king's prisoners *were* bound: **and** he **was** there in the prison." (KJV)

37.) Genesis 39:21 "**But** the LORD **was** with Joseph, and showed him mercy, and gave him favour in the sight of the keeper of the prison." (KJV)

38.) Genesis 41:54 "And the seven years of dearth began to come, according as Joseph had said: **and** the dearth **was** in all lands; but in all the land of Egypt there **was** bread." (KJV)

39.) Genesis 47:28 "And Jacob lived in the land of Egypt seventeen years: **so** the whole age of Jacob **was** an hundred forty and seven years." (KJV)

40.) Genesis 50:9 "And there went up with him both chariots and horsemen: **and** it **was** a very great company." (KJV)

As you can see, when *HAYAH* is used in these passages in the sense of "being," (rather than "having") it expresses dynamic conditions rather than static conditions. ("Coming to be," rather than simple "being.") Famine came upon the land. Esau became a cunning hunter. The rain came upon the land forty days and forty nights. The terror of God came upon these cities. Joseph became a prosperous man. God said, "Light come to be," and light came to be. Again, I know Genesis 1:2 doesn't use the *QAL* Imperfect form of *HAYAH*; it uses the *QAL* Perfect form, but I want to spend some time on this. I want you to see how the ancient Hebrews used *HAYAH*. I want you to begin to get a glimpse of what they thought about *HAYAH*. I want you to think like an ancient Hebrew. Since the *HAYAH* in Genesis 1:2 is in the *QAL* Perfect form, we need to look at what the *QAL* Perfect form means.

The *QAL* Perfect

"The *Qal* Perfect (qpf) indicates, in the active voice, simple perfective **action**, viewed as a whole. 'I will sing unto the Lord, because he hath dealt bountifully with me.' (Psalms 13:6); 'For a nation is come up upon the land...' (Joel 1:6)."[109]

Again we see a form of the *QAL* stem that describes **ACTION**. In this case, the action is usually viewed as completed. This is the form found in Genesis 1:2. Before we look at the *QAL* Perfect, let's examine a sub-category of the *QAL* Perfect, the *WAW* Conjunctive of the *QAL* Perfect. (Are you confused yet?) Let's find out what the *WAW* Conjunctive means.

The *WAW* Conjunctive

"The *Waw* Conjunctive (wcj) The letter *waw* serves as a link between two words, clauses, or sentences, and is affixed inseparably to the word that follows it. It is normally pointed with sh^{e}wa, but may take other vowels depending on which letter of the alphabet it precedes. '… <u>for</u> Joseph was in Egypt *already*' (Exodus 1:5); '… the nobles <u>and</u> princes of the provinces…' (Esther 1:3). Its meaning with verbs is so decisive that some view it as a separate conjunction. '… Be fruitful, <u>and</u> multiply, <u>and</u> fill the waters in the seas…' (Genesis 1:22); 'Behold ye among the heathen, <u>and</u> regard, <u>and</u> wonder marvelously…' (Habakkuk 1:5)"[110]

The *WAW* Conjunctive with the *QAL* Perfect of *HAYAH* in Genesis (KJV)

1.) Genesis 9:13 "I do set my bow in the cloud, **<u>and</u>** it **shall be** for a token of a covenant between me and the earth." (KJV)

2.) Genesis 9:14 "**<u>And</u>** it shall **come to pass**, when I bring a cloud over the earth, that the bow shall be seen in the cloud" (KJV)

3.) Genesis 24:14 "**<u>And</u>** let it **come to pass**, that the damsel to whom I shall say, Let down thy pitcher, I pray thee, that I may drink; and she shall say, Drink, and I will give thy camels drink also: let the same be she that thou hast appointed for thy servant Isaac; and thereby shall I know that thou hast showed kindness unto my master." (KJV)

4.) Genesis 24:43 "Behold, I stand by the well of water; **<u>and</u>** it shall **come to pass**, that when the virgin cometh forth to draw water, and I say to her, Give me, I pray thee, a little water of thy pitcher to drink;" (KJV)

5.) Genesis 30:41 "**<u>And</u>** it **came to pass**, whensoever the stronger cattle did conceive, that Jacob laid the rods before the eyes of the cattle in the gutters, that they might conceive among the rods." (KJV)

6.) Genesis 38:5 "And she yet again conceived, and bare a son; and called his name Shelah: **<u>and</u>** he **was** at Chezib, when she bare him." (KJV)

7.) Genesis 44:31 "It shall **come to pass**, when he seeth that the lad is not with us, that he will die: and thy servants shall bring down the gray hairs of thy servant our father with sorrow to the grave." (KJV)

(Note: The *WAW* is not translated here in the *King James Bible*. The Hebrew actually says, "**And** it shall come to pass," or "**but** it shall come to pass," or "**now** it shall come to pass," *etc*.)

8.) Genesis 46:33 "**And** it shall **come to pass**, when Pharaoh shall call you, and shall say, What is your occupation?" (KJV)

9.) Genesis 47:24 "**And** it shall **come to pass** in the increase, that ye shall give the fifth part unto Pharaoh, and four parts shall be your own, for seed of the field, and for your food, and for them of your households, and for food for your little ones." (KJV)

10.) Genesis 48:21 "And Israel said unto Joseph, Behold, I die: **but** God **shall be** with you, and bring you again unto the land of your fathers." (KJV)

      The only reason I mention the *WAW* Conjunctive of the *QAL* Perfect is because the *King James* translators translated the *HAYAH* in Genesis 38:5 as, "was," and I want to thoroughly examine all the "was" translations of *HAYAH* in Genesis. I don't want to leave out even one, lest I get accused of "cherry-picking" my examples. All the other uses of *HAYAH* in the *WAW* Conjunctive of the *QAL* Perfect are translated in the sense of coming to pass or coming to be; in other words, "become." Even though it is translated, "was," in Genesis 38:5, it describes the dynamic condition of location. The Hebrews did not think of a person's location as being a static, unchanging condition. It was dynamic. As Thorleif Boman said, "the Hebrews thought only in dynamic categories, not static ones."

      The *QAL* Perfect *HAYAH* of Genesis 1:2

      Finally, we get to the *HAYAH* of Genesis 1:2. It is in the *QAL* Perfect Form. I will list all the instances of *HAYAH* in Genesis in the *QAL* Perfect form and translated, "was," in the *King James Bible*. There are other *HAYAH*'s in the *QAL* Perfect form in Genesis translated other ways than, "was," but for now, I want to focus on the argument the *HAYAH* in Genesis 1:2 must mean "was" and cannot mean "became." Following each verse in the KJV (*King James Version*) I will list the PSV (*Peasant Steve Version*) (underlined) to show how a form of "became" makes better sense. I'll save Genesis 1:2 for last. Not all of the *HAYAH*s listed are in the same form as the *HAYAH* in Genesis 1:2. The *HAYAH* (*QAL* Perfect) in Genesis 1:2 is used with the *WAW* Disjunctive, but more on that in the next chapter. For now, I just want you to see how the ancient Hebrews thought when they used the *QAL* Perfect of *HAYAH*.

1.) Genesis 3:1 "Now the serpent **was** more subtil than any beast of the field which the LORD God had made. And he said unto the woman, Yea, hath God said, Ye shall not eat of every tree of the garden?" (KJV)

Genesis 3:1 "Now the serpent **came to be** more subtle than any beast of the field which the LORD God had made. And he said unto the woman, Yea, hath God said, Ye shall not eat of every tree of the garden?"

2.) Genesis 3:20 "And Adam called his wife's name Eve; because she **was** the mother of all living." (KJV)

Genesis 3:20 "And Adam called his wife's name Eve; because she **became** the mother of all living."

3.) Genesis 4:2 "And she again bare his brother Abel. And Abel was a keeper of sheep, but Cain **was** a tiller of the ground." (KJV)

Genesis 4:2 "And she again bare his brother Abel. And Abel became a keeper of sheep, but Cain **became** a tiller of the ground."

4.) Genesis 4:20 "And Adah bare Jabal: he **was** the father of such as dwell in tents, and *of such as have* cattle." (KJV)

Genesis 4:20 "And Adah bare Jabal: he **became** the father of such as dwell in tents, and *of such as have* cattle."

5.) Genesis 4:21 "And his brother's name *was* Jubal: he **was** the father of all such as handle the harp and organ." (KJV)

Genesis 4:21 "And his brother's name *was* Jubal: he **became** the father of all such as handle the harp and organ."

6.) Genesis 6:9 "These *are* the generations of Noah: Noah **was** a just man *and* perfect in his generations, *and* Noah walked with God." (KJV)

Genesis 6:9 "These *are* the generations of Noah: Noah **became** a just man *and* perfect in his generations, *and* Noah walked with God."

7.) Genesis 7:6 "And Noah *was* six hundred years old when the flood of waters **was** upon the earth." (KJV)

Genesis 7:6 "And Noah *was* six hundred years old when the flood of waters **came** upon the earth."

8.) Genesis 10:9 "He **was** a mighty hunter before the LORD: wherefore it is said, Even as Nimrod the mighty hunter before the LORD." (KJV)

Genesis 10:9 "He **became** a mighty hunter before the LORD: wherefore it is said, Even as Nimrod the mighty hunter before the LORD."

9.) Genesis 13:6 "And the land was not able to bear them, that they might dwell together: for their substance **was** great, so that they could not dwell together." (KJV)

Genesis 13:6 "And the land was not able to bear them, that they might dwell together: for their substance **became** great, so that they could not dwell together."

10.) Genesis 15:17 "And it came to pass, that, when the sun went down, and it **was** dark, behold a smoking furnace, and a burning lamp that passed between those pieces." (KJV)

Genesis 15:17 "And it came to pass, that, when the sun went down, and it **became** dark, behold a smoking furnace, and a burning lamp that passed between those pieces."

11.) Genesis 26:1 "And there was a famine in the land, beside the first famine that **was** in the days of Abraham. And Isaac went unto Abimelech king of the Philistines unto Gerar." (KJV)

Genesis 26:1 "And there was a famine in the land, beside the first famine that **came** in the days of Abraham. And Isaac went unto Abimelech king of the Philistines unto Gerar."

12.) Genesis 26:28 "And they said, We saw certainly that the LORD **was** with thee: and we said, Let there be now an oath betwixt us, *even* betwixt us and thee, and let us make a covenant with thee;" (KJV)

Genesis 26:28 "And they said, We saw certainly that the LORD **came to be** with thee: and we said, Let there be now an oath betwixt us, *even* betwixt us and thee, and let us make a covenant with thee;"

13.) Genesis 29:17 "Leah *was* tender eyed; but Rachel **was** beautiful and well favoured." (KJV)

Genesis 29:17 "Leah *was* tender eyed; but Rachel **had become** beautiful and well favoured."

14.) Genesis 30:29 "And he said unto him, Thou knowest how I have served thee, and how thy cattle **was** with me." (KJV)

Genesis 30:29 "And he said unto him, Thou knowest how I have served thee, and how thy cattle **came to be** with me."

15.) Genesis 31:40 "*Thus* I **was**; in the day the drought consumed me, and the frost by night; and my sleep departed from mine eyes." (KJV)

Genesis 31:40 "*Thus* I **became**; in the day the drought consumed me, and the frost by night; and my sleep departed from mine eyes." (KJV)

16.) Genesis 36:12 "And Timna **was** concubine to Eliphaz Esau's son; and she bare to Eliphaz Amalek: these *were* the sons of Adah Esau's wife." (KJV)

Genesis 36:12 "And Timna **became** concubine to Eliphaz Esau's son; and she bare to Eliphaz Amalek: these *were* the sons of Adah Esau's wife."

17.) Genesis 37:2 "These *are* the generations of Jacob. Joseph, *being* seventeen years old, **was** feeding the flock with his brethren; and the lad *was* with the sons of Bilhah, and with the sons of Zilpah, his father's wives: and Joseph brought unto his father their evil report." (KJV)

Genesis 37:2 "These *are* the generations of Jacob. Joseph, *being* seventeen years old, **came** feeding the flock with his brethren; and the lad *was* with the sons of Bilhah, and with the sons of Zilpah, his father's wives: and Joseph brought unto his father their evil report."

18.) Genesis 38:21 "Then he asked the men of that place, saying, Where *is* the harlot, that *was* openly by the way side? And they said, There **was** no harlot in this *place*." (KJV)

Genesis 38:21 "Then he asked the men of that place, saying, Where *is* the harlot, that *was* openly by the way side? And they said, no harlot **came** to this *place*."

19.) Genesis 38:22 "And he returned to Judah, and said, I cannot find her; and also the men of the place said, *that* there **was** no harlot in this *place*." (KJV)

Genesis 38:22 "And he returned to Judah, and said, I cannot find her; and also the men of the place said, *that* no harlot **came** to this *place*."

20.) Genesis 39:22 "And the keeper of the prison committed to Joseph's hand all the prisoners that *were* in the prison; and whatsoever they did there, he **was** the doer *of it*." (KJV)

Genesis 39:22 "And the keeper of the prison committed to Joseph's hand all the prisoners that *were* in the prison; and whatsoever they did there, he **became** the doer *of it.*"

21.) Genesis 41:13 "And it came to pass, as he interpreted to us, so it **was**; me he restored unto mine office, and him he hanged." (KJV)

Genesis 41:13 "And it came to pass, as he interpreted to us, so it **became**; me he restored unto mine office, and him he hanged."

22.) Genesis 41:53 "And the seven years of plenteousness, that **was** in the land of Egypt, were ended." (KJV)

Genesis 41:53 "And the seven years of plenteousness, that **came** in the land of Egypt, were ended."

23.) Genesis 41:54 "And the seven years of dearth began to come, according as Joseph had said: and the dearth was in all lands; but in all the land of Egypt there **was** bread." (KJV)

Genesis 41:54 "And the seven years of dearth began to come, according as Joseph had said: and the dearth was in all lands; but in all the land of Egypt there **came to be** bread."

24.) Genesis 41:56 "And the famine **was** over all the face of the earth: And Joseph opened all the storehouses, and sold unto the Egyptians; and the famine waxed sore in the land of Egypt." (KJV)

Genesis 41:56 "And the famine **came** over all the face of the earth: And Joseph opened all the storehouses, and sold unto the Egyptians; and the famine waxed sore in the land of Egypt."

25.) Genesis 42:5 "And the sons of Israel came to buy *corn* among those that came: for the famine **was** in the land of Canaan." (KJV)

Genesis 42:5 "And the sons of Israel came to buy *corn* among those that came: for the famine **came** in the land of Canaan."

    Here we see the twenty-five instances of *HAYAH* in the *QAL* Perfect form translated, "was," in Genesis in the *King James Bible*. Again, this is the same form as in Genesis 1:2. I can substitute "became," "came," "came to be," or some other form of "become" in all of them, and they make as much sense, or even more sense than the word "was." None of these instances implies a past, static, unchanging condition. All of them imply action rather than being. In other words, every instance of *HAYAH* in the *QAL* Perfect form translated, "was," in Genesis in the *King James Bible* describes a dynamic "becoming" rather than a static "being." Someone tell me again why the *QAL* Perfect form of *HAYAH* in Genesis 1:2 CANNOT be translated as a dynamic condition of becoming.

By now your brain might be a little overworked by all this talk about Hebrew rules of grammar. I know it is confusing and tedious, and you might have been tempted to skim over it. Please, stop for a moment and read this:

IN THE BOOK OF GENESIS, EVERY INSTANCE OF *HAYAH* IN THE *QAL* PERFECT FORM TRANSLATED, "WAS," IN THE *KING JAMES BIBLE*, ACTUALLY DESCRIBES A DYNAMIC CONDITION OF BECOMING AND NOT A STATIC CONDITION OF BEING.

So, what is God telling us in Genesis 1:2? What is the best INFORMATIONAL translation? Only the Gap Theory interprets Genesis with the information God revealed.

Genesis 1:2 "But the earth **had become** without form, and void; and darkness was upon the face of the deep. And the Spirit of God moved upon the face of the waters."

HAYAH and the Preposition *le*

But wait! What about the claim that *HAYAH* cannot mean "became" unless it is followed by the preposition *le*? Over the years, this claim has been made by many creationists who reject the Gap Theory. Both Young-Earth and Day-Age creationists repeatedly insist that since the word *HAYAH* in Genesis 1:2 is not followed by the preposition *le*, (*LAMEDH*, ל, in the Hebrew) then Genesis 1:2 cannot be translated, "But the earth became without form, and void." Go back to Chapter Seven and read Gleason Archer's comments where he refuted this claim. He pointed out why it has no merit; and remember, Archer was not a Gap Theory defender. Arthur Custance, on the other hand, was a Gap Theory defender and he thoroughly destroyed this claim decades ago (1970) in his book, *Without Form and Void*.[111] Nevertheless, this claim has become somewhat of a zombie. It keeps rising out of the grave no matter how much evidence has sealed its coffin. Now, resurrection is a great thing if what comes out of the tomb is good, and pure, and holy. Sadly, this claim was a lie when it was first made, and like a rotting corpse, it remains a filthy lie every time someone digs it up again. I can't tell you how many times I have heard or read someone repeat the mantra, "*HAYAH* cannot be translated, 'became,' unless it is followed by the preposition *le*." More often than should be, this zombie is paraded around by Christians who claim they have read Custance's book.

Looking for *LAMEDH* in All the Wrong Places

The claim is made that the preposition ל must follow the *HAYAH* in order for it to be translated as some form of "became." Here is the real evidence. Along with the English (KJV) words, I will add what *The Complete Word Study Old Testament*[112] reveals about their usage, (grammar codes) and actually show the passages in the Hebrew. I will highlight the specific letters and words in bold and underlined print. (Remember: The Hebrew reads from right-to-left. The Strong's Numbers are included in both the English and the Hebrew to help you find and compare the words.)

First, let me point out that *HAYAH* followed by *LAMEDH* is correctly translated as a form of "became." I will give five examples just to show you what it looks like in the Hebrew. There are many, many more, but my point is not to prove *LAMEDH* following *HAYAH* means "became." My point is to show how *HAYAH* doesn't need the *LAMEDH* to allow it to mean "became."

HAYAH with the *LAMEDH* (ל)

1.) Genesis 2:10 "And a river[H5104] went out[H3318] of Eden[H4480 H5731] to water[H8248 H853] the garden;[H1588] and from thence[H4480 H8033] it was parted,[H6504] and **became**[H1961 wcs,qpf] into four[H702] heads.[H7218]" (KJV)

Genesis 2:10 ונהר[H5104] יצא[H3318] מעדן[H5731] להשקות[H8248] את[H853] הגן[H1588] ומשם[H8033] יפרד[H6504] **והיה**[H1961] **לארבעה**[H702] ראשים[H7218]

You can see how this works. "Became" (*HAYAH*, היה, Strong's Number H1961) is followed by "four" (*ARBA*, ארבעה, Strong's Number H702). But if you look closely you will see that היה is actually והיה and ארבעה is actually לארבעה. Each word has an additional letter tacked onto its front; each word has a prefix. The letter *WAW* (ו) is attached to היה (*HAYAH*) because *WAW* is the conjunction "and." The sentence says, "… it was parted, <u>and</u> became…." The letter *LAMEDH* (ל) is attached to (*ARBA*) because *LAMEDH* is the preposition "to" or "into." The sentence says "… <u>into</u> four heads…." We will look at *WAW* in more detail shortly, but let's look at *LAMEDH* for now. The text literally says the river went out of (or came out of) Eden to water the Garden and from the Garden it parted and "came to" or "came to be" four heads.

2.) Genesis 20:12 "And yet[H1571] indeed[H546] *she is* my sister;[H269] she[H1931] *is* the daughter[H1323] of my father,[H1] but[H389] not[H3808] the daughter[H1323] of my mother;[H517] and she **became**[H1961 wcs,qmf] my wife.[H802]" (KJV)

Genesis 20:12 וְגַם^{H1571} אָמְנָה^{H546} אֲחֹתִי^{H269} בַת^{H1323} אָבִי^{H1} הִוא^{H1931} אַךְ^{H389} לֹא^{H3808} בַת^{H1323} אִמִּי^{H517} **וַתְּהִי^{H1961} לִי לְאִשָּׁה**^{H802}

Sarah was Abraham's half-sister. She had the same father but a different mother. Note that "*is*" is in italics when describing Sarah's relationship to her father Terah and to her brother Abraham; no *HAYAH* is needed in either case because those relationships were static and unchanging. Yet when it comes to her relationship to Abraham as his wife, *HAYAH* is needed; she "came to be" (became) his wife. That was dynamic.

3.) Genesis 32:10 "I am not worthy^{H6994} of the least of all^{H4480 H3605} the mercies,^{H2617} and of all^{H4480 H3605} the truth,^{H571} which^{H834} thou hast showed^{H6213} unto^{H853} thy servant;^{H5650} for^{H3588} with my staff^{H4731} I passed over^{H5674 H853} this^{H2088} Jordan;^{H3383} and now^{H6258} I am **become^{H1961 qpf}** two^{H8147} bands.^{H4264}" (KJV)

Genesis 32:10 קָטֹנְתִּי^{H6994} מִכֹּל^{H3605} הַחֲסָדִים^{H2617} וּמִכָּל^{H3605} הָאֱמֶת^{H571} אֲשֶׁר^{H834} עָשִׂיתָ^{H6213} אֶת^{H853} עַבְדֶּךָ^{H5650} כִּי^{H3588} בְמַקְלִי^{H4731} עָבַרְתִּי^{H5674} אֶת^{H853} הַיַּרְדֵּן^{H3383} הַזֶּה^{H2088} וְעַתָּה^{H6258} **הָיִיתִי^{H1961} לִשְׁנֵי**^{H8147} מַחֲנוֹת^{H4264}

By God's blessing, Jacob's wealth, family, and possessions were large enough to "come to be" (become) two companies of people.

4.) Exodus 7:10 "And Moses^{H4872} and Aaron^{H175} went in^{H935} unto^{H413} Pharaoh,^{H6547} and they did^{H6213} so^{H3651} as^{H834} the L<small>ORD</small>^{H3068} had commanded:^{H6680} and Aaron^{H175} cast down^{H7993 853} his rod^{H4294} before^{H6440} Pharaoh,^{H6547} and before^{H6440} his servants,^{H5650} and it **became^{H1961 wcs,qmf}** a serpent.^{H8577}" (KJV)

Exodus 7:10 וַיָּבֹא^{H935} מֹשֶׁה^{H4872} וְאַהֲרֹן^{H175} אֶל^{H413} פַּרְעֹה^{H6547} וַיַּעֲשׂוּ^{H6213} כֵן^{H3651} כַּאֲשֶׁר^{H834} צִוָּה^{H6680} יְהוָה^{H3068} וַיַּשְׁלֵךְ^{H7993} אַהֲרֹן^{H175} אֶת^{H853} מַטֵּהוּ^{H4294} לִפְנֵי^{H6440} פַרְעֹה^{H6547} וְלִפְנֵי^{H6440} עֲבָדָיו^{H5650} **וַיְהִי^{H1961} לְתַנִּין**^{H8577}

Aaron's rod "came to be" (became) a serpent.

5.) 1 Samuel 25:42 "And Abigail^{H26} hasted,^{H4116} and arose,^{H6965} and rode^{H7392} upon^{H5921} an ass,^{H2543} with five^{H2568} damsels^{H5291} of hers that went^{H1980} after^{H7272} her; and she went^{H1980} after^{H310} the messengers^{H4397} of David,^{H1732} and **became^{H1961 wcs,qmf}** his wife.^{H802}" (KJV)

1 Samuel 25:42 וַתְּמַהֵר^{H4116} וַתָּקָם^{H6965} אֲבִיגַיִל^{H26} וַתִּרְכַּב^{H7392} עַל^{H5921} הַחֲמוֹר^{H2543} וְחָמֵשׁ^{H2568} נַעֲרֹתֶיהָ^{H5291} הַהֹלְכוֹת^{H1980} לְרַגְלָהּ^{H7272} וַתֵּלֶךְ^{H1980} אַחֲרֵי^{H310} מַלְאֲכֵי^{H4397} דָוִד^{H1732} **וַתְּהִי^{H1961} לוֹ לְאִשָּׁה**^{H802}

Abigail "came to be" (became) David's wife.

HAYAH without the LAMEDH (ל)

Now, let me show you some examples to prove *HAYAH* without the *LAMEDH* can still be translated, "became" or "become." Look closely at these examples and you will see that a *LAMEDH* does not follow the *HAYAH*, but it is still translated as a form of "became."

1.) Genesis 3:22 "And the LORD[H3068] God[H430] said,[H559] Behold,[H2005] the man[H120] is **become**[H1961 qpf] as one[H259] of[H4480] us, to know[H3045] good[H2896] and evil:[H7451] and now,[H6258] lest[H6435] he put forth[H7971] his hand,[H3027] and take[H3947] also[H1571] of the tree[H4480 H6086] of life,[H2416] and eat,[H398] and live[H2425] for ever:[H5769]" (KJV)

Genesis 3:22 ויאמר[H559] יהוה[H3068] אלהים[H430] הן[H2005] האדם[H120] **היה**[H1961] כאחד[H259] ממנו[H4480] לדעת[H3045] טוב[H2896] ורע[H7451] ועתה[H6258] פן[H6435] ישלח[H7971] ידו[H3027] ולקח[H3947] גם[H1571] מעץ[H6086] החיים[H2416] ואכל[H398] וחי[H2425] לעלם[H5769]

NO *LAMEDH* FOLLOWS THE *HAYAH*

2.) Genesis 19:26 "But his wife[H802] looked[H5027] back from behind[H4480 H310] him, and she **became**[H1961 wcs,qmf] a pillar[H5333] of salt.[H4417]" (KJV)

Genesis 19:26 ותבט[H5027] אשתו[H802] מאחריו[H310] **ותהי**[H1961] נציב[H5333] מלח[H4417]

NO *LAMEDH* FOLLOWS THE *HAYAH*

3.) Genesis 21:20 "And God[H430] was[H1961] with[H854] the lad;[H5288] and he grew,[H1431] and dwelt[H3427] in the wilderness,[H4057] and **became**[H1961 wcs,qmf] an archer.[H7235 H7199]" (KJV)

Genesis 21:20 ויהי[H1961] אלהים[H430] את[H854] הנער[H5288] ויגדל[H1431] וישב[H3427] במדבר[H4057] **ויהי**[H1961] רבה[H7232] קשת[H7198]

NO *LAMEDH* FOLLOWS THE *HAYAH*

4.) Genesis 37:20 "Come[H1980] now[H6258] therefore, and let us slay[H2026] him, and cast[H7993] him into some[H259] pit,[H953] and we will say,[H559] Some evil[H7451] beast[H2416] hath devoured[H398] him: and we shall see[H7200] what[H4100] will **become**[H1961 qmf] of his dreams.[H2472]" (KJV)

Genesis 37:20 ועתה[H6258] לכו[H1980] ונהרגהו[H2026] ונשלכהו[H7993] באחד[H259] הברות[H953] ואמרנו[H559] חיה[H2416] רעה[H7451] אכלתהו[H398] ונראה[H7200] מה[H4100] **יהיו**[H1961] חלמתיו[H2472]

NO *LAMEDH* FOLLOWS THE *HAYAH*

5.) Genesis 48:19 "And his father[H1] refused,[H3985] and said,[H559] I know[H3045] *it*, my son,[H1121] I know[H3045] *it:* he[H1931] also[H1571] shall become[H1961] a people,[H5971] and he[H1931] also[H1571] shall be great:[H1431] but truly[H199] his younger[H6996] brother[H251] shall be greater[H1431] than[H4480] he, and his seed[H2233] shall **become**[H1961 qmf] a multitude[H4393] of nations.[H1471]" (KJV)

Genesis 48:19 וימאן[H3985] אביו[H1] ויאמר[H559] ידעתי[H3045] בני[H1121] ידעתי[H3045] גם[H1571] הוא[H1931] יהיה[H1961] לעם[H5971] וגם[H1571] הוא[H1931] יגדל[H1431] ואולם[H199] אחיו[H251] הקטן[H6996] יגדל[H1431] ממנו[H4480] וזרעו[H2233] **יהיה**[H1961] מלא[H4393] הגוים[H1471]

NO *LAMEDH* FOLLOWS THE *HAYAH*

6.) Exodus 7:19 "And the LORD[H3068] spake[H559] unto[H413] Moses,[H4872] Say[H559] unto[H413] Aaron,[H175] Take[H3947] thy rod,[H4294] and stretch out[H5186] thine hand[H3027] upon[H5921] the waters[H4325] of Egypt,[H4714] upon[H5921] their streams,[H5104] upon[H5921] their rivers,[H2975] and upon[H5921] their ponds,[H98] and upon[H5921] all[H3605] their pools[H4723] of water,[H4325] that they may **become**[H1961 wcj,qmf] blood;[H1818] and *that* there may be[H1961] blood[H1818] throughout all[H3605] the land[H776] of Egypt,[H4714] both in *vessels of* wood,[H6086] and in *vessels of* stone.[H68]" (KJV)

Exodus 7:19 ויאמר[H559] יהוה[H3068] אל[H413] משה[H4872] אמר[H559] אל[H413] אהרן[H175] קח[H3947] מטך[H4294] ונטה[H5186] ידך[H3027] על[H5921] מימי[H4325] מצרים[H4714] על[H5921] נהרתם[H5104] על[H5921] יאריהם[H2975] ועל[H5921] אגמיהם[H98] ועל[H5921] כל[H3605] מקוה[H4723] מימיהם[H4325] **ויהיו**[H1961] דם[H1818] והיה[H1961] דם[H1818] בכל[H3605] ארץ[H776] מצרים[H4714] ובעצים[H6086] ובאבנים[H68]

NO *LAMEDH* FOLLOWS THE *HAYAH*

---

7. and 8.) Exodus 8:17 "And they did[H6213] so;[H3651] for Aaron[H175] stretched out[H5186] (H853) his hand[H3027] with his rod,[H4294] and smote[H5221] (H853) the dust[H6083] of the earth,[H776] and it **became**[H1961 wcs,qmf] lice[H3654] in man,[H120] and in beast;[H929] all[H3605] the dust[H6083] of the land[H776] **became**[H1961 qpf] lice[H3654] throughout all[H3605] the land[H776] of Egypt.[H4714]" (KJV)

Exodus 8:17 ויעשו[H6213] כן[H3651] ויט[H5186] אהרן[H175] את[H853] ידו[H3027] במטהו[H4294] ויך[H5221] את[H853] עפר[H6083] הארץ[H776] **ותהי**[H1961] הכנם[H3654] באדם[H120] ובבהמה[H929] כל[H3605] עפר[H6083] הארץ[H776] **היה**[H1961] כנים[H3654] בכל[H3605] ארץ[H776] מצרים[H4714]

NO LAMEDHs FOLLOW THE HAYAHs

9.) Exodus 9:10 "And they took[H3947] (H853) ashes[H6368] of the furnace,[H3536] and stood[H5975] before[H6440] Pharaoh;[H6547] and Moses[H4872] sprinkled[H2236] it up toward heaven;[H8064] and it **became**[H1961 wcs,qmf] a boil[H7822] breaking forth[H6524] *with* blains[H76] upon man,[H120] and upon beast.[H929]" (KJV)

Exodus 9:10 ויקחו^H3947 את^H853 פיח^H6368 הכבשן^H3536 ויעמדו^H5975 לפני^H6440 פרעה^H6547 ויזרק^H2236 אתו^H853 משה^H4872 השמימה^H8064 ויהי^H1961 שחין^H7822 אבעבעת^H76 פרח^H6524 באדם^H120 ובבהמה^H929

NO *LAMEDH* FOLLOWS THE *HAYAH*

10.) Exodus 23:29 "I will not^H3808 drive them out^H1644 from before^H4480 H6440 thee in one^H259 year;^H8141 lest^H6435 the land^H776 **become**^H1961 qmf desolate,^H8077 and the beast^H2416 of the field^H7704 multiply^H7227 against^H5921 thee." (KJV)

Exodus 23:29 לא^H3808 אגרשנו^H1644 מפניך^H6440 בשנה^H8141 אחת^H259 פן^H6435 תהיה^H1961 הארץ^H776 שממה^H8077 ורבה^H7227 עליך^H5921 חית^H2416 השדה^H7704

NO *LAMEDH* FOLLOWS THE *HAYAH*

11.) Exodus 32:1 "And when the people^H5971 saw^H7200 that^H3588 Moses^H4872 delayed^H954 to come down^H3381 out of^H4480 the mount,^H2022 the people^H5971 gathered themselves together^H6950 unto^H5921 Aaron,^H175 and said^H559 unto^H413 him, Up,^H6965 make^H6213 us gods,^H430 which^H834 shall go^H1980 before^H6440 us; for^H3588 *as for* this^H2088 Moses,^H4872 the man^H376 that^H834 brought us up^H5927 out of the land^H4480 H776 of Egypt,^H4714 we wot^H3045 not^H3808 what^H4100 is **become**^H1961 qpf of him." (KJV)

Exodus 32:1 וירא^H7200 העם^H5971 כי^H3588 בשש^H954 משה^H4872 לרדת^H3381 מן^H4480 ההר^H2022 ויקהל^H6950 העם^H5971 על^H5921 אהרן^H175 ויאמרו^H559 אליו^H413 קום^H6965 עשה^H6213 לנו אלהים^H430 אשר^H834 ילכו^H1980 לפנינו^H6440 כי^H3588 זה^H2088 משה^H4872 האיש^H376 אשר^H834 העלנו^H5927 מארץ^H776 מצרים^H4714 לא^H3808 ידענו^H3045 מה^H4100 היה^H1961

NO *LAMEDH* FOLLOWS THE *HAYAH*

12.) Exodus 32:23 "For they said^H559 unto me, Make^H6213 us gods,^H430 which^H834 shall go^H1980 before^H6440 us: for^H3588 *as for* this^H2088 Moses,^H4872 the man^H376 that^H834 brought us up^H5927 out of the land^H4480 H776 of Egypt,^H4714 we wot^H3045 not^H3808 what^H4100 is **become**^H1961 wcs,qmf of him." (KJV)

Exodus 32:23 ויאמרו^H559 לי עשה^H6213 לנו אלהים^H430 אשר^H834 ילכו^H1980 לפנינו^H6440 כי^H3588 זה^H2088 משה^H4872 האיש^H376 אשר^H834 העלנו^H5927 מארץ^H776 מצרים^H4714 לא^H3808 ידענו^H3045 מה^H4100 היה^H1961

NO *LAMEDH* FOLLOWS THE *HAYAH*

13.) Exodus 36:13 "And he made^H6213 fifty^H2572 taches^H7165 of gold,^H2091 and coupled^H2266 (H853) the curtains^H3407 one^H259 unto^H413 another^H259 with the taches:^H7165 so it **became**^H1961 wcs,qmf one^H259 tabernacle.^H4908" (KJV)

Exodus 36:13 וַיַּעַשׂ^H6213 חֲמִשִּׁים^H2572 קַרְסֵי^H7165 זָהָב^H2091 וַיְחַבֵּר^H2266 אֶת^H853 הַיְרִיעֹת^H3407 אַחַת^H259 אֶל^H413 אַחַת^H259 בַּקְּרָסִים^H7165 **וַיְהִי^H1961** הַמִּשְׁכָּן^H4908 אֶחָד^H259

NO *LAMEDH* FOLLOWS THE *HAYAH*

14.) Judges 15:14 "*And* when he^H1931 came^H935 unto^H5704 Lehi,^H3896 the Philistines^H6430 shouted^H7321 against^H7125 him: and the Spirit^H7307 of the LORD^H3068 came mightily^H6743 upon^H5921 him, and the cords^H5688 that^H834 *were* upon^H5921 his arms^H2220 **became^H1961 wcs,qmf** as flax^H6593 that^H834 was burnt^H1197 with fire,^H784 and his bands^H612 loosed^H4549 from off^H4480 ^H5921 his hands.^H3027" (KJV)

Judges 15:14 הוּא^H1931 בָא^H935 עַד^H5704 לֶחִי^H3896 וּפְלִשְׁתִּים^H6430 הֵרִיעוּ^H7321 לִקְרָאתוֹ^H7125 וַתִּצְלַח^H6743 עָלָיו^H5921 רוּחַ^H7307 יְהוָה^H3068 **וַתִּהְיֶינָה^H1961** הָעֲבֹתִים^H5688 אֲשֶׁר^H834 עַל^H5921 זְרוֹעוֹתָיו^H2220 כַּפִּשְׁתִּים^H6593 אֲשֶׁר^H834 בָּעֲרוּ^H1197 בָאֵשׁ^H784 וַיִּמַּסּוּ^H4549 אֱסוּרָיו^H612 מֵעַל^H5921 יָדָיו^H3027

NO *LAMEDH* FOLLOWS THE *HAYAH*

15.) 1 Samuel 18:29 "And Saul^H7586 was yet^H5750 the more^H3254 afraid^H3372 of^H4480 H6440 David;^H1732 and Saul^H7586 **became^H1961 wcs,qmf** ^H853 David's^H1732 enemy^H341 continually.^H3605 ^H3117" (KJV)

1 Samuel 18:29 וַיֹּאסֶף^H3254 שָׁאוּל^H7586 לֵרֹא^H3372 מִפְּנֵי^H6440 דָוִד^H1732 עוֹד^H5750 **וַיְהִי^H1961** שָׁאוּל^H7586 אֹיֵב^H341 אֶת^H853 דָּוִד^H1732 כָּל^H3605 הַיָּמִים^H3117

NO *LAMEDH* FOLLOWS THE *HAYAH*

16.) 1 Samuel 28:16 "Then said^H559 Samuel,^H8050 Wherefore^H4100 then dost thou ask^H7592 of me, seeing the LORD^H3068 is departed^H5493 from^H4480 H5921 thee, and is **become^H1961 wcs,qmf** thine enemy?^H6145" (KJV)

1 Samuel 28:16 וַיֹּאמֶר^H559 שְׁמוּאֵל^H8050 וְלָמָּה^H4100 תִּשְׁאָלֵנִי^H7592 וַיהוָה^H3068 סָר^H5493 מֵעָלֶיךָ^H5921 **וַיְהִי^H1961** עָרֶךָ^H6145

NO *LAMEDH* FOLLOWS THE *HAYAH*

17.) 2 Samuel 8:14 "And he put^H7760 garrisons^H5333 in Edom;^H123 throughout all^H3605 Edom^H123 put^H7760 he garrisons,^H5333 and all^H3605 they of Edom^H123 **became^H1961wcs,qmf** David's^H1732 servants.^H5650 And the LORD^H3068 preserved^H3467 (^H853) David^H1732 whithersoever^H3605 H834 he went.^H1980" (KJV)

2 Samuel 8:14 וַיָּשֶׂם^H7760 בֶּאֱדוֹם^H123 נְצִבִים^H5333 בְּכָל^H3605 אֱדוֹם^H123 שָׂם^H7760 נְצִבִים^H5333 **וַיְהִי^H1961** כָל^H3605 אֱדוֹם^H123 עֲבָדִים^H5650 לְדָוִד^H1732 וַיּוֹשַׁע^H3467 יְהוָה^H3068 אֶת^H853 דָּוִד^H1732 בְּכֹל^H3605 אֲשֶׁר^H834 הָלָךְ^H1980

NO *LAMEDH* FOLLOWS THE *HAYAH*

18.) 1 Kings 11:24 "And he gathered^{H6908} men^{H376} unto^{H5921} him, and **became**^{H1961 wcs,qmf} captain^{H8269} over a band,^{H1416} when David^{H1732} slew^{H2026} them *of Zobah*: and they went^{H1980} to Damascus,^{H1834} and dwelt^{H3427} therein, and reigned^{H4427} in Damascus.^{H1834}" (KJV)

1 Kings 11:24 ויקבץ^{H6908} עליו^{H5921} אנשים^{H376} **ויהי**^{H1961} שר^{H8269} גדוד^{H1416} בהרג^{H2026} דוד^{H1732} אתם^{H853} וילכו^{H1980} דמשק^{H1834} וישבו^{H3427} בה וימלכו^{H4427} בדמשק^{H1834}

NO *LAMEDH* FOLLOWS THE *HAYAH*

19.) 1 Kings 13:6 "And the king^{H4428} answered^{H6030} and said^{H559} unto^{H413} the man^{H376} of God,^{H430} Intreat^{H2470} now^{H4994} (^{H853}) the face^{H6440} of the LORD^{H3068} thy God,^{H430} and pray^{H6419} for^{H1157} me, that my hand^{H3027} may be restored me again.^{H7725 H413} And the man^{H376} of God^{H430} besought^{H2470} (^{H853}) the LORD,^{H6440 H3068} and the king's^{H4428} hand^{H3027} was restored him again,^{H7725 H413} and **became**^{H1961 wcs,qmf} as *it was* before.^{H7223}" (KJV)

1 Kings 13:6 ויען^{H6030} המלך^{H4428} ויאמר^{H559} אל^{H413} איש^{H376} האלהים^{H430} חל^{H2470} נא^{H4994} את^{H853} פני^{H6440} יהוה^{H3068} אלהיך^{H430} והתפלל^{H6419} בעדי^{H1157} ותשב^{H7725} ידי^{H3027} אלי^{H413} ויחל^{H2470} איש^{H376} האלהים^{H430} את^{H853} פני^{H6440} יהוה^{H3068} ותשב^{H7725} יד^{H3027} המלך^{H4428} אליו^{H413} **ותהי**^{H1961} כבראשנה^{H7223}

NO *LAMEDH* FOLLOWS THE *HAYAH*

20.) 1 Kings 13:33 "After^{H310} this^{H2088} thing^{H1697} Jeroboam^{H3379} returned^{H7725} not^{H3808} from his evil way,^{H4480 H1870 H7451} but made^{H6213} again^{H7725} of the lowest^{H4480 H7098} of the people^{H5971} priests^{H3548} of the high places:^{H1116} whosoever would,^{H2655} he consecrated^{H4390} (^{H853}) ^{H3027} him, and he **became**^{H1961 wcj,qmf} *one* of the priests^{H3548} of the high places.^{H1116}" (KJV)

1 Kings 13:33 אחר^{H310} הדבר^{H1697} הזה^{H2088} לא^{H3808} שב^{H7725} ירבעם^{H3379} מדרכו^{H1870} הרעה^{H7451} וישב^{H7725} ויעש^{H6213} מקצות^{H7098} העם^{H5971} כהני^{H3548} במות^{H1116} החפץ^{H2655} ימלא^{H4390} את^{H853} ידו^{H3027} **ויהי**^{H1961} כהני^{H3548} במות^{H1116}

NO *LAMEDH* FOLLOWS THE *HAYAH*

21.) Psalms 119:83 "For^{H3588} I am **become**^{H1961 qpf} like a bottle^{H4997} in the smoke;^{H7008} *yet* do I not^{H3808} forget^{H7911} thy statutes.^{H2706}" (KJV)

Psalms 119:83 כי^{H3588} **הייתי**^{H1961} כנאד^{H4997} בקיטור^{H7008} חקיך^{H2706} לא^{H3808} שכחתי^{H7911}

NO *LAMEDH* FOLLOWS THE *HAYAH*

22.) Proverbs 29:21 "He that delicately bringeth up[H6445] his servant[H5650] from a child[H4480] [H5290] shall have him **become**[H1961 qmf] *his* son[H4497] at the length.[H319]" (KJV)

Proverbs 29:21 מפנק[H6445] מנער[H5290] עבדו[H5650] ואחריתו[H319] **יהיה**[H1961] מנון[H4497]

NO *LAMEDH* FOLLOWS THE *HAYAH*

23.) Isaiah 7:24 "With arrows[H2671] and with bows[H7198] shall *men* come[H935] thither;[H8033] because[H3588] all[H3605] the land[H776] shall **become**[H1961] briers[H8068] and thorns.[H7898]" (KJV)

Isaiah 7:24 בחצים[H2678] ובקשת[H7198] יבוא[H935] שמה[H8033] כי[H3588] שמיר[H8068] ושית[H7898] **תהיה**[H1961] כל[H3605] הארץ[H776]

NO *LAMEDH* FOLLOWS THE *HAYAH*

24.) Jeremiah 7:11 "Is this[H2088] house,[H1004] which[H834] is called[H7121] by[H5921] my name,[H8034] **become**[H1961 qpf] a den[H4631] of robbers[H6530] in your eyes?[H5869] Behold,[H2009] even[H1571] I[H595] have seen[H7200] *it,* saith[H5002] the LORD.[H3068]" (KJV)

Jeremiah 7:11 המערת[H4631] פרצים[H6530] **היה**[H1961] הבית[H1004] הזה[H2088] אשר[H834] נקרא[H7121] שמי[H8034] עליו[H5921] בעיניכם[H5869] גם[H1571] אנכי[H595] הנה[H2009] ראיתי[H7200] נאם[H5002] יהוה[H3069]

NO *LAMEDH* FOLLOWS THE *HAYAH*

25.) Jeremiah 22:5 But if[H518] ye will not[H3808] hear[H8085] [H853] these[H428] words,[H1697] I swear[H7650] by myself, saith[H5002] the LORD,[H3068] that[H3588] this[H2088] house[H1004] shall **become**[H1961 qmf] a desolation.[H2723]" (KJV)

Jeremiah 22:5 ואם[H518] לא[H3808] תשמעו[H8085] את[H853] הדברים[H1697] האלה[H428] בי[H428] נשבעתי[H7650] נאם[H5002] יהוה[H3068] כי[H3588] לחרבה[H2723] **יהיה**[H1961] הבית[H1004] הזה[H2088]:

NO *LAMEDH* FOLLOWS THE *HAYAH*

26.) Jeremiah 26:18 "Micah[H4320] the Morasthite[H4183] prophesied[H1961 H5012] in the days[H3117] of Hezekiah[H2396] king[H4428] of Judah,[H3063] and spake[H559] to[H413] all[H3605] the people[H5971] of Judah,[H3063] saying,[H559] Thus[H3541] saith[H559] the LORD[H3068] of hosts;[H6635] Zion[H6726] shall be plowed[H2790] *like* a field,[H7704] and Jerusalem[H3389] shall **become**[H1961 qpf] heaps,[H5856] and the mountain[H2022] of the house[H1004] as the high places[H1116] of a forest.[H3293]" (KJV)

Jeremiah 26:18 מיכיה[H4320] המורשתי[H4183] היה[H1961] נבא[H5012] בימי[H3117] חזקיהו[H2396] מלך[H4428] יהודה[H3063] ויאמר[H559] אל[H413] כל[H3605] עם[H5971] יהודה[H3063] לאמר[H559] כה[H3541] אמר[H559] יהוה[H3068] צבאות[H6635] ציון[H6726] שדה[H7704] תחרש[H2790] וירושלים[H3389] עיים[H5856] **תהיה**[H1961] והר[H2022] הבית[H1004] לבמות[H1116] יער[H3293]

NO *LAMEDH* FOLLOWS THE *HAYAH*

573

27.) Lamentations 1:1 "How^H349 doth the city^H5892 sit^H3427 solitary,^H910 *that was* full^H7227 of people!^H5971 *how* is she **become^H1961 qpf** as a widow!^H490 she *that was* great^H7227 among the nations,^H1471 *and* princess^H8282 among the provinces,^H4082 *how* is she become^H1961 tributary!^H4522" (KJV)

Lamentations 1:1 איכה^H349 ישבה^H3427 בדד^H910 העיר^H5892 רבתי^H7227 עם^H5971 **היתה^H1961** כאלמנה^H490 רבתי^H7227 בגוים^H1471 שרתי^H8282 במדינות^H4082 היתה^H1961 למס^H4522

NO *LAMEDH* FOLLOWS THE *HAYAH*

28.) Lamentations 1:6 "And from^H4480 the daughter^H1323 of Zion^H6726 all^H3605 her beauty^H1926 is departed:^H3318 her princes^H8269 are **become^H1961 qpf** like harts^H354 *that* find^H4672 no^H3808 pasture,^H4829 and they are gone^H1980 without^H3808 strength^H3581 before^H6440 the pursuer.^H7291" (KJV)

Lamentations 1:6 ויצא^H3318 מן^H4480 בת^H1323 ציון^H1323 כל^H3605 הדרה^H1926 **היו^H1961** שריה^H8269 כאילים^H354 לא^H3808 מצאו^H4672 מרעה^H4829 וילכו^H1980 בלא^H3808 כח^H3581 לפני^H6440 רודף^H7291

NO *LAMEDH* FOLLOWS THE *HAYAH*

29.) Lamentations 1:11 "All^H3605 her people^H5971 sigh,^H584 they seek^H1245 bread;^H3899 they have given^H5414 their pleasant things^H4262 for meat^H400 to relieve^H7725 the soul:^H5315 see,^H7200 O LORD,^H3068 and consider;^H5027 for^H3588 I am **become^H1961 qpf** vile.^H2151" (KJV)

Lamentations 1:11 כל^H3605 עמה^H5971 נאנחים^H584 מבקשים^H1245 לחם^H3899 נתנו^H5414 מחמודיהם^H4262 באכל^H400 להשיב^H7725 נפש^H5315 ראה^H7200 יהוה^H3068 והביטה^H5027 כי^H3588 **הייתי^H1961** זוללה^H2151

NO *LAMEDH* FOLLOWS THE *HAYAH*

30.) Lamentations 4:8 "Their visage^H8389 is blacker^H2821 than a coal;^H4480 H7815 they are not^H3808 known^H5234 in the streets:^H2351 their skin^H5785 cleaveth^H6821 to^H5921 their bones;^H6106 it is withered,^H3001 it is **become^H1961 qpf** like a stick.^H6086" (KJV)

Lamentations 4:8 חשך^H2821 משחור^H7815 תארם^H8389 לא^H3808 נכרו^H5234 בחוצות^H2351 צפד^H6821 עורם^H5785 על^H5921 עצמם^H6106 יבש^H3001 **היה^H1961** כעץ^H6086

NO *LAMEDH* FOLLOWS THE *HAYAH*

31.) Ezekiel 19:3 "And she brought up^H5927 one^H259 of her whelps:^H1482 it **became^H1961 qpf** a young lion,^H3715 and it learned^H3925 to catch^H2963 the prey;^H2964 it devoured^H398 men.^H120" (KJV)

Ezekiel 19:3 וַתַּעַל^{H5927} אֶחָד^{H259} מִגֻּרֶיהָ^{H1482} כְּפִיר^{H3715} **הָיָה**^{H1961} וַיִּלְמַד^{H3925} לִטְרָף^{H2963} טֶרֶף^{H2964} אָדָם^{H120} אָכָל^{H398}

NO *LAMEDH* FOLLOWS THE *HAYAH*

32.) Ezekiel 19:6 "And he went up and down^{H1980} among^{H8432} the lions,^{H738} he **became**^{H1961} <u>qpf</u> a young lion,^{H3715} and learned^{H3925} to catch^{H2963} the prey,^{H2964} *and* devoured^{H398} men.^{H120}" (KJV)

Ezekiel 19:6 וַיִּתְהַלֵּךְ^{H1980} בְּתוֹךְ^{H8432} אֲרָיוֹת^{H738} כְּפִיר^{H3715} **הָיָה**^{H1961} וַיִּלְמַד^{H3925} לִטְרָף^{H2963} טֶרֶף^{H2964} אָדָם^{H120} אָכָל^{H398}

NO *LAMEDH* FOLLOWS THE *HAYAH*

33.) Ezekiel 23:10 "These^{H1992} discovered^{H1540} her nakedness:^{H6172} they took^{H3947} her sons^{H1121} and her daughters,^{H1323} and slew^{H2026} [^{H853}] her with the sword:^{H2719} and she **became**^{H1961} <u>wcs,qmf</u> famous^{H8034} among women;^{H802} for they had executed^{H6213} judgment^{H8196} upon her." (KJV)

Ezekiel 23:10 הֵמָּה^{H1992} גִּלּוּ^{H1540} עֶרְוָתָהּ^{H6172} בָּנֶיהָ^{H1121} וּבְנוֹתֶיהָ^{H1323} לָקָחוּ^{H3947} וְאוֹתָהּ^{H853} בַּחֶרֶב^{H2719} הָרָגוּ^{H2026} **וַתְּהִי**^{H1961} שֵׁם^{H8034} לַנָּשִׁים^{H802} וּשְׁפוּטִים^{H8196} עָשׂוּ^{H6213}

NO *LAMEDH* FOLLOWS THE *HAYAH*

34.) Ezekiel 36:35 "And they shall say,^{H559} This^{H1977} land^{H776} that was desolate^{H8074} is **become**^{H1961} <u>qpf</u> like the garden^{H1588} of Eden;^{H5731} and the waste^{H2720} and desolate^{H8074} and ruined^{H2040} cities^{H5892} *are become* fenced,^{H1219} *and* are inhabited.^{H3427}" (KJV)

Ezekiel 36:35 וְאָמְרוּ^{H559} הָאָרֶץ^{H776} הַלֵּזוּ^{H1977} הַנְּשַׁמָּה^{H8074} **הָיְתָה**^{H1961} כְּגַן^{H1588} עֵדֶן^{H5731} וְהֶעָרִים^{H5892} הֶחֳרֵבוֹת^{H2720} וְהַנְשַׁמּוֹת^{H8074} וְהַנֶּהֱרָסוֹת^{H2040} בְּצוּרוֹת^{H1219} יָשָׁבוּ^{H3427}

NO *LAMEDH* FOLLOWS THE *HAYAH*

35.) Jonah 4:5 "So Jonah^{H3124} went out^{H3318} of^{H4480} the city,^{H5892} and sat^{H3427} on the east side^{H4480 H6924} of the city,^{H5892} and there^{H8033} made^{H6213} him a booth,^{H5521} and sat^{H3427} under^{H8478} it in the shadow,^{H6738} till^{H5704} he might see^{H7200} what^{H4100} would **become**^{H1961} <u>qmf</u> of the city.^{H5892}" (KJV)

Jonah 4:5 וַיֵּצֵא^{H3318} יוֹנָה^{H3124} מִן^{H4480} הָעִיר^{H5892} וַיֵּשֶׁב^{H3427} מִקֶּדֶם^{H6924} לָעִיר^{H5892} וַיַּעַשׂ^{H6213} לוֹ שָׁם^{H8033} סֻכָּה^{H5521} וַיֵּשֶׁב^{H3427} תַּחְתֶּיהָ^{H8478} בַּצֵּל^{H6738} עַד^{H5704} אֲשֶׁר^{H834} יִרְאֶה^{H7200} מַה^{H4100} **יִּהְיֶה**^{H1961} בָּעִיר^{H5892}

NO *LAMEDH* FOLLOWS THE *HAYAH*

36.) Micah 3:12 "Therefore^H3651 shall Zion^H6726 for your sake^H1558 be plowed^H2790 *as* a field,^H7704 and Jerusalem^H3389 shall **become^H1961 qmf** heaps,^H5856 and the mountain^H2022 of the house^H1004 as the high places^H1116 of the forest.^H3293" (KJV)

Micah 3:12 לכן^H3651 בגללכם^H1558 ציון^H6726 שדה^H7704 תחרש^H2790 וירושלם^H3389 עיין^H5856
תהיה^H1961 והר^H2022 הבית^H1004 לבמות^H1116 יער^H3293

NO *LAMEDH* FOLLOWS THE *HAYAH*

In all of these passages, NO *LAMEDH* FOLLOWS THE *HAYAH*, but they are ALL translated as some form of "became."

There are thirty-six *HAYAH*s translated, "became" or "become," in the *King James Version* where the preposition ל does not follow the *HAYAH*. And these are just the places where *HAYAH* is translated, "became" or "become." There are many other examples where *HAYAH* is translated into other words, such as, "was," but really mean "became," yet no *LAMEDH* was used. Examples of this are Genesis 3:20, Genesis 4:20, and Genesis 41:13.

Genesis 3:20 "And Adam called his wife's name Eve; because she **was** the mother of all living." (KJV)

Genesis 4:20 "And Adah bare Jabal: he **was** the father of such as dwell in tents, and *of such as have* cattle." (KJV)

Genesis 41:13 "And it came to pass, as he interpreted to us, so it **was**; me he restored unto mine office, and him he hanged." (KJV)

As I mentioned, Arthur Custance revealed this information years ago. Along with these examples, he showed how other translations translated *HAYAH* without the *LAMEDH* as "became" or "become" instead of "was" in many more places than the *King James Bible* does. So, why do Christians make the false claim that *HAYAH* can't be translated as a form of "became" when it isn't true? Those who claim to be Christians, yet repeatedly proclaim such untrue statements as this "*le-HAYAH* zombie," do not present Christ in a fashion that brings Him praise. Rather than being humbled by the truth, they misuse the truth and seek the praise of men for themselves. Once again I find myself needing to apologize to any of my readers who aren't Christians. My hope is you will not listen to Christians who make false claims. Ignore their claims, but take Christ's claims to heart.

Can *HAYETAH* Mean "Became"?

Gap Theory opponents raise another argument in order to convince people our interpretation of *HAYAH* is incorrect. They may grudgingly admit some forms of *HAYAH* can be translated, "became," but not the specific form found in Genesis 1:2. In fact, some accuse Gap Theory proponents of being dishonest when we say *HAYETAH* (The form of *HAYAH* in Genesis 1:2) means "became." They say *HAYETAH* always means "was," and can never be translated, "became." This argument falls into the same category as the "*LAMEDH-HAYAH* Argument." It is repeated so often, so loudly, by so many, it is assumed to be true.

HAYAH is the basic form of the verb, and it has many different forms and spellings. This is also true of our English verb "be." The English verb can be written as "am," "are," "is," "was," "became," "been," and several other forms. As you can see, these spellings vary tremendously, and if you didn't know English, you wouldn't recognize that "am" and "be" and "were" are forms of the same verb. In Hebrew, *HAYETAH* is the specific form in Genesis 1:2. Gap Theory opponents tell us we are wrong to translate *HAYETAH* as "became." In English, this would be like arguing "was" can never mean "became." We know this argument is erroneous. We have looked at my sentence, "I broke my wife's favorite vase, and she was mad." "Was" can mean "became," and it most certainly means "became" in this English sentence. So, can the same be true about *HAYETAH*? Let's look at Genesis 1:2 in the Hebrew.

Genesis 1:2 וְהָאָרֶץ^H776 **הָיְתָה^H1961** תֹהוּ^H8414 וָבֹהוּ^H922 וְחֹשֶׁךְ^H2822 עַל^H5921 פְּנֵי^H6440 תְהוֹם^H8415 וְרוּחַ^H7307 אֱלֹהִים^H430 מְרַחֶפֶת^H7363 עַל^H5921 פְּנֵי^H6440 הַמָּיִם^H4325:

The specific form of *HAYAH* (Strong's H1961) is *HAYETAH* and it looks like this: היתה.

Now look at the forms of *HAYAH* in Genesis 1:3:

Genesis 1:3 וַיֹּאמֶר^H559 אֱלֹהִים^H430 יְהִי^H1961 אוֹר^H216 וַיְהִי^H1961 אוֹר^H216:

As you can see, they are not the same as היתה. Instead, they are יהי and ויהי. As you read through Genesis 1, you will notice *HAYETAH* (היתה) is not used again. Other forms of *HAYAH* are found instead. Does this mean I have been lying to you? Some opponents of the Gap Theory will say I have. My task now is to show you *HAYETAH* can be, and is translated as a form of "became" in other parts of the Bible. Actually, I have shown you this already, but I didn't refer to it as the specific form *HAYETAH*. We have seen the sentences that use *HAYETAH* in Genesis, but now I will show you the Hebrew, so you can see for yourself that *HAYETAH* (היתה) is the form used.

1.) Genesis 1:2 "And the earth **was** (היתה) without form, and void; and darkness *was* upon the face of the deep. And the Spirit of God moved upon the face of the waters." (KJV)

2.) Genesis 3:20 "And Adam called his wife's name Eve; because she **was** (היתה) the mother of all living." (KJV)

3.) Genesis 29:17 "Leah *was* tender eyed; but Rachel **was** (היתה) beautiful and well favoured." (KJV)

4.) Genesis 36:12 "And Timna **was** (היתה) concubine to Eliphaz Esau's son; and she bare to Eliphaz Amalek: these *were* the sons of Adah Esau's wife." (KJV)

5.) Genesis 38:21 "Then he asked the men of that place, saying, Where *is* the harlot, that *was* openly by the way side? And they said, There **was** (היתה) no harlot in this *place*." (KJV)

6.) Genesis 38:22 "And he returned to Judah, and said, I cannot find her; and also the men of the place said, *that* there **was** (היתה) no harlot in this *place*." (KJV)

     You can see how *HAYETAH* expresses the idea of "became," "become," "came to be," "come to pass," *etc.* In fact, it is translated that way in Genesis 47:26 in the *King James Bible*.

7.) Genesis 47:26 "And Joseph made it a law over the land of Egypt unto this day, *that* Pharaoh should have the fifth *part*; except the land of the priests only, *which* **became** (היתה) not Pharaoh's." (KJV)

     There are other examples in the *King James Bible* where *HAYETAH* is translated, "became" or "become."

8.) Exodus 9:24 "So there was hail, and fire mingled with the hail, very grievous, such as there was none like it in all the land of Egypt since it **became** (היתה) a nation." (KJV)

9.) Joshua 14:14 "Hebron therefore **became** (היתה) the inheritance of Caleb the son of Jephunneh the Kenezite unto this day, because that he wholly followed the LORD God of Israel." (KJV)

10.) Psalms 118:22 "The stone *which* the builders refused is **become** (היתה) the head *stone* of the corner." (KJV)

11.) Isaiah 1:21 "How is the faithful city **become** (היתה) an harlot! it was full of judgment; righteousness lodged in it; but now murderers." (KJV)

12.) Jeremiah 50:23 "How is the hammer of the whole earth cut asunder and broken! how is Babylon **become** (היתה) a desolation among the nations!" (KJV)

13.) Jeremiah 51:41 "How is Sheshach taken! and how is the praise of the whole earth surprised! how is Babylon **become** (היתה) an astonishment among the nations!" (KJV)

14.) Lamentations 1:1 "How doth the city sit solitary, *that was* full of people! how is she **become** (היתה) as a widow! she *that was* great among the nations, *and* princess among the provinces, how is she **become** (היתה) tributary!" (KJV)

15.) Ezekiel 36:35 "And they shall say, This land that was desolate is **become** (היתה) like the garden of Eden; and the waste and desolate and ruined cities *are become* fenced, *and* are inhabited." (KJV)

16.) Zephaniah 2:15 "This is the rejoicing city that dwelt carelessly, that said in her heart, I *am*, and *there is* none beside me: how is she **become** (היתה) a desolation, a place for beasts to lie down in! every one that passeth by her shall hiss, *and* wag his hand." (KJV)

In all of these instances, *HAYETAH* (היתה) is translated in the way these Christian scholars say it can't be translated. It is also translated, "came to pass," "come to pass," and other equivalent translations in several other passages. And, that's just in the *King James Version*. There are other versions that translate *HAYETAH* as some form of "became" more times than the *King James* does. So, here again is an argument presented as "TRUTH" that is not true. Here again we have Christian scholars saying things about *HAYAH* that don't agree with God's Word. If you are a Christian, I hope you are beginning to wonder about the integrity of those who make these claims. I will take one final look at *HAYAH* in the next chapter, but before I do that, we need to take a closer look at the Hebrew *WAW*.

Chapter Thirteen: The Meaning of *WAW*

The Hebrew letter/word *WAW* is used as a conjunction. (Remember, *WAW* is actually a single letter, and it looks like this: ו) Conjunctions are words that connect words, clauses, phrases, or sentences. Since there are many different ways such connections can be made, there are many different conjunctions. Some of the most common conjunctions in English are "and," "but," "or," "so," "now," "however," "therefore," *etc*. When we interpret the Hebrew in Genesis 1, we must be sure we understand how the conjunctions are used and what they mean in their specific context. The context is crucial since the exact same word, with the exact same spelling, with the exact same pronunciation, put into the exact same position, can have different meanings based on the context. This is true of English as well. So, what do the different forms of *WAW* mean?

Before I make myself look scholarly, let me quote Allen P. Ross,[113] Th.D., Ph.D., concerning the uses and meanings of *WAW*. Dr. Ross is scholarly! He is a professor of Divinity at Beeson Divinity School, Samford University-Birmingham, Alabama, and his website is:

http://www.christianleadershipcenter.org/exsyntax.htm

This is the *Christian Leadership Center* website, and it contains material about the rules of Hebrew grammar as taught by Dr. Ross. I picked Dr. Ross' material for three reasons. First, he is a well-known and highly respected Hebrew scholar. Second, so you will know I'm not pretending to be a Hebrew scholar, but I really do use material from qualified Hebrew scholars. Third, he just happens to list the uses and forms of the *WAW*s in the first three verses of Genesis. These are the very verses we need to examine. That makes this part of the material very easy and convenient to study. He has provided the answers. Here is what he says about the first three forms of *WAW*:

The *WAW* Coordinative, Consecutive, and Disjunctive

"Hebrew uses the conjunction in a wide number of ways. Apart from the normal conjunction, there also appears the consecutive use, which affects the translation of the verbs, and the disjunctive which breaks the sequence. The following list of uses shows the great many ways Hebrew uses the form.

1.) *Coordination*: words are simply coordinated with 'and.'
'God created the heavens *and* the earth' (Gen. 1:1).

2.) *Sequence*: the *waw* (mostly consecutive) stresses the temporal or logical sequential action between verbs ('and then').
'*And [then]* God said' (Gen. 1:3).

3.) *Disjunction*: the *waw* expresses 'but' or 'now' or some parenthetical translation that breaks away from the sequence; it is signaled by the form on a non-verb at the beginning of the clause.
'*Now* the earth was waste and void' (Gen. 1:2)."

So, according to Dr. Ross:

Genesis 1:1 uses the *WAW* in the *WAW* Coordinative Form.
Genesis 1:2 uses the *WAW* in the *WAW* Disjunctive Form.
Genesis 1:3 uses the *WAW* in the *WAW* Consecutive Form.

It is the same word in all three verses, but the meanings are different. We need to understand these differences if we want to reach the most informationally correct interpretation. Professor Ross goes on to list, define, and explain fifteen other forms of the *WAW*: The Adversative, the Explicative, the Emphatic, the Alternative, the Pleonastic, the Comparative, the Accompaniment, the Resumptive, the Adjunctive, the Distributive, the Noun Clause, the Inferential Clause, the Purpose or Result, the Temporal, the Causal, and finally the Concessive.

The *WAW* Disjunctive Form, the *WAW* Coordinative Form, and the *WAW* Consecutive Form are the only three forms of *WAW* with any connection to the subject in hand, but I wanted to mention the others just to impress you with how well I can copy and paste from web pages. I knew I wouldn't be able to impress you with my knowledge of Hebrew grammar… I thought "Pleonastic" referred to some ancient geological age before the dinosaurs.

One of the arguments Gap Theory opponents often repeat is that *HAYAH* in Genesis 1:2 cannot be translated, "became," because it is connected to a form of *WAW* that prohibits such a translation. They say this because the *WAW* that begins Genesis 1:2 is in the *WAW* Disjunctive Form, and the *WAW* Disjunctive Form does not indicate sequential action. They say the *WAW* would have to be in the *WAW* Consecutive Form for it to indicate sequential or consecutive action. Therefore, they conclude the Gap Theory is not true. Is this true? We need to look at other passages in Genesis with the same syntax. We need to see if other *WAW* Disjunctives prohibit *HAYAH* from being interpreted in a "dynamic-becoming" sense. I know I'm getting in way over my head in this Hebrew grammar stuff, but let me share what little I have learned. First of all, they are correct; the first *WAW* in Genesis 1:2 is not in the *WAW* Consecutive Form. The *WAW* Consecutive Form would read like this in English:

"On my business trip I flew to New York, **AND** London, **AND** Paris, **AND** Moscow, **AND** Beijing."

What does the word "and" imply in this sentence? It indicates a sequence of events over time. It describes consecutive action. One point follows another. It doesn't mean I flew to New York, London, Paris, Moscow, and Beijing all at the same time. That would be impossible. This kind of "and" corresponds to the *WAW* Consecutive Form in the Hebrew. The *WAW* in the *WAW* Consecutive Form implies, "and then."

"On my business trip I flew to New York **AND THEN** to London **AND THEN** to Paris, **AND THEN** to Moscow, **AND THEN** to Beijing."

There are other kinds of "ands" that do not convey sequential actions or conditions. You can see this in the following sentence:

"The cupcake contained flour, **AND** eggs, **AND** milk, **AND** sugar, **AND** cocoa."

Regardless of the order in which the ingredients were added by the baker, the cupcake contained all of the ingredients at once. This kind of "and" corresponds to the *WAW* Coordinative Form in the Hebrew. All the items connected by a *WAW* Coordinative are connected in such a way as to describe some kind of unity, similarity, or equality as a whole. The *WAW* Coordinative implies, "and also."

"The cupcake contained flour, **AND ALSO** eggs, **AND ALSO** milk, **AND ALSO** sugar, **AND ALSO** cocoa."

The Hebrew has a way of differentiating these kinds of "ands." We just use the word "and" in English and leave it to the reader to figure out the specific meaning. That's why we need to see how the ancient Hebrews would have interpreted Genesis 1:2. The *WAW* that begins Genesis 1:2 is not in the Consecutive Form. Opponents to the Gap Theory try to use this as a way of "proving" Genesis 1:2 is not consecutive (does not sequentially follow in a temporal sense) to Genesis 1:1. They interpret this to mean Genesis 1:1 and Genesis 1:2 describe all of creation at the same time and as a unity. The problem with their interpretation is that the *WAW* at the beginning of Genesis 1:2 is not in the *WAW* Coordinative Form either; it is in the *WAW* Disjunctive Form. The *WAW* Disjunctive Form "joins" things together, as do all these different types of conjunctions, but in this case it points out differences, distinctions, variations, dissimilarities, inequalities, or contradictory conditions between the things joined. Here is an example:

"Are you going to eat your cupcake **OR** aren't you?"

In this sentence you can see two sets of possibilities linked together by the conjunction "or," but in this case, the "or" is used as a disjunction.

(Note: Some Hebrew scholars refer to *WAW* as a "*WAW* Alternative" when it is used as an exclusive or.)

The two sets of possibilities are dissimilar. In fact, in this case they are contradictory. You can't do both. You can't eat your cupcake and have it too. Disjunctions show differences between the items connected. The *WAW* Disjunctive in Genesis 1:2 actually begins a parenthetical statement. (A statement enclosed by parentheses that gives additional information about a previous statement... like this one.) In other words, the creative action stops at the end of Genesis 1:1, and what follows in Genesis 1:2 is merely descriptive. This is why some translations render the *WAW* as "NOW." The word "now" calls attention to the description of the earth without making any distinction as to whether it should be an "and" or a "but" condition. It just points out the condition of the earth. Such a translation would look like this:

"In the beginning, God created the heavens and the earth. (**Now** the earth was without form, and void, and darkness *was* on the face of the deep, and the Spirit of God moved over the face of the waters.) And God said, 'Let there be light,' and..."

This translation is grammatically correct, but so are all twenty-seven translations of Genesis 1:1-2 I listed in Chapter Six. Hebrew scholars say so. There are many, many valid translations defended by many, many Hebrew scholars. So, when I hear anti-Gap Theory creationists say a *WAW* Disjunctive makes it IMPOSSIBLE to translate *HAYAH* as "became," I have to ask myself, "Are they telling the truth?" (I just wish they would ask themselves that same question.)

Looking at the contextual meaning of the *WAW* Disjunctive can help us determine the correct informational translation of Genesis 1:1-2. I believe if we seek the truth from God, and we do it with a desire to glorify Christ and not ourselves, then the Holy Spirit will reveal the truth to us. Now, you may think I am about to say something very profound, something so deep it will make me look like a great scholar. You may think I am going to glorify my own brilliance with some kind of deep philosophical pronouncement... Well, I wish! Instead, what I am about to say comes from Mrs. Wyatt's 8th grade English class in Pineville, Missouri, in 1964. Here are her words: "Conjunctions connect; Disjunctions disconnect." Such a declaration must send shockwaves through the ranks of the scholars.

So, if we assume Genesis 1:2 is a parenthetical disjunctive statement containing three descriptive clauses subordinate to the main clause, then what do we know about Genesis 1:2? Well, we know "Conjunctions connect; Disjunctions disconnect." So, what is a disjunction? The word "disjunction" has many meanings depending on whether you're talking about biology, philosophy, logic, music, mathematics, or language. Each discipline has "disjunctions." Its most fundamental concept is one of disjoining, disconnecting, or separating. With this thought in mind, it would seem the purpose for placing a disjunction between two sentences would be to point out a disconnect, a distinction, or a difference between the sentences. It serves to show the two sentences (or the two parts of a single sentence) are not absolutely identical. They have some kind of difference or distinction. It does not seem to be the thing you would place between two statements if they were describing the exact same situation, condition, phenomenon, event, or experience. It would seem a little strange to say something like, "Steven Dill is a veterinarian, but he takes care of sick animals." Since that's what veterinarians do, I think the two parts of the sentence should be co-joined with an "and" rather than dis-joined with a "but." A conjunction rather than a disjunction would make more sense. Likewise, **I find it strange that a disjunction would be used in Genesis 1:2 for a parenthetical description of the earth if it was in the exact same condition as it was in Genesis 1:1.** If the earth was *TOHUW WA-BOHUW* and *CHOSHEK* in Genesis 1:1, and the earth was *TOHUW WA-BOHUW* and *CHOSHEK* in Genesis 1:2, then why join the sentences with a disjunction? Disjunctions disconnect! Genesis 1:2 is disconnected from Genesis 1:1 by the Disjunctive *WAW*. A disjunction implies a "but" condition (dis-joining) more than an "and" condition (co-joining). BUT/AND I am not a Hebrew scholar. Real Hebrew scholars know the proper translation of *WAW* depends on the context, but that's not all that helpful sometimes. It doesn't do any good to claim context proves the translation if you can't prove the context. Real Hebrew scholars also know that if you provide the context you want, you can prove the translation you believe.

I'm sure Gap Theory opponents will accuse me of trying to force a modern English thought into the ancient Hebrew language. They might be right. It is possible that disjunctions in ancient Hebrew bear no resemblance to disjunctions in modern English. Maybe disjunctions in ancient Hebrew do not imply disconnections, separations, dissimilarities, or distinctions. So, rather than trying to persuade you that I know what I am talking about, let me quote a Hebrew scholar, Arthur Custance:[114]

> "Furthermore, in the Masoretic Text in which the Jewish scholars tried to incorporate enough 'indicators' to guide the reader as to correct punctuation there is one small mark which is technically known as *Rebhia* which is classified as a 'disjunctive accent' intended to notify the reader that he should pause before proceeding to the next verse. In short, this mark indicates a **'break'** in the text. Such a mark appears at the end of Genesis 1:1. This mark has been noted by several scholars including Luther. It is one indication among others, that the initial *waw* (ו) which introduces verse 2 should be rendered '**but**' rather than 'and', a **dis-junctive** rather than a con-junctive."

Arthur Custance agreed the *WAW* in Genesis 1:2 is disjunctive. Does this mean he believed the *HAYAH* in Genesis 1:2 couldn't be translated as some form of "became"? Obviously not, since he translated Genesis 1:2 exactly that way. He also explains why:

"'*But the earth **had become** a desolation....*'

The rendering above departs from that to be observed in almost all the better known English translations in three ways:[*] the use of a **disjunctive** (***but*** for *and*), the use of the pluperfect in the place of the simple perfect, and the use of ***become*** in place of the simple ***was***.

Of the disjunctive, little need be said. The Hebrew ו *(waw)* stands for both the conjunctive and the disjunctive particles, and the context alone can determine which is the more appropriate. There is, as we have seen, some reason to prefer the disjunctive in view of the indicated pause in the Hebrew text at the end of verse 1. In Appendix XIV will be found a number of illustrations of this use, including some instances in which the correctness of the disjunctive form is borne out not merely by the obvious sense of the passage quoted but by its reappearance as a quotation in the New Testament where the Greek has 'but', not 'and' (ie., alla rather than kai). [*] *See Appendix III.*"[115]

Custance lists more examples of the *WAW* Disjunctive in Appendix III and Appendix XIV of his book. Again, I encourage you to get his book.

Now that you know what *WAW* Disjunctives do, how would you know if a *WAW* is in the Disjunctive Form? The best way is to invest several years of your life and become a Hebrew scholar yourself. If you don't have the time or the urge to do that, then do what I do. Find some Hebrew study aids (*i.e.* cheat sheets) either in print or on the Internet. Recall what Dr. Ross said about the *WAW* Disjunctive:

"<u>Disjunction</u>: the *waw* expresses 'but' or 'now' or some parenthetical translation that breaks away from the sequence; it is signaled by the form of a non-verb at the beginning of the clause."[116]

To be fair, I really don't know if what Dr. Ross says about *WAW* Disjunctives is accurate or not. He said they are formed when a non-verb (any word but a verb) begins the clause. I checked another Internet site and it agreed. However, another site said *WAW* Disjunctives were formed if the clause following the *WAW* begins with a noun. Well, I believe Dr. Ross because he is such a well-known professor of Hebrew, but I will limit my search of *WAW* Disjunctive clauses in Genesis to just those clauses that begin with a noun. I'm sure if I listed *WAW* Disjunctive clauses that precede *HAYAH* and begin with adjectives, adverbs, pronouns, or other non-verbs, I would be accused of violating some scholar's definition of *WAW* Disjunctive clauses. I limit myself because I want you to see other passages in Genesis, with the exact same syntax as Genesis 1:2, that indicate a dynamic "coming to be" rather than a static "was."

Five examples of *WAW* Disjunctives followed by *HAYAH* in Genesis

I am only listing the *WAW* Disjunctives affixed to nouns followed by *HAYAH*. I am not going to list any *WAW* Disjunctives affixed to pronouns, or other non-verbs, even though these are *WAW* Disjunctives as well. Nor, am I going to list any *WAW* Disjunctives followed by *HAYAH* in any other form but the *QAL* Perfect. I limit myself, not because those other *WAW* Disjunctive-*HAYAH* forms aren't there. I limit myself because even if I showed them, Gap Theory opponents would say those aren't *WAW* Disjunctives affixed to nouns and followed by *HAYAH* in the *QAL* Perfect Form like Genesis 1:2.

Again, I will stay in the Book of Genesis because a complete Scripture search is beyond the purpose of this book. Besides, if I pointed out such examples in Psalms or Isaiah, my opponents would say the rules of Hebrew grammar may have changed over the centuries from the time of Moses to the time of David or Isaiah. They would say we can't count those because they may be in a different socio-geopolitical-cultural-linguistic context. So, I won't use those either. Even after we see the other examples in Genesis, I fear Gap Theory opponents will say there is no other passage in the second verse of Genesis 1 in the *King James Version* that translates the *HAYAH* in any other way but "was." You've got me there; I can't argue that!

There are four other passages in Genesis that fit the exact layout of Genesis 1:2. We have looked at them already and have seen how they are better translated as a dynamic, "became," rather than a static, "was." As I did with the false claim that, "*LAMEDH* must follow the *HAYAH* in order for it to be translated became," I will list the English (KJV) words and add what *The Complete Word Study Old Testament*[117] reveals about their usage. Following that, I will show the Hebrew text, and highlight the specific letters and words in bold and underlined print. This is followed by my comments, delineated by brackets [ ] to illustrate how their syntax is identical. Finally, I will reprint the text in a different layout to show the parenthetical descriptive statements. I think you will see how the information inside the parentheses requires us to interpret the *HAYAH* as some form of "became," "had become," or "came to pass," rather than a static "was." Let's look at Genesis 1:2 first.

1.) Genesis 1:2 "**And the earth**$^{776\ wcj}$ **was**$^{1961\ qpf}$ without form,^{8414} and void;^{922} and darkness^{2822} *was* upon^{5921} the face^{6440} of the deep.^{8415} And the Spirit^{7307} of God^{430} moved^{7363} upon^{5921} the face^{6440} of the waters.^{4325}" (KJV)

Genesis 1:2 **והארץ**^{H776} **היתה**^{H1961} תהו^{H8414} ובהו^{H922} וחשך^{H2822} על^{H5921} פני^{H6440} תהום^{H8415} ורוח^{H7307} אלהים^{H430} מרחפת^{H7363} על^{H5921} פני^{H6440} המים^{H4325}:

["**And**" is a *WAW* Conjunctive followed by "**earth**," (a noun) thereby making it a *WAW* Disjunctive. Our job is to decide if the *QAL* Perfect *HAYAH* that follows can or cannot be translated, "became." (Or "had become" since it is in the pluperfect.)]

Genesis 1:2 "**But the earth had become** without form, and void; and darkness *was* upon the face of the deep, and the Spirit of God moved upon the face of the waters."

2.) Genesis 3:1 "**Now the serpent**[H5175 wcj] **was**[H1961 qpf] more subtil[H6175] than any[H4480] [H3605] beast[H2416] of the field[H7704] which[H834] the LORD[H3068] God[H430] had made.[H6213] And he said[H559] unto[H413] the woman,[H802] Yea,[H637] [H3588] hath God[H430] said,[H559] Ye shall not[H3808] eat[H398] of every[H4480] [H3605] tree[H6086] of the garden?[H1588]" (KJV)

Genesis 3:1 וְהַנָּחָשׁ[H5175] הָיָה[H1961] עָרוּם[H6175] מִכֹּל[H3605] חַיַּת[H2416] הַשָּׂדֶה[H7704] אֲשֶׁר[H834] עָשָׂה[H6213] יְהוָה[H3068] אֱלֹהִים[H430] וַיֹּאמֶר[H559] אֶל[H413] הָאִשָּׁה[H802] אַף[H637] כִּי[H3588] אָמַר[H559] אֱלֹהִים[H430] לֹא[H3808] תֹאכְלוּ[H398] מִכֹּל[H3605] עֵץ[H6086] הַגָּן[H1588]

["**Now**" is a *WAW* Conjunctive followed by "**serpent**," (a noun) thereby making it a *WAW* Disjunctive. Can the following *QAL* Perfect *HAYAH* be translated, "became?" Of course it can! We already looked at how it makes more sense to say the serpent became more subtle. It wasn't always (static-condition) that way. God did not create it with evil thoughts or intentions. The serpent became that way after Satan indwelt it. In fact, the *WAW* is separated from the verb, and if you remember, this is the way the Hebrews indicated the pluperfect tense.]

Genesis 3:1 "**Now the serpent had become** more subtil than any beast of the field which the LORD God had made. And he said unto the woman, 'Truly, has God said, "You shall not eat of every tree of the garden?"'"

3.) Genesis 15:17 "And it came to pass,[H1961] that, when the sun[H8121] went down,[H935] **and it was**[H1961 qpf] **dark,**[H5939 wcj] behold[H2009] a smoking[H6227] furnace,[H8574] and a burning[H784] lamp[H3940] that[H834] passed[H5674] between[H996] those[H428] pieces.[H1506]" (KJV)

Genesis 15:17 וַיְהִי[H1961] הַשֶּׁמֶשׁ[H8121] בָּאָה[H935] וַעֲלָטָה[H5939] הָיָה[H1961] וְהִנֵּה[H2009] תַנּוּר[H8574] עָשָׁן[H6227] וְלַפִּיד[H3940] אֵשׁ[H784] אֲשֶׁר[H834] עָבַר[H5674] בֵּין[H996] הַגְּזָרִים[H1506] הָאֵלֶּה[H428]:

["**And**" is a *WAW* Conjunctive followed by "**dark**" (a noun) thereby making it a *WAW* Disjunctive. If we assume the sun makes the world light, then we can conclude that when the sun goes down, the earth becomes dark. It wasn't dark before the sun went down, but it became dark after it did. The *QAL* Perfect *HAYAH* that follows the *WAW* Disjunctive does not describe a static condition.]

Genesis 15:17 "And it came to pass that when the sun went down, (**and it had become dark**) behold a smoking furnace, and a burning lamp passed between those pieces."

4.) Genesis 29:17 Leah[H3812] *was* tender[H7390] eyed;[H5869] **but Rachel[H7354 wcj] was[H1961 qpf]** beautiful[H3303 H8389] and well[3H303] favored.[H4758] (KJV)

Genesis 29:17 ועיני[H5869] לאה[H3812] רכות[H7390] **ורחל[H7354] היתה[H1961]** יפת[H3303] תאר[H8389] ויפת[H3303] מראה:[H4758]

["**But**" is a *WAW* Conjunctive followed by "Rachel" (a noun) thereby making it a *WAW* Disjunctive. As we have seen previously, this sentence makes much more sense to say Rachel came to be beautiful. Beauty is a dynamic condition. This *QAL* Perfect *HAYAH* describes Rachel's dynamic condition of how she grew to become beautiful in both face and figure.]

Genesis 29:16-18 "And Laban had two daughters: the name of the older *was* Leah, and the name of the younger *was* Rachel. Leah *was* tender eyed. (**But Rachel had become beautiful of form and face**). And Jacob loved Rachel and said, 'I will serve thee seven years for Rachel thy younger daughter.'"

5.) Genesis 41:56 "**And the famine[H7458 wcj] was[H1961 qpf]** over[H5921] all[H3605] the face[H6440] of the earth:[H776] And Joseph[H3130] opened[H6605] [H853] all[H3605] the storehouses,[H834] and sold[H7666] unto the Egyptians;[H4714] and the famine[H7458] waxed sore[H2388] in the land[H776] of Egypt.[H4714]" (KJV)

Genesis 41:56 **והרעב[7458] היה[1961]** על[5921] כל[3605] פני[6440] הארץ[776] ויפתח[6605] יוסף[3130] את[853] כל[3605] אשר[834] בהם וישבר[7666] למצרים[4713] ויחזק[2388] הרעב[7458] בארץ[776] מצרים:[4714]

["**And**" is a *WAW* Conjunctive followed by "famine" (a noun) thereby making it a *WAW* Disjunctive. So, what is the better translation? Had Egypt always been in a static condition of famine or had famine come upon the land? Some anti-gap creationists tell us we can't translate a *QAL* Perfect *HAYAH* as "became" if it follows a noun preceded by a *WAW* Disjunctive. If what they say is true, then Egypt had been in a static condition of famine forever. This not only contradicts the known historical records of ancient Egypt, it contradicts Genesis 12:10. "There was famine in the land, so Abram went to Egypt to live there..." Obviously, there was no famine in Egypt at the time of Abram.]

Genesis 41:55-56 "And when all the land of Egypt was famished, the people cried to Pharaoh for bread, and Pharaoh said to all the Egyptians, 'Go to Joseph. Whatever he says to you, do it.' (**Now, famine had come** to all the face of the land.) And Joseph opened all the storehouses, and sold to the Egyptians. And the famine was severe in the land of Egypt."

So, if what anti-Gap Theory creationists say about "Parenthetical *WAW* Disjunctive statements followed by *HAYAH*" is not true, why do they say it? Like so many other arguments against the Gap Theory, I think this is another example of Applied Mental Inertia. People repeat things other people say as long as it sounds like evidence for their own belief. They don't analyze the claims before they make them. If they did, I don't think they would use this argument. This argument is based on the erroneous assumption that parenthetical statements add only descriptive information but never consecutive-action information. It may be true in most cases, but if the contents inside the parenthesis describe some kind of consecutive-action information, then the parenthetical statement DOES reveal consecutive-action information about the main clause. You have to look at what's inside the parenthesis before you can say whether or not it reveals consecutive action. (And anti-Gap Theory creationists never seem to do that.) True, by using a parenthetical statement, the intent of the author may be to focus on WHAT a condition is, rather than on WHEN or HOW that condition came about. But even if this is the main focus, it doesn't mean the author can't add consecutive-action information inside the parenthesis....

Oh, dear reader, you're giving me a blank stare!

It sounds like a good time for an example in modern English to make this concept a little more apparent:

"I got up early in the morning to take a bag of peanuts to Jumbo the elephant at the zoo. (Now, Jumbo was crazy about peanuts.)"

The parenthetical statement adds no consecutive-action information. It just points out the additional information that Jumbo loves peanuts. This is the emphasis of the parenthetical statement. It doesn't say when or how Jumbo became crazy about peanuts. I could write this in ancient Hebrew... well, no I couldn't, but I am sure a Hebrew scholar could. I'm sure the scholar would use the *WAW* Disjunctive "Now," followed by the noun "Jumbo," followed by the *HAYAH*, "was." In this parenthetical statement about Jumbo, no consecutive-action is included. Anti-Gap Theory creationists would proclaim Jumbo was already crazy about peanuts even before I got up early to go to the zoo. They would insist being crazy about peanuts was something Jumbo already was, not what he came to be. This would be their proof that since the *WAW* in this parenthetical statement is not in the Consecutive Form, it does not contain consecutive-action information. All right, that's true, but now look at this sentence:

"I got up early in the morning to take a bag of peanuts to Jumbo the elephant at the zoo. (But, Jumbo had become gravely ill.)"

The same Hebrew scholar would write this using the *WAW* Disjunctive "But," followed by the noun "Jumbo," followed by the pluperfect *HAYAH* "had become." Even though the main point of the parenthetical statement is to add additional information about Jumbo's condition, it logically imbeds some consecutive-action information. Jumbo had not always been gravely ill. Obviously, he became gravely ill after some point in time. This sentence would have the same Hebrew syntax as the first sentence, and even though it does not use the *WAW* Consecutive Form, it still includes some consecutive-action information. Jumbo came to be gravely ill at some point in time prior to my coming to the zoo. Even if I didn't use the pluperfect, but said, "But Jumbo was gravely ill," in the disjunctive clause, you would still understand it to imply Jumbo hadn't been ill his entire life. His condition of illness was consecutive to his normal condition of health. Consecutive action is revealed even though a consecutive disjunction is not used. Is there a Biblical example like this? Yes. We just looked at an exact parallel:

Genesis 41:55-56 "And when all the land of Egypt was famished, the people cried to Pharaoh for bread, and Pharaoh said to all the Egyptians, 'Go to Joseph. Whatever he says to you, do it.' (**Now, famine had come** to all the face of the land.) And Joseph opened all the storehouses, and sold to the Egyptians. And the famine was severe in the land of Egypt."

The information inside the parenthesis emphasizes there was a famine in Egypt, but logically imbedded in the context is the information the famine had come upon Egypt at some point in time previous to this. Egypt hadn't always been in that condition. Anti-Gap Theory creationists say it is impossible to use *WAW* Disjunctive parenthetical statements to reveal consecutive action, but they forgot to tell the Holy Spirit it was impossible. **There is no justification for claiming Genesis 1:2 cannot describe a changed condition of the earth at some point of time after its original creation in Genesis 1:1.** The anti-Gap Theory creationists didn't think this argument out very well.

A Divinely Revealed Pattern

Most Gap Theory opponents insist Genesis 1:1-2 is part of Day One. They don't believe the Bible describes a creation before the six-day creation. The problem with their belief is Genesis 1:1 comes before Genesis 1:2 chronologically. (And Genesis 1:2 comes before Genesis 1:3, *etc.*) If the Holy Spirit's intent was to give us a chronological account of creation in Genesis 1, (and this is my assumption) then a problem arises with their interpretation. The initial creation comes before Day One started. Day One began when God said, "Let there be light." Day One comes AFTER Genesis 1:1-2. This means there is a chronological gap of time between Genesis 1:1 and Genesis 1:3.

There have been many ways they have tried to "fix" this problem. Some say Genesis 1:1-2 is a summary of the creation account that follows. As we have seen, the beginning and ending conditions of the summary don't match with the beginning and ending conditions of the six days of creation. Okay then, some say Genesis 1:1 is a title. That's fine, but then it means the Bible starts out with the heavens and the earth already in existence and in "chaos." That's why so many translations say things like: "When God began to create the heavens and the earth, the earth was (already) without form, and void." It may be grammatically correct, but it defies the Doctrine of *EX NIHILO* creation. It may even mean "chaos" was co-eternal with God. Furthermore, a title is actually a subset of a summary. Titles tend to be very brief, very succinct summaries with very few details, but the information they give parallels the information that follows; or at least it should. If the title of a story in your morning newspaper reads, "Dog Bites Man," then you would expect somewhere in the story to get the details. If the entire story was about Monarch butterflies migrating to Mexico, and there was nothing mentioned about dogs or dog bites, then it would be a very poor title. The Title-Summary of Genesis 1:1-2 is a very poor Title-Summary since the details do not match the details of Genesis 1:3-31.

Gap Theory proponents believe Genesis 1:1-2 came before Genesis 1:3 chronologically. The easiest way to prove it is to ask this question: How long was it dark before God said, "Let there be light"? No matter what creation theory you believe, you have to admit Genesis says the earth was dark before it was light. It was dark first and then later became light. So, how much later was it? How long of a time period was it? No matter what creation theory you believe, you have to admit there was a gap of time between the earth's initial creation in Genesis 1:1 and the time when God said, "Let there be light," in Genesis 1:3.

The *WAW* Pattern

Many anti-Gap Theory creationists believe Genesis 1:1-2 is a title and/or summary of the Six Days of Creation. They don't believe these two verses describe a creation that came before the Six Days of Creation. It is an interesting thought, but it is not what the context reveals. (Oh, I can hear them throwing my own words back at me: "It doesn't do any good to claim the context proves the translation if you can't prove the context.") Well, I think I can prove the context because the Holy Spirit has given us some clues. His clues consist of a series of *WAW* Consecutives. When we look at the pattern of the *WAW*s, we will discover Genesis 1:1-2 is not part of that pattern; it is not part of the Six Days of Creation. The *WAW* Consecutives lay out a pattern which shows:

1.) When the days began.
2.) What God did during each day.
3.) When the days ended.
4.) Where each day fit into the historic chronology.

Other anti-Gap Theory creationists say Genesis 1:1 describes a creative act, but it was the first creative act on the first day of the Six Days of Creation. They believe the *WAW* Disjunctive clause in Genesis 1:2 is a parenthetical description of the earth's condition when it was created in Genesis 1:1. They believe God created it *TOHUW WA-BOHUW* and *CHOSHEK*. They insist Genesis 1:1 and Genesis 1:2 fit together as one unit. Genesis 1:1 is the main clause and Genesis 1:2 contains three subordinate descriptive clauses. They insist Genesis 1:2 contains no consecutive-action information because it doesn't contain a *WAW* Consecutive. This interpretation puts Genesis 1:1 and Genesis 1:2 into the same time period (no matter how long or short it was) because they describe the same earth in the same condition. Let's look at the Hebrew context to see what the *WAW*s reveal.

When connecting words and sentences together, the Hebrews often put a *WAW* at the beginning of a word to indicate the connection. If you look at the Hebrew of the Bible, you will often see a ו placed as the first letter of a word. This generally indicates some kind of connection or relationship between two words, two parts of a sentence, or two sentences. I will show you the first word of every verse in Genesis 1. Look at the FIRST letter in EACH verse:

1 בראשית

2 והארץ

3 ויאמר

4 וירא

5 ויקרא

6 ויאמר

7 ויעש

8 ויקרא

9 ויאמר

10 ויקרא

11 ויאמר

12 ותוצא

13 ויהי

14 ויאמר

15 והיו

16 ויעש

17 ויתן

18 ולמשל
19 ויהי
20 ויאמר
21 ויברא
22 ויברך
23 ויהי
24 ויאמר
25 ויעש
26 ויאמר
27 ויברא
28 ויברך
29 ויאמר
30 ולכל
31 וירא

Does it look like a pattern? Yes. The first thing you see is that every verse except verse one begins with ו, the letter *WAW*. Now, this is not as amazing as it may seem at first glance. The Hebrews often connected their sentences together with a *WAW*. Since they didn't use punctuation, like periods and commas, this was one way they indicated the start of the next sentence or thought. Still, you can see there is something different about verse 1; it doesn't start with a *WAW*. The next thing you see is that all the initial *WAW*s are *WAW* Consecutives, except verses 18 and 30, which are *WAW* Coordinatives. At least that's what you would see if you are a Hebrew scholar or have a Hebrew "cheat sheet." Why don't verses 18 and 30 fit the pattern? The answer may not be as simple as some creationists think. You see, the meaning of *WAW* is not always a simple "AND" or "BUT." It can also carry the idea of "AND THEN," "BUT THEN," "NOW THEN," "SO THEN," and other kinds of consecutive connections. The *WAW* Consecutive Form reveals these kinds of consecutive actions or conditions. Is the *WAW* Consecutive Form important in Genesis 1? Let's let the context answer that.

First let me explain why verses 18 and 30 don't fit the pattern. I think MAN goofed it up. I think God intended Genesis 1 to reveal the sequence of events of creation in a specific pattern. It is important to note that God did not provide the numbering system. The chapter and verse numbers were supplied by the Council of Old Guys during the reign of Emperor Gluteus Maximus, back in days when there was nothing better to do. Man decided where the breaks are, but man's breaks don't fit God's pattern. The reason verse 18 doesn't fit this pattern is because there shouldn't be a break at verse 18. Verse 18 is actually a continuation of the description of what God did in verse 17. If you look at verses 17 and

18 without any manmade breaks, you can see it makes no sense to break it after the words, "to give light upon the earth…"

Genesis 1:17-18 "**And** God set them in the firmament of the heaven to give light upon the earth, **and** to rule over the day **and** over the night, **and** to divide the light from the darkness: **and** God saw that *it was* good." (KJV)

It just as easily could have been broken after, "and over the night.…" Or you could have broken it after, "the light from the darkness.…" In fact, if you broke the verses at every *WAW*, then you could turn verses 17 and 18 into five verses:

17 **And then** God set them in the firmament of the heaven to give light upon the earth,
18a **and also** to rule over the day
18b **and also** over the night,
18c **and also** to divide the light from the darkness:
18d **And then** God saw that *it was* good.

You can see why verses 18a, 18b, and 18c should be in the same sentence as verse 17. They are *WAW* Coordinatives. They don't describe one action following another. Verse 17 and 18d are *WAW* Consecutive. By breaking the sentences at the *WAW* Consecutives, you see verses 17, 18a, 18b, and 18c all belong to the same sentence.

Verse 17 says God "set" (our old friend *NATHAN*) the lights in the heavens for the purpose of: 1.) giving light upon the earth; 2.) ruling over the day; 3.) ruling over the night; 4.) dividing the light from the darkness. There is no reason to break this purpose clause into chronological segments. It's obvious God was assigning purpose to all of the lights at the same time. While the sun was shining on one part of the earth, the moon and stars were shining on the opposite side of the earth at the same time. No sequence of events is suggested, nor could it be. All this was happening at once. That is why the *WAW* Coordinative rather than the *WAW* Consecutive is used in 18a, 18b, and 18c. Remember, light and dark had been divided since Day One. There was nothing new created here. A new pattern or sequence was not generated. I believe verses 18a, 18b, and 18c should be part of verse 17. The break should be at 18d.

The same thing is true of verses 29 and 30. Verse 30 is a continuation of the purpose clause in verse 29. God didn't give vegetation as food to man, and then later give vegetation as food to the beasts of the earth, and then later give vegetation as food to the birds, and then later give vegetation as food to all the creepy little things. It was all done at the same time. It wasn't as if man needed food first, and then later beasts needed food, and then later birds needed food, and then finally the things that creep on the ground needed food. Everything needed food. Again, why not break verse 30 down into even more verses?

29 **And then** God said, Behold, I have given you every herb bearing seed, which *is* upon the face of all the earth, and every tree, in the which *is* the fruit of a tree yielding seed; to you it shall be for meat.
30a **and also** to every beast of the earth,
30b **and also** to every fowl of the air,
30c **and also** to every thing that creepeth upon the earth, wherein *there is* life, *I have given* every green herb for meat:
30d **And then** it became so.

Verses 30a, 30b, and 30c are all part of God giving vegetation as food for man, beast, bird, and land creature alike. God didn't do this in a consecutive fashion, so the *WAW* Consecutive was not used. Notice He makes no such dietary pronouncement for the creatures of the sea. Only land animals are made vegetarians. Nothing is said about sea creatures being made vegetarians. Do you remember what I said in Chapter Five about plankton-feeding whales being unable to separate microscopic plant-life from microscopic animal-life as they swallowed the nutrient-rich water? This is why God made no such dietary restriction for sea creatures. There was animal death before Adam sinned. This is another pre-scientific clue that God, not man, is the author of the Bible. If this account was a manmade myth created by ancient Hebrews, who feared the sea and had little experience in ocean navigation and marine life, (and who had no microscopes) then I think they would have included a statement that the creatures of the sea were strictly vegetarian too. They can't be, and God knew it, so God didn't say it. (His Words match His work.)

Genesis 1 – Stirred; Not Shaken

So, let's look at the pattern God revealed. I will remove the verse numbers, but the verses will be in the correct order. I will start a new line with each *WAW* Consecutive. If you look at Genesis 1 and translate each *WAW* Consecutive as "AND THEN," rather than as a simple "AND," you get this: (I'll insert titles to denote the days.)

Before Day One

"In the beginning God created the heavens and the earth. (But the earth had become without form, and void, and darkness upon the face of the deep. And the Spirit of God moved upon the face of the waters.")

Day One

"**And then** God said, 'Let light come to be:'
And then light came to be.
And then God saw the light, that *it was* good:
And then God divided the light from the darkness.

And then God called the light Day, and the darkness he called Night.
And then the evening
And then the morning were one day."

Day Two

"**And then** God said, 'Let a firmament in the midst of the waters come to be, and let it divide the waters from the waters.'
And then God made the firmament,
And then divided the waters which *were* under the firmament from the waters which *were* above the firmament:
And then it became so.
And then God called the firmament Heaven.
And then the evening
And then the morning were the second day."

Day Three

"**And then** God said, 'Let the waters under the heaven be gathered together unto one place, and let the dry *land* appear:'
And then it became so.
And then God called the dry *land* earth; and the gathering together of the waters called He Seas:
And then God saw that *it was* good.
And then God said, 'Let the earth bring forth grass, the herb yielding seed, *and* the fruit tree yielding fruit after his kind, whose seed *is* in itself, upon the earth:'
And then it became so.
And then the earth brought forth grass, *and* herb yielding seed after his kind, and the tree yielding fruit, whose seed *was* in itself, after his kind:
And then God saw that *it was* good.
And then the evening
And then the morning were the third day."

Day Four

"**And then** God said, 'Let lights in the firmament of the heaven come to be to divide the day from the night;
And then be for signs, and for seasons, and for days, and years:
And then be lights in the firmament of the heaven to give light upon the earth:'
And then it became so.
And then God made two great lights; the greater light to rule the day, and the lesser light to rule the night, and the stars.

And then God set them in the firmament of the heaven to give light upon the earth, and to rule over the day and over the night, and to divide the light from the darkness:
And then God saw that *it was* good.
And then the evening
And then the morning were the fourth day."

Day Five

"**And then** God said, 'Let the waters bring forth abundantly the moving creature that hath life, and fowl *that* may fly above the earth in the open firmament of heaven.'
And then God created great whales, and every living creature that moveth, which the waters brought forth abundantly, after their kind, and every winged fowl after his kind:
And then God saw that *it was* good.
And then God blessed them, saying, Be fruitful, and multiply, and fill the waters in the seas, and let fowl multiply in the earth.
And then the evening
And then the morning were the fifth day."

Day Six

"**And then** God said, 'Let the earth bring forth the living creature after his kind, cattle, and creeping thing, and beast of the earth after his kind:'
And then it became so.
And then God made the beast of the earth after his kind, and cattle after their kind, and every thing that creepeth upon the earth after his kind:
And then God saw that *it was* good.
And then God said, 'Let us make man in our image, after our likeness: and let them have dominion over the fish of the sea, and over the fowl of the air, and over the cattle, and over all the earth, and over every creeping thing that creepeth upon the earth.'
And then God created man in his *own* image, in the image of God created he him; male and female created he them.
And then God blessed them,
And then God said unto them, 'Be fruitful, and multiply, and replenish the earth, and subdue it: and have dominion over the fish of the sea, and over the fowl of the air, and over every living thing that moveth upon the earth.'
And then God said, 'Behold, I have given you every herb bearing seed, which *is* upon the face of all the earth, and every tree, in the which *is* the fruit of a tree yielding seed; to you it shall be for food. And to every beast of the earth, and to every fowl of the air, and to every thing that creepeth upon the earth, wherein *there is* life, *I have given* every green herb for food:'
And then it became so.

And then God saw every thing that he had made, and, behold, *it was* very good.
And then the evening
And then the morning were the sixth day."

Is Genesis 1 God's chronological account of the creation? Is He telling us the sequence of events? It certainly seems that way to me. The "old guys" created a numbering system to arrange Genesis 1, but if you ignore them and see how God uses each *WAW* Consecutive to begin a new thought or new sentence, you can't miss the pattern. One event follows the next. How could He call the first day a "day" if there hadn't been an evening and a morning? (A day wouldn't have finished until after there was an evening and a morning.) How could there be an evening and a morning if He hadn't already divided the day from night? How could the day be divided from the night if God hadn't already separated the light from the dark? How could light be separated from the dark if light hadn't previously come into being? How could light come into being if God hadn't already commanded it to become? As you go down the list, each event, creation, or condition comes AFTER the preceding event, creation, or condition. Why is this important? What do we learn about the creation if we interpret Genesis 1 as a chronological account of the creation?

The first thing we learn is that Genesis 1:1 does not have a preceding event or condition. Genesis 1:1 does not start with a *WAW*. One of the remarkable doctrines that distinguished the Bible from the cosmogony of the ancient world's religions is the Doctrine of *EX NIHILO* creation. The pagan belief systems of the ancient world believed the universe was created out of pre-existing, eternal "chaos," or from the body parts of dead deities, or something to that effect. The Bible taught "The Beginning" was the absolute beginning of time, space, matter, and energy. Nothing preceded the creation except God. The *WAW* Pattern in Genesis reinforces that doctrine. This is certainly one of the most amazing pre-scientific clues to the Divine authorship of the Bible. Atheists laughed at this idea until the mid-20th century when science finally proved that time, space, matter, and energy had a beginning. They still laugh at the Bible. They laugh because our belief is based on faith without scientific evidence. (Or, so they think.) When Christians say, "God created everything out of nothing," they reply, "That's ridiculous. Everybody knows that nothing created everything out of nothing." (Talk about creation theories based on blind faith! How do they scientifically prove their belief? What scientific test determines what nothing is capable of doing? How do you know it doesn't take two nothings to create something? What if you only had half of a nothing? Would that create a half-universe? What system of measurement do you use to measure nothing: mass; length; charge; color; time; temperature, frequency, flavor? If you can't measure it, how do you know it can create universes? What mathematical formula describes what NOTHING using NOTHING can create? The answer is: $0 + 0 = 0$. Nothing creates nothing. Nothing can't create anything. Nothing has no mass. Nothing has no energy. Nothing emits no forces. Nothing cannot change. Nothing can do nothing… that's why it's called, "nothing.")

What is the next thing we learn by viewing this as a chronological account? We learn Genesis 1:1-2 is not part of Day One. How do we learn this, you ask? All we need to do is determine where Day One starts in the text, and then see if Genesis 1:1-2 is part of that day. Remember, Young-Earth and Day-Age creationists believe Genesis 1:1 and Genesis 1:2 describe the first part of Day/Day-Age One. They base their belief on the fact there is no *WAW* Consecutive in Genesis 1:2. They assume there is nothing in the context that indicates a passage of time between the two verses. But, they overlook the imbedded pluperfect verb that reveals the passage of time. (That's the purpose of the pluperfect—an action is completed **prior** to some past point of time.) An undisclosed period of time transpired between Genesis 1:1 and Genesis 1:2. If we interpret the Genesis Creation Account to be a chronological account, then we see the Holy Spirit used *WAW* Consecutives to divide that account into its sequential steps. Okay, so let me ask, "Where is the FIRST *WAW* Consecutive found IN THE CONTEXT?"

Genesis 1:3 "**And then** God said, 'Let light come to be…'"

Why did the Holy Spirit place a *WAW* Consecutive BETWEEN verses two and three? No matter how you look at it, the Holy Spirit says Genesis 1:1-2 comes BEFORE Genesis 1:3 chronologically. Genesis 1:3 comes AFTER Genesis 1:1-2. That's what a *WAW* Consecutive does. It shows sequential action. If anti-Gap Theory creationists use the lack of a *WAW* Consecutive in Genesis 1:2 as proof there was no gap of time between Genesis 1:1 and Genesis 1:2, then they must admit the presence of the *WAW* Consecutive in Genesis 1:3 proves there is a gap of time between Genesis 1:1-2 and Genesis 1:3. If Genesis 1:1-2 describes one period of time, (Let's call it Time-Period 1.) then any period of time AFTER Time-Period 1 is not part of Time-Period 1. When does the next time-period Start? The next time-period (Time-Period 2) starts after the *WAW* Consecutive. Time-Period 2 starts at Genesis 1:3. Time-Period 2 ends at Genesis 1:5. Time-Period 2 is Day One. Time-Period 1 is not part of Day One. The Holy Spirit placed a *WAW* Consecutive break between the two sentences because there was break in the history of the earth. In addition, the creative acts in Time-Period 1 do not match the creative acts in Time-Period 2, Day One. Nothing is mentioned about God creating the earth in Genesis 1:3-5. The earth is already there. Nothing is mentioned about God creating the waters in Genesis 1:3-5. The waters are already there. Likewise, the creative acts in Genesis 1:3-5 are not mentioned in Genesis 1:1-2. Light is brought forth in Genesis 1:3-5. No light is mentioned in Genesis 1:1-2. Day and Night begin in Genesis 1:3-5. There is no mention of Day and Night in Genesis 1:1-2. There was evening (sunset) and morning (sunrise) in Genesis 1:3-5. There was no evening or morning mentioned in Genesis 1:1-2. God used the word "good" to describe what He did in Genesis 1:3-5. He didn't make that pronouncement in Genesis 1:1-2. In fact, the condition of the earth seems to describe something that wasn't good. Since these two creative acts don't describe the same creative acts, don't possess the same conditions, and since the Holy Spirit separated them with a *WAW* Consecutive, I'm going to interpret the Bible as the Bible reads, and insist that Genesis 1:1-2 is not identical to Genesis 1:3-5. Genesis 1:1-2 is not the same as the first day. It is not a title for the rest of the chapter. It is not a summary of the rest of the chapter. It is not a description of the rest of the chapter. It does not parallel the rest of the chapter. It chronologically comes before the rest of the chapter. Look back at my sentence:

"On my business trip I flew to New York, **AND THEN** London, **AND THEN** Paris, **AND THEN** Moscow, **AND THEN** Beijing."

Because I inserted "and then" (a consecutive AND) between these cities, there is no way you could doubt my trip to New York came before my trips to the other cities. My trip to New York did not happen at the same time as my other trips. That's what the consecutive AND means in English, and that's what it means in the Hebrew. That's why the Holy Spirit put a *WAW* Consecutive there. If Time-Period 1 does not chronologically precede the rest of the chapter, then the Holy Spirit made an error by inserting a *WAW* Consecutive between the two sentences, and He would have flunked Mrs. Wyatt's 8th grade English class.

Here is the pattern: The Bible places God's creative acts into time-periods separated by *WAW* Consecutives. Each time-period follows the previous, except for the first time-period; there was no such thing as time before this time-period began. This means the Bible reveals eight time-periods in Genesis 1. The first time-period was before Day One. Time-periods two through seven are the six days of re-creation. The eighth time-period was the seventh day of rest. I believe the Holy Spirit intended Genesis 1 to be a revelation of the events of creation in their sequential, chronological order. I think this is the context of the chapter. I think He divided the events of creation into eight sequential time-periods so we could learn things we might otherwise miss. If the Holy Spirit did not reveal these things in a chronological sequence, then we might miss the fact Genesis 1:1-2 came before the rest of the chapter chronologically. Without the revelation of this pattern, we might erroneously think Genesis 1:1-2 is a title, a summary, or a parallel of the rest of the chapter. Without the revelation of this pattern, we might mistakenly think Genesis 1:1-2 is part of the first day. **This pattern reveals there was a gap of time between the initial creation and the six days of re-creation that followed.**

This *WAW* Consecutives pattern also reveals something crucial concerning the perspective from which the Genesis Creation Account is viewed. I mentioned early in the book that the description of events is given from an earth-bound perspective. We see what is happening as if we were standing on the surface of the earth looking up, looking around, and looking down. That's why we see stars in the sky; we are looking up. What else do we see by looking up? We see birds flying in the sky. We look around and what do we see? We see trees and plants and cattle and beasts of the field. When we look down, what is there? Fish beneath the surface of the water and things that creep along the ground. God is giving us a view of the six days from a human perspective. He is not telling us what He sees; He is telling us what we would see if we were there. He doesn't give us that same perspective in Genesis 1:1-2. In Genesis 1:1, the perspective is from somewhere beyond/outside/before the universe, looking at the universe being created. Genesis 1:2 is from a perspective "above" the earth looking "down" at the earth. Genesis 1:3-31 is given from an earth-bound perspective as a human would see it. How do I know that? Simple; good science filters out bad theology. Let's look at Genesis 1:3.

Genesis 1:3 "And God said, Let there be light: and there was light." (KJV)

As I mentioned, this is physical/photonic light; not God's eternal light. Now, if you know anything about the four fundamental physical forces of nature, (strong nuclear, weak nuclear, electromagnetism, and gravity) then you understand that physical/photonic light existed before Genesis 1:3. Let me explain: "Light," as we generally think about it, is only a narrow frequency band in the entire electromagnetic spectrum. We can't see ultraviolet light, but it is still light. We can't see infrared light, but it is still light. (Some insects and animals can see in those ranges, however.) We can't see cosmic rays, or x-rays, or microwaves, but they are still light. A fact of physics is that heat is a form of light because it is electromagnetic energy. Any matter with any energy emits light at some frequency. It would have to be Absolute Zero K° to emit no energy. The frequency of the emitted light depends on the temperature of the matter. A cast iron skillet on a stove doesn't have to become visibly red-hot before it emits electromagnetic energy. Just touch a hot skillet and you'll detect it in a very unpleasant way. Even liquid nitrogen emits light at an extremely low frequency. (But don't touch that either because it will be even more unpleasant—as in you would lose a finger or a hand.) So, while we can't see the entire electromagnetic spectrum, God can. In Genesis 1:3, we are seeing light from our perspective, light in our range of perception. God would have seen the entire electromagnetic spectrum in Genesis 1:2. He would have seen the heat being emitted by the earth itself. (He would see it, but if we were there, we wouldn't see it. From our perspective, it would be dark. Darkness would be on the face of the deep.)

What do we know about the earth in Genesis 1:2? It was covered by the abyss, liquid water. This means the water had energy. No one (as far as I know) has ever proposed a creation theory stating the temperature of the earth was Absolute Zero K°, and the ocean covering it was a perfect crystalline solid with no atomic motion. If it was liquid (and it was liquid) then it was emitting light at some frequency. No matter how low that frequency was, God could see it. Genesis 1:3 wasn't the creation of light; it was the revelation of light in the human visible spectrum. Light existed before Genesis 1:3! Because light (outside the visible spectrum) preexisted Genesis 1:3, it proves *HAYAH* is used to describe the experiential, not the existential. This brings up an interesting thought. If *HAYAH* in Genesis 1:3 is the revelation of light, not the creation of light, then how can anyone object to *HAYAH* being used to describe the revelation-but-not-creation of the bodies of light (the sun, moon, and stars) in Genesis 1:14-18? Even though you couldn't see the sun, moon, and stars before Day Four, it doesn't mean they didn't exist. Just as Genesis 1:3 is given from the perspective of what a human would see, so is Genesis 1:14-18. God simply reveals what we would have seen if we had been there. This is from our perspective of creation, not God's. If He were to give us His perception of creation, He would tell us about each fundamental physical particle of nature. He would then describe the different forms of energy He created, and the Laws He established for their interactions with the physical particles. Following that, He would describe where He first placed all 10^{80} fundamental physical particles in the 10^{195} fundamental quantum units of space. Then, He would tell us where each particle was 10^{-43} seconds later; the next fundamental unit of time. Then, the next 10^{-43} seconds. Then, the next 10^{-43} seconds… One second after the universe began, He would have told us 10^{43} times where everything was and what everything had done. I suppose next, He would give us a 3,000-page document describing the mathematical formulas governing the mechanics of the hydrogen atom. It's the simplest atom. Then the helium atom. Then the lithium atom, Then the beryllium atom… To really give His perspective of time, space, matter, and energy, He would write us a description of every individual fundamental particle, where it will be for every fundamental Planck unit of time, what each one will be doing, and how they all interact with each other for fourteen billion years… and even that would be just the introduction to the book on how He "perceives" the creation. No, He does not "experience" the universe like we do. The surface of the deep would not have been dark to God. It would be dark to a human viewing it from inside time and space. That's the perspective of the text.

Not every creationist agrees. Some Day-Age creationists reject this idea because if the creation account is given from the space-time perspective of the earth, then you have to admit we are viewing space and time as if you were standing on the earth. "Evening and morning" would mean one earth day. So, they argue how an astronaut in orbit around the earth will see many evenings and mornings in that same period of time. Therefore, "evening and morning" don't necessarily mean a twenty-four-hour day. Then they add how God is a lot farther out than an astronaut, therefore He wouldn't see these as earth-days either.

This is an argument that arises from the "feeling" centers of the brain, because it certainly doesn't come from the "thinking" centers of the brain. Who do they think God is? Do they think He is some old, white-haired grandfather tottering on His throne looking down at the earth? Yes, God is looking "down" at the earth, provided we accommodate human language and thinking when we use the word "down." But, He is also looking "up" at the earth, and to the "left" of the earth, and to the "right" of the earth, and from "inside" the earth, and from a billion light-years away from the earth, and from a billion years in the past, and from a billion years in the future. This "God-is-Looking-Down" explanation may satisfy the mind of a five-year-old, but it is sadly laughable that any thinking Christian would entertain the thought.

What does it mean when He describes these events using the *WAW* consecutives? One event/condition is described, AND THEN, the next event/condition is described, AND THEN, the next event/condition is described, AND THEN…. God doesn't "experience" events/conditions in a consecutive fashion. He doesn't perceive/experience/create/uphold/control the time-space continuum in a consecutive fashion. The use of the *WAW* Consecutives proves this description of the creation is from the viewpoint of a finite viewer inside the creation. Genesis 1 is not given from God's perspective; it is as if you were standing there watching this happen. Again, the use of the *WAW* consecutives proves He is giving these descriptions from an "inside-time-and-space" perspective. Genesis 1 is viewed from an earthly perspective. This proves the "six days" are six earth days, not ages.

Jack Langford's Picture Frame Pattern

Is there anything else we can learn from this pattern revealed by the Holy Spirit? I say, "we," because it includes me. After my second edition was published, I received an e-mail from Jack Langford, a fellow defender of the Gap Theory… except he refers to it as the Gap Fact, not the Gap Theory. (As far as he is concerned, it is a proven fact.) Jack and I have shared questions and comments back and forth, and he had a comment about my sequential layout of the days of creation. Back in Chapter Eight I laid out the six days as a series. I asked you to work from Day Six back to Day Two, seeing how each day started with, "And God said,…" and each day ended with, "And the evening and the morning were the _____ Day." I then challenged you to tell me when Day One started. The answer was Genesis 1:3, of course. Naturally, Jack agreed, but he told me he had a different illustration. Instead of the layout being a simple linear progression where each day had a beginning and an end, he had a layout where each day was placed inside a "picture frame" of a set duration. Each day had a top, a bottom, and each day had two sides. The top of each day was the phrase, "And God said…" The bottom of each day was the phrase, "were the _____ day." These words were used to describe WHEN each day started and ended. So far, this agreed with my pattern. Jack then added that the sides of each day were the words "evening" and "morning." These words were used to tell us the DURATION of each day. Even though I liked my pattern, I instantly realized my pattern didn't fully explain the words "evening" and "morning." Jack's pattern reveals the significance of these words. This wasn't just a poetic way of expressing the beginning and the ending of an unspecified period of time. This was a way of expressing God's creative acts over the course of each twenty-four-hour day. You see, God didn't create things just during the day; He created things during the night, as well. Jack pointed out how God was creating, day and night, throughout each of the six days. God created things in the dark and God created things in the light. Let's say it was daylight over North America on Day Six. While God was creating the beasts of the earth in the light in North America, He was also creating the beasts of the earth in the dark in China. While it was day on one side of the world, it was night on the other. On Day Five, while He was creating fish and birds on the light side of the globe, He was also creating fish and birds on the dark side of the globe. He didn't create fish and birds on one side, and then wait twelve hours to create fish and birds on the other side. They were all created on the same day, at the same time, whether it was light or dark at any particular spot on the earth. Jack's pattern revealed how God was telling us each twenty-four-hour day on earth consists of a dark zone and a light zone. (EVENING ON ONE SIDE OF THE EARTH, MORNING ON THE OTHER SIDE OF THE EARTH—AT THE SAME TIME, ON THE SAME DAY) Jack's pattern showed us God was giving us a pre-scientific view of our rotating globe. God didn't use the words "evening" and "morning" just to tell us about light intensity. He used these words to tell us about the simultaneous light-and-dark-nature of each twenty-four-hour day. God used the words the ancient Hebrews used to designate a literal, twenty-four-hour day. This was the way the ancient Hebrews designated a twenty-four-hour day. Each day did not last FROM evening to morning; that would be only about twelve hours. Each day consisted OF an evening and a morning—dark on one side of the globe; light on the other side. One evening and one morning equaled on day. ("There was evening and there was morning, one day.")

I liked my linear layout of the days of creation, but as soon as I read Jack's illustration, I realized mine fell short. For that reason, and much more, I encourage you to read his book, *The Gap is Not a Theory*.[118] What really impressed me was that he gave a real-life illustration of this pattern. He explained how he visited a Jewish community center in Dallas, Texas, and saw a series of paintings depicting the traditional Jewish view of the creation week. There was a painting for Day One, a painting for Day Two, a painting for Day Three, *etc.* The creation events of each day fit into the frame of its own painting. What struck me was Jack described EIGHT paintings, not SEVEN. There was a painting that came BEFORE the Day One painting. This painting was of the earth as a "chaos." Jack went on to explain how the Jews traditionally viewed Day One as coming AFTER an unspecified period of time in which the earth was without form, and void. The Genesis 1:1-2 painting came before the seven paintings that followed. The Genesis 1:1-2 painting revealed a period of time before the seven days of (re)creation. His Picture-Frame illustration of the days of creation fit the Jewish traditional view perfectly. This prompted me to go back and look at the *WAW* Consecutives in Genesis 1 again to see what I had missed. I had missed the pattern inside the pattern.

The only thing I felt might be wrong with using each *WAW* Consecutive as a new line in Genesis 1, was the pronouncements of the evenings and the mornings didn't fit very well. In the Hebrew, it says, "And then there was evening. And then there was morning." The problem was this layout put both of these statements toward the end, just before declaring the day of the week. If my linear illustration was correct, then the text should read something like this:

And then there was evening.
And then God said, "…."

And then there was morning,
The _____ day.

    The text didn't read that way, but it was close. I had the right idea, but a weak illustration. My problem was I saw this only as a linear progression. I had a one-dimensional view, and the *WAW* Consecutives didn't fit my view as well as I would have liked. My view wasn't wrong if you considered the pronouncement of the evenings and mornings as an indicator for the end of each day. But, as soon as I read Jack's Picture Frame illustration, I saw the pattern in the pattern. God wasn't laying out just the "tops" and "bottoms" of the days; He was laying out their "sides" as well. One side was: "And then there was evening." The other side was: "And then there was morning." The words "evening and morning" were not telling us WHEN the days began and ended, but HOW LONG the days were. Each day had a dark period and a light period because the earth had a dark side and a light side on each day. On Day One, the earth had a dark side and a light side at the same time. On Day Two, the earth had a dark side and a light side at the same time. So did the rest of the days. **These were earth-days.** These "sides" did not fit my one-dimensional approach, but they did fit Jack's two-dimensional approach. Everything God created, made, and formed for each of the twenty-four days fit within the borders of those frames. If we look at Jack's Picture Frame Pattern we learn:

1.) We learn the Young-Earth Theory can't be true. Those who defend it believe Genesis 1:1-2 is part of the first day. Yes, you can lump Genesis 1:1 and Genesis 1:2 together, but the description of Genesis 1:1-2 is different from the descriptions of the six days of creation. Genesis 1:1-2 was given no "top" or "bottom," (God never speaks the words, "Let…; and it doesn't end with the statement, "it was the ___ day." Genesis 1:1-2 had no "sides." (There is no mention of an evening and a morning.) **Genesis 1:1-2 did not describe a twenty-four-hour day.** Instead, it was an unspecified period of time that came before Day One. We know this because each of the Six Days of Restoration consisted of an evening and a morning; light and dark. It was light on one side of the globe and it was dark on the other side of the globe on the same day. If you were an observer in space looking at the earth, you would see the earth on Day One had a light side and a dark side. The earth on Day Two had a light side and a dark side. The earth on Day Three had a light side and a dark side. Each of the days consisted of an evening and a morning because there was a light side of the earth and a dark side of the earth. God described the days this way. Each had light on one side of the earth and each had dark on the other side of the earth. Day One had light. Day Two had light. Day three had light, *etc*. All the days had light.

    Now, what does the Bible say about the earth in Genesis 1:2? It was dark; There was no light. It wasn't light on one side and dark on the other. There was NO LIGHT at all. The earth is described as being without any light. Darkness was upon the face of the deep. (Genesis 1:2) The entire ocean on both sides of the globe was dark. It was wrapped in a swaddling band of darkness. (Job 38:9) There was no light (Jeremiah 4:23). The earth in Genesis 1:2 didn't have a light side and a dark side. Both sides were dark at the same time. The earth in Genesis 1:2 is different than the earth during the six days. Genesis 1:1-2 does not describe the six days of Genesis 1:3-31. Since Genesis 1:3 comes after Genesis 1:2, and Genesis 1:2 comes after Genesis 1:1, we know the initial creation came before the six days of creation. There were two creations, two beginnings.

2.) We learn the Day-Age Theory doesn't work. The "sides" of the picture frames won't allow it. One side says, "And then there was evening." It means "evening" in the Hebrew chronological sense. The other side says, "And then there was morning," It means "morning" in the Hebrew chronological sense as well. If the Day-Age Theory were true, then you couldn't put these words into that context. The placement of the "sides" reveals why that can't happen. For each day, the earth is dark on one side and light on the other side at the same time. This is why an evening and a morning designate one day. The beginning of the first evening starts the first day and it goes through the next morning, and then ends with the next evening. The duration of the first day is from one evening to the next. The second day is marked off by these same boundaries, as are all the days that follow. This is how the Hebrews reckoned their days. A new day starts at sundown. One day goes from sunset, then to sunrise, and then ends at the next sunset. The DURATION of each day is one evening and one morning, one dark period and one light period. This, however, requires that the days each have a single period of darkness and a single period of light. Jack's pattern in the pattern reveals this. No Day-Age Theory proposes that each AGE had a single period of darkness followed by a single period of light. One side of the earth wasn't light for an age while the other side of the earth was dark for an age. Each day has one period of dark and one period of light. In Genesis 1, the first day started with the first evening, it went through the morning, and it ended when Day Two started at the next evening. The pattern in the pattern in Genesis 1 is this: **The events of each dark-and-light-at-the-same-time day fit into the time-reckoning system of Hebrew days**. The sides God put on the Picture-Frames were ordinary Hebrew days. The length of each day was from sunset to sunset. The Day-Age Theory doesn't fit into ordinary Hebrew days. God used the Hebrew language to tell the Hebrew people the days of (re)creation fit into their Hebrew system of measuring days. I assume if God had intended to reveal this to the Romans, He would have said the days went from midnight to midnight. If He had intended to reveal the time periods to nuclear physicists, He would have said, "And then there were 794,243,849,928,000 vibrations of a cesium-133 atom; the first day." These were ordinary Hebrew days.

3.) We learn the Repeated Days/ Framework Theory cannot be true. Day Four cannot be the same as Day One because the context reveals Day Four came after Day Three, Day Three came after Day Two, and Day Two came after Day One. The Picture Frames are not repeated. The Picture Frames are sequential. This is the purpose of the *WAW* Consecutive.

4.) We learn the Days of Divine Decrees Theory cannot be true as well. These days did not take place before time began. You might argue the period before Day One was before time started. (It wasn't, but you might argue it.) However, the *WAW* Consecutive at the beginning of Genesis 1:3 shows that time started before that. Remember my illustration: "On my business trip I flew to New York AND THEN to London AND THEN to Paris, AND THEN to Moscow, AND THEN to Beijing." Placing "AND THEN" before London shows my trip didn't begin in London. My trip had already started BEFORE London. By placing "AND THEN" at the beginning of Day One, we know time existed BEFORE Day One. Day One wasn't the first day of time any more than London was the first city of my trip. Time had already started. The Picture Frame Pattern reveals how each day was a one-day period of time that followed the previous one-day period of time, and there was an unspecified period of time before Day One. These were not "days" that existed before time began.

5.) The Days of Relativity Theory also fails in the light of the Picture Frame Pattern revealed in Genesis 1. These Picture Frames are viewed from an earthly perspective. They are time periods designated by the earth's evenings and mornings; dark on one side, light on the other. These are not "days" as viewed by some astronaut supposedly traveling through space at near the speed of light.

6.) The Days of Revelation Theory fails as well. This is the theory God met with Moses over a seven-day period to dictate the first chapter of Genesis to him. (Moses was a very slow writer; this works out to less than five words per hour.) The Bible refers to these days as "accounts," *TOWLEDAH*, but the Picture Frame Pattern put God's WORKS, not just His WORDS inside these frames. However long it took God to reveal this account to Moses, His creative acts still fit into six literal, twenty-four-hour days.

7.) The Picture Frame Pattern reveals something I missed about Genesis 1:1-2. I have to admit I would have guessed the *WAW* in Genesis 1:2 would be a *WAW* Consecutive instead of a *WAW* Disjunctive. After all, I believe the earth became without form, and void AFTER its initial creation in Genesis 1:1. "In the beginning, God created the heavens and the earth, but THEN the earth had become without form, and void..." would seem to fit the Gap Theory better. That's not what the Bible says, and as soon as I saw the pattern in the pattern Jack's Picture Frame Illustration revealed, I realized why it didn't. The Bible doesn't assign a "top" to Genesis 1:1-2. It doesn't give it "sides." It doesn't furnish a "bottom." In other words, Genesis 1:1 doesn't tell us when it started, when it ended, or how long it was. BUT, it does set it apart as vastly different from what is about to happen. This was the purpose of the disjunction. When I saw this, I realized God was telling us the period of time described by Genesis 1:1 was much different from what was about to take place. Of course! That was another Age. That was the angelic realm. The Holy Spirit was revealing that it wasn't just a gap of raw time between Genesis 1:1 and Genesis 1:2; there was something different, disconnected, disjoined about the previous Age. If this were just the passage of billions of years of time since the Big Bang, then there would be no need for a *WAW* DISJUNCTION. A *WAW* Consecutive would have been more appropriate. No, there was something about the Last Age that made it different (disconnected) from This Age. The point God was making by including the *WAW* Disjunctive in Genesis 1:2 before the days started, was that the dark, dead, and desolate earth was part of the Last Age. It was disjoined from This Age. It wasn't meant to be part of This Age. Something happened in the Last Age that God intended to separate from This Age. God made it clear He intentionally DISJOINED This Age from the Last Age. I think this provides strong evidence that from the time sin was first introduced by Lucifer until the end of Genesis 1:2, there was an age of unspeakable evil. We don't know how long it was after the initial glorious creation in Genesis 1:1 that Lucifer rebelled, but his rebellion introduced death into a previously perfect universe. The universe needed a rebirth, a restoration. The Picture Frame Pattern points to the Ruin-Restoration Theory as opposed to Just-a-Gap-of-Raw-Time Theory.

The Holy Spirit used a series of *WAW* Consecutives to reveal a pattern in Genesis 1. The Picture Frame Pattern reveals when each day started, when each day ended, how long each day lasted, what was created, made, and formed during each day, and how the days fit together in sequential order. Jack's Picture Frame Pattern destroys all the other theories of creation. Only the Gap Theory remains standing when compared to what the Holy Spirit revealed in Genesis 1. (Sorry Jack, I still call it the Gap Theory. However, I agree with you; it is a fact. It's just that I've called it the Gap "Theory" for so long, I find it hard to change. Besides, I don't use the word "theory" in its common, non-scientific fashion. Many people think "theory" means something that may or may not be true. "Theory" in scientific terms means a set of rules or principles that explain a phenomenon. We talk about the Law of Gravity, but science still fits that Law within the larger framework of the Gravitational Theory. It simply means we don't know all there is to know about gravity. The same is true about the creation. We don't know all there is to know about creation, but I think the Gap Theory best explains how creation happened.)

Jonah 3:3

Jonah 3:3 "So Jonah arose, and went unto Nineveh, according to the word of the LORD. Now Nineveh was an exceeding great city of three days' journey." (KJV)

Many anti-Gap Theory creationists have used Jonah 3:3 as an example of why the *HAYAH* in Genesis 1:2 should not be translated, "became." Jonah 3:3 uses *WAW* and *HAYAH* the same way they are used in Genesis 1:2. They say if you translate Genesis 1:2, "and the earth became," then you must translate Jonah 3:3, "and Nineveh became." Since it makes no sense to translate *HAYAH* as "became" in Jonah 3:3, (they say) then it makes no sense to translate *HAYAH* as "became" in Genesis 1:2. They ridicule Gap Theory believers by saying we should translate Jonah 3:3 this way if we were consistent:

"So Jonah arose, and went unto Nineveh, according to the word of the LORD. And Nineveh became an exceeding great city of three days journey."

In other words, they say Gap Theory believers must believe Nineveh became a great city after Jonah went there. They laugh at the idea by pointing out how the description of Nineveh's size was not a sequential event following Jonah's arrival. Instead, it is a parenthetical description of what Nineveh already was. From this they conclude "without form, and void" is a parenthetical description of what the earth already was; not what it became. They say Jonah 3:3 proves the Gap Theory is wrong. Unfortunately for them, their argument fails to prove what they think it does, because Jonah 3:3 doesn't say what they think it says. We need to look at the Hebrew of Jonah 3:3 to see how it compares to Genesis 1:2. Here is what *The Complete Word Study Old Testament*[119] reveals about the Hebrew words and the Hebrew parts of speech of Jonah 3:3. (I will show the ***HAYAH*s** in bold print, and the **_WAW_s** in bold, underlined print.):

Jonah 3:3 "**So** Jonah^H3124 arose,^H6965 **and** went^H1980 unto^H413 Nineveh,^H5210 according to the word^H1697 of the LORD.^H3068 **Now** Nineveh^H5210 wcj **was**^H1961 qpf an exceeding^H430 great^H1419 city^H5892 of three^H7969 days'^H3117 journey.^H4109" (KJV)

Note there are three *WAW*s in Jonah 3:3. The first is translated, "So" ("**So** Jonah arose"). The second *WAW* is translated, "and" ("**and** went unto Nineveh"). The third *WAW* is translated, "Now" ("**Now** Nineveh was"). Now, look very closely: The first two *WAW*s aren't used with the verb "was." (*HAYAH*) They are used with the verbs "arose" and "went" instead. This means they aren't part of the *WAW-HAYAH* controversy. However, they do reveal something important about the word order. We must look at the Hebrew word order before we look at the third *WAW* in Jonah 3:3. Here is Jonah 3:3a:

Jonah 3:3a וַיָּ֣קָם ^H6965 יוֹנָ֗ה ^H3124 וַיֵּ֛לֶךְ ^H1980 אֶל־ ^H413 נִֽינְוֵ֖ה ^H5210 כִּדְבַ֥ר ^H1697 יְהוָֽה׃ ^H3068

Jonah 3:3a [**So** arose]^H6965 [Jonah]^3124 [**and** went]^H1980 [unto]^H413 [Nineveh]^H5210 [according to the word]^H1697 [of the Lord.]^H3068

Note very carefully how both of these *WAW*s are connected to verbs. ("**so** arose" "**and** went") The word order is: *WAW*-Verb. Now look at the third *WAW* in Jonah 3:3b:

Jonah 3:3b וְנִֽינְוֵ֗ה ^H5210 **הָיְתָ֤ה** ^H1961 עִיר־ ^H5892 גְּדוֹלָה֙ ^H1419 לֵֽאלֹהִ֔ים ^H430 מַהֲלַ֖ךְ ^H4109 שְׁלֹ֥שֶׁת ^H7969 יָמִֽים׃ ^H3117

Jonah 3:3b [**Now** Nineveh]^H5210 [**was**]^H961 qpf [a city]^H5892 [great]^H1419 [an exceeding]^H430 [journey]^H4109 [of three]^H7969 [days.]^H3117

It is connected to a noun. ("**Now** Nineveh") There is a difference in word order. The word order in Jonah 3:3b is *WAW*-Noun. The third *WAW* in Jonah 3:3 is translated, "Now," because it is a *WAW* Disjunctive. Is the word order important in Hebrew? Yes. Here again is what Dr. Ross said about *WAW* Disjunctives:

> "*Disjunction*: the *waw* expresses 'but' or 'now' or some parenthetical translation that breaks away from the sequence; it is signaled by the form on a non-verb at the beginning of the clause."[120]

The third *WAW* is a *WAW* Disjunctive. Furthermore, by making the word order *WAW*-Noun, the *WAW* is separated from the verb. What happens to a verb when the *WAW* is separated from it? Remember what Martin Anstey said:

> "the separation of the *Vav* from the verb being the Hebrew method of indicating the pluperfect tense."[121]

When *WAW* (or *VAV* as some write it) is separated from the verb, it means we should translate the verb in the pluperfect tense. The third *WAW* in Jonah 3:3 is not in the same word order as the first two *WAW*s. The third *WAW* in Jonah 3:3 is connected to a noun and separated from the verb. This means it expresses a difference with respect to the tense of the verb. The first two *WAW*s in Jonah 3:3 are *WAW* Consecutives connected to verbs in the Perfect tense. We could translate the first part of Jonah 3:3 as, "**And then** Jonah arose, **and then** went to Nineveh…," because that's exactly what happened. That's exactly what he did. The third *WAW* is a *WAW* Disjunctive connected to a verb in the Pluperfect tense. The third *WAW* has to be translated, "had become," because that's what the pluperfect implies. It does not say, "Nineveh **became** a great city." It says, "Now, Nineveh **had become** a great city." This destroys the argument that Jonah 3:3 disproves the Gap Theory. Instead, it proves it. *HAYAH* is translated, "**had become**," in Jonah 3:3, and the same should be true in Genesis 1:2.

Jonah 3:3 "And Jonah is rising and going to Nineveh, according to the word of Yahweh. **Now** Nineveh **had become** a great city to Elohim, of three days walking." (CVOT)

Let's compare Genesis 1:2 with Jonah 3:3 to see for ourselves how this works.

Genesis 1:2 and Jonah 3:3

Genesis 1:2 "**And** the earth **was**…" (KJV)
Jonah 3:3b "**Now** Nineveh **was**…" (KJV)

You can see the similarities between the *WAW*s and the *HAYAH*s in Genesis 1:2 and Jonah 3:3b. The similarities are quite striking, even in English. However, we aren't trying to figure out what some English-speaker thinks about the English. We need to see what the Hebrew reveals. What are the similarities in the Hebrew?

1.) Both *WAW*s are followed by a noun subject, followed by the verb *HAYAH*, followed by a description of the subject. ("without form, and void…" and "an exceeding great city…")

2.) Both passages use the same form of *HAYAH* (*HAYETAH*) in the *QAL* Perfect.

3.) Both connect *WAW* to a noun at the beginning of each clause, making them both *WAW* Disjunctives that provide parenthetical descriptions of their subjects.

4.) In both Genesis 1:2 and Jonah 3:3b the *WAW*s are separated from the verb *HAYAH*, which means they both express the pluperfect tense.

This means Jonah 3:3 is exactly like Genesis 1:2. The fact each verse uses a *WAW* Disjunctive is important. A disjunction indicates a break, a disconnect, a dissimilarity, or a distinction between the parts connected. The *WAW* Disjunctive in Jonah 3:3b points to a difference between what Nineveh once was and what it was when Jonah went there. That's also what the *WAW* Disjunctive in Genesis 1:2 implies. It points out a difference between what the earth was in Genesis 1:1 and what the earth was in Genesis 1:2. Let's look again at Genesis 1:2 according to *The Complete Word Study Old Testament*.[122]

Genesis 1:2

Genesis 1:2 "**And** the earth[H776] [wcj] **was**[H1961] [qpf] without form,[H8414] and void;[H922] and darkness[H2822] *was* upon[H5921] the face[H6440] of the deep.[H8415] And the Spirit[H7307] of God[H430] moved[H7363] upon[H5921] the face[H6440] of the waters.[H4325]" (KJV)

Genesis 1:2 וְהָאָרֶץ[H776] **הָיְתָה**[H1961] תֹהוּ[H8414] וָבֹהוּ[H922] וְחֹשֶׁךְ[H2822] עַל[H5921]־פְּנֵי[H6440] תְהוֹם[H8415] וְרוּחַ[7307] אֱלֹהִים[H430] מְרַחֶפֶת[H7363] עַל[H5921]־פְּנֵי[H6440] הַמָּיִם[H4325]

As we have seen, the *WAW* in Genesis 1:2 is in the *WAW* Disjunctive Form which indicates some kind of difference, distinction, disconnect, or dissimilarity between the earth in Genesis 1:1 and the earth in Genesis 1:2. The ancient Hebrew reveals a difference between the earth of Genesis 1:1 and the earth of Genesis 1:2. That's why the *WAW* Disjunctive form was used. Something had changed. How do we know it had changed? The syntax of Genesis 1:2 is the same as the syntax of Jonah 3:3b. Again, this is why the anti-gap creationists have gone to Jonah 3:3 to make their point about Genesis 1:2. The only problem is they don't prove their point; they prove the opposite of what they believe. Rather than proving Genesis 1:2 says, "**and** the earth **was**…," they actually prove Jonah 3:3 says, "**Now** Nineveh **had become**…"

^{H1961}**היתה** ^{H776}וְהָאָרֶץ Genesis 1:2
^{H1961}[**had become**] ^{H776}[**But** the earth]

^{H1961}**היתה** ^{H5210}וְנִינְוֵה Jonah 3:3b
^{H1961}[**had become**] ^{H5210}[**Now** Nineveh]

The *WAW* in Genesis 1:2 is separated from the *HAYAH*. The *WAW* in Jonah 3:3b is separated from the *HAYAH*. Separating the *WAW* from the *HAYAH* creates the pluperfect form of the verb. The *HAYAH* in Jonah 3:3 is better translated: "had become." A more accurate translation of Jonah 3:3b is:

Jonah 3:3b "**Now** Nineveh **had become** an exceeding great city of three days' journey."

This parenthetical description is a thumbnail sketch of Nineveh's history. It explains what Nineveh had become. So, why would the Holy Spirit give the readers a parenthetical, thumbnail sketch of Nineveh's history at this point? The answer is easily understood if you think like an ancient Hebrew in the culture of Jonah's time. We 21st century people often face two problems when we read the Bible. First, we fail to look at the Old Testament from the perspective it was a growing collection of books that began with Genesis around 1445-1400 B.C. and ended with Malachi around 450-400 B.C. That means if you were living during the time of Jonah, (circa 760 B.C.) you wouldn't have had the entire Old Testament. You would have not heard of Ezekiel, Daniel, Jeremiah, and a whole host of other Biblical prophets. The other thing we modern people often forget is the order of the books we use is not the same order the Hebrews used. Theirs was chronologically correct. In our Bible, the Book of Jonah is the 32nd book. In the Hebrew Bible it is the 18th. Assuming you had all the books of the Bible written up to the time of Jonah, what would you know about Nineveh from God's Word? Of all the books of the Bible you had, Nineveh was last described in Genesis 10.

Genesis 10:8-12 "Now Cush became the father of Nimrod; he became a mighty one on the earth. {9} He was a mighty hunter before the LORD; therefore it is said, 'Like Nimrod a mighty hunter before the LORD.' {10} The beginning of his kingdom was Babel and Erech and Accad and Calneh, in the land of Shinar. {11} From that land he went forth into Assyria, and built Nineveh and Rehoboth-Ir and Calah, {12} and Resen between Nineveh and Calah; that is the great city." (NASB)

The last time Nineveh was described in the Bible was the story of its beginning. The last time the Bible mentioned Nineveh, it was a tiny town making up part of the kingdom Nimrod was beginning to build. It wasn't a great city at that time. In fact, it was Calah that was called, "the great city." If that was all you knew about Nineveh, and you were now reading about Jonah going to Nineveh, you might erroneously believe Jonah went to a tiny town of pagans about 500 miles northeast of Israel. You would miss the significance that by the time of Jonah, Nineveh had become an exceedingly great city. While Nineveh had been there hundreds of years, it really began to grow when the Assyrian Empire began its great rise to super-power status around 900 B.C. It had changed. God called Jonah to take the Word of God to the super-power of his day. I think that's why the Holy Spirit inspired the writer of the Book of Jonah to use the pluperfect form of *HAYAH*. He wanted His readers to know that since the last time Nineveh was described in the Bible, it had changed. (Its condition was dynamic, not static.) At one time, Nineveh wasn't an exceeding great city. Since the last time Nineveh was described in the Bible, it had become an exceedingly great city. The Holy Spirit gave His readers a thumbnail sketch of Nineveh's history so they would know what Nineveh had become. The Holy Spirit used the pluperfect form of *HAYAH* to indicate a long gap of time between Genesis 10:8-12 and Jonah 3:3, and the change that had occurred in that gap. The Holy Spirit didn't want His readers making erroneous conclusions about Nineveh. The Holy Spirit didn't want His readers thinking Jonah was sent to a small, insignificant village. If Nineveh had become an exceeding great city over the centuries, why not tell people Nineveh had become an exceeding great city? Should we Christians be surprised when God's Words in Scripture match His works in history? No! If the Bible uses the pluperfect form of *HAYAH* to describe what had become of Nineveh, then what must we say about the history of Nineveh? Nineveh had become something it wasn't before. It had become an exceedingly great city. So, when the Bible uses that very same pluperfect form of *HAYAH* to describe the earth in Genesis 1:2, what are we to say about the history of the earth?

I bet you think I am going to say, "the earth had become without form, and void." You are right; I will say it. However, even with all we have discovered about Jonah 3:3, there are still anti-gap creationists who won't agree. Oh, they agree it's okay to translate it "had become" concerning Nineveh, but they still insist it can't be translated, "had become," concerning the earth. What Hebrew grammar rules do they use? What passages of Scripture do they quote? What pieces of scientific or historic evidence do they reveal? None! They say it's okay to translate it "had become" in reference to Nineveh because Nineveh had time to change. There had been a long history of Nineveh. Nineveh had been there hundreds of years. Because there had been a long gap of time between Genesis 10:8-12 and Jonah 3:3, it's perfectly proper to say, "Nineveh had become...." BUT, they say you can't say the same thing about the earth in Genesis 1:2 because it had been created instantly that same day. There is no gap of time between Genesis 1:1 and Genesis 1:2. Earth had no history. Earth could not "become" anything because there was no gap of time for it to do so. It couldn't have become without form, and void and covered by water and darkness because that was the way it was created. They say there can't be a gap of time between Genesis 1:1 and Genesis 1:2 because there was no gap of time between Genesis 1:1 and Genesis 1:2.

Do you see what they do? They use their conclusion as proof for their assumption. They use their belief the earth is young as the "context" out of which they develop their interpretation the earth is young. Rather than using the rules of Hebrew grammar, rather than comparing Scripture to Scripture, rather than believing what history and science prove, they use their preconceived ideas as a way of interpreting God's Word. They don't worry about what the Holy Spirit inspired the ancient Hebrew writers to write in the ancient Hebrew. They insist they know better. What do they do when they confront Genesis 1:2, a passage of Scripture that uses a *WAW* Disjunctive combined with *HAYAH* in its Pluperfect, Dynamic-Becoming Form? They translate it as a *WAW* Coordinative combined with *HAYAH* in its simple Perfect, Static-Being Form. In spite of that, they still say their interpretation is the literal interpretation.

Closing comment on *HAYAH*

I want to say one last thing about *HAYAH*. In truth, the exact translation of *WAW* in Genesis 1:2 is not as important in this issue as the correct translation of *HAYAH*. Look at these six possible translations:

1.) In the beginning, God created the heavens and the earth, **AND** the earth **WAS** without form, and void.

2.) In the beginning, God created the heavens and the earth, **BUT** the earth **WAS** without form, and void.

3.) In the beginning, God created the heavens and the earth. **NOW** the earth **WAS** without form, and void.

As you can see, examples 1, 2, and 3 say essentially the same thing. Each translation implies the earth being "without form, and void" was its initial condition. That was the way God created it. Whether the word is "AND," "BUT," or "NOW" makes little difference.

All three sentences imply the earth was created *TOHUW WA-BOHUW*. Now look at examples 4, 5, and 6.

4.) In the beginning, God created the heavens and the earth, **AND** the earth **HAD BECOME** without form, and void.

5.) In the beginning, God created the heavens and the earth, **BUT** the earth **HAD BECOME** without form, and void.

6.) In the beginning, God created the heavens and the earth. **NOW** the earth **HAD BECOME** without form, and void.

Again, the exact translation of *WAW* makes little difference to the overall thought of the passage. All three of these translations indicate the condition of being "without form, and void" was something that came to be after the initial creation. All three sentences say the earth had become *TOHUW WA-BOHUW*.

As far as the Hebrew grammar is concerned, the most important factor in this issue is the exact meaning of *HAYAH* in Genesis 1:2. Virtually all creationists who reject the Gap Theory believe *HAYAH* means "was" as a past, static "being." They reject the idea it can mean a past, active "coming to be." Many other creationists insist on their definition, and accuse anyone who believes otherwise of being a false teacher, a liar, or even a heretic. Their emotions run high because their prejudice runs deep. They fail to investigate the various meanings of the Hebrew word in all the various passages where it is used. Even if it is translated, "was," in the English, they still fail to investigate all the various meanings of "was" in all the various passages where it is used. Virtually every word in every language has a range of meanings (linguistic range) that must be understood before correct communication is possible. When you remember we are dealing with a language that has a relatively small number of different words, you must be willing to accept the fact *HAYAH* can mean more than one thing. Anti-Gap Theory creationists have convinced themselves, and others, that *HAYAH* can mean only one thing; a past, static, unchanging condition. They want us to think the earth ALWAYS WAS without form and void since its creation. But, the word "was" doesn't necessarily imply something has always been that way; not even in the English. Look at these sentences:

The dog WAS sick.
The road WAS icy.
The cabin WAS deserted.
The woman WAS pregnant.
The temperature WAS 102°F in the shade.
The little boy WAS five years old.

Are we to assume the dog was sick its entire life? Are we to believe the road was always icy? If the cabin had been deserted forever, who built it? If you insist "was" always means "forever and unchanging," then I feel very sorry for that pregnant woman. Where has it always been statically 102°F in the shade? When the little boy was born, was he five years old and remained that age? You can see what these other creationists do. They assume their definition is true, but they do so without considering the possibility that "was" has a linguistic range of meanings. Just because it may say, "WAS without form and void," it doesn't mean it WAS ALWAYS without form and void, any more than, "the woman WAS pregnant," means she WAS ALWAYS pregnant. Their definition of "was" has no grammatical or contextual defense. There are three positive Hebrew Grammar indicators in the context that prove it doesn't mean what they say it means.

1.) Genesis 1:2 is a disjunction from Genesis 1:1. That means there is some kind of difference or disconnect between the earth in Genesis 1:1 and the earth in Genesis 1:2.

2.) The very use of the word *HAYAH* indicates it is not meant to be a copula, a mere connecting word. The Hebrews usually left it out when they expressed that concept.

3.) The verb is in the pluperfect form, "had become," instead of the simple form, "was." This indicates a past change had been completed prior to what follows the verb. (Before Day One.)

God has given us three grammatical clues in the context, but anti-Gap Theory creationists reject His clues. And, that's not counting all the other clues He gives from other parts of Scripture. If you do a little research on your own, it won't take long to find an uncountable number of comments by experts and non-experts alike who say the Gap Theory is wrong because *HAYAH* is never translated, or very rarely translated, "become." They insist Genesis 1:2 cannot be translated, "But the earth became (or had become) without form, and void." Now, I've presented several arguments showing you why their claim is false, and you may think I've run that horse into the ground. But, like a good jockey on a good horse, I've saved the best for last. The correct interpretation of *HAYAH* in Genesis 1:2 is THE key issue in this debate. **If I can absolutely prove *HAYAH* means "became" or "had become" in Genesis 1:2, then ALL the non-Gap Theories lose the race.** Well, hang on to your hats, boys and girls, I'm about to leave them in the dust.

That's Very Un-Becoming of You

So, if you still hate the Gap Theory and still believe *HAYAH* cannot be translated, "became" or "had become," I've got some bad news for you. The computer age has arrived! Back in the "old days" it would have been virtually impossible for us non-scholars to compare every single Hebrew word in the Bible, with how it is used in every single place in the Bible, taking into consideration all the forms of the words, all the variations in tenses or stems, all the prefixes and suffixes that alter the meanings, all the prepositional attachments, and all the other factors, INCLUDING THE CONTEXT, that give each word its linguistic range of meanings. Just the word *HAYAH* alone would have taken years to study. It is used over 3,500 times in the Bible. Looking at what it means in every place it is found, and comparing it to every other place it is found, would have been a task few would have attempted. Fewer still would have completed it. We had to take the scholars at their word, even though they rarely agreed on what *HAYAH* meant in Genesis 1:2. Today, thanks to the computer, Hebrew texts have been scanned, digitalized, and can be searched in seconds. Words, parts of words, phrases, and whole sentences can be instantly found, compared, and contrasted. If only there were some people who had enough knowledge of the Hebrew and Greek languages, enough reverence for the Holy Scriptures, enough desire to glorify Jesus Christ by helping us understand God's Holy Word, and enough computer power to digitally analyze every single word in the Bible, then it might be possible for those people to provide a way for us non-scholars to know what God actually said in His Word. Such people, with such computer prowess, could help make us less dependent on the scholars and the so-called scholars.

Hallelujah, those people exist, and they have done exactly that! Even more amazing is they offer their labor of love as a gift of love. The greatest Bible Language study tool I have seen is the *Interlinear Scripture Analyzer* or *ISA*. It is a freely offered computer software package that can be downloaded at:

http://www.scripture4all.org

While it is free, I strongly encourage you to send a donation if you use the *ISA*… and if you are a student of God's Word, believe me, you will want to use it. The *Interlinear Scripture Analyzer* is an Interlinear Bible and Concordance Search tool that gives you the opportunity to do an in-depth study of EVERY word in the Bible. I downloaded the program because I wanted to do a study of the word *HAYAH*. I wanted to see what an exhaustive computer-analysis would reveal. Now that I've done that, I want to share my findings.

By clicking on the word *HAYAH* in Genesis 1:2, the *ISA* calls up a screen showing all the uses of *HAYAH*, in all of its forms, in the entire Bible. According to the *ISA*, *HAYAH* is used 3,575 times (Based on the *Westminster-Leningrad Codex*, the oldest complete Hebrew Bible we have.) with 247 meanings/variations in the Hebrew. (Yes, Hebrew really is a "rubber" language.) The *ISA* also shows all the various Hebrew spellings, with all the prefixes, suffixes, vowel-points, *etc.*, as well as the Strong's Number. The following images are screen-shots of what I found concerning *HAYAH*. I have limited the information to four items: The first column is the number of times that particular Hebrew variation is found in the Bible. The second column is the Strong's Number. In this case, they are all "H1961," Strong's Number for *HAYAH*. The third column is the spelling of the word in

Hebrew, including the prefixes, suffixes, and vowel points from the *Westminster-Leningrad Codex*. The last column is the meaning of the word according to the *Concordant Hebrew English Sublinear* (*CHES*), which is the *ISA* rendering based on the vocabulary of the *Concordant Version of the Old Testament* (*CVOT*) translation of the Masoretic Text. It sounds complicated but it isn't. Now, first of all, don't get confused by the use of "he" and "she." Hebrew words, like many non-English languages, have gender. This may or may not have any connection to gender in the sexual sense, but it is used to help identify the objects of verbs, modifiers, *etc.* The "he" and the "she" are not as important as the actual definitions and usages of the word.

Let me explain how this works for the first three *HAYAH*'s on the list. The first *HAYAH* in this same stem, with this same spelling, with these same prefixes and suffixes, with these same vowel-points, *etc.*, is found in the Scripture 709 times. (I won't list them, but the *Interlinear Scripture Analyzer* lists all 709. If you want to see them for yourself, in their context, then download the *ISA* software.) This form of *HAYAH* means, "and is becoming." Again, don't worry about the "he" because it applies to inanimate objects as well as to people or animals. The second *HAYAH* on the list is found in 363 places in the Scriptures in that exact same form. It means, "and becomes." The third *HAYAH* on the list is found in 220 places in Scripture, and it means, "shall become."

So, the task before you is to look down the list at the meanings of *HAYAH*, and see if "became," "become," "becoming," *etc.* are ever used. Remember, there are numerous Young-Earth and Day-Age scholars who say *HAYAH* can't be translated as a form of "become." Here are the screen-shots: (Note: I have underlined the 13th listing of *HAYAH* because it is the form of *HAYETAH* used in Genesis 1:2. It means, "became," and is used 65 times in Scripture that way.)

	Strong	WLC_V	CHES2
709	H1961	וַיְהִי	and·he-is-becoming
363	H1961	וְהָיָה	and·he-becomes
220	H1961	יִהְיֶה	he-shall-become
152	H1961	הָיָה	he-became
134	H1961	הָיָה	he-was[bc]
109	H1961	יִהְיֶה	he-shall-be[bc]
107	H1961	וְהָיוּ	and·they-become
89	H1961	וְהָיְתָה	and·she-becomes
73	H1961	יִהְיוּ	they-shall-become
70	H1961	וַתְּהִי	and·she-is-becoming
66	H1961	וַיְהִי	and·he-was[bc]
65	H1961	הָיוּ	they-became
65	H1961	הָיְתָה	she-became
65	H1961	תִּהְיֶה	she-shall-become
61	H1961	הָיוּ	they-were[bc]
60	H1961	יִהְיֶה	he-is-becoming
60	H1961	וַיִּהְיוּ	and·they-are-becoming

	Strong	WLC_V	CHES2
42	H1961	וַיִּהְיוּ	and·they-were[bc]
41	H1961	לִהְיוֹת	to·to-become-of
33	H1961	הָיָה	he-becomes
30	H1961	הָיְתָה	she-was[bc]
29	H1961	אֶהְיֶה	I-shall-become
28	H1961	הָיוּ	they-become
28	H1961	יְהִי	he-shall-become
26	H1961	הָיִיתִי	I-became
26	H1961	תִּהְיֶה	she-shall-become
26	H1961	יִהְיוּ	they-shall-be[bc]
26	H1961	לִהְיוֹת	to·to-be[bc]-of
26	H1961	וְהָיָה	and·he-became
25	H1961	וְהָיִיתָ	and·you-become
21	H1961	יִהְיֶה	he-is[bc]
21	H1961	וִיהִי	and·he-shall-become
18	H1961	וְהָיִיתִי	and·I-become
16	H1961	הָיָה	he-is[bc]
16	H1961	תִּהְיֶה	she-shall-be[bc]
15	H1961	הָיִיתָ	you-became

	Strong	WLC_V	CHES2
15	H1961	תִּהְיֶה	you-shall-become
15	H1961	יְהִי	he-shall-be[bc]
15	H1961	וִהְיִיתֶם	and·you(p)-become
12	H1961	הֱיוֹת	to-become-of
12	H1961	הָיוּ	they-are[bc]
12	H1961	הָיְתָה	she-becomes
12	H1961	יִהְיוּ	they-are-becoming
11	H1961	הָיִיתִי	I-was[bc]
11	H1961	תִּהְיֶה	she-shall-be[bc]
11	H1961	וַתְּהִי	and·she-was[bc]
10	H1961	תִּהְיֶה	she-is-becoming
9	H1961	וְהָיָה	and·he-is[bc]
9	H1961	וְיִהְיוּ	and·they-shall-become
8	H1961	הָיִיתִי	I-am[bc]
7	H1961	בִּהְיוֹת	in·to-be[bc]-of
7	H1961	תְּהִי	she-shall-become
7	H1961	תִּהְיֶיןָ	they-shall-become
7	H1961	תִּהְיֶינָה	they-shall-be[bc]
7	H1961	תִּהְיֶינָה	they-shall-become
6	H1961	בִּהְיוֹת	in·to-become-of
6	H1961	הֱיִיתֶם	you(p)-became
6	H1961	תִּהְיוּ	you(p)-shall-become
6	H1961	יְהִי	he-is-becoming

	Strong	WLC_V	CHES2
6	H1961	יָהָיָה	he-was^{bc}
6	H1961	וַיְהִי	and·he-is-becoming
6	H1961	וַתִּהְיֶינָה	and·they-are-becoming
6	H1961	וּתְהִי	and·she-shall-become
5	H1961	אֶהְיֶה	I-shall-be^{bc}
5	H1961	הֱיִיתֶם	you(p)-were^{bc}
5	H1961	הָיִינוּ	we-became
5	H1961	תִּהְיֶה	she-is-becoming
5	H1961	תִּהְיֶה	you-shall-become
5	H1961	יִהְיֶה	he-shall-become
5	H1961	נִהְיָתָה	she-has-become
5	H1961	וְהָיִינוּ	and·we-become
5	H1961	וִהְיוּ	and·be^{bc}-you(p) !
5	H1961	וִיהִי	and·he-shall-be^{bc}
5	H1961	וָאֱהִי	and·I-was^{bc}
5	H1961	וָאֶהְיֶה	and·I-am-becoming
5	H1961	וּתְהִי	and·she-shall-be^{bc}
4	H1961	אֶהְיֶה	I-am-becoming
4	H1961	הֱיֵה	become-you !
4	H1961	הֱיוֹת	to-be^{bc}-of
4	H1961	הָיִיתָ	you-were^{bc}
4	H1961	הֱיוֹ	to-become
4	H1961	תִּהְיוּ	you(p)-shall-become
4	H1961	תִּהְיֶינָה	they-shall-become
4	H1961	תְּהִי	she-is-becoming
4	H1961	תְּהִי	she-shall-be^{bc}
4	H1961	תְּהִי	you-are-being^{bc}
4	H1961	תִּהְיוּ	you(p)-are-becoming

	Strong	WLC_V	CHES2
4	H1961	לִהְיֹ֣ת	to·to-become-of
4	H1961	מִהְיֹ֣ות	from·to-be^(bc)-of
4	H1961	מִהְיֹ֣ות	from·to-become-of
4	H1961	וְהָי֣וּ	and·they-became
4	H1961	וְהָיָ֣ה	and·he-was^(bc)
4	H1961	וִהְיִיתֶ֣ם	and·become-you !
4	H1961	וַיְהִ֣י	and·he-is^(bc)
4	H1961	וָאֱהִ֣י	and·I-am-becoming
3	H1961	אֶהְיֶ֣ה	I-was^(bc)
3	H1961	בִּהְיֹתֹ֣ו	in·to-be^(bc)-of·him
3	H1961	בִּהְיֹותָ֣ם	in·to-become-of·them
3	H1961	הֱיֵ֣ה	be^(bc)-you !
3	H1961	הָיְתָ֣ה	she-is^(bc)
3	H1961	הָיִ֣יתָ	you-become
3	H1961	הָיִ֣יתִי	I-become
3	H1961	הָיִ֣יתָ	you-are^(bc)
3	H1961	תִּהְיֶ֣ה	you-are-becoming
3	H1961	תִּהְיֶ֣ה	you-shall-be^(bc)
3	H1961	תְּהִ֣י	you-are-becoming
3	H1961	תִּהְיֶ֣ה	you-are-becoming
3	H1961	נִהְיֶ֣ה	we-shall-become
3	H1961	נִהְיָ֣ה	he-^(n)became
3	H1961	וּתְהִ֣י	and·she-shall-become
3	H1961	וָאֶהְיֶ֣ה	and·I-was^(bc)
3	H1961	שֶׁהָיָ֣ה	who·he-was^(bc)
3	H1961	שֶׁיִּהְיֶ֣ה	which·he-shall-become
2	H1961	אֶהְיֶ֣ה	I-am^(bc)
2	H1961	בִּהְיֹותָ֣ם	in·to-be^(bc)-of·them

	Strong	WLC_V	CHES2
2	H1961	בִּהְיוֹתוֹ	in·to-be^bc-of·him
2	H1961	בִּהְיוֹתוֹ	in·to-become-of·him
2	H1961	הֱיוֹתְךָ	to-be^bc-of·you
2	H1961	הֱיוֹתָם	to-become-of·them
2	H1961	הֲיִהְיֶה	?·he-shall-become
2	H1961	הָיִיתָ	you-were^bc
2	H1961	הָיִינוּ	we-are^bc
2	H1961	הָיִינוּ	we-become
2	H1961	הָיִינוּ	we-were^bc
2	H1961	הָיְתָה	she-becomes
2	H1961	הֱיֵה	to-become
2	H1961	תִּהְיוּ	you(p)-shall-be
2	H1961	תִּהְיֶיןָ	they-shall-be^bc
2	H1961	תִּהְיֶינָה	they-are-becoming
2	H1961	יִהְיוּ	they-were^bc
2	H1961	לִהְיוֹת	to·to-be^bc-of
2	H1961	מִהְיוֹת	from·to-become-of
2	H1961	נִהְיָה	he-is-become
2	H1961	וְאֶהְיֶה	and·I-shall-become
2	H1961	וְהָיְתָה	and·she-became
2	H1961	וַיִּהְיוּ	and·they-are-becoming
2	H1961	וְלִהְיוֹת	and·to·to-be^bc-of
2	H1961	וְנִהְיָתָה	and·she-has-become
2	H1961	וִהְיוּ	and·become-you(p) !
2	H1961	וִהְיִיתֶם	and·you(p)-are^bc
2	H1961	וֶהֱיֵה	and·be^bc-you !
2	H1961	וַתְּהִי	and·you-are-becoming
2	H1961	וַתִּהְיֶיןָ	and·they-are-becoming
2	H1961	וִיהִי	and·he-shall-be^bc
2	H1961	וַיִּהְיוּ	and·they-are^bc

	Strong	WLC_V	CHES2
2	H1961	וַיְהִי	and·he-is-becoming
2	H1961	וַנְּהִי	and·we-are-becoming
2	H1961	וָאֱהִי	and·I-am^bc
2	H1961	וָאֱהִי	and·I-shall-become
2	H1961	וְאֶהְיֶה	and·I-shall-be^bc
2	H1961	וּתְהִי	and·you-are-becoming
2	H1961	שֶׁיִּהְיוּ	who·they-shall-become
2	H1961	שֶׁהָיָה	which·he-became
1	H1961	בִּהְיוֹת	in·to-be^bc-of
1	H1961	בִּהְיֹת	in·to-become-of
1	H1961	בִּהְיוֹתְכֶם	in·to-be^bc-of·you
1	H1961	בִּהְיוֹתְכֶם	in·to-become-of·you(p)
1	H1961	בִּהְיוֹתָךְ	in·to-be^bc-of·you
1	H1961	בִּהְיוֹתֵנוּ	in·to-be^bc-of·us
1	H1961	הָיוּ	be^bc-you(p) !
1	H1961	הָיוּ	become-you(p) !
1	H1961	הֱיִתֶם	you(p)-were^bc
1	H1961	הֱיִיתֶם	you(p)-become
1	H1961	הֱיֵה	to-become-of
1	H1961	הֱיוֹתְכֶם	to-become-of·you(p)
1	H1961	הֱיוֹתִי	to-become-of·me
1	H1961	הֱיוֹתָךְ	to-become-of·you
1	H1961	הֱיוֹתֵנוּ	to-be^bc-of·us
1	H1961	הֱיוֹתָם	to-be^bc-of·them
1	H1961	הֱיוֹתָהּ	to-become-of·her
1	H1961	הֱיוֹתוֹ	to-become-of·him
1	H1961	הֱיִי	become-you !
1	H1961	הֲנִהְיָה	?·he-^noccurred
1	H1961	הֲהָיְתָה	?·she-became

	Strong	WLC_V	CHES2
1	H1961	הָיְתָה	she-becomes
1	H1961	הָיוּ	they-are
1	H1961	הָיְתָה	she-occurred
1	H1961	הָיִיתִי	you-become
1	H1961	הָיִיתָ	you-became
1	H1961	הָיִיתָ	you-become
1	H1961	הָיִיתָה	you-were[bc]
1	H1961	הָיְתָה	she-became
1	H1961	הָיְתָה	she-was[bc]
1	H1961	ה וְיָה	becoming
1	H1961	תְהִי	she-is-becoming
1	H1961	תְהִי	she-shall-be[bc]
1	H1961	תִהְיוּ	you(P)-are-becoming
1	H1961	תִהְיִי	you-shall-become
1	H1961	תִהְיֶיןָ	they-are-becoming
1	H1961	תִהְיֶיןָ	they-shall-become
1	H1961	תְהִי	you-shall-become
1	H1961	תִהְיוּן	you(P)-shall-become
1	H1961	תִהְיֶה	you-are-becoming
1	H1961	תִהְיֶה	she-is[bc]
1	H1961	תִהְיֶה	you-shall-be[bc]
1	H1961	תִהְיֶיןָ	they-are-becoming
1	H1961	יִהְיוּ	they-are[bc]
1	H1961	יִהְיֶה	he-is-being[bc]
1	H1961	יְהִי	he-is-becoming
1	H1961	יִהְיוּ	they-shall-become
1	H1961	יִהְיֶה	he-is[bc]
1	H1961	כְּשֶׁהָיָה	as·which·he-was[bc]
1	H1961	לִהְי וּתְכֶם	to·to-become-of·you(P)
1	H1961	מִהְי ת	from·to-be-of

	Strong	WLC_V	CHES2
1	H1961	מִֽהְיֽוֹתְךָ֖	from·to-be_bc_-of·you
1	H1961	מִֽהְי֥וֹתָ֖ם	from·to-become-of·them
1	H1961	נִהְיָ֔תָה	she-_n_occurred
1	H1961	נִהְיֵ֔יתִי	I-was-become
1	H1961	נִהְיֵ֖יתָ	you-_n_have-become
1	H1961	נִהְיִ֑וּ	we-are-becoming
1	H1961	נִהְיֶ֖ה	we-are_bc_
1	H1961	נִהְיָ֑ה	being-become
1	H1961	נִהְיָ֑ה	he-was_bc_
1	H1961	נִהְיָ֖תָה	she-has-become
1	H1961	נִהְיָ֔תָה	she-has-become
1	H1961	וְהָי֖וּ	and·they-are_bc_
1	H1961	וְהָי֖וּ	and·they-were_bc_
1	H1961	וְהָיְתָ֖ה	and·she-was_bc_
1	H1961	וְהָיִ֑תָ	and·you-become
1	H1961	וְהָיְתָ֖ה	and·you-become
1	H1961	וְהָיִ֖יתָ	and·you-become
1	H1961	וְהָיִ֖יתָ	and·you-become
1	H1961	וְהָיִ֖יתָה	and·become-you !
1	H1961	וְהָיִ֑ת	and·she-becomes
1	H1961	וְתִהְיֶ֖ינָה	and·you(P)-shall-become
1	H1961	וְתִהְיֶ֖ינָה	and·they-shall-become
1	H1961	וְיִהְי֖וּ	and·they-shall-be_bc_
1	H1961	וְלִהְיֹ֥ת תְךָ֖	and·for·to-be_bc_-of·you
1	H1961	וְנִהְיֶ֖ה	and·we-shall-become
1	H1961	וִהְיִתֶ֖ם	and·you(P)-become
1	H1961	וַתִּהְי֖וּ	and·you(P)-are-becoming
1	H1961	וַתְּהִ֖י	and·you-are-becoming
1	H1961	וַתִּהְיֶ֖ינָה	and·they-were_bc_
1	H1961	וַתִּהְיֶ֖ינָה	and·they-are-becoming

	Strong	WLC_V	CHES2
1	H1961	וַתְּהִי	and·she-is-becoming
1	H1961	וִיהִי	and·he-shall-become
1	H1961	וַיִּהְיוּ	and·they-are-being[bc]
1	H1961	וְנִהְיָה	and·we-are-becoming
1	H1961	וְנִהְיָה	and·we-are-being[bc]
1	H1961	וּתְהִי	and·she-is-becoming
1	H1961	שֶׁהָיוּ	who·they-were[bc]
1	H1961	שֶׁהָיָה	which·he-was[bc]
1	H1961	שֶׁיִּהְיוּ	which·they-are-becoming
1	H1961	שֶׁיִּהְיֶה	who·he-shall-become
1	H1961	שֶׁהָיָה	which·he-is[bc]
1	H1961	שֶׁהָיָה	which·he-was[bc]
1	H1961	שֶׁיִּהְיֶה	which·he-shall-become

Do you remember Arthur Custance said "had become" was the best translation? And do you remember Thorleif Boman said *HAYAH* was never used as a static condition? And do you remember James Strong said it was not a mere copulative? And do you remember Martin Anstey agreed? And do you remember Gleason Archer told us this was true? And do you remember A.W. Pink, John Darby, Alfred Edersheim, Charles Spurgeon, James Montgomery Boice, and a whole list of other scholars nodded in approval? Against their claims, we have scholars who say *HAYAH* never or rarely means "became" or "become." So, who is telling the truth?

If you are still a Gap Theory hater, you are probably saying, "Oh Yeah, well I see 'am' and 'are' and 'is' and 'was' in that list, so I'm still going to reject the Gap Theory." Okay, go back over the list, and at each so-called copulative use, you will see two little letters as a superscript: [bc]. What does [bc] mean? The answer is found in the Abbreviation Key in the *Concordant Hebrew English Sublinear* help-file. The [bc] means *HAYAH* is actually used in the sense of "become" or "became" even though it is translated another way in English. Again, this is like my example of saying, "I broke my wife's favorite vase, and she was mad." Yes, it is "was," but we understand from the context it means she "became" mad. It's not static. So, go back and look at all the little [bc] markers.

Let me do the number-crunching for you. Of the 3,575 times *HAYAH* is used in the sense of the verb "to be," it is in some form of "became" 2,776 times. It is used by words marked by the little [bc] indicator another 792 times. That means *HAYAH* indicates a state of dynamic being ("becoming," "coming to be," "coming to pass," or some other form of "became") 3,568 times. That leaves only 7 times it is used in some other sense. The first four of those seven describe conditions/events that will happen in the future. (In other words, they don't describe past, static conditions.)

1.) Genesis 44:10 "And he said, Now also *let* it *be* according unto your words: he with whom it is found **shall be** my servant; and ye shall be blameless." (KJV)

2.) Leviticus 26:12 "And I will walk among you, and will be your God, and ye **shall be** my people." (KJV)

3.) Leviticus 26:13 "I *am* the LORD your God, which brought you forth out of the land of Egypt, that ye **should not be** their bondmen; and I have broken the bands of your yoke, and made you go upright." (KJV)

4.) Daniel 12:1 "And at that time shall Michael stand up, the great prince which standeth for the children of thy people: and there **shall be** a time of trouble, such as never was since there was a nation *even* to that same time: and at that time thy people shall be delivered, every one that shall be found written in the book." (KJV)

The next two describe past dynamic actions rather than past static conditions.

5.) Deuteronomy 4:32 "Indeed, ask now concerning the former days which were before you, since the day that God created man on the earth, and *inquire* from one end of the heavens to the other. Has *anything* **been done** like this great thing, or has *anything* been heard like it?" (NASB)

6.) 1 Kings 11:11 "So the LORD said to Solomon, 'Because you **have done** this, and you have not kept My covenant and My statutes, which I have commanded you, I will surely tear the kingdom from you, and will give it to your servant.'" (NASB)

These two verses translate *HAYAH* as "done." "Done" defines a completed ACTION, not a static BEING. Even these two verses show us Genesis 1:2 doesn't describe what the earth WAS; it describes what the earth BECAME. This leaves only one *HAYAH* listed in the *ISA* as a form of "to be" not marked with a [bc] notation. That passage is Lamentations 1:16.

7.) Lamentations 1:16 "For these *things* I weep; mine eye, mine eye runneth down with water, because the comforter that should relieve my soul is far from me: my children **are** desolate, because the enemy prevailed." (KJV)

I don't know why this *HAYAH* is not marked with a [bc] notation. His children (Israel) became desolate because the enemy prevailed. They weren't always desolate. It may be an oversight or computer quirk on the part of the *ISA*. It is obvious the writer is speaking about what had happened (action) to Israel; how Israel's condition had changed. It wasn't a past static, unchanging condition; it was dynamic. Israel wasn't always desolate.

The final tally is this: Out of 3,575 times *HAYAH* is used in the sense of "to be," it is used 3,575 times in a dynamic sense. That's 100% of the time. **HAYAH is never used for "was" in the sense Young-Earth and Day-Age creationists say it is**. It is never used in the static, copulative sense. (That's what Boman, Strong, Custance, Anstey, and others said.) The Young-Earth and Day-Age claims are not true. In fact, they are the exact opposite of the truth. (They believe the truth is a lie, and a lie is the truth.) We know their theories are not true because they create contradictions between science and the Bible. We know their theories are not true because they erect barriers to the Gospel of Jesus Christ. All I ask of my readers is to believe the truth.

Summary of the Evidence for the Duo-Genesis Principle

1.) Qualified Hebrew scholars confirm *HAYAH* can be translated, "became." The Restoration Theory is not based on an unscholarly interpretation.

2.) Job 38:4-6 describes the creation of the earth as a process over time. The Restoration Theory agrees.

3.) The Restoration Theory has been believed and defended by theologians for hundreds, if not thousands of years. It is not something dreamed up to compromise the Bible with evolution.

4.) Isaiah 45:18 reveals God did not create the earth a desolate waste. This is what the Restoration Theory teaches.

5.) Job 38:7 shows the angels rejoiced over the creation of the earth, thus indicating the earth wasn't created a desolate waste. The Restoration Theory agrees with this.

6.) Job 38:8-11 reveals there was a global flood accompanied by global darkness that happened before Adam was created. This is one of the beliefs of the Gap Theory.

7.) Paul indicates in 2 Corinthians 4:6 that physical light existed before Genesis 1:3 in the same way that Spiritual Light existed before we experience it in our souls. It was not a new creation. The Gap Theory is in agreement.

8.) According to the Bible, the creation of the earth came before the first day of creation. Genesis 1:1-2 is not a title or summary of creation. This is at the heart of the Restoration Theory.

9.) Jeremiah 4:23-26 reveals the Pre-Adamic earth was made *TOHUW WA-BOHUW* by God's fierce anger. The Restoration Theory says the earth was judged by God's fierce anger.

10.) Isaiah 34:11 confirms *TOHUW* and *BOHUW* describe Divine judgment. The Restoration Theory agrees again.

11.) Interpreting *TOHUW WA-BOHUW* to mean something other than Divine judgment violates accepted rules of letting Scripture interpret Scripture. The Restoration Theory doesn't violate this rule. Rather, it enforces it.

12.) The Restoration Theory explains why God pronounced His works of restoration were, "very good," but did not say that of the heavens and the earth in Genesis 1:2.

13.) The writings of Job and Ezekiel combined with the teachings of Jesus and John show how the earth had two separate beginnings. The Restoration Theory prevents a contradiction between what Jesus and John taught about Lucifer and what Job and Ezekiel taught.

14.) The descriptions of what Lucifer did to the earth match with the descriptions of what God did to the Pre-Adamic earth as a result of sin. This fits with the Restoration Theory.

15.) Both Haggai 2:6 and Hebrews 12:25-27 reveal God has judged (shaken) the Pre-Adamic heavens and earth. Only the Restoration Theory mentions a Pre-Adamic judgment.

16.) The Restoration Theory explains the discrepancy between the order of fossils seen in the Geological Column and the order of creation/restoration mentioned in Genesis 1:3-31. God did not restore life in the same order He had originally created it.

17.) The Restoration Theory explains the phenomenon of Living Fossils. Some things had died millions of years ago and God restored them recently.

18.) The Restoration Theory explains why some dating techniques indicate a Young-Earth while other dating techniques indicate an Old-Earth.

19.) The Gap Theory explains the appearance of Pre-Adamic death as revealed in the fossil record.

20.) The meaning of *YOM* when used for the six days in Genesis 1 can only mean a literal twenty-four-hour day. The Restoration Theory and the Young-Earth Theory agree with the Bible on this meaning, but the Day-Age Theory doesn't.

21.) The observations of science indicate the universe is very old. The Restoration Theory and the Day-Age Theory agree with these scientific observations, but the Young-Earth Theory doesn't.

22.) The Restoration Theory reveals there were intelligent beings on the earth before man. This is what paleontologists have discovered. Science doesn't disagree with Scripture.

23.) The Ruin-Restoration Theory shows how the judgment and restoration of the earth was a foreshadow of what Christ would do for fallen man. The visible heavens declare the invisible glory of our Redeemer. Redemption is not seen in the heavens if they were never redeemed.

24.) Jeremiah saw the earth in a condition of having dry land but no light while Genesis shows the earth in a condition of having light but no dry land. There is no contradiction here; the Gap Theory explains the proper historical sequence of events.

25.) Hebrews 11:3 reveals God created an age before our present age. This was the Pre-Adamic age the Gap Theory presents.

26.) Paul created a parallel between the light God shines into the hearts of restored sinners, and the light He shone into the restored earth. Fallen man and the fallen earth have both been restored, but both are awaiting a future perfection. The Gap Theory reveals God as the God of restoration.

27.) The argument *HAYAH* cannot be translated as a form of "became" because it is not followed by the preposition *le* is easily disproved by several examples in Genesis.

28.) The argument *HAYAH* cannot be translated as a form of "became" because it is part of a *WAW* Disjunctive parenthetical statement is also disproved by several examples in Genesis.

29.) Interpreting Genesis 1 as a sequential, chronological account of the events of creation, as is suggested by the Hebrew word *TOWLEDAH*, reveals a pattern of creation that excludes both the Day-Age and the Young-Earth Theories of creation.

30.) The phrase *KATABOLE KOSMOS* used in the New Testament refers to a time before the Age of Men, when the earth was catabolized for the purpose of being rebuilt. This is the Gap Theory.

    Something terrible happened to the earth between Genesis 1:1 and Genesis 1:2. The earth HAD BECOME without form, and void. Arthur Custance was right!

To Those Who Haven't Put Their Trust in Jesus

I think you now see my motive for believing in the Restoration Theory. I think you understand why I believe what I believe, not just what I believe. It's not a matter of being able to manipulate Hebrew grammar rules. It is not a matter of trying to make the Bible agree with a human-contrived theory. It is a matter of trying to find an explanation that agrees with all the Bible. It is a matter of seeing how Scripture agrees with Scripture. It is a matter of showing how God's Works agree with God's Words. It is a matter of giving Jesus Christ all the Glory He so richly deserves. He is the God of Mercy, Grace, Forgiveness, and most of all, the God of Restoration.

It is amazing how the Gap Theory is rejected as a weak argument by Young-Earth and Day-Age creationists. Their theories have far less evidence. Their theories create problems and confusion. If you study the other creation theories carefully, I think you will discover they have little Biblical and scientific evidence in their favor. Why then does the Restoration Theory receive such criticism? Satan doesn't want us to see how the handiwork of God reveals His invisible attribute of Redeemer/Restorer. The Gap Theory glorifies God by revealing how His restoration of the fallen earth foreshadows His restoration of fallen man. **Unbelievers, please listen to me.**

Believe on the Lord Jesus Christ, and you will be RESTORED.

Dear unsaved friends: I know some of you have rejected the Bible because you believed it was full of lies and errors. I understand your rejection. I wouldn't believe it either if it taught things that weren't true. If you have read this book with an open mind, then I think you now realize the Bible doesn't teach many of the things you have been told were true, things you objected to, things you knew weren't true! The Bible reveals the truth. The Bible reveals the truth about the origin of man, and more importantly, the Bible reveals the truth about the destiny of man. Most importantly, the Bible reveals the truth about YOUR destiny. God will not tolerate sin. He will not tolerate your sin and He will not tolerate my sin. We all have sinned, and we are all doomed to face God's eternal judgment if we reject His gift of forgiveness and salvation through Jesus Christ. All of us are fallen beings in need of restoration, and that restoration comes only from the God who restores. That restoration comes only by faith in Jesus Christ.

Here is the most important truth you need to know: Jesus loved you enough to take upon Himself the judgment and the punishment for your sins. He became a human, born in the most humble of circumstances. He became a Dirt-Man. He lived a human life full of the same suffering, sorrow, pain, and temptations we all face. However, He did it without succumbing to sin. He lived a sinless life, but then died a sinner's death. When Jesus went to the cross, it wasn't a symbolic act of self-sacrifice. It wasn't an act of martyrdom-for-a-cause. He went to the cross to ransom us from sin and death. It was to pay the price for all our sins. When He screamed out, "My God, My God, why have you forsaken Me," it wasn't because of the nails in His hands and feet; it wasn't because of the crown of thorns on His head; it wasn't because of the lashes that had ripped open His flesh. He cried out because at that moment, the Father was judging Him in our place. That was your torment you never need to experience. That was your pain you never need to feel. That was your judgment you never need to face. That was your blood you never need to bleed. That was your death you never need to die. For three hours the Father forsook His Beloved Son. For three hours God caused darkness to cover the land. He caused the same darkness that covered the Pre-Adamic earth and the Pre-Exodus Egypt; the darkness of judgment. In those three hours of darkness, Jesus was judged in our place, died our death, and bore an eternity of hell for each and every one of us. He did this for you because He didn't want you to have to bear it. He didn't want you to suffer eternal death. You are a fallen sinner, but He wants to restore you today. The Bible is very clear about what you must do. Believe that Jesus died for your sins, and you will be saved.

"How could He do that," you ask? "How could He pay for all the sins of all men in three hours, when the wages of the sins of even one man is eternity in hell?"

Do you remember I told you back in Chapter Two the point of 2 Peter 3:8 and Psalms 90:4 was to tell us something about God, not something about the passage of time during the Creation Days? I told you I would repeat the point one more time. Here it is:

THE POINT OF THESE PASSAGES IS
TO TELL US SOMETHING ABOUT GOD

You will miss this next point if you think these verses are merely telling us something about the passage of time. Let's look at those verses again:

2 Peter 3:8 "But, beloved, be not ignorant of this one thing, that one day *is* with the Lord as a thousand years, and a thousand years as one day." (KJV)

Psalms 90:4 "For a thousand years, in thy sight, are as yesterday when it is past, and *as* a watch in the night." (KJV)

Do you remember I told you these verses reveal that God doesn't experience time as we experience it? Do you remember I told you that being outside of time, God causes/experiences all time, at the same time? These verses (one from the Old Testament and one from the New Testament) reveal something about God that is extremely important in understanding what Jesus did for us on the cross. God didn't reveal this about Himself so we would know something about our origin. He revealed this to us so we would know something about our destiny. **In <u>three hours</u>, Jesus experienced <u>eternity</u> in hell so we**

could experience eternity in heaven. This is "The Deeper Magic" C. S. Lewis spoke of in the *Chronicles of Narnia*. Only as man could Jesus experience the pain and suffering of hell. Only as God could Jesus experience an eternity of time in a three-hour period. ONLY A BEING WHO CAUSES/EXPERIENCES ALL TIME AT THE SAME TIME COULD CAUSE/EXPERIENCE AN ETERNITY OF HELL IN THREE HOURS. Only The God-Man could accomplish both. This is why only God could be our Savior.

Isaiah 43:11 "I, *even* I, *am* the LORD; and beside me *there is* no saviour." (KJV)

This is why God had to become a human. There was no other way to save us.

John 1:14 "And the Word was made flesh, and dwelt among us, (and we beheld his glory, the glory as of the only begotten of the Father,) full of grace and truth." (KJV)

He did this for you because He didn't want you to suffer eternal death. He didn't want you to suffer eternal torment. He didn't want you to suffer the eternal darkness of judgment. He didn't want you to suffer eternal separation from the Father. This is what you deserve. This is what I deserve. But, it is not what He wants for us. He wants to restore us, and He has done that for me. He will do that for you today, this very moment, if you put your trust in Him. The Bible is very clear about what you must do. Turn away from your rejection of Christ. Believe that Jesus died for your sins, and you will be saved. He will take you from Ruin to Restoration. **He is the God of Restoration.** You will have a second beginning!

Bible Translations

(ABP) = Scriptures quoted from the Holy Bible, *APOLOSTOLIC BIBLE POLYGLOT*. Copyright 1995-2003 by Charles Lynn VanderPool, Sr. Used by permission. All rights reserved.

(AKJV) = Scriptures quoted from the Holy Bible, *AMERICAN KING JAMES VERSION*. Translated by Michael Peter (Stone) Engelbrite. Public Domain.

(AMP) = Scriptures quoted from the Holy Bible, *AMPLIFIED BIBLE*. Copyright © 2015 by The Lockman Foundation, La Habra, CA 90631. Used by permission. All rights reserved.

(ASV) = Scriptures quoted from the Holy Bible, *AMERICAN STANDARD VERSION*. Copyright © 1901 by Thomas Nelson, Inc. Used by permission. All rights reserved.

(BBE) = Scriptures quoted from the Holy Bible, *BIBLE IN BASIC ENGLISH*. Translated by S. H. Hooke. Copyright © 1965 by Cambridge University Press. Used by permission. All rights reserved.

(BISHOPS) = Scriptures quoted from the Holy Bible, *BISHOP'S BIBLE*. Translated by The Church of England 1568. Public Domain.

(BRENTON) = Scriptures quoted from the Holy Bible, *BRENTON BIBLE*. Translated by Charles Lee Brenton. Published by Samuel Bagster & Sons, London, 1844. Public Domain.

(BV) = Scriptures quoted from the Holy Bible, *BERKELEY VERSION*. Copyright © 1959 by Zondervan Publishing House. Used by permission. All rights reserved.

(CEB) = Scriptures quoted from the Holy Bible, *COMMON ENGLISH BIBLE*. Copyright © 2012 Common English Bible Committee. Published by The Christian Resources Development Corporation. Used by permission. All rights reserved.

(CEV) = Scriptures quoted from the Holy Bible, *CONTEMPORARY ENGLISH VERSION*. Copyright © 1995 American Bible Society. Used by permission. All rights reserved.

(CJB) = Scriptures quoted from the Holy Bible, *COMPLETE JEWISH BIBLE*. Translated by David H. Stern. Copyright © 1998 Jewish New Testament Publications, Inc. Used by permission. All rights reserved.

(CVOT) = Scriptures quoted from the Holy Bible, *CONCORDANT VERSION OF THE OLD TESTAMENT*. Copyright © 2007 by Concordant Publishing Concern, Santa Clarita, CA. Used by permission. All rights reserved.

(DBY) = Scriptures quoted from the Holy Bible, *DARBY'S 1884 BIBLE*. Translated by John Nelson Darby. Public Domain.

(DRB) = Scriptures quoted from the Holy Bible, *DOUAY-RHEIMS BIBLE*. Translated by English College at Rheims and Douay. 1610. Public Domain.

(EMP) = Scriptures quoted from the Holy Bible, *EMPHASIZED BIBLE* (*ROTHERHAM BIBLE*) by Joseph Bryant Rotherham. 1902. Public Domain.

(ERRB) = Scriptures quoted from the Holy Bible, *EXEGESIS READY REFERENCE BIBLE*, Copyright © 1993 by Herb Jahn. Published by World Bible Publishers. Used by permission.

(ERV) = Scriptures quoted from the Holy Bible, *THE EASY TO READ VERSION*. Copyright © 1987 by The World Bible Translation Center. Used by permission. All rights reserved.

(ESV) = Scriptures quoted from the Holy Bible, *ENGLISH STANDARD VERSION*. Copyright © 2007 by Crossway Bibles, a ministry of the Good News Publishers of Wheaton, IL. Used by permission. All rights reserved.

(EXB) = Scriptures quoted from the Holy Bible, *EXPANDED BIBLE*. Copyright © 2011 by Thomas Nelson, Inc. Used by permission. All rights reserved.

(GN-TEV) = Scriptures quoted from the Holy Bible, *GOOD NEWS TRANSLATION* (*TODAY'S ENGLISH VERSION*), 2nd Edition. Copyright © 1992 American Bible Society. Used by permission. All rights reserved.

(GNV) = Scriptures quoted from the Holy Bible, *GENEVA BIBLE*. 1560. Public Domain.

(GW) = Scriptures quoted from the Holy Bible, *GOD'S WORD TRANSLATION*. Copyright © 2003 Baker Publishing Group, Grand Rapids, MI. Used by permission. All rights reserved.

(HCSB) = Scriptures quoted from the Holy Bible, *HOLMAN CHRISTIAN STANDARD BIBLE*. Copyright ©1999 by Holman Bible Publishers, Nashville, TN. Used by permission. All rights reserved.

(ISV) = Scriptures quoted from the Holy Bible, *INTERNATIONAL STANDARD VERSION*. Copyright © 2011 International Standard Version Society. Used by permission. All rights reserved.

(JPSB) = Scriptures quoted from the Holy Bible, *THE JEWISH PUBLICATION SOCIETY BIBLE*. Copyright © 2011 Jewish Bible Society, Philadelphia, PA. Used with permission. All rights reserved.

(JUB) = Scriptures quoted form the Holy Bible, *JUBILEE BIBLE*. Copyright © 2013 Life Sentence Publishing, Abbotsford, Wisconsin. Used with permission. All rights reserved.

(KJV) = Scriptures quoted from the Holy Bible, *KING JAMES VERSION*. 1769. Public Domain.

(KJV-1611) = Scriptures quoted from the Holy Bible, *KING JAMES VERSION*. 1611. Public Domain.

(KJ21) = Scriptures quoted from the Holy Bible, *21st CENTURY KING JAMES VERSION*. Copyright © 1994 by Deuel Enterprises, Inc. Used by permission. All rights reserved.

(LESSER) = Scriptures quoted from the Holy Bible, *LEESER JEWISH BIBLE*. Translated by Isaac Leeser. 1853. Public Domain.

(LEX) = Scriptures quoted from the Holy Bible, *LEXHAM ENGLISH BIBLE*. Copyright © 2014 Logos Bible Software. Used by permission. All rights reserved.

(LTV) = Scriptures quoted from the Holy Bible, *LITERAL TRANSLATION VERSION*. Copyright © 1976-2000. Translated by Jay P. Green, Sr. Used by permission. All rights reserved. Courtesy of Sovereign Grace Publishers and Christian Literature World.

(MB) = Scriptures quoted from the Holy Bible, *THE MOFFAT BIBLE*. Translated by James Moffatt. Copyright © 1954 by James Moffatt. Published by Kregel Publication. Used by permission.

(MKJV) = Scriptures quoted from the Holy Bible, *MODERN KING JAMES VERSION*. Copyright © 1962-1998 by Jay P. Green, Sr. Used by permission. All rights reserved. Courtesy of Sovereign Grace Publishers and Christian Literature World.

(NASB) = Scriptures quoted from the Holy Bible, *NEW AMERICAN STANDARD BIBLE*, Copyright © 1960, 1962, 1963, 1968, 1971 by The Lockman Foundation. Used by permission. All rights reserved.

(NBV) = Scriptures quoted from the Holy Bible, *NEW BERKELEY VERSION*. Copyright © 1964 by Zondervan Publishing House. Used by permission. All rights reserved.

(NCV) = Scriptures quoted from the Holy Bible, *NEW CENTURY VERSION*. Copyright © 1987, 1988, 1991 by Thomas Nelson, Inc. Used by permission. All rights reserved.

(NET) = Scriptures quoted from the Holy Bible, *NEW ENGLISH TRANSLATION*. Copyright ©1996-2006 by Biblical Studies Press, L.L.C. Used by permission. All rights reserved.

(NHEB) = Scriptures quoted from the Holy Bible, *NEW HEART ENGLISH BIBLE*. Edited by Wayne A. Mitchell and Mark D. Harness. Published 2008. Public Domain.

(NIRV) = Scriptures quoted from the Holy Bible, *NEW INTERNATIONAL READER'S VERSION*. Copyright © 1995, 1996, 1998, 2014 by Biblica, Inc.®. Used by permission. All rights reserved worldwide.

(NIV) = Scriptures quoted from the Holy Bible, *NEW INTERNATIONAL VERSION*. Copyright © 1973, 1978, 1984 International Bible Society. Used by permission. All rights reserved.

(NJB) = Scriptures quoted from the Holy Bible, *NEW JERUSALEM BIBLE*. Copyright © 1985 by Darton, Longman, and Todd, Ltd. and by Doubleday, a division of Bantam Doubleday Dell Publishing Group. Used by permission. All rights reserved.

(NKJV) = Scriptures quoted from the Holy Bible, *NEW KING JAMES VERSION*. Copyright © 1979, 1980, 1982 by Thomas Nelson, Inc. Used by permission.

(NLT) = Scriptures quoted from the Holy Bible, *NEW LIVING TRANSLATION*. Copyright © 1996, 2004, 2015 by Tyndale House Foundation. Used by permission. All rights reserved.

(NLV) = Scriptures quoted from the Holy Bible, *NEW LIFE VERSION*. By Gleason and Kathryn Ledyard. Copyright © 1986 by Christian Literature International. Used by permission. All rights reserved.

(NOG) = Scriptures quoted from the Holy Bible, *NAMES OF GOD BIBLE*. Copyright © 2011 by Baker Publishing Group. Used by permission. All rights reserved.

(NRSV) = Scriptures quoted from the Holy Bible, *NEW REVISED STANDARD VERSION*. Copyright © 1989 by The Division of Christian Education of The National Council of the Churches of Christ in the United States of America. Used by permission. All rights reserved.

(OJB) = Scriptures quoted from the Holy Bible, *ORTHODOX JEWISH BIBLE*. Copyright © 2002, 2003, 2008, 2010, 2011 by Artists for Israel International. Used by permission. All rights reserved.

(RSV) = Scriptures quoted from the Holy Bible, *REVISED STANDARD VERSION*. Copyright © 1946, 1952 by The Division of Christian Education of The National Council of the Churches of Christ in the United States of America. Used by permission. All rights reserved.

(S&G) = Scriptures quoted from the Holy Bible, *AN AMERICAN TRANSLATION*, by J. M. P. Smith and Edgar J. Goodspeed. Copyright © 1931 by the University of Chicago. Used by permission. All rights reserved.

(SCRIP) = Scriptures quoted from the Holy Bible, *THE SCRIPTURES '98*. Copyright © 1998 by the Institute for Scripture Research, Randburg, The Republic of South Africa. Used by permission. All rights reserved.

(SPEIS) = Scriptures quoted from the Holy Bible, *Genesis*. Translated by Ephraim A. Speiser; Volume One of *An Anchor Bible*, Copyright Doubleday and Company, Inc., Published September 1964. Used by Permission. All rights reserved.

(TLB) = Scriptures quoted from the Holy Bible, *THE LIVING BIBLE*. Copyright © 1971 by Tyndale House Foundation. Used by permission. All rights reserved.

(TLV) = Scriptures quoted from the Holy Bible, *TREE OF LIFE*. Copyright © 2015 by The Messianic Jewish Family Bible Society. Used by permission. All rights reserved.

(TYN) = Scriptures quoted from the Holy Bible, *TYNDALE BIBLE*, by John Tyndale. 1534. Public Domain.

(VOICE) = Scriptures quoted from the Holy Bible, *THE VOICE BIBLE*. Copyright © 2012 Thomas Nelson, Inc. The Voice™ translation © 2012 Ecclesia Bible Society. Used by permission. All rights reserved.

(WEB) = Scriptures quoted from the Holy Bible, *WORLD ENGLISH BIBLE*. Public Domain.

(WEBSTER) = Scriptures quoted from the Holy Bible, *WEBSTER BIBLE*. By Noah Webster. 1833. Public Domain.

(WYC) = Scriptures quoted from the Holy Bible, *WYCLIFFE BIBLE*. By John Wycliffe. 1395. Public Domain.

(YLT) = Scriptures quoted from the Holy Bible, *YOUNG'S LITERAL TRANSLATION*. By Robert Young. 1898. Public Domain.

Hebrew and Greek Definitions
With Strong's Numbers
(H = Hebrew; G = Greek)

ABAD (H5647)—work, labor, cultivate, serve
AION (G165)—age
APO (G575)—from, out from, proceeding from
APOLLUMI (G622)—destroyed
ARBA (H720)—four
ARCHE (G746)—beginning
ARUWM (H6175)—crafty, cunning, prudent
ASAH (H6213)—make
BAL (H1077)—not; never
BARA (H1254)—create
BOHUW (H922)—void, emptiness, waste, wilderness
BOQER (H1242)—morning, dawn, sunrise
CAMESH (H2568)—five
CHAMIYSHIY (H2549)—fifth
CHAY (H2416)—life, living
CHOSHEK (H2822)—dark, darkness
ECHAD (H259)—one, once, first
ELOHIM (H430)—God, gods
EN (G1711)—in
EPO (G2036)—speak, say, call, command
EREB (H6153)—evening, dusk, sunset
ERETS (H776)—earth, land, field, ground
GAN (H1588)—garden, enclosure
GANAN (H1589)—to protect, to surround, to defend
HAYAH (H1961)—be, is, am, was, became, come to pass
HEYLEL (H1966)—the morning star, Lucifer
KATABALLO (G2598)—catabolize, tear down, lay down
KATABOLE (G2602)—catabolism, destruction
KATARTIDZO (G2675)—prepare, perfect, restore, mend
KOSMOS (G2889)—world, world-system
KTISIS (G2937)—formation, building, creation
KTIZO (G2936)—create
LAMEDH (The 12th letter in the Hebrew Alphabet; used as a preposition)—to, for
LAYIL (H3915)—night
LUO (G3089)—loosen, untie, break
NATHAN (H5414)—set, put, appoint

NEPHESH (H5315)—creature, soul
NESHAMAH (H5397)—breath, spirit
OTH (H226)—sign, mark, signal, miracle
OWD (H5750)—again, more, yet
OWR (H216)—light
PARADIDOMI (G3860)—surrender, betray, yield, seize
PNEUMA (G4151)—wind, spirit
POIEO (G4160)—make
RAAH (H7200)—to see, to appear, to expose, to display
RAASH (H7493)—shake, tremble, make afraid
RACHAPH (H7363)—hover, brood
RAQIYA (H7549)—firmament, expanse
REBIY'IY (H7243)—fourth
RESHITH (H7225)—beginning
RISHON (H7223)—first
SHALOSH (H7969)—three
SHAMAR (H8104)—guard, protect, keep
SHAMAYIM (H8064)—heavens, sky
SHEBAH (H7651)—seven
SHEBIY'IY (H7637)—seventh
SHELIYSHIY (H7992)—third
SHENAYIM (H8147)—two
SHENIY (H8145)—second
SHESH (H8337)—six
SHISHSHIY (H8345)—sixth
SPERMA (G4690)—seed
STOICHEION (G4747)—elements, rudimentary particles, atoms
SULLAMBANO (G4815)—conceive
TEHOM (H8425)—deep, abyss, sea, ocean
THEMELIOS (G2310)—foundation
TOHUW (H8414)—chaos, desolation
TOWLEDAH (H8435)—accounts, generations
TRITOS (G5154)—third, one-third
WAW (or *VAV*) (6th Letter of the Hebrew Alphabet, used as a conjunction/disjunction)—and, but, now
YAHWEH (H3068)—LORD
YATSAR (H3335)—form
YOM (H3117)—day

Index

A Divinely Revealed Pattern 591
ABAD
    work, labor, cultivate, serve 446
Actual Age 376
AION
    age 484, 485, 486, 502
Alcuin of York 339
Anderson, Sir Robert 488
Anstey, Martin 332, 527, 611, 630
Ape-Men 518, 519
APO
    away from, out from, proceeding from
    .... 424, 426, 427, 434
APOLLUMI
    destroyed 494
Apparent Age 216, 235, 236, 238, 239, 249, 376, 507
Aquinas, Thomas 339
ARBA
    four 566
ARCHE
    beginning 426, 427, 434, 493
Archer, Gleason .. 271, 330, 331, 565, 630
ARUWM
    crafty, cunning, prudent 538
ASAH
    make 301, 347, 352, 353, 354, 355, 356, 357, 367, 376, 377, 386, 415, 424, 425, 471, 512
Astronomy 101 238
Augustine 339
Australopithecus 519, 524
Baker, Warren 333
BAL
    not 476
BARA
    create ... 299, 301, 342, 343, 346, 347, 348, 349, 352, 353, 354, 355, 356, 357, 365, 367, 370, 375, 376, 377, 386, 390, 415, 424, 425, 469, 471, 512
BARA vs. *ASAH* 352
Barnes, Albert 322, 338
Barnhouse, Donald Grey ... 329, 330, 337, 338
Baylee, Robert 318
Biblical Order of Appearance
    Figure 1 58
Biblical Order vs. Scientific Order
(Part 1)
    Figure 4 62
Biblical Order vs. Scientific Order
(Part 2)
    Figure 5 63
Big Bang Theory 22, 39, 41, 44, 51, 75, 285, 303, 304, 305, 366, 427, 511, 512, 514, 609
BOHUW
    void, emptiness, waste, wilderness
    .... 287, 288, 290, 291, 292, 294, 297, 298, 352, 413, 414, 416, 632
Boice, James Montgomery 337, 338, 630
Boman, Thorleif 528, 630
BOQER
    morning, dawn, sunrise 102, 112, 113, 116, 118, 125, 126, 129, 130, 131, 132, 133, 138, 214, 216
Brown, David 326
Buckland, William 317, 338
Burgon, John William 325, 326
Caedmon 339
Canopy Theory 379, 381, 382
Carbon 14 253
Carbon Dating 253, 254
Cardinal Numbers 157, 162

Carpenter, Eugene.............................333
Cassuto, Umberto 268, 286
Chafer, Lewis Sperry 329
Chalmers, Thomas.....317, 318, 323, 337, 339
Chaos 55
Chaos Theory.....................................22
CHAY
   life, living..226
CHOSHEK
   dark, darkness....76, 77, 138, 144, 214, 287, 288, 351, 352, 416, 507, 511, 515, 516, 517, 518, 585, 593
Coates, Charles Andrew 335
Coelacanth 72, 510
Co-Eternal Matter and Energy.......38, 50
Coniah
   See Jehoiachin 466, 467
Conkin, Paul Keith.............................321
Conybeare, William Daniel 319
Coral Reefs 249, 250, 251
Crampon, Augustin....................269, 286
Custance, Arthur........269, 282, 286, 337, 339, 340, 410, 411, 492, 493, 494, 497, 565, 585, 586, 630
Cuvier, Georges 317
Dake, Finis Jennings..........................336
Darby, John Nelson 325, 338, 630
Darwin, Charles.....67, 70, 317, 318, 321, 322, 323, 325, 339
Dathe, Johann August........................339
Day-Age Solutions..............................75
Days of Divine Decrees 48
Days of Relativity 45
Days of Revelation 47
Death before Adam...........................225
Dillman, August.................268, 282, 286
Dual-Creation: Gap Theory 43
DUO
   two 178

ECHAD
   one, once, first.......162, 163, 164, 169, 170, 461, 463, 464
Edersheim, Alfred......................326, 630
Edgar, King of England 338
Einstein, Albert.....................32, 46, 241
EN
   in 424
Episcopius, Simon 338
EPO
   speak, say, call, command 455
EREB
   evening, dusk, sunset.....102, 110, 112, 113, 131, 133, 138, 214, 216
EREB and *BOQER*
   evening and morning 133, 216
ERETS
   earth, land, field, ground........277, 281, 365, 411, 469, 471
Evolution and the Geologic Ages
   Figure 3 61
EX NIHILO
   out of nothing..........38, 50, 52, 54, 299, 301, 302, 303, 304, 354, 355, 356, 365, 370, 592, 599
Fausset, Andrew Robert.....................326
Fee, Richard.......................................488
Fine-Tuning 305, 396, 397
Flat-Earth Theory...............................300
Flood-Geology.....45, 219, 221, 222, 244, 245, 247, 252, 264
Fossil Index System..69, 70, 72, 251, 252
Four Characteristics of the Gap Theory 54
Framework Theory 38, 48, 607
Functional Age...................................238
Gaebelein, Arno Clement 335
Galileo..301, 302
GAN
   garden, enclosure 447

GANAN
    to protect, to surround, to defend .. 447
Garden of Eden 234, 353, 445, 447, 448, 469
Ginzberg, Louis 28, 336
Grant, Frederick William 335
Greenland Ice Sheet Project Two 264
Harris, John 339
Harris, R. Laird 331
HAYAH
    be, is, am, was, became, come to pass ...282, 283, 284, 307, 315, 322, 331, 332, 333, 334, 335, 338, 339, 368, 370, 371, 375, 376, 377, 410, 419, 472, 479, 487, 527, 528, 529, 530, 531, 532, 533, 534, 536, 537, 538, 539, 540, 541, 542, 543, 544, 545, 546, 547, 548, 549, 550, 551, 552, 553, 554, 555, 558, 559, 560, 564, 565, 566, 567, 568, 576, 577, 579, 582, 584, 585, 586, 587, 588, 589, 590, 591, 602, 609, 610, 611, 612, 613, 614, 615, 616, 617, 618, 619, 630, 631, 632, 634
HAYAH and the Preposition *le* 565
HAYAH in Genesis (KJV) 534
HAYAH in Genesis 1:2 548
HAYAH in Genesis as Some Form of "Became" 307
HAYAH Translated as "Was" or "Wast" in the KJV 536
HAYETAH
    A form of *HAYAH* 577, 578, 579, 612, 619
Hayward, Alan 264
HEMERA
    day 178, 179, 186
HEMERA DUO
    two days 178
HEYLEL
    The morning star, Lucifer 431

Higgins, William Mullinger 320
Historic Young-Earth Theory 44, 219, 220
Hitchcock, Edward 321, 338
Hole, Frank Binford 336
Hugo St. Victor 339
Ice-Age 383, 384, 420, 421, 422
In God (Can) We Trust? 237
Instantaneous/Intact Creation Theory 301, 302, 303
Instantaneous-Creation 302
Jahn, Herb 282
James Strong 527, 630
Jamieson, Robert 326
Japanese Plesiosaur 256
Jeconiah
    See Jehoiachin 466
Jehoiachin 466
Jehoram 173, 176, 177, 178
Johanson, Donald 524
Johnson, Gaines 263, 264
Justin Martyr 339
KATABALLO
    catabolize, tear down, lay down ... 493, 494, 502, 505
KATABALLO in the Septuagint 502
KATABOLE
    catabolism, destruction 492, 493, 494, 495, 496, 500, 502, 505
KATABOLE KOSMOS
    catabolism/destruction of the world 493, 494, 495, 496, 500, 501, 505, 506, 634
KATABOLE SPERMA
    catabolism of seed 495, 496, 497, 498, 499, 500
KATARTIDZO
    prepare, perfect, restore, mend 483, 484
Kelly, William 335
King of Tyre 433, 438

KOSMOS
    world, world-system 231, 493, 494
KTISIS
    formation, building, creation..426, 427
KTIZO
    create..375
Kurtz, J. H. 339
LAMEDH
    ל The 12th letter in the Hebrew alphabet, the preposition *le* 565, 566, 568, 576, 587
Langford, Jack 604
Large Magellanic Cloud 239, 240, 376
Larkin, Clarence 316
LAYIL
    night 76, 77, 92, 96, 97, 214, 216
Lazarus Fossils..............................72, 73
Leupold, Herbert Carl 268, 286
Lewis, C. S...............................337, 441
Limestone 234, 257
Living Fossils......43, 44, 71, 72, 73, 252, 510, 633
Lowrance, James......................475, 483
Lucifer.......229, 306, 329, 335, 354, 379, 380, 397, 398, 414, 415, 417, 418, 431, 432, 433, 434, 435, 436, 437, 438, 439, 440, 441, 442, 443, 444, 445, 447, 448, 449, 450, 451, 452, 453, 454, 459, 465, 477, 480, 482, 501, 505, 510, 515, 516, 519, 520, 521, 522, 523, 524, 538, 609, 633
Lucifer's Rebellion 433, 437
Lucy 524
LUO
    loosen, untie, break 509
Luther, Martin...........................267, 286
Lyell, Charles....................................317
Macro-Evolution..................................25
Magnetic Field Decay.......................257
Martins, Joaozinho............................432
Masoretic Text 487, 585, 619

Merism......................................276, 277
Micro-Evolution 25
Mississippi River Delta......................258
Modern Young-Earth Theory.....44, 219, 220, 319
Moffatt, James 52, 272
Morgan, G. Campbell 328, 338
Mosaic Covenant 500
Mount of Olives..................165, 166, 485
Multiple Creation Theory 44
Multiple-Gaps Theory 38
My Sentiments on Sediments 251
Nahmanides 28, 32, 513, 514, 515
NATHAN
    set, put, appoint......390, 396, 398, 595
Neanderthal Man 518, 519, 523, 524
NEPHESH
    creature, soul.................................226
NESHAMAH
    breath, spirit 226
Nicodemus 456, 457, 458, 459
Non-Adaptive Radiation.......................73
Ontological Language........................237
Ordinal Numbers 157
Origen 339
OTH
    sign, mark, signal, or miracle.......388, 396, 397
OWD
    again, more, yet..............461, 463, 464
OWR
    light 76, 77, 144, 156, 214
Paluxy River Footprints.....................256
PARADIDOMI
    surrender, betray, yeild, seize 452
Pember, George H. 337
Pererius, Benedict.............................339
Petavius, Dionysius............................339
Phenomenological Language..............237
Phillips, William................................319
Picture Frame Pattern 604

Pink, A. W. 329, 337, 338, 630
Planck time 514
Planck units 251
PNEUMA
   wind, Spirit 457
POIEO
   make 424
Pre-Adamic Cities 416
Preposition *le* 331, 565, 634
Price, George McCready 222
Prince of Tyre 438
Process-Creation 302
Progressive Creation Theory 38
Punctuated Creation Theory 38, 43, 44
Punctuated Equilibria 43, 70, 71
Pusey, Edward Bouverie 324
QAL
   The simple form of Hebrew verbs 548, 549, 558
QAL Imperfect
   Hebrew verb form indicating simple incomplete action 549, 550, 554, 555
QAL Imperfect of *HAYAH* 551, 552, 553, 554
QAL Perfect
   Hebrew verb form indicating simple complete action 549, 550, 558, 559, 560, 564, 565, 587, 588, 589
RAAH
   to see, to appear, to expose, to display 385
RAASH
   shake, tremble, make afraid 459, 460, 465
RACHAPH
   hover, brood 384
Ramm, Bernard 338
RAQIYA
   firmament, expanse 275, 276

Rebhia
   Hebrew Disjunctive Accent Mark 487, 585
Repeated-Days Theory 38
RESHITH
   beginning 169
Riemannian Space 242, 243, 374, 391, 499
Rimmer, Harry 337
RISHON
   first 166, 167, 168, 169, 170
Rosenmuller, J. G. 338
Ross, Allen P. 581, 586
Ross, Hugh 305, 391
Rotherham, Joseph Bryant 282
Satan 186, 223, 228, 229, 230, 231, 274, 329, 338, 356, 399, 416, 418, 435, 438, 439, 440, 441, 442, 443, 447, 448, 449, 450, 451, 452, 453, 467, 501, 509, 510, 520, 521, 522, 523, 524, 588, 635
Satan's World 414
Sauer, Erich 337
Schaeffer, Francis 337
Schroeder, Gerald 514
Scientific Order of Appearance
   Figure 2 59
Scofield, C. I. 315
Septuagint ... 177, 178, 269, 287, 502, 505
SHAMAR
   guard, protect, keep 446, 447
SHAMAYIM
   heavens, sky 272, 273, 277, 469, 471
SHAWNAW
   year 172, 174
Shealtiel 466
SHELIYSHIY
   third 189
SHENAYIM
   both, second, two, more 172, 174, 175

SHENIY
- second 171, 172, 175

Simeon ben Jochai 28, 318, 339
Single Gap Theory 38
Single-Creation: Young-Earth Theory
.... 44
Smith and Goodspeed Bible 272
Smith, J. Pye 338
Speciation 25, 26
Specimen Ridge 244, 245, 246, 247, 248
Speed of Light 241, 242, 243, 373, 499
Speiser, Ephraim A. ... 268, 272, 282, 286
Spurgeon, Charles Haddon 322, 323, 338, 630
St. Basil 324
St. Gregory Nazianzen 339
St. Jerome 324

STOICHEION
- elements, rudimentary particles, atoms 509

SULLAMBANO
- conceive 495, 500

Sumner, John Bird
- Archbishop of Canterbury 318

Supernova 239, 240, 376
Targum of Onkelos 339

TEHOM
- deep, abyss, oceasn, sea 516, 517

The "Day" Ages Compared to the Geological Ages
- Figure 6 66

The Biblical Meaning of "DAY" 75
The Invisible Attributes of God ... 390, 391
The Rainbow Painting 68
Theistic evolution 39

THEMELIOS
- Foundation 490, 491, 492, 494

Theodoret 339

Thieme, Robert B 268, 272, 282, 285, 286, 336

TOHUW
- chaos, desolation 287, 288, 290, 291, 292, 298, 341, 342, 343, 347, 348, 349, 350, 352, 413, 414, 416, 632

TOHUW WA-BOHUW
- without form, and void 50, 56, 287, 306, 317, 338, 351, 352, 397, 402, 405, 406, 407, 408, 409, 411, 413, 422, 431, 448, 450, 507, 511, 514, 515, 516, 517, 518, 585, 593, 616, 632

Torrey, R. A. 326, 338

TOWLEDAH
- generations 48, 468, 469, 470, 608, 634

Traditional-Geology 244, 252

TRITOS
- third, one-third 274

Turner, Sharon 320
Two Creation Accounts 468
Two Global Floods 471
Unger, Merrill F. 333, 334
Ussher, James 223
Varves 248
Von Bohlen, Peter 268, 272, 286
Waltke, Bruce K. 331

WAW
- Hebrew conjunction
  and, but, now 279, 280, 281, 333, 554, 555, 559, 560, 566, 579, 581, 582, 583, 584, 585, 586, 588, 590, 592, 593, 594, 595, 599, 608, 609, 610, 611, 612, 613, 615, 616

WAW Alternative 584
WAW Conjunctive 558, 559, 560, 587, 588, 589
WAW Consecutive 554, 555, 582, 583, 591, 592, 593, 594, 595, 596, 599, 600, 601, 605, 606, 607, 608, 609, 611

WAW Coordinative....582, 583, 594, 595, 615
WAW Disjunctive......487, 554, 560, 582, 583, 584, 585, 586, 587, 588, 589, 590, 591, 593, 608, 609, 611, 612, 613, 615, 634
WAW Pattern 592
White, Ellen............... 220, 221, 222, 255
White, William, Jr. 334
Wilson, William 334, 335
YALAD
   begat, born.................................... 223
YATSAR
   form.....301, 347, 354, 370, 371, 425, 512
Yellowstone National Park 244
YOM
   day......75, 76, 77, 97, 102, 129, 130, 157, 158, 162, 163, 164, 165, 167, 168, 170, 171, 172, 173, 174, 175, 178, 179, 189, 194, 212, 213, 214, 215, 216, 377, 432, 633
YOM and *LAYIL*
   day and night............................ 97, 216
YOM CHAMIYSHIY
   fifth day 196, 197, 212
YOM ECHAD
   first day/one day....158, 161, 162, 163, 165, 166, 170, 212, 463
YOM REBIY'IY
   fourth day 195, 196, 212

YOM RISHON
   first day................................ 166, 170
YOM SHEBIY'IY
   seventh day.................... 199, 203, 212
YOM SHELIYSHIY
   third day 186, 195, 212
YOM SHENIY
   second day..................... 170, 178, 212
YOM SHISHSHIY
   sixth day 197, 199, 212
YOMIM
   days........158, 166, 167, 168, 169, 170, 172, 174, 175
YOMIM ARBA
   four days... 196
YOMIM CAMESH
   five days 197
YOMIM SHALOSH
   three days 190, 194, 195
YOMIM SHEBAH
   seven days 204, 212
YOMIM SHENAYIM
   two days...172, 173, 176, 177, 178, 186
YOMIM SHESH
   six days.................................. 198, 199
Young, Robert 268, 272, 282, 286
Young-Earth Solutions....................... 219
Zedekiah... 466
Zerubbabel......................... 465, 466, 467
Zohar
   The Book of Light......................... 318
Zona Pellucida 497, 498

Scripture References

1 Chronicles 9:25	210
1 Chronicles 9:27	125
1 Chronicles 9:33	87
1 Chronicles 10:12	210
1 Chronicles 12:39	192
1 Chronicles 16:30	237
1 Chronicles 16:40	110, 125, 135
1 Chronicles 17:3	87
1 Chronicles 21:12	192
1 Chronicles 23:30	110, 126, 135
1 Chronicles 29:11	443
1 Corinthians 2:14	455
1 Corinthians 3:10-12	490
1 Corinthians 6:3a	453
1 Corinthians 10:8	179
1 Corinthians 15	233
1 Corinthians 15:4	183
1 Corinthians 15:21	225
1 Corinthians 15:21-22	232, 233
1 Corinthians 15:21-23	231
1 John 1:5	367, 368
1 John 3:8	434, 442, 452, 501
1 John 5:19	440
1 Kings 1:1	175
1 Kings 1:2	555
1 Kings 2:11	488, 489
1 Kings 3:5	86
1 Kings 3:18	188
1 Kings 3:19	86
1 Kings 3:20	86
1 Kings 3:21	124
1 Kings 4:22	159
1 Kings 6:1	487, 488, 489
1 Kings 8:29	87, 99
1 Kings 8:59	87, 99
1 Kings 8:65	196, 210
1 Kings 11:11	631
1 Kings 11:24	572

1 Kings 12:5	192
1 Kings 12:12	188
1 Kings 13:6	572
1 Kings 13:33	572
1 Kings 16:15	210
1 Kings 17:6	109, 124, 135
1 Kings 17:17-24	458
1 Kings 18:26	124
1 Kings 19:8	87, 99
1 Kings 20:29	159, 203, 210
1 Kings 22:8	461
1 Kings 22:35	110
1 Peter 1:20	492
1 Samuel 1:19	122
1 Samuel 2:9	139
1 Samuel 2:19	174
1 Samuel 2:34	159
1 Samuel 3:15	122
1 Samuel 4:16	333
1 Samuel 5:4	122
1 Samuel 9:15	159
1 Samuel 9:19	122
1 Samuel 9:20	192
1 Samuel 10:8	209
1 Samuel 11:3	209
1 Samuel 11:11	122
1 Samuel 12:21	288
1 Samuel 13:8	209
1 Samuel 14:24	109
1 Samuel 14:27	146
1 Samuel 14:29	146
1 Samuel 14:34	84
1 Samuel 14:36	84, 122, 146
1 Samuel 15:11	84
1 Samuel 15:12	122
1 Samuel 15:16	85
1 Samuel 17:20	122
1 Samuel 18:29	571
1 Samuel 19:2	123
1 Samuel 19:10	85
1 Samuel 19:11	85, 123

Reference	Pages
1 Samuel 19:24	85, 98
1 Samuel 20:5	109
1 Samuel 20:34	171
1 Samuel 20:35	123
1 Samuel 25:16	85, 99
1 Samuel 25:22	123
1 Samuel 25:34	123, 146
1 Samuel 25:36	123, 146
1 Samuel 25:37	123
1 Samuel 25:42	567
1 Samuel 26:7	85
1 Samuel 27:1	159, 163
1 Samuel 27:7	174
1 Samuel 28:8	85
1 Samuel 28:16	571
1 Samuel 28:20	85, 99
1 Samuel 28:25	85
1 Samuel 29:10	123, 146
1 Samuel 29:11	123
1 Samuel 30:1	188
1 Samuel 30:12	85, 99, 192
1 Samuel 30:13	192
1 Samuel 30:17	109
1 Samuel 31:12	85
1 Samuel 31:13	210
1 Timothy 6:19	490
2 Chronicles 1:7	87
2 Chronicles 2:4	110, 126, 135
2 Chronicles 6:20	88
2 Chronicles 7:8	210
2 Chronicles 7:9	210
2 Chronicles 7:12	88
2 Chronicles 10:5	193
2 Chronicles 10:12	189
2 Chronicles 13:11	110, 126, 135
2 Chronicles 18:7	461
2 Chronicles 18:34	110
2 Chronicles 20:20	126
2 Chronicles 20:25	193
2 Chronicles 20:26	195
2 Chronicles 21:9	88

Reference	Page(s)
2 Chronicles 21:12-15	176
2 Chronicles 21:16-19	173
2 Chronicles 21:18	176
2 Chronicles 21:19	172, 173, 175, 176, 177, 178, 186
2 Chronicles 28:6	159
2 Chronicles 29:17	199
2 Chronicles 30:21	210
2 Chronicles 30:22	210
2 Chronicles 30:23	211
2 Chronicles 31:3	110, 126, 135
2 Chronicles 32:21	503
2 Chronicles 35:14	88
2 Chronicles 35:17	211
2 Corinthians 4:4	440
2 Corinthians 4:6	454, 455, 632
2 Corinthians 4:9	493, 494
2 Corinthians 5:17	454
2 Corinthians 12:2	274
2 Kings 2:17	192
2 Kings 3:9	210
2 Kings 3:19	502
2 Kings 3:20	125
2 Kings 3:22	125
2 Kings 3:25	502
2 Kings 4:18-37	458
2 Kings 6:5	503
2 Kings 6:14	87
2 Kings 7:9	125, 147
2 Kings 7:12	87
2 Kings 7:20	333
2 Kings 8:21	87
2 Kings 10:8	125
2 Kings 10:9	125
2 Kings 13:21	458
2 Kings 16:15	110, 125, 135
2 Kings 19:7	503
2 Kings 19:35	87, 125
2 Kings 20:5	188
2 Kings 20:8	188
2 Kings 25:4	87, 447
2 Peter 1:20	297

Reference	Page(s)
2 Peter 3	480
2 Peter 3:1-18	480
2 Peter 3:4	434
2 Peter 3:5	386, 481, 482
2 Peter 3:5-6	386
2 Peter 3:7	408
2 Peter 3:8	39, 40, 45, 179, 222, 636
2 Peter 3:10	402, 509
2 Peter 3:13	234
2 Samuel 1:1	172, 176
2 Samuel 1:2	188
2 Samuel 1:12	109
2 Samuel 2:27	123
2 Samuel 2:29	86
2 Samuel 2:32	86, 146
2 Samuel 4:7	86
2 Samuel 7:4	86
2 Samuel 8:14	571
2 Samuel 11:2	109
2 Samuel 11:13	109
2 Samuel 11:14	123
2 Samuel 12:18	203
2 Samuel 13:4	124
2 Samuel 13:23	174
2 Samuel 14:26	175
2 Samuel 14:28	175
2 Samuel 17:1	86
2 Samuel 17:16	86
2 Samuel 17:22	124, 147
2 Samuel 18:9	277
2 Samuel 19:7	86
2 Samuel 19:20	168
2 Samuel 19:34	172
2 Samuel 20:4	192
2 Samuel 20:15	502
2 Samuel 21:10	86
2 Samuel 22:12	139
2 Samuel 22:16	517
2 Samuel 22:29	139
2 Samuel 23:4	124, 147
2 Samuel 24:11	124

2 Samuel 24:13	192
2 Samuel 24:15	124
2 Timothy 2:19	490
2 Timothy 3:1	179
Acts 1:3	186
Acts 1:9-12	165
Acts 7:8	185
Acts 7:54	440
Acts 9:9	181
Acts 10:30	183
Acts 10:40	183
Acts 13:17-21	487, 488, 489
Acts 16:26	490
Acts 17:26	221
Acts 20:6	183, 184
Acts 20:18	180
Acts 21:4	184
Acts 21:7	179
Acts 21:27	184
Acts 24:1	183
Acts 24:11	185
Acts 25:1	181
Acts 25:6	185
Acts 27:33	185
Acts 28:7	181
Acts 28:12	181
Acts 28:13	179
Acts 28:14	184
Acts 28:17	182
Amos 4:4	132, 175, 193, 194
Amos 4:13	346
Amos 5:8	96, 101, 132
Amos 5:18	143, 156
Amos 5:20	143, 156
Amos 8:9	156
Daniel 5:3	530
Daniel 8:14	113, 131, 137
Daniel 8:26	113, 131, 138
Daniel 9:17	155
Daniel 9:21	113
Daniel 10:12	168

Daniel 10:13	161, 162
Daniel 11:12	505
Daniel 11:20	161, 162
Daniel 12:1	630
Deuteronomy 1:33	82
Deuteronomy 4:11	139
Deuteronomy 4:32	168, 344, 631
Deuteronomy 5:13	199
Deuteronomy 5:14	203
Deuteronomy 5:23	139
Deuteronomy 9:9	82, 98
Deuteronomy 9:11	82, 98
Deuteronomy 9:18	82, 98
Deuteronomy 9:25	82, 98
Deuteronomy 10:10	82, 98, 168
Deuteronomy 16:1	82
Deuteronomy 16:3	209
Deuteronomy 16:4	108, 120, 134, 168, 209
Deuteronomy 16:6	108
Deuteronomy 16:7	120
Deuteronomy 16:8	199, 203
Deuteronomy 16:13	209
Deuteronomy 16:15	209
Deuteronomy 17:15	30
Deuteronomy 18:10-14	389
Deuteronomy 23:10	82
Deuteronomy 23:11	108
Deuteronomy 28:66	82
Deuteronomy 28:67	108, 120, 135
Deuteronomy 32:10	288
Ecclesiastes 1:4-5	236
Ecclesiastes 2:13	152
Ecclesiastes 2:13-14	142
Ecclesiastes 2:23	93, 100
Ecclesiastes 5:17	142
Ecclesiastes 6:4	142
Ecclesiastes 6:6	222
Ecclesiastes 7:10	168
Ecclesiastes 8:1	153
Ecclesiastes 8:16	93, 100
Ecclesiastes 10:16	129

Reference	Pages
Ecclesiastes 11:6	112, 129, 137
Ecclesiastes 11:7	153
Ecclesiastes 11:8	142
Ecclesiastes 12:1	344
Ecclesiastes 12:2	153
Ephesians 1:4	491
Ephesians 1:18-21	485
Ephesians 2:2	440
Ephesians 2:8	454, 455
Ephesians 2:20	190
Esther 1:3	559
Esther 1:5	211
Esther 1:10	203
Esther 2:14	111, 126, 136
Esther 3:13	160
Esther 4:16	89, 99, 193
Esther 5:1	189
Esther 5:14	126
Esther 6:1	89
Esther 7:2	171
Esther 8:12	160
Esther 9:15	196
Esther 9:17	193
Esther 9:19	196
Esther 9:21	196, 197
Exodus 1:5	559
Exodus 2:13	170
Exodus 3:18	190
Exodus 5:3	190
Exodus 7:10	567
Exodus 7:15	115
Exodus 7:19	569
Exodus 7:25	205
Exodus 8:17	569
Exodus 8:20	115
Exodus 8:27	190
Exodus 9:10	569
Exodus 9:13	115
Exodus 10:13	79, 98, 115
Exodus 10:21-22	138
Exodus 10:22	191, 378

Reference	Pages
Exodus 10:23	145, 191
Exodus 11:1	461
Exodus 11:4	79
Exodus 12:6	103
Exodus 12:8	79
Exodus 12:10	115
Exodus 12:12	79
Exodus 12:15	162, 166, 200, 205
Exodus 12:16	166, 200
Exodus 12:18	103, 159, 162
Exodus 12:19	205
Exodus 12:22	115
Exodus 12:29	80
Exodus 12:30	80, 333
Exodus 12:31	80
Exodus 12:42	80
Exodus 13:6	200, 205
Exodus 13:7	205
Exodus 13:10	174
Exodus 13:21	80, 145
Exodus 13:22	80
Exodus 14:20	80, 138, 145
Exodus 14:21	80
Exodus 14:24	116
Exodus 14:27	116
Exodus 15:22	191
Exodus 16:5	197
Exodus 16:6	103
Exodus 16:7	116
Exodus 16:8	103, 116, 133
Exodus 16:12	103, 116, 133
Exodus 16:13	104, 116, 133
Exodus 16:19	116
Exodus 16:20	116
Exodus 16:21	116
Exodus 16:22	197
Exodus 16:23	116
Exodus 16:24	117
Exodus 16:26	198, 200
Exodus 16:27	200
Exodus 16:29	197, 200

Reference	Pages
Exodus 16:30	200
Exodus 18:13	104, 117, 133
Exodus 18:14	104, 117, 133
Exodus 19	464
Exodus 19:4	287
Exodus 19:11	187
Exodus 19:15	191
Exodus 19:16	117, 187
Exodus 20:9	198
Exodus 20:10	200
Exodus 20:11	48, 49, 198, 200, 352, 353, 354, 355, 356, 357, 358, 359, 360, 361, 362, 424, 425
Exodus 22:30	205
Exodus 23:12	198, 200
Exodus 23:15	205
Exodus 23:18	117
Exodus 23:29	570
Exodus 24:4	117
Exodus 24:16	198, 200
Exodus 24:18	80, 98
Exodus 25:37	145
Exodus 27:21	104, 117, 134
Exodus 29:30	205
Exodus 29:34	117
Exodus 29:35	205
Exodus 29:37	205
Exodus 29:39	104, 117, 134
Exodus 29:41	104, 117, 134
Exodus 30:7	117, 118
Exodus 30:8	104
Exodus 31:15	198, 201
Exodus 31:17	198, 201
Exodus 32:1	570
Exodus 32:1,23	333
Exodus 32:23	570
Exodus 34:2	118
Exodus 34:4	118
Exodus 34:10	343
Exodus 34:18	206
Exodus 34:21	198, 201
Exodus 34:25	118

Exodus 34:28	80, 98
Exodus 35:2	198, 201
Exodus 36:3	118
Exodus 36:13	570, 571
Exodus 40:2	159, 161
Exodus 40:38	80
Ezekiel 3:15	211
Ezekiel 3:16	211
Ezekiel 6:4	504
Ezekiel 8:12	143
Ezekiel 12:4	112
Ezekiel 12:7	112
Ezekiel 12:8	131
Ezekiel 19:3	574, 575
Ezekiel 19:6	575
Ezekiel 21:30	346
Ezekiel 23:10	575
Ezekiel 23:25	504
Ezekiel 24:18	112, 131, 137
Ezekiel 26:4	504
Ezekiel 26:9	504
Ezekiel 26:12	504
Ezekiel 28:1-10	438
Ezekiel 28:2	438
Ezekiel 28:11-19	329, 438
Ezekiel 28:12	438
Ezekiel 28:12-15	433
Ezekiel 28:13	346, 432
Ezekiel 28:13-14	443
Ezekiel 28:13-16	438
Ezekiel 28:13-17	444
Ezekiel 28:15	346
Ezekiel 29:5	504
Ezekiel 30:22	505
Ezekiel 31:12	505
Ezekiel 32:7	155
Ezekiel 32:8	143, 155
Ezekiel 32:12	505
Ezekiel 33:22	112, 131, 137
Ezekiel 36:35	575, 579
Ezekiel 38:18-20	460

Ezekiel 38:20	459
Ezekiel 39:3	505
Ezekiel 43:2	155
Ezekiel 43:22	171
Ezekiel 43:25	211
Ezekiel 43:26	211
Ezekiel 44:26	211
Ezekiel 45:21	212
Ezekiel 45:23	212
Ezekiel 45:25	212
Ezekiel 46:1	199
Ezekiel 46:2	112
Ezekiel 46:13	131
Ezekiel 46:14	131
Ezekiel 46:15	131
Ezra 3:3	111, 126, 135
Ezra 3:6	160, 161, 162
Ezra 6:22	211
Ezra 8:15	193
Ezra 8:32	193
Ezra 8:33	195
Ezra 9:4	111
Ezra 9:5	111
Ezra 9:8	147
Ezra 10:8	193
Ezra 10:9	193
Ezra 10:13	160
Ezra 10:16	160, 161
Ezra 10:17	160, 161
Galatians 1:18	185

Genesis 1...48, 49, 75, 76, 97, 101, 102, 132, 136, 137, 138, 157, 158, 169, 170, 174, 175, 179, 212, 215, 219, 276, 285, 290, 327, 329, 336, 340, 368, 374, 385, 410, 411, 415, 421, 427, 428, 437, 468, 469, 470, 471, 479, 577, 581, 587, 591, 593, 594, 596, 599, 601, 604, 605, 606, 607, 608, 609, 633, 634

Genesis 1:1...13, 32, 37, 43, 44, 51, 52, 53, 54, 157, 158, 169, 219, 224, 264, 272, 273, 274, 275, 276, 277, 278, 279, 280, 281, 285, 290, 299, 303, 306, 317, 319, 323, 324, 325, 326, 327, 329, 330, 337, 339, 342, 343, 348, 350, 351, 353, 354, 355, 356, 364, 365, 366, 367, 369, 370, 372, 374, 377, 403, 413, 415, 423, 424, 425, 430, 435, 437, 448, 470, 471, 487, 489, 501, 512, 514, 515, 581, 582, 583, 584, 585, 591, 592, 593, 599, 600, 602, 606, 607, 608, 609, 612, 613, 615, 617, 634

Genesis 1:1-2....52, 53, 157, 169, 269, 270, 276, 284, 290, 339, 340, 365, 366, 367, 416, 471, 502, 554, 584, 591, 592, 600, 601, 602, 605, 606, 607, 608, 632

Genesis 1:1-2a 267
Genesis 1:1-5 157
Genesis 1:1-31 436
Genesis 1:1-2:3 .... 469, 470
Genesis 1:2....51, 52, 55, 64, 138, 144, 228, 276, 277, 279, 280, 281, 282, 283, 284, 285, 288, 290, 291, 292, 297, 298, 317, 319, 322, 323, 324, 325, 326, 327, 328, 329, 330, 331, 332, 333, 334, 337, 339, 340, 341, 342, 348, 349, 350, 351, 353, 365, 366, 369, 370, 374, 380, 383, 384, 385, 402, 403, 405, 407, 408, 410, 411, 413, 414, 415, 421, 432, 448, 461, 471, 472, 473, 478, 479, 482, 487, 489, 514, 516, 517, 527, 528, 529, 531, 534, 536, 538, 541, 542, 544, 547, 548, 550, 554, 558, 560, 564, 565, 577, 578, 582, 583, 584, 585, 586, 587, 588, 591, 593, 600, 602, 606, 607, 608, 609, 610, 611, 612, 613, 614, 615, 616, 617, 618, 619, 631, 633, 634

Genesis 1:3....53, 145, 317, 324, 329, 333, 334, 339, 364, 366, 367, 368, 369, 370, 372, 373, 375, 377, 378, 384, 401, 402, 418, 420, 432, 448, 455, 479, 515, 536, 537, 555, 577, 581, 582, 591, 592, 600, 602, 603, 604, 608, 632

Genesis 1:3-5 .... 157, 158, 162, 600, 601
Genesis 1:3-8 479
Genesis 1:3-13 371
Genesis 1:3-31...13, 44, 51, 52, 53, 136, 158, 219, 228, 275, 281, 290, 298, 301, 306, 337, 353, 354, 355, 365, 366, 367, 368, 384, 385, 398, 415, 418, 424, 425, 437, 471, 502, 592, 602, 607, 633

Genesis 1:3-2:3 .... 426, 428, 429, 471
Genesis 1:4 .... 145, 366
Genesis 1:4-5 138
Genesis 1:5 .... 76, 77, 97, 102, 113, 133, 145, 158, 161, 162, 169, 463, 600
Genesis 1:5b 76
Genesis 1:6 380
Genesis 1:6a 418
Genesis 1:6b 418
Genesis 1:6-7 552
Genesis 1:6-8 379
Genesis 1:7 .... 356, 384, 471, 537, 555
Genesis 1:7,9 333
Genesis 1:8a 76
Genesis 1:9 .... 64, 385, 386, 420, 537, 552, 555
Genesis 1:9a 418
Genesis 1:9b 418
Genesis 1:9-10 479
Genesis 1:10 .... 366, 479

Reference	Pages
Genesis 1:10a	76
Genesis 1:10b	76
Genesis 1:11	302, 355, 419, 537, 555
Genesis 1:11-13	409
Genesis 1:12	366
Genesis 1:13	102, 114, 133, 186
Genesis 1:14	77, 97, 372, 373, 375, 377, 388, 389, 396, 397
Genesis 1:14a	419
Genesis 1:14b	419
Genesis 1:14-16	375
Genesis 1:14-18	101, 372, 377, 461, 602, 603
Genesis 1:14-19	372
Genesis 1:15	145, 419, 537, 555
Genesis 1:16	77, 97, 277, 367, 369, 370, 377, 471
Genesis 1:16-17	272
Genesis 1:17	145, 390
Genesis 1:17-18	595
Genesis 1:18	77, 97, 138, 145
Genesis 1:19	102, 114, 133, 195
Genesis 1:20	273, 419
Genesis 1:20-22	482
Genesis 1:20-23	409
Genesis 1:21	225, 343, 366
Genesis 1:22	419, 559
Genesis 1:23	102, 114, 133, 196
Genesis 1:24	225, 303, 419, 537, 555
Genesis 1:25	471
Genesis 1:26	443, 471
Genesis 1:26a	419
Genesis 1:26b	419
Genesis 1:26-27	417
Genesis 1:27	343
Genesis 1:27-31	444
Genesis 1:30	231, 232, 537, 555
Genesis 1:31	102, 114, 133, 197, 353, 365, 415, 471
Genesis 2:1-3	426
Genesis 2:2	199
Genesis 2:3	199, 242, 343, 430, 470
Genesis 2:4	47, 48, 343, 428, 437, 468, 469, 470, 471
Genesis 2:4a	469, 470
Genesis 2:4b	469

Reference	Page(s)
Genesis 2:4-6	318
Genesis 2:5-25	428, 429, 430, 469
Genesis 2:7	225, 307, 425
Genesis 2:7-9	429
Genesis 2:9	303
Genesis 2:10	307, 566
Genesis 2:10-14	262
Genesis 2:11-14	530, 531
Genesis 2:14	262
Genesis 2:15	445
Genesis 2:16-17	232, 233
Genesis 2:17	231
Genesis 2:19	41, 225, 303
Genesis 2:21	42
Genesis 3:1	229, 538, 560, 561, 588
Genesis 3:4	229
Genesis 3:5	229
Genesis 3:6a	230
Genesis 3:6b	230
Genesis 3:6c	231
Genesis 3:7	355, 386
Genesis 3:14-16	230
Genesis 3:17	167, 232, 465
Genesis 3:17-19	501
Genesis 3:20	331, 539, 561, 576, 578
Genesis 3:22	307, 568
Genesis 3:24	447
Genesis 4:2	539, 555, 556, 561
Genesis 4:3	307
Genesis 4:8	307
Genesis 4:14	308
Genesis 4:15	388
Genesis 4:20	331, 539, 561, 576
Genesis 4:21	539, 561
Genesis 4:23	278
Genesis 4:25	463
Genesis 5:1	343, 468
Genesis 5:2	343
Genesis 5:4	167
Genesis 5:32	539, 556
Genesis 6:1	308

Genesis 6:4	167
Genesis 6:7	261, 343
Genesis 6:9	533, 540, 561
Genesis 6:14	355
Genesis 6:20	446
Genesis 7	476, 477
Genesis 7:4	77, 97, 204
Genesis 7:6	540, 561
Genesis 7:10	204, 308
Genesis 7:10-24	246
Genesis 7:11	260, 473
Genesis 7:12	77, 97, 540, 556
Genesis 7:17	540, 556
Genesis 7:19-20	246
Genesis 7:20	260
Genesis 8:1-5	247, 475
Genesis 8:6	308
Genesis 8:10	204
Genesis 8:11	103
Genesis 8:12	204, 463
Genesis 8:13	308
Genesis 8:22	78, 97, 391, 409
Genesis 9:3	553
Genesis 9:11	476
Genesis 9:13	559
Genesis 9:13-17	388
Genesis 9:14	308, 559
Genesis 9:15	308, 463
Genesis 9:16	333
Genesis 10	613
Genesis 10:1	468
Genesis 10:8-12	614, 615
Genesis 10:9	540, 562
Genesis 10:10	540, 556
Genesis 10:19	540, 556
Genesis 10:30	540, 556
Genesis 11:1	541, 542, 556
Genesis 11:2	308
Genesis 11:6	542
Genesis 11:10	468
Genesis 11:27	468

Genesis 11:30	542, 556
Genesis 12:10	543, 556, 589
Genesis 12:11	308
Genesis 12:14	308
Genesis 13:6	543, 562
Genesis 13:7	543, 556
Genesis 14:1	167, 308
Genesis 14:15	78
Genesis 15:1	308
Genesis 15:5	553
Genesis 15:17	309, 543, 562, 588
Genesis 16:11-12	553
Genesis 16:15	497
Genesis 17:1	531, 543, 556
Genesis 18:6	355, 356
Genesis 18:18	309
Genesis 19:1	103
Genesis 19:5	78
Genesis 19:17	309
Genesis 19:26	309, 334, 568
Genesis 19:27	114
Genesis 19:29	309
Genesis 19:33	78
Genesis 19:34	78, 309
Genesis 19:35	78
Genesis 20:3	78
Genesis 20:8	114
Genesis 20:12	309, 566, 567
Genesis 20:13	309
Genesis 21:14	114
Genesis 21:20	309, 543, 556, 568
Genesis 21:22	309
Genesis 22:1	309
Genesis 22:3	114
Genesis 22:4	186
Genesis 22:20	309
Genesis 23:1	543, 556
Genesis 24:11	103
Genesis 24:14	310, 559
Genesis 24:15	310
Genesis 24:20	464

Genesis 24:22	310
Genesis 24:30	310
Genesis 24:43	310, 559
Genesis 24:52	310
Genesis 24:54	114
Genesis 24:63	103
Genesis 24:67	310
Genesis 25:1-2	497
Genesis 25:11	310
Genesis 25:20	543, 557
Genesis 25:27	543, 557
Genesis 26:1	544, 557, 562
Genesis 26:8	310
Genesis 26:24	78
Genesis 26:28	544, 562
Genesis 26:31	114
Genesis 26:32	310
Genesis 26:34	544, 557
Genesis 27:1	311
Genesis 27:30	311, 544, 557
Genesis 27:40	311
Genesis 27:44	158, 162
Genesis 27:45	158
Genesis 28:12	273
Genesis 28:15	446
Genesis 28:18	114
Genesis 29:10	311
Genesis 29:13	311
Genesis 29:16-18	589
Genesis 29:17	532, 533, 544, 562, 578, 589
Genesis 29:20	158, 162
Genesis 29:23	103, 311
Genesis 29:25	114, 311
Genesis 30:15	78
Genesis 30:16	78, 103
Genesis 30:25	311
Genesis 30:29	544, 545, 562, 563
Genesis 30:31	446
Genesis 30:36	190
Genesis 30:41	311, 559
Genesis 31:10	311

Reference	Page(s)
Genesis 31:14	464
Genesis 31:22	186
Genesis 31:23	204
Genesis 31:24	78
Genesis 31:39	79, 97
Genesis 31:40	79, 97, 545, 563
Genesis 31:55	115
Genesis 32:10	312, 567
Genesis 32:13	79
Genesis 32:21	79
Genesis 32:22	79
Genesis 33:9	554
Genesis 33:13	159
Genesis 34:16	312
Genesis 34:25	187, 312
Genesis 35:3	545, 557
Genesis 35:5	545, 557
Genesis 35:16	545, 557
Genesis 35:17	312
Genesis 35:18	312
Genesis 35:22	312
Genesis 36:12	545, 563, 578
Genesis 37:2	545, 563
Genesis 37:20	312, 568
Genesis 37:23	312
Genesis 38:1	312
Genesis 38:5	529, 545, 559, 560
Genesis 38:7	545, 557
Genesis 38:9	312
Genesis 38:21	546, 563, 578
Genesis 38:22	546, 563, 578
Genesis 38:24	312
Genesis 38:27	312
Genesis 38:28	313
Genesis 38:29	313
Genesis 39:2	530, 531, 546, 557
Genesis 39:5	313, 546, 557
Genesis 39:6	546, 557
Genesis 39:7	313
Genesis 39:10	313
Genesis 39:11	313

Genesis 39:13	313
Genesis 39:15	313
Genesis 39:18	313
Genesis 39:19	313
Genesis 39:20	546, 558
Genesis 39:21	546, 558
Genesis 39:22	546, 563, 564
Genesis 40:1	313
Genesis 40:5	79
Genesis 40:6	115
Genesis 40:12	190
Genesis 40:13	190, 532, 547
Genesis 40:18	190
Genesis 40:19	190
Genesis 40:20	187, 313
Genesis 41:1	314
Genesis 41:8	115, 314
Genesis 41:11	79
Genesis 41:13	314, 546, 564, 576
Genesis 41:53	547, 564
Genesis 41:54	547, 558, 564
Genesis 41:55-56	589, 591
Genesis 41:56	547, 564, 589
Genesis 42:5	547, 564
Genesis 42:17	190
Genesis 42:18	187
Genesis 42:35	314
Genesis 43:2	314
Genesis 43:21	314
Genesis 44:3	115, 145
Genesis 44:10	630
Genesis 44:17	549
Genesis 44:24	314
Genesis 44:31	314, 559
Genesis 46:2	79
Genesis 46:33	314, 560
Genesis 47:20	314
Genesis 47:24	314, 560
Genesis 47:26	315, 578
Genesis 47:28	547, 558
Genesis 48:1	315

Reference	Pages
Genesis 48:19	315, 568, 569
Genesis 48:21	560
Genesis 49:1	167
Genesis 49:15	315
Genesis 49:27	103, 115, 133
Genesis 50:9	547, 558
Genesis 50:10	205
Habakkuk 1:5	559
Habakkuk 1:8	113
Habakkuk 3:4	156
Habakkuk 3:11	156
Haggai 1:1	161
Haggai 2:6	460, 461, 462, 463, 465, 633
Haggai 2:20-23	465
Haggai 2:21	460, 466, 467
Hebrews 1:3	241, 242
Hebrews 1:10	434
Hebrews 2:14-16	453
Hebrews 4:3	492
Hebrews 4:4	184
Hebrews 6:1	491, 493, 494
Hebrews 9:19-26	500
Hebrews 9:26	492
Hebrews 10:5	483, 484
Hebrews 11:3	328, 483, 484, 485, 486, 634
Hebrews 11:10	491
Hebrews 11:11	495, 496
Hebrews 11:30	184
Hebrews 12:25-27	464, 633
Hebrews 12:27	424
Hosea 2:16	333
Hosea 4:5	96, 101
Hosea 6:1-3	189
Hosea 6:2	189
Hosea 6:4	132
Hosea 6:5	155
Hosea 7:6	96, 132
Hosea 13:3	132
Isaiah 1:21	579
Isaiah 2:5	153
Isaiah 4:5	93, 344

Isaiah 5:11	129
Isaiah 5:20	142, 153
Isaiah 5:30	142, 153
Isaiah 7:18,21	333
Isaiah 7:24	573
Isaiah 9:2	142, 153
Isaiah 9:6	30
Isaiah 9:14	160
Isaiah 10:17	153, 160
Isaiah 13:9-11	378
Isaiah 13:9-13	459
Isaiah 13:10	153
Isaiah 13:13	459
Isaiah 14	448
Isaiah 14:12	431
Isaiah 14:12-17	448
Isaiah 14:13-15	439
Isaiah 14:17	520
Isaiah 15:1	93
Isaiah 16:3	93
Isaiah 16:9	504
Isaiah 17:7-11	129
Isaiah 17:11	129
Isaiah 17:14	112, 130, 137
Isaiah 21:8	93
Isaiah 21:11	93
Isaiah 21:12	93, 130
Isaiah 24:10	289, 329
Isaiah 26:5	504
Isaiah 26:9	93
Isaiah 27:3	94, 100
Isaiah 27:11	153
Isaiah 28:10,13	425
Isaiah 28:19	94, 100, 130
Isaiah 29:7	94
Isaiah 29:18	142
Isaiah 29:21	289
Isaiah 30:26	153, 211
Isaiah 30:29	94
Isaiah 33:2	130
Isaiah 34	292, 413

Isaiah 34:1-11	292
Isaiah 34:8-11	413
Isaiah 34:10	94
Isaiah 34:11	289, 291, 292, 297, 298, 326, 327, 413, 414, 632
Isaiah 37:36	130
Isaiah 38:12	94, 101
Isaiah 38:13	94, 101, 130
Isaiah 40:17	289
Isaiah 40:22	511
Isaiah 40:23	289
Isaiah 40:26	344
Isaiah 40:28	344
Isaiah 41:20	345
Isaiah 41:29	289
Isaiah 42:5	345, 511
Isaiah 42:6	154
Isaiah 42:7	142
Isaiah 42:13	45, 278
Isaiah 42:16	154
Isaiah 43:1	345
Isaiah 43:7	345, 354
Isaiah 43:11	30, 637
Isaiah 43:15	299, 345
Isaiah 44:9	289
Isaiah 45	341, 412
Isaiah 45:3	142
Isaiah 45:7	142, 154, 345, 368, 369, 370
Isaiah 45:8	345
Isaiah 45:12	345
Isaiah 45:18	325, 327, 332, 336, 341, 342, 343, 347, 348, 349, 350, 352, 354, 401, 425, 632
Isaiah 45:18-19	289
Isaiah 45:19	142, 349, 350
Isaiah 47:5	143
Isaiah 47:9	160
Isaiah 48:7	345
Isaiah 49:4	289
Isaiah 49:6	154
Isaiah 49:9	143
Isaiah 50:4	130
Isaiah 51:4	154

Reference	Pages
Isaiah 54:16	299, 345
Isaiah 57:19	346
Isaiah 58:8	154
Isaiah 58:10	143, 154
Isaiah 59:4	289
Isaiah 59:9	143, 154
Isaiah 60:1	154
Isaiah 60:2	143
Isaiah 60:3	154
Isaiah 60:11	94
Isaiah 60:19	154
Isaiah 60:20	155
Isaiah 62:6	94, 101
Isaiah 65:17	346
Isaiah 65:18	299, 346
Isaiah 66:8	161
Jeremiah 4	292, 401
Jeremiah 4:1-31	293
Jeremiah 4:23	155, 289, 291, 292, 297, 298, 401, 402, 408, 410, 411, 413, 414, 606
Jeremiah 4:23-24	410
Jeremiah 4:23-26	329, 401, 403, 404, 405, 408, 409, 412, 415, 479, 480, 519, 632
Jeremiah 4:23-27	412
Jeremiah 4:24	449, 459
Jeremiah 4:25	417, 538
Jeremiah 4:26	449
Jeremiah 4:27	407
Jeremiah 6:4	112
Jeremiah 6:5	94
Jeremiah 7:11	573
Jeremiah 9:1	94
Jeremiah 10:12	511
Jeremiah 13:16	155
Jeremiah 14:17	95
Jeremiah 16:13	95
Jeremiah 19:7	504
Jeremiah 20:16	130
Jeremiah 21:12	130
Jeremiah 22:5	573
Jeremiah 22:24-30	466
Jeremiah 25:10	155
Jeremiah 26:18	573

Jeremiah 31:22	346
Jeremiah 31:35	155
Jeremiah 31:35-36	95, 407
Jeremiah 33:20	95, 101
Jeremiah 33:25	95
Jeremiah 35:4	446
Jeremiah 36:30	95, 101
Jeremiah 39:4	95, 447
Jeremiah 41:4	171
Jeremiah 49:9	95
Jeremiah 50:23	579
Jeremiah 51:15	290
Jeremiah 51:41	579
Jeremiah 52:7	95, 447
Job 1:5	127
Job 1:6-7	440
Job 2:13	89, 99, 211
Job 3:3	89, 99
Job 3:4-5	139
Job 3:6	89, 100
Job 3:7	89
Job 3:9	147
Job 3:16	147
Job 3:20	147
Job 4:7	432
Job 4:13	89
Job 4:20	111, 127, 136
Job 5:14	89, 139
Job 6:18	288
Job 7:3	89
Job 7:4	111
Job 7:18	127
Job 10:21	139
Job 11:17	127
Job 12:14	503
Job 12:22	139, 147
Job 12:24	288
Job 12:25	139, 148
Job 15:22-23	139
Job 15:30	140
Job 16:9	503

Reference	Page(s)
Job 16:14	503
Job 17:12	90, 100, 148
Job 17:12-13	140
Job 18:5	148
Job 18:6	148
Job 18:18	140, 148
Job 19:8	140
Job 20:8	90
Job 20:26	140
Job 22:11	140
Job 22:28	148
Job 23:17	140
Job 24:13	148
Job 24:14	90, 148
Job 24:16	140, 148
Job 24:17	127
Job 25:3	148
Job 26:7	288
Job 26:10	140, 148
Job 27:20	90
Job 28:3	140
Job 28:11	148
Job 29:3	140, 148
Job 29:24	148
Job 30:17	90
Job 30:26	149
Job 31:26	149
Job 33:15	90
Job 33:28	149
Job 33:30	149
Job 34:20	90
Job 34:22	140
Job 34:25	90
Job 35:10	90
Job 36:20	90
Job 36:30	149
Job 36:32	149
Job 37:3	149
Job 37:11	149
Job 37:15	149
Job 37:19	140

Job 37:21	149
Job 38	316, 431, 474, 476, 477, 478, 479, 480
Job 38:1-7	473
Job 38:1-11	472
Job 38:4-6	299, 301, 632
Job 38:4-7	431
Job 38:7	127, 632
Job 38:8	473
Job 38:8-11	473, 632
Job 38:9	369, 383, 479, 606
Job 38:10-11	479
Job 38:12	127
Job 38:15	149
Job 38:16	517
Job 38:19	141, 149
Job 38:24	149
Job 40:3-5	244
Job 41:18	149
Job 41:32	150
Joel 1:6	558
Joel 2:2	143
Joel 2:10	459, 460
Joel 2:31	143
Joel 2:31-32	408
Joel 3:13-17	460
Joel 3:16	459, 460
John 1:1	275
John 1:1-2	434
John 1:1-3	285
John 1:3	275
John 1:14	637
John 2:1	183
John 2:19	181
John 2:20	181
John 3:1-12	456
John 4:40	180
John 4:43	180
John 8:44	433, 434
John 9:7	389
John 11:6	180
John 11:17	183

John 11:43	42
John 12:1	184
John 12:23-24	227
John 12:24	226
John 12:31	440
John 14:30	440
John 16:8-11	441
John 17:24	491
John 19:10-11	442
John 19:15	30
John 20:26	185
Jonah 1:17	96, 101, 195
Jonah 2:5-6	517
Jonah 3:3	195, 609, 610, 611, 612, 613, 614, 615
Jonah 3:3a	610
Jonah 3:3b	610, 611, 612, 613
Jonah 3:4	161
Jonah 4:5	575
Jonah 4:10	96
Joshua 1:8	82
Joshua 1:11	191
Joshua 2:2	82
Joshua 2:5	139
Joshua 2:16	191
Joshua 2:22	191
Joshua 3:1	120
Joshua 3:2	191
Joshua 4:3	83
Joshua 5:10	108
Joshua 6:3	199
Joshua 6:4	203
Joshua 6:12	120
Joshua 6:14	171, 199
Joshua 7:6	108
Joshua 7:14	120
Joshua 7:16	120
Joshua 8:3	83
Joshua 8:9	83
Joshua 8:10	120
Joshua 8:13	83
Joshua 8:29	108

Joshua 9:16	192
Joshua 9:17	188
Joshua 10:9	83
Joshua 10:26	108
Joshua 10:32	171
Joshua 13:1	174
Joshua 14:14	578
Judges 1:3	554
Judges 3:7-8	488
Judges 3:12-14	488
Judges 4:1-3	489
Judges 6:1	489
Judges 6:25	83
Judges 6:27	83
Judges 6:28	121
Judges 6:31	121
Judges 6:40	83
Judges 7:9	83
Judges 9:32	83
Judges 9:33	121
Judges 9:34	83
Judges 11:40	196
Judges 13:1	489
Judges 14:12	209
Judges 14:14	192
Judges 14:15	203, 204
Judges 14:17	203, 209
Judges 14:18	203
Judges 15:14	571
Judges 16:2	83, 121, 146
Judges 16:3	84
Judges 17:10	174
Judges 19:4	192
Judges 19:5	121, 195
Judges 19:8	121, 197
Judges 19:16	108
Judges 19:25	84, 121
Judges 19:26	121, 146
Judges 19:27	121
Judges 20:5	84
Judges 20:19	121

Judges 20:22	168
Judges 20:23	109
Judges 20:24	171
Judges 20:25	171
Judges 20:26	109
Judges 20:30	188
Judges 21:2	109
Lamentations 1:1	574, 579
Lamentations 1:2	95
Lamentations 1:6	574
Lamentations 1:11	574
Lamentations 1:16	631
Lamentations 2:18	96
Lamentations 2:19	96
Lamentations 3:2	143, 155
Lamentations 3:23	131
Lamentations 4:8	574
Leviticus 4:3	549
Leviticus 6:9	81, 118
Leviticus 6:12	118
Leviticus 6:20	104, 118, 134
Leviticus 7:15	118
Leviticus 7:17	187
Leviticus 7:18	187
Leviticus 8:33	206
Leviticus 8:35	81, 98, 206
Leviticus 9:17	118
Leviticus 11:24	104
Leviticus 11:25	104
Leviticus 11:27	104
Leviticus 11:28	104
Leviticus 11:31	105
Leviticus 11:32	105
Leviticus 11:39	105
Leviticus 11:40	105
Leviticus 11:44-45	533
Leviticus 12:2	206
Leviticus 12:4	191
Leviticus 12:5	199
Leviticus 13:4	206
Leviticus 13:5	170, 172, 201, 206

Leviticus 13:6	201
Leviticus 13:21	206
Leviticus 13:26	206
Leviticus 13:27	201
Leviticus 13:31	206
Leviticus 13:32	201
Leviticus 13:33	170, 172, 206
Leviticus 13:34	201
Leviticus 13:50	206
Leviticus 13:51	201
Leviticus 13:54	170, 172, 207
Leviticus 14:8	207
Leviticus 14:9	202
Leviticus 14:38	207
Leviticus 14:39	202
Leviticus 14:46	105
Leviticus 15:5	105
Leviticus 15:6	105
Leviticus 15:7	105
Leviticus 15:8	105
Leviticus 15:10	105
Leviticus 15:11	105
Leviticus 15:13	207
Leviticus 15:16	105
Leviticus 15:17	106
Leviticus 15:18	106
Leviticus 15:19	106, 207
Leviticus 15:21	106
Leviticus 15:22	106
Leviticus 15:23	106
Leviticus 15:24	207
Leviticus 15:27	106
Leviticus 15:28	207
Leviticus 17:15	106
Leviticus 19:6	187
Leviticus 19:7	187
Leviticus 19:13	119
Leviticus 22:6	106
Leviticus 22:27	207
Leviticus 22:28	159
Leviticus 22:30	119

Leviticus 23:3	199, 202
Leviticus 23:5	106
Leviticus 23:6	207
Leviticus 23:7	166
Leviticus 23:8	202, 207
Leviticus 23:24	162
Leviticus 23:32	106
Leviticus 23:34	207
Leviticus 23:35	166
Leviticus 23:36	207
Leviticus 23:39	166, 208
Leviticus 23:40	166, 208
Leviticus 23:41	208
Leviticus 23:42	208
Leviticus 24:3	106, 119, 134
Leviticus 25:29	174
Leviticus 26:12	630
Leviticus 26:13	630
Luke 1:7	179
Luke 1:18	179
Luke 1:24	495
Luke 1:31	495
Luke 1:59	185
Luke 2:21	184
Luke 2:46	181
Luke 4:2	186
Luke 4:5-6	335
Luke 4:5-8	451
Luke 6:48-49	490
Luke 7:19-23	31
Luke 9:22	182
Luke 9:28	185
Luke 11:50	491
Luke 13:14	184
Luke 14:29	490
Luke 18:33	182
Luke 20:34-35	486
Luke 22:51	42
Luke 24:7	183
Luke 24:21	183
Luke 24:46	183

Malachi 1:10	156
Malachi 2:10	346
Mark 1:13	186
Mark 8:2	181
Mark 8:31	181
Mark 9:2	184
Mark 9:31	182
Mark 10:34	182
Mark 12:1	447
Mark 14:1	180
Mark 14:12	180
Mark 14:58	181
Mark 15:29	181
Matthew 1:13-16	467
Matthew 2:1	179
Matthew 4:2	186
Matthew 4:8-10	441
Matthew 4:12	453
Matthew 4:21	483
Matthew 10:4	452
Matthew 12:32	485
Matthew 12:40	180, 217
Matthew 13:22	485
Matthew 13:30	288
Matthew 13:35	491
Matthew 13:39	485
Matthew 13:40	485
Matthew 13:41-42	440
Matthew 13:41-43	408, 449
Matthew 13:49	485
Matthew 15:32	180
Matthew 16:21	182
Matthew 17:1	183
Matthew 17:23	182
Matthew 19:4	423, 424, 434
Matthew 20:19	182
Matthew 21:33	447
Matthew 24:3	485
Matthew 25:34	491
Matthew 26:2	180
Matthew 26:61	181

Reference	Page(s)
Matthew 27:40	181
Matthew 27:45	378
Matthew 27:63	181
Matthew 27:64	182
Micah 2:1	132, 156
Micah 3:6	96, 101
Micah 3:12	576
Micah 7:4	333
Micah 7:8	144, 156
Micah 7:9	156
Nahum 1:8	144
Nehemiah 1:6	88, 99
Nehemiah 2:11	193
Nehemiah 2:12	88
Nehemiah 2:13	88
Nehemiah 2:15	88
Nehemiah 3:5	447
Nehemiah 4:9	88
Nehemiah 4:22	88, 99
Nehemiah 5:18	160
Nehemiah 6:10	89
Nehemiah 6:15	173, 176
Nehemiah 8:2	160, 161
Nehemiah 8:3	147
Nehemiah 8:13	171
Nehemiah 8:18	168, 211
Nehemiah 9:1	195
Nehemiah 9:3	195
Nehemiah 9:12	89, 147
Nehemiah 9:19	89, 147
Numbers 1:53	446
Numbers 3:32	446
Numbers 6:9	202
Numbers 6:12	167
Numbers 6:25	145
Numbers 7:11	159, 162, 163
Numbers 7:12	168
Numbers 7:18	170
Numbers 7:24	187
Numbers 7:30	195
Numbers 7:36	196

Numbers 7:42	197
Numbers 7:48	202
Numbers 7:78	172, 176
Numbers 8:2	146
Numbers 9:3	107
Numbers 9:5	107
Numbers 9:11	107
Numbers 9:12	119
Numbers 9:15	107, 119, 134
Numbers 9:16	81
Numbers 9:21	81, 107, 119, 134
Numbers 10:33	191
Numbers 11:9	81
Numbers 11:19	159, 197
Numbers 11:32	81, 98
Numbers 12:14	208
Numbers 12:15	208
Numbers 14:1	81
Numbers 14:14	81
Numbers 14:40	119
Numbers 16:5	119
Numbers 16:30	343
Numbers 19:7	107
Numbers 19:8	107
Numbers 19:10	107
Numbers 19:11	208
Numbers 19:12	187, 202
Numbers 19:14	208
Numbers 19:16	208
Numbers 19:19	107, 188, 202
Numbers 19:21	107
Numbers 19:22	107
Numbers 22:3	549
Numbers 22:8	81
Numbers 22:13	119
Numbers 22:19	81
Numbers 22:20	81
Numbers 22:21	119
Numbers 22:41	119
Numbers 28:4	108, 120, 134
Numbers 28:8	108, 120, 134

Numbers 28:17	208
Numbers 28:18	168
Numbers 28:23	120
Numbers 28:24	208
Numbers 28:25	202
Numbers 29:12	208
Numbers 29:17	170
Numbers 29:20	188
Numbers 29:23	195
Numbers 29:26	196
Numbers 29:29	198
Numbers 29:32	202
Numbers 31:19	188, 202, 209
Numbers 31:24	202
Numbers 33:8	191
Obadiah 1:5	96
Philippians 1:5	180
Proverbs 2:13	141
Proverbs 4:18	152
Proverbs 6:23	152
Proverbs 7:9	92, 112
Proverbs 7:18	128
Proverbs 7:26	503
Proverbs 8	478, 479
Proverbs 8:22-29	478
Proverbs 13:9	152
Proverbs 16:15	152
Proverbs 18:8	504
Proverbs 20:20	141
Proverbs 25:28	504
Proverbs 27:14	128
Proverbs 29:13	152
Proverbs 29:21	573
Proverbs 31:15	92
Proverbs 31:18	92
Psalms 1:2	90
Psalms 4:6	150
Psalms 5:3	127
Psalms 6:6	90
Psalms 8:3	251
Psalms 8:4-8	444

Psalms 13:3	150
Psalms 16:7	90
Psalms 17:3	90
Psalms 18:11	141
Psalms 18:28	141, 150
Psalms 19:1	275, 276
Psalms 19:1-3	35, 389
Psalms 19:1-6	236
Psalms 19:2	91, 100
Psalms 19:8	150
Psalms 21:7	237
Psalms 22:2	91
Psalms 27:1	150
Psalms 30:5	111, 127, 136
Psalms 31:16	150
Psalms 32:4	91
Psalms 35:6	141
Psalms 36:9	150
Psalms 37:6	150
Psalms 37:14	503
Psalms 38:10	150
Psalms 42:3	91, 100
Psalms 42:8	91
Psalms 43:3	150
Psalms 44:3	150
Psalms 46:5	127
Psalms 49:14	127
Psalms 49:19	150
Psalms 51:10	344
Psalms 55:10	91
Psalms 55:17	111, 127, 136
Psalms 55:22	237
Psalms 56:13	151
Psalms 59:6	111
Psalms 59:14	111
Psalms 59:16	128
Psalms 65:8	111, 128, 136
Psalms 67:1	151
Psalms 68:8	460
Psalms 73:14	128
Psalms 73:18	503

Psalms 74:16	91, 100
Psalms 76:4	151
Psalms 77:2	91, 100
Psalms 77:6	91
Psalms 77:18	151
Psalms 78:14	91, 151
Psalms 78:44	476
Psalms 80:3	151
Psalms 80:7	151
Psalms 80:19	151
Psalms 88:1	91, 100
Psalms 88:12	141
Psalms 88:13	128
Psalms 89:12	344
Psalms 89:15	151
Psalms 89:47	344
Psalms 90	137
Psalms 90:1-6	136
Psalms 90:4	40, 91, 100, 136, 222, 636
Psalms 90:5	128
Psalms 90:6	111, 128, 136
Psalms 90:14	128
Psalms 91:5	91
Psalms 92:2	92, 128
Psalms 93:1	237
Psalms 95	406
Psalms 95:8-11	406
Psalms 96:10	237
Psalms 97:4	151
Psalms 97:11	151
Psalms 101:8	128
Psalms 102:18	344
Psalms 102:26	33
Psalms 104	475, 476, 477, 479, 480
Psalms 104:1-2	511
Psalms 104:1-9	474
Psalms 104:2	151
Psalms 104:7	475
Psalms 104:9	474, 475, 476, 478
Psalms 104:20	92, 141
Psalms 104:23	112

Psalms 104:30	344
Psalms 105:28	141
Psalms 105:39	92, 151
Psalms 106:26	503
Psalms 106:27	503
Psalms 107:10	141
Psalms 107:14	141
Psalms 107:40	289
Psalms 112:4	141, 151
Psalms 118:22	578
Psalms 118:27	152
Psalms 119:55	92
Psalms 119:62	92
Psalms 119:83	572
Psalms 119:105	152
Psalms 119:130	152
Psalms 119:135	152
Psalms 121:6	92
Psalms 130:6	128
Psalms 134:1	92
Psalms 136:7	152
Psalms 136:9	92
Psalms 139:11	92, 152
Psalms 139:11-12	141
Psalms 139:12	92, 100, 152
Psalms 140:10	503
Psalms 141:2	112
Psalms 143:8	128
Psalms 148:3	152
Psalms 148:5	344
Revelation 2:10	185
Revelation 4:1	274
Revelation 11:3	186
Revelation 11:9	182
Revelation 11:11	182
Revelation 12:4	415
Revelation 12:6	186
Revelation 12:10	494
Revelation 13:8	492
Revelation 17:8	492
Revelation 18:8	180

Reference	Page(s)
Revelation 20:2-7	223
Revelation 21:14	491
Revelation 21:19	491
Romans 1:20	35, 390
Romans 5	233
Romans 5:12	225, 228, 231, 232
Romans 5:12-19	232
Romans 6:16	452
Romans 8:22	232
Romans 9.10	495
Romans 14:5	179
Romans 15:20	490
Ruth 1:12	84
Ruth 2:7	121
Ruth 2:17	109
Ruth 3:2	84
Ruth 3:8	84
Ruth 3:13	84, 122
Ruth 3:14	122
Song of Solomon 3:1	93
Song of Solomon 3:8	93
Song of Solomon 5:2	93
Titus 3:5	454, 459
Zechariah 1:8	96
Zechariah 3:9	161
Zechariah 12:1	512
Zechariah 14:4	165
Zechariah 14:6	156
Zechariah 14:7	97, 101, 113, 156, 161, 163, 164, 165, 166
Zephaniah 1:15	144
Zephaniah 2:15	579
Zephaniah 2:7	113
Zephaniah 3:3	113, 132, 138
Zephaniah 3:5	132, 156

Bibliography

[1] Custance, Arthur C., *Without Form and Void*
Copyright: Arthur C. Custance, 1970
Brockville, Ontario: Doorway Publications

[2] Kimball, John W.: *Biology* 2nd Edition
Copyright: Addison-Wesley Publishing Co., 1969

[3] http://www.itsgila.com/tipsbibheb.htm

[4] Carl. F. Keil, and Delitzsch, Franz
Commentary on the Old Testament, Vol. 3, 1 Kings to 2 Chronicles, 1878
(Public Domain)

[5] National Centers for Environmental Information, National Oceanic and Atmospheric Organization. https://www.ngdc.noaa.gov/mgg/sedthick/sedthick.html

[6] White, Ellen G. (1864). *Spiritual Gifts*, Volume 3. Chapter 10: The Flood. p. 75. Online Edition.

http://www.gilead.net/egw/books/spiritual-gifts/Spiritual_Gifts._Volume_3/index.htm

[7] Hayward, Alan: *Creation and Evolution*, Page 128
Copyright: Alan Hayward, 1985
Minneapolis: Bethany House Publishers

[8] Hayward, Alan: *Creation and Evolution*, Page 88
Copyright: Alan Hayward, 1985
Minneapolis: Bethany House Publishers

[9] Dyni, John R. Geologist, USGS
Verification that Green River Varves are Annual Layers, 26 June 2000
http://www.indiana.edu/~ensiweb/lessons/varve.ev.pdf

[10] Hayward, Alan: *Creation and Evolution*, Page 85
Copyright: Alan Hayward, 1985
Minneapolis: Bethany House Publishers

[11] Carpenter, Kenneth: *Eggs, Nests, and Baby Dinosaurs*
Copyright: Kenneth Carpenter, 1999
Bloomington, Indiana: Indiana University Press

[12] Hayward, Alan: *Creation and Evolution*, Page 137
Copyright: Alan Hayward, 1985
Minneapolis: Bethany House Publishers

[13] Hayward, Alan: *Creation and Evolution*, Page 83
Copyright: Alan Hayward, 1985
Minneapolis: Bethany House Publishers

[14] Johnson, Gaines: *The Bible, Genesis & Geology*
Copyright: Gaines Johnson, 2010
Published by CreateSpace Independent Publishing (www.CreateSpace.com)

[15] Johnson, Gaines: *The Bible, Genesis, and Geology*, 2nd Edition
Copyright: Gaines Johnson, 2013
Published by CreateSpace Independent Publishing (www.CreateSpace.com)

[16] Hayward, Alan: *Creation and Evolution*
Copyright: Alan Hayward, 1985
Minneapolis: Bethany House Publishers

[17] Quoted by Arthur C. Custance, *Without Form and Void*, Page 130
Copyright: Arthur C. Custance, 1970
Brockville, Ontario: Doorway Publications

[18] Quoted by Arthur C. Custance, *Without Form and Void*, Page 130
Copyright: Arthur C. Custance, 1970
Brockville, Ontario: Doorway Publications

[19] Quoted by Arthur C. Custance, *Without Form and Void*, Page 131
Copyright: Arthur C. Custance, 1970
Brockville, Ontario: Doorway Publications

[20] Dillman, August, *Genesis Critically and Exegetically Expounded*
(Translation by William B. Stevenson)
Edinburgh: T. & T. Clark, 1897, (Public Domain)

[21] Young, Robert, *Literal Translation of the Bible*,
1898, (Public Domain)

[22] Thieme, Robert B., Jr., *Creation, Chaos, and Restoration*, Page 23
Copyright: Robert B. Thieme, Jr., 1974
Houston: Berachah Tapes and Publications

[23] Custance, Arthur C., *Without Form and Void*, Page xi
Copyright: Arthur C. Custance, 1970
Brockville, Ontario: Doorway Publications

[24] Quoted by Arthur C. Custance, *Without Form and Void*, Page 131
Copyright: Arthur C. Custance, 1970
Brockville, Ontario: Doorway Publications

[25] Custance, Arthur C., *Without Form and Void*, Page xi
Copyright: Arthur C. Custance, 1970
Brockville, Ontario: Doorway Publications

[26] Quoted by Arthur C. Custance, *Without Form and Void*, Page 131
Copyright: Arthur C. Custance, 1970
Brockville, Ontario: Doorway Publications

[27] Quoted by Arthur C. Custance, *Without Form and Void*
Copyright: Arthur C. Custance, 1970
Brockville, Ontario: Doorway Publications, page 132

[28] Strong, James, *Strong's Dictionary of the Hebrew Language*
Copyright: James Strong, 1890
London: Hodder and Stroughton

[29] *The New American Standard Exhaustive Concordance of the Bible*
Copyright 1981: The Lockman Foundation

[30] Strong, James, *Strong's Dictionary of the Hebrew Language*
Copyright: James Strong, 1890
London: Hodder and Stroughton

[31] http://www.hebrew4christians.com/Grammar/Unit_Ten/Introduction/introduction.html

[32] Ross, Hugh, *The Improbable Planet*
Copyright © 2016 by Reasons to Believe
Published by Baker Books, Grand Rapids, MI

[33] *The Complete Word Study Old Testament King James Version*
Copyright: 1994 AMG International, Inc. D/B/A AMG Publishers
Chattanooga, TN 37422, U.S.A.

[34] Scofield, C. I., *The New Scofield Reference Bible*
Copyright: Oxford University Press, Inc., 1967
New York, London, Toronto

[35] Larkin, Clarence, *Dispensational Truth*
Copyright: Clarence Larkin, 1920
Philadelphia: Rev. Clarence Larkin Est.

[36] Joseph Baylee, D. D.
Principal of St. Aidan's Theological College, Birkenhead, England
Holy Word of God Defended From Its Assailants, Footnote Page 133
Liverpool: Adam Holden, (Late W. Grapel.)
London: Arthur Hall and Company, 1857 (Public Domain)

[37] Sumner, John Bird, *A Treatise on the Records of the Creation*,
Volume 1, 2nd Edition, Corrected, Pages 357-358
London: 1818 (Public Domain)

[38] Conybeare, William Daniel (1787-1857) and Phillips, William (1775-1828),
Outlines of the Geology of England and Wales (1822), Introduction, Pages lix-lx
Publisher: William Phillips (Public Domain)

[39] Higgins, William Mullinger, *Mosaical and Mineral Geologies Compared*, Pages 133-134
London: John Scoble, 1832 (Public Domain)

[40] Higgins, William Mullinger, *Mosaical and Mineral Geologies Compared*, Page 137
London: John Scoble, 1832 (Public Domain)

[41] Higgins, William Mullinger, *Mosaical and Mineral Geologies Compared*, Page 159
London: John Scoble, 1832 (Public Domain)

[42] Turner, Sharon, *Sacred History of the World* (1833), Page 461
(Public Domain)

[43] Hitchcock, Edward, *Elemental Geology*, 25th Edition, 1855,
Section IX (Connection Between Geology and Natural and Revealed Religion), page 350
Publisher: Ivison and Phinney, New York (Public Domain)

[44] Conkin, Paul Keith, *The Uneasy Center: Reformed Christianity in Antebellum America*, Page 283
Copyright 1995, The University of North Carolina Press

[45] Barnes, Albert, (1798-1870), *Notes on the Bible*: Genesis 1:2
1834 (Public Domain)

[46] Spurgeon, Charles Haddon, Sermon Delivered on Sunday, June 17, 1855
New Park Street Chapel, Southwark (Public Domain)

[47] Spurgeon, Charles Haddon, Sermon Delivered on Sunday, July 7, 1889
The Metropolitan Tabernacle, Newington (Public Domain)

[48] Spurgeon, Charles Haddon, *The Teachings of Nature in the Kingdom of Grace*, Page 7
Passmore and Alabaster, London, 1896 (Public Domain)

[49] Pusey, Edward Bouverie, *Daniel the Prophet*, Preface, Pages xvii-xviii
James Parker and Company, Oxford (377 Strand. London) and Rivingtons (London, Oxford, Cambridge), 1868 (Public Domain)

[50] Darby, John Nelson, (1800-1882) *The Collected Writings in 34 Volumes*,
Edited by William Kelly (Public Domain)

[51] Burgon, John William, (1813-1888) *Inspiration and Interpretation Seven Sermons Preached Before the University of Oxford*, 1861, Pages xciii-xciv
J. H. and Jas. Parker, Oxford and London (Public Domain)

[52] Temple, Frederick; Williams, Rowland; Powell, Baden; Wilson, Henry Bristow; Goodwin,
C. W.; Pattison, Mark; and Jowett, Benjamin, *Essays and Reviews*, 1860 (Public Domain)

[53] Jamieson, Robert; Fausset, A. R.; Brown, David,
Commentary Critical and Explanatory on the Whole Bible, 1871 (Public Domain)

[54] Edersheim, Alfred, *Bible History, Old Testament*, (1890) Public Domain
Book 1: The World Before the Flood, and the History of the Patriarchs.
Hendrickson Publishers, Inc. 1995

[55] Torrey, Reuben Archer, *Difficulties in the Bible: Alleged Errors and Contradictions*, Fleming H. Revell, 1907 (Public Domain)
Kindle Locations 352-381; Heraklion Press. Kindle Edition. (2014-07-20).

[56] Morgan, George Campbell, *Exposition on the Whole Bible*,
http://www.studylight.org/commentaries/gcm/genesis-1.html

[57] Morgan, George Campbell, *In the Beginning God*,
http://articles.ochristian.com/article14135.shtml

[58] Pink, Arthur Walkington, *Gleanings in Genesis*, Page 10
Moody Bible Press, 1922 (Public Domain)

[59] Chafer, Lewis Sperry, *Systematic Theology, Volume 2*, Page 39
Copyright: Lewis Sperry Chafer, 1947
Dallas: Dallas Seminary Press, Sixth Printing, December 1969

[60] Barnhouse, Donald Grey, *The Invisible War*, pages 9-10
Copyright: Zondervan Publishing House, 1965
Grand Rapids, Michigan

[61] Archer, Gleason, *A Survey of Old Testament Introduction*, Page. 184
Copyright: Gleason Archer, 1974
Chicago: Moody Press

[62] Laird, R. Harris, Archer, Gleason, and Waltke, Bruce K., *Theological Wordbook of the Old Testament*
Copyright: 2003 Moody Publishers, Moody Bible Institute
Chicago, Illinois

[63] Anstey, Martin, *The Romance of Bible Chronology*, Page 62
Copyright: Marshal Brothers, LTD., London, Edinburgh, and New York, 1913

[64] Baker, Warren and Carpenter, Eugene,
The Complete Word Study Dictionary: Old Testament, Page 262
Copyright: 2003 AMG Publishers
Chattanooga, TN 37421

[65] *Nelson's Expository Dictionary of the Old Testament*, Page 21
Edited by Merrill F. Unger, Th.M., Th.D., Ph.D. and William White, Jr., Th.M., Ph.D.
Copyright 1980, Thomas Nelson Publishers, Nashville, TN

[66] *Nelson's Expository Dictionary of the Old Testament*, Page 22
Edited by Merrill F. Unger, Th.M., Th.D., Ph.D. and William White, Jr., Th.M., Ph.D.
Copyright 1980, Thomas Nelson Publishers, Nashville, TN

[67] Wilson, William, *Wilson's Old Testament Word Studies*, Page 30
Copyright: Mac Donald Publishing Company, McLean, Virginia 22102, 1975

[68] Coates, Charles Andrew, (1862-1945) *An Outline of the Book of Genesis*
Copyright: Kingston-on-Thames, Surrey: Stow Hill Bible and Tract Depot, 1921

[69] Kelly, William, (1821-1906), *Lectures on the Pentateuch*
London: W. H. Broom, 1871 (Public Domain)

[70] Gaebelein, Arno Clement, (1861-1945), *The Annotated Bible, the Book of Genesis*
Copyright 1919: Arno Clement Gaebelein (Public Domain)

[71] Grant, Frederick William, (1834-1902), *Genesis in the Light of the New Testament*
New York: Loizeaux Brothers. (Public Domain)

[72] Hole, Frank Binford (1874-1964) *Old and New Testament Commentary*: Genesis 1:1-13
(Public Domain)

[73] Ginzberg, Louis, (1873-1953) *The Legends of The Jews*, The Creation of the World, Page 4
Copyright 1912: The Jewish Publication Society, Philadelphia

[74] Thieme, Robert B., Jr., *Creation, Chaos, and Restoration*, Pages 1-12
Copyright: Robert B. Thieme, Jr., 1974
Houston: Berachah Tapes and Publications

[75] Dake, Finis Jennings, *Dake's Annotated Reference Bible*
Copyright: Finis Jennings Dake, 1963
Lawrenceville, Georgia: Dake Bible Sales, Inc.

[76] Sauer, Erich, (1898-1959) *The King of the Earth*
Copyright: Grand Rapids, Michigan: William B. Eerdmans Publishing Co., December 31, 1996

[77] Pember, G. H., (1837-1910) *Earth's Earliest Ages*
London: Hodder and Stroughton, 1876 (Public Domain)
Grand Rapids: Kregel Publications, 1975

[78] Boice, James, *The Gap Theory*, The Bible Study Hour,
http://www.oneplace.com/ministries/the-bible-study-hour/listen/the-gap-theory-310249.html

[79] Ramm, Bernard, *The Christian View of Science and Scripture*,
Copyright: Wm. B. Eerdmans Publishing Co. (June 1954)

[80] Custance, Arthur C., *Without Form and Void*
Copyright: Arthur C. Custance, 1970
Brockville, Ontario: Doorway Publications

[81] *The Complete Word Study Old Testament King James Version*
Copyright: 1994 AMG International, Inc. D/B/A AMG Publishers
Chattanooga, TN 37422, U.S.A.

[82] Ross, Hugh, *The Improbable Planet*
Copyright © 2016 by Reasons to Believe
Published by Baker Books, Grand Rapids, MI

[83] http://calumsblog.com/apologetics/arguments-for-gods-existence/finetuning

[84] Anil Ananthaswamy on PBS *NOVA*
http://www.pbs.org/wgbh/nova/blogs/physics/2012/03/is-the-universe-fine-tuned-for-life/

[85] Collins, Robin, Distinguished Professor of Philosophy and chair of the Department of Philosophy at Messiah College in Grantham, Pennsylvania
http://worldview3.50webs.com/mathprfcosmos.html

[86] Ashton, Goeff
http://somethingpersonal.typepad.com/something_personal-deleted-20141015-lzduv/2012/08/a-universe-precision-tuned-for-life-by-what-or-by-whom.html

[87] Davies, Paul, *God and the New Physics*
Copyright: Paul Davis, 1983
London: J. M. Dent and Sons

[88] Ross, Hugh, *The Creator and the Cosmos*, page 115
Copyright: Hugh Ross, 1995
Navpress

[89] Edward L. Wright, Ph.D.
Professor of Astronomy, U.C.L.A.
http://www.astro.ucla.edu/~wright/cosmo_03.htm#FO
[90] http://www.reasons.org/articles/fine-tuning-for-life-on-earth-june-2004

[91] Custance, Arthur C., *Without Form and Void*
Copyright: Arthur C. Custance, 1970
Brockville, Ontario: Doorway Publications

[92] Custance, Arthur C., *Without Form and Void*, Page 102
Copyright: Arthur C. Custance, 1970
Brockville, Ontario: Doorway Publications

[93] Martins, Joaozinho, *Pre-Historic Pre-Adamic Theology*
Copyright: Joaozinho Martins, 2016
Published by Xulon Press, U.S.A.

[94] Lewis, C. S., *The Lion, the Witch, and the Wardrobe*, Chapter 15
Copyright: C. S. Lewis, 1950
Published by Geoffrey Bles, London

[95] Lowrance, James M., *Why Christianity, and Bible-Belief Makes Sense: Does Faith Give Hope Beyond this Life?*
Copyright: James M. Lowrance, 2010
Published by CreateSpace Independent Publishing (www.CreateSpace.com)

[96] Han, Nathan E., *A Parsing Guide to the Greek New Testament*, (Sixth Printing)
Copyright: Herald Press, 1971
Scottsdale, Pennsylvania

[97] Anderson, Sir Robert, *The Coming Prince*, 1894 (Public Domain)

[98] Custance, Arthur C., *Without Form and Void*, Page 18 and Appendix XIX
Copyright: Arthur C. Custance, 1970
Brockville, Ontario: Doorway Publications

[99] William R. Newcott, "A Short History of the Universe" *National Geographic*, Vol. 185 No. 1 Jan. 1994, Page 12
Copyright: The National Geographic Society, 1994
Washington D.C.

[100] Gerald L. Schroeder, *Genesis and the Big Bang*, Page 65
Copyright: Gerald L. Schroeder, 1990
New York, Toronto, London, Sydney, Auckland; Bantam Books

[101] M. Krings, A. Stone, R. W. Schmitz, H. Krainitzki, M. Stoneking, and S. Pääbo, July 1997. Neanderthal DNA Sequences and the Origin of Modern Humans
Cell 90:19-30.

[102] Igor Ovchinnikov, A. Götherström, G. P. Romanoval, V. M. Kharitonov, K. Lidén, and W. Goodwin, March 2000.
Molecular Analysis of Neanderthal DNA from the Northern Caucasus
Copyright: *Nature* 404:490-493.

[103] James Strong, *Strong's Dictionary of the Hebrew Language*
Copyright: James Strong, 1890
London: Hodder and Stroughton

[104] Anstey, Martin, *The Romance of Bible Chronology*, Page 62
Copyright: Marshal Brothers, LTD., London, Edinburgh, and New York, 1913

[105] *The Complete Word Study Old Testament King James Version*, Page 2311
Copyright: 1994 AMG International, Inc. D/B/A AMG Publishers
Chattanooga, TN 37422, U.S.A.

[106] *The Complete Word Study Old Testament King James Version*, Page 2282
Copyright: 1994 AMG International, Inc. D/B/A AMG Publishers
Chattanooga, TN 37422, U.S.A.

[107] *The Complete Word Study Old Testament King James Version*, Page 2282
Copyright: 1994 AMG International, Inc. D/B/A AMG Publishers
Chattanooga, TN 37422, U.S.A.

[108] *The Complete Word Study Old Testament King James Version*, Page 2283
Copyright: 1994 AMG International, Inc. D/B/A AMG Publishers
Chattanooga, TN 37422, U.S.A.

[109] *The Complete Word Study Old Testament King James Version*, Page 2283
Copyright: 1994 AMG International, Inc. D/B/A AMG Publishers
Chattanooga, TN 37422, U.S.A.

[110] *The Complete Word Study Old Testament King James Version*, Page 2283
Copyright: 1994 AMG International, Inc. D/B/A AMG Publishers
Chattanooga, TN 37422, U.S.A.

[111] Custance, Arthur C., *Without Form and Void,*
Copyright: Arthur C. Custance, 1970
Brockville, Ontario: Doorway Publications

[112] *The Complete Word Study Old Testament King James Version*,
Copyright: 1994 AMG International, Inc. D/B/A AMG Publishers
Chattanooga, TN 37422, U.S.A.

[113] Ross, Allen P., Th.D., Ph.D.,
http://www.christianleadershipcenter.org/exsyntax.htm
Copyright: Allen P. Ross
Samford University, Birmingham, Alabama

[114] Custance, Arthur C., *Without Form and Void*, Page 14
Copyright: Arthur C. Custance, 1970
Brockville, Ontario: Doorway Publications

[115] Custance, Arthur C., *Without Form and Void*, Page 41
Copyright: Arthur C. Custance, 1970
Brockville, Ontario: Doorway Publications

[116] Ross, Allen P., Th.D., Ph.D.
http://www.christianleadershipcenter.org/exsyntax.htm
Copyright: Allen P. Ross
Samford University, Birmingham, Alabama

[117] *The Complete Word Study Old Testament King James Version*
Copyright: 1994 AMG International, Inc. D/B/A AMG Publishers
Chattanooga, TN 37422, U.S.A.

[118] Langford, Jack, *The Gap is Not a Theory*
Copyright: Jack Langford, 2011
Published by Xlibris Corporation

[119] *The Complete Word Study Old Testament King James Version*
Copyright: 1994 AMG International, Inc. D/B/A AMG Publishers
Chattanooga, TN 37422, U.S.A.

[120] Ross, Allen P., Th.D., Ph.D.
http://www.christianleadershipcenter.org/exsyntax.htm
Copyright: Allen P. Ross
Samford University, Birmingham, Alabama

[121] Anstey, Martin, *The Romance of Bible Chronology*, Page 62
Copyright: Marshal Brothers, LTD., London, Edinburgh, and New York, 1913

[122] *The Complete Word Study Old Testament King James Version*
Copyright: 1994 AMG International, Inc. D/B/A AMG Publishers
Chattanooga, TN 37422, U.S.A.

www.ingramcontent.com/pod-product-compliance
Lightning Source LLC
Chambersburg PA
CBHW081102080526
44587CB00021B/3412